THE GREAT
HIGHLAND FAMINE

THE GREAT HIGHLAND FAMINE

Hunger, Emigration and the Scottish Highlands in the Nineteenth Century

T.M. DEVINE

Research Assistant
WILLIE ORR

JOHN DONALD PUBLISHERS LTD
EDINBURGH

This edition first published in 1995 by
Birlinn Limited
West Newington House
10 Newington Road
Edinburgh EH9 1QS

www.birlinn.co.uk

Reprinted 2004

First published by Victor Gollancz Ltd 1980

ISBN 1-904607-42-X

British Library Cataloguing-in-Publication Data
A Catalogue record for this book is available from
the British Library

Printed and bound by Antony Rowe Ltd, Eastbourne

Introduction

The primary purpose of this book is to provide an account of the potato famine in the Scottish Highlands in the middle decades of the nineteenth century through a consideration of its origin, nature and effects. This was the last great subsistence crisis on the British mainland and potentially the most devastating to affect any region of Scotland since the notorious Lean Years of the 1690s. Events in the Highlands at the time also suggest interesting parallels and contrasts with the Great Famine in Ireland. Yet the Highland famine has not thus far attracted much systematic attention from historians, and even its existence is not widely known outside the relatively small number of those with a serious interest in the Scottish past.[1] This may be partly because the crisis in the Highlands did not have the same horrendous impact on death rates as the much greater catastrophe in Ireland. Some might even argue that the absence of a major crisis in mortality suggests that the emergency in the Highlands does not deserve the description of 'famine'. There are, for instance, social scientists who assert that only excess mortality defines the existence of such a crisis.[2] But this is probably too narrow a view and is only one of several definitions to be found in the modern literature on famine.[3]

The term 'Highland Famine' can be justified on at least three counts. First, for almost a decade between 1846 and 1855 the potato, the main subsistence crop of the population of the Western Highlands and Islands, failed in whole or in part and threatened a large number of the region's inhabitants with both malnutrition, severe destitution and the killer diseases associated with these conditions. Second, massive external assistance was required to reduce the real danger posed to the lives of many thousands of people. Third, the subsistence crisis had a fundamental impact on such crucial social indicators as birth, marriage, emigration and migration. The famine caused a huge exodus from the stricken region on a quite unprecedented scale. The Highland Famine did not directly cause the deaths of many people, except in 1846 and 1847, but it had momentous demographic consequences for the inhabitants of the north of Scotland.

The aim of this study, however, is not confined to a straightforward historical assessment of the potato famine itself. It also seeks to bridge some of the gaps in current literature on the nineteenth-century Highlands which exist in the periods covered by Malcolm Gray's *Highland Economy* (1957) and James Hunter's *Making of the Crofting Community* (1976). Gray's volume is restricted to the decades before *c*. 1840. The main thrust of Hunter's book is towards the last quarter of the nineteenth century, though he also surveys earlier periods. The middle decades, some of the most crucial in the society's development, have not hitherto been explored in any depth.

The book also devotes considerable attention to emigration and migration and seeks to make a contribution to an understanding of an important phase in the movement of the Scottish people to overseas destinations. The treatment here, however, is restricted to an examination of the indigenous causes, nature and process of emigration, and no attempt is made to determine the pattern of life eventually adopted by the emigrants in either Canada or Australia. Effective pursuit of the emigrant trail would require another volume concerned with the diaspora itself.

Finally, the study endeavours to contribute to the methodology of Highland history. Scholarly examination of the society after *c.*1840 has tended towards a kind of duality. On the one hand, there is the statistical treatment favoured by the historical demographers led by M.W. Flinn; on the other, the traditional historical approach using contemporary correspondence, government files and newspapers to construct an essentially impressionistic account of social development. This study tries to combine both methods. The core of the book rests on a foundation of numerical materials: rentals, the published and unpublished census, summonses of removal, emigration records and statistical series produced by both government and destitution committees. Throughout the attempt is made to quantify the issues and problems under discussion, not because of an obsession with number for its own sake but because only through some reckoning of the order of magnitude do patterns become apparent, trends reveal themselves and the fundamental questions come more clearly into focus. Systematic analysis inevitably rests on the greater precision which comes from elementary quantification. A more elaborate manipulation of the data is not attempted, not merely because of the inadequacies of much of the source materials but also because of the limitations of the expertise of the author. 'Softer' evidence, of the type mentioned above, is also an essential element. From it derives the information on motivation, attitudes, values and perceptions which are vital to a meaningful understanding of causation and the ideologies and assumptions which drove men to action.

It must be stressed from the outset that there are a number of intractable problems associated with some of the major sources which have been used in the analysis. An effort has been made to locate all important, relevant materials for the period and region of study. Where omissions remain it can normally be assumed that the source in question did not provide much useful information or that it is not presently recorded in record office guides, National Register of Archive (Scotland) surveys or in bibliographical literature. The specific difficulties involved in using some of the data which are available for examination and the gaps in much of the materials consulted are explored in detail in Chapters 2, 3 and 8. Here, however, attention should be drawn to the general problems associated with three sources which in theory might have yielded hard information of a quantitative nature but which in practice were somewhat disappointing.

The *Agricultural Statistics* for Scotland only started to appear in the 1850s, near the end of the potato famine. They do not initially record any information on tenants paying less than £20 per annum and so exclude from coverage the vast majority of landholders in the Western Highlands and Islands. Because of this, it is impossible to calculate precise and comprehensive long-run series of changing acreage, cropping systems, tenancy structures and yields from the official returns in the way that can be done for parts of Ireland. The Irish *Agricultural Statistics* and other official sources are not only more detailed but are available from the 1840s and thereafter. Again, Highland demographic history before civil registration must be constructed on the basis of fragile materials and on the understanding that yawning gaps exist in the evidence. Recording of births, marriages and deaths was not only erratic in the region during the

1840s and early 1850s but was artificially distorted by the Disruption of 1843 and the emergence of the Free Church of Scotland. After that date entries in some Church of Scotland registers declined dramatically or disappeared altogether. Customs returns for the Highland ports, the key source for the determination of changing patterns of regional trade during the famine period, have not survived. They were undoubtedly collected in such ports as Stornoway, Tobermory, Portree and Inveraray because extracts from the returns were occasionally produced in evidence before official enquiries. Tragically, however, for the period of this study at least, the originals seem to have been destroyed. The historian of the Highland famine, therefore, is forced to grapple with imperfect materials, base many of his conclusion on imprecise measures and rely also on tentative estimates of what might have happened. The only justification that can be offered is that, at the present time at least, there is no alternative to such an approach.

The study itself is set in three coherent parts. Chapters 1 to 3 identify the origins, nature and demographic effects of the crisis. The analytical perspective of dividing the Highlands into two distinctive social formations, the Western Highlands and Islands on the one hand, the eastern, central and southern zone on the other, is here explained and developed. This structure forms the basic organising principle of the entire study. Secondly, Chapters 4 to 7 examine the varied responses of landlords, government, lowland charities and the people themselves to the emergency. The main purpose of this section is to explain how the Highlands managed to escape a tragedy of Irish proportions. Finally, Chapters 8 to 12 consider the pattern of emigration and migration, the forces which shaped the outward movement and the impact of the famine on the development of Highland society in the medium and long terms.

A project on this scale based on an array of original sources, many of them very demanding of time and labour, would not have been possible without external funding. I am therefore happy to acknowledge the generous support provided by the Economic and Social Research Council (Grant No. B00232099) and the University of Strathclyde Research and Development Fund in 1985 and 1986, when most of the gathering and processing of information was carried out. This financial help allowed me to employ a first-class research assistant, my former graduate student, Mr. W. Orr. By his careful, thorough and meticulous work, he made a major contribution to the successful completion of the project.

In 1986 and early 1987 parts of the study were read as papers at Research Seminars in the Universities of Aberdeen, Glasgow, Strathclyde and St. Andrews and given as lectures at the Annual Conference of the British Agricultural History Society (University of Ulster, 1987) and First Residential Conference of the Economic and Social History Society of Scotland (University of Aberdeen, 1987). These meetings not only gave me the opportunity to clarify my thoughts on complex issues but comments and criticisms made on each occasion benefited the development of the entire project.

Acknowledgement is made to the following for permission to consult and cite original material in their care: the Keeper of the Records of Scotland; the Controller of H.M. Stationery Office; the Keeper and Trustees of the National Library of Scotland; the Keeper of the Public Records, Public Record Office; Fr. Mark Dilworth, Catholic National Archives; the Duke of Argyll; the Duke of Hamilton; Cameron of Lochiel;

John Macleod of Macleod; John Mackenzie of Gairloch.

I am particularly grateful to Mr. John Mackenzie for his hospitality when examining the Mackenzie of Gairloch MSS; to Mr. C.C. Johnston, Registrar of the National Register of Archives (Scotland) for his efficient and speedy processing of several queries; and to Alastair Lorne Campbell Jr. of Airds, of Argyll Estates, Inveraray Castle, for his generous assistance, often at considerable inconvenience to himself, when research on the immensely valuable Argyll Estate Papers was undertaken.

The following helped by answering queries or providing information: Jeanette Brock; Margaret Buchanan; Fr. Mark Dilworth; Pat Gibb; Liam Kennedy; Mairhi Macarthur; Ann Morton; John Robertson; Willie Sloan; Christopher Smout; Neil Tranter; James Treble; John Tuckwell; Peter Vasey. The maps were drawn by Dr. Miles Oglethorpe.

Mrs. Irene Scouller typed all the successive drafts of a long and difficult manuscript. I thank her not only for her skilful work but for her powers of endurance and patience when continuously confronted by my idiosyncratic handwriting.

The volume could not have been completed without the constant support and encouragement of Catherine Mary Devine. To her and our children this book is dedicated with love.

Tom Devine, University of Strathclyde.

NOTES

1 The background to the events of the 1840s is discussed in M. Gray, *The Highland Economy, 1750-1850* (Edinburgh, 1957) and 'The Highland Potato Famine of the 1840s', *Economic History Review*, 2nd ser., vii (1955). James Hunter, *The Making of the Crofting Community* (Edinburgh, 1976) devotes a chapter to the famine though his conclusions differ in some respects from those of this volume. M.M. Flinn *et al* eds., *Scottish Population History from the Seventeenth Century to the 1930s* (Cambridge, 1977), is concerned almost exclusively with some of the demographic aspects of the crisis.

2 See, for example, M. Alamgir, *Famine in South Asia: the Political Economy of Mass Starvation* (Cambridge, Mass., 1980), 24; D.G. Johnson, 'Famine', in *Encyclopaedia Britannica* (14th ed., 1973), 58; G.B. Masefield, *Famine: Its Prevention and Relief* (Oxford, 1963), 3-4. For a historian's use of this measure see Andrew B. Appleby, *Famine in Tudor and Stuart England* (Liverpool, 1978), 7-8.

3 They are, *inter alia*, periods of extreme incidence of hunger and malnutrition; food emergencies identified by an increase in external assistance to relieve the affected population; shortfalls in food production leading to demographic and other changes in the social order. For a recent review of these definitions see Alamgir, *Famine in South Asia*, and Masefield, *Famine*; see also P.M.A. Bourke, 'The Potato Blight, Weather and the Irish Famine', Unpublished Ph.D. thesis, National University of Ireland, 1965.

Abbreviations

Destitution Papers	Free Church Destitution Committee, *Statements and Reports* (Edinburgh, 1847)
	Reports of Central Board of Management of the Fund raised for the Relief of the Destitute Inhabitants of the Highlands and Islands of Scotland, 1847-50
	Reports of Edinburgh Section of the Central Board (Edinburgh, 1847-50)
	Reports of the General Assembly of the Free Church of Scotland regarding Highland Destitution (Edinburgh, 1847)
	Report on Mull, Tiree etc. by a Deputation of the Glasgow Section of the Highland Relief Board (Glasgow, 1849)
	Report on the Outer Hebrides by a Deputation of the Glasgow Section of the Highland Relief Board (Glasgow, 1849)
GRO	General Register Office, Edinburgh
McNeill Report	*Report to the Board of Supervision by Sir John McNeill on the Western Highlands and Islands,* Parliamentary Papers, 1851, XXVI
N.C.	(Napier Commission) *Report and Evidence of the Commissioners of Inquiry into the Condition of the Crofters and Cottars in the Highlands and Islands of Scotland,* Parliamentary Papers, 1884, XXXII-XXXVI
NLS	National Library of Scotland, Edinburgh
N.S.A.	*New Statistical Account of Scotland.* 15 Vols. (Edinburgh, 1845)
O.S.A.	*Statistical Account of Scotland.* Edited by Sir John Sinclair. 21 Vols. (Edinburgh, 1791-99)
PP	Parliamentary Papers
PRO	Public Record Office, London
RGS	Registrar-General for Scotland
Relief Correspondence	*Correspondence relating to the Measures adopted for the Relief of Distress in Ireland and Scotland,* Parliamentary Papers, 1847, LIII
S.C. on Emigration	*Report from the Select Committee appointed to inquire into the Condition of the Population of the Highlands and Lowlands of Scotland, and into the practicability of affording the People relief by means of Emigration,* Parliamentary Papers, 1841, VI
SRO	Scottish Record Office, Edinburgh

Tables

Contents

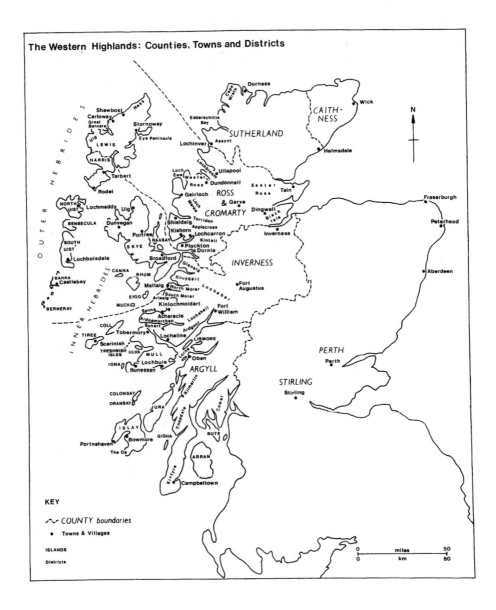

The Western Highlands: Counties, Towns and Districts

KEY

~~ COUNTY *boundaries*

• Towns & Villages

ISLANDS

Districts

| 0 | miles | 50 |
| 0 | km | 80 |

N

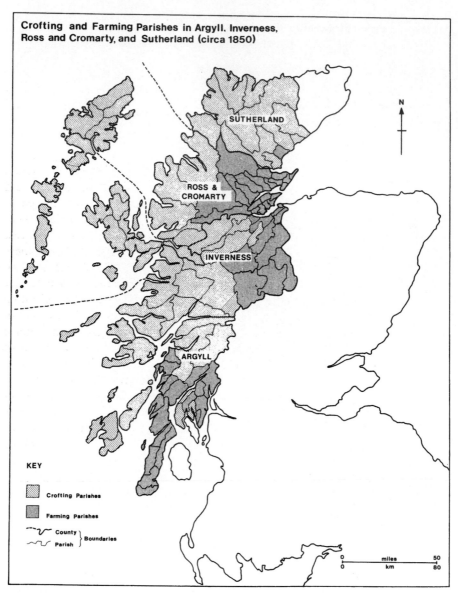

Crofting and Farming Parishes in Argyll, Inverness,
Ross and Cromarty, and Sutherland (circa 1850)

SUTHERLAND

ROSS &
CROMARTY

INVERNESS

ARGYLL

N

KEY

Crofting Parishes

Farming Parishes

County ⎱ Boundaries
Parish ⎰

miles   50
km   80

Note: See Appendix 1 for lists of Crofting and Farming Parishes.

1

A Vulnerable Society:
The Western Highlands and Islands, c.1800-1846

Two Highland Societies

By the 1840s two broadly divergent social and economic systems had emerged in the Highland counties of Scotland. In the southern and eastern districts, which included central and eastern Inverness-shire, Easter Ross and the greater part of mainland Argyllshire, a type of social structure had developed which will be referred to throughout this volume as 'farming society'.[1] It had several characteristics which, though not equally uniform in all areas, served to differentiate the south and east from the far western mainland and the islands.[2] As in most of the Lowlands, there had occurred a widespread consolidation of land between c.1780 and c.1840. The number of rent-paying tenants declined, holdings were enlarged and a greater proportion of the population than had been the case in the old order fell into a dependent position as farm servants, labourers, cottars and crofters. The extent of consolidation and its social effects varied between districts. In the coastal strip north of Inverness, large units of over 100 acres were general, whereas in southern Argyllshire and Highland Perthshire 'family'-sized holdings of forty to sixty acres were often more common. Throughout all these areas, however, there was a general tendency towards the concentrated control of tenancies in the hands of a smaller number of men.[3] In a group of four parishes in Argyll in the later 1830s, no more than one quarter of all families rented directly from the proprietor, while in the Easter Ross parish of Killearnan only five per cent of those engaged in agriculture were classified as 'farmers'.[4]

Agrarian specialisation varied. Large pastoral farms existed alongside holdings where mixed agriculture was dominant.[5] Along the east coast rim, arable cultivation was also to be found on a considerable scale. It followed, therefore, that in several districts within the region there was a continued demand for labour as both the area of cultivated land and productivity per acre increased within an unmechanised system of food production. Some of the labouring classes in certain localities were entirely landless. For example, fifty-four per cent of the employed population of the parish of Kilmartin in Argyll were either farm servants or labourers.[6] The more common pattern, however, in central and eastern Inverness-shire and parts of Ross, was for farmers to draw their labour supply from a semi-landless class of crofters and cottars. These groups possessed small lots of land, but most primarily depended for a living on the work they could obtain in the neighbourhood from the larger farmers. In many coastal districts this pattern varied, with the produce of the small holding taking second place to the earnings from fishing as the prime source of subsistence.

This was a social system in which the decisive influence on the standard of life for most of the population was the demand for labour in the bigger holdings which specialised in arable or mixed husbandry and the health of the fishing industry along the north-east coast. While distress was not unknown and the labouring classes only achieved at best a modest standard of comfort, there was little experience here of the persistent levels of acute destitution which characterised the much poorer society to the west and north.

The relative resilience of the new social order was apparent in a number of ways. There was a diverse structure of cropping and food supply. The potato was certainly a prime element in rotation systems and in the diet of the smallholding and labouring classes. But in most districts grain was either as significant or even more important in the structure of production and consumption. In the parish of Nigg, according to the *New Statistical Account*, the value of the acreage in grain crops and potatoes was eighty-three per cent and seventeen per cent respectively; in Tain, eighty-nine per cent and eleven per cent; in Craignish, sixty per cent and forty per cent; in Strachur, sixty-eight per cent and thirty-two per cent.[7] Again, though profound levels of poverty existed within the region, especially in such villages as Kingussie and Newtonmore, material standards in general were measurably higher than those of the Western Highlands.[8] Food shortages were not unknown, yet the majority of the population did not live continuously close to the basic minimum of subsistence. The harvest failure of 1836-7 brought many in the Western Highlands and Islands to the brink of starvation. But there was much less need for destitution committees established during the crisis to come to the aid of the people of the central and eastern areas.[9] The modest material improvements characteristic of much of the region were visibly demonstrated in the extensive construction of new houses built of timber, mortar, slates and glass.[10]

Above all this was a society where the majority no longer depended mainly on their own smallholding for survival. This is not to say that most people in all areas had become entirely detached from the land in the manner characteristic of so many Lowland regions. But the money economy was well developed. Cottars and crofters who worked for bigger farmers were partly paid in kind and cash. Fishermen sold their catch in the markets of the south. Pools of money income existed to provide a source of savings and something of an insurance against the worst economic or natural disasters. Perhaps the most telling indicator of the erosion of the old subsistence society was the vast increase in the importation of goods from the Lowland towns in the first half of the nineteenth century. The local manufacturers of cloth and even the production of shoes had virtually disappeared from many parishes in the farming region by the 1840s.[11]

These material changes were influenced by two main factors. Many localities, especially in eastern Inverness, Easter Ross and parts of southern Argyllshire were blessed with a relatively favourable natural endowment. The Highland massif is a great tableland which tilts slightly towards the east. This provides good drainage systems for the land surface of the eastern zone, affords protection against heavy rainfall and, through the great straths or river valleys which intersect the mountain range, facilitates communication with the economic heart of Scotland to the south.

The climatic and topographical advantages of many parishes, at least in relation to the poor circumstances of the west, help to explain the early development of arable surpluses, larger holdings and the modest capital accumulation which eventually allowed for greater economic diversification in the nineteenth century.

The demographic history of the region during the era of population increase from the later eighteenth century was also important. Between 1755 and 1851 there was a sustained haemorrhage of people. From 1755 to the 1790s this was so great that sixty per cent of the region's parishes failed to increase population at all. Between 1801 and 1841, the net rise in numbers was a mere seven per cent. These heavy rates of out-migration, markedly higher than those of the Western Highlands and Islands, were the combined result of proximity to alternative sources of employment in the Lowlands and the expulsive effects of a social system based on consolidation of smaller tenancies and effective controls over subdivision of holdings.[12] With a much larger and increasing arable acreage than the far west and a higher rate of out-migration, the ratio of population to available cultivable land was greater than anywhere along the western mainland. In the early 1840s, for instance, arable acreage per head in mainland Argyllshire was an estimated 2.18 but a mere 0.5 in Wester Ross and Skye.[13]

By the 1840s, a relatively balanced, more secure and much more productive economic régime had developed in many of the 'farming' districts of the Highlands, although it is also important to emphasise that 'prosperity' was distributed very unevenly across both the population and the localities of the region. The system had much in common with some of the improved regions of the Lowland countryside. A moderate degree of consolidation had produced a new farming élite employing an increased number of semi-landless and landless wage labourers who derived their subsistence partly from income at work and partly from their smallholdings. In both the south-west and north-east corners, prosperous fishing communities were well established. More arable land than existed elsewhere in the Highlands and an easing of demographic pressure as migration creamed off surplus population permitted the rise of a class of enterprising farmers in several districts throughout the region. This group, normally natives of the area and renting holdings at from £20 to £100, formed the economic backbone of the farming zone and gave it a resilience notably lacking in the poorer districts of the Western Highlands and Islands.

Along the western seaboard north of Fort William and extending to all the Inner and Outer Hebrides, a quite different social and economic structure had developed by the 1840s. At the census of 1841, while the farming districts contained a population of 121,224, the crofting region, as it will be described throughout this volume, had 167,283 inhabitants.[14] Like their counterparts in the south and east, they depended primarily on the produce of the land and sea to make a living. Both regions were almost entirely devoid of major manufacturing industry. Yet, this similarity apart, they differed considerably in material standards, income levels, demographic behaviour, social structure and economic specialisation. These fundamental contrasts go a long way to explain the varied impact of the potato famine on the two regions after 1846. Crofts also existed throughout the east and south, but in the west they were, in numerical terms, the dominant social formation. By the 1840s, the Western Highlands and Islands were still a peasant society. The overwhelming majority of the inhabitants depended to a significant extent on smallholdings and tiny patches of land for subsistence.

The Structure of Crofting Society

When he visited the Western Highlands in 1847, Robert Somers drew attention to the 'peculiar construction' of the society. It was one where '. . . there are only two ranks of people – a higher rank and a lower rank – the former consisting of a few large tenants all occupying nearly the same level; and the latter consisting of a dense body of small cottars and fishermen.'[15] Somers' observations are confirmed by the data presented in Table 1.1. This sets out the proportion of total rent paid by 'big' farmers in a sample of fifteen West Highland districts. Clearly in several areas, landlords relied on tenants paying rents of £20 per annum or more for the bulk of rental income by the 1840s. Many of these tenants, especially those renting at £100 or more per annum, operated large sheep farms which by the middle decades of the nineteenth century had penetrated virtually all the Western Highlands and Islands with the exception of Tiree, Islay, parts of Lewis, Barra and some other localities.[16] Large-scale pastoral husbandry in most districts had become the basis of estate economies and the major source of increasing rentals. It was a form of land use which was well suited to the climatic and topographical conditions of the area, reflecting the development of regional specialisation within the British economy, and the systematic exploitation of the comparative advantage of the Western Highlands as a low-cost source of wool and mutton for the industries and urban populations of the south.

Table 1.1. Percentage Share of Total Rental Paid by Tenants with Holdings Valued at Over £20 per Annum, Crofting Districts, c.1850

Parish/Estate	%
Kilfinichen (Mull)	68
Kilmuir (Skye)	54
Snizort (Skye)	71
Portree (Skye)	43
Strath (Skye)	54
Sleat (Skye)	59
North Morar	73
Knoydart	90
Glenelg	87
Glenshiel	97
Lochalsh	70
Kintail	77
Lochcarron	58
Applecross	52
Torridon	70
Average	74

Source: McNeill Report, Appendix A, *passim*

The very rapid development of commercial sheep farming demonstrated that the Western Highlands were just as responsive to 'improvement' and market opportunity as the southern and eastern areas. But the economics of sheep farming ensured that the vast income stream accruing from the development of pastoral husbandry failed to benefit the population as a whole. Specialist sheep farms existed throughout the southern and eastern Highlands, but in Argyll and eastern Inverness they often developed alongside mixed and arable farms which had a considerable demand for both permanent and seasonal supplies of labour.[17] In the west, however, sheep farms were not only more extensive, there was also little of the variegated structure of middling holdings, practising mixed agriculture, which might have created secure employment opportunities for the majority of the population. Sheep farming was both land- and capital-intensive.[18] It was organised mainly by incomers who alone possessed the financial resources necessary to stock large units. The profit accrued directly to landowners, farmers and middlemen. It was basically an alien penetration offering little to a society rich in underemployed labour resources but poor in capital. Only small numbers of regular wage-earners were required. One typical farm of 3000 sheep had a manager and six shepherds.[19] Labour costs were also pared to a minimum to ensure maximum efficiency. The new pastoral husbandry further reduced the slim resources available to the indigenous population as a whole. Sheep farming absorbed much of the scarce arable in certain districts and intensified congestion in coastal areas, marginal land and in slum villages as displacement of peasant communities accelerated throughout the region. It also debilitated the old cattle economy, traditionally the vital source of cash income for the peasantry. In the southern and eastern Highlands the new agriculture had brought a modest prosperity to the native farming class and provided a more secure standard of life for the labouring poor, albeit at the expense of heavy rates of migration. In the west, however, agrarian capitalism perpetuated the chronic poverty of the area and contributed to the social crisis which emerged after the end of the Napoleonic Wars.[20]

Below the level of the tenants of the large farms the population consisted principally of two classes, small tenants, or crofters, and cottars. The primary distinction between the two groups was that crofters were recognised tenants of land whereas cottars were either subtenants or had no legal claim to land at all and simply existed on many properties as squatters. The vast majority of tenants on most West Highland estates were crofters paying £10 per annum or less (see Table 1.2) although, as earlier discussion has suggested, they no longer necessarily contributed the major proportion of rental by the 1840s. The small tenancies were laid out in 'townships' or crofting settlements. These varied considerably but had certain common characteristics. At the centre of the township was an area of arable land divided into a number of separate smallholdings. These were surrounded by grazing or hill pasture, which was held in common by the township's tenants. The grazing land was a vital resource as the rental was normally calculated on the basis of the numbers of cattle per tenancy. A conventional ratio, for example, was one cow for each £1 sterling of annual rental.

There is a tendency in some historical writing on crofting to view these communities simply as uniform, undifferentiated masses of small tenants, all living close to the margin of subsistence in conditions of extreme poverty. There is, of course, considerable truth in this description. Certainly there was little evidence in the west of the graduated hierarchy of small and medium-sized holdings characteristic of many districts in the south and east. Nevertheless there were social differences and degrees of poverty within the ranks of the small tenants and they help to explain the different spatial and social impact of the famine after 1846 within the crofting region. The ability to sell an extra cow, plant a larger grain crop when the potatoes failed or draw on savings could make the difference between complete destitution and basic adequacy. In turn, these two possibilities depended on the position of the small tenant within the social hierarchy and the size and location of his croft.

Table 1.2. Tenants Paying £10 per Annum Rental or Less as Percentage of All Tenants, Crofting Districts, c.1850

Parish/Estate	%
Kilfinichen (Mull)	86
Kilmuir (Skye)	67
Snizort (Skye)	92
Portree (Skye)	86
Strath (Skye)	88
Sleat (Skye)	93
North Morar	67
Knoydart	82
Glenelg	71
Glenshiel	14
Lochalsh	91
Kintail	86
Lochcarron	86
Applecross	93
Torridon	90
Average	80

Source: McNeill Report, Appendix A, passim

Table 1.3 brings these points into sharper focus. It indicates the different economic levels which coexisted within a community where most lived in conditions of considerable poverty. The data suggest a wide range of cattle stocks among those tenants who paid annual rentals of £15 to £5. They also imply that the relative volume of potatoes as a percentage of cultivated acreage tended to increase proportionately in the smaller holdings and decline in the larger. It seems that holdings with rentals of £6 to £15 had a more varied pattern of cropping than those below them in the social scale.

But even this evidence presents too simple a picture. There was no necessary correlation between the size of holding, as defined by rental, and the economic standing of the tenant. Much depended, for example, on the quality of land. Townships which existed on moorland, wasteland or on mosses were notoriously among the most impoverished.[21] Economic opportunities also played a part. Earnings from temporary migration in the Lowlands were increasingly important to the population of the Western Highlands in the first half of the nineteenth century. However, the extent of dependence on this source of income varied markedly between districts.[22] Again, in areas such as Lewis, western Sutherland and Wester Ross, the key factor in economic status was often not acreage of land but the returns which accrued from fishing. In Lewis, for instance, crofting townships with fishing traditions were more able to maintain rental payment in years of distress than others, while, in Wester Ross, fishermen tenants renting tiny holdings at £3 per annum or less were often better off than crofters elsewhere with larger holdings and more cattle stock.[23] At the other extreme, communities which had specialised in kelp manufacture were very vulnerable by the 1840s due to the contraction of that industry and the associated decline in earnings. A detailed investigation into the rentals of the estates of Lord Macdonald in Skye between 1820 and 1855 reveals that the total of rent arrears tended to be markedly higher in townships where kelp production had concentrated than in other areas of the property.[24]

Table 1.3. Social Stratification of West Highland Crofting Townships, c.1850

Annual rental (£)	No. of references	Average cattle stock of tenancies	Average potatoes planted (barrells)	Average oats planted (barrells)
15	5	11.25	5	8.5
10	4	6.25	5.25	4.75
7	4	4.5	6	6.25
6	2	2	?	5
5	17	2.5	4.75	3
2-4	15	1.84	3.23	2.85

Source: McNeill Report, Appendix A, *passim*

Notes: (i) 1 'barrell' = 4 bushels.
    (ii) 'Average cattle stock' refers to numbers recorded on croft holdings in 1851. They almost certainly suggest depletion in numbers of cattle as a result of the famine.
    (iii) Evidence cited from Mull, Skye, Wester Ross, Lewis, Harris, North Uist, South Uist and Barra.

The problems associated with defining standards in any simple fashion are compounded by the vicissitudes of changes over time. Material conditions varied profoundly with alterations in climate, the erratic movement of the herring in the sea lochs and the fluctuating returns from temporary migration. Yet there can be little doubt that many crofters endured an existence of profound insecurity. For the smaller men in particular destitution was always a threat and often a reality even in favourable climatic circumstances. But not all were in this position. There were considerable differences in economic standards from area to area, township to township and even within the social fabric of individual townships. This complexity forms the essential background to the varied impact of the potato famine after 1846 throughout the crofting region.

In an even more hazardous position than most crofters was the cottar class. In 1847 the main organisation responsible for famine relief described them thus:

The cottars possess nothing but the cottage which shelters them, and depend on the kindness of neighbours for a few patches of ground for potatoes, and supply their other wants by fishing, and such work as they may obtain at home or abroad. The latter class live at all times in a constant struggle for the means of bare subsistence, and do not rise above the lowest scale of living necessary for existence, not to talk of comfort. In some seasons they are frequently reduced to live upon such shell-fish as they can collect, with a little milk etc.[25]

The main defining characteristic of the cottars was that they were not recognised tenants of land. Yet the distinction between the poorer crofters and the cottars was often blurred.[26] Even those who were described as officially 'landless' usually possessed a small patch of land which they normally devoted to potato cultivation. Their origins were varied. Small colonies of cottars were attached to the larger farms to supply the seasonal labour force.[27] Others were subtenants of crofters who paid a rental direct to them rather than the landlord. Some were allocated land in the 'half-foot' system by which the main tenant furnished a patch of land and seed corn to the cottar. He in turn provided the labour for cultivation of the crop which, when harvested, was divided between tenant and subtenant.[28] Cottars were also often the kinsmen of tenants. Sons and sons-in-law were allowed to build houses on the family lot.[29] Control over such subdivision was beginning to occur in the 1820s and 1830s but apparently only became widespread and really effective during and after the potato famine itself.[30]

Again, some cottars were former tenants who had suffered eviction and descended the social scale as a result. Many of those dispossessed in the early nineteenth century tended to congregate in the scattered villages of the West Highland region.[31] Colonies of impoverished cottars were to be found by the 1840s in Tobermory in Mull, Lochaline in Morvern, Arnisdale in Glenelg, Ullapool, Lochcarron and Scoraig in Wester Ross and in many other similar settlements. These villages all suffered grievous distress during the potato famine.[32] Finally, the small artisan class of the Highlands – carpenters, blacksmiths, shoemakers and weavers – were invariably also cottars with a small plot of land and the possibility of growing a potato crop.[33]

The cottar class was very numerous. On Lord Macdonald's Skye estates there were 1300 families who did not pay rent, '. . . chiefly relatives of the tenants, such as sons and sons-in-law, sometimes two or three of them are on the lot'.[34] On Macleod of Macleod's property on the same island, it was estimated that for every tenant family there were two cottar families.[35] In Harris 450 tenants paid rent but a further 400 families existed as cottars on the estates.[36] Similarly in Barra, more than half of those who held some land were not registered in the rental book.[37] In Skye in the later 1840s there were 1900 crofter families and 1531 cottars.[38] The majority of the inhabitants of Glenelg, North Morar and Knoydart were also nominally landless.[39] On the Duke of Argyll's estate in Mull cottars outnumbered tenants. There were 1455 members of tenant families and 1533 members of cottar families. In Tiree, sixty-three per cent of the population belonged to tenant families and thirty-seven per cent (1838) to cottar families.[40] It is plain that the number of cottars varied significantly between estates but in many of the Hebridean islands they often comprised as much as half and sometimes more of the entire population.

The cottars contributed in a significant way to the vulnerability of West Highland society. Even in good seasons, they eked out a precarious existence close to the margin of subsistence. They were unlikely to possess much in the way of savings to tide them over bad seasons. Their patches of land were so small that only the potato, the highest yielding crop available, was normally cultivated. Of all the inhabitants of the crofting region, the cottars were most committed to monoculture.[41] Again, the small tenant class could not necessarily remain detached from the plight of the cottars. On some estates, the distinction between the two groups was wholly artificial. In many districts, cottars were simply members of extended families living in separate households but gaining a living from the same small area of land. In bad seasons, it was common for cottars to obtain assistance from the rent-paying tenants, a custom which was often seen as the discharge of kinship obligation.[42] It followed, therefore, that when subsistence crisis occurred the resources of the tenant class in some districts were likely to be partially shared, not simply within the tenant household but with kinfolk whose plots of land were not enough to maintain an entirely secure existence even in favourable seasons. Almost certainly this obligation extended beyond the ranks of family members. Contemporary observers stressed how marginal elements in the society could only survive because of the widespread assistance they received from their neighbours in time of need. This they attributed to an active tradition of community concern for the maintenance of the poor in a society which, as late as the 1840s, still lacked a meaningful public provision funded from legal assessment of the region's ratepayers.[43]

The Origins of Crofting

Crofting preserved the traditional peasant connection with the land. This has tended to convey the impression that it was an archaic remnant from an older era, a reflection of Highland conservatism and social inertia. In fact, the croft system was as innovative in the Highland context as consolidated farms and Lothians husbandry in the Lowlands. It emerged in the second half of the eighteenth century and by *c*.1820 had changed the entire social map and settlement pattern of the Western Highlands and Islands.[44] In the early eighteenth century the dominant social formation in the region was the joint tenancy with land cultivated in runrig, pasture held in common and strong communal traditions associated with the varied tasks of herding, harvesting, peat-cutting, building and repair. Over two or three generations the joint farms were removed from most west Highland estates and replaced by a structure of small, separate, single smallholdings or 'crofts'. In all parishes in the region for which we have detailed records, at least eighty-six per cent and in most ninety-five per cent of holdings were rented at £20 per annum or less by the 1840s.[45]

There were a number of reasons why 'improvement' in the north-west produced this type of land fragmentation rather than the consolidation of holdings characteristic of most districts in the eastern Highlands. In the far west the proportion of cultivated to uncultivated land was estimated at between nine and fifteen per cent in 1800 and the tiny patches of arable were often separated by extensive stretches of moor and rough grazing.[46] The fashionable system of bigger farms based on mixed husbandry, which brought increasing prosperity to other areas of Scotland, was not technically possible in the Western Highlands. Crofting was a response both to the natural limitations and to the assumed economic potential of the region. Late eighteenth-century publicists argued that the maritime resources of the Western Highlands in both fish and kelp (an alkali extract from seaweed used in the manufacture of soap and glass) were richer by far than those of the land. It became common to emphasise the benefits of a division of labour, of a dual economy which would efficiently combine the pastoral potential of the interior and the quasi-industrial potential of the coast.[47] The impoverished population of the inner straths should be relocated in the maritime districts and there encouraged both to earn a living and produce higher rentals by engaging in the labour-intensive activities of fishing and kelping. The rich grazing available inland might at the same time be laid down to large sheep farms.

Such a programme of action had powerful theoretical and practical attractions. In the 1790s and early 1800s demand for Highland kelp reached hitherto unknown levels as industrialisation widened markets and the Napoleonic Wars restricted the supply of cheaper Spanish barilla. The herring fishery also flourished as the shoals began to visit the sea lochs on a regular basis. Moreover, the crofting system was in theory an attractive solution to the problem posed by an increasing population in an era of agrarian rationalisation. Resettlement seemed in the short term to promise a reduction in the social costs of outright eviction. It transformed communities made redundant by the development of a more efficient form of pastoral husbandry into a productive asset and significant source of revenue.

It had three particular advantages. First, like their counterparts in the north-eastern counties of Aberdeen and Banff and some other parts of Scotland, Highland landlords viewed the settlement of colonies of crofters at nominal rents as an economical way of bringing into cultivation some part of the large stretches of waste and moor land which dominated whole areas of their estates.[48] It was characteristic of late eighteenth-century optimism that these tracts were deemed ripe for reclamation. They seemed to present a major challenge for an area rich in abundant and underemployed resources of labour but poor in arable land.[49] Expansion of small-holdings into waste land was likely anyway as numbers increased and areas of existing settlement no longer sufficed for all the people who now had to be fed. Second, the increasing prosperity of illicit whisky-making in the later eighteenth century encouraged landlords in some districts to divide holdings and encourage subdivision among kinfolk in order to accommodate a larger population able to sustain a higher rental from 'industrial' earnings.[50] Third, during the great wars of the later eighteenth century, there was a huge expansion in the recruitment of Highlanders to regiments of the British army. Several proprietors became military entrepreneurs, raising family regiments from the men of their estates in return for payment from the state. It became common on the properties of Lord Macdonald, the Duke of Argyll and the Duke of Sutherland, among others, for land to be allocated in return for service. In the process, the division of holdings accelerated.[51] One reason given for the proliferation of subdivision in Tiree in the 1820s was that 'four fencible regiments of men' had been raised during the Napoleonic Wars by the Duke of Argyll. Plots were carved out of existing tenancies to accommodate those who had served in them.[52]

Between the middle decades of the eighteenth and early nineteenth centuries, numerous communities of joint-tenants were displaced and moved to form the crofting townships which have formed the characteristic settlement pattern of the Western Highlands and Islands ever since that time. Since both kelping, whisky-making and fishing were highly seasonal, some land had to be made available to provide food and fuel for a part of the year. But too much land would act as a powerful distraction from other more profitable tasks. These crofters were to be labourers first and agriculturists only second. The townships in which they lived were essential quasi-industrial communities in which rents were raised beyond their limited agricultural potential in order to force dependence on the produce of the sea, the loch and the shore. The central weakness in the entire system was that most smallholdings were simply not designed to provide enough for the needs of a normal-sized family from subsistence cultivation. It was reckoned in the early 1850s that only crofts rented at £15 per annum could produce secure self-sufficiency from agricultural activity in average seasons.[53] The overwhelming majority of holdings in the Western Highlands were valued at £10 per annum or less.

The scenario for potential disaster only became clear after the Napoleonic Wars. Until the second decade of the nineteenth century, earnings from the non-agricultural employments had been on the increase. There is little evidence, however, that the flow of income to the regional economy promoted either much in the way of social mobility or a rising level of savings within the peasant community. It seems more likely that much of what was earned was absorbed in higher rental payments, the funding of a rising population and expenditure on meal imports from the Lowlands in times of scarcity.[54] But by the 1820s the entire economic edifice on which the croft system had been first constructed was crumbling rapidly. The renewal of trade with Spain, allowing the importation of Spanish barilla, the repeal of the salt duties and new production refinements within the chemical industry, destroyed the prosperity of kelp manufacture. Illicit whisky-making on a commercial scale had virtually disappeared in most areas by the 1830s as a result of changes in revenue legislation and greater efficiency on the part of the excise service. Earnings from military employment fell away rapidly after 1815 and instead there was considerable return migration of both demobbed soldiers and sailors which added further to the demographic pressures already present in several districts. Although the herring fishery survived and in some years in the 1830s managed to equal the good times of the 1790s, activity was much more sporadic and the fish disappeared from several lochs for long periods. On the eve of the potato famine, the fishing villages of Plockton, Dornie, Tobermory, Lochcarron and Shieldaig, the fruits of the era of high optimism in the later eighteenth and early nineteenth centuries, were regarded as among the poorest communities on the west coast.[55]

By the 1840s, then, the fatal weakness of the crofting system had finally been exposed. The non-agricultural sources of income on which its success depended had either evaporated completely or had become too precarious to maintain a secure living. The numbers dependent on kelp manufacture itself were variously estimated at between 25,000 and 40,000 people, and several thousands in addition had relied on other occupations for a livelihood. Whole communities had been established on narrow tracts of marginal land which were not intended to provide enough to feed their inhabitants and at the same time produce a surplus to pay rents from agriculture alone. There was a parallel here between the plight of the handloom weavers of Lowland Scotland and the peasantry of the Western Highlands. Both were victims of a wider economic process which concentrated industrial production in fewer centres and undermined the traditional employment structure of peripheral districts. The ebbing of 'industrial' employment from the Highlands after *c*.1815 reflected the fact that, like many rural areas, it did not possess the resources, the markets or the entrepreneurship to compete against the manufacturing towns of the central Lowlands. In the view of some contemporary observers only one crop, the potato, stood between the people of the Western Highlands and Islands and even greater calamities.

A Potato Economy?

The chronology of development of the potato as a food crop in the Scottish Highlands is relatively well documented.[56] The first specific reference occurs in Martin Martin's account of the Hebrides in 1695, although by 1750 cultivation of the crop was still relatively uncommon. The period of greatest expansion was probably the last quarter of the eighteenth and first few decades of the nineteenth centuries. By 1790 potatoes were being grown widely as a subsistence crop. Their importance was highlighted during the grain harvest failures of 1782-3 when they helped to save many communities from complete starvation. Potato cultivation seems also to have developed in acreage and intensity after the end of the Napoleonic Wars. Dr. John Macculloch, who travelled annually in the Western Highlands between 1811 and 1821, was only one of several observers to comment on its increasing significance.[57] In 1811, James Macdonald claimed that potatoes constituted four-fifths of the nourishment of Hebrideans.[58] In 1798 the parish of Kilmuir in Skye produced 1600 bolls of oats and bere and 5000 barrels of potatoes. By 1840 there had been a slight increase in grain cultivation to 1618 bolls but the volume of potatoes produced had multiplied more than sixfold to 32,000 barrels.[59] It is hardly surprising, therefore, that R.N. Salaman could describe the crop as 'the cornerstone of the social structure of the Western Highlands in the first half of the nineteenth century'.[60] It is probable that the productivity of the potato helps to explain why, despite economic collapse after *c*.1820, there was still a larger population living in the crofting region by the 1840s than three decades earlier.

The Scottish Highlands, like Ireland, seem to have adopted the potato relatively quickly and earlier than many other parts of Europe. The new crop faced much resistance both from customers and peasant farmers on the Continent.[61] In the Baltic provinces in the early nineteenth century, people regarded it as a danger to health. In Russia, determined efforts by the state to require peasants to plant potatoes set off a train of violent opposition known as the 'potato revolts'. As late as 1788 Arthur Young found considerable resistance to potatoes in many areas of France. The plant's rapid conquest of the Highlands depended to some extent on its intrinsic advantages.

Potatoes grow in virtually any soil, adjust to different climates but flourish best where the weather is cool and moist. They also allow for a dramatic increase in food supply without the need for radical changes in traditional methods of cultivation, technology or social organisation. In the Western Highlands the crop was grown in the lazy-bed system.[62] Soil was turned with the *caschrom*. Earth from ditches dug between different ridges was cast on top. Seeds were broadcast and the ridges well manured with seaweed, of which there was an abundant supply in the maritime districts, and animal manure. Once dug, potatoes were ready for the pot and unlike the staple grains did not require any additional labour to make them edible. They were easy to store but quickly lost their nutritional content if kept over long periods. The calorific content of a given quantity of potatoes was considerably less than the same amount of grain. But since potatoes had a much greater yield, an acre under potatoes provided as much as three to five times as many calories as an acre in grain crop.[63] They can provide all human nutritional needs. As two modern nutritionists have put it, 'Potatoes are the only single cheap food that can support life when fed as the *sole* (their italics) article of diet'.[64]

But the widespread adoption of the potato in the Highlands cannot be explained simply in terms of the basic advantages of the crop. Only in the crofting region did potatoes assume overall dominance in the diet of the majority of the population.[65] This suggests that they suited the natural limitations but also met the social and economic needs of the region. In the eighteenth century, the people of the Western Highlands and Islands lived close to the very margin of subsistence. Famine was always a threat and, in several years, a reality.[66] Any food resource which would provide more security was a welcome addition. One significant factor was that oats tended to ripen later in the Western Highlands than elsewhere in Scotland. The earliest potatoes, however, were available in August, two to three months earlier than the oat crop. They therefore helped to fill part of the gap in the period between the consumption of the old grain harvest and the collection of the new. The grain crop was notoriously vulnerable and yields in most areas were relatively low. One Highland proprietor graphically described in 1851 the climatic obstacles which frustrated grain cultivation in the Hebrides:

> Seasons no doubt vary; but it will scarcely be controverted by any one who has resided for years in these regions – winter as well as summer – that in three out of every five seasons, the springs are wet – the summers cold – and the harvest abounding with drenching tempests of rain. Referring to cases where the land has been thoroughly drained, as on many large farms, it often happens that from the long and continued heavy drenching rain of winter, the land is too wet for the plough until the middle of March, but it is chiefly in harvest that the principal danger to the corn crops arises, particularly in slopes and exposed places from the effects of the tempests of wind and rain, in shaking and lodging the corn, in its late ripening, and the great uncertainty of drying and securing it in any tolerable condition when cut . . .[67]

Yields from the oat crop, and to a lesser extent from bere, varied both over time and space. But, as Table 1.4 indicates, they were usually abysmally low and often of a standard comparable with peasant agriculture before the eighteenth century. In 1814 it was estimated that oat yields in Scotland as a whole varied between ten and sixteen pecks per boll and in 'the best cultivated counties' from thirteen to eighteen pecks per

Table 1.4. Oat Yields, Western Highlands and Islands, c.1851

Parish/District	Yield from Seed
Iona	
Kilfinichen	4-5
Kilfinan	6
Portree	3-4
Snizort	1½
Snizort	2
Snizort	4
Duirnish	3
Duirnish	3
Duirnish	2
Sleat	3½
Lochcarron	2
Applecross	3
Applecross	4
Gairloch	3
Stornoway	3½-4
Stornoway	3
Barvas	4
Lochs	2½
Uig	2
Uig	6
Harris	3
Harris	4
Harris	3½
S. Uist	3
Benbecula	3
Tiree	3-4
	3½
Average	3.29

Source: McNeill Report, Appendix A, *passim*

boll. But in the Western Highlands the average was a return of four to six pecks.[68] In this respect, the potato had a crucial advantage. The produce of grain in the Hebrides was often no more than one-third of land elsewhere in Scotland, but the return from the potato was equal or superior.[69] The heavy rainfall and high winds which harassed grain farmers were often a positive advantage to potato cultivation in the crofting districts. They provided a natural protection against the 'curl', the most destructive potato disease of the eighteenth century. It is now known that the greenfly which spreads the disease rarely moves from a host plant when the wind rises above eight miles per hour. Heavy rainfall washes plants clear of the parasite altogether.[70] The potato was not invulnerable, but until the partial failure of 1836-7, the crop was mainly damaged by early frosts. In the first few decades of the nineteenth century at least it promised a much more secure return than grain.

Yet the major attraction of the potato lay not simply in the fact that it lowered the threshold of risk. It also had an extraordinarily high yield. In Mull a normal yield would be twelve barrels for each one planted.[71] In parts of Skye it was between eight and ten barrels and in Lochalsh six to eight.[72] Sir John Sinclair estimated that four times as many people could be supported by an acre of potatoes as by an acre of oats.[73] As the greatest yielder of food of any crop known in the early nineteenth century it therefore formed an integral part of the social and economic changes which spread through the Highlands between 1750 and 1840. The cultivation of the potato expanded with such speed not simply because of its intrinsic merits but because the development of crofting, the movement of communities into areas of waste and marginal land and the subdivision of holdings could not have occurred on the same scale without widespread adoption of the new crop. It was almost a precondition of the social revolution which swept over the Scottish Highlands in this period.

Four factors were fundamental. First, the minuscule holdings formed to support kelpers, whisky producers and fishermen could only provide a subsistence living because of the high yields derived from potato cultivation. Both communities depended on seasonal work. The potato provided support for much of the rest of the year and especially during the winter and spring. Second, the further fragmentation of lots among cottars and kinsmen was facilitated by the adoption of the potato. The evidence suggests that the smaller the holding, the greater the reliance placed on the crop.[74] Third, potatoes were very well suited to the policies of clearance and relocation pursued by Highland landlords. They could be grown in all soils except stiff clay. It was partly because of the potato that new communities could be established on narrow strips of land on coast, moorland and mosses.[75] One contemporary claimed that, 'It is by the potato crop that all the wild land has hitherto been reclaimed'.[76] The capacity of the potato to support evicted people on small patches of land helps to explain why clearance in the Western Highlands resulted in much dispossession but did not necessarily produce wholesale regional depopulation in the short term.

Fourth, the potato became even more vital after the Napoleonic Wars. Sir John Sinclair estimated that the typical crofter had to be able to obtain at least 200 days of additional work outside his holding to escape destitution.[77] But external employment within the Highlands contracted in the 1820s and 1830s in some areas and disappeared entirely in others. At the same time, there was a slump in cattle prices. The price of a three-year-old, which in 1810 had stood at about £6, had, by the 1830s, fallen to around £3.10/-.[78] Black cattle had traditionally been the peasant's store of value and an important means of both paying rental and covering the costs of meal imports in seasons of scarcity. Modern research suggests that cattle stocks were diminishing over time and that many small tenants and cottars by the 1830s had only one or two beasts or none at all.[79] In a survey of holdings of stock in thirty-four tenancies, in a wide sample of areas, rented at £6 per annum or less, the average number of cattle ranged between 2.5 and 1.84 per holding.[80] This was substantially less than was allowed for in rental agreements. Almost certainly these difficulties in the pastoral sector dictated a greater reliance on the arable patch than hitherto and hence on the potato.

The pressures making for increased dependence on the crop were so great that A.J. Youngson has been able to describe the Highlands in the first decades of the nineteenth century as '. . . almost a potato economy'.[81] The remark has some validity in that it brings out the crucial importance of the crop in the life of the population as a principal source of food. However, generalisation about any aspect of Highland experience is difficult in this period and Youngson's phrase disguises the diversity of diet and cropping which still existed despite the popularity of the potato. As one contemporary noted, '. . . the state of the Highlands varies so much in different places, that it is not easy to form any estimate of the relative proportion in which grain and potatoes enter into the food of the people'.[82] In broad terms, the potato seems to have been of most significance in the poorest and most congested districts where alternative employments to agriculture were few. Thus the Central Relief Board concluded in 1847 that the potato throughout the Highlands was 'the principal produce of the ground under tillage, and the principal article of food for the people'. But in the eastern and central Highlands it reckoned that it formed one-half of the subsistence of the people, in the western districts 'fully three-quarters' and, in the islands, the potato was 'the principal means of subsistence'.[83]

But there was also considerable variation within the western and insular zone itself. In 1846 the Free Church conducted its own detailed investigation into the relative importance of potatoes in the diet of the people in forty-four representative areas within the western region.[84] In fifteen, or thirty-four per cent, of the localities surveyed, they formed between one-half to three-quarters of food consumption. These included five parishes in Sutherland, where the great clearances of the early nineteenth century had markedly reduced population density and so possibly diminished reliance on the crop. On the other hand, in thirty-two per cent of the areas examined, potatoes accounted for up to four-fifths of the diet of the people. These included one Sutherland parish, Assynt, where population congestion was much greater than elsewhere in the county, not least because numbers in it had grown as a result of the resettlement of evictees from the interior straths. Such villages as Plockton, Lochcarron and Shieldaig, which contained large populations of semi-landless people, likewise had a high potato dependency. But there was little uniformity even within the same island or mainland area. According to the Free Church inquiry, potatoes formed half the subsistence in the parish of Kilmuir in Skye but eleven-twelfths of the diet in Bracadale, an adjoining parish on the same island. In general terms, however, they were most important in the Hebrides. Of thirteen districts most reliant on potatoes, nine were islands or within islands. Overall the relative significance of the crop varied in relation to local economic specialisation, population pressure, availability of land and social structure. Where the number of cottars was greatest there also the potato would be most crucial to food supply.[85]

It is reasonably clear, however, that few districts had the overwhelming reliance on potatoes which characterised some sections of the population in parts of the poor west of Ireland. The diet of most of the peasantry was meagre (though nutritious) but was not restricted to any one food. Dr. John Macculloch in the 1820s noted how in some areas potato consumption was equal to that of grain, in a few even greater and in some others less. However, he '. . . found no place where, as in Ireland, the potato is the exclusive article of vegetable diet'.[86] Macculloch's comments are confirmed from the data assembled in Table 1.3 (p.7) and by contemporary comments on dietary patterns in the Western Highlands. Thus after the crop failures of 1836-7, two of the leading members of the relief committees which brought aid to the distressed region reported that, 'The food of the great proportion of the people is both poor and scanty. It consists chiefly of potatoes, meal made of oats and barley, prepared in different forms, with herrings and milk in its natural or coagulated state. Butcher meat or tea are luxuries which they seldom or never enjoy'.[87] Again, in one of the poorest communities on the west coast, the inhabitants of the village of Lochcarron (Jeantown) consumed potatoes and herring twice a day and oatmeal gruel for supper.[88] In many areas, it was common for potatoes to form the main source of food for a part of the year and meal with fish for the remainder.[89]

Grain supplies plainly continued to be widely available despite the increasing scale of potato cultivation. They derived not simply from domestic sources but from the meal trade which had existed from time immemorial between the pastoral Highlands and the more arable Lowlands.[90] Meal imports continued to flow annually into the region. They were paid for by sales (albeit at lower prices than those current between *c*.1795 to *c*.1810) of black cattle, earnings from the increasing volume of temporary migration and the occasional bonanza of a good year's herring fishery.[91] It should also be remembered that grain prices fell on trend during the 1820s and early 1830s, and while the crofter's purchasing power may have declined at this time, so also did the cost of this most vital import. In the early 1840s, an 'immense quantity of meal' was imported annually into Wester Ross. It was reckoned that about 2000 bolls were purchased by the people of the Ullapool district and a similar quantity by those of Gairloch.[92] The great grain imports which took place during the potato famine years represented the expansion of this well-established and important commerce.

Furthermore, the relative failure or stagnation of commercial herring fishing in many areas in the 1820s and 1830s should not obscure the enduring significance of the commercial white fishery for cod and ling and subsistence fishing. Ironically, the same shifts of population and changes in land tenure which promoted potato cultivation probably also encouraged greater dependence than before on the produce of the sea. Some observers noted how the movement of population to the coast and the creation of the system of maritime crofts had substantially increased fish consumption: '. . . the facility of taking fish is generally very great all along the coasts of the maritime Highlands and there are very few cottages without a share, at least, in a boat . . .'.[93] Coal fish or cuddy were the staple diet because they could be caught throughout the year, in many places without boats. Rods or landing nets sufficed in the sheltered bays and sea lochs of many insular and mainland areas.[94] Cod and herring were also extensively fished. Sir John McNeill reported of the crofters: 'Of fresh fish they can almost always command a supply, for in those districts there are few crofts that are far from the coast'.[95] In scarce seasons it was noted in Sutherland that '. . . in general the maritime inhabitants suffered little, compared to those who have no access to fish'.[96] Communities with more reliance on white fishing than on pastoral farming included Durness and Edderachillis in Sutherland, Gairloch, Applecross and Lochcarron in Wester Ross and parts of Skye, Lewis and Barra.[97] The disappearance of the herring from several districts had reduced some communities to deep poverty but it had not entirely deprived them of the opportunity to obtain a subsistence from the sea by fishing for other species. Moreover, the collection of shellfish, not simply in seasons of scarcity, but as a necessity in normal times during the summer months before the grain and potato crops were harvested, was very common in South Uist, Barra, parts of Skye and some localities in Sutherland.[98]

Throughout the region, then, the potato had become a central component of the diet of the people. Its failure between 1846 and the early 1850s was likely to threaten a social catastrophe on a huge scale. Yet, the continued significance of meal and fish would at least help to diminish if not entirely eliminate the dangers of widespread starvation.

Sheep Clearances and Subsistence Crisis

Some contemporary commentators and later polemicists claimed that the main origin of destitution in the Highlands lay in the great clearances carried out to establish sheep farms before 1840.[99] They asserted that these at once deprived the peasantry of their lands and, at the same time, forced the people to eke out an existence on uneconomic holdings on the coast which left them vulnerable to the disastrous consequences of the potato blight. The problem with this question is that it is very difficult to resolve in precise or unequivocal terms. No authoritative aggregate figures yet exist of the scale of land losses during the removals, and not all land under sheep farms had previously been cultivated. Enumeration of the number and location of evictions is problematic because most observers and the contemporary press were primarily interested in large-scale clearances and ignored for the most part the less dramatic but probably more typical process of gradual thinning of the population in relatively small numbers over long periods of time. Equally intractable is the task of separating out and weighing the 'clearance variable' from the other influences which caused Highland poverty in the first half of the nineteenth century. The effects of individual clearances also varied over time, space and in relation to prevailing economic conditions. Those which occurred in the 1800s when the bi-employments were still in an expansionist phase, were not likely to have the same social consequences as the evictions which took place in the era of economic deflation after the end of the Napoleonic Wars. For these reasons no final, convincing quantitative balance sheet of the impact of clearance or of its significance in the origins of famine can be drawn up.

It is clear, nevertheless, that the sheep clearances must be considered in any analysis of the background to the disasters of the 1840s. By that decade widespread evictions to establish large pastoral farms had occurred throughout most parts of the region which experienced the most acute levels of distress during the potato famine. From *c*.1820 to *c*.1840 as kelping profits receded, commercial pastoralism took an even greater hold than hitherto throughout the Hebrides. On the island of Harris, seven townships 'were cleared at one stroke'. The whole of the west side, a stretch of forty miles from Rodel to Loch Eisort, was depopulated. 'Hundreds were dispossessed'.[100] A detailed survey of Harris carried out by the estate factor in 1846 described the effect on the island's social structure:

> This Country seems occupied by four classes. 1st. Large tenants of Pasture Farms, varying from 35,000 acres downwards, of whom there are only 4 or 5. 2nd. A very poor class of small tenants, with rents varying from 50/- to £9 per annum, these huddled together on the island of Bernera and the East Bays on ground generally of the most miserable description or quite insufficient in extent for their support, but who hitherto

maintained themselves by such potatoes and grain as they could raise in their small-holdings . . .[101]

Similarly in 1826 and 1828 large sheep farms were established in Rhum and Muck.[102] In 1841, eleven townships were cleared by Lord Macdonald's factors in North Uist: '. . . unfortunately the fall in the value of kelp renders . . . a change in the management of the North Uist property necessary . . . it becomes necessary that a number of the small tenants be removed and the land let for grazing'.[103] Clearances were also very extensive in this period in Mull, parts of Lewis, South Uist and Skye, especially in the parish of Bracadale.[104] Only the islands of Barra, Tiree, Jura and several areas in Lewis apparently remained relatively insulated from the marked increase in eviction and land consolidation which took place in the 1820s and 1830s.[105]

However, one must resist the temptation to draw a simple and automatic connection between these clearances and the onset of the great crisis of the 1840s. For a start, the Western Highlands was a society already close to the margin of subsistence before the removals took place. Low agricultural productivity, poor climate and primitive transport systems ensured that scarcity and local famines were endured almost as a fact of life in the eighteenth and early nineteenth centuries. The severe shortages of the 1690s, 1740, 1751, 1756, 1782-3, 1806-7, 1811 and 1816-17 emphasised the vulnerability of the Highlands to climatic deterioration and 'exposed the Achilles heel of the regional economy.'[106] The strain of population on resources was already so great that in some districts an estimated one-third to one-half of the gross income from cattle sales was expended on the purchase of meal.[107] In addition, during the famine of the 1840s there was no necessary or obvious correlation between areas which had experienced sheep clearances and those which experienced the worst levels of distress. In the opinion of the Central Relief Board, the islands of Barra and Tiree suffered most. Yet neither experienced major removals for sheep farming before 1846.[108] Similarly, the plight of the people in the interior townships of Knockan and Elphin in Assynt was more serious than that of any of the other communities on the Sutherland estate. However, they had been left untouched by the major evictions which took place on that property in the second and third decades of the nineteenth century.[109]

Nor can large-scale eviction *per se* necessarily be regarded as a cause of destitution. The growth of the new system of farming throughout the Scottish Lowlands was itself prefaced by the wholesale removal of many communities of small tenants and cottagers. These 'clearances' were the necessary precondition for the régime of more efficient farms which released employment opportunities for some of the dispossessed in the short term and, in the long run, contributed to the growth of both rural and national levels of income.[110] It was the same pattern in several parishes in the central and eastern Highlands. The removal of people was accompanied by heavy migration and agrarian improvements which sustained a more secure existence for the minority who remained. The Rev. Thomas Maclauchlan, a bitter critic of the clearance system in the Western Highlands, stressed its different effects elsewhere:

There are districts where eviction has relieved the population who remain, by leaving room for judicious management on the part of the landowners, improving the condition of their tenantry by furnishing them with suitable holdings. In the valleys of the Spey, the Findhorn and the Nairn, the effect of this is very manifest. A declining population had led to a marked amelioration in the appearance of the country and in the condition of the people. In these extensive districts the lands are chiefly held by the native tenantry, but these have received at the hands of judicious and considerate landlords such treatment, as that they have risen rapidly with the general improvement of the country and all parties have been gainers.[111]

Even in the Western Highlands and Islands, the effects of clearances were very varied. Each series of evictions had its own particular micro-history. Where the bulk of the people who were cleared also emigrated, either at their own expense or supported by their landlords, the social impact would obviously be less damaging than where communities were resettled in already congested townships. Thus 400 left Rhum when their lands were consolidated in 1826.[112] Clearances on the estates of Lord Macdonald in Skye and North Uist were also followed by the emigration of 3250 people between 1838 and 1842.[113]

The social problems associated with clearance did not directly or necessarily derive from evictions alone but depended ultimately on the prevailing local economic conditions and the response of the dispossessed. When examined over the long term and in a broader historical context, the Clearances were the *result* rather than the *cause* of Highland economic weakness and the absence of a structure of employment which would absorb more of the region's inhabitants in relative economic security. But conditions in the Western Highlands were such that clearances to create sheep farms did at least aggravate social problems. No secure sector of employment emerged to absorb those who lost their land. Indeed, many evictions took place as a response to the contraction of kelping and the uncertainties of fishing. In addition, clearances were not always followed by a fall in local population. Where they were, as in Sutherland and the islands of Rhum and Muck, the impact of the potato blight was much less severe than elsewhere.[114] Many estates, however, tried to exploit the labour power of the cleared populations by settling them on waste land, on patches of land on the coast and in fishing villages.[115] Even when such policies were not enforced there was a generally permissive attitude to subdivision and squatters were allowed to occupy poor tracts of land and scrape a bare subsistence through potato cultivation. Many of those who had lost their holdings clung on at the fringes of the great sheep farms, on inferior land, in congested townships and villages, as cottars rather than tenants.

What made matters worse was that in the view of some contemporary observers it was often the poorest who remained.[116] They claimed that those with some means preferred to emigrate to North America or Australia. Some confirmation of the impoverished condition of the victims of clearance who remained at home is available in the evidence of the period. Eleven townships were cleared in Glenelg and large farms created in their place.[117] In 1841 the parish's census enumerator described how, 'Within the last fifty years all the more affluent inhabitants have emigrated . . . and few remained behind, except such as have not the means of removing, but these are now crowded together on limited portions of the soil, whose produce is entirely inadequate to their support'.[118] A few years later an analysis of the social composition of part of the parish population revealed that thirty-five per cent of families had no land, fifty-one per cent had one acre or less and only four per cent more than five acres. Seventy-one per cent of families were classified as cottars.[119] Evictions seem to have produced similar results in Glenshiel, Arisaig, Lochaber and Torridon.[120] Many of those at the bottom of the social scale sought refuge in the small towns of the Western Highlands such as Oban, Tobermory and Stornoway or in the villages of Plockton, Dornie and Ullapool originally built to act as the centres for the great expansion in herring fishing predicted in the later eighteenth century.[121]

There is little doubt, therefore, that the sheep clearances intensified congestion and promoted destitution in certain districts. But even if the analysis is confined to their short-term effects they were not the only or even the principal causes of poverty. Later analysis will demonstrate that there was a more convincing correlation between areas which had specialised in kelp manufacture and the most profound level of destitution after 1846. This pattern helps to explain why islands such as Tiree and Barra, where there were few large sheep farms before the 1840s, suffered so much during the great destitution while counties like Sutherland, where large-scale pastoral husbandry was dominant, escaped relatively lightly. The fundamental weakness of the society was that indigenous employment opportunities ebbed away while population continued to rise. The sheep clearances aggravated this problem but did not cause it.

Overpopulation

To several observers at the time and some later historians the essential problem of Highland society was the increase in population which had taken place since the later eighteenth century. In this view the crisis which beset the region had been brought about by Malthusian pressures. As Allan Fullarton and Charles Baird argued in 1837: 'We do not profess to be unqualified Malthusians, yet we much fear that the comparative statement of the population of the Highlands and Islands . . . will strongly tend to confirm the leading doctrines of that unpopular and much maligned sect. At all events it proves that the population has increased with a degree of rapidity seldom exemplified in an old and poor country . . .'.[122] In fact, as Table 1.5 demonstrates, the real rate of growth in West Highland population was in relative terms comparatively modest and in most years between 1801 and 1841 lower than that of England and Wales, Ireland and Scotland as a whole. Only between 1811 and 1821 was the annual average growth rate almost as great as that of Scotland but this was essentially an artificial pattern, temporarily inflated by the return of demobilised soldiers to their homes after the end of the Napoleonic Wars.

Table 1.5. Annual Percentage Population Increase by Region and Country, 1801-40

Region	1801-10	1811-20	1821-30	1831-40
Ireland	1.34	1.34	1.34	0.51
England & Wales	1.34	1.67	1.48	1.36
Scotland	1.16	1.48	1.23	1.03
West Highlands	0.72	1.46	0.51	−0.03

Source: After Richards, *Highland Clearances*, I, 99

Note: The 'West Highlands' in these figures refers to the West Highland Survey Area as defined by F. Fraser Darling, *West Highland Survey*, (Oxford, 1955), 15-17. This is a marginally larger area than the 'crofting region' defined above and contains more parishes in Argyllshire than the latter.

Table 1.6. Emigration from West Highland Parishes noted by 1841 Census Enumerators

Parish	Total Emigration	Period
Tiree	200	'within these few years past'
N. Uist	'about 300 annually emigrated from the Island to Cape Breton'	
Gairloch	150-160	Since 1831
Edderachallis	333	Since 1831
Loth	65	Since 1831
Applecross	20-30 families	Since 1831
Glenshiel	37	Since 1831
Lochbroom	'Almost every year for a considerable time back a greater or less number have left for British North America' c.50	'last six months'
Glenelg	700	'last 30 years'
Bracadale	c.70	?
Harris	43 families	?
Kilmuir	c.600	Since 1831
Ardnamurchan	138	Since 1831
Morvern	12 families	'Within last 4 years'

Source: GRO, Census Enumerators' Schedules, Relevant Parishes, 1841

As Table 1.6 indicates the census enumerators in 1841 noted that emigration was occurring widely throughout the crofting region. The area's decadal growth rate, which stood at 7.5 per cent, 1801-1811, fell to 6.9 per cent, 1821-31, and 0.2 per cent, 1831-41. Of the sixty parishes in the crofting region, twenty-seven (forty-five per cent) had already reached their maximum population size by the census of 1831. The haemorrhage of people concentrated in specific years of crisis. One recent estimate suggests that between 1840 and 1842, in the aftermath of the poor harvests of 1837 and 1838, the Western Highlands lost three per cent of their 1841 population.[123]

The experience of a number of different areas, for example Ulster in the eighteenth century and north-east Scotland in the nineteenth century, is a reminder that in itself a growing population of smallholders need not necessarily result in social destitution. The problem in the Western Highlands was not so much a slow increase in population in the early nineteenth century as the development of a gross imbalance between numbers, resources and employment opportunities. The major drawback was the absence of viable industry to provide an alternative to the insecurities of peasant agriculture for the inhabitants of the region. In addition, between 1810 and 1846 some land resources, and especially the arable tracts available to the peasant population, contracted with the expansion of commercial pastoralism. The amount of land which went out of cultivation varied enormously but could be of considerable extent in certain areas. In the parish of Duirnish in Skye, for example, it was estimated that sixty-one per cent of arable once cultivated had disappeared from the holdings of the tenantry by *c.*1840.[124]

It may well be that the position was partly alleviated by the gathering pace of emigration. As has been recently argued, 'Had it not been so, the famine of 1846 . . . would probably have been as uncontrollable as it was in parts of Ireland'.[125] But the point ought not to be pressed too far. Assisted emigration was often associated with clearance and land consolidation. Not all the dispossessed were able to fund themselves or gain assisted passage to North America and Australia.[126] The lands of emigrants were not normally redistributed among the remaining small tenants when their neighbours departed. Emigration, therefore, need not necessarily relieve population pressure. It might, in certain circumstances, intensify it as the poor remnant of cleared communities was moved to inferior land.[127] The pace of the exodus also varied significantly between districts.[128] Of those parishes which reached their maximum level of population before the census of 1841, the great majority, sixty-three per cent, were on the western mainland and only thirty-seven per cent were in the islands. In the early 1840s, emigration was extensive from North Uist, but limited from the neighbouring island of Lewis. The population of the Small Isles fell from 1620 in 1821 to 993 in 1841 while South Uist rose from 6038 to 7327 over the same period. Congestion and depopulation could clearly coexist side by side as a result of the complicated interplay of landlord policies, clearances and schemes of assisted emigration.[129]

Despite the increasing volume of emigration there was no mass desertion from the land during the economic crisis which followed the end of the Napoleonic Wars. In 1841 there were 85,342 more people living in the West Highland Survey Area than the total recorded in the region at Webster's Census in the 1750s.[130] This represented a rise of seventy-four per cent over the period. The growth in emigration was significant, but equally relevant is the fact that depopulation was still limited to Sutherland and a few other districts. Even in areas of heavy emigration, such as Skye and parts of Wester Ross, numbers continued to rise until the 1840s.[131] A vital question, therefore, is not simply why the exodus of people began to gather speed after 1815 but why it did not do so more rapidly and so ease to a greater extent the social problems of certain parishes of the crofting region.

In the half-century before the potato famine the grip of the majority of the population on the land had not been completely broken. Eviction was more often than not followed by resettlement rather than outright expulsion. No entirely landless class emerged in this period. By the 1840s the Western Highlands was still a peasant society and its members possessed that tenacious attachment to land which is characteristic of all such societies. As the French historian, Pierre Goubert, has remarked, 'No peasant will voluntarily give up his land, be it only half a furrow'.[132] In similar vein, the parish minister of Duirnish in Skye explained how the people '. . . feel a blind and, therefore, a very powerful attachment to the rocks and glens amid which they were brought up – an almost invincible aversion to abandon them'. [133] Even grinding poverty could not easily or quickly dissolve these powerful social attitudes. After all, those who lived in the West Highlands had always had to contend with hardship and insecurity. They sought to achieve little more than a modest standard of subsistence. It was usually only in periods of harvest failure and great distress that there was evidence of a marked acceleration in the numbers leaving the region.

Moreover, the productivity of the land continued to increase because of a continued expansion in potato cultivation. As one contemporary noted, '. . . the potato has done more to prevent emigration than any device whatever'. [134] Temporary migration for work in the Lowlands also became increasingly important. [135] It peaked during the months of summer and autumn, the period of greatest hardship in the Highlands, the phase when the old grain and potato harvest had often been consumed and the new had yet to be gathered. While ensuring that there were fewer mouths to feed at this critical time, temporary migration also produced a flow of cash income into the north-west (since seasonal migrants had a very high propensity to save) which was used to buy meal and, to a lesser extent, defray rental payments. This support of the peasant way of life was, however, as insecure as any other and income from temporary migration fluctuated dramatically over time. Those who went south and east found jobs mainly in casual agricultural or industrial employment, the very sectors in which the labour market was most unstable.

The role of the landlord classes was also relevant. Their control over the land was absolute and they were in a powerful position to promote the movement of people out of the region by eviction, assisted emigration and prevention of subdivision. As has been seen, many proprietors did act in this way and their pursuit of these policies helps to explain the acceleration in out-migration characteristic of the decades after 1815. On the other hand, if all landlords had been intent on maximising their economic opportunities, the exodus of people would undoubtedly have been much more rapid and extensive. Only commercial pastoralism guaranteed secure rentals in the 1820s and 1830s. If the landlord class had placed the profit motive above all else, the crofting sector would have been crushed to an even greater extent than it actually was to accommodate more sheep. Sheep farming would not simply have become dominant but, in theory, might have quickly obtained a virtual monopoly of all Highland land. Emigration did not occur on a greater scale partly because several landlords refused to exploit their economic opportunities to the full and settled instead for a muddled response of partial clearance, inaction, indirect and direct subsidy to the people who lived on their estates and occasional attempts to sponsor assisted emigration.

The reasons why they were unwilling before 1846 to put into effect a strategy of fundamental economic rationalisation varied. Some were reluctant for paternalistic and humanitarian reasons and were discouraged by the unacceptable social costs of total clearance. [136] Others could not afford to incur the likely expenses of supporting emigration to North America. By c.1830, most hereditary estates in the Western Highlands were burdened with heavy debts and a process of massive transfer of ownership to new proprietors was already underway. Again, the crofting population had become less vital to the economic health of some properties. As the large sheep farms became established, so the small tenants furnished but a small and declining fraction of total rental.[137] Even this minor contribution fell in real terms as arrears accumulated among them in times of hardship. The threat of increased expenditure on famine relief or on poor rates to support the destitute could, and eventually did, compel action to remove the impoverished communities of smallholders.[138] As one of the officials associated with Highland relief measures in 1836-7 put it: 'It is absolutely necessary to have a compulsory provision for the poor . . . not merely that the really necessitous of all classes should be sustained, but also to force landlords and wealthier classes to look more to the improvement of the poor around them, to encourage migration, by paying at least part of the expense thereof, and to make them watch more carefully and take means to prevent in future an increase of a pauper population'.[139] But throughout the Western Highlands the Poor Law before 1840 was '. . . little more than a dead letter'.[140] As elsewhere in Scotland, the able-bodied had no legal right to relief. In the crofting region even discretionary relief was minimal because only one per cent of crofting parishes had a legal assessment in the early 1840s and only twenty-three per cent a voluntary assessment.[141] Any real pressure to thin the population in order to reduce poor law rates in the Western Highlands only became imperative after the Poor Law Amendment Act of 1845 and, even more so, during the potato famine itself.

In the event, therefore, some landlords ironically became associated with policies which indirectly inhibited migration rather than promoted it. Three specific factors merit comment. First, on several estates there was considerable tolerance of increasing rent arrears. In effect, this was an indirect subsidy to the small tenantry at the cost to them of increasing insecurity and indebtedness. Table 1.7 identifies the scale of rent arrears on the western section of the Sutherland estate. The pattern there was not exceptional. In Ardnamurchan, in 1838, total arrears had reached £7101 or £133 more than the annual book rental.[142] In Coigach, arrears varied between 169 per cent and 121 per cent of total rental between 1834 and 1841.[143] They had increased to £8121 by 1839 on the Skye estates of Lord Macdonald.[144] The widespread incidence of arrears suggests that a considerable part of the reduction in regional income after the Napoleonic Wars was being passed on to the landlord class by the small tenants whose principal aspiration remained the traditional one of maintaining a basic level of subsistence. Second, many landlords continued to provide grain in scarce years at cost price, which was initially credited against the rental account but eventually submerged among the accumulation of arrears.[145] Third, the decline in the profitability of kelp manufacture did not always have the anticipated demographic consequences because, despite falling returns, kelp continued to be made in several areas until the 1840s. In North Uist, in 1837, 400 families were still engaged in kelping and, in South Uist, 1872 persons.[146] Production continued in Tiree, Harris and Lewis on a major scale until the later 1830s.[147] One commentator explained:

> The price of Kelp bounded downwards; but the fall of price did not tell so rapidly upon the condition of the people as might have been expected, because considerable quantities were continued to be made long after it had ceased to afford a fair immediate profit. The employment enabled the labourer to pay his rent, that rent however consequently to be paid in work, or in the draft of fish, and not in money. The circulating medium of

exchange has become greatly diminished in the country; and in many cases the society is gradually going backwards into a state of barter.[148]

The maintenance of kelp production in some districts therefore reduced the mobility of the population. It probably also contributed to the perpetuation of subdivision. Since labour power paid the rent and kelping was highly labour-intensive, the small tenantry had a continued vested interest in providing a patch of land for kinfolk who could augment the labour team.[149] Landlords were endeavouring to control sub-division in Islay, parts of Skye, Coigach, Canna, Loch Broom and Barra by the 1830s but it continued to flourish in many other areas of the Inner and Outer Hebrides, not least because kelp manufacture endured in several districts.[150] Elsewhere it was alleged that the reduction in cattle prices encouraged many small tenants to subdivide their holdings in order to spread the burden of maintaining their rent payments. In western Inverness-shire, '. . . when a man becomes unable to pay his rent or to manage his loss, he seeks to lighten his burden without parting with all his interest and accordingly takes a partner into the concern. This is the way in which subdivision has mainly arisen . . .'[151] It is not hard to understand why some proprietors connived at a practice fraught with potential danger for the future in the hope of extracting a more favourable return from the small tenantry in the short term. But by allowing many of the new generation even a tenuous connection with the land they helped to dissuade large numbers from permanently leaving the Highlands.

Table 1.7. Sutherland Small Tenants, Western Parishes, 1836–46

	Assynt				Edderachillis				Durness			
	No. Ten- ants	Rent (£)	Arr- ears	(%)	No. Ten- ants	Rent (£)	Arr- ears	(%)	No. Ten- ants	Rent (£)	Arr- ears	(%)
1836	379	929	1832	197	233	733	1247	170	65	236	382	162
1837	373	967	2466	255	235	783	1848	237	70	271	661	244
1838	399	964	2243	233	237	779	2161	277	70	248	575	232
1839	409	968	2187	226	249	777	2206	283	73	255	565	222
1840	401	957	4	14	241	757	8	1	74	246	–	0
1841	376	960	29	3	233	731	86	12	70	239	92	38
1842	376	959	104	11	229	775	339	44	70	253	117	46
1843	375	953	205	22	230	743	462	62	70	253	145	57
1844	376	953	370	39	228	737	476	65	71	251	153	61
1845	377	967	175	18	231	735	292	40	72	259	118	46
1846	374	955	169	18	230	748	427	57	72	259	121	47

Source: NLS, Sutherland Estate Papers, Dep. 313/2283-2302

Note: (i) Arrears were written off in 1840
  (ii) % = arrears as per cent of annual rental

A Vulnerable Society

The inherent weakness in crofting society was brutally exposed in 1836 and 1837 when two partial but successive failures in the potato and grain crops pushed many of the population to the very edge of mass starvation.[152] The deficiency in potatoes ranged from one quarter to one half of the normal crop. Oats failed from one half to two thirds throughout the region. This was a classic subsistence crisis reminiscent of pre-industrial times and entirely foreign to the dynamic world of Victorian Britain. A concerned and alarmed government sent a special emissary to the north-west to report on the extent and causes of the disaster. He was Robert Grahame, Professor of Botany in Glasgow University, an early enthusiast of social medicine and a close associate of the social reformer, William Alison. Grahame's detailed letters to the Treasury in London and his final report provide an authoritative guide to West Highland society in the later 1830s.

He reckoned that the total population of the distressed districts was around 105,000 people. Many communities faced the risk of starvation though conditions varied markedly between areas and social groups. Sutherland had escaped relatively lightly as had much of Wester Ross. The worst affected localities were in Skye and the Outer Hebrides. The cottar classes were most vulnerable but many small tenant families also suffered to a considerable extent.

Grahame recognised that the crop failures were simply the immediate cause of the crisis. The more fundamental factors were long-term influences. The 'grand cause of the evil' was that 'the Population of this part of the country has been allowed to increase in a much greater ratio than the means of subsistence which it affords'. Although emigration was an important safety valve, the number of people in some areas had continued to grow or did not decline rapidly enough in relation to the diminished employment opportunities available in the 1820s and 1830s. The people depended on a narrow and fragile economic structure supported by the potato, subsistence fishing, temporary migration and occasional landlord assistance. It was a precarious way of life which did not produce enough savings in the good years to provide a margin of security in seasons of scarcity. The whole system was likely to be threatened with total collapse when crop failure, even of a partial nature, occurred. In times of shortage the majority of the inhabitants of the distressed districts did not possess the purchasing power to obtain enough alternative supplies of food to avoid severe malnutrition without external assistance. In the event, disaster was averted in 1836-7 by the combined efforts of government, landlords and Lowland charitable agencies. The crisis was a harbinger of the even greater calamity triggered by the potato blight in the following decade.

NOTES

1. For the parishes and population figures of this region see Appendix 1, Crofting and Farming Parishes.
2. This brief analysis of 'farming society' is based mainly on M. Gray, *The Highland Economy, 1750-1850* (Edinburgh, 1957), 68-79, 223-236; I.R.M. Mowat, *Easter Ross, 1750-1850* (Edinburgh, 1980); *New Statistical Account of Scotland* (15 vols., Edinburgh, 1834-45); *PP*, XXVII-XXXVI (1844), *Report from the Commissioners appointed for inquiring into the Administration and Practical Operation of the Poor Laws in Scotland*.
3. Gray, *Highland Economy*, 224.
4. *N.S.A.*, Ross and Cromarty, 67.
5. R. Somers, *Letters from the Highlands* (Glasgow, 1848), 28-9.

6. *N.S.A.*, VII, 562.
7. *PP*, VI (1841), *S.C. on Emigration* (Scotland), Q.821; *Destitution Papers*, Reports of Central Board (1847), 11; Gray, *Highland Economy*, 223-236.
8. Somers, *Letters from the Highlands*, 25-9.
9. PRO, T1/4201, Correspondence, Robert Grahame to Fox Maule, 6 March-6 May 1837.
10. *N.S.A.*, XIV, 109, 326, 377.
11. *Ibid.*, 233.
12. T.M. Devine, 'Highland Migration to Lowland Scotland, 1760-1860', *Scottish Historical Review*, 62 (1983) considers these points in more detail.
13. Gray, *Highland Economy*, 259.
14. See Appendix 1 for parishes included in this region.
15. Somers, *Letters from the Highlands*, 65
16. See below, pp.18-21; 314-316.
17. *Destitution Papers*, First Report of Central Board of Management (1847), 10.
18. The most recent discussion of these issues is to be found in Eric Richards, *A History of the Highland Clearances*, Vols. I-II (London, 1982 and 1985).
19. Gray, *Highland Economy*, 200.
20. See below, pp.11-12; 20-27, for a fuller discussion.
21. Somers *Letters from the Highlands*, 134; PRO, T1/4201, R. Grahame to Fox Maule, 6 April 1837; *McNeill Report*, Appendix A, 11, 125.
22. See below, pp.147-9
23. MS. Diary of J.M. Mackenzie, 1851; Conon House, Conon, Mackenzie of Gairloch MSS, Bundle 53, Correspondence *re* estate affairs, 1847-53.
24. SRO, Lord Macdonald Papers, GD221/122/1, 4, 11, 19 and below, Table 2.9.
25. *Destitution Papers*, First Report of Central Board of Management (1847), 10.
26. For evidence that in a few localities cottars were better off than some tenants see *McNeill Report*, Appendix A, 43, 64, 128.
27. *N.C.*, 1196, Q.18075; PRO, T1/4201, R. Grahame to Fox Maule, 25 March, 1837.
28. *N.S.A.*, XIV, 278; Sir J. Sinclair, *General Report of the Agricultural State and Political Circumstances of Scotland* (Edinburgh, 1814), 396.
29. PRO, T1/4201, R. Grahame to Fox Maule, 6 April 1837; A. Fullarton and C.R. Baird, *Remarks on the Evils at Present Affecting the Highlands and Islands of Scotland* (Glasgow, 1838), 16, 78.
30. See below, pp.279-82.
31. GRO, Census Enumerator's Schedule, Parish of Kilfinichen (Mull), 1841; SRO, HD21/35, Petition of the Inhabitants of Glenelg; *N.C.*, 1176, Q.17840, 2010, Q.31526; SRO, Lord Macdonald Papers, GD221/43, Report by Mr. Ballingall for Mr. Brown, 1851; *McNeill Report*, Appendix A, 110.
32. See below, p.49.
33. PRO, T1/4201, R. Grahame to Fox Maule, 6 April 1837.
34. *Ibid.*, 14 April 1837.
35. *Ibid.*, 20 April 1837.
36. *PP*, VI (1841), *S.C. on Emigration (Scotland), 1841*, 95.
37. *Ibid.*
38. *McNeill Report*, x.
39. Catholic Archives, Columba House, Edinburgh, Oban Letters, OL 1/29/15, Dr. Coll Macdonald to Dr. Scott, 22 December 1839.
40. Inveraray Castle, Argyll Estate Papers, Bundle 1529, List of families, Tiree and Ross of Mull, 1841.
41. *Destitution Papers.*, Report on the Islands of Mull, Tiree etc. (1849), 7; Fullarton and Baird, *Remarks*, 10; SRO, Lord Advocate's Papers, AD58/84, W.H. Sitwell to Countess of Dunmore, 1 October 1846.
42. PRO, T1/4201, R. Grahame to Fox Maule, 25 March, 6 May 1837; NLS, Sutherland Estate Papers, Dep. 313/1165, R. Horsburgh to James Loch, 27 April 1841.

43. See, for example, *N.S.A.*, XIV, 320. For the operation of the Poor Law in the Highlands see below, pp.182-3

44. James Hunter, *The Making of the Crofting Community*, (Edinburgh, 1976), 15-33; M. Gray, 'The Consolidation of the Crofting System', *Agricultural History Review*, V (1957).

45. Gray, *Highland Economy*, 197.

46. Sinclair, *General Report*, IV, 92.

47. See, for example, James Anderson, *An Account of the Present State of the Hebrides and Western Coasts of Scotland* (Edinburgh, 1785); John Knox, *A View of the British Empire, especially Scotland* (London, 1785), 2 vols.

48. Ian Carter, *Farm Life in Northeast Scotland, 1840-1914* (Edinburgh, 1979); T.M. Devine, ed., *Farm Servants and Labour in Lowland Scotland, 1770-1914* (Edinburgh, 1984), 20.

49. J. Loch, *An Account of the Improvements on the Estates of the Marquis of Stafford* (London, 1820), 72-3.

50. T.M. Devine, 'The Rise and Fall of Illicit Whisky-Making in Northern Scotland', *Scottish Historical Review*, 54 (1975).

51. S.D.M. Carpenter, 'Patterns of Recruitment of the Highland Regiments', Unpublished M.Litt. Thesis, University of St. Andrews, 1977.

52. *PP*, VI (1841), *S.C. on Emigration, 1841*, 68.

53. *McNeill Report*, Appendix A, 110.

54. Gray, *Highland Economy*, 41-56.

55. Somers, *Letters from the Highlands*, 58-84.

56. See R.N. Salaman, *The History and Social Influence of the Potato* (Cambridge, 1949), 347-374; M.W. Flinn, ed., *Scottish Population History from the Seventeenth Century to the 1930s* (Cambridge, 1977), 421-436; W.G. Burton, *The Potato* (London, 1948).

57. Dr. J. Macculloch, *The Highlands and Western Islands of Scotland* (London, 1824), IV, 338.

58. James Macdonald, *General View of the Agriculture of the Hebrides* (Edinburgh, 1811), 232.

59. *Destitution Papers*, Second Report of Committee of Management to the Edinburgh Section (1850), 46.

60. Salaman, *History and Social Influence of the Potato*, 362.

61. Jerome Blum, *The End of the Old Order in Rural Europe* (New Jersey, 1978), 272-3.

62. Macdonald, *Agriculture of the Hebrides*, 240.

63. Blum, *Old Order in Rural Europe*, 273.

64. S. Davidson and R. Passmore, *Human Nutrition and Dietetics* (3rd. ed., Cambridge), 269-270.

65. Ian Levitt and Christopher Smout, *The State of the Scottish Working Class in 1843* (Edinburgh, 1979), 22-53.

66. Richards, *Highland Clearances*, I, 74-110.

67. *McNeill Report*, Appendix A, 39.

68. Sinclair, *General Report*, I, 405.

69. Macdonald, *Agriculture of the Hebrides*, 253.

70. Flinn, *Population History*, 430.

71. *McNeill Report*, Appendix A, 1.

72. *N.C.*, 365; 1930-1, Q.30056.

73. Sinclair, *General Report*, I, 437.

74. Somers, *Letters from the Highlands*, 72; *N.C.*, 1993; Sir John Sinclair, *An Account of the System of Husbandry in Scotland* (Edinburgh, 1812), 269; *Destitution Papers*, Second Report by the Committee of Management to the Edinburgh Section (1850), 42-3; SRO, AD58/84, Lord Advocate's Papers, Conditions in Harris.

75. *N.C.*, 854, Q.13256; 1177, Q.17844; 1196; 2142, Q.33607; 2891, Q.4273; T. Mulock, *The Western Highlands and Islands of Scotland Socially Considered* (Edinburgh, 1850), 10-11, 68; SRO, Brown MSS, TD80/100/4, John Paterson to Robert Brown, 29 October 1844; Macdonald, *Agriculture of the Hebrides*, 236; Macculloch, *Highlands and Islands of Scotland*, 115.

76.   Macdonald, *Agriculture of the Hebrides*, 236.
77.   Quoted in *N.C.*, 470.
78.   PRO, T1/4201, R. Grahame to Fox Maule, 22 March 1837; PP, VI (1841).
79.   Gray, *Highland Economy*, 182, 245.
80.   *McNeill Report*, Appendix A, *passim*.
81.   A.J. Youngson, *After the '45* (Edinburgh, 1973), 164.
82.   Macculloch, *The Highlands and Western Islands*, 338.
83.   *Destitution Papers*, First Report of the Central Board of Management (1847), 10.
84.   *Ibid.*, Second Statement of the Destitution Committee of the Free Church, 6-12.
85.   Fullarton and Baird, *Remarks*, 17; PRO, T1/4201, R. Grahame to Fox Maule, 3 April 1837; *PP*, 1844, XX, *R.C. On Scottish Poor Laws*, Part 1, Q.12605; SRO, AD58/84, Lord Advocate's Papers, W.H. Sitwell Esq., to Countess of Dunmore, 1 October 1846.
86.   Macculloch, *Western Highlands and Islands*, 338.
87.   Fullarton and Baird, *Remarks*, 15.
88.   *N.S.A.*, Ross and Cromarty, 1101-111.
89.   Macdonald, *Agriculture of the Hebrides*, 258.
90.   For grain cultivation see Table 1.3 (above, p.7); PRO, T1/4201, Grahame-Fox Maule Correpondence; *McNeill Report*, Appendix A, *passim*; Sinclair, *General Report*, I, Appendix I, 49-105. Several parish reports in the *New Statistical Account* (1837-42) testify to the continuation of the cultivation of oats and bere (barley) viz:

Parish	% Value of Cattle	% Value Grain	% Value Potatoes
Harris	21	36	43
N. Uist	23	37	40
Applecross	45	24	31
Glensheil	47	16	37
Morvern	24	32	44

91.   For a detailed analysis of the increasing flow of cash income from temporary migration, see below, pp.147-150.
92.   *PP*, VI (1841), *S.C. on Emigration (Scotland)*, *1841*, 122, Q.1322.
93.   Macculloch, *Highlands and Western Islands*, IV, 341.
94.   Fullarton and Baird, *Remarks*, 16; PP, XXVIII (1847), *First Annual Report of the Board of Supervision for the Relief of the Poor*, 39; *N.S.A.*, XIV, 204, 293, 311.
95.   *McNeill Report*, IX.
96.   Macculloch, *Highlands and Western Islands*, IV, 350.
97.   Gray, *Highland Economy*, 214-217.
98.   PRO, T1/2401, R. Grahame to Fox Maule, 26 April 1837; *McNeill Report*, Appendix A, 46; Sinclair, *General Report*, 104; *N.S.A.*, XIV, 254.
99.   See, for example, Eric J. Findlater, *Highland Clearances: the Real Cause of Highland Famines* (Edinburgh, 1855); A. Robertson, *Where are the Highlanders?* (Edinburgh, n.d.), 7.
100.   *N.C.*, 1172, Q.17782-17813.
101.   SRO, Lord Advocate's Papers, AD58/84/3, W.H. Sitwell to Countess of Dunmore, 1 October 1846.
102.   *PP*, VI (1841), *S.C. on Emigration (Scotland)*, 1841, 71.
103.   *N.C.*, 787, QQ. 12248-2266; SRO, Lord Macdonald Papers, GD221/43, Report by Duncan Shaw, 1838-9.
104.   *McNeill Report*, xv; PRO, T1/4201, Grahame-Fox Maule Correspondence, 1837; SRO, Seaforth Papers, GD46/17/71, K. Macleod to Seaforth, 11 Feb. 1823; GD46/17/72, List of Townships lotted Whit. 1826; *N.C.*, QQ.49986-7; QQ.13850- 13852; *N.S.A.*, XIV, 349; SRO, Clanranald Papers, GD201/1/338, Report of D. Shaw, 19 November 1827; *PP*, VI (1841), *S.C. on Emigration (Scotland)*, 1841, Q.1012.
105.   MS. Diary of J.M. Mackenzie, Chamberlain of the Lews, 1851; Inveraray Castle, Argyll Estate Papers, Bundle 1529, Report by Chamberlain of Tiree, July 1845.
106.   Richards, *Highland Clearances*, I, 87-9.

107. Gray, *Highland Economy*, 43-4.
108. See below, Appendix 7 and p.184.
109. NLS, Sutherland Estate Papers, Dep. 313/877, E. Maciver to Tenants of Knockan and Elphin, Height of Assynt, 7 January 1843.
110. This issue is discussed in more detail in T.M. Devine, 'Social Stability and the Agricultural Revolution in the Eastern Lowlands of Scotland, 1780-1840' in T.M. Devine, ed., *Lairds and Improvement in the Scotland of the Enlightenment* (Dundee, 1979), and in T.M. Devine, 'Social Responses to Agrarian Improvement: the Highland and Lowland Clearances in Scotland', in R. Houston and I. Whyte, eds., *Scottish Society, 1600-1800* (forthcoming, Cambridge University Press).
111. Rev. T. McLauchlan, 'The Influence of Emigration on the Social Condition of the Highlands', *Trans. of National Association for Social Science* (1864), 608.
112. Fullarton and Baird, *Remarks*, 32.
113. SRO, Lord Macdonald Papers, GD221/21, Emigration, 1839-41.
114. See below, p.46.
115. See above, pp.9-12.
116. *N.C.*, 2024, Q.31749.
117. *N.C.*, 2024-2055.
118. GRO, Census Enumerator's Schedules, 1841, Parish of Glenelg.
119. SRO, HD21/35, Petition of the Inhabitants of Glenelg.
120. *Ibid.*, 1932-2010.
121. Fullarton and Baird, *Remarks*, 44, 46; Somers, *Letters from the Highlands*, 58-9; PRO, T1/4201, Grahame-Fox Maule Correspondence, 1837, *passim*; *PP*,VI(1841), *S.C. on Emigration (Scotland)*, 95.
122. Fullarton and Baird, *Remarks*, 14.
123. Levitt and Smout, *State of the Scottish Working Class*, 238.
124. *N.S.A.*, XIV, 349.
125. Levitt and Smout, *State of the Scottish Working Class*, 239.
126. GRO, Census Enumerator's Schedules, Parish of Glenelg, 1841, See also, *inter alia, PP*, VI (1841), *S.C. on Emigration (Scotland)*, 1841, 110; *McNeill Report*, X; SRO, Clanranald Papers, GD201/40/10/97, Report of D. Shaw: '. . . the most wealthy and industrious part of our population left'; *N.C.*, Q37858; PP, IV (1826), *Reports from the Select Committee appointed to inquire into the expediency of encouraging Emigration from the United Kingdom*, QQ.725-27; *Destitution Papers*, Second Report of the Committee of Management to the Edinburgh Section, 42-3.
127. *N.C.*, 841, Q.13036; 854, Q.13256; 2057, Q.32330; Findlater, 'Highland Clearances', 8-9.
128. See, for example, Inveraray Castle, Argyll Estate Papers, Bundle 1529, Report by Chamberlain of Tiree, August 1845.
129. SRO, Lord Macdonald Papers, GD221/21, Skye and North Uist Emigrations.
130. As defined in Darling, *West Highland Survey*, 15-17.
131. GRO, Census Enumerator's Schedules, Parish of Applecross, 1841; SRO, Lord Macdonald Papers, GD221/21, Skye and North Uist Emigrations.
132. P. Goubert, *The Ancien Régime: French Society, 1600-1740* (London, 1973), 44.
133. *N.S.A.*, XIV, 344.
134. James Robertson, *General View of the Agriculture in the Southern Districts of the County of Perth* (London, 1794), 39.
135. See below, ch. 6, for a detailed discussion.
136. *PP*, VI(1841), *S.C. on Emigration (Scotland)*, *1841*, Q.95: 'A strong feeling exists among the proprietors to make no great or sudden change, with reference to throwing their small farms into great, until they can get rid of the redundant population'. See also *Ibid.*, 70-72.
137. See below, pp.95-100.
138. See below, pp.188-9.
139. *PP*, VI (1841), *S.C. on Emigration (Scotland)*, *1841*, 111.

140.   Fullarton and Baird, *Remarks*, 64.
141.   Levitt and Smout, *State of the Scottish Working Class*, 195.
142.   SRO, Riddell Papers, AF49/4, Ardnamurchan and Sunart Rentals.
143.   SRO, Cromartie Papers, GD305/2-84-121, Estate Rentals, 1834-1855.
144.   SRO, Lord Macdonald Papers, GD221/70, List of Arrears due on Skye, 31 August 1839.
145.   PRO, T1/4201, Grahame-Fox Maule Correspondence, 1837, *passim*; SRO, Lord Macdonald Papers, GD221/43, Report by D. Shaw, factor for North Uist, 1839; *PP*, VI (1841), *S.C. on Emigration (Scotland)*, 1841, 154, Q.1881; SRO, Clanranald Papers, GD201/27, Report by Factor, 1826; *McNeill Report*, Appendix A, 107, 118.
146.   *N.S.A.*, XIV, 178, 194.
147.   *PP*, VI (1841), *S.C. on Emigration (Scotland)*, *1841*, 214; SRO, Lord Macdonald Papers, GD221/76, List of sums due to tenants for kelp manufacture, 1850; *N.S.A.*, XIV, 158; PRO, T1/4201, R. Grahame to Fox Maule, 6 May 1837.
148.   PRO, T1/4201, R. Grahame to Fox Maule, 6 May 1837.
149.   Fullarton and Baird, *Remarks*, 77; SRO, Riddell Papers, AF49/2, Report by Thomas Anderson, 1829.
150.   *PP*, IV (1841), *S.C. on Emigration (Scotland)*, *1841*, 120, 150; Q.1935, 41; SRO, Lord Macdonald Papers, GD221/62, Minute *re* Macdonald Affairs, 28-30 October 1831; PRO, T1/4201, R. Grahame to Fox Maule, 6 May 1837.
151.   *North British Daily Mail*, 13 September 1847.
152.   What follows is based on PRO, T1/4201, Grahame-Fox Maule Correspondence, March-May 1837.

2

Anatomy of the Potato Famine

1

The potato blight was caused by the fungus *Phytophthora Infestans*.[1] It first makes its appearance as a white mould surrounding the decaying parts on the leaves of the plants. The mould consists of numerous filaments each containing the spores of the fungus. When the spore containers are mature, they are detached by rain or gentle winds, and countless numbers then fall to the ground or become airborne. However, infection of a healthy potato plant only occurs when germination of the spores takes place. For this to happen moisture is necessary. There is no certainty about how blight originated or how it came to Europe. A potato disease similar to blight was reported in northern Germany in 1830, and in parts of the Hebrides in the same decade, and a major outbreak occurred along the Atlantic coast of North America in 1842. These, however, were minor compared to the international disaster of 1845-6 when blight destroyed the potato crop throughout many countries in western Europe and Britain.

The disease was likely to have a lethal effect on the agriculture of the Western Highlands and Islands. The climatic conditions of wind and rain which gave the region protection from the 'curl' actually encouraged the rapid spread of blight. The severity of the disease ultimately depends on weather. Cool, rainy nights and moderately warm cloudy days are most suitable for propagation and germination of the spores. This was the type of climatic condition most common during the summer months in the West Highlands. The reproductive cells of the fungus are distributed by splashing rain or by wind and in water films on both plant and soil. The disease does not spread in dry weather and has less impact on dry soils than on heavy wet ground. The climate and terrain of the crofting districts were therefore ideal for the spread of the disease. This may explain why the western region of the Highlands was not only more widely affected by blight than the eastern zone in 1846 but also why the disease continued to infect the potato crops of the crofting area for several years after it had either died out entirely or very much abated elsewhere in Scotland.

This was the other major problem associated with blight. Unlike the grain crop, which might be devastated by harsh climatic conditions over one or two consecutive seasons before weather improved, the potato could remain vulnerable to the deadly fungus for many years. In 1846 there was no accepted explanation of the cause of the blight. Not until 1861 was it finally acknowledged that a fungus was responsible and only in 1885 was a chemical treatment for the disease shown to be effective. The catastrophic failure of the crops in 1845 and 1846 in Britain and the devastating impact that this had on Ireland in particular produced numerous publications on the subject. But no meaningful consensus as to cause or cure emerged.[2] Given the appropriate conditions, therefore, blight could flourish virtually unchecked over long periods of time. The relatively mild weather of the Hebrides allowed the spores of the fungus to survive the winter months in the soil and wreak havoc on the crop the following year. Through both ignorance and accident, the disease persisted because slightly infected potatoes were planted alongside healthy tubers. The fungus grew within the stem, diseased shoots developed and as soon as weather conditions were favourable, spore production commenced.

Once this began, the blight fungus spread with extraordinary rapidity: 'in moist, warm conditions, one diseased plant within a day or two releases several million spores, each one of which is capable of dividing itself and producing a swarm of smaller spores . . . countless millions of spore containers germinate hourly; germ-tubes work their way into leaf and tuber, reducing green and healthy plants to decay; fields are seen to turn black, tubers, hastily dug, collapse into stinking masses, and the fearful stench of decomposition hangs over the land'.[3] The fact that even healthy potatoes could be vulnerable after digging added to the bewilderment of those who saw their main source of food destroyed over a matter of days or weeks. Even if the fungus had not attacked the tuber when it was in the soil, it could still shower healthy potatoes with spores from the leaves of infected plants as they were dug out. Thus, it was a common occurrence in the Highlands for apparently disease-free potatoes to be placed in pits for storage only to be found to be rotten when finally dug for consumption.

It was a considerable irony, in the light of the subsequent development of the potato famine in the Western Highlands from 1846, that the north-west region was one of the few areas in Britain to escape the first devastating impact of the blight in 1845. The disease destroyed potato fields all over the country, and in Ireland and continental Europe in that year, but most areas of the Highlands were unaffected. Indeed, in 1845, the potato crops in several districts of the north were particularly abundant and increased exports to the Lowlands fetched scarcity prices.[4]

As late as February 1846, there was a thriving trade in seed potatoes from the Highlands, '. . . where the disease happily has not yet penetrated or at least has only shown itself to a very partial extent'.[5] In April 1846, 5000 barrels of potatoes were exported from North Uist to Glasgow and were sold at 4s. to 5s. a barrel or almost double the going rate in the Hebrides.[6] It would appear, however, that the partial infection of the summer of 1845 had tainted some of the tubers pitted for winter and spring consumption. In Skye, in late February 1846, for instance, it was reported ominously that 'the potatoes are giving way in various localities'.[7] Across the Minch, in Harris, pitted potatoes dug up in June '. . . turned out all but a complete failure'.[8] The acreage under potatoes had actually been increased to take advantage of the anticipated continuation of scarcity prices in 1846. Throughout August and September, alarm and consternation spread across the Highlands as it rapidly became apparent in many districts that the crop of 1846 was likely to be a complete failure.

The full enormity of the disaster revealed itself by the autumn and contemporary observers were stunned into apocalyptic utterances. The Free Church newspaper, the *Witness*, regarded the calamity as '. . . unprecedented in the memory of this generation and of many generations gone by, even in any modern periods of our country's history'.[9] Over two centuries had passed since a crisis of such magnitude had occurred: 'The hand of the Lord has indeed touched us'.[10] The Highland and Agricultural Society observed how the disease was causing 'very general alarm' because the plants appeared to grow well initially and only became seriously affected as the tubers advanced towards maturity.[11] The Rev. Dr. Norman Macleod, a veteran of the earlier subsistence crisis in the Highlands in 1837-8, asserted at the end of 1846 that 'the present year certainly marks the most momentous calamity in the condition of the Highlands that has occurred for a century – that has taken place since 1746'.[12]

In the latter part of 1846, the Free Church issued a questionnaire to its ministers and catechists in the distressed districts. Among other queries, it asked them to estimate the extent of potato failure in their area. This information allows a more systematic test to be carried out of the validity of the contemporary response to the onset of the potato blight.

Table 2.1. Estimated Extent of Potato Failure, 74 Highland Districts, December 1846

Extent of Failure	Per Cent of Total Crofting Districts	Per Cent of Total Farming Districts	Per Cent of Highland Districts
Entirely	76	59	67
Almost Entirely	15	24	20
Partially	9	12	10
Half	—	5	3
	100	100	100

Source: Calculated from *Destitution Papers*, Second Statement of the Destitution Committee of the Free Church, 6-13

Table 2.1 suggests that in 1846 there was indeed very serious failure of the potato crop throughout the Highlands. No less than sixty-seven per cent of reporting districts indicated that total failure had occurred and only thirteen per cent estimated that partial loss had taken place. However, the tabulation also suggests that there was considerable variation between regions. Seventy-six per cent of reporting districts in the crofting zone described a complete failure but only fifty-nine per cent of those in the farming region indicated a total loss. Though few districts in the Highlands as a whole escaped, the blight had its most destructive effects on the poorer western districts where dependence on the potato as a subsistence crop was greatest. The blight was most lethal in that region which had fewest resources and least resilience. Literary evidence also suggests that there was some variation in the extent of the disease within the crofting zone itself. Some parishes in Sutherland were less seriously affected than elsewhere.[13] Government relief officials also reported that 'The loss of crop does not, however, appear to be quite so general or so complete . . .' along the western mainland of Argyll, Inverness and Ross.[14] From the first year of the blight, therefore, the most acute levels of distress concentrated in the Hebrides where potato dependency was greatest and where the failure of the crop was more widespread than in any other Highland regions.

It was not, however, the incidence of one year of potato blight, no matter how devastating, which posed the gravest threat to the welfare of the people of the Highlands. The failure of 1846 was only the first of a continuous series of attacks by the disease which endured for a decade until 1857. Appendix 2, which has been compiled from press reports, estate correspondence, and destitution information, reveals the pattern of failure over that period. Inevitably the extent of loss varied both over time and space but the data indicate failures of at least half of the annual potato crop in many districts from 1847 to 1850 and again in 1852. The evidence suggests that the impact of the blight was almost as serious in 1854 as in 1846. In 1851, 1855 and 1856 failure was partial. Only in 1853 did most observers conclude that crops returned to near normal. However, it was not until 1857 that the regular pattern of abundant potato harvests became established once again. The compilers of the Agricultural Statistics for Scotland observed in that year that, in western Inverness, '. . . for years there has not been so sound a crop of potatoes'. In the Hebrides, the crop had been so good that the population '. . . has rarely been so well prepared to encounter the wants and trials of the winter'.[15] The information presented in Appendix 2 also shows that blight concentrated even more than in 1846 on the parishes of the crofting region from 1848 to 1856. The disease became less vigorous and disappeared entirely from some eastern and southern districts, yet remained very active in the Western Highlands and Islands.

It was not simply the impact of blight which temporarily reduced the significance of the potato in the Highland diet. There was also a very considerable decline in the acreage of the crop planted. The government's principal relief official in August 1847 reckoned that 'a small proportion . . . not exceeding probably one-fifth of the common average' had been planted and '. . . the inferior productiveness of the grain and green crops substituted for them, the return must fall greatly short of the quantity of food produced in ordinary seasons'.[16] A similar pattern was maintained in subsequent years. In 1848, there was less concern about the spread of the blight because 'the breadth of potatoes planted was small', and as late as 1851 it was estimated that in some Hebridean parishes 'few' potatoes were now sown.[17] Even in seasons of great scarcity many small tenants tried to reserve some potatoes for seed. Indeed it was the habit of planting partially diseased tubers which helped to perpetuate the blight. Both landlords and relief committees, the latter after much initial reluctance, also dispensed seed potatoes.[18] But their efforts were likely to have only marginal impact. It was impractical to provide seed potatoes in sufficient quantity to make up for the deficiency in each locality. One estimate suggested that nearly one ton of seed potatoes per acre would be required to do so. Bulk transportation on that scale was obviously out of the question.[19]

Such was the variety in conditions both over time and space that it is impossible to be certain about the exact extent to which the indigenous supply of food diminished in the Western Highlands as a consequence of the failure of the potatoes. Experienced government relief officers who had seen service in Ireland and had participated in other famine emergencies in Asia were in no doubt, however, that a massive contraction had occurred. They estimated in the summer of 1847 that the failure of the potatoes resulted '. . . in the destruction of two-thirds of the supply of food ordinarily raised by the cultivation of the labouring classes for their own subsistence'.[20] Two years later a detailed investigation carried out by the Glasgow Section of the Central Board for Highland Relief considered the result of the series of potato failures on food production in Harris.[21] Before 1846, each small tenant planted about twelve barrels of potatoes which gave a return of eighty barrels, sowed about fifteen pecks of barley, which yielded four bolls of meal, and five barrels of oats, with a return of three bolls of meal. By 1849, the quantity of potatoes planted had fallen to only two barrels which produced a return of about eighty per cent fewer potatoes than was common before 1846. Ten pecks of barley and three barrels of oats were also sown. All in all, there had also been a decline of twenty-five per cent in grain production.

Obviously such a dramatic collapse in indigenous food production was the principal factor responsible for distress in the period 1846 to 1856. Nevertheless, it is important to stress that the destitution was aggravated by a number of other influences which interacted with the impact of the potato blight to deepen the intensity of the crisis. The most important of these was the decline in earnings from the cattle trade which was the principal source for the crofting class of the purchasing power to buy meal. This was almost as great a disaster as the failure of the potatoes. With the main subsistence crop destroyed in some districts and badly diseased in others the small tenants had an even greater need than before to fall back on earnings from the sale of black cattle, their principal insurance in bad seasons. Appendix 3 assembles the known data on the market reports for and prices of small Highland cattle between 1845 and 1853. They suggest that the period opened well. In both 1845 and 1846 prices were buoyant and the good returns in these years probably help to explain the very significant increases in the purchase of meal which many communities were able to make in 1846 and 1847.[22] For instance, in June 1846, it was reckoned that there had not been a better spring market in Portree than for several years past.[23] The Falkirk tryst of October 1846, '. . . for amount of prices and extent of sales, is the best that has occurred since 1810, both for sheep and cattle'.[24] From 1847, however, the market slumped badly. A reduction of ten per cent on 1846 prices took place by August 1847, and over the period 1847 to 1851 prices on average declined by between one third and one half.[25] In 1849 and 1850, in particular, there were many reports of West Highland cattle being left unsold at market partly because their condition was poor as grain formerly fed to them was now being consumed by their owners.

Some observers regarded this not simply as a predictable downturn in an unstable market but as a manifestation of a basic structural change in demand for Highland cattle. One commentator described how the Highland breed was 'entirely out of favour with the graziers and butchers'.[26] It was argued that they now supplied their needs more profitably by the improved methods of stall-feeding the younger stock of the heavier and larger Lowland breeds. The contraction in demand for Highland beasts was also due to a marked increase in the importation of Irish cattle brought across the Irish Sea more cheaply than from the Hebrides and to the Repeal of the Corn Laws in 1846 which encouraged an extension of permanent grazing in the south at the expense of arable husbandry. These arguments were somewhat exaggerated because, as is demonstrated in Appendix 3, prices did recover again in 1852 and 1853. Nevertheless, between 1847 and 1851, the depression in the market for Highland cattle added very substantially to the social and economic problems of the crofting region. It meant that the inhabitants of the area were assailed not just by a biological disaster, which removed a vital part of their food supply, but by an economic crisis which made it more difficult for them to purchase alternative supplies of meal. Not surprisingly, it became impossible in many districts both to buy grain and to pay rent.[27]

The welfare of the population also depended fundamentally on three other factors, the health of the fisheries, the market for temporary migrants and the attitude and actions of the landlord class. Appendix 4 describes the pattern of activity in the commercial fishing sector of the west coast and Hebrides. It is obviously extremely difficult to generalise about fishing because of the extraordinary local fluctuations in herring catches, the conflicting contemporary evidence and the different experiences of white fishing for cod and ling and herring fishing. No clear pattern emerges from the data. In 1846 there was a considerable range of experience from high to low activity, while in 1849 the herring fishery was generally unusually productive. But there is no evidence to indicate any sustained expansion or even vigour in commercial fishing of such an extent to make up for the deficiency in purchasing power resulting from the stagnation of the cattle trade. Undoubtedly, subsistence fishing helped to keep people alive and the commercial sector in such areas such as eastern Lewis, Wester Ross and the western parishes of Sutherland bestowed some resilience on a number of fortunate communities. Overall, however, commercial fishing could not protect the majority of the population from the destructive impact of the combined subsistence and economic crisis. Appendix 4 shows plainly, for instance, that the herring fishery in 1847 was in the doldrums and, in other years, such areas as Harris, Lochcarron, Glenelg and Arisaig suffered profoundly as the herring temporarily deserted the neighbouring lochs or the adjacent coast.[28]

Probably more significant as a source of vital cash earnings was temporary migration for work in Lowland society. The whole subject of temporary movement and its significance during the famine years is of crucial importance and is examined in detail in Chapter 6. Here it is only proposed to provide a brief summary of its development and the extent to which it alleviated the crisis in crofting society. It is argued later that in 1846 and 1847 the labour market in the Lowlands was of major consequence to the population of the distressed regions. There was a very substantial increase in these years in the scale of temporary migration for work on railway construction, the fisheries and in agricultural employment. Throughout the famine it remained significant. Yet, despite its importance, the earnings from temporary migration could not provide a panacea for the problems of the destitute districts. In 1848 and 1849 the industrial recession in the Lowlands reduced opportunities in all areas of casual employment, and not until after 1853 did the labour market for temporary migrants return towards the level of the earlier periods.

The response of the landed classes is another topic to which considerable attention is devoted later in this book.[29] As that analysis demonstrates, many proprietors, especially in the first two years of the potato famine, devoted considerable resources to providing relief, developing employment schemes on their estates and dispensing meal at cost price to their needy tenants. Several continued with these provisions into the early 1850s. For some, however, this was less possible. During and after the financial crisis of 1848 the estates of Lord Macdonald in Skye and North Uist, Macleod on Skye, Campbell of Islay and Sir James Riddell in Ardnamurchan were placed under trusteeship. This especially reduced landlord relief in Skye. From the same period it is possible to detect a hardening of attitudes among other sections of the landed classes. The reasons for this are explored in depth in Chapters 4 and 12. The strategy on some estates moved decisively from the provision of relief to the promotion of the expulsion of the destitute population through a massive increase in clearance, removal and assisted emigration. In several districts, these policies simply exacerbated the sufferings of the poor and contributed to the persistence of acute levels of destitution especially in those cases where no support was provided to evicted families to enable them to emigrate. In 1846-8 there had been a widespread tolerance of accumulating rent arrears which represented a net subsidy to the small tenantry and allowed them to devote their scanty resources to the purchase of meal. A policy of rigorous exaction of rental became more common thereafter.

It is clear, then, that the Highland famine was a much wider, longer and deeper crisis than a simple failure of the potato crop in 1846. The blight continued to a greater or lesser extent for almost a decade. The damage done to the society's major source of subsistence was compounded by a collapse in cattle prices and the impact of a major wave of clearances beginning in the later 1840s. Fishing and temporary migration, especially the latter, provided both income and employment in some years but neither could expand sufficiently to compensate entirely for the decline in food supply and the contraction in income as a result of the slump in the cattle trade. The magnitude and duration of the emergency necessitated a massive expansion in external assistance in addition to the resources contributed by many of the proprietors in the Western Highlands. The Free Church of Scotland was the first to mount a major relief operation by raising subscriptions in its churches in the autumn and winter of 1846 to supply meal to the distressed districts. It was quickly followed by the formation of relief committees in Edinburgh in December 1846 and in Glasgow in January 1847. By February of that year these three bodies had combined to form the Central Board of Management for Highland Relief, with two constituent sections, based on the original Edinburgh and Glasgow committees, and each responsible for particular areas of the famine-stricken region. The Central Board maintained its operations during the spring, summer and early autumn months from 1847 until its activities terminated in 1850. From the winter of 1846-7 until the end of August 1847, the Government stationed a team of relief officers under the command of Sir Edward Pine Coffin, a veteran of famine relief in Ireland, Mexico and India, in the Western Highlands. Two meal depots were established at Portree in Skye and Tobermory in Mull to supply the distressed districts with grain at controlled prices. Coffin and his men also carefully monitored the progress of destitution and the relief measures implemented by individual landlords. The roles of both Government and the Central Relief Board are considered in Chapter 5.

The reports of these agencies illustrate the persistence of severe distress in most districts of the Western Highlands and Islands into the early 1850s. The potato failure in 1846 was followed by renewed difficulties in 1847 and 1848. The Central Board explained this as a result of five influences.[30] First, it estimated that only about one sixth of the usual quantity of potatoes had been planted. Second, the crop which had been planted was partially destroyed by blight, and in 1847 the grain crop was 'much injured by severe and boisterous weather'. Third, much of the ground formerly planted with potatoes had been sown with grain using seed supplied by the landlords and Central Board. But this could not supply the deficiency because three acres under oats and bere were required to produce the same amount of food as could be derived from one acre of potatoes. Fourth, many cottars found it difficult to obtain potato plots in the customary way, because small tenants now often sowed the whole of their possessions with grain. Fifth, in many districts, savings had been used to purchase grain in 1846 and by 1848 these were exhausted: 1849 was regarded as one of the worst years. Only about a quarter of the usual crop of potatoes was planted, 'the hoarded means of the people are exhausted' and the collapse of the southern labour market in 1848 had left less cash available in 1849 to purchase grain.[31] In 1850, when the Central Board ended its relief operation, its funds being virtually exhausted, it concluded that the condition of the people was even more miserable than when it commenced activities four years earlier.[32]

2

The scale of the crop failure in 1846 provoked strong reactions. One writer saw it as '. . . society now smitten at its base' and added that 'No political revolution ever effected such a thorough social change as the potato failure will assuredly accomplish'.[33] The Free Church, alarmed at the fate of so many of its flock in the northern districts of Scotland, drew an analogy with a possible urban calamity: 'a parallel more easily realised than, perhaps, Highland Destitution would be that of the population of one of our largest cities, by some dreadful and sudden visitation deprived – not merely of their household stores, not merely of their family resources, but also, together with those, deprived of their commerce and ordinary business – of all and whole, the sources by which their whole bodily sustenance was wont to be maintained'.[34] One result of the widespread shock produced by the extent of the blight and its ominous implications for the future of the Highland population was the publication of a wide range of contemporary estimates of the numbers threatened with starvation. These varied from 650,000 to 150,000, the Free Church itself suggesting that in December 1846, 200,000 were already 'destitute of food' and a further 200,000 were likely to be in this condition in a matter of months.[35] These alarming figures gave real impetus both to the relief operation and to the energetic and highly successful efforts which were made to raise funds for the distressed districts. The realisation that tens of thousands were in grave danger powerfully stimulated philanthropic sentiment in both the Lowlands, England, the British Empire, the U.S.A, and throughout western Europe.[36] The estimates were of considerable propaganda value but they offer only a guide to contemporary thinking about the scale of the famine and do not provide a real indicator of the numbers who were actually at serious risk. In the remainder of this chapter the extent, spatial variation and social distribution of distress will be probed in order to try to determine the reality behind conflicting contemporary claims.

It is important to begin by stressing the key differences between the crofting region and the eastern, central and southern Highlands. The latter region did not escape entirely unscathed in 1846 and 1847.[37] Relief committees were established all over the Highlands. The potato failure caused distress in certain localities in the central and eastern zone, especially among the poor, large families of the labouring classes and village populations. Some destitution also prevailed along the Caithness coast, from Wick to Helmsdale. The eruption of food riots in several areas testified to the hardship endured by the people.[38] However, there were two fundamental differences between the experience of the inhabitants of the farming region and those of the crofting zone. First, the distress which developed in the central, eastern and southern Highlands posed less of a serious threat to life itself. The problem there derived principally from a temporary imbalance between sharp increases in grain prices and slower rises in wages. Second, in these areas the crisis was confined to the years 1846 and 1847. From 1847 the Central Relief Board terminated its operations in the south and east and restricted its efforts after 1848 to the western maritime and insular districts.[39]

The contrasting experiences of the two regions are highlighted in Tables 2.2 to 2.4. Table 2.2 indicates that, with the exception of the special case of the county of Sutherland, which will be discussed below, the numbers estimated as 'destitute of food' were much higher in the crofting region than in the farming zone. Similarly, Table 2.3 suggests that while seventy-one per cent of the population of the crofting districts sampled were likely to have consumed or had consumed their grain crops by the end of February 1847, only nineteen per cent of farming districts were in the same hazardous position. Finally, the sharp contrast in the scale of 'remunerative employment' provided in the two regions by landlords or relief committees is a clear indication that the population in the western districts required much more external assistance to survive in the later months of 1846 than the inhabitants of the south and west.

Table 2.2. Estimated Percentage of Families in Highland Districts, by County, 'not paupers, but now destitute of food', December 1846

County	No. of Districts in Sample	Percentage of families destitute of food	
		Crofting Districts	*Farming Districts*
Sutherland	6	3	3
Ross	17	14	10
Inverness	18	30	8
Argyll	15	16	4
Average		16	6

Source: Destitution Papers, Second Statement of the Destitution Committee of the Free Church, 6-13

Note: (i) In the source total numbers in districts are given as total population and total numbers 'destitute of food' in families. 'Population' has been converted to 'families' by dividing total numbers by five.
(ii) Districts estimating those 'destitute of food' in non-quantitative terms have been excluded from the samples.

Table 2.3. Estimated Length of Time Corn Crops Might Support Rent-Paying Families, 74 Highland Districts, December 1846

Estimated Period	Per cent of Total Crofting Districts	Per cent of Total Farming Districts
Grain crop already consumed	13	6
1 month	28	7
2 months	30	6
3 months	22	24
4 months	7	30
5 months	0	5
6 months	0	10
1 year	0	9
2 years	0	3
	100	100

Source: Destitution Papers, Second Statement of the Destitution Committee of the Free Church, 6-13

Table 2.4. 'Remunerative Employment Provided', Crofting and Farming Districts, December 1846

	All Districts	Crofting	Farming
Per cent of districts providing 'some' employment	47	68	37
Per cent of districts providing 'not much' employment	3	0	4
Per cent of districts providing 'very little' employment	6	5	12
Per cent of districts providing no employment	44	27	47
	100	100	100

Source: Destitution Papers, Second Statement of the Destitution Committee of the Free Church, 6-13

The relative resilience of the farming areas derived from a number of advantages. Potato dependency was not only less but, as already seen, crop failure was not as extensive in 1846 and 1847 as elsewhere.[40] Again, a substantial proportion of the population derived their living from labouring and only partially from the produce of their smallholdings. It was therefore a considerable advantage to them that the labour market in agriculture in 1846-7 was very active.[41] Table 2.5 illustrates that the proportion of the population of cottar status, the most vulnerable class in the west, was also much lower in the central and eastern Highlands. Finally, the balance of supply of labour and employment opportunities differed radically. In 1850, the Central Board summed up the advantages of the farming region thus:

> The population of these districts was in an entirely different position from that of the Western Districts. The different classes of society were in their proper place. There was a labouring class supporting themselves and their families by remunerative employment – a fishing population, carrying on that branch of industry as a permanent resource – and there were all the appliances of an advanced state of society, in which purchased food

forms a principal feature of the subsistence of the people. The distress among them had been occasioned by a temporary disproportion between the wages of labour and the price of food, and the loss of the potato, which formed but a subordinate element in their means of subsistence.[42]

It was among the cottar and crofter population of the western maritime and insular districts that the most acute levels of distress occurred in 1846 and 1847 and endured to a greater or lesser extent until the middle years of the following decade. In the first two years of the potato failure there were unambiguous signs of imminent famine and mortality crisis. During the winter months consumption of seed corn occurred in Lewis, Barra, South Uist, Harris, Skye, Arisaig and Moidart.[43] Reports of diseases related to vitamin deficiency and malnutrition began to proliferate in the Scottish press.[44] The evidence that these illnesses were beginning to push up mortality rates is considered in Chapter 3. At the same time, sheep-stealing was reported to be on the increase in certain areas, and in the islands larger numbers than usual were gathering shellfish from the shores.[45] This was a normal occurrence in certain districts during the summer months but was less common during the winter. The fact that it was more frequent in 1846-7 suggested that, in some areas at least, the people were rapidly approaching the limit of their sparse food resources. Confirmation of this came from the reports of experienced government relief officers and correspondents of the Central Board. Some were reduced to a diet consisting almost entirely of fish and shellfish, to one meal per day and to sending their children to bed early to reduce the pangs of hunger.[46] Table 2.6 indicates the scale of the problem in statistical terms.

Table 2.5. Average Cottar Population (Estimated) as Percentage of Total Population, Crofting and Farming Districts, 1846

County	Cottar Population as Per cent of Total Population Crofting Districts	Cottar Population as Per cent of Total Population Farming Districts
Ross	28	9
Inverness	43	27
Argyll	38	24

Source: *Destitution Papers*, Second Statement of the Destitution Committee of the Free Church, 6-13
Note: Estimated cottar population = number of cottar families × 5.

The weight of the anecdotal evidence and the demographic data considered in Chapter 3 suggest that in late 1846 and early 1847 the Western Highlands and Islands came very close to suffering a mortality crisis of major proportions. That it was contained was due primarily to a huge increase in both landlord and charitable assistance which, by February-March 1847, had apparently managed to stabilise the situation.[47]

From then until the Central Board brought its activities to a close in 1850 many people in several districts of the crofting region depended on external support to maintain a basic level of subsistence. Table 2.7 outlines the largest numbers receiving relief from the Central Board in a variety of mainland and insular districts in 1848 and 1849. It does not include the unknown number who were supported by individual landlords or by kinfolk. The data are a useful means of indicating the scale of destitution in the crofting region for two reasons. First, other evidence suggests that 1848 and 1849 were typical years of the crisis. The danger of starvation was not as menacing as in 1846 and 1847. On the other hand, conditions were apparently worse than in such years as 1853 and 1855. Second, in 1848, the Central Board operated the 'destitution test' in order to ensure that those who sought relief were really in need of it.[48] Able-bodied male applicants were required to carry out specified work for an entire day of eight hours in return for a total 'payment' at the rate of 1lb. of meal. The theory was that only those entirely devoid of the means of subsistence would accept such a pittance, the minimum to sustain life, on this basis. During 1848 and 1849, therefore, there was a consistent imbalance in the number of relief applicants and the number who finally received it.[49] This probably implies that many were unwilling to accept assistance through the destitution test. It is therefore likely that the figures in Table 2.7 are restricted to those who had no choice but to accept the Board's help and who might have been in danger of starving but for the meagre assistance which they received.

Table 2.6. Estimated Percentage of Families, Insular Districts, 'not paupers but destitute of food', December 1846

District	Total Population in Districts Sampled	Per Cent Families Destitute of Food
Skye districts	6410	21
Small Isles (Eigg & Muck) districts	557	33
N. Uist (Trumsgarry)	1100	36
Coll and Mull districts	6055	32

Source: *Destitution Papers*, Second Statement of the Destitution Committee of the Free Church, 6-13

Note: (i) In the source total numbers in districts are given as total population and total numbers 'destitute of food' in families. 'Population' has been converted to 'families' by dividing total numbers by five.
(ii) Districts estimating those 'destitute of food' in non-quantitative terms have been excluded from the samples.

An average of thirty-five per cent of the population of the mainland districts, thirty-two per cent of the population of Inner Hebridean districts and seventy-one per cent of the people of the Outer Hebrides featured in the relief list at these periods of most acute hardship. The averages concealed great disparities. At such times, for instance, a staggering eighty-nine per cent of the inhabitants of Barra were supported by the Central Board. In several areas, especially in the islands, serious levels of destitution persisted until the mid-1850s. These were aggravated by the cessation of the efforts of the Central Board in 1850 and the impact of the clearances which increased in intensity from the later 1840s. As late as 1855 the administration of the Duke of Argyll in Tiree and Mull was still providing meal and relief work for the needy. As the Duke's Chamberlain emphasised, this assistance was vital '. . . to keep the people from starving'.[50]

Table 2.7. *Abstract of Largest Numbers Receiving Relief from Central Board as Percentage of Total Population, 1848-1849*

Year	Mainland Districts							Inner Hebrides				Outer Hebrides			
	Morvern	Mainland Inver-ness	Ardna-murchan	Glenelg	W. Ross	Kilmallie	Arisaig	Islay	Skye	Tiree	Mull	Barra	S. Uist	N. Uist	Harris
1848	?	30	49	44	37	15	?	10	23	50	57	89	62	48	70
1849	14	13	43	67	20	?	55	11	33	41	44	85	67	50	72

Source: Destitution Papers, Tenth Report of Glasgow Section (1848), Abstract Statement of Persons Receiving Aid, 1 January-1 October 1848; Report on the Islands of Mull etc. (1849), 32.

3

It is now possible to provide a clearer numerical estimate of the scale of the subsistence crisis. The numbers likely to be directly affected during the decade 1846 to 1856 have been estimated from the records of the Central Board to 1850 and, thereafter, from estate and Poor Law records and the files of the contemporary press. In 1851 the total population of the four Highland counties was 239,961. The population of the parishes which required a consistent supply of external aid or, in the case of Sutherland and the Island of Lewis, considerable landlord subsidy, numbered 117,000 or forty-nine per cent of the total. The number of inhabitants of parishes 'seriously at risk' (defined as having up to one third of their populations on the relief lists at any point between 1847 and 1850) was 66,705 or twenty-eight per cent of the region's population. The fact that only about one third of the region's inhabitants were in grave danger implied considerable social suffering in the affected districts but it enabled relief resources to be concentrated and emergency measures managed effectively. The contrast with Ireland, where several millions of people were at risk from outright starvation or from hunger-related diseases, is immediately and obviously apparent.

There was considerable variation in the extent of destitution within the distressed region. Virtually from the first year of the potato blight, conditions were worst on the islands. The mainland parishes in serious distress had a total population of 22,214 in 1851 or nineteen per cent of the inhabitants of the stricken region as a whole. When the Free Church correspondents in December 1846 estimated the families who were 'not paupers but were destitute of food', they reckoned that ten per cent of those in mainland districts were in this plight compared with twenty-one per cent of those living on the islands.[51] There were, therefore, several areas, even in the crofting zone, which escaped profound distress. In Sutherland, few localities suffered badly in 1846-7, because the potato blight was less extensive than elsewhere and a major relief operation was launched by the Duke of Sutherland.[52] Thereafter, serious distress was confined to the poorer western parishes of Assynt and Edderachillis. This pattern is apparent in the rentals of the Sutherland estate. The arrears of small tenants in the eastern districts of the property never reached more than ten per cent of rental in the later 1840s but climbed to eighty-five per cent of the total in Edderachillis and sixty-one per cent in Assynt.[53]

Almost all of Wester Ross was badly affected in 1846 and 1847 but from then the northern district, comprising the parishes of Lochbroom and Gairloch, escaped relatively lightly. In the view of the relief officials this was because of the resilience of the area's fishing activities and the greater dependence of the population on the sea than the land.[54] The varying incidence of distress in this district is clarified in Table 2.8. Other mainland areas in the crofting region where destitution levels were relatively low included the parishes of Appin, Ardchattan and Morvern in northern Argyllshire and Lochaber in Inverness. Acute distress concentrated in the Ardnamurchan peninsula and the parishes of Arisaig, Moidart, Glenelg, Kintail and Lochcarron.

As the famine persisted, the epicentre of destitution began to focus even more strongly on the Hebrides. When the Highland and Island Emigration Society commenced its major programme to assist the poor to emigrate to Australia from 1851, seventy-nine per cent of those who received aid were inhabitants of the islands.[55] Even in the insular districts, however, there was great diversity. The eastern parishes of Lewis, Islay, Jura and some of the Small Isles had much lower numbers of relief applicants than Tiree, South Uist, Barra, Skye, Harris and Mull. In general terms, conditions were worse in the Long Island than in the Inner Hebrides. Relief officials acknowledged that the inhabitants of Barra, Tiree, South Uist and parts of Skye endured the most acute suffering of all the areas under their care.[56]

Table 2.8. Relief Recipients, Wester Ross Districts and Villages, 1848

	Population	Per Cent of Population Receiving Relief
Districts		
Lochbroom, Gairloch, Torridon	10,700	13
Villages		
Shieldaig	800	25
Plockton	1,200	52
Dornie	1,500	45

Source: *Destitution Papers*, Capt. H.B. Elliot, 1 May 1848

It is difficult to determine any clear pattern behind the varying incidence of distress: so much depended on the diversity of natural endowment, landlord initiative, the ratio of cottars to rent-paying tenants and the local scale of emigration after 1846. It seems reasonably clear, however, that there was often a very close correlation between severe difficulty and areas which had been major centres of kelp manufacture in earlier decades. Barra, Tiree and South Uist, for instance, were the most prominent kelping districts. Most destitution in Lewis concentrated in the areas around Loch Roag, another kelping centre.[57] Table 2.9, which is calculated from the rentals of the estates of Lord Macdonald in Skye, indicates that the scale of rent arrears tended to be higher in crofting townships with kelping traditions than in others. The potato famine exposed even more clearly than before the vulnerability of communities which had grown to depend on a source of income and employment which had experienced rapid contraction since the 1820s.

At the same time, several districts which relied more on the sea than on the land were often in a better position to resist the worst consequences of the potato blight. It was perhaps above all the complex interrelationship between fishing and agriculture, which often varied from township to township *within* estates, which makes generalisation about the impact of the famine so hazardous. Table 2.10 describes the range of fishing activity in Argyllshire and demonstrates how neighbouring localities often had quite different traditions. The western areas of Lewis, especially the parish of Uig, suffered much more than the rest of the island, simply because fishing was virtually impossible along the stormy Atlantic coast which lacked suitable harbours.[58] Communities which depended on the white fishery, such as Lewis and, to a lesser extent, Harris, where catches were regular, were more favourably placed than those which

Table 2.9. Rent Arrears, Kelp and Crofting Townships, Lord Macdonald Estates, Isle of Skye, 1830-1854

Average Rents etc.	1830/31	1838/39	1845/46	1846/47	1847/48	1848/49	1850/51	1851/52	1852/53	1853/44
No Kelp £5 or less										
No. of Tenants	146	149	154	155	155	155	165	165	159	153
Rent (£)	649	644	636	636	636	636	647	647	627	602
Arrears (£)	623	533	307	397	421	330	319	366	273	239
% Rent/Arrears	96.0	82.8	48.3	62.4	66.2	51.9	49.3	56.6	43.5	39.7
£5 or less										
No. of Tenants			26	26	26	26				
Rent (£)			58	58	58	58				
Arrears (£)			54	54	36	33				
% Rent/Arrears			25.9	93.1	62.1	56.9				
Kelp £5 or less										
No. of Tenants	110	105	116	116	116	116	139	139	138	133
Rent (£)	364	352	368	368	368	368	400	400	399	399
Arrears (£)	434	279	229	395	392	337	216	333	243	250
% Rent/Arrears	119.2	79.3	62.2	107.3	106.5	91.6	54.0	83.3	60.9	62.9
Kelp (£)	39	20	42	42	42	42				
% Kelp/Rent	10.7	5.7	11.4	11.4	11.4	11.4				
No Kelp £5-£10										
No. of Tenants	45	47	53	53	53	53	65	65	65	43
Rent (£)	355	357	357	357	357	357	340	340	331	259
Arrears (£)	331	275	193	264	295	230	138	185	139	76
% Rent/Arrears	93.2	77.2	54.1	73.9	82.6	64.7	40.6	54.4	42.0	29.5
Kelp £5-£10										
No. of Tenants	56	59	60	60	60	60	75	75	67	58
Rent (£)	482	496	502	502	502	502	508	508	503	408
Arrears (£)	650	555	267	427	474	355	298	432*	299	267
% Rent/Arrears	135.0	111.9	53.2	85.1	94.4	70.7	58.7	85.0	59.4	65.4
Kelp (£)	10.5	8.0	15.5	15.5	15.5	15.5				
% Kelp/Rent	2.2	1.6	3.1	3.1	3.1	3.1				

Sources: SRO, Lord Macdonald Papers, GD221/122/4; GD221/122/19; GD221/123/1; GD221/122/11

relied on the chance appearance of a herring shoal in the loch or off the coast. Robert Somers, for instance, in his tour of the Western Highlands in 1847, noted how some of the most destitute localities were the Ross-shire fishing villages of Dornie, Plockton, Shieldaig and Lochcarron because they simply could not rely on the herring appearing on a regular annual basis.[59] Table 2.11 confirms Somers' observations by outlining the very large numbers who claimed relief in these villages in 1848. Lochcarron, for example, experienced a cycle of despair and prosperity during the famine due to the agonising fluctuation in the herring fishery. In October, 1846, it was reported, 'Hopes are blighted . . . not a single herring now in the loch'.[60] Three years later conditions had altered dramatically: 'Never in the memory of man was there such an appearance of herring'.[61]

Table 2.10. Argyll Fishing District Survey, 1851

Tiree: 70 boats engaged in cod and ling fishery. Only 13 properly equipped with long lines.
Coll: No herring fishery; in general not much fishing activity. Only two crews.
Tobermory: No regular fishing except by handline for small white fish. Sound of Mull too narrow for drift net fishing; bottom too rocky for line fishing.
Ulva: Scarcely prosecutes fishing at all.
Loch Scridain (Mull): 20-30 boats. Good for herring, cod and ling.
Iona: Only fishing by handline.
Lochbuie (Mull):Excellent cod and ling fishery from February to May.
Sunart: No fishing of any consequence for several years.
Loch Eil: Last season (1849) the best herring fishery for several years.
Lismore: Several crews of successful fishermen.
Ballachulich: Little or no fishing because of work on the slate quarries.
Gigha: Cod fishing actively pursued.
Islay: Cod fishing exploited with great success, especially from Portnahaven. No herring fishery around Islay.

Source: SRO, AF7/85, Report of a Survey of Inveraray District, 8 April 1851

The pattern of distress which has been described cannot easily resolve the vexed question of the relationship between the sheep clearances and social destitution already referred to in Chapter 1. Contemporary observers drew attention to the fact that some of the most acute conditions of hardship existed in the villages of Wester Ross, Western Inverness-shire, Skye and Mull where many of the evicted congregated as cottars and lodgers in the wake of the clearances.[62] Almost certainly, too, the escalation in eviction from 1849 also did much to exacerbate the suffering of the poor in some areas.[63] On the other hand, there was no inevitable or automatic correlation between clearance and destitution. On the mainland, districts such as the county of Sutherland and Morvern in Argyllshire, which had experienced widespread eviction in earlier decades, suffered less distress than other areas.[64] Similarly, the population of the 'uncleared' Ross of Mull was more destitute than that of other parts of the island.[65] Conditions in North Uist were not as bad as Barra at least partly because many people had left the island between 1838 and 1842 in a combined programme of clearance and assisted emigration.[66] The terrible sufferings of the inhabitants of the 'uncleared', congested islands of Barra and Tiree during the famine suggest that mass eviction, when associated with assisted emigration, was sometimes a necessary if often brutal method of correcting a chronic and dangerous imbalance between population and local opportunities for employment and subsistence.

Table 2.11. Numbers on Relief, Wester Ross, April 1848

District	Population	Numbers on Relief	Numbers on Relief as Per cent of Total Population
Shieldaig & Kishorn	800	311	39
Applecross	1,100	590	54
Lochcarron	1,600	397	25
Plockton	1,200	668	55
Lochalsh & Dornie	1,500	746	50
Glenshiel	1,110	698	63
Totals	7,310	3,410	48

Source: *Destitution Papers*, Report by Capt. Rose, Resident Inspector, W. Ross, 1 April 1948

Not all social groups in the Western Highlands and Islands were equally affected by the crisis. Three groups in particular were most vulnerable, widows with families, elderly spinsters and the cottar class. There seems little doubt that the plight of many of these was due in part to the weaknesses of the Poor Law in the Highlands. Several relief officials pointed out that many of those widows and spinsters in receipt of assistance ought to have been supported instead by the official Poor Law. But these, '. . . the most indigent and the most to be pitied of the Highland population', always formed a significant proportion of those who claimed relief from the agencies of the Central Board.[67] Table 2.12 indicates, for example, that they formed no less than twenty-eight per cent of those likely to require relief in Skye in 1848.

Reports from all over the Highlands suggested that the cottars were also a vulnerable class.[68] Only in some localities, such as parts of Wester Ross, where many scraped a living principally from the sea rather than the land, were they able to exist without official support.[69] The serious distress which they experienced derived mainly from the factors considered in Chapter 1.[70] But, in addition, reports also circulated from several districts that some tenants were repossessing the tiny cottar holdings in order to extend grain cultivation for their own needs.[71] It was also the case that some landlords only felt an obligation to assist their rent-paying tenants and specifically excluded cottars from relief.[72] Partly this was because many of this class lived in the small villages of the crofting region, sometimes as squatters and lodgers, and so were outside the direct responsibility of any one proprietor. Craftsmen-cottars were also regarded as most indigent during the famine as their former customers now devoted any scanty cash resources to the purchase of meal.[73] There is also some evidence that landlords in Skye, Mull, Barra and South Uist were endeavouring to weed out many cottar families as part of a general programme of clearance in the latter stages of the famine and, at the same time, pursue a more effective policy of prohibiting subdivision.[74] The failure of the potato was the trigger which released a whole series of other pressures on this marginal class and eventually forced many of them to emigrate.

Table 2.12. Numbers Likely to Seek Relief, Skye, December 1847

District	Crofters	Able Cottars	Widows inc. Families	Single Women	Part Disabled	Total
Bracadale	120	60	40	10	60	290
Duirnish	–	80	40	6	40	166
Kilmuir	70	60	90	20	50	290
Snizort	350	200	200	60	180	990
Portree	130	150	55	20	40	395
Strath & Strathaird	150	90	100	50	60	450
Sleat	100	125	150	50	54	475
Raasay	–	very few other than some women				
Total & Per cent	920 (30%)	765 (26%)	675 (22%)	216 (6%)	484 (16%)	3056

Source: *Destitution Papers*, Report from Capt. E.G. Fishbourne, Resident Inspector, Skye, 2 December 1847

The plight of the cottars, however, should not obscure the fact that the impact of the famine reached also into the ranks of the small tenantry. Previous discussion has shown that their condition and that of the cottars were often intimately connected because many cottars were close kindred of the crofters.[75] Where such kin links did not exist, the land available to the cottar class, as indicated above, may have been reduced during the course of the famine as the small tenantry also struggled to survive. But there is evidence from other areas that kinship obligations were still maintained between crofter and cottar families even after 1848. In Glenorchy in November 1846 it was reckoned that many cottars would have died but for the assistance of the small tenants. The Free Church referred to the tenants '. . . sharing their own little stores most liberally with the destitute', and similar reports came from Tiree, Mull and Moidart.[76]

For this reason alone, the crofter class could not remain unscathed. As one factor on the Sutherland estate put it, '. . . in bad seasons, the cottars eat up the too scanty subsistence of the tenants'.[77] Yet, despite their marginally greater resources – the possibility of cultivating more oats and bere to partially compensate for the lost potatoes and the ability to sell a cow and to buy meal – many small tenants throughout the Western Highlands found themselves in a similar condition to the cottars. The evidence for this assertion comes from two sources, the rapid rise in rent arrears among the small tenantry, even in estates outside the most distressed region, and the fact that the families of crofters swelled the ranks of those who received relief from the Central Board after 1847.

Arrears on the Gairloch estate in Wester Ross, a part of the Highlands not unusually afflicted by the famine, stood at £877 in 1846. By 1848 they had risen to £1,831. In 1846 twenty-two per cent of all tenants were in arrears. Two years later the proportion had risen to sixty per cent.[78] Rental income on the Macdonald estate on Skye collapsed by a spectacular 125 per cent between 1845 and 1850.[79] Arrears on Sir James Riddell's

Table 2.13. *Largest Numbers on Relief, Skye and Wester Ross, 1847-1850*

	1847	1848	1849	1850
Skye	13,471 (56%)	5,559 (22%)	8,162 (30%)	6,952 (26%)
Wester Ross (North)	7,010	997	No figures	No figures
Wester Ross (South)	6,260	2,579	1,984	1,763
Wester Ross	13,270 (67%)	3,576 (18%)	1,984 (10%)	1,763 (8%)

Source: Destitution Papers, Second Report of Edinburgh Section (1850), 20.
Notes: (i) Figures in brackets refer to numbers relieved as per cent of total population.
(ii) Wester Ross (North) = Ullapool, Laigh, Gairloch, Poolewe; Wester Ross (South) = Shieldaig, Applecross, Kishorn, Lochcarron, Lochalsh, Plockton, Kintail, Letterfearn, Inversheil.

Ardnamurchan estate soared from £269 in 1847 to £3,219 in 1852.[80] Arrears among tenants on Cameron of Locheil's property in central Inverness were almost double the book rental of £555 in 1847.[81] Even in the three western parishes of the Sutherland estate, where conditions were better than in many parts of the Hebrides, the trend was similar. Arrears as a proportion of small tenant rental moved from eleven per cent in Assynt in 1842 to sixty-one per cent by 1849; from forty-four per cent in Edderachillis in 1842 to eighty-five per cent in 1849; and from forty-six per cent in Durness to eighty-six per cent seven years later.[82] These data tend to confirm the accuracy of Sir John McNeill's observation in 1851 that the twin impact of the potato blight and the collapse in cattle prices rendered it virtually impossible for those with rentals of £5 per annum or less to maintain payment and feed their families at the same time.[83] The evidence also suggests that, in the first few years of the famine at least, many crofters benefited from an indirect subsidy from their landlords. A tolerance of rising rent arrears for a period of time allowed the small tenant to divert much of his meagre income and resources to the purchase of meal. Despite this the evidence presented in Tables 2.7 and 2.10 to 2.12 above and the comparative figures outlined in Table 2.13 above show plainly that the numbers on relief were so large in certain districts that crofters and their families must have been included among them. In late 1847, for example, thirty per cent of those estimated as likely to require relief in Skye were small tenants.[84] It was unlikely, nonetheless, that as a class they suffered the same privation as the cottars in all areas. In addition, the known variations in material standards within the group make generalisation hazardous. But the effect of the famine obviously had a major effect throughout virtually all social strata below the level of landlords and large tenants in the Western Highlands and Islands and was not confined to any one section.

NOTES

1. This survey of blight is based on W.G. Burton, *The Potato* (London, 1948), 104-100; C. Woodham-Smith, *The Great Hunger* (London, 1962), 94-102; K.S. Chester, *The Nature and Prevention of Plant Diseases* (Philadelphia, 1942); 'Report on the Disease of the Potato Crop in Scotland in the Year 1845' in *Trans. Highland and Agricultural Society*, new ser., 1845-7, 437-555.

2. See, for example, 'Report on the Disease of the Potato Crop'; 'Continuation of Reports', *Trans. Highland and Agricultural Society*, new ser., 1847-9, 102-123 ; Donald Bain, *Observations upon the Potato Disease of 1845 and 1846* (Edinburgh, 1848); F.J. Graham, *On the Potato Disease* (London, 1847); Laurence Rostone, *The Cause of the Potato Disease Ascertained by Proofs* (London, 1847)

3. Woodham-Smith, *The Great Hunger*, 101.

4. *Inverness Courier*, 29 April 1846; 5 November 1845; *Glasgow Herald*, 4 February 1846; 10 June 1846.

5. *Glasgow Herald*, 4 February 1846.

6. *Inverness Courier*, 29 April 1846.

7. *John O'Groats Journal*, 6 March 1846.

8. *Glasgow Herald*, 22 June 1846.

9. *Witness*, 21 November 1846.

10. *Ibid.*, 25 November 1846.

11. 'Report on the Disease of the Potato Crop', 437.

12. *Extracts from Letters to the Rev. Dr. McLeod regarding the Famine and Destitution in the Highlands of Scotland* (Glasgow 1847), 71.

13. *Scotsman*, 29 August 1846; 8 August 1846.
14. *Relief Correspondence*, Sir E. Coffin to Mr. Trevelyan, November 1846.
15. 'Agricultural Statistics for Scotland 1857', in *Trans. Highland and Agricultural Society*, 1857-59, 203.
16. SRO, HD6/2, Sir E. Coffin to Mr. Trevelyan, 16 August 1851.
17. *Witness*, 12 February 1848; *Inverness Courier*, 6 February 1851.
18. See below, pp.128-129.
19. Sir Charles Trevelyan, *The Irish Crisis* (London, 1880), 7.
20. SRO, HD6/2, Sir E. Coffin to Mr. Trevelyan, 16 August 1847.
21. *Destitution Papers*, Report on the Outer Hebrides (1849), 20.
22. See below, pp.303-305.
23. *Inverness Courier*, 13 June 1846.
24. *Ibid.*, 21 October 1846; *Edinburgh Evening Courant*, 3 October 1846.
25. *McNeill Report*, Appendix A, 75.
26. *Ibid.*, 38-9.
27. See below, pp.122-3.
28. *Inverness Courier*, 14 January 1846; *Witness*, 9 September 1846; *Inverness Advertiser*, 2 October 1849.
29. See below, pp. 91-105.
30. *Destitution Papers*, Report of Committee on Disposal of Funds (1847-8), 7.
31. *Ibid.*, Papers of Central Board (1849), Capt. R. Eliot to W. Skene, 30 June 1849.
32. *Ibid.*, Second Report of the Edinburgh Section for 1850, 37.
33. Mulock, *Western Highlands and Islands*, 78.
34. *Destitution Papers*, Second Statement of the Destitution Committee of the Free Church, 3.
35. For contemporary estimates see *Relief Correspondence*, Sir J. Riddell to Sir G. Gray, 24 August 1846; Speirs to Lord Advocate, 28 August 1846; Sir J. McNeill to Sir G. Gray, 27 September 1846; *Scotsman*, 19 December 1846; *Destitution Papers*, Second Statement of Destitution Committee of the Free Church, 3; *Witness*, 25 November 1846; SRO, HD6/2, Treasury Correspondence. Sir J. McNeill to Trevelyan, 8 March 1847.
36. See below, pp.117-118.
37. These generalisations on conditions in the central and eastern Highlands are based on SRO, HD19/1-28, Minutes and Papers of Easter Ross, Inverness and Argyll Destitution Committees, 1846-7; *Destitution Papers*, Central Board Reports (1847), Reports by Captain Eliot, April-May 1847, 1-51; SRO, HD6/2, Treasury Correspondence, Sir E. Coffin to Mr Trevelyan, 28 September 1847.
38. E. Richards, *The Last Scottish Food Riots* (London, 1982).
39. *Destitution Papers*, Third Report of the Edinburgh Section of the Central Board for 1848, 5.
40. See above, pp.1-3 for an assessment of the economic and social structure of the farming region.
41. SRO, HD19/1 (Alness); HD19/3 (Avoch); HD19/4 (Boleskine); HD19/6 (Dores); HD19/9 (Fort Augustus); HD19/12 (Kincardine).
42. *Destitution Papers*, Second Report by the Committee of Management to the Edinburgh Section for 1850, 11.
43. *Glasgow Herald*, 21 December 1846; *Witness*, 27 January 1847; SRO, HD6/2, Treasury Correspondence, Major Halliday to Trevelyan, 7 March 1847; SRO, HD 20/187, Return from the Island Glass Lighthouse, January 1847; *Relief Correspondence*, Capt. Rose to Sir E. Coffin, 27 January 1847.
44. See below, Appendix 5.
45. *Glasgow Herald*, 19 October 1846; *Witness*, 27 January 1847; SRO, Lord Advocate's Papers, AD58/86, Conditions in Barra and South Uist, 1846-49; *Glasgow Herald*, 6 November 1846; *Destitution Papers*, First Statement appointed by Edinburgh Public Meeting, 2-3.

46. SRO, HD6/2, Sir E. Coffin to Mr. Trevelyan, 28 September 1847; *Destitution Papers*, Central Board and Glasgow Section Reports, 1847, *passim*; *Witness*, 9 October 1848; 27 January 1847; *Scotsman*, 19 December 1846; *Witness*, 13 February 1847.

47. See below, pp.120-132.

48. *Destitution Papers*, Fourth Report of the Edinburgh Section, 69. For an examination of the 'destitution test' and its effects see below, pp. 130-137.

49. *Ibid.*, H.B. Rose to W. Skene, 22 February 1848. In Wester Ross (South District), 4230 applied for relief in the period March-May 1848. Only 2257 were willing to accept it under the terms of the test.

50. Inveraray Castle, Argyll Estate Papers, Bundle 1806, John Campbell to Duke of Argyll, 21 February 1855.

51. *Destitution Papers*, Second Statement of the Destitution Committee of the Free Church, 7-12.

52. NLS, Sutherland Estate Papers, Dep. 313/1173, James Loch to Duke of Sutherland, 4 September 1846; to W. Mackenzie, 20 February 1847; Dep. 313/2021, Scourie Account, 1838-49.

53. *Ibid.*, Dep. 313/2207-15; 2216-22, Sutherland Small Rents (Eastern); Dep. 313/2234-2249, Sutherland Small Rents (Western).

54. *Destitution Papers*, Capt. H.B. Rose to Capt. Eliot, 1 May 1848.

55. SRO, HD4/5, Papers of Highland and Island Emigration Society, 1851-57. See also below, pp. 246-247.

56. *Relief Correspondence*, Sir E. Coffin to Mr. Trevelyan, 14 November 1846; *Destitution Papers*, Report on the Outer Hebrides by the Glasgow Section (1849), 9; Second Statement by Free Church Destitution Committee (1847), 24.

57. MS Diary of John M. Mackenzie, Chamberlain of the Lews, 1851.

58. *Ibid.*

59. Somers, *Letters from the Highlands*, 58-9, 80-5.

60. *Inverness Courier*, 23 September 1846.

61. *John O'Groats Journal*, 27 July 1849.

62. *McNeill Report*, Appendix A, 16, 20; *Destitution Papers*, Second Statement by Free Church Destitution Committee, 17; Report on Mull etc. by Glasgow Section (1849), 8, 12.

63. See below, pp. 176-80.

64. For relief applications in Morvern see Table 2.7 above, p.45.

65. Inveraray Castle, Argyll Estate Papers, Bundle 1522, A. McGregor, Minister of Iona to Duke of Argyll, 1 February 1847; *Destitution Papers*, Statement of Numbers receiving Relief from Glasgow Section, Mull, 1849. The largest number of relief recipients in the island in 1849 accounted for 42 per cent of total population. In the Ross, recipients totalled 63 per cent of total population.

66. SRO, Lord Macdonald Papers, GD221/21, Emigration Papers. In all, 841 were assisted to leave the island, 1839-41, most of them of the poorer class. For the background to the evictions see SRO, GD221/43, Report by Duncan Shaw, factor for North Uist, 1839.

67. *Destitution Papers*, Sixth Report of the Committee of Management of the Edinburgh Section (1848), Extract from Capt. Elliot's Journal, June 1848, 18.

68. *Relief Correspondence*, Sir E. Coffin to Mr. Trevelyan, 22 October 1846. See, *inter alia*, *Witness*, 13 March 1847; 21 October 1846; *McNeill Report*, Appendix A, 48; *Letters to Rev. Dr. Macleod*, 32; *Destitution Papers*, Report on Mull etc. by Glasgow Section, 7.

69. *Ibid.*

70. See above, p.8.

71. *Witness*, 6 October 1847; 9 February 1848; SRO, HD6/2 Treasury Correspondence, Sir E. Coffin to Mr. Trevelyan, 28 September 1847; *Destitution Papers*, Seventh Report of the Edinburgh Section (1847), 18.

72. SRO, HD6/2, Treasury Correspondence, Sir Godfrey Webster to Coffin, 28 February 1847; Rev. J. Macrae to Mr. Ellice, 3 March 1847.

73. SRO, Lord Advocate's Papers, AD14/47/628, C. Shaw to J.C. Brodie, 23 March, 1847.

74. See below, pp.291-4.
75. See below, pp.7-9.
76. *Witness*, 21 November 1846; *Destitution Papers*, Second Statement by Destitution Committee of the Free Church, 4.
77. NLS, Sutherland Estate Papers, Dep. 313/1165, R. Horsburgh to James Loch, 27 April 1841.
78. Conon House, Mackenzie of Gairloch MSS, Rentals, 1846-49.
79. SRO, Lord Macdonald Papers, GD221/82, 46, 43, 70, 62, Macdonald Rentals, 1796-1858.
80. SRO, Riddell Papers, AF49/6, Report of T.G. Dickson for Trustees, 1852.
81. Achnacarry Castle, Cameron of Lochiel Papers, R.H. Top Drawer, Bundle 15, List of Arrears due by crofters to Lochiel.
82. NLS, Sutherland Estate Papers, Dep. 313/2283-2302, Small Tenant Rentals, Eastern and Western Districts.
83. *McNeill Report*, xii.
84. *Destitution Papers*, Reports from Capt. E.G. Fishbourne, Resident Inspector, Skye, 2 December 1847.

3

The Demographic Consequences

1

The tragic consequences of the Great Irish Famine, when an estimated 800,000 to over one million people died, raises the major question of the impact of the Highland subsistence crisis on regional rates of mortality.[1] This problem has only been addressed directly before by M.W. Flinn and his colleagues as part of their wider investigation of nineteenth-century Scottish population history.[2] The result of their inquiries was essentially tentative because of the inadequacy of the source materials with which they had to deal. The demographic effects of the Highland famine are very difficult to assess because civil registration only became compulsory towards the end of the crisis in 1855. The decadal census does provide a glimpse of the key social determinants but does not record, nor does it indicate, natural growth, decline or emigration. Prior to statutory registration records of mortality for the Highlands are particularly sparse and even those which do survive are incomplete. The Flinn team, for instance, were only able to assemble hard data from the burial register of the tiny parish of Gigha, an island which was not located within the distressed districts which suffered most during the famine.

It was possible in this investigation to establish a slightly stronger statistical basis for analysis. The registers of the Catholic parishes of Arisaig and Moidart were apparently well kept and contain an annual list of deaths. Unlike the Church of Scotland registers, which recorded burials when the parish mortcloth was used, the Catholic registers are enumerations of deaths, with the names inserted by the priest after he had carried out the rites of the dead. It is not known for certain whether only those who had been confirmed were listed, as seems to have been the practice in Catholic Ireland. If this was the procedure, then the Catholic registers do not record the deaths of infants and young children, two of the most vulnerable groups during the famine. Both the Catholic parishes were in areas badly affected by the famine. Furthermore, the Old Parish Registers of Iona and the Sutherland parish of Dornoch also recorded burials. This somewhat bigger sample allows for a closer examination of those localities which experienced the most acute distress and at the same time permits an evaluation of one district in Sutherland which escaped the full rigours of the famine. It has to be admitted, however, that the materials are very frail. The Church of Scotland registers do not necessarily record all burials. Still-born babies and infants may not have been recorded. On the other hand, the data derived from the registers do provide a guide, if not to total mortality, at least to changes in the number of deaths within registered groups. Unfortunately, however, it is not possible to determine the age, sex or social status of the dead in any consistent fashion from the materials which have been used.

Because of the relatively small number of areas in the sample of burial registers, three additional measures were employed to monitor the cycle of mortality in those parishes not included in the detailed study. First, in two representative Hebridean parishes, Kilfinichen in Mull and Barvas in Lewis, 'deaths' of heads of household were estimated from the enumerators' returns across the three censuses of 1841, 1851 and 1861. The estimate was based on the following technique. If only one partner in a married couple listed in one census appeared in a subsequent census, it was assumed that the other partner had died. A significant increase in losses of marital partners between each census might then suggest a mortality crisis. In the calculation, these 'deaths' were listed as a proportion of total households rather than total population. Second, the pattern of enrolment of 'permanent' paupers supported by the Scottish Poor Law in the Highlands can provide an indirect guide to any marked increase in sickness or disease among destitute families. At some point in the cycle of deprivation and illness these people would have a legal right to the support of the Poor Law. There is some evidence by the later 1840s that due to the intervention of the Board of Supervision the standard of administration of the Poor Law in the Highlands marginally improved over the period of the famine though abuses still occurred. Third, both the government from August 1846 to August 1847 and the Central Board thereafter devoted a considerable effort to the monitoring of deaths through hunger or diseases related to malnutrition in the Western Highlands. Their reports were not normally couched in quantitative terms but they nevertheless provide useful insights from the perspective of experienced relief officials who were very concerned about the possible impact of food deficiency on mortality rates. Two other public bodies, the Lord Advocate's Office in Edinburgh and the Board of Supervision of the Scottish Poor Law, also carried out official inquiries whenever any claim was made that death had occurred through starvation or malnutrition.

Table 3.1. Annual Deaths, Moidart, 1838-1855

Year	Deaths
1838	7
1839	6
1840	6
1841	8
1842	7
1843	8
1844	no entry
1845	12
1846	4
1847	10
1848	12
1854	8
1855	7

Source: SRO, RH21/48/2

Table 3.2. Annual Deaths, Arisaig, 1838-1860

Year	Deaths	Average for period
1838	14	
1839	20	
1840	8	
1841	17	
1842	23	14.87
1843	10	
1844	18	
1845	9	
1846	17	
1847	24	
1848	20	
1849	13	
1850	5	13.3
1851	11	
1852	12	
1853	6	
1854	9	
1855	16	
1856	13	
1857	7	
1858	8	10
1859	8	
1860	14	

Source: SRO, RH21/44/1

Table 3.3. Annual Burials, Iona, 1835-1854

Year	Deaths	Average for period
1835	13	
1836	8	
1837	30	18.4
1838	16	
1839	25	
1840	21	
1841	21	
1842	11	
1843	3	14.5
1844	13	
1845	18	
1846	17	
1847	29	
1848	12	
1849	4	
1850	14	11.55
1851	12	
1852	9	
1853	5	
1854	5	

Source: GRO, Old Parish Registers, Iona

Table 3.4. Annual Burials, Dornoch, 1835-1854

Year	Deaths	Average for period
1835	33	
1836	36	
1837	65	40.25
1838	34	
1839	26	
1840	36	
1841	37	
1842	44	35.5
1843	25	
1844	33	
1845	38	
1846	38	
1847	44	
1848	41	
1849	28	37.44
1850	33	
1851	32	
1852	40	
1853	42	
1854	39	

Source: GRO, Old Parish Registers, 47/2, Dornoch

The evidence presented in Tables 3.1 to 3.4 suggests certain patterns. There was a perceptible increase in deaths in all four areas in 1847 and this was maintained in Moidart and Arisaig in 1848. In Iona, the number of burials in 1847 was almost double the annual average for the period 1840 to 1845. On the other hand, deaths in Arisaig and burials in Iona in 1847 were not substantially greater than the previous crisis of 1837-8, and in Dornoch they were considerably lower. Burials in the Sutherland parish did rise above the average for the previous years in 1847 and 1848 but the scale of the increase was much less than in the other districts and moderated more quickly. The main conclusion from all the areas examined seems to be that a crisis in mortality may have been likely in 1847, and to a lesser extent in 1848, but that it was successfully contained. For the remainder of the famine period, annual deaths and burials returned to relatively 'normal' levels. In the case of deaths in Arisaig and burials in Iona, the average between 1846 and 1854 was actually lower than the preceding five years, though it has to be remembered that this figure was considerably affected by the substantial increase in emigration which occurred from both areas during the decade of the famine.

The three other indicators point in a similar direction. Estimated 'deaths' of heads of household in Kilfinichen were 4.8 per cent of all households from 1841 to 1851 and 8.5 per cent between 1851 and 1861. In Barvas, the figures were 7.9 per cent and 5.7 per cent respectively. These estimates hardly suggest a great surge in mortality of the type which characterised subsistence crises in Scotland in the seventeenth century.[3]

As might be anticipated during the potato famine, the numbers of the 'poor on roll' (though not occasional poor) did rise in the four Highland counties from 1846 to 1853 (see Table 3.5). The total climbed from 8086 in 1846 to 11,875 in 1849 and again to 13,132 in 1853. But even this increase, which reflects greater efficiency in Poor Law organisation as well as rising demand, hardly suggests that famine-related diseases were rampant in the Highlands. The marked expansion in the number of poor was also mainly confined to the counties of Inverness and Argyll. The other official sources support the conclusion that significant increases in mortality were restricted to the later months of 1846, early 1847 and, to a lesser extent, 1848. Sickness and unusual numbers of deaths were reported from Coll, Barra, North Uist, Arisaig, Iona, Skye and Mull.[4] By the spring of 1847, seven deaths were alleged to have been caused by absolute starvation, two in Glensheil, three in Barra, one in South Uist and one in Harris. In only two cases in Barra, however, did judicial investigation indicate that death was 'the immediate result of lack of food'.[5]

Table 3.5. Poor on Roll, Highland Counties, 1846-1853

County	1846	1847	1848	1849	1850	1851	1852	1853
Inverness	2433	3458	3538	3664	3845	3932	4100	4117
Argyll	2213	2774	3009	3321	3552	3585	3859	4173
Ross and Cromarty	2598	3759	3663	3850	3756	3686	3692	3743
Sutherland	842	1005	1006	1040	1039	1056	1103	1099
Total	8086	10997	11213	11875	12192	12259	12754	13132

Sources: *PP*, *Annual Reports of the Board of Supervision for Relief of the Poor in Scotland*, XXVIII (1847); XXXIII (1847-8); XXV (1849); XXVI (1850); XXIII (1852); L (1852-3); XXIX (1854); XLV (1854-5).

There remains the possibility that death was 'exported' as many of the inhabitants of the Western Highlands fled to the southern cities and died there or took ship across the Atlantic, like the Irish, to fall victim to disease either *en route* or when they arrived in North America. The first hypothesis seems unlikely. A later chapter argues that there is little evidence of a massive *permanent* migration from the Highlands to the urban areas of the Lowlands during the course of the famine.[6] Nor is there any indication in the press of reports of unusually high mortality among Highland migrants despite the considerable interest shown by several southern journals in their plight. In 1847 and 1848 the Scottish cities themselves suffered an outbreak of cholera and a savage epidemic of typhus which was exacerbated by the industrial recession of these years. Highland migrants were just as likely to be as vulnerable as any others to these diseases.[7]

During the 1840s most emigrants from the Western Highlands made for Canada. There were some reports of tragedies on board ships and of high death rates among some emigrant parties when they reached North America. In 1849, seventy emigrants out of a group of 300 from Lochalsh, who sailed on the *Circassian*, died during the voyage.[8] In the same year, cholera claimed many deaths among 600 emigrants from Tiree and the Ross of Mull.[9] The Canadian press estimated that only a third reached their final destination.[10] Typhus was rife among a party of emigrants from the Duke of Sutherland's estate when they arrived on the *Vesper* at Quebec in 1850.[11] However, though these incidents attracted considerable publicity, they seem to have been relatively isolated and unrepresentative. Immigration officials regularly complained about the deep poverty, lack of clothing and destitute condition of many Highland emigrants but they did not very often refer to their poor health.[12] In statistical terms, mortality rates in vessels carrying emigrants from the Highlands to Canada were much lower than on ships from Ireland. In 1847, no less than fifteen per cent of those who sailed for Quebec from Liverpool, the vast majority of whom were Irish, failed to survive the voyage.[13] The mortality rate in ships which sailed direct from Ireland was eight per cent but only three per cent in vessels from Scottish ports to Canada.[14] There was indeed a huge increase in Highland emigration at this time but, in general, the 'coffin ships' of Irish folk tradition were not associated with the Hebridean exodus.[15]

The conclusion, therefore, seems inescapable that the potato famine in the Highlands did not have the same devastating consequences on death rates as the Great Famine in Ireland. Much of the remainder of this volume directly or indirectly explores the reasons for this outcome. Here, however, it needs to be stressed that West Highland society may have come very close to a major disaster. The most critical phase seems to have been the winter and early spring of 1847, the period when the initial consequences of the potato blight were first experienced but before either the relief programmes operated by government, landlords and charities had taken full effect or the labour markets for temporary migrants in the Lowlands had opened up with full vigour.[16] Evidence from the burial registers considered earlier suggests these were the months when the number of deaths rose sharply. An insight into the possible imminence of disaster can also be gained from Appendix 5. This reports information on both disease and mortality from a wide variety of sources covering the Highlands between 1846 and 1854.

The data assembled in Appendix 5 support the conclusion that 1846-7 were the years of most serious risk. Of forty-two separate reports of disease, thirty-two derive from 1846-7 and, of these, twenty-nine were from the crucial period November 1846 to March 1847.[17] The type of sickness reported was often associated with malnutrition, vitamin deficiency and intestinal disorders. 'English cholera', or *cholera nostra*, a form of extreme diarrhoea, was both widespread and potentially fatal. Significantly, it flourished during the winter of 1846 and 1847 although diarrhoea itself was normally confined to the summer months. Young children and infants were most vulnerable. *Purpura*, akin to scurvy, was also widely reported. It was almost certainly caused by the effects of deficiency in the traditional potato diet, which was relatively rich in vitamin C, and the increasing consumption of salt fish. The patient was attacked with exhaustion, ulcers, pains in the mouth and throat, and large blotches on the skin. More ominously, there were signs in some districts that food supplies were also approaching exhaustion. As food intake becomes less, bloody diarrhoea begins as starvation approaches. This is sometimes described as if it were an infectious disease but it is basically the result of the intestinal tract ceasing to function properly.[18] From Skye in February 1847 and the Ross of Mull in March

1847 it was reported that 'bloody stools' were always present as 'English cholera' spread among the people.[19]

Typhus, the disease which was the major killer in Ireland, though not caused by poor diet, thrived on conditions of severe destitution. Reports suggest it was on the increase in parts of mainland Argyll, Mull, Harris and Skye and remained a threat to life in several districts into the early 1850s.[20] The famine may have helped to spread this disease indirectly. The year 1847 saw a severe typhus epidemic in urban Scotland. The subsistence crisis promoted a marked increase in seasonal migration to the Lowland areas. It is very possible, though difficult to prove, that typhus may have been disseminated in part by temporary migrants returning to the north-west after being infected during their sojourn in the southern cities. The observations reported in Appendix 5 also confirm the mortality increases noted earlier in the burial registers. The age and social class of the victims are rarely mentioned, but when they are they are normally children, the old and members of cottar families. As might be expected, hunger-related illnesses flourished mainly in the Hebrides in early 1847 and not in every Highland district. Thirty-six of the forty-two references were from insular areas and no reports of serious disease came from the central and eastern Highlands. The information does suggest, however, that if external intervention on a large scale had not taken place, many parishes in the Western Highlands and Islands might well have seen death rates maintain the increase in subsequent years that they achieved in late 1846 and early 1847.

There is, however, a real irony here. In Scotland as a whole mortality rates rose to a high level in 1847 and very high rates were sustained for a further four years. The crisis had two central features, a severe typhus epidemic in 1847 and the second great cholera epidemic of 1848. Sharp increases in mortality were not confined to the large towns and cities alone but they were mainly concentrated there. Rapid urbanisation together with the inadequacy of water supplies and public health measures had created a lethal environment in which disease thrived. The Highlands, on the evidence presented in this chapter, not only escaped starvation but also the worst effects of the epidemics of the later 1840s which raged elsewhere in Scotland. Despite contemporary anxieties it was clearly safer to endure the privations of life in the Western Highlands than a hazardous existence in the perilous conditions of the wynds and alleyways of Glasgow and Dundee.

2

The recording of marriages and baptisms features more regularly than deaths in the Old Parish Registers of the Highlands. However, the registers are often affected by the Disruption of 1843 and the emergence thereafter of the Free Church which attracted its most loyal and largest following in the Western Highlands. The records of the parishes of Clyne, Kilfinichen and Bracadale, for example, show a marked decline in marriages in the early 1840s, almost certainly as a result of this factor, and the registers for Barvas and Dornoch fade out altogether. The baptismal registers also present a considerable problem. They were not only distorted by the Disruption, but they also did not necessarily record all births which occurred in a particular area. Baptisms often took place some years after birth, and where the date of birth is not recorded the discrepancy cannot be allowed for. Both marriages and baptisms were also likely to be affected profoundly by the marked expansion in emigration already mentioned. For example, the *permanent* decline in marriages and baptisms which took place in Kilfinichen in Mull after 1847 may simply reflect heavy and sustained emigration and little else.

At best, then, the Old Parish Registers can only offer a very tentative and partial guide to the vicissitudes of some of the crucial social indicators during the famine. The tabulations and analysis which follow are based on the Catholic registers of Arisaig and Moidart together with those of sixteen parishes where the records were not obviously affected by the Disruption and where baptisms can be redistributed to year of birth.

Table 3.6. Baptisms and Marriages, Iona, 1829-1854

Year	Baptisms	Average for Period	Marriages	Average for Period
1829	15		1	
1830	22		5	
1831	38		7	
1832	26		3	
1833	43	28.8	3	3.8
1834	16		–	
1835	34		6	
1836	12		5	
1837	20		3	
1838	33	23	3	3.4
1839	41		3	
1840	36		3	
1841	31		7	
1842	26	33.5	4	4.25
1843	24		7	
1844	16		2	
1845	23		10	
1846	14		5	
1847	14	18.2	5	5.8
1848	30		8	
1849	22		6	
1850	22		5	
1851	19		3	
1852	20	22.6	3	5
1853	17		3	

Source: GRO, Old Parish Registers, Iona

Despite the limitations of the sources, the trends outlined in Tables 3.6 to 3.9 are not without significance. All the districts shared the common experience of a decline in both marriages and baptisms. In some cases this was very substantial. In Iona, for example, baptisms fell from an annual average of 32.2 between 1839 and 1842 to 18.2 from 1843 to 1847. In both 1846 and 1847 baptisms and marriages declined to fourteen and five respectively. Marriage fees amounted to a sum of between three and ten

Table 3.7. *Baptisms and Marriages, Moidart and Arisaig, 1830-1860*

	Moidart				Arisaig			
Year	Marriages	Average	Baptisms	Average	Marriages	Average	Baptisms	Average
1830	8		23					
1831	2		18					
1832	13		27					
1833	6		16					
1834	5	6.8	8	18.4				
1835	4		29					
1836	1		9					
1837	5		32					
1838	3		26		6		31	
1839	8	4.2	33	25.8	4		32	
1840	7		26		7		35	
1841	4		30		11		31	
1842	6		26		5		36	
1843	6		14		5		37	
1844	2	5	32	25.6	11	7.8	27	33.2
1845	6		26		5		42	
1846	5		25		2		29	
1847	2		25		4		20	
1848	3		12		2		27	
1849	4	4	18	21.2	1	2.8	23	28.2
1850	3		14		6		25	
1851	None		14		7		28	
1852	5		14		1		24	
1853	1		15		8		19	
1854	7		14		1		22	
1855	2	3.6	13	16.8	2	5	16	26.8
1856	2		16		3		18	
1857	3		15		2		16	
1858	2		16		6		16	
1849	4		18		3		20	
1860	4	3	14	15.8	3	3.4	21	25

Source: SRO, RH21/48/2; RH21/44/1

Table 3.8. Baptisms and Marriages, Tiree, 1835-1854

Year	Baptisms	Average for Period	Marriages	Average for Period
1835	137		24	
1836	149		16	
1837	110		23	
1838	145		32	
1839	149	138	27	24.4
1840	122		23	
1841	137		31	
1842	117		22	
1843	131		23	
1844	112	124	38	27.4
1845	130		28	
1846	111		17	
1847	80		10	
1848	79		20	
1849	103	100	27	20.4
1850	69		13	
1851	90		11	
1852	63		24	
1853	69		15	
1854	81	74	21	16.6

Source: GRO, Old Parish Registers, Tiree

shillings which might be thought too much in times of hardship. Marriage rates may also have been affected by the increased incidence of both temporary and permanent migration which altered the balance of the sexes in some localities. The general pattern indicated from Tables 3.6 to 3.8 was that baptisms fell more rapidly than marriages. Indeed, in Iona, the marriage rate was relatively stable while the baptismal rate experienced a sharp decline. This might imply increased mortality among infants, a rising rate of miscarriages, a loss of sexual appetite, or amenorrhoea, an interruption of the female menstrual cycle which is triggered by malnutrition.[21] Unfortunately, however, the data are too fragile and the variables too uncertain to come to any firm conclusion on precise causation.

Table 3.9, which is a summation of the baptismal registers of sixteen West Highland parishes, confirms the conclusions suggested by the individual parish tabulations. It can be seen that the first radical depletion occurred in 1843 and the second in 1847. There was, however, no return to the number of baptisms common in the period prior to the Disruption. The first depletion was about eighteen per cent on the average of the previous eight years and the second thirty-one per cent on the average of the previous four years. If the period 1835 to 1855 is divided into three, 1835-42, 1843-46 and 1847-54, and averages computed for each of the three phases, thirty-two per cent

Table 3.9. Annual Baptisms, Sixteen Crofting Parishes, 1835-1854

Year	Baptisms	Average for Period
1835	805	
1836	735	
1837	637	
1838	780	
1839	712	734
1840	718	
1841	700	
1842	713	
1843	595	
1844	502	645
1845	443	
1846	441	
1847	341	
1848	364	
1849	363	390
1850	329	
1851	341	
1852	328	
1853	302	
1854	334	327

Source: GRO, Old Parish Registers for relevant parishes
Note: The Parishes were Kilfinichen, Tiree, Ardchattan, Glenorchy, Iona, Ardnamurchan, Dornoch, Creich, Clyne, Stornoway, Portree, N. Uist, Moidart, Arisaig, Bracadale, Strontian.

depletion first occurs, followed then by a further reduction, also of around thirty-two per cent. There were, then, two steps downward in the number of recorded baptisms, the Disruption and the famine. Even allowing for the weakness of the data, these figures must have some significance.

3

Precise and certain evaluation of emigration (leaving the country of one's birth) and migration (changing permanent residence within the country of one's birth) is even more difficult than examination of the other demographic measures which have been surveyed. In the 1841 returns census enumerators were asked to estimate the scale of emigration from their parishes in the six months prior to registration. Some not only provided this information but also recorded emigration from 1831. Unfortunately, however, this practice was not followed either in 1851 or 1861. An analysis of out-migration (the combined measure of emigration and migration) during the famine years depends, therefore, on establishing a series of estimates derived from imperfect materials. Estimation of net out-migration is possible; more problematic, as will be seen in Chapter 8, is the division of the outward flows into those who moved to other areas of Scotland and those who left the country altogether.[22]

The method adopted here to estimate net out-migration involves a comparison of the *actual* change in population, as recorded in the census with the estimated *natural* change as indicated by the excess of births over deaths. If the actual change falls short of natural growth, net migration was assumed to have taken place and can then be calculated in numerical terms. It is important to emphasise the problems associated with this technique. First, before 1861, the recordings of births and deaths in the Highlands are scattered and unreliable. They also, therefore, have to be estimated. For the pre-1861 period, natural increase was assumed to be at the level of ten per cent per decade. When the rate does become measurable after 1861 it is not at first much below this figure. However, it is possible, in the light of the discussion earlier in this chapter, that due to increased mortality among infants, reduction in baptism and a decline in marriages, the assumption of a ten per cent increase in all parishes from 1841 to 1851 is too high. However, no allowance was made for this because of the likely diversity between parishes. For certain parishes, therefore, the assumptions on which the calculations are based may exaggerate the 'rate' of out-migration in the first decade of the famine but probably not in the second. Secondly, the calculations only provide snapshots of estimated out-migration because they are derived from the decadal census and cannot provide any insight into fluctuation in annual rates between the census years.

Thirdly, the printed census may underestimate the number of permanent residents in some parishes. This is because of the incidence of temporary migration to the Lowlands which tended to increase in spring, rise through the summer months and reach its peak in August and September, the period when there was most work in grain harvesting and fishing in the south and north-east. The censuses of 1841, 1851 and 1861 were taken in March, April and June respectively. They probably understate the number of parish inhabitants and, in particular, young adult males and females, many of whom were working elsewhere when the census was taken but returned to the parish of their birth later in the year. The extent of distortion which this factor could cause could be very great and has perhaps not been sufficiently recognised by some who have written on the demography of the nineteenth-century Highlands.[23] In this regard it is a salutary lesson for the unwary scholar to read the entry for the Wester Ross parish of Lochbroom in the *New Statistical Account*. Here the local minister carried out his own private census in November 1834 and compared his count with that of the official census taken three years earlier. According to his calculations the total parish population was 5206, a figure which was 1409 more than the official count! The discrepancy was explained by the fact that 'some hundreds of parishioners' were omitted from the government census as they were away at sea, the Caithness fishery and 'south country labouring of various kinds' when it was taken.[24] In the famine period, under-recording was, if anything, likely to be even more serious because of the considerable increase in temporary migration which occurred at the time.[25] This weakness in the basic source material cannot easily be overcome. It has to be admitted, therefore, that some of the estimates which follow may exaggerate the 'real' levels of permanent out-migration from certain Highland parishes. To partially compensate for this problem, two additional measures were employed. The rate of loss of *households* rather than individuals was calculated for three censuses from the original enumerators' returns for the representative parishes of Kilfinichen (Mull) and Barvas (Lewis). It was assumed that the disappearance of entire households would indicate permanent migration while the 'loss' of individuals might not necessarily do so. At the same time, estate records often contain useful numerical information on assisted emigration and these can also be used to build up a partial analysis of the scale of movement from certain districts.

The calculation of out-migration is therefore necessarily an approximate one. It rests on some assumptions which cannot be conclusively proven to be correct and on source materials which are partially flawed. At best it provides a provisional rough guide to migration and emigration and suggests orders of magnitude rather than precise and final judgements. The exercise was carried out for twenty-eight West Highland insular and mainland parishes. The results are presented in Table 3.10. These data, and other calculations which follow, suggest three types of conclusions about out-migration during the famine period: (i) the scale of migration, (ii) variation over time, (iii) variation over space. Each of these will now be probed in detail in the remainder of this chapter.

(i)   The estimates imply that an enormous loss of population took place from many West Highland parishes between 1841 and 1861. Uig in Lewis lost almost one half of its total population over the period, Jura almost one third, 1841-51, the Small Isles, almost one half, 1851-51, Kilfinichen (Mull), one third, 1841-51, and a further one quarter, 1851-61, Barra, one third, 1841-51, and several parishes in Skye, around a quarter or more, 1851-61. In some cases the level of out-migration was so great that it eliminated the entire actual growth in parish population which had occurred since 1801. Table 3.11 provides another perspective on the scale of the exodus. For twenty-one mainland parishes within the crofting region the estimated loss, 1841 to 1861, has been calculated as a percentage of estimated net out-migration for the nineteenth century as a whole. The result demonstrates the extent to which very heavy migration in several parishes concentrated in the famine decades. For example, in five of the twenty-one parishes, about one half of all estimated net migration, 1801 to 1891, took place in the years 1841 to 1861. Of all the losses sustained by the eleven insular parishes between 1801 to 1891 an estimated forty-seven per cent occurred between 1841 and 1861.

These estimates cannot be dismissed as a mere statistical mirage. They are broadly consistent with other evidence from the period of the famine. For example, an analysis of the enumerators' returns for 1841, 1851 and 1861 reveals a huge haemorrhage of people from the two representative crofting parishes. By 1851 Kilfinichen 'lost' 45.5 per cent of all households enumerated in 1841 and 43.6 per cent of those listed in 1851 by the next census. In Barvas, migration was less extensive but still significant: 24.4 per cent of all households disappeared by 1851 and 26.5 per cent of 1851 households by 1861.[26] In neither parish is there any evidence of excessively high mortality between 1851 and 1861 which might offer an alternative explanation for these figures. It is also

Table 3.10. *Net Out-Migration, Crofting Parishes, 1801-1891*

Parish & District	1801-11 M	%	1811-21 M	%	1821-31 M	%	1831-41 M	%	1841-51 M	%	1851-61 M	%	1861-71 M	%	1871-81 M	%	1881-91 M	%
Outer Hebrides																		
Barvas	291	13.0	+186	+8.6	+186	+7.2	+583	+17.9	46	11.9	+1	0.0	535	11.6	478	9.7	630	11.8
Lochs	136	7.3	+549	+28.5	+279	+10.5	+238	+7.8	+219	+6.0	+489	+11.5	229	6.4	360	8.6	643	14.2
Uig	+205	+9.8	+125	+0.1	122	4.2	29	1.0	439	13.2	1523	47.7	165	8.2	190	8.8	129	5.7
Harris	+273	+9.1	17	0.5	400	10.2	+139	+3.6	622	14.0	592	11.6	661	16.1	83	2.0	558	11.8
N. Uist	+552	+18.3	+722	+18.7	865	17.4	635	13.8	953	21.5	351	9.0	406	10.3	415	10.1	568	13.3
S. Uist	230	5.0	+730	+15.1	+248	+4.1	246	3.6	1893	25.8	1432	23.2	281	5.2	318	5.5	780	12.8
Barra	4	0.2	22	1.0	436	18.9	56	2.7	726	30.7	207	11.1	154	8.3	63	3.2	166	7.7
Inner Hebrides																		
Snizort	83	3.9	+286	+12.6	+419	+15.0	616	17.7	441	13.7	772	24.9	488	18.7	314	13.6	293	13.9
Strath	+184	+10.5	+301	+14.3	+81	+3.1	108	3.6	222	7.0	903	27.8	335	12.6	227	8.9	345	13.2
Torosay	+174	9.9	37	1.8	628	27.4	462	24.5	417	25.8	117	8.6	261	26.5	144	17.1	106	15.0
Kilninian	+103	+2.9	113	2.8	+37	+0.8	978	20.2	815	18.8	916	23.2	818	21.5	153	4.9	312	10.7
Jura	165	13.7	9	0.8	78	6.2	123	9.4	388	29.4	118	11.1	349	24.0	138	11.2	230	19.3
Small Isles	108	21.6	17	3.8	64	13.6	+49	+10.8	140	25.6	198	43.0	96	16.9	16	3.1	136	24.7
Kilfinichen	286	9.0	+441	+13.8	546	13.7	88	2.3	1470	35.7	841	27.5	311	12.3	626	25.4	392	22.5
Tiree	259	6.5	375	9.1	146	3.5	507	11.4	1121	25.5	438	11.8	598	18.6	294	10.4	455	16.6
Duirnish	299	9.0	+450	+13.4	203	4.9	259	5.4	151	3.0	1088	20.4	787	16.5	581	13.1	750	17.4
Kilmuir	59	2.3	+360	+13.1	310	9.2	135	4.0	811	22.4	649	20.4	478	16.6	298	11.5	404	15.7
Wester Ross																		
Lochbroom	132	3.7	+411	+10.9	379	8.3	278	6.0	466	9.7	432	9.0	793	16.3	581	13.2	622	14.8
Gairloch	+1174	+81.7	+1487	+54.0	525	11.6	10	0.2	206	4.2	229	4.4	829	15.6	1293	26.3	565	12.6
Applecross	+211	+11.1	+216	+9.4	180	6.4	320	11.1	438	15.3	436	16.1	231	8.6	325	12.5	309	13.1
Lochcarron	+18	+16.0	+298	+20.1	+11	+0.6	390	18.3	544	27.8	181	11.2	30	1.9	227	13.9	158	10.9

(continued overleaf)

Table 3.10 (continued)

Sutherland

	M	%	M	%	M	%	M	%	M	%	M	%	M	%	M	%	M	%
Assynt	156	6.5	+76	+3.1	+78	+2.8	299	9.5	507	16.0	110	3.7	339	10.7	374	12.4	269	9.7
Edderachillis	231	18.4	33	2.9	+613	+47.9	463	23.6	293	17.2	93	5.9	255	15.5	134	8.8	277	18.2
Clyne	168	10.2	+71	+4.3	350	18.7	117	6.8	9	0.5	240	12.4	235	12.5	+1	+0.1	231	12.7
Creich	202	10.2	+188	+9.5	27	1.1	236	9.2	126	4.9	78	2.9	134	5.3	401	15.9	308	13.9
Dornoch	+83	+3.5	+151	−5.6	30	1.0	1004	29.7	4	0.1	394	13.2	324	11.2	362	13.1	317	12.6
Farr	241	10.0	655	27.2	120	6.0	63	3.0	236	10.6	320	14.5	220	10.5	216	10.7	169	8.8
Kildonan	10	0.7	1166	74.1	365	64.6	27	10.5	+2006*	+83.6	365	16.8	365	17.1	112	5.8	281	14.5

Source: Census to 1861; thereafter RGS.
Notes: M = Estimated Net Numbers of Migrants
  % = Estimated percentage of net migration between censuses
  * = Boundary change

Table 3.11. Estimated Net Migration Loss, Selected West Highland and Hebridean Parishes, 1841-1861, as Proportion of Net Migration Loss, 1801-1890

Parish	Total Population Loss, 1801-90 (Estimated)	Loss, 1841-61 (Estimated)	1841-51 Loss as Per Cent of 1801-90 Loss
Insular			
Jura	1598	506	32
Kilfinichen	4559	2311	51
Lismore	3587	1427	40
Barra	1778	933	52
Bracadale	2081	831	40
Strath	2140	1125	53
S. Uist	5180	3325	64
Harris	2833	1114	39
Snizort	3007	1213	40
Uig	1726	1091	63
Lochs	1368	+708	–
Mainland			
Glenelg	3461	1406	41
Applecross	2239	874	39
Gairloch	3657	435	12
Kintail	1218	496	41
Lochalsh	2131	902	42
Lochbroom	3683	898	24
Lochcarron	1530	725	47
Morvern	2581	880	34
Clyne	1278	249	19
Durness	1165	226	19

Source: Census to 1861; thereafter RGS

the case that much of the estimated loss in Tables 3.10 and 3.11 may be accounted for in part by a major increase in the scale of assisted emigration which can be documented from estate records and will be considered in Chapter 8. For the Highlands as a whole, then, the decades of the famine represent a turning-point between the era of significant growth in numbers from the early decades of the eighteenth century and the sustained decline in population which occurred in the second half of the nineteenth (see Table 3.12).

(ii)   The data presented in Tables 3.10 to 3.12 show that the famine accelerated a migration trend which was well-established before 1840. Fifty-one per cent of parishes in the crofting and fifty-six per cent in the farming zone had already reached their maximum levels of population by the census of 1831. Over half the Highland parishes (fifty-three per cent) had attained their maximum population size by that year. As suggested earlier, the heavy rate of out-migration which was taking place before 1841 may, with some qualifications, help to explain why the Western Highlands escaped the demographic catastrophe suffered by Western Ireland during the potato famine.[27] The crisis of the 1840s and 1850s can therefore be regarded as a powerful new stimulus

Table 3.12. *Highland Crofting and Farming Parishes, Populations, 1801-1901*

	1801	1811	1821	1831	1841	1851	1861	1871	1881	1891	1901
Crofting Parishes											
Sutherland	20,636	21,377	21,747	23,356	22,501	23,191	22,542	21,494	20,820	19,522	19,775
Argyll	39,146	41,639	47,243	51,250	47,884	42,597	37,064	32,445	30,606	29,112	27,559
Ross	20,566	24,203	30,301	33,017	36,044	37,888	39,291	40,571	41,129	41,959	41,674
Inverness	45,272	47,794	56,859	59,328	60,854	58,032	52,017	49,882	49,968	47,873	46,278
Total	125,620	135,013	156,150	166,951	167,283	161,708	150,914	144,392	142,523	138,466	135,286
		(+7.5)	(+15.7)	(+6.9)	(+0.2)	(−3.3)	(−6.7)	(−4.3)	(−1.3)	(−2.8)	(−2.3)
Farming Parishes											
Sutherland	1,616	1,391	1,036	1,149	1,214	1,529	1,615	1,804	1,556	1,451	1,665
Argyll	37,800	40,141	45,534	45,456	45,411	43,040	39,912	40,872	43,765	44,033	45,223
Ross	36,352	36,650	38,461	41,803	42,620	44,819	42,115	40,384	37,418	35,851	36,624
Inverness	22,894	25,138	28,251	30,404	31,979	33,865	32,653	31,645	34,583	35,667	38,341
Total	98,662	103,320	113,282	118,812	121,224	123,253	116,295	114,705	117,322	117,002	121,853
		(+5.0)	(+9.4)	(+4.9)	(+2.0)	(+1.7)	(−5.6)	(1.4)	(+2.3)	(−0.3)	(+4.2)
Highland Counties	224,282	238,603	269,432	280,233	288,507	284,961	267,205	205,615	261,711	255,488	257,139

Source: Census
Note: Figures in brackets refer to per cent increases or decreases between censuses

to a rising volume of emigration which had its origins in the depression of the 1820s and had also probably been fuelled by the harvest failures of 1816-17, 1825 and 1837-8.

Equally, in the long run, there was no simple pattern of response to the pressures of the period 1846 to 1856. The population of the majority of parishes declined consistently after 1851 but in some of the insular districts there was a dramatic divergence from this trend. The Outer Hebrides, which experienced much privation during the famine, had a complex demographic history after 1851. Only two of the eight parishes there, North and South Uist, showed an absolute decline in numbers in the second half of the nineteenth century. The majority recovered after the 1850s and Lewis, Harris and Barra did not achieve their maximum population until the census of 1891. Even North and South Uist experienced a temporary increase in numbers between 1871 and 1891 (see Table 3.13). The famine, therefore, was manifestly not a watershed in the demographic history of the Outer Hebrides. The possible reasons for this important regional variation are explored in Chapter 12.

There were also significant differences over the two decades of the famine period itself. The statistical analysis suggests that estimated out-migration was greater from 1851 to 1861 than from 1841 to 1851. Crofting parishes lost an estimated 11.75 per cent of their populations in the first decade but 15.75 in the second. The population losses in farming parishes were significantly greater between 1851 and 1861, with net out-migration calculated at 15.6 per cent, but at eight per cent from 1841 to 1851. Several factors probably help to account for these differences. The relief programmes of both landlords and the Central Board, which were implemented most effectively from 1846 to 1850, could have reduced some of the need for mass emigration. Again, in the early 1850s the labour markets in the receiving countries of Canada and Australia were more buoyant than they had been in the 1840s due to the effect of a railway construction boom and the gold discoveries respectively.[28] The acceleration in emigration in the 1850s may therefore reflect the fact that both 'push' forces at home and 'pull' forces overseas interacted to create even more powerful pressures for movement than had existed hitherto. The recovery of the Lowland industrial economy from the serious recession of 1847 to 1849 could also have encouraged migration. Again, not only was relief from the Central Board terminated after 1850 but, partly as a result, both individual landlords and a new philanthropic agency, the Highland and Island Emigration Society, began a major programme of assisted emigration from the Western Highlands to Canada and Australia.[29] Sixty-one per cent of the grand total of 16,533 known to have taken advantage of these assisted passages left the Highlands between 1850 and 1857. Chapter 7 also demonstrates that it was in the latter phase, after c.1849, that most of the major clearances occurred which did much to stimulate and reinforce the underlying tendency towards emigration. Finally, however, it is important not to overemphasise the differences between the two periods. Clearly, the size and absolute scale of the exodus of people was also very great in the 1840s. What happened in many districts in the 1850s was simply a further stimulus to an accelerating outward flow.

(iii) General consideration of the pattern of out-migration at the regional level conceals the marked variations which existed within the Highlands. The famine was more significant as a factor which promoted migration from the crofting zone than

Table 3.13. Population of Outer Hebridean Parishes, 1801-1921

Parish	1801	1811	1821	1831	1841	1851	1861	1871	1881	1891	1901	1911	1921
Barvas	2495	2435	2941	3440	4361	4785	5226	5742	6133	6494	6722	*6953*	6660
Uig	2349	2770	3249	3471	3828	3805	3630	4112	4476	*4621*	4463	4462	3956
Lochs	1350	1387	1922	2208	2630	3064	3529	4118	4489	4675	4733	*4750*	4396
Stornoway													
(a) Landward	–	–	–	–	4864	5666	6060	6975	7696	8413	9131	*9632*	9287
(b) Burgh	–	–	–	–	1333	2374	2587	2498	2627	3287	3711	3735	*3946*
Harris	2996	3569	3909	3900	4429	4250	4178	4095	4784	4980	5249	*5427*	5255
N. Uist	3010	3863	*4971*	4603	4428	3918	3910	4107	4264	4187	3891	3677	3223
S. Uist	4595	4825	6038	6890	*7327*	6173	5346	5749	6063	5821	5490	5383	4839
Barra	1925	2114	2303	2097	2363	1873	1853	1997	2141	2359	2545	*2620*	2345

Source: Census
Note: Year of maximum population in italics

from farming districts. This is indeed the outcome which might be anticipated in the light of previous discussion which demonstrated that the subsistence crisis had a much more devastating and protracted effect in the Western Highlands than in the central, southern and eastern areas.[30] Table 3.14 indicates that migration had been occurring from farming parishes *before* 1841 more rapidly and over a longer time-scale than from crofting parishes. The estimated numbers leaving the farming region accelerated in the 1850s but there was not the same decisive change in trend that can be detected in several crofting, and especially insular, districts. Higher actual rates of population increase (and hence lower rates of net out-migration) were achieved in the crofting zone from 1801 to 1841. The average decadal rise in population over that period was 7.5 per cent compared to 5.25 per cent for the farming zone. From 1841 to 1861, on the other hand, the number of inhabitants in the crofting region fell by five per cent but only by 1.9 per cent in farming parishes. In the first decade of the famine the differences were even more perceptible. While population declined by 3.3 per cent in the Western Highlands and Islands, it marginally rose by 1.7 per cent in the south and east. It is argued in Chapter 8 that these distinctive patterns cannot be explained, as M.W. Flinn *et al* suggest, by movement of people from west to east within the Highland region during the famine years. What they probably do reveal, however, is the much greater resilience of the farming districts to the impact of the potato blight and its associated effects. Population pressure was not only more acute in the far west but, in addition, the crofting economy did not possess the material resources to resist the shock of crop failure. A massive increase in the exodus of people from the region was the inevitable consequence.

There was also substantial diversity within the crofting area itself which makes facile generalisation very hazardous. Extremes of demographic experience can be observed. At least three trends can be identified. First, Sutherland had a distinctive population history. Only three parishes, Assynt, Loth and Lairg, show exceptional losses for the famine period. The rate of estimated out-migration for the county as a whole was much higher between 1831 and 1841 than in either of the famine decades. The emigration history of Sutherland was plainly primarily determined by the great clearances of the early nineteenth century and not by the subsistence crisis of the middle decades. The heavy migration of adult males produced by the clearances before 1841 is confirmed by the evidence of the grossly imbalanced sex ratios (the number of males per 100 females) which became a major feature of the county's population structure. In 1841, for the age group 20 to 29, the ratio was as low as 43 in Farr, 48 in Rogart and 64 in Clyne. Only the two 'uncleared' parishes of Assynt and Edderachillis on the west coast had sex ratios approaching the national average, at 82 and 80 for ages 20 to 29.

A second discrete area was the three coastal north-west Ross-shire parishes of Lochbroom, Gairloch and Applecross. They probably lost more people through migration than Sutherland between 1841 and 1861 but less than other crofting districts. Estimated rates of net out-migration were higher from these parishes between 1821 and 1841 and after 1861 than in the famine decades. These districts generally suffered much less than some Hebridean parishes during the crisis, partly because of their dependence on fishing, not simply in local waters, but through

Table 3.14. Estimated Net Out-Migration, Crofting and Farming Regions by County, 1801-1891

Crofting Parishes	1801	1811	1821	1831	1841	1851	1861	1871	1881	1891
Argyll (16)	39,146	41,639	47,243	51,250	47,884	42,597	37,455			
Actual %*		+6.4	+13.5	+8.5	-6.6	-11.0	-12.1	-12.5	-5.4	-5.2
Natural %*		+10	+10	+10	+10	+10	+10	+7.4	+7.0	+7.2
Migration %		-3.6	+3.5	-1.5	-16.6	-21.0	-22.1	-19.9	-12.4	-12.4
Inverness (19)	45,272	47,794	56,859	59,328	60,854	58,032	52,017			
Actual %*		+5.6	+19.0	+4.3	+2.6	-4.6	-10.4	-4.4	-0.2	-4.4
Natural %*		+10	+10	+10	+10	+10	+10	+9.5	+9.4	+8.2
Migration		-4.4	+9	-5.7	-7.4	-14.6	-20.4	-13.9	-9.6	-12.6
Ross & Cromarty (12)	20,566	24,203	30,301	33,017	36,044	37,888	39,291			
Actual %*		+17.7	+25.2	+9.0	+9.2	+5.1	+3.7	+3.3	+1.4	+2.0
Natural %*		+10	+10	+10	+10	+10	+10	+13.3	+12.7	+12.5
Migration		-7.7	+15.2	-1.0	-0.8	-4.9	-6.3	-10	-11.3	+10.5
Sutherland (12)	20,636	21,377	21,747	23,356	22,501	23,191	22,542			
Actual %*		+3.6	+1.7	+7.4	-3.7	+3.1	-2.8	-4.7	-3.1	-6.1
Natural %*		+10	+10	+10	+10	+10	+10	+6.3	+6.2	+6.4
Migration		-6.4	-8.3	-2.6	-13.7	-6.9	-12.8	-11.0	-9.3	-12.5
Farming Parishes										
Argyll (18)	37,800	40,411	405,534	45,456	45,411	43,040	39,912			
Actual %*		+6.9	+12.7	-0.2	-0.1	-5.2	-7.3	+2.3	+6.2	+0.4
Natural %*		10	10	10	10	10	10	10.1	7.9	9.4
Migration		-3.1	+2.7	-10.2	-10.1	-15.2	-17.3	-7.8	-1.7	-9.0
Inverness (11)	22,894	25,138	28,251	30,404	31,979	33,865	32,653			
Actual %*		+9.8	+12.4	+7.6	+5.2	+5.9	-3.6	+5.7	+8.4	+2.5
Natural %*		10	10	10	10	10	10	9.6	7.8	9.3
Migration		-0.2	+2.4	-2.4	-4.8	-4.1	-13.6	-3.9	+0.6	-6.8

(continued overleaf)

Table 3.14 (continued)

Crofting Parishes	1801	1811	1821	1831	1841	1851	1861	1871	1881	1891
Ross &										
Cromarty (22)	36,352	36,650	38,461	41,803	42,620	44,819	42,115			
Actual %*		+0.8	+4.9	+8.7	+2.0	+5.2	-6.0	-3.8	-7.7	-4.3
Natural %*		10	10	10	10	10	10	8.0	5.9	6.3
Migration		-9.2	-5.1	-1.3	-8.0	-4.8	-16.0	-11.8	-13.6	-10.6
Sutherland (1)	1,616	1,391	1,034	1,149	1,214	1,529	1,615	1,804	1,556	1,451
(Golspie)										
Actual %*		-13.9	-25.5	+10.9	+5.7	+25.9	+5.6	11.8	-13.7	-6.7
Natural %*		10	10	10	10	10	10	13.4	8.9	8.4
Migration		-23.9	-35.5	+0.9	-4.3	+15.9	-6.4	-1.6	-22.6	-15.1

Sources: Census to 1861; RGS from 1861

Notes: (i) * = increase

(ii) Bracketed figures refer to number of parishes

Table 3.15. Net Out-Migration (Estimated) from Selected West Highland and Hebridean Parishes as Percentage of Starting Population, 1841-1851

Parish	Estimated out-migration, 1841-51, as percentage of 1841 population
Kilfinichen (Mull)	−35.7*
Barra	−30.7*
Jura	−29.4*
Lochcarron	−27.8
S. Uist	−25.8*
Kintail	−23.6
Bracadale (Skye)	−22.4*
N. Uist	−21.5*
Lochalsh	−21.5
Glenelg	−19.5
Kilninian (Mull)	−18.8*
Kilfinan (Mull)	−16.7*
Sleat (Skye)	−16.5*
Applecross	−15.3
Harris	−14.0*
Snizort (Skye)	−13.7*
Uig (Lewis)	−13.2*
Lismore	−12.3*
Portree (Skye)	−10.5*
Lochbroom	−9.7
Strath (Skye)	−7.0*
Gairloch	−4.2
Lochs (Lewis)	+6.0*
Stornoway (Lewis)	+19.6*
Average	16.08

* = insular parish

temporary migration to the industries of the Caithness and Aberdeenshire coasts.

Finally, the biggest loss through emigration was concentrated in a small number of mainland parishes in western Inverness and Wester Ross and, in particular, in the islands. Lochcarron, Kintail, Lochalsh and Glenelg were at the top of the migration league on the western mainland. But between 1841 and 1851 six of the nine parishes estimated to have lost twenty per cent or more of their starting populations were insular. From 1851 to 1861 ten of the twelve parishes losing twenty per cent or more were also located in the Hebrides (see Tables 3.15 and 3.16).

The detailed analysis which has been carried out of estimated out-migration suggests a number of general conclusions. Before the census of 1841 the population of the four Highland counties rose in absolute terms. After 1851 the number of their inhabitants began a long-term decline. In this perspective, therefore, the famine was a turning-point in the demographic history of Highland society. But closer examination reveals this to be an essentially superficial judgement. Migration from the whole region was already occurring on a substantial scale before 1846. The crisis

Table 3.16. *Net Out-Migration (Estimated) from Selected West Highland and Hebridean Parishes as Percentage of Starting Population, 1851-1861*

Parish	Estimated out-migration, 1841-51, as percentage of 1841 population
Glenelg	−35.4
Strath (Skye)	−27.8*
Kilfinichen (Mull)	−27.5*
Bracadale (Skye)	−26.4*
Snizort (Skye)	−24.9*
S. Uist	−23.2*
Kilninian (Mull)	−23.2*
N. Uist	−23.2*
Lismore	−23.2*
Kintail	−22.3*
Portree (Skye)	−21.8*
Uig (Lewis)	−21.2*
Sleat (Skye)	−20.3*
Applecross	−17.9*
Lochalsh	−16.1
Harris	−15.0*
Lochcarron	−11.6*
Jura	−11.2*
N. Uist	−9.0*
Lochbroom	−9.0
Gairloch	−4.4
Stornoway (Lewis)	−2.4*
Kilfinan (Mull)	+1.5*
Lochs (Lewis)	+11.5*
Average	15.87

* = insular parish

caused it to accelerate further though the increase was significantly greater in the crofting region than in the farming zone. Within the crofting districts, Sutherland was distinctive. It apparently lost many more people in the 1820s and 1830s than in the 1840s and 1850s. Massive haemorrhage was confined to most of the Outer and Inner Hebrides and to certain mainland parishes in western Inverness and parts of Wester Ross. The majority of parishes in this area suffered a continuous decline in population thereafter. However, there was a recovery in the Outer Hebridean districts of Lewis, Harris and Barra and numbers rose once again into the early twentieth century. The analysis also suggests a very close correlation between those localities which endured the most extreme levels of distress and the areas which suffered the heaviest rates of loss of population through migration and emigration during the famine. Both serious destitution and massive emigration were confined to the Hebrides and particular parts of the western mainland. This implies that the great exodus was principally driven on by the pressure of privation and economic stress. It also suggests that the major increase in emigration was probably a significant factor helping to reduce the threat of an even more serious demographic catastrophe in the stricken region.

NOTES

1. For the varying Irish mortality estimates see E.M. Crawford, 'Dearth, Diet and Disease in Ireland, 1850', *Medical History*, 28 (1984), 151.
2. Flinn, *Scottish Population History*, 421-438.
3. GRO, Census Enumerators' Schedules, Parishes of Kilfinichen (Mull) and Barvas (Lewis), 1841, 1851, 1861.
4. SRO, HD6/2, Treasury Correspondence, Sir E. Coffin to Mr. Trevelyan, 28 June 1847, 16 August 1847.
5. *Ibid.*, Sir John McNeill to Sir G. Grey, 3 May 1847; SRO, Lord Advocate's Papers, AD 14/47/628, Precognition as to the alleged death of Widow Anne Gillies, 18 March 1847; AD 58/81, Reports on Conditions on various Highland estates, 1846-7; AD 58/80, Conditions in Barra and South Uist, 1846- 49.
6. See below, Chapter 8.
7. Flinn, *Scottish Population History*, 387-420.
8. *Witness*, 3 November 1849; *PP*, XL (1850), *Papers relative to Emigration*, 22; *PP*, XXIII (1850), *Tenth Report of Colonial Land and Emigration Commissioners*, 23.
9. *Witness*, 27 October 1849; Inveraray Castle, Argyll Estate Papers, Bundle 1533, List of Emigrants from Mull and Tiree, June 1849.
10. *Witness*, 27 October and 29 December 1849.
11. *PP*, XXXIII (1852), *Papers relative to Emigration*, 575.
12. See, for example, *PP*, XXXVIII (1849), *Papers relative to Emigration*, 40 (South Uist emigrants); *PP*, XXXIII (1852), *Papers relative to Emigration*, A.C. Buchanan to Earl Grey, 31 December 1851 (South Uist, Barra and Benbecula emigrants); 568, 578 (Glenelg and Lewis emigrants).
13. *Ibid.*, *PP*, XLVII (1847-8), 14.
14. *Ibid.*
15. See below, Chapter 8.
16. See below, Chapter 5 for a detailed discussion of the timing and scale of relief measures.
17. Discussion of the symptoms, nature and classification of disease is based on A.W. Blyth, *A Dictionary of Hygiene and Public Health* (London, 1876), and A. Macaulay, *Popular Medical Dictionary* (11th ed., Edinburgh, 1852).
18. A. Kemp *et al*, *The Biology of Human Starvation* (Minneapolis, 1950), I, 587-90; Appleby, *Famine in Tudor and Stuart England*, 8.
19. *Witness*, 13 March 1847; SRO, HD6/2, Treasury Correspondence, Hope to Coffin, 6 March 1847.
20. See Appendix 5.
21. E. Le Roy Ladurie, 'L'Aménorrhée de famine (XVIIe- XXe siècles)', *Annales*, 24 (1969), 1589-1601.
22. See below, pp.193-197.
23. This is a weakness in Ruth Hildebrandt, 'Migration and Economic Change in the Northern Highlands during the Nineteenth Century with particular reference to the period 1851-91', Unpublished Ph.D. thesis, University of Glasgow, 1980. M.W. Flinn *et al* show awareness of temporary migration but do not emphasise the effect which it could have in undermining several of their calculations.
24. *N.S.A.*, Ross and Cromarty, 83-4.
25. See below, Chapter 6.

26. GRO, Census Enumerators' Schedules, Kilfinichen (Mull) and Barvas (Lewis), 1841, 1851, 1861.
27. See above, pp.23-4.
28. See below, p.203.
29. See below, Chapter 11.
30. See above, pp.41-3.

4

The Landed Classes

1

On the face of it, the recurrent failure of the potato crop posed as great a threat to the Highland landed classes as to the peasantry. For the people it was a tragedy of massive proportions bringing in its train hunger, poverty and sickness. Proprietors, however, were more likely to be hit in their pockets than in their stomachs. As Chapter 2 has shown, there was an enormous and rapid contraction in rental income from the small tenant class on several estates as arrears accumulated after 1846.[1] The failure of the potatoes meant that funds normally devoted to rent payment were instead diverted to the purchase of grain. Traditional sources of cash income, such as from the sale of cattle and earnings from temporary migration, were also affected, the former by a persistent decline in the prices of stock throughout the famine years and the latter for a shorter period by the economic recession of 1848 to 1851.[2] The depression which began in the latter months of 1847 also posed a grave threat to the security of some landed families in the Highlands. Several proprietors were deeply in debt and their finances depended on fluctuating interest charges on their extensive loans. For instance, the gross income of the Macdonald estates in Skye and North Uist, after payment of public burdens, was £11,269 in 1846. But no less than £7971, or about seventy-one per cent of gross annual income, was absorbed to fund interest charges on the family's huge accumulated debt of £140,676. In times of economic stability these payments could be managed. However, in periods when interest rates rose, the solvency of the entire property was immediately placed at risk. It was reckoned that an increase at half of one per cent in rates would necessitate a rise in interest payments of £560 or seventeen per cent of the net annual income of the estates.[3] Creditors were also likely to be concerned as the value of the properties to which their loans were attached fell as deficits mounted on rental account.

The problems of the landed classes were compounded by the fact that other costs seemed set to rise irresistibly as income from small rents collapsed. Initially, most proprietors had anxiously proclaimed the need for government assistance if a major human disaster in the Highlands was to be avoided. As the Marquis of Lorne asserted: 'Highland landlords are not generally so rich as to be able to relieve the crisis to any great degree'.[4] However, the government was resolutely opposed to any action that relieved landlords of personal responsibility for the population on their estates. As pressure for government assistance built up, the Lord Advocate of Scotland penned a highly critical letter to the Home Secretary, Sir George Gray, in September 1846, which laid the blame for the destitute condition of the Highlands on the proprietors. The economic crisis had been caused by their inability to manage their properties efficiently. He therefore urged that government should not be too prompt or liberal in coming to their aid. To do so would relieve landlords of their obligations and encourage them and their tenants to rely on public relief. This would be an 'injudicious though most humane interference which would leave the future as bad as the past or the present'. It was therefore to be avoided at all costs.[5]

The Lord Advocate need not have worried. Government had no intention of coming to the direct assistance of the Highland élite. Charles Trevelyan at the Treasury laid down the broad guidelines of policy the following month: '. . . it is by no means intended to afford relief in such a way as would relieve the landowners and other persons of property from the obligations they are under to support the destitute poor . . . any assistance contemplated would be rather in the form of giving a proper organisation and direction to the efforts of the proprietors . . .'.[6] Thereafter, far from providing direct aid, much of government activity was devoted to ensuring that Highland landlords did assume the responsibility of relieving destitution. With growing alarm, several proprietors contemplated the probability of having to support the people of their estates at a time when their own limited sources of rental income were drying up.[7]

The second potential source of increasing costs was legal rather than political in origin. A year before the potato blight the Act of Parliament (8 and 9 Vic. *c.* 83) 'For the amendment and better administration of the laws relating to the relief of the poor in Scotland' had come into force. Each parish remained responsible for its own poor. A parochial board was annually appointed and could itself decide whether to raise funds by imposing a poor rate or by continuing to rely on voluntary contribution. Relief was to continue to be discretionary. As was noted in Section 68 of the Act, '. . . nothing herein contained shall be held to confer a right to demand relief on able-bodied persons out of employment'. Adequate help had to be provided for 'paupers' but the Act did not define this term and so the previous criteria for destitution, themselves ambiguous, remained in force. A central Board of Supervision was created to administer the new legislation.[8]

In itself the Poor Law Amendment Act did not automatically threaten the imposition of a new financial burden on Highland proprietors. In the early 1840s few parishes in the Western Highlands were assessed for a poor rate. Indeed, contemporary observers argued with only some exaggeration that '. . . the poor law of Scotland is, in fact, so far as the greater part of the Highlands and Islands are concerned, little more than a dead letter'.[9] In 1843 when the expenditure on the poor per head of population was £1.81 per annum in Scotland as a whole, it was a derisory £0.34 in the crofting areas.[10] Yet such was the scale of destitution and the likely sharp increase in sickness and disability after 1846 that Highland expenditure on poor relief was expected to rise dramatically.[11] As the famine persisted, the Board of Supervision, government law officers and the Court of Session began to provide both guidance and legal judgements which emphasised that the able-bodied destitute poor, while having no right to relief, could and should be assisted in accordance with the discretion allowed in the 1845 Act. As early as January 1847, the Lord Advocate had indicated that while this class had no claim which they could enforce in law the local parochial board could legitimately apply an increased assessment for them as 'occasional poor'.[12] Both government law officers and eventually the Board of Supervision itself not only stated that this was possible at the discretion of local interests but began to insist that it amounted almost to a requirement. Thus the Lord Advocate himself emphasised:

> The resident factors should well consider not only the moral responsibility they incur in refusing assistance at this period but even *their own most selfish interest* in the matter, looking not merely to the discretionary power in the parochial board . . . but to the clear liability they will incur if the sickness and disease consequent upon the general state of destitution shall reduce many persons or families to the condition of being proper objects of legal relief.[13]

The same message was communicated by Sir John McNeill, chairman of the Board of Supervision in Scotland, to all Highland proprietors in early 1847. It also became the basis of the strategy of the government relief officers when they were dealing with individual landlords who were not responding to the perceived needs of the destitute on their estates.[14]

2

It would appear, then, that at the end of the first year of the potato famine the landed class was likely to be caught in an inescapable vice of contracting revenue and soaring costs. Financial ruin for many seemed inevitable. Yet a review of the evidence does not support this pessimistic conclusion. A search was carried out for the period 1846-60 of the press, estate papers and petitions of sequestration in the Court of Session in order to determine the extent of financial crisis among Highland land-owners during and in the years following the potato famine.[15] The phrase 'financial crisis' is ambiguous. It is used here for properties (a) which were put on the market or sold as a result of a proprietor's difficulties or (b) of estates which came to be administered by trustees because of the owner's increasing indebtedness. Of course, these are only crude measures of pressure and cannot provide a guide to the stresses and anxieties of families who, while assailed by difficulty, did manage to survive without selling lands or experiencing personal bankruptcy. On the other hand, they do furnish a reasonable estimate of the extent of crisis among the landed classes. There is little hard evidence that the sources might be biased because the condition of the land market inhibited creditors from enforcing landowners into sales. Several Highland estates were bought and sold during the famine, and though the market was sluggish until c.1854 it became much more vigorous thereafter.[16] Nor does the problem of entail necessarily complicate any conclusions reached on the basis of the evidence. Most West Highland landed families possessed both unentailed and entailed property. These legal controls could inhibit land sales in certain areas but not in all.

Some landed families did suffer acute distress. Probably the most spectacular example of bankruptcy was that of Walter Frederick Campbell who owned most of the island of Islay. In April 1847 Joseph Mitchell, at that time Engineer to the Fishery Board Commissioners, stayed with Campbell and his family while preparing a report on harbour improvements on the island. He recollected how: 'The poor laird

. . . appeared despondent beyond measure. We attributed this to the dreadful potato blight, so disastrous to the country and his people; but he was depressed by what was to him a more serious calamity. Owing to the general distress, the rents were not forthcoming, and the holders of bills and bonds were not paid their interest. The banks also became alarmed, and stopped further advances. Hence, in a few months after this the creditors seized the property of Islay and Mr. Campbell was declared bankrupt . . .'.[17] The Islay estate was sequestrated and managed by trustees for Campbell's creditors from 1848 until 1853 when it was finally sold to James Morrison of Basildon Park in Wiltshire.[18] The property was burdened with debts to the extent of £185,000.[19]

The case of Norman Macleod of Macleod in Skye was probably the one which most stirred contemporary imagination and sympathy. All commentators were agreed that he had worked with great vigour and generosity to protect the population on his Skye estates from the worst effects of the potato blight. In an Address to his People of December 1846, he stressed that 'no exertions on my part have been, or will be spared to alleviate your distress . . . I deem it my duty to place it in every man's power to employ himself. It is also my duty to take care that the country is supplied with a sufficiency of good and wholesome food'.[20] By March 1847, Macleod had imported nearly 3500 bolls of oatmeal and advanced more than £5 each to between three and four hundred families. He had very little hope of repayment in the short term because of the destitute condition of the people.[21] The pressures eventually became too great for a landlord who was described by government relief officers as 'first in respect of his active benevolence, and his personal and practical exertions to improve the land'.[22] In the spring of 1847 he was obliged to sell the unentailed parts of his estate and finally obtained employment as a clerk in London.[23] Thirty-six years later in evidence to the Napier Commission, he gave his own version of the events of that time:

> The famine years of 1847 and 1848 found me at Dunvegan. Every morning, when food became scarce, hundreds of people awaited my appearance at the Castle door. I had at the time large supplies of meal for my work-people, but these were soon exhausted and I went to Aberdeen for more. I only did what every other man similarly circumstanced would have done; but the strain was too great, and although largely aided at first by many friends and afterwards by the government, I was myself utterly ruined, and forced to get work in London and to live there.[24]

The other major estate in Skye, that of Lord Macdonald, was under similar intense pressure. The properties were already managed by trustees because of the extensive debts attached to them. But these escalated in the famine years from £140,676 in 1846 to £200,000 in 1850.[25] Eventually, in 1856, the family estates in North Uist had to be sold to meet the demands of creditors.[26] Similarly, the Ardnamurchan estate of Sir James Riddell was placed under the administration of trustees in 1852 and put up for sale in three lots in July 1854, at an upset price of £81,000.[27] The trustees were informed in a report of 1852 that the estate had suffered through 'a very great increase in arrears' which was primarily due to 'the failure of the potato crop and fall in the price of black cattle together with the cessation of drainage works since 1848'.[28]

Finally, in the 1850s, Knoydart, the last remaining property of the Macdonnels of Glengarry, was sold by the estate trustees, after a series of notorious clearances, to James Baird, a member of the lowland iron-manufacturing dynasty.[29]

In these areas where the potato blight wreaked most havoc there were eight-six individual landowners. Yet in only five known cases, according to the evidence consulted, were financial pressures severe enough to cause sale of properties, sequestration or judicial management by trustees.[30] Indeed, even in the five instances quoted, the famine was almost certainly the final stage in a much more extended economic agony, which in several cases stretched back to the 1820s and before. Lord Macdonald already had an accumulated debt burden in 1846 of £140,676, with £7971 out of a gross rental of £11,269 absorbed in interest payments.[31] He was clearly teetering on the edge of financial ruin long before the onset of the crisis of the 1840s completed his discomfiture. In the same way Macleod of Macleod owed his plight not simply to increased costs and expenditure during the famine but to the contraction of income from kelp in the 1820s and 1830s together with some unsuccessful investments in fishing.[32] Even in the case of Campbell of Islay, Joseph Mitchell contended that his 'pecuniary difficulties . . . arose mainly from previous embarrassments on the estate, but unfortunately Mr. Campbell was no man of business'.[33] The famine aggravated his problems but did not cause them. Campbell was widely described as 'a man of kind heart and generous nature' intent on doing everything within his means to bring his tenantry through the crisis, unaided by either government or the lowland charities. But as early as the winter of 1846, government officials were reporting that his means were probably unequal to the task of relief and that he had grossly underestimated the extent of destitution.[34] In his case, too, the financial strain of the crisis accelerated the collapse of his fortunes.

Examined over the long run, therefore, there seemed little especially significant about the crises of the 1840s and 1850s in landlord fortunes. Since the end of the Napoleonic Wars Highland property had been changing hands on an unprecedented scale as the old proprietors surrendered family estates in the wake of the fall in kelp prices, the malaise in fishing and the stagnation in cattle markets.[35] At most, the famine brought about a short-term increase in an ongoing process of changing patterns of ownership. The evidence of the relatively small number of bankruptcies and estate sales does, nevertheless, point to a central paradox in the history of the period. The scenario seemed set for a massive transfer of ownership of land in a context of rising cost and diminishing income. This did not occur. Much of the remainder of this chapter will attempt to explain why the overwhelming majority of Highland proprietors managed to survive despite the suggestion presented earlier that they were likely to face an unacceptable increase in expenditure and an alarming collapse in revenue.

3

One possible answer might be found in the thesis advanced by James Hunter, who asserts that the majority of landowners did little to assist their tenantry and, with a few

noted exceptions, were indifferent to their plight. He refers to 'examples of pro-
prietorial apathy' which 'could be multiplied endlessly'. Landlords were 'reluctant'
and displayed 'a general and evident lack of enthusiasm'.[36] The problem with this
thesis, however, is that it is not supported by adequate or convincing evidence.
Argument 'by example' is a particularly unrewarding approach when dealing with
such a diverse social group as the Highland landed classes. The difficulty is to establish
who were 'active' or 'inactive' landlords, how many belonged to each group and to
determine, however roughly, the typicality of the 'good' or 'bad' landlord. What
complicates the problem and makes any simple assessment impossible is the different
circumstances of individual proprietors. A failure to provide adequate relief may not
necessarily reflect negligence but rather financial embarrassment or the constraint of
strict entail arrangements which could effectively prohibit the raising of adequate relief
funds in the money market. One government relief officer proposed five possible
variations in the strategy and circumstances of individual proprietors:

> In my late tour through a large district I met living proof of all that I have stated above. I
> met proprietors of various dispositions; the proprietor who was jealous of his people's
> sufferings, and claimed the right of providing for them without possessing the ability to
> do so efficiently; the proprietor who was able to provide for his tenants, and was doing so
> on principle not derived from hereditary impulse; the proprietor who was willing to
> provide for his people, and being unable, would not confess it; the proprietor who was
> willing and admitted his inability; and lastly, the proprietor who, with the power, was
> neglecting to provide for his people.[37]

It proved possible to assemble documentation on the activities of fifty-nine (or
sixty-seven per cent) of the total of eighty-six landlords in the distressed districts. This
is a much bigger sample than that considered by Dr. Hunter who refers to only eleven
individual proprietors in the course of his discussion.[38] Furthermore, this evidence
comes from a variety of sources and allows for some cross-checking. In most cases
commentators were often government officials independent of landlord influence.[39]
Sir Edward Pine Coffin carried out two detailed investigations himself at the beginning
and end of government relief operations. His subordinates, Captains Pole and Rose
and Commissary-General Dobrée, made several tours of inspection in order to
monitor the effect of the government's policy in 1846 and early 1847 of relying on local
landlords as the fundamental basis of the relief effort. Their exhaustive and sometimes
highly critical reports are a major source for the evaluation of landlord strategies in the
first year of the famine. To these can be added information derived from local and
national destitution committees which also undertook regular investigations of the
stricken areas, statements from law officers, such as sheriffs and procurators-fiscal,
and from the Free Church and established Church of Scotland.[40] The estate papers of
eight of the twelve landlords on whose properties eighty-six per cent of the famine-
stricken population lived are extant and have also been consulted in this survey.[41]
What follows are the general conclusions derived from evaluation of these varied
sources of information.

In the late summer and early autumn of 1846 many proprietors, but by no means all,
seem to have shown a reluctance to assume responsibility for the population of their

estates.[42] Instead, by drawing attention to the scale of the crisis they put most of their efforts into an attempt to attract government aid. However, when it became clear that no direct assistance in the form of cheap food or public-work schemes was likely to be forthcoming, the vast majority of Highland landowners began to accept that they had at least a moral responsibility to ensure the welfare of their people. Coffin, who was critical of the initially sluggish response of certain proprietors, admitted that a change of heart had taken place as early as October 1846.[43] He explained: 'The recent origin of the cause for alarm, the uncertainty of its extent, and an indefinite expectation of the intervention of the Government must . . . have tended to retard the proceedings of the landholders in districts threatened with famine . . . as the crisis approaches I am in hopes that no highland proprietor will be found wanting in the discharge of an obligation, which I found all with whom I communicated ready to acknowledge'.[44]

Inevitably, there was no necessary correlation between the acceptance of a moral duty and the implementation of the action necessary to ensure the survival of the people through the crisis.[45] Yet some landowners won golden opinions from all quarters for their efforts in 1846 and 1847. The Duke of Sutherland was determined to be 'the legal and natural protector' of his people.[46] Large supplies of meal were laid in, including 3000 bolls of grain for the two western parishes of Assynt and Edderachillis alone. They were retailed at below market price, 24/– per boll compared with 27/– at the Glasgow market, and sold to those who had cash or in return for labour to the destitute. £1 was offered to each young adult male to assist travel to the south for work on the railways.[47] The Duke was anxious to maintain his people from his own resources and in 1846 and 1847 did not draw meal from government stores or allow the inhabitants of the estate to be relieved by the Free Church or its successor the Central Board.[48] As a result it was said in early 1847 that no unrelieved case of destitution existed on the Sutherland estate.[49] During the summer of that year the ministers of both the Established and Free Churches in Assynt visited the Duke 'as a joint deputation on behalf of their congregations, to thank him for the noble exertions which he had made for their benefit'.[50] Sir Edward Coffin, when he visited Sutherland in July 1847, could not suggest any improvement in the estate's scheme of relief for 'the preservation of the people from severe want'.[51] By that time, £18,000 had been spent on alleviating distress, with most of the resources devoted to the poor parishes of the west.[52]

In their scale and comprehensiveness, the efforts of the Duke of Sutherland were only surpassed by James Matheson, the proprietor of Lewis. From 1846-51 he expended £30,000 on meal and seed for crofters. At the same time extensive improvement works took place on the island, involving draining, fencing, reclamation and harbour construction, which provided employment for many of the destitute. During the 1840s and 1850s no less than £259,248 was spent by Matheson on these projects and in supporting emigration. Probably, however, his most dramatic intervention was the provision of his yacht, the *Mary Jane*, to enable seasonal migrants from the Hebrides to travel to the labour markets of the south free of charge in 1847. Matheson was knighted for his services during the famine.[53]

The Duke of Sutherland and James Matheson were men of colossal wealth and exceptional in the scale of their expenditure. But they were not alone in making energetic efforts to provide relief. Lady Mackenzie of Gairloch was 'deserving of the highest praise for her benevolent care of the poor'.[54] Captain Pole's impression of the two main proprietors in Skye in October 1846, Lord Macdonald and Macleod of Macleod, was that they were 'anxious to do all in their power to relieve their people'.[55] Campbell of Islay assured government relief officers in April 1847 that 'not a man on his property shall want employment during the summer', though there were fears that he was likely to endanger his own financial position by assuming such a responsibility.[56] Sir James Riddell, the owner of the extensive Ardnamurchan estate, was extensively involved in relief operations throughout the winter of 1846 and 1847.[57] Other proprietors who attracted special mention or praise for their efforts from government officials in these years included William Lillingston of Lochalsh,[58] Mackenzie of Applecross,[59] Maclean of Ardgour,[60] Lord Lovat,[61] Lady Dunmore (Harris),[62] Campbell of Jura,[63] Lord Ward,[64] Edward Ellice,[65] Sir Duncan Cameron of Fassiefern,[66] and Lord Compton (Mull).[67]

A list of energetic landlords does not of itself reveal much about the response of the landed class as a whole. A more systematic approach is necessary. Three rough categories of performance can be designated: A, where a landowner was especially singled out for praise in contemporary sources (it is relevant to note here that there was an unusual unanimity between independent observers, whether from the press, government or destitution committees, about those who deserved positive comment); B, where a proprietor's activities were adequate although improvement was possible; C, where a landlord was singled out for censure because of his negligence. Seventeen landowners (twenty-nine per cent of the sample and twenty per cent of the total of all landlords in the distressed districts) were placed in category A; thirty in category B (fifty-one per cent of the sample and thirty-six per cent of the total); and twelve (twenty per cent of the sample, fourteen per cent of the total) in category C.[68]

This pattern strongly suggests that in the first year of the famine most Highland landowners had developed a satisfactory strategy in the view of experienced and informed contemporaries to meet the crisis. What adds force to this conclusion is that some proprietors who initially attracted condemnation later improved their efforts. The best example was the notorious Colonel John Gordon of Cluny, the wealthy owner of Barra, South Uist and Benbecula, whose neglect in the winter of 1846 of his starving tenantry caused widespread criticism in both the press and Parliament and forced government to send emergency grain supplies to his estates. However, by the summer of 1847, even Sir Edward Coffin, one of Gordon's most bitter critics, acknowledged that there had been a change for the better:

. . . he [Gordon] has, in fact, done more for their benefit than many of the proprietors who have obtained credit for their exertions. He has expended large sums in works of improvement . . . Large arrears of rent were remitted by him previously to the commencement of the present distress. Considerable quantities of food were sent by him for the supply of the people, which, though insufficient, much exceeded similar efforts of many others; and his factor admitted to me that he had now authority to draw on him for the like purpose to the extent of nearly £2000, the food purchased with which is all, I apprehend, to be applied in payment of labour of different kinds . . . So much has been said to Col. Gordon's disparagement, that I think it but just to call attention to these facts, which if they do not prove that he has done all that might have been expected from him, certainly remove him out of the class of proprietor showing utter neglect of their people.[69]

The evidence also indicates that in 1846 and the early months of 1847, most of the West Highland population, whatever the diversity of response of individual proprietors, lived on the estates of greater landlords where work was made available and meal distributed either in return for labour, money or by grain being credited to rental payments. About 97,000 persons dwelt on the properties of twelve 'big' landlords. These were the Duke of Sutherland, James Matheson, Lord Macdonald, Lord Dunmore, Macleod of Macleod, George Rainy, Sir Kenneth Mackenzie, Sir James Riddell, the Duke of Argyll, Campbell of Islay, Mr. J. Bankes and Gordon of Cluny. Only the latter two were censured by government relief officers. These estates accounted for 10,500 people (Gordon, 8500; Bankes, 2000) of the total population of 97,000. It was relatively rare for the greater landowners to attract much reproach. In Skye and Mull vigorous criticism was reserved for the smaller proprietors who were often absentee speculators and had only recently acquired their lands.[70] This view is supported by both the Free Church and the government, neither of whom were necessarily sympathetic to the landlord class. The *Witness* could report in March 1847 that 'the landlord proprietors are, with some exceptions, attending to the destitute on their respective estates'.[71] Sir Charles Trevelyan, who was also in direct control of government relief operations in Ireland, as well as being Assistant Secretary to the Treasury, admitted in private that the government was well satisfied with the relief operations of Highland landlords. In a meeting with the Marquis of Breadalbane's agent in the spring of 1847 he observed that: '. . . the Treasury have been quite delighted with the whole conduct of the Highland proprietors in the present crisis – that it was a source of positive pleasure to them to turn from the Irish to the Scotch case – in the former every thing both with regard to the people and proprietors is sickening and disgusting'.[72] A year later in correspondence with William Skene, Secretary of the Edinburgh Section of the Central Relief Board, he once again drew a comparison between Irish and Scottish proprietors: '. . . there is this important difference in the Proprietors and larger class of Farmers, that in Ireland the general disposition of these classes is to do nothing while in Scotland they are disposed to do what is in their power . . . If Skye were in the west of Ireland, the people would be left to starve in helpless idleness'.[73]

This more positive conclusion about the role of the Highland landowners during the early years of the famine begs two questions: First, why were they prepared to assume these responsibilities? Second, and in relation to the main theme of this chapter, why were the vast majority able to escape financial disaster despite the increased outlay on relief as rental income from the small tenantry collapsed?

4

Some landlords had a distinct awareness of their traditional responsibilities. It was what their people and peers expected of them, and to shirk their duties would have offended both family honour, pride and social position. These sentiments come through strongly in Macleod of Macleod's *Address to his People* in 1846 and in the correspondence of such grandees of elevated rank and social prominence as the

Marquis of Breadalbane and the Duke of Sutherland.[74] Breadalbane's estate chamberlain was appalled when he learned that one of his subordinate factors had asked for
assistance from the Glasgow Relief Committee to feed the people under his care. This
would cause 'mortification' to his lordship: 'it would never do to let it go abroad that
Lord Breadalbane's people depended on the Relief Committee for their sustenance'.[75] Similar sentiments and an acute sensitivity to public opinion explain the
decision by the Sutherland estate to assume the burden of relieving all destitution on
the property without recourse to government or external charitable aid. James Loch
asserted to the second Duke: 'I find that several who are most sincerely attached to you
are of the opinion that it would lower your proud position to let any relieve your people
but yourself – this is felt deeply'. He maintained also that if any other organisation
distributed meal in Sutherland the Duke's authority 'would be both infringed on' and
he would not continue to be 'their legal and natural protector . . .'.[76] The need for the
estate to assume responsibility for the people was therefore vital. If this course was not
followed, the family's reputation would inevitably be damaged: '. . . the public and
newspapers will say, here is a person rich enough to maintain his people, capable to
ward off the pressure of want, and yet he takes a portion of that which was intended for
the starving tenants of needy and poverty-stricken landlords . . . the complaint of the
public would be unanswerable in the House of Commons'.[77] Later Loch was even to
go so far as to advise that the Duke should reduce his application for financial aid under
the Drainage Act from £90,000 to £7500, so that there would be more for others. He
stressed that '. . . you would do a very gracious act which would be most highly
appreciated by all in the House of Commons and by all Scotchmen . . .'.[78] It should
be remembered that the famine initially attracted massive publicity, with detailed
newspaper reports and fund-raising meetings of the churches and charities ensuring
that events in the north-west attracted a large and attentive audience. This must have
placed effective pressure on aristocratic proprietors such as Sutherland and Breadalbane who had both the means to provide relief from their own resources and a jealous
concern to defend the good name, honour and reputation of their families.

Not all landowners, however, had an equally keen sense of their responsibilities. But
government was determined that they would all honour their obligations: to do so was
nothing less than the fulfilment of the contract between tenant and proprietor. As
Trevelyan stressed: 'It is part of the duty of the landlord to give his small tenants the
necessary assistance in provision of food and seed. In every country the party entitled to
receive the rent, or surplus produce of the soil, is expected to remit a portion of his
ordinary demands when that produce fails, and in extreme cases he is likewise expected
to make advances of seed and other necessary means of enabling his underholders to
carry on the cultivation – his outlay in the last-mentioned case being returned to him in
the produce of the next harvest, which must otherwise fall short'.[79] A careful strategy
was conceived in order to bring maximum pressure to bear on the truculent, lazy or
irresponsible proprietor.[80] It had three elements. First, circulars were addressed to all
owners of land, inviting them to describe their relief measures. If the response was
unsatisfactory, government relief officials were sent to the property to carry out a
detailed inspection. They also returned at regular intervals to discover how far matters
had improved. None but officers in whom Sir Edward Coffin had the highest

confidence were employed on these missions and a steamer of the Royal Navy was always at hand to provide transport. Second, a proprietor unwilling to do his duty was to be formally exhorted to assume his responsibilities. Trevelyan himself was of the opinion that this pressure would be sufficient: 'We may reasonably expect that no proprietor will have the hardihood to fly in the face of the well-pronounced opinion of his countrymen, brought home to him by authoritative and able intervention'.[81] Third, if a landowner refused to cooperate and government had to intervene by sending meal to avoid starvation, two penalties could be exacted. The proprietor was threatened with being charged the cost of the grain either directly or by government selling a portion of his estate to recoup the outlay. On the other hand, if sickness developed among his people because of malnutrition, they would be entitled to claim poor relief because of their disability. This in turn, asserted Sir John McNeill, Chairman of the Board of Supervision, would 'entail a very heavy burden on proprietors whose people have been allowed to suffer from want'.[82] Sir Edward Coffin wrote to Gordon of Cluny, Lord Cranstoun, Mrs Stewart Mackenzie, Mr Bankes of Loch Broom, Mr Baillie of Glenelg, Macdonald of Locheil and others in the winter of 1846 outlining the grave consequences of any inattention to duty. In the case of Gordon, Bankes and Baillie at least these tactics did bring rapid results.

Yet even government, despite its insistence that estate owners should do their duty, had to acknowledge that some of the proprietors '. . . are more or less embarrassed' and could not provide relief indefinitely. This was one reason why it refused to provide them with meal on credit because it feared that several would be unable to make repayments.[83] Moreover, the convention that landowners had a direct responsibility for the tenants of their estates had in the past been associated with harvest failures of one or at most two seasons. It was likely to break down in the crisis of the 1840s when successive years of blight ensured that serious levels of destitution endured from 1846 until the mid 1850s. Why, therefore, in this context was there not more evidence of landlord bankruptcy or of estates being taken over and administered by trustees as their internal debts escalated? To answer this question adequately four factors must be considered: (i) The Social Composition of the Landed Class; (ii) The Economic Structure of Highland Estates; (iii) The Drainage Act and Landlord Funding of Relief; (iv) The Role of Charity.

The Social Composition of the Landed Class

By 1846 the landed class of the Western Highlands and Islands had undergone a radical change in personnel and structure. Before 1800 the Highland land market was very sluggish.[84] In the subsequent fifty years it probably became one of the most active of all the regions of the United Kingdom. Improved transport facilities (especially the expansion of steam navigation), the new scenic and sporting attractions of the Highlands, the shortage of estates around the lowland cities, the rise of a larger and richer urban middle class and the failure of many landed families in the north-west, were all factors in this process. For the purposes of this discussion, however, the results of land purchase are more crucial than its causes. Many of the old, impoverished families were swept away and their places taken by men who had made fortunes in trade, the law, banking, industry and the professions. By the 1840s all of the Outer Hebrides, with the exception of North Uist (still, until 1854, under Macdonald ownership), were held by new landowners. Two millionaires, John Gordon of Cluny Castle in Aberdeenshire, reckoned the richest commoner in Scotland, and James Matheson of the giant East India trading firm of Jardine, Matheson and Co., had acquired Barra, South Uist, Benbecula and Lewis. Harris was owned by the Dunmore family, lowland lairds with estates near Falkirk. Seventy-six per cent of estates in Mull were possessed by new men who had purchased their properties since *c*.1820. Between then and 1850, several estates changed hands more than once.[85] Only the lands of the Duke of Argyll at Iona and the Ross of Mull and those of the Maclaines of Lochbuie were still held by their original owners. Across the Sound of Mull, in the parish of Morvern in mainland Argyllshire, every single property was put on the market from 1813 to 1838. By 1844 there was scarcely a proprietor left who had any traditional association with the area.[86] Few localities elsewhere were unaffected. Raasay, Ulva, Arisaig, Loch Broom, Kinloch, Moidart, Appin, Eigg, and Glenelg were all held by new owners. By 1846 the old, hereditary estates were mainly limited to those of the grandees, the Dukes of Sutherland and Argyll and the Marquis of Breadalbane, or to those of the less wealthy such as Lord Macdonald, Macleod of Macleod, Sir James Riddell, Maclean of Coll, Macdonald of Lochsheil and Macdonnel of Knoydart. Significantly several of these were under trust and were to be either sold or subjected to rigorous judicial management during the famine. All in all, of the total of eighty-six landowners in the distressed districts in 1846, at least sixty-two (seventy per cent) were new purchasers who had not owned Highland property before 1800.[87]

In 1848 William Skene described how 'the whole stretch of Country from Fort Augustus to Fort William and Arisaig is in the possession of rich English capitalists'.[88] He may have exaggerated the scale of penetration by men from south of the Border – the majority were in fact successful lowland Scots – but he was entirely correct when he stressed the wealth of the new élite. They belonged to families who did not exclusively or mainly depend on Highland land or crofters' rents for income. That came principally from the profits of their industrial and commercial interests, their legal firms or their banking businesses. As a class they were broadly insulated from the stresses which oppressed Lord Macdonald, Macleod of Macleod, Maclean of Coll and others, who did have to rely mainly on the revenue from their estates. A telling indication of the depth and breadth of their resources was the ease with which such 'new' proprietors as Sir James Matheson, Baillie of Glenelg and Gordon of Cluny were able to personally finance large-scale schemes from their properties in the early 1850s despite the collapse of estate income in the previous decade.[89]

The Economic Structure of Highland Estates

There was a prevalent assumption in both government circles and among the ranks of contemporary publicists that the accumulation of rent arrears among the small peasantry would inevitably bankrupt the Highland landlord class. This belief depended on the unquestioned premise that by the 1840s the main source of estate income was the petty payments of an impecunious tenantry. It is this assumption which must now be scrutinised.

Obviously the stereotype had some basis in fact in certain areas. Thus, of the £2629.7.0 paid by the Duke of Argyll's tenants on the island of Tiree, £1312.11.8 (or fifty-two per cent) derived from those occupying land at an annual rent not exceeding £10 while only £364.5.0 (or fourteen per cent) came from tenants with an annual rental exceeding £100.[90] On the Coigach section of the Cromartie estate in Ross-shire, sixty-seven per cent of total rental was paid by tenants with rentals of £10 per annum or less.[91] The seven tacksmen or large tenants on the Ardnamurchan estate of Sir James Riddell contributed £1223, or thirty-nine per cent of the rental, but the remaining £1897 (or sixty-one per cent) was paid by small joint tenants and crofters.[92] There were broadly similar rental structures on the Clark estate on Ulva, Gordon of Cluny's properties on Barra and South Uist and the Duke of Argyll's lands on Mull.[93] Estates such as these were particularly vulnerable unless their owners had other assets or properties with a different tenant composition.

But it is important to emphasise that not all lands in the Western Highlands had this rental pattern by the 1840s. The principal though by no means the only reason for this was the rapid advance of large-scale commercial sheep farming. The Central Board in 1847 described the territorial expansion of the sheep ranches: 'In the eastern and central parts of these districts, the country is partly occupied as large sheep or store farms, and partly as small farms or crofts, and a considerable portion of the country is under tillage; but towards the west, the country becomes more and more exclusively occupied as large sheep-walks and the great mass of the population are clustered round the shores, and either occupying small crofts, or subsisting by labour, fishing etc.'[94] By the time of the *New Statistical Account*, which was mainly compiled in the later 1830s, at least eighty-five per cent of the parishes in Sutherland, sixty-one per cent of those in Ross and Cromarty, sixty per cent of those in Inverness-shire, and thirty-five per cent of those in Argyllshire had experienced large-scale sheep-farm development which resulted in the emergence of bigger tenancies and land consolidation. The pattern of growth, however, was far from complete by that date. In the following decade sheep-farming penetrated further into many other parishes in the Inner and Outer Hebrides. Most estates on Mull were under sheep by the 1840s.[95] From the 1830s extensive grazing farms were established in North Uist and by the 1840s sixty per cent of Lord Macdonald's rental of £3536 from that island was paid by seventeen large tenants paying over £10 a year. This group also accounted for ninety-eight per cent, seventy-four per cent, ninety-one per cent and ninety-two per cent of the rental on the estates of Glenshiel, North Morar, Knoydart and Glenelg respectively.[96] Sixty-four per cent of the total rental of £15,073 on six estates in Skye derived from tenants paying over £10 a year for their holdings. The emigration of 500 from Rhum had left behind a population of fifty and accelerated the island's conversion into a great sheep ranch.[97] By the 1840s there were five large sheep-farms on Harris, varying from 35,000 acres downwards, which occupied over ninety per cent of the land area of the island.[98] Sheep-farming was also described as on the increase in Skye in the 1830s, and by 1850 the Sheriff-Substitute for the island claimed that it was the dominant economic activity: 'The greater part of the island being in the hands of a small number of tacksmen, and the great bulk of the population on the remainder, the holdings of the latter are necessarily circumscribed . . .'[99] Furthermore, as will be argued in Chapters 7 and 13, clearance and consolidation continued to accelerate during the famine itself and its immediate aftermath. In the process, while causing profound social suffering, it helped to transform formerly insolvent properties into more profitable enterprises. By 1851, eighty-six per cent of the rental of the parish of Kilfinichen in Mull, formerly mainly paid by crofters, was contributed by tenants holding land at £20 or above.[100]

Table 4.1. Sheep Prices, 1838-1865
A. Cheviots

Year	Wethers	Ewes	Lambs	Average (to nearest s.)
	s.d. s.d.	s.d. s.d.	s.d. s.d.	s.
1835	22 0 to 27 6	18 0 to 20 6	8 0 to 11 0	18
1836	24 0 to 31 6	16 0 to 19 0	10 0 to 14 0	19
1837	19 0 to 28 0	14 0 to 19 0	10 0 to 13 0	17
1838	23 0 to 30 6	17 0 to 22 0	12 0 to 14 0	19
1839	23 0 to 31 0	14 0 to 19 0	0 0 to 13 0	16
1840	24 0 to 33 0	15 0 to 23 0	7 0 to 11 6	19
1841	23 0 to 30 0	14 0 to 22 0	8 0 to 12 0	18
1842	22 6 to 28 0	13 0 to 17 0	7 6 to 10 0	16
1843	19 0 to 25 0	8 0 to 12 0	7 0 to 8 0	13
1844	21 0 to 29 0	10 0 to 16 0	8 0 to 10 5	15
1845	23 0 to 33 0	13 0 to 20 0	8 0 to 13 0	18
1846	24 0 to 33 6	14 6 to 21 6	10 0 to 14 6	*20*
1847	24 0 to 35 0	13 0 to 24 0	11 6 to 15 0	*20*
1848	23 0 to 34 6	13 0 to 28 0	11 6 to 15 0	*21*
1849	21 0 to 30 2	12 0 to 21 0	0 0 to 14 0	*16*
1850	20 6 to 29 6	12 0 to 21 0	8 0 to 13 0	*17*
1851	21 6 to 31 0	12 0 to 20 0	8 9 to 14 0	*18*
1852	21 0 to 32 0	13 0 to 21 0	8 0 to 14 0	*19*
1853	26 6 to 38 0	15 0 to 28 0	9 0 to 17 0	22
1854	25 0 to 36 0	17 0 to 26 0	9 0 to 16 6	*21*
1855	23 6 to 36 0	16 0 to 25 0	10 0 to 17 0	*21*
1856	22 0 to 35 6	15 6 to 24 0	10 0 to 15 0	20
1857	24 0 to 36 0	14 6 to 26 0	10 6 to 14 5	21
1858	24 0 to 34 6	14 0 to 24 6	10 6 to 14 0	20
1859	25 0 to 34 6	16 0 to 25 0	10 3 to 14 9	21
1860	26 0 to 38 0	17 6 to 27 6	12 6 to 17 6	23
1861	25 0 to 38 6	16 0 to 28 0	9 0 to 16 0	22
1862	27 0 to 37 6	17 6 to 28 0	10 0 to 16 0	23
1863	25 0 to 38 6	19 0 to 28 6	10 0 to 16 0	26
1864	31 0 to 41 0	21 0 to 31 6	14 0 to 18 0	27
1865	32 6 to 44 0	22 6 to 33 6	14 6 to 20 0	

Source: Transactions of the Highland Agricultural Society, 1921
Notes: (i) The average for each year has been obtained by averaging annual prices of wedders, ewes and lambs.
(ii) Famine years are italicised.
(iii) Average 'cheviot price', 1838-1865 = 19s; average price, famine years, 1846-52 = 19s.

B. Blackface

Year	Wethers	Ewes	Lambs	Average (to nearest s.)
	s.d. s.d.	s.d. s.d.	s.d. s.d.	s.
1835	15 0 to 18 9	10 0 to 13 0	7 0 to 8 0	12
1836	15 0 to 21 0	9 0 to 12 0	8 6 to 11 0	12
1837	13 0 to 16 0	8 0 to 12 0	8 0 to 9 6	11
1838	15 0 to 20 6	10 0 to 13 0	not quoted	14 (of 2)
1839	15 0 to 22 0	10 0 to 12 0	7 0 to 8 3	12
1840	15 0 to 22 6	11 0 to 12 0	7 0 to 9 3	12
1841	16 0 to 20 0	9 0 to 11 0	6 0 to 8 0	11
1842	14 0 to 19 0	7 6 to 8 0	5 6 to 7 0	10
1843	not quoted	4 9 to 6 6	not quoted	–
1844	15 0 to 21 0	6 6 to 10 0	5 0 to 8 0	11
1845	14 0 to 23 0	8 0 to 12 0	6 0 to 8 0	12
1846	13 0 to 24 0	10 0 to 13 0	8 0 to 9 0	*13*
1847	20 6 to 25 0	10 0 to 14 0	8 6 to 9 6	*14*
1848	20 0 to 24 0	11 3 to 12 0	8 6 to 10 0	*14*
1849	not quoted	not quoted	7 0 to 7 6	–
1850	not quoted	not quoted	7 0 to 0 0	–
1851	17 6 to 28 0	9 0 to 12 0	6 6 to 8 0	*13*
1852	18 6 to 22 0	9 6 to 12 0	4 6 to 7 0	*12*
1853	23 0 to 27 0	14 6 to 16 6	8 0 to 11 6	*16*
1854	20 0 to 26 0	11 0 to 16 6	8 0 to 10 6	*15*
1855	23 6 to 26 6	14 0 to 16 0	10 0 to 11 0	*16*
1856	17 0 to 24 0	10 0 to 20 0	7 6 to 10 0	14
1857	20 0 to 29 0	10 6 to 15 0	9 3 to 11 0	15
1858	20 0 to 27 0	9 9 to 18 9	8 3 to 10 6	16
1859	20 0 to 25 0	10 0 to 14 0	8 9 to 11 0	14
1860	21 0 to 27 3	11 0 to 16 0	10 0 to 13 6	16
1861	21 0 to 29 0	12 0 to 22 0	6 3 to 14 0	17
1862	16 9 to 27 0	12 0 to 18 8	6 0 to 12 0	15
1863	20 0 to 30 6	13 0 to 16 0	8 0 to 11 6	16
1864	25 0 to 30 0	15 0 to 19 0	10 0 to 13 6	18
1865	15 6 to 32 6	15 0 to 25 0	10 0 to 17 0	19

Source: Transactions of the Highland and Agricultural Society, 1921

Notes: (i) The average for each year has been obtained by averaging average annual prices for wedders, ewes and lambs.

(ii) Famine years are italicised.

(iii) Average 'blackface price', 1835-65 = 14s; average price, famine years = 13s. (average of 1846-8, 1851-2. Figures for 1849-50 incomplete).

The expansion of commercial pastoralism therefore gave a resilience to a number of estates during the famine. As Tables 4.1 and 4.2 demonstrate, the prices of sheep and wool not only held up well but increased very substantially in the first few years of the crisis. It is not therefore surprising that properties where the bulk of rent payment derived from bigger tenancies, dependent partly on large-scale pastoral farming, saw only a modest decline rather than a catastrophic collapse in their revenue yield. Two examples will be given for the purposes of illustration: the estates of the Mackenzies of Gairloch in Wester Ross and the great Sutherland estate where sheep-farming had expanded most notoriously earlier in the nineteenth century.

Table 4.2. Prices of Wool (Laid Cheviot and Laid Highland), 1840-1860

Year	Laid Cheviot s.d. s.d.	Laid Highland s.d. s.d.	Average (to nearest s.) s.
1840	15 0 to 20 0	7 0 to 10 0	13
1841	15 0 to 16 9	6 0 to 7 5	11
1842	12 6 to 14 0	not quoted	–
1843	9 0 to 11 6	5 0 to 6 0	8
1844	15 0 to 18 0	7 6 to 8 6	12
1845	14 6 to 17 6	8 0 to 8 6	12
1846	12 0 to 14 6	not quoted	11
1847	12 6 to 14 0	4 9 to 10 0	–
1848	9 6 to 14 0	6 0 to 6 3	10
1849	12 0 to 16 6	8 0 to 8 6	10
1850	15 0 to 17 6	8 0 to 9 3	12
1851	12 0 to 16 0	8 0 to 9 0	11
1852	13 0 to 15 0	11 0 to 12 6	11
1853	19 0 to 22 0	7 6 to 8 6	16
1854	12 0 to 15 0	8 6 to 9 0	11
1855	14 6 to 19 0	11 0 to 10 0	13
1856	19 0 to 21 6	13 0 to 14 3	15
1857	19 0 to 21 6	8 9 to 10 0	17
1858	15 0 to 17 0	10 9 to 11 6	12
1859	18 6 to 24 0	10 0 to 11 3	16
1860	22 0 to 32 0		19

Source: Transactions of the Highland and Agricultural Society, 1921
Notes: (i) Average for each year has been obtained by averaging annual prices per laid cheviot and laid highland.
　　　(ii) Famine years are italicised.
　　　(iii) (a) Average 'wool price', 1840-60 = 12s;
　　　　　(b) Average price, famine years = 11s;
　　　　　(c) Average price, 'pre-famine', i.e. 1840-5 = 11s;
　　　　　(d) Average price, 'post-famine', i.e. 1853-60 = 15s.

The number of small tenants in arrears in Gairloch rose steeply from 1847.[101] In 1846, 24.9 per cent of all tenants were in arrears; by 1848 this figure had increased to sixty-one per cent. However, this was very much a crisis which was mainly restricted to the crofter class, the eighty-four per cent of tenants who in the first year of the famine paid a rental of £5 per annum or less. The estate did not depend upon this group for most of its revenue. In 1846, a small élite of thirty-five bigger tenants, paying £20 or more per annum in rental, accounted for eighty-four per cent of total rental income. Arrears among this group remained at a consistently low level. In 1846, six were in arrears but only to a total of £89.7.0 which represented 10.4 per cent of all arrears in that year. The following year the number of these indebted tenants fell by one and the arrears accounted for by this class rose marginally to £119 of the total of £877.3.3½. By 1848 the value of arrears on the estate had climbed dramatically to £1831.2.7, an increase of forty-eight per cent, but only £214, or twelve per cent, was accounted for by the larger tenants. On the whole they were able to sustain rental payments throughout the later 1840s. This helps to explain why despite the difficulties of the smaller men there was only an overall deficit of £467 or twelve per cent in 1848 of the annual rental of

£3881.17.0. £3012 of this was contributed by tenants paying £20 or more per annum.

The Sutherland estate covered such a vast area that the economic impact of the potato blight varied not only between large and small tenants but between the poor areas of the far west, especially the parishes of Assynt and Edderachillis, and the more favoured localities of the eastern sections.[102] Thus arrears among the small tenants in the east increased only marginally between 1846 and 1850, reaching a total of £223 or ten per cent of the small tenant rental of £2319. Small rents on the eastern part of the estate show a change in the later 1830s, possibly as a result of the harvest failure of 1837-8. Arrears increased, the rental declined and the number of holdings fell. Yet, in the later 1840s, the number of holdings rose, arrears were kept to a minimum and there was slight evidence of crisis conditions. Even more significantly, the rental of the larger tenants was maintained. The bigger men accounted for eighty-five per cent of the total rental of £14,951 and their arrears never rose to more than £629. In the case of the eastern parts of the Sutherland estate, it was the resiliency of *both* the small *and* the larger tenants (the former's favourable position being due to a combination of fishing opportunities, the Duke's relief schemes and temporary migration earnings),[103] which helps to explain why, quite remarkably, arrears actually *fell* from six per cent of total rental in 1845 to five per cent in 1850.

There was a quite different pattern in the poorer western parishes of Assynt, Edderachillis and Durness. The rental data point self-evidently to a crisis among the small tenants. By 1849, arrears in all three parishes had risen to sixty-one per cent, eight-five per cent and eighty-six per cent respectively of total rental. There was a broadly similar trend in the parishes of Farr and Tongue although the pattern in Reay was more akin to that of the eastern side of the estate. Even in the west, however, the bulk of rental payment depended mainly on the larger tenantry. In 1845, they accounted for seventy-two per cent of the accumulated rental of small and large tenants in the western district. The arrears of these bigger men never reached more than ten per cent of their annual rental.

Table 4.3. Tenant and Rental Structure, Parish of Lochbroom, Wester Ross, 1851

	Per cent of Total Holdings Occupied by Tenants of less than £10 rental	Per cent of Total Rental Paid by Tenants of less than £10 rental
Marchioness of Stafford	86	28
Mr. Davidson	90	16
Mr. Mackenzie (Ardross)	93	31
Sir Alexander Mackenzie	82	8
Sir James Matheson	95	74

Source: McNeill Report, Appendix A, 86, Return for Parish of Lochbroom of Number of Persons assessed for the Poor rate

The economic strength of the Sutherland estate did not entirely depend on the prosperity of sheep-farming. The family's massive wealth was able to absorb both limited reduction in rental and the increased costs of relief with relative ease.[104] However, both its experience and that of the Gairloch estate underscores the significance of tenant composition during the famine. There were several other properties with a similar dependence on large tenancies which had grown because of the scale of consolidation and the expansion of sheep farms which had occurred in the Western Highlands before 1846 (see, for example, Table 4.3 and above, Table 1.1, p.4). This structure helped prevent rental income falling to unacceptable levels despite the ruinous impact of the potato blight on the small tenantry.

The Drainage Act and Landlord Funding of Relief

As has been seen, government was determined to ensure that in 1846 and early 1847 the major responsibility for famine relief should rest with local landowners. However, from as early as August 1846, it conceded that this would place a substantial financial burden on them. Government therefore advised needy proprietors to draw on drainage loans which had been available from the Exchequer since 1846 in order to provide employment for their tenants.[105] An 'Act to authorise the Advance of Public Money to promote the Improvement of Land in Great Britain and Ireland' (9 and 10 Vic. cap. C1 (1846)) was part of Sir Robert Peel's declared policy of compensating British agriculture for the loss of protection after the repeal of the Corn Laws. Government loans would be made available for drainage purposes at an interest rate of 6½ per cent per annum. Repayment could take place over twenty-two years. £2 million was allocated for this purpose in the original Act and a further £2 million was made available by the Treasury from 1850.[106]

As pleas and petitions for Government assistance poured in from the Western Highlands, all interested parties were referred to the Drainage Act as an obvious existing source of financial aid. However, there were initially at least several major obstacles to widespread use of this facility. The process of application was lengthy while the emergency was immediate. By the eighth clause no advance could be made until a detailed application had been submitted to and sanctioned by the Treasury. By the sixteenth clause, if the Commissioners did sanction the application, then the plan, estimate and specification of the proposed works had to be lodged with the Government surveyor while no advance would be issued until two months had elapsed from publication of the proposal in the *London Gazette*. This was to ensure that 'persons having charges upon the land should have the opportunity of dissenting from such application if they should think fit'.[107] Even government relief officers admitted it was 'an unwieldy and complex process . . . while the present pressure admits of no delay'.[108] Moreover, it was widely believed that estates under trust or under a minority could not apply for such loans. Even if an application was contemplated, the scheme seemed irrelevant to the needs of the impecunious landowner. The Act made allowances only for sums spent on drainage, a pointless expenditure if the proprietor could not furnish from his own resources funds for trenching and fencing. Without these additional works, no real improvement in the land was anticipated. As one observer in Skye concluded in October 1846: '. . . the statute [the Drainage Act] may be good and judicious in its enactments, but is in no way calculated to afford that *immediate* relief which is now so very urgently required. Its machinery is too complicated, its provisions too contracted, and its operations far too tedious and restricted for the present crisis'.[109]

Because of these problems the potential of the Drainage Act was not fully realised in 1846. Landowners had to rely mainly on their own resources to meet the crisis. Only in December 1846 did the Scottish press provide clear indication that some proprietors were willing to apply.[110] At the same time government was being informed about the ineffectiveness of the legislation not only by correspondents from the north but by its own relief officers.[111] It soon became apparent that if the basic policy of dependence on landlord efforts was to be maintained the Drainage Act would have to be adapted to the conditions prevailing in the Western Highlands. Thus, from November 1846, it was decided that applicants could commence work without awaiting the end of the two-month period and that Commissioners would include all works done as carried out under the provisions of the Act when examining applications. A month earlier the Chancellor of the Exchequer had emphasised to the Lord Advocate that in order to bring the Act into operation he was 'willing to strain it to the uttermost'.[112] Thus trenching and fencing could be included as long as they were 'subordinate to and connected with a system of drainage'.[113] Estates under trust were also invited to make application, the Lord Advocate having expressed his conviction that 'the Courts would exonerate any trustee who should exercise a fair discretion in meeting the present emergency . . .'[114]

These adjustments were widely publicised and soon brought forth a major increase in applications from the Highlands.[115] Between September 1846 and September 1847 Highland applications to the value of £281,810 were lodged; during February and March a further series of applications of £206,901 in value were submitted. By the end of March 1847 the Highland total had reached £488,711 which was eighteen per cent of the sum for Britain as a whole and twenty-two per cent of all Scottish applications. £84,472 came from Argyll, £74,748 from Inverness, £281,262 from Ross and Cromarty and £52,000 from Sutherland. Quite clearly the level of applications from the Highland counties was out of all proportion to the value of land in the region compared to the rest of Britain. It primarily reflected the exigencies of the subsistence crisis in the north-west and must have had a remarkable effect on the availability of employment and income in the distressed districts. The final sum of almost half a million pounds was considerably more than that available to the Central Relief Board, although it must be admitted that not all drainage money was channelled into areas of the Highlands where destitution was most acute.

For many landlords, however, the advantages were enormous. The factor of Lord Macdonald's estate admitted that while 'It [the Drainage Act] is not, however, altogether adapted to our circumstances . . . we have, like drowning men catching at a straw, been obliged to lay hold of it as the only means within our reach of keeping the working-classes from starvation'.[116] Sir Edward Coffin agreed, after his tour of inspection of the distressed areas, that the loans obtained under the Drainage Act, rather than landowners' own resources, had become the major source of funding employment from early 1847.[117] The wages gained in the course of drainage and trenching work were also employed to directly pay off arrears while the landowner was assisted in the payment of interest and the principal to government by charging interest

of 6½ per cent to tenants on improvements to crofts carried out under the Act.[118] The
funds, in this way, amounted to an indirect subsidy from the state to the Highland
landed class. An insight into the way the Drainage Act worked to landlord advantage
can be obtained from the examples of the Macdonald estates in Skye and the Mackenzie estates in Wester Ross. Angus Macdonald, Lord Macdonald's ground-officer in
Sleat, noted how rents had begun to be 'generally well paid' from 1850. The payment of
the Whitsun rent he attributed in particular to the availability of wages received for
draining and trenching under the Drainage Act. Crofters simply worked until they had
obtained enough to pay the rent and then stopped.[119] Essentially, then, much of the
loan was simply a book transfer directly to Lord Macdonald's account. In Gairloch, in
Wester Ross, a form of truck operated. The crofters were paid a daily wage of from 1s.
to 1s.6d. from the drainage grant. They were supplied with meal on a weekly basis on
account of their wages. The residue of their wages went to pay arrears of rent and the
balance was then given in cash.[120] What had been designed as a measure to avert mass
starvation was becoming one which indirectly diverted funds into the pockets of some
landed families.

The Role of Charity

The formation of the Central Relief Board in January 1847 which brought together the
combined efforts of the Free Church and the Glasgow and Edinburgh Destitution
Committees, was of even greater significance for the landed class. The object of the
Board, through its local committees, was to provide relief 'to any party who is ascertained to be in a destitute state, who is willing to work, but cannot find employment,
but not to parties on the ordinary poor roll . . . or able immediately to obtain such
relief'.[121] This implied that as soon as the structure of relief began to function effectively the Board would take responsibility for all destitute persons in the Western
Highlands and, by so doing, relieve proprietors of much of their responsibility. Most
landowners quickly realised their good fortune. Sir Edward Coffin noted how their
hopes 'were excited' by the formation of the relief associations and that 'what many aim
at evidently is to shift the burden from their own shoulders on any others that will bear
it'.[122] For its part government, while still continuing to acknowledge the moral
responsibility of the proprietors, in practice accepted that the main burden of the relief
operation would henceforth fall upon the Central Board.[123] In 1847 and 1848 some
landowners, such as James Matheson in Lewis, the Duke of Sutherland and Campbell
of Jura, continued to support the destitute on their estates without assistance from the
relief committees.[124] In 1849 and 1850, however, even Lewis and Sutherland were
included in the relief operation. Not all proprietors entirely ceased relief activity.[125]
Many supplied seed grain in 1847, though their efforts were powerfully supported by
and, in the view of some observers at least, outdone by those of the British Association
for the Relief of Distress in Scotland and Ireland.[126] Drainage work continued and on
some estates became concentrated in the late autumn and winter months because
during those seasons the Central Board suspended its activities.[127] Eventually, in
1849, some landowners, especially in Wester Ross, Skye, Sutherland and Lewis,

became partners with the Central Board in work schemes through the so-called Cooperative System.[128] For the most part, however, most proprietors ceased to assume the main responsibility for the destitute on their estates from the spring of 1847 until 1850.[129]

Table 4.4. Poor on Roll and Occasional Poor by County, 1846-1851

County	1846		1847		1848		1849		1850		1851	
	(1)	(2)	(1)	(2)	(1)	(2)	(1)	(2)	(1)	(2)	(1)	(2)
Inverness	2433	296	3458	1498	3538	746	3664	715	3845	573	3982	2099
Argyll	2213	553	2774	932	3009	838	3321	719	3552	716	3585	843
Ross and Cromarty	2598	169	3759	380	3663	416	3850	383	3756	406	3686	417
Sutherland	842	34	1006	26	1003	39	1040	52	1039	70	1056	120

Source: PP, XXVII (1847); XXXIII (1847-8); XXV (1849); XXVI (1850); XXIII (1852)
Note: Col. 1 refers to regular poor on roll; col. 2 to occasional poor.

It was also due to the operations of the Central Board that the landed class managed to avoid the crippling increase in poor law assessments which many feared in the early months of the famine. Table 4.4 indicates that the major burden for relief of destitution between 1846 and 1850 was not borne by the official poor law. After a marginal increase in 1847 the number of 'occasional' poor actually fell slightly until 1851 in a region where a significant proportion of the population was living in conditions of great destitution. But the law allowed discretionary payments to be made. Sir John McNeill succinctly stated the legal position in 1851: '. . . while the statute of 1845 did not recognise in able-bodied persons out of employment a right to demand relief, it recognised in parochial boards a discretionary power to apply the funds raised by assessment to the temporary relief of occasional poor; and (on the authority of a joint opinion for the late Lord Advocate and the late Dean of Faculty) they were told that this power extended to the temporary relief of able-bodied persons in absolute want of the means of subsistence'.[130] That action was not taken until after 1850 was partly due to the primitive condition of the Poor Law in some parts of the Highlands. In Barra, for example in 1846-7, no records were kept and no doctor attended the poor; it was a regulation of the parish that any person renting land or owning a horse or a cow was not placed upon the poor roll.[131] The Poor Law Board was not legally constituted and no member 'felt at liberty to interfere actively for fear of giving umbrage to the factor or the proprietor'. The Inspector did 'not know how to act and entirely lent (*sic*) upon the factor by whom alone he was guided'.[132] Barra and the adjacent parish of South Uist were the most notorious examples. Yet, from elsewhere in the Western Highlands and Islands there came other reports of the inadequacy of relief, landlord and factor opposition to the raising of assessments and a basic ignorance of the 1845 legislation and administrative procedure.[133] Edward Ellice, M.P., himself a landlord in Inverness-shire, was of the opinion that '. . . the aged, the sick and the helpless . . . have their legal claims, but the obstacles placed in the way of enforcing these claims are almost insuperable'.[134] One of the most telling pieces of evidence which tends to confirm the accuracy of Ellice's observation was the surprisingly large number of appeals against Inspectors of the Poor's decisions not to grant relief which can be found in Sheriff Court Processes.

In the later 1840s, for example, much of the business of the Court at Portree in Skye was concerned with these actions. [135]

Nevertheless, there were signs that the sheer scale of the crisis in 1846 forced even inert parochial boards dominated by vested interests to take more action. Several in the Western Islands had begun to give temporary relief to 'able-bodied persons in absolute want' from that year. [136] This probably explains the increase in the numbers of poor between 1846 and 1847 recorded in Table 4.4. Yet Sir John McNeill admitted that this flexibility had been temporary. The policy came to an end during the operations of the Central Board and only resumed when it ceased its activities in 1850. [137] This analysis exactly fits the pattern in Table 4.4 of a significant rise in the numbers of official paupers occurring from 1851.

The destitution committees, therefore, came to the rescue not simply of the starving in the Highlands but of those proprietors who dreaded the crushing burden of a massive increase in poor law assessments. In 1849 the Central Board supported for a period 8162 people in Skye or about one third of the total population. [138] In the same year only 1045 regular and occasional poor were relieved by the parochial boards of the island. [139] At the peak of the relief operations in 1848, 7893 – or forty-seven per cent of the population of Mull – were receiving relief from the destitution committees compared to only 385 from the parochial boards. [140] Similar figures could be produced from all over the Highland region. There is also evidence from independent witnesses and the Central Board itself that some individuals who were entitled to relief from the parish were forced instead to rely on the charities. William Skene, Secretary of the Edinburgh Section, admitted that many who had the right to relief were not on the poor's roll: 'The proprietors undertake the management of their own poor and in the Highlands, with the large properties and the dense population where sometimes there is but one proprietor in the Parish, this is almost equivalent to leaving matters as they were before the Poor Law Act was passed . . .'. [141] Captain Rose, his Resident Inspector in Wester Ross, confirmed that there were many aged and infirm persons who were assisted from the relief fund but who ought to have been dependent on the poor law. Their transfer from one to the other had been facilitated in 1847 because the parochial boards and the local destitution committees often shared a similar membership. [142]

Critics of the landlords argued, however, that the Central Board not only allowed them to shirk their legal and moral responsibilities, but that it also provided opportunities to them for improving their properties at the expense of a great charitable fund. As will be seen in Chapter 5, the systems of relief practised by the Central Board almost inevitably meant that this would happen. A central principle was that gratuitous relief should be avoided and work demanded in return for meal. The labour involved covered a range of activities including trenching, road-building and pier construction. [143] Necessarily, all this added to the infrastructure of Highland estates and meant that 'the proprietors would prosper at the expense of public benevolence'. [144]

The Cooperative System attracted even more opprobrium. The Central Board began to operate this from 1848. The Board contributed a sum limited to the estimated cost of relieving destitution in a given area on a public work. The proprietor, in return, bore a proportion of the cost and was bound to support his people during the period of the contract. It was also possible for the money to be made available for 'reproductive labour' or improvement to crofts. In this case, the people had to be provided with leases by the proprietors in order to realise the benefits of their labour. By 1850 most properties in Skye, the northern parishes of Wester Ross, Lewis and the great Sutherland estate were involved in these cooperative arrangements.[145] The major achievements of the policy were a series of important roads in Wester Ross and the route from Lairg to Loch Laxford in Sutherland. They undoubtedly raised the value of property in these areas, and some estates also took advantage of the employment afforded to the population to reduce rent arrears in exactly the same manner as they exploited the Drainage Act. In the parish of Gairloch, for instance, 'a great part of the labour performed under a cooperative arrangement with the relief committee . . . went to liquidate arrears of rent. It was in no doubt of great assistance to the people, who were supplied with meal while working, and were also enabled in that manner to pay off part of their arrears'.[146] The editor of the *Inverness Advertiser* passed his own verdict on these schemes: 'This so-styled co-operative system, stripped of Mr. Skene's mystifying verbiage, is neither more nor less than a monstrous malversation of a charitable fund, by giving largesse to noblemen and gentlemen, who may be truly said to have improved their estates by means of public subscriptions'.[147]

It was indeed a nice irony that a crisis which had been regarded in its initial stages as a serious threat to the survival of many landed families ended with angry accusations that they were exploiting the disaster which had overtaken the people of their estates to gain advantage for themselves at public expense. There can be little doubt, however, that for several proprietors the famine was an experience of great economic difficulty. For a few it was a disaster which finally destroyed their personal fortune and social position. Yet the vast majority of landed families came through the crisis, if not unscathed, then with their possessions intact and livelihood secure. This was in stark contrast to the ordeal suffered by the mass of the inhabitants of the Western Highlands and Islands in the 1840s and 1850s.

NOTES

1. See above, pp.50-3.
2. See below, pp.161-6; 303-5.
3. SRO, Lord Macdonald Papers, GD221/62, General view of the affairs of Rt. Hon Lord Macdonald, 3 February 1846.
4. *Relief Correspondence*, July 1846-February 1847, Marquis of Lorne to Sir George Gray, 25 July 1846. See also similar pleas in this collection from Sir James Riddell, 24 August 1846 and Dr. John Mackenzie, 27 August 1846.
5. *Relief Correspondence*, July 1846-February 1847, Lord Advocate to Sir G. Gray, 2 September 1846.
6. *Ibid.*, Mr. Trevelyan to Sir E. Coffin, 11 September 1846. This basic policy was reiterated until government disengaged from direct involvement in August 1847. See *ibid.*, Sir G. Gray to Sir John McNeill, 11 September 1846; Trevelyan to Earl of Auckland, 19 November 1846; Sir John McNeill to Sir E. Coffin, 22 December 1846; SRO, HD6/2, Treasury Correspondence, Sir E. Coffin to Trevelyan, 28 September 1847.

7. SRO, HD7/26, Miscellaneous correspondence from Highland landowners, 18467-7.

8. See Audrey Paterson, 'The New Poor Law in Nineteenth Century Scotland', in Derek Fraser, ed., *The New Poor Law in the Nineteenth Century* (London, 1976), 171-93 for a discussion of the nature of the legislation and its implementation.

9. Fullarton and Baird, *Remarks on the Evils at Present Affecting the Highlands and Islands*, 64.

10. Levitt and Smout, *State of the Scottish Working Class*, 183.

11. *Witness*, 17 October 1846.

12. SRO, Lord Advocate's Papers, AD58/86, Lord Advocate to Mr. Tytler, 5 January 1847.

13 *Ibid.*

14. See, for example, *Relief Correspondence*, Sir E. Coffin to Mr. Trevelyan, 1 January 1847.

15. For newspapers and estate papers consulted see Bibliography. The Court of Session data were examined in SRO, CS277, Sederunt Books in Sequestration and SRO, CS279, Petitions in Sequestration, 1839-56.

16. For example, Arisaig was sold by Lord Cranstoun and purchased by Mr. Mackay of Bighouse in early 1848. (*The Scotsman*, 29 January 1948). The estate of Lynedale in Skye was purchased by Alexander McDonald of Thornbank, Falkirk, at a price of £9,000 in July 1849. This represented an advance of 10 per cent on its 1837 price (*Scotsman*, 11 August 1849).

17. Joseph Mitchell, *Reminiscences of My Life in the Highlands* (1883, reprint. Newton Abbot, 1971), 299-300.

18. SRO, CS277, Sederunt Books in Sequestration, W.F. Campbell of Islay; SRO, Campbell of Jura Papers, GD64/1/347/1, Report to the Creditors of W.F. Campbell, Esq., of Islay; Margaret C. Storrie, *Islay: Biography of an Island* (Port Ellen, 1981), 135-6.

19. SRO, Campbell of Jura Papers, GD64/1/347/1, Report to the Creditors of W.F. Campbell, Esq. of Islay.

20. Dunvegan Castle, Skye, Macleod of Macleod Muniments, 659/23/4, Macleod's Address to his People, 26 December 1846.

21. SRO, HD20/31, Report of Committee on the Case of Macleod of Macleod, 5 March 1847.

22. SRO, HD6/2, Treasury Correspondence, Major Halliday to Mr. Trevelyan, 6 February 1847.

23. NLS, Sutherland Estate Papers, Dep. 313/1174, James Loch to Duke of Sutherland, 8 March 1847.

24. *N.C.*, Appendix A, 28. See also I.F. Grant, *The Macleods: the History of a Clan, 1200-1956* (London, 1959), 584-5.

25. SRO, GD221/62, General View of the Affairs of Lord Macdonald, 3 February 1846; GD221/160/4, State of Debts due by Lord Macdonald, November 1849.

26. Cameron, 'Scottish Emigration', 367.

27. *North British Advertiser*, 15 July 1854; SRO, Riddell Papers, AF49/6, Report of T.G. Dickson for Trustees, 1852.

28. SRO, Riddell Papers, AF49/6, Report of T.G. Dickson for Trustees, 1852.

29. Cameron, 'Scottish Emigration', 388-9; Anon., *The State of the Highlands in 1854* (Inverness, 1855), 21-44.

30. SRO, HD6/1, Map of the Distressed Districts of Scotland by D.W. Martin, including lists of proprietors.

31. SRO, Lord Macdonald Papers, GD221/62, General View of the Affairs of Lord Macdonald, 3 February 1846.

32. Dunvegan Castle, Skye, Macleod of Macleod Muniments, Box 51, C.E. Gibbons to Macleod of Macleod, 27 December 1833.

33. Mitchell, *Reminiscences*, 299-300.

34. *Relief Correspondence*, Sir John McNeill to Mr. Trevelyan, 21 November 1846; 30 November 1846; SRO, HD6/2, Treasury Correspondence relating to Highland Destitution,

Deputy-Commissioner Dobrée to Sir Edward Coffin, 21 April 1847; Correspondence from Highland landowners.

35. See, for example, numerous references to land sales in the *Inverness Courier*, reported in J. Barron, *The Northern Highlands in the Nineteenth Century* (Inverness, 1907), 320-30.

36. Hunter, *Crofting Community*, 61-2.

37. *Relief Correspondence*, Capt. Pole to Mr. Trevelyan, 28 December 1846.

38. Hunter, *Crofting Community*, 61-2.

39. Reprinted in *Relief Correspondence, passim*, and SRO, HD6/2, Treasury Correspondence relating to Highland Destitution, February-September 1847.

40. *Destitution Papers* (1849), Report on the islands of Mull . . .etc., (1849); Free Church Destitution Committee, *Statements*; Anon., *Letters to the Rev. Dr. Macleod regarding the Famine in the Highlands and Islands* (Glasgow, 1847); SRO, Lord Advocate's Papers, AD58/81, Reports on conditions on various estates in the Highlands and Islands, 1846-7.

41. NLS, Sutherland Estate Papers, Dep. 313; Inveraray Castle, Inveraray, Argyll Estate Papers; SRO, Lord Macdonald Papers, GD221; Dunvegan Castle, Skye, Macleod of Macleod Muniments; Conon House, Conon Bridge, Mackenzie of Gairloch MSS.; Islay Estate Office, Islay Estate Papers; SRO, Riddell Papers, AF49/6; MS. Diary of J.M. Mackenzie, Chamberlain of the Lews, 1851.

42. *Relief Correspondence*, Lord Advocate to Sir G. Grey, 2 September 1846.

43. *Ibid.*, Sir Edward Coffin to Mr. Trevelyan, 5 October 1846.

44. *Ibid.*, 14 November 1846.

45. *Ibid.*, Capt. Pole to Mr. Trevelyan, 28 December 1846.

46. NLS, Sutherland Estate Papers, Dep. 313/1174, James Loch to the Duke of Sutherland, 6 January 1847.

47. *Ibid.*, James Loch to W. Mackenzie, 20 February 1847.

48. *Ibid.*, James Loch to Duke of Sutherland, 6 and 20 January 1847.

49. SRO, HD19/5, Minutes and Correspondence of Local Committees of Creich, Notes of Statement by R. Rutherford, meal-dealer, Helmsdale.

50. SRO, HD6/2, Treasury Correspondence relating to Highland Destitution, Sir E. Coffin to Mr. Trevelyan, 16 July 1847.

51. *Ibid.*

52. NLS, Sutherland Estate Papers, Dep. 313/2021, Scourie account, 1838-48.

53. *N.C.*, Appendix A, Memorandum as to Expenditure incurred by the late Sir James Matheson, 124; *John O'Groats Journal*, 7 May 1847; *North British Daily Mail*, 11 May 1847. See also below, Ch. 9 for a fuller consideration of Matheson's relief programme.

54. *Relief Correspondence*, Mr. Trevelyan to Sir E. Coffin, 28 December 1846.

55. *Ibid.*, Capt. Pole to Sir E. Coffin, 13 October 1846. See also SRO, HD20/31, Report of Committee on Macleod's Case, 5 March 1847, for an examination of Macleod's relief schemes.

56. SRO, HD6/2, Treasury Correspondence relating to Highland Destitution, Deputy-Commissary Dobrée to Sir E. Coffin, 21 April 1847.

57. *Ibid.*, Mr Fraser to Mr. Skene, 26 January 1847. See also *Destitution Papers*, Tenth Rept. of Glasgow Section of the Central Board, 13-14 for a summary of Riddell's activities.

58. SRO, HD6/2, Treasury Correspondence relating to Highland Destitution, Sir E. Coffin to Mr. Trevelyan, 16 August 1847; *Letters to Rev. Dr. Macleod*, 61.

59. *Scotsman*, 27 December 1848.

60. *Destitution Papers*, Tenth Rept. of Glasgow Section (1848), 11.

61. *Relief Correspondence*, Capt. Pole to Sir E. Coffin, 21 December 1846.

62. SRO, HD6/2, Treasury Correspondence relating to Highland Destitution, Capt. Halliday to Sir E. Coffin, 31 January 1847; SRO, Lord Advocate's Papers, AD58/54, Conditions on the Island of Harris.

63. *Destitution Papers*, Seventh Report of Glasgow Section of the Central Board (1847), David Boyter to C.R. Baird, 11 September 1847, 9-10.

64. *Inverness Courier*, 27 January 1847.

65. SRO, HD19/9, Minutes and Correspondence of the Local Committee of Fort Augustus, 10 March 1847.

66. *Inverness Advertiser*, 5 March 1850; *Destitution Papers*, Tenth Rept. of Glasgow Section (1848), 11.

67. *McNeill Report*, Appendix A, 12-13.

68. The 'negligent' were Col. Gordon of Cluny, Mr. Bankes of Lochbroom, McDonald of Glengarry, Mr. Baillie of Glenelg, McDonald of Lochsheil, Mrs. Stewart Mackenzie, Lord Cranstoun, Lord Abinger, McIntosh of McIntosh (Keppoch), F.W. Caldwell, J. Stewart of Penabbanach, Clark of Ulva.

69. SRO, HD6/2, Treasury Correspondence relating to Highland Destitution, Sir E. Coffin to Mr. Trevelyan, 28 June 1847.

70. *Ibid.*, Major Halliday to Mr. Trevelyan, 6 February 1847; Commander Maclean to Sir E. Coffin, 2 April 1847; *Relief Correspondence*, Major Halliday to Sir E. Coffin, 3 February 1847. Some landowners, however, reserved assistance only for rent-paying tenants, arguing that they had no obligation to cottars who simply squatted on their estates.

71. *Witness*, 24 March 1847.

72. SRO, Breadalbane Papers, GD12/14/19, Alex. Campbell to Breadalbane, 23 April 1847.

73. SRO, HD7/46, Trevelyan-Skene Correspondence, 1847-9, 2 March 1848. For similar comments at an earlier stage see SRO, Lord Advocate's Papers, AD58/81, C. Trevelyan to Sir E. Coffin, 28 December 1846.

74. Dunvegan Castle, Skye, Macleod of Macleod Muniments, 659/23/4, Macleod's Address to his People, 26 December 1846.

75. SRO, Breadalbane Papers, GD112/41/18, Alexander Campbell to Mudie, 30 March 1847.

76. NLS, Sutherland Estate Papers, Dep. 313/1174, James Loch to Duke of Sutherland, 6 January 1847.

77. *Ibid.*, 23 January 1847.

78. *Ibid.*, 8 March 1847.

79. *Relief Correspondence*, Mr. Trevelyan to Sir J. McNeill, 29 January 1847.

80. Its development can be followed in *ibid.*, Mr. Trevelyan to Sir E. Coffin, 28 December 1846; Sir J. McNeill to Mr. Bankes, 12 November 1846.

81. *Ibid.*, Mr. Trevelyan to Sir J. McNeill, 29 January 1847.

82. *Ibid.*, Sir J. McNeill to Mr. Bankes, 12 November 1846.

83. *Relief Correspondence*, Mr. Trevelyan to Sir E. Coffin, 28 December 1846.

84. L. Timperley, 'The Pattern of Landholding in Eighteenth Century Scotland', in M.L. Parry and T.R. Slater, eds., *The Making of the Scottish Countryside* (London, 1980), 137-54.

85. *McNeill Report*, XV.

86. P. Gaskell, *Morvern Transformed* (Cambridge, 1968), 23.

87. This estimate is derived from an examination of the sources cited in notes 39-40 above, and the *Inverness Courier*, 1810-46.

88. SRO, HD7/74, Skene-Trevelyan Correspondence, 21 February 1848.

89. This topic is examined in detail in Chapter 8.

90. Inveraray Castle, Argyll Estate Papers, Bundle 1522, Abstract of Accounts, Tiree, 1843-50.

91. SRO, Cromartie Estate Papers, GD305/2/84, rental series.

92. SRO, Riddell Papers, AF49/6, Report of T.G. Dickson for Trustees, 1852.

93. MS. Diary of John Munro Mackenzie, Chamberlain of the Lews, 1851 (in private hands); *McNeill Report*, Appendix A, 7; Inveraray Castle, Argyll Estate Papers, Bundle 1522, Abstract of Accounts, Mull property, 1843-50. In the latter case the dependence on small tenant rental was not as great as in Tiree. 25 per cent of rental income was paid by tenants occupying land of £10 annual rental or less and 27 per cent by those with an annual rental of £27 or above.

94. *Destitution Papers*, First Report of Central Relief Board (1847), 2.

95. *Destitution Papers*, Report on the Islands Mull, Ulva etc. (Glasgow, 1849), 8, 10; *PP*, VI (1841), *S.C. on Emigration* (1841), 215.

96. SRO, Lord McDonald Papers, GD221/43, Report by D. Shaw, Factor for N. Uist, 1839; GD221/70, Rental N. Uist, 1853-4; *McNeill Report*, Appendix A, 31, 68. The six estates were those of Lord Macdonald, Skeabost, Lyndale, Raasay, Strathaird, Clachamish.

97. *PP*, VI (1841) *S.C. on Emigration* (1841), 17, Q.207.

98. SRO, Lord Advocate's Papers, AD58/84/3, Copy Letter, W.H. Sitwell to Countess of Dunmore, 1 October 1846.

99. *McNeill Report*, Appendix A, Evidence of Thomas Fraser, 45.

100. *Ibid.*, 8.

101. This analysis of the finances of the Gairloch estate is based on the Mackenzie of Gairloch MSS., Conon House, Conon Bridge and especially on the Account of Charge and Discharge of the Intromission of Dr. J. Mackenzie as Factor for Mackenzie estates; Rental of Entailed Estates of Gairloch etc. 1846-8; Report by Thomas Scott on accounts of Dr. Mackenzie as factor, 1843-6.

102. The generalisations which follow are based on a systematic examination of Sutherland estate rents, 1827-1854, in Sutherland Estate Papers, NLS, Dep. 313/2159-260; 2198-9; 2256-62; 2207-15; 2216-22. A mass of documents has been scrutinised to compile the long-run series. Because of the different times of collecting rents over the years concerned and the different procedures involved – on some occasions rents being collected in advance, on others in arrears – it is difficult to maintain consistency. Nevertheless, a reasonably accurate representation of the pattern in the first half of the century can be obtained.

103. NLS, Sutherland Estate Papers, Dep. 313/867, Capt. Eliot to Duke of Sutherland, 19 June 1847.

104. *Ibid.*, Dep. 313/2021, Scourie Account, Charge and Discharge 1838-48; Dep. 313/2039, Scourie Potatoes and Meal Book.

105. *Relief Correspondence*, Mr Ellice to Chancellor of the Exchequer, 31 August 1846.

106. J.B. Denton, 'Land Drainage etc. by Loans', *Journal of the Royal Agric. Soc. of England*, 4 (ii), 1868.

107. *Glasgow Herald*, 19 October 1846.

108. *Relief Correspondence*, Capt. Pole to Sir Edward Coffin, 13 October 1846.

109. *Ibid.*, Rev. Alex. Macgregor to Sir G. Gray, 27 October 1846.

110. *Glasgow Herald*, 21 December 1846.

111. See, for example, SRO, HD7/14, Report on the property of Sir James Riddell; SRO, HD7/26, Correspondence from Highland landowners, 1846-7, especially W. Campbell of Islay to Sir E. Coffin, 28 October 1846.

112. *Relief Correspondence*, Chancellor of the Exchequer to Lord Advocate, 13 October 1846.

113. *Ibid.*, 17 October 1846.

114. *Ibid.*, Sir E. Coffin to Mr. Trevelyan, 22 October 1846.

115. Data are taken from *PP*, XXXIV (1847), Return of Number of Applications under the Drainage Act. For a detailed list of applicants see Appendix 6. From a review of individual cases there appears to have normally been a close relationship between the sum applied for and the value of the grant received.

116. *Relief Correspondence*, Mr McKinnon to Capt. Pole, December 1846.

117. SRO, HD6/2, Treasury Correspondence relating to Highland Destitution, Sir E. Coffin to Mr. Trevelyan, 28 September 1847.

118. *Witness*, 28 July 1849; *Inverness Courier*, 6 February 1851; *N.C.*, Q.5564, 302; Conon House, Conon, Mackenzie of Gairloch MSS., Black Deed Box, Bundle 53, Report by Mr. Inglis on Management, 1854-7; SRO, Lord Macdonald Papers, 221/46, Charge/Discharge, 1850-51.

119. *McNeill Report*, Appendix A, Evidence of Angus Macdonald, 8 March 1851, 60.

120. *Ibid.*, Evidence of Charles Macleod, 20 March 1851, 81.

121. *Destitution Papers*, First Rept. by Central Board of Management (1847), 3-4.

122. *Relief Correspondence*, Sir Edward Coffin to Mr. Trevelyan, 2 February 1847.

123. SRO, HD6/2, Treasury Correspondence relating to Highland Destitution, Sir E. Coffin to Mr. Trevelyan, 28 September 1847.

124. *Scotsman*, 8 January 1848; *Destitution Papers*, Tenth Rept. of Glasgow Section (1848), Appendix IV, 8-9.

125. See, for example, *Inverness Advertiser*,. 23 April 1850; SRO, HD7/46, Trevelyan to W.F. Skene, 13 May 1848; *Destitution Papers*, Seventh Rept. by Glasgow Section (1847), Appendix II; Report on the Outer Hebrides ((1849), 21, 23; Report on Mull, Iona, Ulva etc. (1849), 12-13 for details on 'active' landowners after 1847.

126. The following proprietors were purchasing seed grain in the spring of 1847, viz: Mackenzie of Gairloch; Marquis of Lorne, Tiree and Mull; Cameron of Lochiel; Gordon of Cluny, South Uist and Barra; Lady Dunmore, Harris; eleven other unnamed landowners. See SRO, HD6/2, Treasury Correspondence relating to Highland Destitution, Sir E. Coffin to Mr. Trevelyan, 19 March 1847; Trevelyan to Coffin, 7 April 1847; Dr. Boyter reported after visiting Tiree, Ulva, Eigg and Skye that all proprietors there were to secure seed. *Ibid.*, Boyter to Coffin, 12 April 1847.

127. Inveraray Castle, Argyll Estate Papers, Bundle 1522, J. Campbell to Duke of Argyll, 14 July 1847, 3 September 1848; *McNeill Report*, Appendix A, 130-1.

128. See below, pp.134-5; 139-140.

129. See, for example, evidence from the following areas, viz: South Uist and Barra, *Destitution Papers*, Sixth Rept. by Glasgow Section, Appendix II, 17-18; Skye, *Destitution Papers*, First Rept. by Central Board, Appendix I, *passim*; Mull, Inveraray Castle, Argyll Estate Papers, J. Campbell to Duke of Argyll, 10 June 1847.

130. *McNeill Report*, 111.

131. SRO, Lord Advocate's Papers, AD14/47/628, Precognition as to the death of Widow Anne Gillies, 18 March 1847.

132. *Ibid.*, Charles Shaw to J.C. Brodie, 23 March 1847.

133. *PP*, 1847-8, XXIII, *Second Annual Report of the Board of Supervision for the Relief of the Poor in Scotland*, 60-71.

134. Anon., *The State of the Highlands in 1854* (Inverness, 1855), E. Ellice to Viscount Palmerston, 4 December 1854.

135. SRO, Sheriff Court Records, SC32/5/1, Portree, *passim*.

136. *McNeill Report*, VII.

137. *Ibid.*

138. *Destitution Papers*, Second Report of Committee of Management to the Edinburgh Section, 21 June 1849.

139. *PP*, XXVI (1850), *Annual Report of the Board of Supervision*.

140. *Destitution Papers*, Tenth Report of Glasgow Section (1848), Appendix III.

141. SRO, HD7/47, Skene-Trevelyan Correspondence, 21 February 1848.

142. *Destitution Papers*, Fifth Report by Committee of Management to the Edinburgh Section, 33-4.

143. See below, pp.134-5, 139-140.

144. *Scotsman*, 8 January 1848.

145. See below, pp.134-5.

146. *McNeill Report*, Appendix A, 82.

147. Mulloch, *Western Highlands and Islands*, 91.

5

The Provision of Relief

1

The impact of the potato blight in Western Ireland and in Highland Scotland was similar in that the crises in both societies stimulated a huge increase in emigration.[1] But the differences were more significant. In Ireland, between 1,000,000 and 1,200,000 died during the Great Famine.[2] In the Scottish Highlands, mortality rates did start to climb but eventually the crisis was successfully contained. The basic reason for the contrasting fates of the Irish and the Highlander was the difference in the scale of the two disasters. Several millions were affected by crop failure in Ireland while in the Western Highlands and Islands the numbers seriously at risk were never more than 150,000 and often much less. Because of this the Highland crisis was more manageable. It could be controlled by the famine relief measures which were put into effect from the later months of 1846. The massive difference in the scale of the two disasters is most obviously demonstrated in the response of government. Despite their strong adherence to the principles of classical political economy, which advocated minimum state interference whenever possible, successive British governments failed to extricate themselves from the Irish problem until the early 1850s. They had to continue to provide relief, organise public-work schemes and supervise the administration of medical aid throughout the famine years. In Scotland, however, as will be seen in more detail below, the state was compelled only to intervene to a marginal extent in 1846 and 1847. It quickly terminated its limited operations in August 1847, leaving the administration of relief to the Central Board.[3] There was much philanthropic effort in Ireland also, principally as a result of the energetic activities of the Quakers and the British Association for Relief of Distress. However, the catastrophe in Ireland was simply too huge to be left to charitable action even by mid-Victorian governments thoroughly imbued with *laissez-faire* principles. In Scotland, on the other hand, the crisis was much more confined and the state was therefore able and willing to allow the detailed organisation of assistance to become the responsibility of the benevolent societies of the Lowlands, although government officials still felt the need to influence the direction of their policies.[4]

The adverse effects of the potato famine in the Highlands were also more easily controlled for other reasons. Not all Irish landowners were indifferent to the fate of their tenants but in general it would appear that Highland proprietors were much more active as a class in famine relief measures. They also seem to have exploited the advantages of the grants available under the Drainage Act for relief purposes more rapidly. An analysis of applications lodged for assistance under the Act at January 1847 reveals that seventy-six per cent (£803,804) were from Scotland, twenty per cent from England (£211,843) and a mere four per cent (£39,171) from Ireland.[5] Again, the stricken region in Scotland lay in a maritime environment. This not only provided

111

alternative sources of food from the sea and the shore but also did much to facilitate relief operations. In the Western Highlands and Islands it was the land which divided and the sea which united. By the 1840s the widespread introduction of steam navigation made speedy access possible to most parts of the area in virtually all weather conditions.

It may also be that dependence on the potato was less in the Highlands than in most parts of Western Ireland. The cottar class in Scotland was similar in one way to the poor cottiers of Ireland. Both groups eked out a living on patches of land suitable only for potato cultivation. But the Highland cottars were much fewer in number; in several districts they were more likely to be fishermen than small farmers, and they usually did not pay an annual money rental for the smallholdings which they occupied. The majority were either squatters, kinfolk of the small tenants, or families who held land in return for labour services on bigger farms but who were settled permanently in the neighbourhood. They were therefore not quite as insecure as many Irish cottiers. It was from their destitute ranks that the hordes of Irish vagrant poor were drawn and among whom were numbered most of the dead during the Great Famine.

There was another final and crucial difference between the conditions of the Irish and the Highland Scots. The Scottish famine took place in a society which by the 1840s had experienced a massive change in economic structure. Industrialisation and urbanisation had produced a new order in which agriculture, though still significant, was no longer the most dynamic and influential sector in the economy. It was a society which was not only much wealthier than Ireland's but also offered a greater range of employment opportunities in general and casual labouring in lowland centres not far distant from the distressed districts of the north-west. Through temporary migration for work on the railways, fisheries, domestic service and the great construction programmes of the Scottish cities, the poorest classes in the Highlands could escape the threat of starvation in the north and, at the same time, contribute modest sums to the income of their families. Seasonal employment was low-paid, insecure and in some years, such as 1848 to 1850, difficult to obtain, but it could still mean the difference between getting by and falling into complete destitution. The western counties of Ireland also sent out many seasonal migrants for work in other areas of the country and in Britain but their range of outlets was neither so varied nor so accessible as those of the Highland Scots.

The differences between the Highland famine and earlier Scottish subsistence crises also help to place the relief operations of the 1840s and 1850s in perspective. When measured by the rate of emigration, the potato famine had probably a more significant demographic impact than that of the harvest failure of 1782-3 and at least as profound an effect as the notorious 'Lean Years' at the end of the seventeenth century. Yet, as with the Irish comparison, mortality rates were certainly lower in the 1840s than in the 1690s and, literary evidence would suggest, probably also not as great as in the distressed years in the Highlands of 1782-3.[6] The reasons why the potato famine did not push up death rates in the manner characteristic of previous Scottish subsistence crises are primarily to be found in some of the main features of the economic and social development of Scotland over the period concerned.

The potato failure temporarily destroyed one subsistence crop throughout Scotland in 1846. But the corn crop was not affected and after 1846 the blight was mainly limited to the maritime districts of the Highlands, Hebrides and Northern Isles. Unlike previous great failures, therefore, the potato famine was eventually confined to one peripheral region of the country and did not place a strain on the national food supply for any extended period. Since the early eighteenth century, too, the productivity of Scottish agriculture had been transformed both by new cropping systems and the improved organisation of farming technique and labour supply. The wider marketing of grain and the process by which areas of shortage were fed by regions of surplus was already far advanced in the decades following the Union of 1707. The Repeal of the Corn Laws in 1846 in the long term further facilitated the international exchange of foods. Scotland was also a much richer society with the purchasing power to acquire from overseas essential commodities in periods of shortage.

Because of all these factors the failure of the potatoes in the 1840s did not significantly push up grain prices except briefly in late 1846 and early 1847. On the contrary, United Kingdom average prices for barley and oats actually fell in the five-year period, 1848-52, relative to the previous quinquennium. Between 1843 and 1847, barley per imperial quarter averaged 34.4s. In the following five years it declined to 27.2s. Similarly oats stood at 22.8s in the first quinquennium but at 18.4s between 1848 and 1852.[7] In 1846 and early 1847 there was also heavy importation of Indian corn into Scotland from the United States.[8] This sold at an average price about one fifth lower than oats but, significantly, the relief organisations in the Highlands only bought it in the first two years of the emergency and relied thereafter on domestic grain.[9] Even in 1847, several Highland landlords and meal merchants imported oatmeal from the north-east counties rather than from further afield because the harvest that year had been a bumper one.[10] The Scottish and British system of food production and distribution had apparently become so efficient by the 1840s that it would easily cope with a regional crisis of subsistence without pushing prices up beyond the resources of the relief agencies.

This was but one aspect of the greater strength of the Scottish economy by the middle decades of the nineteenth century. Three results of this fundamental development are worthy of note. First, as has already been stressed, the Lowland industrial and agrarian economy had now more capacity to provide job opportunities for Highland seasonal migrants. Second, the transformation of the landed structure in the Highlands and the large-scale penetration of new proprietors described in Chapter 4 can be regarded as one result of rapid capital accumulation among the urban élites of Lowland Scotland and England. It was the prosperous merchants, financiers, professional men and industrialists who had grown wealthy on the proceeds of revolutionary economic growth who were buying up Highland estates. All were in a better financial position to offer famine relief to the people of their properties than the old families with their burden of multiple trusts and historic indebtedness. Of course, there was no necessary correlation between the possession of resources and the implementation of measures of relief. Some of the proprietors criticised by government officials for inertia were very wealthy, absentee *arrivistes*. But many others did make a real effort. Their relief programmes can be regarded as net subsidies from the urban economy of the Lowlands to the distressed districts of the Highlands. Even the much-maligned Col.

John Gordon of Cluny claimed in 1848 that during the previous nine years he had derived £37,403 from his Hebridean estates in rental but had paid out £26,983 '. . . for endeavouring to improve the condition of the people'.[11] Third, the new wealth generated by the Victorian economy was the essential precondition for the growth of a great philanthropic agency of relief. The extraordinary profusion of public and private charities in nineteenth-century Scotland which provided the context for the development of a relief organisation was in part a manifestation of the growing resources of the benevolent middle classes.[12]

By the 1840s there had also been a revolution in communications. The potato famine in the Highlands was successfully relieved partly because news of the disaster was spread rapidly outside the distressed areas and vital food supplies were transported into the region with commendable speed. It was probably primarily through the contemporary press that most of those who later contributed so handsomely to the relief funds were first informed of the crisis. Press coverage was intensive during the first two years of the famine. The *Times* sent a 'commissioner' to the Western Highlands in 1846 and again in 1851. His first dispatches appeared as early as September 1846 and alerted the nation to the real possibilities of an Irish-type disaster occurring on British soil. The *Guardian* also provided sustained coverage and the *Morning Chronicle* sent a special correspondent. All these journals were published in England and had a mainly southern readership. Their interest was a telling illustration of the attraction which the Scottish Highlands now had for a very wide middle- and upper-class readership both at home and abroad.

Press coverage on this scale and the effective provision of relief would not have been possible without the transport revolution which took place in the Western Highlands in the decades before the potato famine. It was modern technology in the form of steam propulsion for ships which helped to save the people of the region from the full horrors of a pre-industrial subsistence crisis.[13] As a contemporary observer put it in graphic terms, 'a bridge of boats now unites the southern mainland with the northern coast and very specially with the Western Isles'.[14] One traveller took five weeks going and returning from Edinburgh to Tiree in the 1770s using the most expeditious route. In 1846, however, the round trip from Glasgow to Mull by steamship took less than three days.[15] The steamer for Portree in Skye also called at Mull, Glenelg and Lochalsh.[16] Lewis had a regular service from 1845.[17] By that year there was also a link to Lochmaddy in North Uist.[18] When Mendelssohn set out on his romantic tour, including the trip to Staffa, in 1829, he found in Glasgow 'seventy steam-boats, forty of which start every day'.[19]

Perhaps even more crucial than the regular services was the role of the powerful steam vessels of the Royal Navy. These were used by government in early 1847 and were made available on request to the relief committees thereafter to convey vital supplies to the most destitute communities. Their particular advantage was their speed and the fact that they could carry out their function in virtually all climatic conditions. It was due mainly to them that the Outer Hebrides could be sure of relief supplies during the stormy winter months. Again, the regular tours of inspection carried out by Sir Edward Coffin and his officers in the localities experiencing the most acute distress, which both served to provide intelligence of those areas requiring emergency supplies and maintained pressure on inactive landowners, would not have been possible without the systematic employment of the naval steamers. The winter gales no longer isolated the islands as easily as they had done in the very recent past.[20]

Nineteenth-century society therefore possessed the technical expertise to overcome the natural obstacles which had plagued the efforts of those who in earlier times had tried to bring relief to the Hebrides in years of food scarcity and shortage. But it also had a much more fully developed tradition of philanthropic intervention and endeavour. This is not to say that the provision of charitable aid was unique to the Victorian period. Private charity had also been a vital social cement in earlier centuries. In the eighteenth century, for instance, it was common for both landlords and townspeople to subscribe funds for those in distress in time of harvest failure.[21] However, by the 1840s, the formation of official charities, seeking to respond to virtually every social need, had expanded as never before. In Glasgow, for instance, two charitable societies were founded between 1801 and 1810. In the following decade the number rose to eleven and, from 1821 to 1830, to fifteen.[22] Each industrial slump produced an array of philanthropic agencies to bring some assistance to the able-bodied unemployed who had no legal right to relief under the Scottish Poor Law. Relief committees were formed in the major towns in 1816-17, 1819-20, 1826-7 and again in 1829.[23] In 1836 and 1837 the Highlands benefited from Lowland philanthropy when, in association with government, relief organisations in Glasgow dispensed meal and clothing in the distressed districts.[24] This was almost a rehearsal for the much greater intervention which took place after 1846. Individuals such as Charles Baird and the Rev. Dr. Norman Macleod, who were heavily involved in 1836, also played a leading role in the formation of the Glasgow Section of the Central Board in the following decade.[25]

The reasons for the extraordinary expansion in all forms of official philanthropy are not the primary concern here.[26] Among other factors it came about because of the powerful influence of the Evangelical movement in the Church of Scotland, which stressed the Christian duty of charity to one's less fortunate neighbours, and the need to respond to the social problems crystallised and aggravated by urbanisation and industrialisation. Philanthropy also became a recognised part of the lifestyles of the urban middle classes. The charities offered opportunities for mixing socially with the great, making one's mark in polite society and providing suitable and acceptable work for the underemployed wives of the well-to-do. Philanthropy was at once a response to urban unrest and social dislocation, an assertion of Christian values which were seen to be under challenge by the forces of economic and social change and an accepted and integral part of the Victorian code of respectability. By the 1840s, to be philanthropic and respond with due generosity to worthy causes was expected of all who could afford it. The potato famine therefore occurred in a society which had the wealth, the social attitudes and the experience to launch and organise a great philanthropic endeavour.

But the response to the crisis in the Highlands was unusually generous even by contemporary standards. By the end of 1847 the Central Board had at its disposal a massive £209,376 available for famine relief, probably the greatest single cash sum ever raised voluntarily in nineteenth-century Scotland for the relief of distress.[27] In 1846, for instance, the total amount paid out by the official Poor Law, *throughout* Scotland, was only £80,000 more than the funds available to the Central Board in the Highlands. These were much greater than the amounts collected during periods of heavy unemployment and mass destitution in the towns. In Glasgow in 1816-17 nearly £10,000 was raised and distributed among 23,000 people; in 1826-7, £9,000 was contributed for relief.[28] Even the sums collected during the great depression of 1841-2 in Paisley, which forced almost a quarter of the town's population on to relief schemes, did not match the resources of the Central Board during the potato famine.[29] The General Relief Committee in Paisley finally disposed of £28,000 of charitable money.

Yet the official resources of the Highland relief fund were only part of the total volume and value of charitable resources which flowed into the north of Scotland in these years. Unrecorded, individual sums of cash were sent through private channels and distributed through the agency of ministers of the Free Church and the established church.[30] Even more important was the arrival of relief in kind from the United States.[31] In 1847, a series of vessels from Savannah, Charlestown, New York and other ports in North America brought cargoes of wheat, rice and maize to help feed the hungry of the Western Highlands: 'The munificence and generosity of the citizens of the United States towards the destitute population in Scotland has been unexampled'.[32] How is this unusual level of charitable response to be explained?

Three factors were probably important. First, the population of the Highlands probably indirectly gained from the great tragedy which engulfed the people of Ireland. The potato blight struck a year earlier there and very quickly produced serious social effects. By early 1847 the two disasters were linked in charitable appeals. The British Association, for instance, which eventually raised the enormous sum of £434,251 for relief, was established to bring succour to 'the remote districts' of both Ireland and Scotland.[33] Press reports also stressed that unless assistance was provided on a considerable scale the Highlanders would quickly suffer the same terrible fate as the Irish.[34] So horrendous was the Irish tragedy that it achieved publicity on a world-wide scale and this also helped to awaken international interest in the Highland crisis. On 13 January 1847, Queen Victoria issued a personal letter of appeal on behalf of 'our brethren in many parts of this United Kingdom who are suffering extreme famine'.[35] This raised over £170,000 which, together with £263,000 collected under its own auspices, was distributed through the British Association.[36] The total sum was divided in the proportion of five sixths to Ireland and one sixth to the Scottish Highlands. In the light of the great difference in the number seriously at risk and in danger of starvation in each society, it is patently clear that the population of the Highlands did rather well out of this division. The Edinburgh Section of the Central Board obtained £31,000 from the British Association, a sum which amounted to twenty-six per cent of all the funds at its disposal.[37]

Secondly, the infant Free Church of Scotland was in an excellent position to both collect funds and guide them in appropriate directions. In its own right it represented an embryonic relief organisation which through its local parishes, synods and ministers could be activated to provide assistance. Not surprisingly, therefore, as early as September 1848 it was the first agency in the field to gather funds.[38] The Free Church had two advantages. A large number of its followers lived in the region where distress was most acute. It therefore had a powerful motivation to action. In addition, however, the Church also had a loyal following among congregations in the cities who could be expected to respond to the plight of their co-religionists in the north-west. By the end of December 1846, the Free Church congregations in the Lowlands, after five Sunday collections, had already managed to raise over £10,400.[39]

Third, the changed perception of Highland society which took place over the century between the Jacobite defeat at Culloden and the potato famine also had a major impact on the collection of relief funds: 'Before 1745 the Highlanders had been despised as idle, predatory barbarians . . . but after 1746, when their distinct society crumbled so easily, they combined the romance of a primitive people with the charm of an endangered species'.[40] Between 1800 and 1846 a series of influences combined both to sentimentalise the Highlander and place the Highlands not simply in the consciousness of the middle and upper classes of Britain but also firmly on the world map. This extraordinary process took place precisely at the same time as the inhabitants of this fictitious romantic world were enduring the trauma of the Clearances and the collapse of the peasant economy after 1815. Scott's *Waverley Novels* and the fame of the Highland regiments captured the imagination of Europe. The most distinguished members of the Romantic Movement visited the southern Highlands and were both stunned and thrilled by their dramatic and picturesque scenery. The Highlanders were now represented in some quarters as 'a pure peasantry', noble rustics whose martial virtues had not been contaminated either by urban vices or mischievous radicalism.[41] It was in this period, too, that the 'traditional' *Highland* culture, so recently despised, came to be regarded as the final remnant of ancient *Scottish* culture.[42] By the 1830s, the sporting attractions of the Highlands were also coming to be highly regarded and their future role of providing outdoor recreation for the rich and titled was given even greater prominence when Queen Victoria decided to build her castle at Balmoral.[43]

It is difficult now to appreciate the enormous appeal which the 'romantic' Highlands had for the British upper and middle classes by the 1840s. In 1853, the *Illustrated London News* described how 'The desolate grandeur of the scenery of Skye annually attracts to it crowds of tourists. Every phase of our society is duly represented in the course of each season, at the Stor, Quiraig, Coruisk, and the Cuchuillin or Coollen Hills. They returned delighted as well as they may, with the wildest and most impressive scenery in the kingdom'.[44] Another observer pointed to the irresistible attraction of the Highlands for the rich and famous:

> Within the last forty years scarcely one of any note in the world of letters that has not left footprints on Benledie, Benlomand, Benevis, and Cairn Gorum, and wandered by the lakes and scenes rendered dear to heart and eye by the songs and stories of Ossian and Scott; while the most celebrated of these classic scenes have been transferred to canvas by the pencils of Williams, Landseer, MacCulloch and others – the first artists of the age.
>
> Instead of wandering on the banks of the Rhine, the Mediterranean, the Missilonghi, the Tiber, the Po and the Seine, which formerly formed the grand tour . . . a visit of some weeks' duration to the mountains and rivers of the Tay, the Dee, the Avon, the Spey, the Caledonian Canal and the Western Islands now constitutes the grand tour of fashionable life.[45]

Highland society had a popular image, a renown and an appeal which was familiar across both Europe and America by the middle decades of the nineteenth century. It is, therefore, hardly surprising that there was a very lively international response to the requests for help which came after 1846. One basic reason why the relief fund for the Highlands raised so much more than similar efforts during industrial crises in the cities was that more money was collected for the victims of the potato famine *outside* Scotland. This is suggested in Table 5.1 which records the sources of funds collected by the Edinburgh Section of the Central Board after 1846 and the sums raised by the General Relief Committee in Paisley in 1841-2. What is also striking, however, is the very great diversity of the sources of funds.[46] Scottish expatriates in Canada, India and the East Indies were very prominent and contributed a total of almost £25,000 to the Edinburgh Section alone. The Celtic Society Ball in Edinburgh yielded £180. Edinburgh advocates and Writers to the Signet were also well represented on the subscription lists.

Table 5.1. Source of Relief Funds, Edinburgh Section, 1846-1847 and General Relief Committee, Paisley, 1841-1842

	Edinburgh Section (%)	General Relief Committee (%)
Local (Edinburgh, Paisley)	9	5
Scotland	26	31
England	34	42.5
Overseas	29	5
Miscellaneous	2	17
Total	£119,043	£28,000

Source: *Destitution Papers*, Seventh Report of Edinburgh Section (1847), 13; Smout, 'Strange Intervention of Edward Twistleton', 228.
Note: The 'Overseas' percentage in Column 1 is a minimum figure as all funds collected by the British Association have been placed under 'England'.

Highland regiments raised a total of £347. Collections in local parish churches produced substantial sums. Equally revealing, however, are the small amounts raised from working people: servants, Cramond House, £2; workmen at Cockpen, £2.7s; inmates of Crichton Institution, £18; Dalkeith Colliery, £24; 'a few Scotchmen on the South-East Railway Company', £3. The Highland potato famine apparently captured the imagination of all social classes.

The organisers of the relief funds were able to exploit public sympathy with considerable skill. They made their appeal to both the hearts and minds of potential subscribers. Highly emotive descriptions of the suffering poor of the Highlands were published in both newspapers and contemporary pamphlets.[47] The unprecedented nature of the calamity and its scale was constantly emphasised. Invariably the numbers affected by the potato failure were claimed to be between 400,000 and 600,000. In the initial stages of the appeal at least both the Free Church and the Glasgow and Edinburgh Committees persistently exaggerated the extent of the crisis. Letters to the Rev. Dr Norman Macleod from Highland parish ministers were published. These pleaded for aid and contained graphic descriptions of the ravages of hunger and disease in local communities.[48] A strong religious theme also ran through the campaign. The disasters in both Ireland and the Highlands were depicted as the awful signs of God's wrath, 'the Chastisement of the Lord'. A National Day of Fasting was proclaimed by Queen Victoria and subscriptions to the relief funds were advertised as a necessary form of atonement to an angry Creator.[49]

Much was made of the comparisons and contrasts with the crisis in Ireland. On the one hand, the Irish example was used to demonstrate the horrific consequences of famine on a poor, peasant population.[50] It vividly showed what might happen in the Highlands unless relief came swiftly and effectively. On the other hand, the 'virtuous' Highlanders were contrasted with the unregenerate Irish as a race who were far more deserving of assistance.[51] The romantic associations of Highland society were fully exploited. The Scottish Highlanders, suggested one contemporary, '. . . instead of being rude and unprincipled depredators, were possessed of many accomplishments and virtues . . . and, in respect of poetry and music, and national literature, were equal, if not superior, as a community to any similar class of their fellow subjects'.[52] The people of the Highlands were not only brave and daring in war but also 'peaceful, patient and submissive' in the face of the great disaster which had overwhelmed them.[53] No mention was made of the increase in sheep stealing which was widely reported in the winter of 1846-7.[54] In contrast, the Irish were 'unruly and turbulent' and did not have the same claim on the generous feelings of the philanthropic.[55]

Such images, however, were unlikely in themselves to convince the hard-headed businessmen and professional classes of the cities of Britain who eventually not only contributed much to the relief funds but were among the dominant influences on the Central Board when it was formally constituted in February 1847. As late as December 1846, for instance, the Free Church approached the Lord Provost of Edinburgh to promote a joint church and civic effort to raise funds: 'Contrary to expectation they met with a somewhat cold reception. His Lordship seemed to think that the time for movement had not arrived; spoke of the necessity of complete statistics'. Again, from the earliest months of the crisis, the *Scotsman*, true to its Whig principles, systematically and scathingly criticised the 'Ossianic sentimentality' which obscured the reality of the problem 'like a mist'.

The Free Church soon recognised the need for convincing information to support its claims and circulated a 'schedule of enquiries' to its parishes in the Highlands with detailed questions on the extent of food supply, crop failure, numbers at risk, and availability of employment. The answers to these queries were then published in full.[56] In addition, both the Church and the Central Board, which eventually took over its responsibilities, appealed to the dominant social philosophy of the Victorian middle classes and their hatred of the demoralising effects of gratuitous relief. From the very beginning of the operations of the Central Board in early 1847 it was established as a cardinal principle that relief should be given only in return for labour: 'The Local Committee shall hold it as a general rule, that work of some kind should be given in exchange for relief; and shall impress upon the people that food given is not a gratuitous gift, but is to be paid for in one way or another'.[57] Despite this commitment, however, the Board's regulation was persistently breached in the first year of its operations and these failures help to explain why even more uncompromising policies were eventually implemented in 1848 and thereafter.

2

During the Scottish harvest failures of the 1690s and again in 1782 and 1783 the state had been heavily involved in relief measures. 'Mercantilist' governments in the seventeenth century sought to regulate the economy in a variety of ways and intervention in times of dearth was an inevitable extension of general state functions in this period. It was also at a more practical level designed to minimise the dangers of political and social unrest which the threat of starvation or a rapid rise in the cost of meal might bring about. Thus between 1695 and 1699 the state introduced a series of measures designed to combat or alleviate the problems of food shortage. The duty-free import of victual was allowed and bounties were paid to encourage the meal trade. Government also moved against forestallers and regraters, introducing searches for hoards of corn held in private warehouses and directing burghal authorities to control prices.[58] Again, almost a century later, in 1782-3, the government intervened by making funds available in the form of a grant of £10,000 for grain to be distributed by sheriffs and another sum to allow food to be sold 'at prime cost'. The relief supplies in most areas consisted of white peas, surplus naval stores which could be boiled into a heavy porridge. The year 1783 was accordingly long remembered in the Highlands as *bliadhna na peasrach*, the peasemeal year.[59]

By the middle decades of the nineteenth century, however, the intellectual basis of such intervention had been destroyed and a new view of the role of the state had emerged. No government, of course, could entirely remove itself from the normal processes of civil and economic life. But in the 1840s and 1850s the state 'strove purposefully for the minimum: it abjured any right to direct the national economy. The sole concern . . . was to make every element in the economy free to carve out its own path to prosperity.'[60] The intellectual critique of the classical economists and the extraordinary growth in national wealth produced by industrialisation combined to bring about a new consensus: that an economy thrives best when left to the free play of market forces, and any unnecessary interference with them is bound eventually to cause much more harm than good. This, then, was the conventional wisdom which governed the responses of the state to the potato famines in both Ireland and the Western Highlands.[61]

But government attitudes and the policies which were eventually implemented were far from simple. There was too much at stake and too serious a threat to the lives of thousands in the Highlands and millions in Ireland for the orthodoxies of political economy to be followed entirely to the letter. In Ireland, the state was quickly drawn into the administration of a huge famine relief operation. In the Highlands, too, government officials adhered to one fundamental line of policy throughout the crisis. This was expressed by Charles Trevelyan as early as September 1846: 'The people cannot, *under any circumstances*, be allowed to starve'.[62] Equally, however, there was also a strong desire to limit involvement to the very minimum consistent with the saving of life and to evolve techniques of intervention which would do least damage to the functioning of the 'natural' economic system. There was also an eagerness to disengage government agencies from famine relief at the earliest opportunity.

This overall strategy was resolutely maintained despite the great stream of petitions which poured in from landlords, official bodies and the churches for increased government assistance in 1846 and 1847 to aid the distressed districts.[63] Clearly, much influential opinion in Scotland was less concerned to preserve the purity of the axioms of political economy during a crisis of this magnitude than government ministers and their officials. But it is clear from the correspondence of the latter that the heavy claims made on the state during the first year of the Irish famine in 1845 and early 1846 had if anything hardened attitudes and made government even more reluctant to respond to requests for aid from the Highlands. There was a strong feeling that once intervention took place, at however modest a level, the sheer enormity of the problem would force further interference until the state was hopelessly embroiled in a disaster which it did not have the resources or expertise to handle and from which it might not be able to extricate itself without causing irreparable damage to the 'normal' social and economic fabric of northern Scotland.[64] At the same time, however, there was the awareness of the responsibility to preserve life. Total detachment was never regarded as a serious option.[65]

In September 1846, the very experienced relief officer, Commissary-General Sir Edward Pine Coffin (1784–1862), was sent to the Highlands to report on the extent of the potato failure and its social consequences. Coffin had seen active service during the Napoleonic Wars and had taken part in famine relief operations in China and Mexico. More recently he had been responsible for the administration of relief at Limerick in the west of Ireland and had been knighted for his services there.[66] In the same month as Coffin was ordered north, secret plans were also set in motion to augment the food supply of the Highlands. Government had to be prepared to fulfil its fundamental responsibility of saving life but with as little damage to the market economy as possible. Thus secrecy was vital, '. . . from fear of creating a false dependence on what we were prepared to do, and interfering with private efforts'. It was also necessary to avoid undue interference with the normal retail trade.[67] A series of requests for immediate state support for a variety of famine relief measures were denied on the grounds that they would either involve the government in huge expense or distort the efficient operation of the 'natural' economic system.[68]

Public works, such as the construction of a railway from Oban to Glasgow and the enlarging of the Crinan Canal, were suggested. Another petition included the proposal that loans at low rates of interest should be made available to railway companies. Government assistance for a massive scheme of emigration was also sought. The Free Church tried to obtain Royal Navy vessels to help transport men from the Hebrides to the south as part of its scheme for encouraging temporary migration and placing Highlanders in the employment of lowland railway construction companies. Finally, several proposals came from a number of quarters in Scotland that government should undertake an inquiry into the social and economic conditions of the Highlands in order to probe the reasons for the disaster which had overwhelmed its society. After due consideration, all these suggestions were rejected. For instance, much as they welcomed the Free Church scheme, government ministers and officials were loath to become involved. They feared that the state might be expected to maintain responsibility for the labourers when they arrived in the Lowlands and were alarmed above all that such an action would be deemed a gross interference in the workings of the southern labour market.[69]

By the end of 1846 the main lines of the policy to be pursued by government during the potato famine had become clear. As indicated in Chapter 4, a prime element was 'the assertion, and practical enforcement, as far as possible, of the landowner's obligation to provide for the necessary subsistence of the people residing on his property as tenants'.[70] Secondly, those who received assistance were either obliged to pay for it or carry out work of some kind in return. Finally, the role of government would be residual: 'collateral assistance . . . in the fulfilment of these respective obligations', as it was officially described.[71] Every effort was made to avoid any innovative measure which could be regarded as a precedent which might lead to an unacceptable extension of the field of government action.

Loans were indeed made available, but under *existing* legislation: the Drainage and Public Works Act and the measures which were already on the statute book to encourage fishing. Inspectors of the Poor were given 'great discretion' on the advice of the Board of Supervision, 'with respect to casual relief in meal to destitute families'.[72] Two government vessels were to be stationed as meal depôts at Portree in Skye and Tobermory in Mull. The grain made available from these shops, however, was only to be retailed for cash at 'market prices'. The decision to send storeships into the famine area created a dilemma for officials. The basic reason for establishing such an emergency grain supply was to avoid the danger of spiralling scarcity prices. But subsidised meal also manifestly offended against the canons of political economy. Government therefore tried to steer a middle course between necessary assistance on the one hand and on the other the grave danger of destroying the 'private trade' by forcing meal merchants out of business as demand concentrated on cheaper grain from the depôt ships. The compromise was to charge purchasers at the rates prevailing in the nearest large markets of Glasgow and Liverpool which, so the argument ran, would not be as vulnerable to massive price increases as the stricken districts of the north-west.[73] Finally, Royal Navy steamers would be made available to assist in the distribution of food and seed throughout the distressed areas.

The government function in the Highland famine was therefore seen as that of a great enabling agency which left the direct administration of relief to others. Furthermore, official government involvement in the Highlands was short-lived and lasted for less than a year. The two storeships at Mull and Skye were withdrawn in August 1847. The role of the state in the Scottish famine was both more limited and transient than in the Irish crisis. This was noted at the time and various commentators complained bitterly that the 'turbulent' Irish were receiving more aid than the 'peaceful' Highlanders.[74] The reason, however, was probably the different scale and circumstances of the two crises. The regional focus of the Highland famine, the rapid response of the Lowland charities and the Free Church, both of whom were active in relief work by early 1847, the more energetic participation of Highland landowners and the buoyancy of the labour market for seasonal workers in the Lowlands, were all significant. Also of importance was the fact that the grain trade was more highly developed in such areas as Sutherland, Wester Ross, Skye and several other of the Inner Hebrides than in the far west of Ireland. Relief officials estimated that most of these districts imported meal in 'normal' times. Proprietors kept grain stores as did several large tenants. Fish merchants provided meal on credit and income from temporary migration was also used to buy grain from local meal merchants. There was therefore a commercial mechanism through which additional emergency supplies could penetrate as long as supply was maintained and cash resources remained available.[75]

These factors not only allowed government to keep a relatively low profile but gave the state the opportunity to disengage itself, officially at least, from famine relief from the end of the summer of 1847. It must be stressed that it was as much these fortunate circumstances as ideological hostility to involvement as such that was crucial. Trevelyan informed Coffin that news was to be relayed promptly of any district which required immediate relief and steps would then have to be taken to provide it.[76] The impression given throughout the correspondence of government officials is that in the last resort the free distribution of food might be necessary to preserve life. But every other option was to be exhausted before any such action was seriously contemplated.[77] Favourable circumstances ensured that ideological commitment was not in the event put fully to the test.

Between the autumn of 1846 and the summer of 1847, however, government was far from irrelevant to the relief effort. The provision of meal depôts was important but not of critical significance. By August 1847, they had carried out sales to the value of £58,000; £22,000 was spent by the Free Church and then the Central Board, £12,000 by proprietors and £24,000 by consumers for their own use.[78] Nevertheless, a much greater volume of meal was imported through established channels. Of the 34,850 bolls of oatmeal imported into Tobermory between 1846 and 1850, only 14,027 were landed in 1846 and 1847, and not all of this came through the government depôt ships.[79] In addition, most landlords apparently acquired their grain from the north-east ports in 1846 and 1847, because it was alleged that prices there were lower than those current in Glasgow and Liverpool which were the rates which governed the sale price from the government ships.[80] The main significance of the state's efforts lay rather in three other areas. First, the careful monitoring of landlord policies and the pressure brought to bear on inactive proprietors had, as seen earlier, significant effect.[81] Second, in the long term, the relief works made possible under the Drainage Act introduced much employment to the distressed region and helped to complement the efforts of the Central Board. The Board's operations were mainly confined to the spring and summer months while drainage and land improvement schemes were usually concentrated in autumn and winter. Third, the availability of powerful naval steamships to convey grain and seed assisted in maintaining reliable communications throughout the Hebrides and ensured that no community was prevented from receiving aid because of remoteness or the hazards of winter storms. This facility did help to save life in the Outer Hebrides in the winter of 1846-7.[82]

3

The formation of the Central Board of Management for Highland Relief in February 1847 gave the government the opportunity to surrender official responsibility for the distressed districts of the Western Highlands. The Central Board was established to carry out the aims of the three existing Relief Committees, that of the Free Church, the

Edinburgh Committee, founded at a public meeting on 18 December 1846, and the Glasgow Committee, formed on 6 January 1847. It almost certainly came about through government pressure. As early as 8 December 1846, Trevelyan had written to Sir Edward Coffin, indicating that 'It is to be hoped the Free Kirk and the general subscription will come to our aid'.[83] Detailed discussions took place in January and early February 1847 between government officials and the Edinburgh Committee.[84] Coffin, for instance, approvingly noted the appointment of William Skene, Secretary of the Edinburgh Committee, to the new position of Secretary of the Central Board and hoped for continued cooperation with him.[85] Trevelyan praised the sound views of the leadership of the Edinburgh Committee. He described it as representing 'in a very fair degree the intelligence and benevolence of Scotland' and stressed that of the three bodies absorbed within the Central Board it was the most powerful.[86] It will also become clear later in this chapter that the most prominent members of the Edinburgh Committee shared the same principles about the general management of famine relief as government officials.

Not surprisingly, therefore, Trevelyan decided a mere twelve days after the first meeting of the new Central Board that '. . . we are to depend on the Edinburgh Committee and its affiliated bodies for carrying out the detail of relief in the cases not provided for by the exertions of the proprietors'.[87] Skene and his colleagues were asked to prepare and submit a plan for the organisation of relief. Yet while the charities were to actually administer the assistance, they were not to be allowed complete independence. Their strategy was to be checked and vetted by Trevelyan and his colleagues. Government obviously hoped for the best of both worlds. The charitable organisation would bear the burden of responsibility and any adverse criticism of the relief operations; government meanwhile successfully extricated itself from a difficult situation but at the same time continued to exert considerable influence on an 'independent' body. It was an arrangement similar to that in Paisley during the depression of 1841-4 when relief was dispensed through a charity activated by government and administered by a civil servant, Edward Twistleton.[88] In 1846-7, however, the problem in the Highlands was infinitely greater in scale while the charities had first emerged autonomously and then had their independence usurped by government. But the political and intellectual pressures in Paisley and the Highlands were identical: the distaste for intervention founded on a *laissez-faire* ideology but, at the same time, the compelling need to intervene to some extent because of the danger to life and the threat to stability caused by social crisis. Allowing the charities to run the operations, as long as they paid due attention to government views, allowed for a neat compromise between the constraints of political economy and the obligations of humanity.

It is plain that the government officials who were prominent in famine relief in 1846 and 1847 did not suddenly leave the centre of the stage at the end of that year. Trevelyan, Coffin and Sir John McNeill remained of vital significance throughout the period until the mid 1850s. All of them had a crucial effect on the policies adopted by the Central Board. Even when its operations came to an end in 1850, Trevelyan and McNeill retained a strong interest in the Highland problem.[89] It was McNeill's *Report to the Board of Supervision in Scotland* of 1851 which finally discredited charitable relief as a solution to Highland destitution and made a powerful case for assisted emigration as the only remaining solution. McNeill's *Report* in turn led to the passage of the Emigration Advances Act which provided loans at low rates of interest to proprietors who wished to assist the emigration of the destitute population of their estates. Both McNeill and Trevelyan then became deeply involved in the formation and administration of the Highland and Island Emigration Society which between 1851 and 1856 supported the movement of almost 5,000 people to Australia. Trevelyan was the principal organising force in the Society and McNeill was his trusted Scottish lieutenant. It is essential, therefore, to sketch in some of the background, attitudes and values of these men who were to have such a profound and enduring impact on the lives of the people of the Western Highlands and Islands during the whole of the potato famine and its immediate aftermath.

Sir John McNeill (1795-1883) was of Highland birth and ancestry.[90] He was born at Colonsay, the third son of the laird of that island, John McNeill. He studied medicine at Edinburgh University and between 1816 and 1835 saw service with the East India Company in both India and Persia. He later became a diplomat and was special envoy to the Shah of Persia until 1841. In 1845, he was appointed first chairman of the Board of Supervision of the Scottish Poor Law, a post which he held until 1868.

Charles Trevelyan (1807-1886) had also served in the East Indies.[91] He entered the employment of the East India Company service in 1826 as a writer, rising eventually to be assistant to Sir Charles Metcalfe, commissioner at Delhi. He was appointed Assistant Secretary to the Treasury in 1840, a position he held at the time of the potato famine. His official title, however, gives a false impression of his real authority. In essence, Trevelyan might be better described as Permanent Head of the Treasury with a very considerable influence over policy as well as administration. He was also a member of the 'Clapham Sect', a man of intense religious beliefs, renowned for his iron integrity, strong principles and commitment to duty.

Both these men shared many similar attitudes to Highlanders and the Highland problem. Their values were firmly grounded on the teachings of classical political economy and the writings of Thomas Malthus. They both gave tacit support to the contemporary individualist consensus: that poverty was a reflection of personal failure and economic success an achievement which merited moral approval. McNeill argued that 'except actual want' there was '. . . nothing so injurious to the people and to the country as the gratuitous distribution of food'.[92] Such misplaced charity would encourage the cancer of pauperism, the habit of the poor depending on the help of others rather than on their own efforts. Instead, McNeill stressed that rather than inflict such 'demoralisation', the charitable funds should be used to 'promote habits of industry and self-dependence by increasing the productive powers of the soil'.[93] In other words, the crisis was to be used as an opportunity to teach the Highlanders more industrious habits and bring about moral and material regeneration. It was a point of view which echoed the policies of James Loch, William Young and Patrick Sellar on the Sutherland estate a few decades before and derived from the same intellectual roots as their formulae for Highland improvement.[94] Men like McNeill did not share the romantic notion of Highland society. To him the Highlanders to a very large extent had brought the calamity of the potato famine upon themselves.

Trevelyan was even more outspoken in his condemnation of the Highland population. He viewed the inhabitants of the north as racially inferior. They were Celts exactly the same as the inferior Irish, 'except that they are not turbulent or blood-thirsty'.[95] Only through prolonged social and economic intercourse with Anglo-Saxon society might the indolent and feckless Celts become 'practical men'. He re-garded himself as being the result of such a process of improvement because his family belonged to the class of 'reformed' Cornish Celts who had benefited by close and long contact with Anglo-Saxon civilisation. The inferior and uncivilised Highlanders might also benefit if communications between their barbarous society and the rest of Britain were more fully developed. He believed also that both the Highland and Irish famines represented the judgement of God on an indolent people. Relief should not therefore be too lavish because the lazy had to learn their lesson so that eventually improvement could take place: 'Next to allowing the people to die of hunger, the greatest evil that could happen would be their being habituated to depend upon public charity. The object to be arrived at, therefore, is to prevent the assistance given from being produc-tive in idleness and, if possible, to make it conducive to increased exertion'.[96]

Both McNeill and Trevelyan regarded gratuitous relief as a curse, saw the Highland population as inadequate and shared the belief that they had to be taught a 'moral' lesson in order to bring about the economic revolution which alone would permanently end destitution. The essential point was that the attitudes and values of the people had to be changed and this could only be accomplished by a stringent system of relief which would produce moral benefit rather than social harm. The careers of both men in India had brought into even sharper focus for them the gulf between 'civilised' and 'uncivil-ised' races. Indians, Irish and Highlanders were all inferior but could be raised to acceptable Anglo-Saxon standards by appropriate forms of education and social improvement. As the Central Board evolved different policies between 1847 and 1850 both Trevelyan and McNeill, and also Sir Edward Coffin, were to exert a major influence on the strategy of relief. By using the Board as a front they were able to implement their grand plan for moral and material regeneration without directly incurring the public opprobrium and criticism which it eventually provoked in many quarters.

The first relief organisation to make an impact on the distressed districts was the Free Church of Scotland.[97] Eventually the Church's Destitution Committee raised more than £15,000 throughout Scotland and its schooner, *Breadalbane*, built to carry ministers around the Hebrides, was used to ship provisions into the region. The Free Church's Destitution Committee, though it lasted as an independent operation for only a few months from November 1846 to February 1847, attracted much widespread and deserved praise. It was the only agency active in the field at the most critical time; through its superb intelligence network of local congregations and ministers it was able to direct aid to the areas where destitution was most pressing; and its activities were entirely free of any sectarian bias. Grateful thanks for help received came from such Catholic areas as Arisaig and Moidart.[98] The Church also concentrated its relief measures on the cottars, the most vulnerable group by far – '. . . as a general rule, no food shall be distributed to the families of rent-paying tenantry, but to the families of cottars' – and through its parish communities was able to organise *ad hoc* relief commit-tees to dispense aid. It also had the advantage of having Charles Baird and Allan

Fullarton of Glasgow, who had been prominent in the relief committees in 1836-7, as key members of its organising committee. Not the least of the Free Church's contributions was its highly imaginative plan to transport over 3000 able-bodied men from the Highlands for work on the railway construction gangs of the Lowlands in 1846-7. This very successful strategy, its significance and impact are considered more fully in Chapter 6.

When the Central Board assumed overall control in February 1847, the responsibility for different regions of the Highlands was delegated to the Glasgow and Edinburgh Committees, or 'Sections' as they were now known. Each had considerable independence from the parent body. The Edinburgh Section eventually assumed responsibility for Skye, Wester Ross, the Northern Isles and the Eastern Highlands; the Glasgow Section was entrusted with Argyll, western Inverness, the Outer Hebrides and the Inner Hebrides, apart from Skye. The Central Board itself had 117 members, including the Moderators of the Church of Scotland, the Free Church and the Relief Church, the Provosts of all the major Scottish towns, several landowners, Bishop Murdoch of the Roman Catholic Church, and the Principals of Edinburgh and Glasgow Universities as 'extraordinary members'.[99] The most significant characteristic of this group, however, was the presence of two government law officers, the Lord Advocate and the Solicitor General, within it. The 'ordinary' members of each Section consisted mainly of the business and professional classes of Glasgow and Edinburgh. The occupations of twenty-seven of the forty-three Edinburgh members can be identified. Thirteen were lawyers or advocates, and there were five ministers, three merchants, three landowners, two doctors and an accountant. Of the thirty-five members of the Glasgow Section whose occupations can be traced, seventeen were merchants, eight were ministers and there were six landowners, two 'manufacturers', one professor and one accountant. These bodies were therefore dominated by the urban upper middle classes and their policies would obviously be shaped by their principles and values.

The most important and influential figures, however, were the two organising secretaries. Charles Baird held the position in the Glasgow Section and William Skene in the Edinburgh Section. As noted earlier, Baird had played a key role in the relief operations of 1836-7. He had also published with Allan Fullarton a pamphlet in 1838 entitled *Remarks on the Evils at Present Affecting the Highlands and Islands of Scotland*, in which the authors acknowledged the Highlander's many virtues, his valour, his religious loyalties and his kindness to kinfolk and poor. But they also stressed that the people of the Western Highlands were feckless, guilty of overbreeding to an alarming extent, were too fond of 'ardent spirits' and were notoriously indolent. Like McNeill and Trevelyan, they saw the Highland population as 'uncivilised' and lacking the proper values which only education and closer communication with the world to the south and east could instil. The Highland work cycle, which involved considerable effort in the spring, summer and autumn but less activity in the winter, was an inevitable result of the nature of subsistence agriculture, the pastoral economy, and the climatic patterns of the north-west. But it was deeply offensive to these observers since it jarred with their own profound belief in the moral and material value of regular and disciplined toil. More than any other single factor the middle-class Victorian commitment to the work ethic played a central part in influencing the shaping of relief policies in the Highlands during the famine.

William Forbes Skene (1809-1892), the powerful Secretary of the Edinburgh Section, was a member of the family of the Skenes of Rubislaw, lairds in Aberdeenshire.[100] He had strong Highland connections and interests and was actually born in Knoydart, the property of Macdonnel of Glengarry, and lived for a time in the household of the Rev. Mackintosh Mackay, minister of Laggan in Inverness-shire. His interests in the Highlands were further stirred by his association with Sir Walter Scott. Indeed, it was on Scott's personal recommendation that he was able to obtain lodgings with the Rev. Mackay. He trained as a lawyer, achieving the rank of Writer to the Signet in 1832, and became clerk of the bills in the bill chamber of the Court of Session, a position which he occupied until 1865.

From his earliest manhood, Skene developed a consuming interest in Highland society and quickly became a recognised expert on Celtic culture, publishing successively *The Highlanders in Scotland* (1837), an introduction to the Dean of Lismore's *Collection of Gaelic Poetry* (1862) and finally his three-volume *magnum opus, Celtic Scotland: a History of Ancient Alba* (1876-80). He was eventually appointed Historiographer Royal for Scotland in 1881.

But Skene's regard for the traditional culture of the Highlands did not dilute his moral disapproval of the habits and customs of the Highlanders of the nineteenth century. His attitude encapsulated the dualism which enabled some of the Scottish middle classes to sentimentalise the world of the 'old' Highlands and, at the same time, vigorously and stridently condemn the way of life of the contemporary inhabitants of the region. Thus, several of Skene's statements echoed the comments of McNeill, Trevelyan and Baird. The population was 'secluded . . . from all intercourse with an advanced state of society and, in general, is "reposing in the bosom of two graceless sisters – sluggishness and ignorance"!'.[101] From 1847 to 1850 he was also in constant communication with Sir Charles Trevelyan, and from their letters it is clear that they both agreed about the 'inadequacy' of the Highland people and the need to reform their way of life and habits of work.[102] This stereotyping of the population of the distressed districts as both morally and racially inferior was the essential precondition for the enactment of a series of extraordinary schemes of 'improvement' during the famine on a scale which would scarcely have been contemplated for the population of any other region of mainland Britain. To a significant extent, by the spring of 1847, the management of the relief funds had fallen under the control of the officers of the Central Board and a small group of government officials who shared similar views and were determined to use the opportunity of the great subsistence crisis to carry out a social revolution in northern Scotland.

In early 1847, however, all this lay in the future. The distribution of meal was managed initially under the Sections' Local Committees who were appointed from each district or parish from lists of names supplied by local clergymen. The aim was to do enough to prevent starvation, and so allowances were limited to 1½ lbs. of meal per adult male per day and ¾lb. per female. Children under twelve received ½lb. each.[103] According to the rules of distribution, gratuitous relief was to be avoided and work extracted in return for meal. All over the Western Highlands and Islands in the spring and summer of 1847, gangs of men, women and children could be seen labouring at such 'public' works as the repairing and building of walls and the construction of roads and quays. Independent contemporary observers acknowledged that in this period the Central Board's meal supplies saved many in the most distressed areas from malnutrition and even worse.[104] In spring 1847, the Glasgow Section alone dispatched 7047 bolls of wheatmeal, 5696 bolls of oatmeal, 1980 bolls of peasemeal and 690 bolls of Indian corn.[105] The Central Board also continued to implement the Free Church's policy of assisting the movement of able-bodied men and women to the labour market of the Lowlands.[106]

When judged by the simple and vital criterion of how far it had saved life, the relief programme in the first half of 1847 had been remarkably successful. Mortality rates which, as shown in Chapter 3, had started to climb from the latter months of 1846, were quickly stabilised. Reports of disease became fewer. But this achievement did not satisfy all contemporary opinion and, in particular, some sections of the press, several of the relief officers and their committees or government officials, who had been monitoring the actual implementation of the Central Board's policies at the local level with increasing concern. By the early summer of 1847 the critics were proclaiming that the Highlanders were being encouraged to depend upon 'pauperising' assistance rather than their own efforts.[107] The 'labour test' was everywhere being disregarded.[108] Stories were recounted in the press of lavish distribution of meal, often to people who had no need of assistance, and 'evidence' was produced purporting to demonstrate that many were returning from work in the south to take advantage of the liberal provision of food in the north.[109] It was also alleged, with much more foundation, that the works established as part of the 'labour test' were useless, added little of value to the local economy and were carried out in a slipshod manner.[110] The *Final Report* of Sir Edward Coffin, while praising the relief initiative, further added to the developing controversy by arguing that the people were actually better fed than in normal times during the spring and summer of 1847, traditionally the 'hungry' period of the year, and appeared to be much healthier as a result.[111]

All these accusations caused much alarm among members of the Central Board. As early as June 1847, the Edinburgh Section recruited a half-pay Royal Naval officer, Captain Robert Eliot, to inspect the Local Committees and 'purify' them. His report provided further evidence of broken regulations, liberal provision of relief and maladministration.[112] Three further factors ensured that there would inevitably be radical changes in the relief system in 1848 and thereafter. First, it soon became obvious that the potato failure was likely to persist and destitution would have to be relieved for at least one further year. The opportunity had to be taken now to ensure a radical change in the way of life of the inhabitants of the Highlands so that they would be able to support themselves in the future. Second, adverse publicity provoked a vitriolic campaign in the pages of the *Scotsman* and in pamphlet literature against the 'lazy' Highlander who was taking advantage of the charity and benevolence of the 'industrious' Lowlander.[113] Those who countered with evidence of the hard labour which went into eking out a living in the harsh climate and barren lands of the north went unheeded.

A 'Friend lately pedestrianising in Skye' pointed out the paradox of the poverty of the population coexisting alongside the potential riches of the sea. The explanation was obvious to him: the 'sloth' of the people. '. . . the evil is in the character and inveterate habits of the race'.[114] The *Scotsman* condemned the 'rash enthusiasm about "the Highlanders" ' which had promoted such indulgent philanthropy in the first place. The Central Board should now either use its remaining funds to help the hospitals of the Scottish cities or in the next season of relief be as 'sparing and rigid to the utmost limits that common humanity will permit'.[115]

Even more remarkable were the views propounded by John Bruce in *Letters on the Present Condition of the Highlands and Islands of Scotland* which were serialised in the newspapers and eventually published as a pamphlet. Bruce toured some of the distressed areas in early 1847, and this personal contact lent a spurious credibility to his opinions. One of the key assumptions throughout his lengthy diatribe was the familiar taunt of the racial inferiority of the Highlander: 'In the inns of the Highlands, the Saxon language – the language of civilisation – is keeping its own with the Celtic and the latter is happily doomed to be supplanted by the former'. It was now 'a fact that morally and intellectually the Highlanders are an inferior race to the Lowland Saxon'. Their habits had to be changed by southern example. Instead the 'industrious' Lowlanders were supporting the 'idle and lazy' Highlanders through the agency of the Central Board. These views were not characteristic of all Lowland opinion. Journals such as the *North British Daily Mail*, the *Inverness Advertiser* and pamphleteers like Thomas Mulock and Donald Ross argued just as vehemently that the Highlands required more liberal aid and support. However, by the autumn of 1847 the critics had the advantage of having the ear of some key officers in the Central Board itself.

Thirdly, and most decisively of all, government officials began to play a more direct role in influencing the strategy of relief. In early 1848, James Loch, the Duke of Sutherland's principal factor, described the close relationship which by that time had grown up between the government and the Edinburgh Section. He referred to it as the organisation which 'communicates with Sir John McNeill and the Government'.[116] From the start of its operations, the Central Board had worked closely with them. McNeill had several meetings with members of the Glasgow Section in the spring of 1847.[117] He encouraged them to form a paid inspectorate to supervise relief, to publicise their proceedings in order to gain the confidence of their subscribers and to ensure that the labour test was implemented with full rigour. When the Glasgow officials voiced their concern that work schemes might benefit Highland proprietors he reassured them that in the circumstances this was inevitable and the only alternative to the moral disease of gratuitous relief.[118] In addition, both McNeill and Sir Edward Coffin were present at a 'private meeting' of members of the Central Board with Charles Baird, William Skene and Captain Eliot when the key principles in the new system of relief for 1848 were decided.[119] Indeed, it is plain that its main elements derived not from the members of the Board but partly from a *Memorandum* written by Coffin himself in August 1847 and also subsequent correspondence from Trevelyan to William Skene, the Secretary of the Edinburgh Section.[120] It was the two government officials who produced the detailed blueprint which was to direct the entire course of relief operations from early 1848 until they ceased in 1850.

The central component of this system was the idea of the 'destitution test'. Skene defined this as follows: '. . . the Committee took the whole labour of the recipient, and paid for it at the rate of a pound of meal for a day's work'.[121] The theory was that only those truly in a condition of severe destitution would accept relief on these terms. The meagre allowance provided but a bare subsistence and only those with no food resources of their own or who did not have the possibility of obtaining gainful employment would endure such a harsh régime for so little in order to avoid starvation. In one sense, it represented the ethic of the new English Poor Law carried to an extreme and transferred to the Highlands. In 1834, the revision of the English Poor Law organised relief under stricter conditions. Outdoor relief was to be abolished and all recipients were to be made to enter the workhouse. Conditions in the workhouse were made 'less eligible', i.e. more miserable, than the condition of the lowest-paid worker outside, and a rigorous workhouse test was applied to all applicants for relief in order to deter all but the really 'deserving'. The only differences between the 'workhouse test' and the 'destitution test' were that the latter was applied to outdoor relief and the pittance of one pound of meal per day was even less than the allowances dispensed under the New Poor Law.

But the idea did not come directly from the English experience alone. The allocation of one pound of meal a day was first used in Ireland in 1846 and 1847 and it was Sir Charles Trevelyan himself who pressed its advantages on the Central Board: 'In Ireland we found by the result of our experience which comprehended the feeding of upwards of three millions of persons for several months, that one pound of good meal properly cooked was amply sufficient for the support of an able-bodied person'.[122] He also insisted that only by this bare subsistence could 'pauperism' be avoided: '. . . the pound of meal and the task of at least eight hours hard work is the best régime for this moral disease'.[123] Trevelyan also urged upon Skene the vital need for a paid inspectorate which would not favour the people or sympathise with them and could be relied upon to implement the test with full vigour. The idea of cooperation between the Central Board and local proprietors was also suggested.[124] Out of this came the 'cooperative system' by which the Board and individual landlords shared the burden of relief but the work carried out was devoted to estate improvement and the development of roads.

But Trevelyan, and to a lesser extent Coffin and McNeill, were not only the main sources of inspiration of the new system of relief. All new initiatives were also sent to London for personal approval by Trevelyan before they were implemented. Skene admitted to him in March 1848, 'I do not anticipate that any proposal will be sanctioned by the Committee which is not in accordance with your views'.[125] He was even consulted over the issue of what should be done with the balance of the relief funds when operations came to an end. He replied in characteristic fashion that it should be employed to establish correction 'Union Houses' (workhouses) in the Highlands to enable the important work of the moral reformation of the Highland Celts to continue.[126] It was partly due also to his disapproval in 1849 that the Central Board rescinded its original decision to provide emigration assistance in the distressed areas.[127]

Trevelyan also found time despite his many other responsibilities to write to the subordinate officials of the Board encouraging them in the resolute execution of the destitution test which he passionately believed was the only effective defence against social and moral disintegration in the Western Highlands.[128] But government influence was not only confined to his enthusiastic supervision of the Board's efforts. The posts of paid inspectors required under the new system were filled by Royal Navy officers on half pay, who had had experience of government service during the relief operations in Ireland or who were previously employed by the Board of Supervision of the Scottish Poor Law.[129] Thomas Mulock described them scathingly as 'heroes of the quarter deck, accustomed to rule by means of a boatswain's whistle, to effect at land what they had never tried at sea viz. to exact the *maximum* of work for the *minimum* of food'.[130] Captain Eliot was appointed to the post of Inspector-General of the Edinburgh Section. All the officers were selected on the recommendations of McNeill and Trevelyan.[131]

It is difficult to avoid the conclusion that the Central Board and, in particular, the Edinburgh Section had been virtually transformed by early 1848 almost into a quasi-government agency. Its principal policies were inspired by government officials who maintained a close supervision of the Board's activities. Its relief inspectors were on leave of absence from government employment. The Board had become an organisation for the 'improvement' of the Highlands along the ideological lines defined by Trevelyan, McNeill and Coffin in close cooperation with Skene, Baird and others. But the costs of the programme now to be executed were not borne by the state or by the ratepayers of the region but by those both at home and abroad who had contributed to the great Relief Fund of 1846 and 1847. It was an extraordinary outcome. But the major influence of the government officials remained covert. Little explicit reference to their role was made in the published reports and correspondence of the Central Board. Indeed, Skene's original correspondence with Trevelyan is prefaced with the instruction in Skene's hand: 'Pray do not let these find their way into print'.

5

Relief was suspended in September 1847 in anticipation of the coming grain and potato harvests. The intention was that even if a programme of relief was found to be necessary it would not commence again until the spring of 1848 as the people could be expected to survive on their own resources until then. But the continued failure of the potatoes and the fact that the southern labour market became depressed from the latter months of 1847 meant that the Central Board was forced to start the provision of relief again from January 1848. When it did so, however, the nature of the system had altered radically from that of 1847.

The Local Committees, long discredited for their lack of stringency, were replaced by 'a paid agency', an elaborate bureaucracy consisting, in the case of the Edinburgh Section, of an Inspector-General, one resident inspector in Skye and another in Wester Ross, and, below these, relief officers and work overseers. The Board acknowledged that this management structure was expensive but that it was necessary 'in order to secure the efficient application of the Test', the central element in the new system.[132] Only staff unconnected with the relief districts were selected for this duty; officers with local connections might be too sympathetic: 'They must be men of intelligence and firmness, who will do their duty as representing the Board and not sympathise with the

People'.[133] The resident inspector in Skye was one Captain E.J. Fishbourne, a man who was enthusiastically committed to the moral value of the destitution test with an almost religious zeal and who justified it in terms of Christian doctrine. Trevelyan corresponded with him in 1848, giving him 'all the support and encouragement possible' in his important task.[134] Both were fond of quoting Biblical texts at one another. Trevelyan's favourites were, 'In the sweat of thy face shalt thou eat Bread' and 'If any provide not for his own, and especially for those of his own house, he hath denied the Faith *and is worse than an Infidel*' (underlined in original).[135] Fishbourne replied with a quotation from St. Paul: 'If any would not work, neither should he eat'.[136]

The relief inspectors and officers were charged above all else with the implementation of the destitution test. The allowance of one pound of meal per adult male was parsimonious even by the standards of other schemes established in Scotland to relieve distress. Relief works for destitute handloom weavers in Glasgow in 1819 paid 7s.6d. per week for married men with three dependants.[137] In Paisley in 1841-2, men with similar responsibilities received 7s., single males 4s., and unmarried women 1s.9d.[138] But the meagre pittance, reckoned by Trevelyan as only enough to sustain life, was not the only unusual aspect of the system imposed on the inhabitants of the Western Highlands and Islands after 1848. The aim was more to change the values and assumed moral weaknesses of the people than support them through a major subsistence crisis. Relief officers were instructed to become 'the hardest taskmasters of and worst paymasters in the district'.[139] They had to select the groups who were to be permitted to obtain relief through the destitution test with great care: 'the parties who are the primary objects of relief are those who are destitute, but who have no legal claim to subsistence from the Parish or who are not able-bodied labourers'.[140] The able-bodied were not 'primary objects' of relief if they were in a position to obtain employment. This instruction explains why young single men and women and, eventually, married men with three or less children, were struck off the relief lists from early summer.[141] It was assumed that the labour market in the south was sufficiently buoyant by that time to allow them to obtain work there. By August 1848, the relief officers in Skye were informed: 'Every able-bodied man to be struck off it matters not how many in the family. They must either go to Gairloch or Ullapool [for work]'.[142] Again, the criterion of destitution was clearly spelt out: 'Parties who possess means of their own, or who have not consumed the produce of their ground or stock, or whose property is sufficient to enable them to render their credit available are not destitute until their means are exhausted'.[143] Those who were eligible for relief, if fit for outdoor work should be employed in the construction of roads, piers, fishing, enclosure of townships or improvement of land. The unfit worked at spinning, knitting and making fishing nets.

Children under twelve years of age would only receive meal if they attended school regularly.[144] The Board viewed education as an important agency for curing the barbarous and lazy habits of the Highlanders. Special attention was devoted to the 'aged and infirm poor' who had been assisted by the Local Committees in 1847 but who ought to have depended on the official Poor Law. They were to be driven back on to the parish by an especially stringent régime.[145] Their allowances of meal were fixed in April 1848 'at the lowest possible scale' in Wester Ross of one half pound of meal per person per day, 'cautioning them that even this aid was irregular, and could only be continued for a short time, and as an interim measure'.[146] Meal allowances for both the able-bodied and the infirm were issued once a fortnight in order to inculcate 'habits of prudence' by teaching the poor to spread their means over an extended period rather than depend upon being fed on a daily basis. Labour books were kept by the overseers in which the hours of work of each recipient were recorded. The fortnight's allowance for each family was calculated and a ticket was then issued to the labourer which he presented to the local meal dealer for his supply. The work books were kept with great care and the correspondence of the Resident Inspectors shows plainly that the destitution test was resolutely put into effect by relief officers who saw it as their sacred duty to teach the people of their districts a moral lesson which they would never forget.[147]

The Cooperative System, first begun in 1848, became the dominant method of relief provision in several areas of the Western Highlands and Islands by 1850.[148] In Skye, for example, virtually all the proprietors had entered into cooperative arrangement with the Central Board by 1850. In that year, therefore, while a substantial proportion of the population was still employed in relief works, Test Relief was limited to 1840 out of a total island population of over 23,000. On the other hand, in Wester Ross, 8906 people were still covered by Test Relief when the Central Board terminated its operations.[149] The Cooperative System has already been referred to both in this chapter and in the previous one but it is appropriate to look at it in more detail here.

It combined the financial contributions of two parties, the Board and local landowners, in the employment of all the population in a given district deemed qualified for relief in 'some public work of recognised advantage to the whole community'. The Board provided a sum equal to the estimated cost of relief in the area in question; the proprietor, in the case of public works, bore a proportion of the cost, 'equal to the advantage he could derive' from the improvement. In return, he was 'bound to support and take charge of his people'. Later the system was extended to land reclamation or 'reproductive labour'. In this case the bargain was that the small tenants should be provided with long leases in order that they might obtain the long-term benefit of the improvements which they had carried out.

The system was attacked almost as vigorously as the destitution test as one which diverted monies from a great charity into the pockets of Highland landowners.[150] But to the Central Board it had several advantages. It allowed it to partly withdraw from the direct supervision and administration of relief and, as it became popular in more districts, the large and expensive staff necessary to enforce the destitution test could be reduced. Again, it fitted neatly into the general strategy of stimulating economic improvement in the distressed areas and enabling their inhabitants to support themselves when the relief operations ceased. Above all, it re-established what the Board saw as the 'natural relations' in the society which were distorted by the very nature of a system of relief:

> A relief system affecting the food and labour of the people inverts the connection of work and payment, and disturbs to a certain extent the natural relation between superior and dependent, employer and employed. The labourers are paid, not according to the value of the work done, but according to their wants and the number and position of those dependent upon him; and relief being extended to the latter, withdraws the ordinary

stimulus of the labourer being dependent on his earnings for the support of his family. Where the Committee must undertake useful works for the employment of the people, it naturally produces the tendency to throw works upon them which might otherwise have been undertaken and to add those to their list of recipients who might otherwise have been employed.[151]

In the cooperative arrangement, however, the labourer was once again supported by wages for piece work done, restored to his 'natural' employer, the landlord, and received legitimate encouragement to improve his holding. Finally, since the Cooperative System first developed to assist in road construction in Wester Ross, it exactly suited another of the ideological and intellectual assumptions of those who controlled the policies of the Central Board: that the society of the Western Highlands could only be roused from its 'primitive' condition by better access to the markets of the Lowlands and 'immediate contact with a more advanced state of society' by the development of an improved system of communications.

The full implementation of the destitution test from early 1848 provoked anger and hostility in the distressed areas and widespread criticism from sections of the press. Skene observed that opposition 'was almost universal'.[152] The system which was imposed upon the people of the Highlands did not reflect any Lowland or middle-class consensus about the roots of the social problems of the north-west or the steps that should be taken to remove them. The policy adopted from 1848 was agreed only by a small group and implemented with the tacit approval of members of the Central Board. The most scathing critic was Thomas Mulock, the editor of the *Inverness Advertiser*.[153] He recognised Trevelyan's role in the whole affair: 'Sir Charles was invited to try his hand in starving the poor Highlanders according to the most approved doctrines of political economy . . . the Highlanders upon grounds of Catholic affinity, were to be starved after the Irish fashion'. Mulock poured scorn on 'the enlightened doctrines of the Economists' which were now used to justify inflicting further misery on a people already ravaged by famine.

The response of the Highland population itself was inevitably hostile. The execution of the policies of the Central Board ensured that two entirely different value systems came into direct and open conflict. The inhabitants of the Western Highlands practised subsistence husbandry. Their patterns of work were determined by season and climate, the limitations of the land they cultivated and the seas which they fished. They laboured to gain a sufficiency of food, fuel and clothing and for their very basic needs, not to maximise income. Such scanty evidence as survives suggests that in years of scarcity they felt they had a right to be relieved by their landlords in return for rental payment in 'good' years. It was a kind of 'moral economy' totally at variance with the ideology of relief officers of the Central Board.[154] Landlord assistance had been the pattern in earlier crises, and as the previous chapter showed, was also common in the first year of the potato famine. Support from proprietors was not purely charitable: 'It was much cheaper for a landowner, particularly a non-resident one, to give generously in an emergency . . . rather than find his estate permanently rated for poor relief'.[155] By the 1840s, some communities apparently felt that the provision of assistance amounted not only to a moral but almost to a legal obligation. In Lewis, for instance, it was noted that, 'The people generally are under an impression that the proprietor is bound in law to support them'.[156] When relief supplies were sent to the region in 1846, the distressed population also felt they had a justifiable right to 'the Committee meal' and to 'the public bounty' which had been collected for their benefit.[157] Even the enforcement of a milder labour test in Mull, in 1847, brought widespread opposition: 'The people had been led to imagine that it was an act of oppression, emanating from the proprietors, to require work as a condition of relief, and that the contributors to the fund never contemplated that work should be exacted'.[158] This attitude was anathema to the key members of the Central Board and their staff and provided unambiguous proof of the corrupt state of the people whom it was now their responsibility to lead to moral enlightenment.

The destitution test brought into even sharper focus the conflict between the expectations of the inhabitants of this peasant society and the ethos of zealots steeped in the orthodoxies of classical political economy. Skene recorded that 'A storm of local vituperation burst upon us for not giving enough'.[159] Local Free Church ministers, who had been in the vanguard of the relief effort in 1846, protested vigorously.[160] Skene noted that the strength of the opposition was even affecting members of the Board itself. At the end of February he confided in Trevelyan that 'the principle of a bare subsistence for a full amount of labour is threatened with revision'.[161] This would be disastrous because it was the core of the entire system. He sought Trevelyan's *public* support (which he declined to give) but found comfort in the 'stern determination' of the Resident Inspectors who, despite hostility, were carrying out their duties efficiently and were 'beyond all praise'. To him the basic problem was that the critics did not comprehend what the Board was trying to achieve. The 'stringent nature of the test may appear harsh and unfeeling . . . yet we are consulting the best interests of the people in enforcing it and they will in time find their permanent advantage in what we are now doing'.[162]

Not surprisingly the population of the distressed areas did not see it in these terms. One critic called the test 'systematised starvation'.[163] There was considerable and vocal hostility in Skye and Wester Ross. Meetings were held to petition for an increase in allowances.[164] In Kilmuir and Snizort in Skye there was collective opposition to accepting relief under the terms of the test. In Kilmuir, only ten men out of a population of 1740 were employed at road works in April 1848, while in Sleat 'some people were subject to such ridicule for accepting the test and would not accept work in the village though they did out of it'.[165] One observer noted how the relief officials 'are more likely to do harm than good, they raise and breed an evil spirit of irritation and vengeance in the poor's mind by not giving a reasonable allowance for labour'. He likened it to 'gradual starvation' to labour from 6 a.m. to 6 p.m., including walking to and from the task works for 1lb. of meal.[166] By April 1848 it was reported that in Skye 'the people are disgusted at them' (the Central Board), especially since their unacceptable system was being implemented by a well-paid group of relief officers who had no sympathy with the plight of the poor.[167]

The immediate result of the policy was a sharp decline in the numbers on the relief lists, a development which the Board's Resident Inspectors took as certain proof of the efficiency of the system. In Wester Ross, sixty-seven per cent of the population received relief at the peak period in 1847; in 1848, the proportion on relief at the same time slumped to eighteen per cent. In Skye, the comparable figures were fifty-six per cent of the population in 1847 and twenty-two per cent in 1848.[168] Captain Rose reported from Wester Ross that the test had provoked 'so strong a feeling of opposition' that it was widely refused. This, he reported with satisfaction, was 'a very wholesome symptom'.[169] It was suggested that very few young able-bodied men and women would accept relief under the test and, in consequence, there had been a vast increase in the temporary migration of this group to the Lowlands, despite the contraction of opportunities for employment in the south as a result of the depression of 1848.[170] During that year, at least, in the districts supervised by the Edinburgh Section, most of those relieved under the test were older men and women, the semi-infirm and children.[171] Despite this, one fifth of the population of Wester Ross and one quarter of the inhabitants of Skye were still forced to accept the destitution test at some point in 1848. It was striking confirmation of the fact that only the allowance dispensed by the Section's officials in return for eight hours of closely supervised physical effort stood between many and possible starvation.

The sufferings of the people of Strathaird in Skye may have been typical of the plight of the poorer communities.[172] Many 'were sometimes unable to come to work from defective nourishment'. In such cases, their allowances were always withheld while they were absent. Their 'payment' of one pound of meal per day compared with 'the ordinary allowance in Scotland for a working man' of 17lbs. of meal or bread weekly together with milk and fish. At first the test works were situated four miles away from their homes. Later on they had to travel a distance of ten miles which meant rising normally at 4 a.m. The roads they were required to build 'did not lead to any place of importance'. A pier which they were constructing and which might have been of some practical benefit was suddenly abandoned and eventually entirely destroyed by winter storms. The heads of families by the end of 1848 were close to despair. But, as was shown in Chapter 2, the continued failure of the potatoes and the depressed condition of the market for temporary labour in the Lowlands in 1848 ensured that many more of the population of the Western Highlands had to submit to the destitution test if they were to survive in 1849.

6

In its concluding report of 1850, the Edinburgh Section of the Central Board summed up its contribution over the previous four years, in tones of self-congratulation: 'They believe that some of their labours will be found to remain in the works of permanent improvement they have left behind them, and in the stimulus to industry and self-exertion their measures were calculated to give'.[173] A major mortality crisis had indeed been averted.[174] But even this achievement had been won at very considerable social cost during the years when the destitution test formed the cornerstone of the Board's policies. External observers for the most part regarded it as adding unnecessarily to the sufferings of the poor and through the expensive administration which it required diverted funds from areas where they were most needed. The foolishness of the rule that only those devoid of property could claim relief in 1848 was acknowledged as a factor which actually increased destitution by forcing the people to sell off their possessions.[175] There was no evidence either that the Board's strategy had increased 'habits of industry'. This was hardly surprising since the main premise behind the policy, that the people of the Highlands were indolent, was manifestly false and based on a complete lack of comprehension of the labour rhythms and social values of a peasantry practising subsistence husbandry. Even Sir John McNeill, in his *Report* of 1851, concluded, not surprisingly, that the work patterns of the society had not altered in any obvious way. All that the Board had apparently accomplished by the stringent enforcement of the test was to instil a sullen resentment and deep hostility among the people. This must have obviously reduced any possibility of their enthusiastic cooperation in the Board's more positive initiatives in textile work and fishing. Nor should it be forgotten that the charities were only one source of relief to the distressed region. The role of the landlord class, the provision of employment under the Drainage Act and the increased dependence on earnings from temporary migration were also important in saving life.

The Edinburgh Section, in particular, claimed considerable success for its strategy of economic development which was intended to render the districts under its control better able to support themselves when relief finally came to an end. There were four elements in this programme, most of which were undertaken as part of the cooperative system.[176] First, help was given for improvement of tenancies through drainage work and the taking in of waste land. In return for support from the Section in these activities, landlords promised leases to the small tenants. By 1850 the Edinburgh Section had concluded such agreements with the two largest estates in Skye and several properties in Wester Ross. Second, much attention was devoted to the construction of roads to make the region more open to 'civilising' influences and southern markets. As noted earlier, it was assumed that their poverty was in part caused by poor communications. Road-building, of both short and long routes, had been carried on by the Central Board throughout the Western Highlands since 1847, but the Edinburgh Section's initiatives in Wester Ross between 1848 and 1850 were the most ambitious schemes. By 1850, a direct route along the south bank of Loch Maree connected Gairloch in the west with Dingwall in Easter Ross. The road from Ullapool via Garve also linked west to east at Dingwall. The Dundonnel and Strathcannaird roads extended the connection up the west coast through the wilds of Coigach to Assynt in Sutherland. These 'destitution roads' stand to this day as the basis of the modern communications system in this part of the Highlands, a lasting monument to the famine relief programme of the 1840s. Eventually ninety miles of road were completed: 'Two great lines of communication with the east country are opened up, the entire circle of internal communications established, and this large population brought within the range of those benefits arising from facility of communication access to markets, and immediate contact with a more advanced society.'[177]

Third, the manufacture of hosiery in Skye was promoted. Funds were made available under favourable terms to an Aberdeen woollen manufacturer, William Hogg, to establish a wool spinning factory on the island. The building was completed in 1849. In that year, Skye produced almost 16,000 pairs of stockings. In 1850, Hogg was making 137 dozen stockings per month, employing ten women in the mill and over 1000 outworkers or knitters. The Section optimistically concluded in its final report that 'a hosiery trade is now permanently established in Skye'.[178] Finally, investment was also used in an attempt to expand the white fishery. The reason why this particular sector was chosen gives yet another insight into the ideological assumptions of the Section's officials. The herring fishery should not be encouraged since, being active at only one season, it '. . . is not calculated to promote habits of industry'. The white fishery, however, was continuous throughout the year, requiring 'more patient and continuous industry', and so was consistent with the broader aims of the relief strategy.[179] Eight boats with full crews from Cellardyke in Fife were engaged in 1849 'to instruct the natives' and fishing stations were established at Soay, Stein and Uig in Skye and at Badachro, near Gairloch, in Wester Ross. The Badachro station was by far the most elaborate with a pier, curing house and smoking house. In its plan to encourage the fisheries, the Section was following a long tradition of Highland 'improvement' which stretched back into the eighteenth century.

Despite its claim, however, there is no evidence that the strategy of economic regeneration had any significant effect. The famine persisted for almost five years after 1850. Numbers on the official Poor Law rose sharply when the Central Board ceased its activities. When recovery did eventually come after 1855 it was because of the decline in the potato blight and the revival in cattle prices rather than the efforts of the relief committees before 1850.[180] In the districts where the Edinburgh Section's investment concentrated there was little evidence of permanent improvement. It did admit that its experiments in fishing had been 'most unsatisfactory'. This was the nearest it came to a public admission of failure. The textile enterprises do not appear to have survived for long after 1850. The land improvement schemes promised security of tenure for the crofters on those estates where cooperation agreements had been established. Yet the arrangements were so qualified by legal conditions that most proprietors felt little compulsion to enforce their side of the agreement and, anyway, the contracts could not be made to apply to succeeding proprietors. In Skye, therefore, where the cooperative system was most common, the small tenants complained before the Napier Commission in the 1880s that insecurity of tenure was still one of their principal grievances.

The development of communications was probably the most enduring result of the Central Board's activities but even here the results were far from decisive. The fishing piers which were built in Wester Ross attracted scathing criticism from the Scottish Fishery Board. Those at Lochs Torridon and Kishorn were 'small and insubstantial erections. The first had been erected too far up the loch to be of service to them. The second had been left unfinished'.[181] The new network of roads in Wester Ross failed to produce an economic renaissance. The Board seemed not to comprehend that the most efficient, speediest and cheapest form of communication in the area was by sea and that the population of the west coast, far from being isolated, was already well connected by steamship to the Clyde by 1846. The whole transport system was geared to trade between the major towns of the western Lowlands and the north-west, while the Board's roads merely facilitated better contacts with the east coast, which were less important in economic terms. The assumption that the problems of the crofting region could be solved if access was improved to the Lowlands had been a common fallacy since the eighteenth century. Better communications often simply exposed the north-west even more to the competitive pressures from the industrial economy to the south. The powerful forces of regional specialisation and comparative advantage had already gone too far to be reversed by the puny efforts of the Central Board.

The failure of the Board's programme of economic regeneration was therefore inevitable. The policy of changing attitudes through the destitution test and the plan to promote economic reform in partnership with people and proprietors were mutually inconsistent. The first incited opposition and alienation among the population and ensured that they would not contribute with any enthusiasm to the success of the second. The Board's intention of implementing an elaborate development plan with modest resources in the middle of the greatest Highland economic crisis of the nine-teenth century meant that its schemes were probably doomed from the start. The whole story, indeed, has a familiar ring. It recalls the Sutherland experiments of the early nineteenth century and the series of futile schemes for Highland improvement which were launched in the second half of the eighteenth century. But the Board's officials seem to have learned little from these previous failures. Their lack of success had, however, profound and ominous significance for the people of the Western Highlands and Islands. Their vain attempt to solve fundamental economic and social problems together with the continuation of destitution totally discredited charitable relief.[182] The Central Board's failure ensured that only the emigration option now remained in the continuing search for a simple solution to Highland distress.

NOTES

1. The Irish evidence on which this analysis depends is based mainly on the following: R.D. Edwards and Desmond T. Williams, eds., *The Great Famine: Studies in Irish History* (Dublin, 1956); Society of Friends, *Transactions of the Central Relief Committee of the Society of Friends during the Famine in Ireland 1846-7* (Dublin, 1852); C. Woodham-Smith, *The Great Hunger* (London, 1962); S. Kierse, *The Famine Years in the Parish of Killaloe, 1845-51* (Killaloe, 1984); Joel Mokyr, *Why Ireland Starved* (London, 1982); G. O'Tuathaig, *Ireland before the Famine, 1798-1848* (Dublin, 1972); L.M. Cullen, *An Economic History of Ireland since 1660* (London, 1972); L.M. Cullen and T.C. Smout, eds., *Comparative Aspects of Scottish and Irish Economic and Social History, 1660-1900* (Edinburgh, 1977); T.M. Devine and D. Dickson, eds., *Ireland and Scotland 1600-1850* (Edinburgh, 1983); James S. Donnelly, *Land and People of Nineteenth Century Cork* (London, 1975); works by S.M. Cousens, E.M. Crawford, J.M. Goldstrom and C. O'Gráda listed in the bibliography.

2. E.M. Crawford, 'Dearth, Diet and Disease in Ireland, 1850', *Medical History*, 28 (1984).

3. See below, pp.119-124.

4. *Ibid.*

5. *PP*, XXXIV (1847), *Returns of Number of Applications under the Drainage Act.*

6. Flinn, ed., *Scottish Population History*, 164-186; 233-237.

7. B.R. Mitchell, *Abstract of British Historical Statistics* (Cambridge, 1962), 488-90.

8. *Witness*, 29 September 1847.

9. SRO, HD6/2, Treasury Correspondence, Sir E. Coffin to Mr. Trevelyan, 28 September 1847.

10. *Witness*, 20 February 1847; *Relief Correspondence*, Major Halliday to Sir E. Coffin, 31 January 1847.

11. *Witness*, 22 November 1848.

12. Olive Checkland, *Philanthropy in Victorian Scotland* (Edinburgh, 1980).

13. C.L.D. Duckworth and G.E. Langmuir, *West Highland Steamers* (Glasgow, 1967).

14. Mulock, *Western Highlands and Islands*, 160.

15. E.R. Cregeen, ed., *Argyll Estate Instructions, 1771-1805* (Edinburgh, 1964), xx; J. Bruce, *Letters on the Present Condition of the Highlands and Islands of Scotland* (Edinburgh, 1847), 5.

16. Mulock, *Western Highlands and Islands*, 159.

17. *Inverness Courier*, 13 August 1845.

18. Bruce, *Letters on the Present Condition of the Highlands*, 42.

19. D. Jenkins and M. Visocchi, *Mendelssohn in Scotland* (London, 1978), 85.

20. SRO, HD00/2, Treasury Correspondence, Coffin to Trevelyan, 28 September 1847; *Scotsman*, 23 January 1847; *Destitution Papers*, Sixth Report by Central Board (1847), Appendix 16.

21. T.C. Smout, 'Famine and famine-relief in Scotland', in L.M. Cullen and T.C. Smout, eds., *Comparative Aspects of Scottish and Irish Economic and Social History, 1600-1900* (Edinburgh, 1977), 21-31.

22. L.J. Saunders, *Scottish Democracy, 1815-1840* (Edinburgh, 1950), 415.

23. Norman Murray, *The Scottish Handloom Weavers, 1790-1850: A Social History* (Edinburgh, 1978), 130-151.

24. PRO, T1/4201, Papers relating to Distress in the Highlands, 1836-7.

25. Fullarton and Baird, *Remarks on the Evils at Present affecting the Highlands*, *passim*.

26. This discussion of philanthropy is primarily based on the following: Saunders, *Scottish Democracy*, 222-240; Checkland, *Philanthropy in Victorian Scotland*; B. Harrison, 'Philanthropy and the Victorians', *Victorian Studies* (1966); Derek Fraser, *The Evolution of the British Welfare State* (London, 1973), 115-122.

27. *Destitution Papers*, Third Report of the Edinburgh Section (1849), 265. Curiously, however, it is not mentioned in Checkland, *Philanthropy in Victorian Scotland*.

28. Saunders, *Scottish Democracy*, 222-240.

29. T.C. Smout, 'The Strange Intervention of Edward Twistleton: Paisley in Depression, 1841-3', in T.C. Smout, ed., *The Search for Wealth and Stability* (London, 1979).

30. PRO, HO45/1794, J.B. Standish Hay to Sir George Gray, 30 April 1847; *McNeill Report*, Appendix A, 36, 50-1.

31. *Inverness Advertiser*, 18 February, 10 June 1851.

32. *Destitution Papers*, Fourth Report by Edinburgh Section (1847), 6; *Witness*, 25 August 1847; *North British Daily Mail*, 11 May 1847.

33. PRO, HO45/1794, Papers of the British Association for the Relief of Distress in Ireland and Scotland.

34. *Glasgow Herald*, 11 December 1846; *Witness*, 3 October 1846.

35. Sir Charles Trevelyan, *Irish Crisis* (London, 1880), 85.

36. *Ibid.*

37. *Destitution Papers*, Seventh Report of Edinburgh Section (1847), 13.

38. *Destitution Papers*, Second Statement of the Destitution Committee of the Free Church, 4.

39. *Witness*, 30 December 1846.

40. H.R. Trevor-Roper, 'The Invention of Tradition: the Highland Tradition of Scotland', in Eric Hobsbawm and Terence Ranger, eds., *The Invention of Tradition* (Cambridge, 1983), 25.

41. Bruce, *Letters on the Present Condition of the Highlands*, 19, 33, 63; *NSA*, XIV, 344; J. Steill, *The Wrongs and Rights of the Scottish Gael* (Edinburgh, 1854).

42. Trevor-Roper, 'Invention of Tradition', 27.

43. Orr, *Deer Forests, Landlords and Crofters*, 28-43; Christopher Smout, 'Tours in the Scottish

Highlands from the Eighteenth to the Twentieth Centuries', *Northern Scotland*, 5 (1983), 99-122.
44. *Illustrated London News*, 15 January 1853.
45. W.G. Stewart, *Lectures on the Mountains or the Highlands and Highlanders as they were and as they are* (London, 1860), 309-310.
46. SRO, HD16/170, List of Subscriptions to Edinburgh Section.
47. See, for example, Free Church of Scotland, *Highland Destitution: to the Inhabitants of Edinburgh* (1846); *Destitution Ppapers*, Second Statement of the Destitution Committee of the Free Church; *Glasgow Herald*, 21 December 1846; *Times*, 9 October 1846.
48. Anon., *Extracts from Letters to Rev. Dr. McLeod*, passim.
49. Trevelyan, *Irish Crisis*, 85.
50. *Relief Correspondence*, Mr Ellice to Chancellor of the Exchequer, 31 August 1846.
51. Stewart, *Lectures on the Mountains*, 5.
52. *Ibid*.
53. Anon., *Extracts from Letters to Rev. Dr. Norman McLeod*, passim.
54. SRO, HD7/26, Correspondence from Highland landowners.
55. *Relief Correspondence*, Marquis of Lorne to Sir G. Gray, 25 July 1846.
56. *Destitution Papers*, Second Statement of the Free Church of Scotland.
57. *Ibid*., Plan of Operation for the Distributing Committee, 3-4.
58. Flinn, ed., *Scottish Population History*, 169.
59. *Ibid*., 235.
60. Arthur J. Taylor, *Laissez-faire and State Intervention in Nineteenth-Century Britain* (London, 1972), 59.
61. R.D.C. Black, *Economic Thought and the Irish Question* (Cambridge, 1960).
62. *Relief Correspondence*, Trevelyan to Mr. Horne, 20 September 1846. The phrase is italicised in the original source.
63. SRO, HD7/26, Correspondence from Highland landowners.
64. *Relief Correspondence*, Lord Advocate to Sir G. Gray, 2 September 1846; Trevelyan to Sir John McNeill, 20 October 1846.
65. *Ibid*., Trevelyan to Horne, 20 September 1846.
66. *Gentleman's Magazine*, 3rd ser., XIII, 372.
67. *Relief Correspondence*, Sir G. Gray to Sir John McNeill, 28 September, 1847.
68. *Ibid*., Sir John McNeill to Sir G. Gray, 15 September 1846; 12 October 1846; Trevelyan to Coffin, 6 October 1846; Trevelyan to Marquis of Lorne, 28 January 1847; SRO, HD6/2, Treasury Correspondence, Coffin to Baird, 18 March 1847; *Witness*, 25 September 1847.
69. *Relief Correspondence*, Trevelyan to the Lord Advocate, 14 December 1846.
70. SRO, HD6/2, Treasury Correspondence, Coffin to Trevelyan, 28 September 1847.
71. *Ibid*.
72. *Relief Correspondence*, Ellice to Chancellor of the Exchequer, 20 September 1846.
73. *Ibid*., Trevelyan to McNeill, 13 October 1846.
74. See, for example, *Witness*, 25 September 1847.
75. *Relief Correspondence*, Sir J. McNeill to Sir G. Gray, 27 September 1836; *Destitution Papers*, First Report of Edinburgh Section (1849), 20, 46.
76. *Relief Correspondence*, Trevelyan to Coffin, 16 October 1846.
77. See, for instance, SRO, HD6/2, Treasury Correspondence, Coffin to Commander Maclean, 15 February 1847.
78. *Ibid*., Coffin to Trevelyan, 28 September 1847.
79. *McNeill Report*, Appendix A, 25.
80. NLS, Sutherland Estate Papers, Dep. 313/1174, James Loch to Sutherland factors, 6 January 1847.
81. See above, pp.92-3.
82. SRO, HD6/2, Treasury Correspondence, Mr Shaw to Sir E. Coffin, 1 February 1847.
83. *Relief Correspondence*, Trevelyan to Coffin, 28 December 1846.
84. *Ibid*., 17 February 1847.

85. SRO, HD6/2, Treasury Correspondence, Coffin to Trevelyan, 26 February 1847.
86. *Relief Correspondence*, Trevelyan to Coffin, 17 February 1847.
87. *Ibid.*
88. Smout, 'Strange Intervention of Edward Twistleton', 218-239.
89. For their later activities see below, Ch. 11.
90. *Dictionary of National Biography* (London, 1909), XII.
91. Details on Trevelyan are derived from *Dictionary of National Biography* (London, 1909), XIX; Jenifer Hart, 'Sir Charles Trevelyan at the Treasury', *English Historical Review*, LXXV (1960), 94-110; C. Woodham-Smith, *The Great Hunger* (London, 1962), 58-61, 415.
92. SRO, HD6/2, Treasury Correspondence, Sir J. McNeill to Trevelyan, 8 March 1847.
93. *Ibid.*, 15 March 1847.
94. Richards, *Leviathan of Wealth*, esp. Part III.
95. SRO, HD7/46, Trevelyan-Skene Correspondence, 2 March 1848.
96. SRO, HD6/2, Treasury Correspondence, Trevelyan to Baird, 19 March 1847.
97. This account of the Free Church's activities is based on: *Destitution Papers*, First and Second Statements of the Free Church, *passim*, 1846; *Witness*, 1846-7, *passim*.
98. Bruce, *Letters on the Present Condition of the Highlands*, 30-1.
99. SRO, HD6/2, Membership of Central Board of Management (1847).
100. *Dictionary of National Biography* (London, 1909), XVIII, 338.
101. *Destitution Papers*, Second Report by the Committee of Management to the Edinburgh Section (1850), 48.
102. SRO, HD7/46, Trevelyan-Skene Correspondence, 1848-50.
103. *Destitution Papers*, First Report of the Central Board (1847).
104. SRO, HD6/2, Treasury Correspondence, Coffin to Trevelyan, 2 September 1847.
105. *Destitution Papers*, Second Report of Central Board (1847), 10-11.
106. SRO, HD6/6, Note of Men sent to Railway Contractors, 1847; HD16/57, Employment Committee Minutes.
107. *Destitution Papers*, Reports of Edinburgh Section (1848), 2.
108. SRO, HD21, Reports on Local Committees, Wester Ross (1847), *passim*.
109. *Scotsman*, 21 July 1847; 3 February 1847.
110. *Destitution Papers*, Case for the Edinburgh Section (1847), 20.
111. SRO, HD6/2, Treasury Correspondence, Coffin to Trevelyan, 2 September 1847.
112. SRO, HD21, Reports on Local Committees, Skye and Wester Ross.
113. *Scotsman*, 10 February 1847; 1 September 1847.
114. *Ibid.*, 21 July 1847.
115. *Ibid.*, 1 September 1847.
116. NLS, Sutherland Estate Papers, Dep. 313/1176, James Loch to Duke of Sutherland, 21 January 1848.
117. SRO, HD6/2, Treasury Correspondence, McNeill to Trevelyan, 15 March 1847.
118. *Ibid.*, 13 March 1847; Baird to McNeill, 16 March 1847; McNeill to Coffin, 20 March 1847.
119. *Destitution Papers*, Memorandum of Points Discussed at a Private Meeting held within the Highland Destitution Committee Rooms, 1 October 1847.
120. *Ibid.*, Memorandum by Sir E.P. Coffin (1847); SRO, HD7/46, Trevelyan-Skene Correspondence.
121. *Ibid.*, Second Report by the Committee of Management of the Edinburgh Section for 1850, 15.
122. SRO, HD7/46, Trevelyan to Skene, 2 March 1848.
123. *Ibid.*
124. SRO, HD7/46, Skene to Trevelyan, 21 February 1848.
125. *Ibid.*, 1 March 1848.
126. *Ibid.*, Trevelyan to Skene, 26 March 1848.
127. *Destitution Papers*, Special Report by the Committee of Management to the Edinburgh Section, 29 March 1849, 249; *Witness*, 12 June 1847.

128. SRO, HD7/46, Trevelyan to Fishbourne, 17 January 1848; Captain Fishbourne to Trevelyan, 31 January 1848.
129. *Destitution Papers*, Second Report by the Committee of Management for the Edinburgh Section (1850), 10.
130. Mulock, *Western Highlands and Islands*, 81.
131. *Destitution Papers*, Report of the Edinburgh Section for 1848, 3, 8.
132. *Ibid.*, Second Report of the Edinburgh Section (1850), 10.
133. *Ibid.*, Memorandum as communicated to Sir E.P. Coffin, 3 September 1847.
134. SRO, HD7/46, Trevelyan to Capt. Fishbourne, 24 January 1848.
135. *Ibid.*, 17 January 1848.
136. *Ibid.*, Fishbourne to Trevelyan, 31 January 1848.
137. Murray, *Scottish Handloom Weavers*, 130-151. Compare the régime in some Scottish prisons in the early 1860s. Breakfast: 8oz. oatmeal (porridge), ¾pt. milk; Dinner: 2 pts. broth with 8oz wheaten bread or 2½lbs. potatoes with ¾pt. milk and 4oz. bread; Supper: 1½lbs. potatoes or 4oz. oatmeal made into porridge with ½pt. buttermilk. *Edinburgh Medical Journal* (1865). I owe this reference to Prof. Christopher Smout.
138. Smout, 'Strange Intervention of Edward Twistleton', 235.
139. *Destitution Papers*, Second Report to the Edinburgh Section, 14 January 1848, 31.
140. *Ibid.*, Instructions to the Resident Inspectors for the Discharge of their Permanent Duties (1848), 12.
141. SRO, HD3/10, Portree Letterbook, 1847-8.
142. *Ibid.*
143. *Destitution Papers*, Instructions to the Resident Inspectors for the Discharge of their Permanent Duty (1848), 12.
144. *Ibid.*, 13.
145. *Ibid.*, Report by Capt. Rose, Resident Inspector, Wester Ross, 1 April 1848, 33-4.
146. *Ibid.*, Instructions to Resident Inspectors (1848).
147. SRO, HD10/1-47, Letters from and to Capt. Fishbourne; HD11/1-12, Correspondence of H.B. Rose; HD15/1-12, Correspondence of Capt. Ewan Ross (Ullapool); HD3/10, Portree Letterbook, 1847-8.
148. *Destitution Papers*, Second Report by the Committee of Management for the Edinburgh Section (1850), *passim*.
149. *Ibid.* The following description of the System is based on this source.
150. Mulock, *Western Highlands and Islands*, 97.
151. *Destitution Papers*, Second Report by the Committee of Management for the Edinburgh Section (1850), 25.
152. SRO, HD7/47, Skene to Trevelyan, 21 February 1848.
153. Mulock, *Western Highlands and Islands*, 81-2.
154. *McNeill Report*, Appendix A, 13, 103.
155. Flinn, ed., *Scottish Population History*, 234.
156. *McNeill Report*, Appendix A, 103.
157. *Destitution Papers*, Second Report to the Edinburgh Section (1848), 31.
158. *McNeill Report*, Appendix A, 13.
159. SRO, HD7/47, Skene to Trevelyan, 21 February 1848.
160. *Ibid.*
161. *Ibid.*
162. *Ibid.*
163. Mulock, *Western Highlands and Islands*, 81.
164. *Destitution Papers*, E.J.Fishbourne to W. Skene, 26 February 1848.
165. *Ibid.*, Fishbourne to Eliot, 29 April 1848.
166. Dunvegan Castle, Macleod of Macleod Muniments, 659/8/1, N. Ferguson to Miss Macleod, 2 June 1848.
167. *Ibid.*, 659/8/2, N. Ferguson to Miss Macleod, 4 April 1848.
168. *Destitution Papers*, Second Report by Edinburgh Section (1850), 19-20.

169. *Ibid.*, Capt. H.B. Rose to Capt. Eliot, 1 May 1848.

170. Dunvegan Castle, Macleod of Macleod Muniments, 659/11/3, E. Gibbons to Miss Macleod, 27 June 1849.

171. *Destitution Papers*, Capt. Fishbourne to Capt. Eliot, 29 April 1848.

172. SRO, HD20/36, Memorandum as to the State of Strathaird (1848).

173. *Destitution Papers*, Second Report by Edinburgh Section (1850), 52.

174. *Ibid.*, Seventh Report by the Glasgow Section (1847), Extracts from Dr. Boyter's Reports, 31.

175. *Ibid.*, Report on the Outer Hebrides (1849), 2, 32.

176. The Section's initiatives in this area are suitably summarised in *Destitution Papers*, Second Report by Edinburgh Section (1850), 8-36. Unless otherwise indicated, all references hereafter in this chapter are to this source.

177. *Ibid.*, 26.

178. *Ibid.*, 32.

179. *Ibid.*, 33.

180. See below, pp.285-6.

181. SRO, AF7/85, Survey by Laurence Lamb, Assistant Inspector of the Fishery, 30 September 1850.

182. SRO, Home Office (Scotland), Domestic Entry Books, RH2/4/240, H. Waddington to Macleod of Macleod, 7 December 1850; *Illustrated London News*, 28 May 1853; *Witness*, 20 September 1851.

6
Temporary Migration

Historians are now more aware of the pivotal significance of seasonal and temporary migration for nineteenth-century Highland society.[1] The annual movement to seek work in the Lowland economy had a number of vital effects on the Highlands as a whole. The income which accrued helped to support the maintenance of a precarious existence in the north and contributed to the payment of rental when returns from cattle, kelp and fish declined from the 1820s. It allowed more people to survive in the crofting region than might otherwise have done if they had had to depend entirely on the slender and contracting economic resources of the indigenous peasant economy. In this way, temporary migration helped to slow down the rate of permanent movement which could have occurred on a much greater scale, especially from the north-west and the islands, if such opportunities had not grown in significance.

Yet, despite its importance, we know little in detail about the nature, scale and form of temporary migration. Reference to it appears only fleetingly and occasionally in contemporary sources. The national census is a most unsatisfactory guide. Within the census categories, it is not possible to differentiate in a meaningful way between 'temporary' and 'permanent' migrants, especially since there is evidence that some 'temporary' migrants, such as seamen, stayed away for several years before returning to the household of their birth. Again, two of the most popular types of temporary movement, for work at the fisheries or the grain harvest, tended to peak in the late summer and early autumn. The census, however, was normally taken in the spring or early summer months of March, April or June. Even, therefore, when enumerators were asked to estimate the numbers 'temporarily absent' at the time of the census they were likely, because of the date when the count was taken, to under-record the annual scale of temporary migration. Because of the inadequacies of the census this form of migration defies precise quantitative analysis.

One of the advantages, however, of exploring temporary migration in the 1840s and 1850s is that it is possible to gain more insight into it then than for most other periods of the nineteenth century. The famine generated much valuable data in the press, government and other sources which enable the historian to piece together a fuller profile of this vital aspect of Highland social history than has been available hitherto. In the first section of the chapter, the general characteristics of temporary migration on the eve of the potato famine are examined. The rest of the discussion explores the movements which took place during the subsistence crisis and analyses their increasing scale, their impact on peasant society and the overall significance of temporary migration in the economic and social history of the famine period.

1

By the early 1840s, the income earned by temporary migrants had become a key component of the local economies of many crofting districts. The census enumerators on census day 6 June 1841 were asked to estimate the numbers 'temporarily absent' from their normal place of residence. The figures they collected then and in the subsequent censuses of 1851 and 1861 are assembled in Appendix 8. They reveal that temporary migration was occurring from a significant number of areas. Of fifty-six designated 'crofting' parishes, thirty-two had a proportion of their resident populations living elsewhere on census day, and in a majority of cases the enumerator recorded that those absent were 'at work in the south'. The number of individuals involved could be very considerable: 568, or fourteen per cent, of the total parish population of Kilfinichen in Mull were absent as were 495, or twelve per cent, of the inhabitants of Tiree. Temporary migration also seems to have been more common in the poorer crofting districts of the west than in the farming region of the central and eastern Highlands. Of fifty 'farming' parishes listed in Appendix 8, only ten had significant numbers 'temporarily absent' on census day.

The enumerators' estimates, however, though valuable, undoubtedly under-record the real scale of temporary migration. This was partly for the reason given earlier: that the census was taken before the main period for movement. But it was also because the zeal and accuracy of the enumerators varied when they were asked to compile supplementary estimates of this type, especially since the criteria for deciding who should be counted among the 'temporarily absent' was inevitably a matter of personal judgement. It is evident from the books themselves that several simply ignored the instruction to record this group. When a broader range of source material is examined, the number of crofting parishes with traditions of temporary migration rises substantially from thirty-two to forty-four of the total of fifty-six.[2] The information on which this figure is based is presented in Appendix 9. Of the twelve parishes unaccounted for, evidence was lacking in the case of eight, making it impossible to determine whether this form of migration was occurring or not.

On the basis of the data assembled in both Appendices 8 and 9 it is apparent that temporary migration was common throughout most parts of the crofting region by the early 1840s. Only in some parts of the Outer Hebrides was it still relatively underdeveloped. While there was extensive migration to the fisheries of the east coast and Caithness from Lewis and, to a lesser extent, from Harris, there was little evidence of movement to the mainland from Barra, South Uist and Benbecula at the southern tip of the Long Island. Partly this may have been because, unlike Lewis, these parishes did not yet have regular steamship or other shipping connections to the mainland. In addition, however, there was a more serious obstacle. In both Barra and South Uist, kelp manufacture was substantially maintained into the 1840s by the proprietor to provide employment for the people. The kelp season endured throughout the summer until the end of August and so effectively prevented an exodus of people from these parishes, precisely at the time when demand for seasonal labour on the mainland was on the increase.[3] Elsewhere on the Long Island, notably in Lewis, it was reported that the contraction of kelp manufacture from 1826-7 had given the initial impetus to the great migration to the east-coast fisheries which had become a characteristic feature of life there by the 1840s.[4]

With the exception of these areas, however, the ability of most communities in the crofting region to pay rent and buy grain in years of shortage had come to depend in large part not only on cattle sales but on earnings from temporary movement. The very fact of the absence of large numbers of people in the summer and early months was a great boon. It meant fewer mouths to feed at the most critical time of the year, the period when the old grain and potato harvests were almost exhausted and the new had yet to be gathered. The Free Church of Scotland was broadly correct when it maintained in 1847 that, from '. . . the central and northern districts of the Highlands and from the Islands nearest the mainland considerable numbers have been in the habit of resorting to the Lowlands for employment'.[5] But there was also much variation in the scale of migration between parishes in this region. Of all the areas he visited in 1851, Sir John McNeill estimated that the island of Skye 'depended more upon employment at a distance than any other district'.[6] On the Skeabost estate there the crofts in good years could maintain a family in food but all rents were paid by working in the south.[7] So extensive had temporary migration become in the Skye parish of Strath that, '. . . in consequence of the constant intercourse held by the natives with the low country, language is very much corrupted with a mixture of English words and phrases'.[8] Of a parish population of 3243 men, 500 were reckoned to leave annually for the Lowlands.[9] From the area of Corrie on Lord Macdonald's estate, at least ninety young men went to the south from the four townships of the district.[10] Several other parts of the crofting region had similar traditions. 'Almost all the young men' of Applecross and the vast majority of those from the other Wester Ross parishes of Gairloch, Lochbroom and Lochcarron went to the east-coast fishing.[11] In Lewis, 'of the class of small crofters there are few families in which there is an able-bodied man who do not send one member to the Caithness fishery'.[12] Temporary migration was the chief support of crofting families in the Tongue and Dunrobin districts of the Sutherland estate.[13] On the island of Tiree the small tenants and cottars relied mainly on earnings from work on the mainland to buy meal and pay rent.[14]

Yet there were curious anomalies. Even in Skye there was considerable variation within the islands in the extent of temporary movement. The clerk to Lord Macdonald's chamberlain noted the effect that this diversity had on rent yields. In parts of the parishes of Kilmuir in Snizort and in Sleat rents were paid more regularly than in Portree and Strath. He attributed this to the fact that in the first three parishes 'a larger proportion of persons go from those districts to the south, and there earn the means of paying rent'.[15] Again, in Sutherland, it was common for young people to go to the Lowlands from the central and eastern districts of the estate, but the custom was not as strong in the far western parishes.[16] Migration to the east-coast fisheries was very popular in Lewis, but occurred on a much smaller scale from the adjacent parish of Harris in the Outer Hebrides.[17] Glenelg had weak traditions of temporary migration but neighbouring districts in mainland western Inverness-shire had strong connections with the labour markets of the south.[18]

No simple explanation can be offered for this range of different experiences within the same geographical zone. Temporary migration was induced by the pressure of want, the collapse or decline of alternative local sources of income and employment and the stress of rising population. Obviously these forces could vary enormously in their impact within the confines of a single parish or even an individual estate. In addition, the nature of local economic specialisations often dictated the extent to which different communities participated. There could be a problem of conflicting claims for claims for labour. In the case of both Harris and the western parishes of Sutherland, for instance, the success of the local fishery in some years rendered a great migration to the Caithness, Aberdeen and Moray coasts at once less necessary and more difficult.[19] The persistence of kelp manufacture in some parts of the Outer Hebrides has already been noted as a factor limiting temporary migration from that area.[20]

Evidence on the social composition of temporary migrants is both fragile and vague. However, it is reasonably clear that not all social classes took part in equal numbers. Contemporary sources place special emphasis on the role of young, unmarried males and females, though increasingly heads of household, especially those of the cottar class, felt the need to trek south and east in search of employment. Local officers of the Central Board during the famine noted that single men did not often appear in the relief lists during spring and summer because the majority had gone for work elsewhere.[21] In Applecross, Colonsay, Glenelg, Islay, Lochbroom, Mull, Skye and Sutherland the largest number of temporary migrants were single men and women.[22] However, married men did feature in the movement. It was specifically reported of Ardnamurchan, where there was substantial migration for work in the dye-works of Glasgow, that 'a very large number . . . leave *their wives and families* for a great portion of the year'.[23] Again, in Tiree, while 'a great portion of the young, unmarried population, especially of females, found harvest work in the south', the Argyll estate also estimated that about one third of the heads of tenant households paying rent of less than £5 per annum also travelled to the low country.[24] Similar evidence of the movement of married men comes from the parishes of Lochbroom and Gairloch.[25] The crop failures of the 1840s ensured that heads of household would play an even greater part in temporary migration than they had done in most years before.[26]

Migration to the Lowlands for seasonal work seems also to have been mainly associated with the poorest classes in the Highlands. Virtually every observer who commented on the movement of people to the south and east stressed that most migrants came from the smaller tenantry and the cottar class. With limited land available to them, these groups suffered most from underemployment and had therefore both the need and the opportunity to venture elsewhere in search of work. They were also less restricted by the annual routine of preparing the soil, of sowing, harvesting and supervision of stock than the better-off crofters. Cottars, for instance, normally only had a small patch of land devoted exclusively to potato cultivation. In their case, their very survival depended on the local opportunities for fishing or on work elsewhere. A typical pattern was described in the Kishorn area of the parish of Lochcarron. It was estimated that about one in every four crofting families sent a member to the east-coast fishery. There were in addition thirty-three cottar families who 'hire a piece of ground, by the year, from one of the tenants, in which they plant potatoes'. Almost all the young men of this class and 'such of the heads of household who are young and active' went to Caithness or elsewhere for work.[27] Again, in the Torridon and Sheildaig districts of the parish of Applecross, the vast majority of temporary migrants were also drawn from the semi-landless class. The ground officer of the local estate described how their subsistence depended on wages earned in other parts of the country. An entire way of life was built on the foundations of earnings acquired in the south and east. Some 'who had not numerous families' engaged in rural labour in different parts of Easter Ross and other districts. The majority, however, relied on the annual herring fishery along the Caithness and Aberdeen coasts for employment. As soon as their children were old enough, they went to service in Morayshire or elsewhere.[28] Here was a social system in which both young and old were forced to leave for long periods and where the home and the land did not provide enough for a basic existence even in good years.

2

In the middle decades of the eighteenth century, the dominant form of temporary migration was for harvest work in the Lowlands.[29] By and large most migrants were women and the majority came from the southern and eastern Highlands. The period spent away from home was limited to the three to four weeks it normally took to cut the grain harvest in late August and early September. Other forms of migration, to the Clyde fisheries, domestic service, industrial employment on the printfields and, especially later in the eighteenth century, army and navy, had also developed. But in the 1750s and 1760s temporary migration in most years was mainly seasonal, limited to those parts of the Highlands closest to the Lowlands, and overwhelmingly related to agricultural employment.

A century later the pattern had altered in a quite fundamental fashion. As already shown, temporary movement had spread to virtually all parts of the Highlands and Islands. Only in some districts of the Long Island was it limited in scale. In the 1750s, income from seasonal employment was but a marginal element in the economies of a few areas. A century later, the economic and social structure of entire regions had come to depend on it. There had also been a remarkable expansion in the range of jobs taken by migrants from the Highlands. It was this extension in the number of employments which gradually altered the nature of migration itself. In many cases, it was no longer confined to short, seasonal phases and restricted to agriculture. The growing industrial and urban economy had spawned a new series of tasks, each with its own peak periods of demand for labour in the year. It became possible to move between different occupations and so extend the period away from home for several months and even years. In this way 'seasonal' migration became 'temporary' in nature and so developed as an even more significant source of income for the deprived areas of the north. Unfortunately, however, it was far from being a panacea. Temporary migrants were concentrated in the poorest-paid jobs and were exceedingly vulnerable to the ebb and flow of the trade cycle. As will be seen in more detail below, the market for temporary labour could be very depressed at the time when Highland society had most need of the earnings of its migrant workers.[30]

Agriculture

By the 1840s, agricultural employment no longer maintained the dominance of earlier periods but it was still a very important outlet for seasonal workers. Examination of Appendix 9 reveals that a rough regional division of labour had evolved. Migrants from the Inner Hebrides, mainland Argyll and parts of western Inverness-shire tended by and large to seek rural employment in the central and south-eastern Lowlands. Indeed, for the inhabitants of Mull, Tiree, Coll, Islay and Colonsay, agricultural work in the south seems still to have been the main type of temporary employment in the mid-nineteenth century. Skye presents a more complex pattern. Migration for the harvest and other agricultural tasks was still very significant especially for young females, but in some parishes it was balanced by an additional flow of people to the fisheries of the east coast. Elsewhere, in the Western Highlands and Islands, notably in Lewis, Harris, Sutherland and most parishes in Wester Ross, temporary migration to the Caithness and Aberdeenshire fisheries was most important. Even here, however, there was a subordinate movement for work in the farms of Easter Ross, Caithness and Moray. In any case, agricultural and fishing employment were not mutually exclusive. One contemporary traveller met women on the roads leading from Wick, 'returning from the herring harvest and now going to that of the corn'.[31] On the east coast, the herring season lasted from July through to August, thus fitting neatly into the period immediately before the grain harvest. Thus, at the end of the fishing season in 1849, it was reported that '. . . the multitudes of gutters and packers are taking a fortnight's rest after their profitable labours and are preparing to go to the harvest field'.[32]

The continued significance of agricultural employment reflected the labour requirements of the farming classes of Lowland Scotland. The Agricultural Revolution had massively increased the productivity of the land. One estimate by the contemporary expert on rural affairs, George Robertson, suggested that between 1740 and 1829 corn production had doubled while that of animal food had multiplied sixfold.[33] But agriculture still remained an essentially labour-intensive activity, a matter of sweat and muscle rather than new machinery. Despite some experimentation in mechanised reaping, new technology did not become significant until the 1850s and 1860s.[34] Indeed, the major innovation before the 1840s in harvesting was a revolution in hand-tools, with the scythe becoming more popular at the expense of the sickle. At the same time the spread of green crops, a vital element in the new agriculture, ensured that the farmer's busy season, and hence his need for seasonal workers, extended for a longer period in the year. Clover and turnips required an almost gardenly care.[35] From May until harvest, turnip fields were subjected to dunging, a double hoeing and thinning. As a result, 'High farming of the present day requires and actually pays for, more manual labour than at any former period'.[36]

While improved agriculture had more need of reliable seasonal workers, organisational changes from the later eighteenth century made it more difficult to recruit an adequate supply in some districts from local sources. Two factors were important. First, before c.1820, subtenancy was eliminated in most lowland areas outside the north-east counties. In the old world, the families of the subtenants had been the main reservoir of seasonal labour for the bigger farmers of the neighbourhood. As subtenancy was crushed, many farmers looked to the Highlands, Ireland and local towns and villages to make up the supply. By using seasonal workers from distant regions with a labour surplus, farmers effectively reduced their costs. They were able to cut their permanent labour force to a minimum. There was less need to employ additional workers for long periods simply to ensure a reliable supply at critical times. In addition, they saved on accommodation costs because seasonal migrants lived rough, in barns and farm outbuildings.[37] Thus, during the first half of the nineteenth century the young men and women of the Highlands and Ireland formed the main reserve army of labour for the prosperous agriculture of central and southern Scotland.

Secondly, by the middle decades of the nineteenth century, increased migration from country to town in the Lowland countryside was making recruitment of seasonal workers in parts of the eastern counties more difficult. The families of handloom weavers and linen spinners had in the past been key sources of harvest labour. But as industry gradually concentrated in the coalfields of the central lowlands and factory organisation in the larger towns hastened the demise of many textile village communities it became more difficult to maintain this supply.[38] As one parliamentary inquiry concluded in the 1860s: 'Increased means of locomotion and improved machinery are putting an end to the village tradesman, the handloom weavers . . . They are no longer near to aid the small staff of the farm in times of pressure nor to keep up the supply of young men and women necessary for that staff'.[39] The problem was by no means a general one. In Lanarkshire, Renfrewshire, Ayrshire, Fife and Dunbartonshire, farmers still drew on the families of industrial workers for harvest labour.[40] But in some other districts there was even more reason to depend on areas such as the Highlands with their abundant population of underemployed workers.

This suggestion is, however, difficult to reconcile with the traditional belief that after *c*.1820 Lowland agriculture came to rely more on Irish than Highland migrants. It has been asserted that the Irish flooded the rural labour market in the nineteenth century. According to this view, they worked harder, accepted lower wages and, with the extension of steam navigation from Ulster to the Clyde, reached the hiring fairs more quickly than their northern rivals.[41] It is true that Irish seasonal migration markedly increased in the 1830s and 1840s but it is more difficult to accept that they monopolised seasonal agricultural tasks in the manner described. One obvious reason for scepticism is the evidence already presented both in this chapter and in Appendix 9 of the continuation and expansion of temporary migration from the Highlands for agricultural work in the Lowlands. There are a number of additional arguments which suggest that the traditional view is at least exaggerated in its claims.

The thesis is almost exclusively based on evidence submitted to the Select Committee on the State of the Irish Poor in Great Britain (1836) and the Select Committee on Emigration, Scotland (1841). Both sources must be treated with caution. The 1836 Report drew mainly on the opinion of those who had a vested interest in reducing Irish immigration and who tended therefore to exaggerate its adverse effect on Scottish society. The majority of witnesses were from the western counties. Irish dominance in these districts might be anticipated for reasons of geographical proximity and because of the traditional migrant connection between Ayr, Wigtown and Ireland in the eighteenth century. Several witnesses to the Select Committee on Emigration in 1841 had another axe to grind. Many were determined to demonstrate that mass emigration was the only possible solution to the Highland problem. Not surprisingly, therefore, to support their case, they asserted that even agricultural work in the Lowlands was no longer a realistic option for the unfortunate population of the north because of Irish competition.

The impact of the Irish on the harvest labour market was directly related to the growing popularity of the scythe at the expense of the sickle.[42] The scythe could cut most grains more quickly than the sickle as long as the corn was standing undisturbed by heavy winds or rain and on level ground. It was, however, a man's tool, requiring considerable physical strength. The sickle, on the other hand, could easily be used by women. Indeed, some contemporaries argued that it was more suited to females because the corn was cut low down and so necessitated much bending and stooping. Since the majority of Irish migrants were male, and most Highland harvesters were female, the victory of the scythe might ensure the supremacy of the Irish over the Highlanders.

But this notion is too simple. Highland migration for work in the Lowland countryside was able to survive despite the greater Irish presence for a variety of reasons. Irish and Highland harvest labour was partly complementary. Even in districts where the scythe was adopted (and this did not occur in all areas at the same pace), grain was sometimes cut by the Irish and then collected, bound and stacked by Gaelic-speaking lasses from the Western Isles.[43] Again, young men from the Highlands found jobs as day labourers on Lowland farms. The expansion in the construction of more effective drainage systems in the 1840s and 1850s yielded much employment of this type.[44] Competition to obtain work in the grain harvest fields may have become more acute but this was partly balanced by the additional requirements for seasonal labour in spring and summer associated with the preparation, sowing and thinning of an extended acreage of green crops.[45] There seems also to have been something of a regional division of labour between the Irish and Highland migrants. The Irish were strongly represented in most parts of the central Lowlands and south-east region. But they do not appear to have penetrated in any numbers north or west of the Tay. As late as the 1830s, it could be said, '. . . the Irish labourers, wanderers as they are never penetrate so far and the Highland mountaineers who "rush like a torrent down upon the vale" at the beginning of harvest receive a momentum, that cannot be arrested until they arrive at the Lothians'.[46] The northern counties of Aberdeen and parts of Banff derived their own indigenous seasonal labour force from the crofts of the north-east region. Elsewhere, however, in Caithness, Easter Ross, eastern Inverness-shire, southern Argyllshire, Perthshire, Stirling, Angus and Forfar, there was still much opportunity for the seasonal migrants of the crofting region. Indeed, close study of harvest wage rates for other areas in the contemporary press suggests that the size of the grain harvest and the speed with which it ripened were almost as significant as the supply of labour in dictating demand for Highland and all other types of seasonal labour in the 1840s and 1850s.[47]

Fishing

The ambitious plans to promote a prosperous and successful herring fishery in Hebridean waters in the eighteenth century developed by the British Fisheries Society, southern commercial interests and Highland landlords did not bear enduring fruit.[48] By the 1820s it was apparent that such progress as had been achieved in the later eighteenth and early nineteenth centuries was likely to be short-lived. Fishing remained an integral part of the way of life in the Western Highlands but in most areas it was carried on to satisfy local needs. The white fishery had a continuing importance, and from time to time the herring shoals did visit the northern sea lochs but the commercial sector remained a pale shadow of the flourishing industry of the early 1800s. Over time, the herring fishery became more concentrated than ever before along the lochs of the Clyde estuary and an even bigger and successsful enterprise developed in Caithness, Aberdeen and Moray. Yet, although the commercial centre of herring fishing lay elsewhere, the communities of the Western Highlands and Islands were able to gain in some degree because they provided an essential supply of seasonal labour both for the north-east and south-west industries.

Even in the eighteenth century, there had been a significant connection between the Clyde fisheries and the population of the Western Highlands. On one estimate, some eighty-nine per cent of the crew members of herring 'busses' based at Greenock in the 1790s were Highland-born.[49] It was said that '. . . along the coasts where the busses resort, many of the inhabitants come every year from one or two hundred miles to hire on board the busses at Rothesay, Campbeltown and other fishing ports'.[50] In the nineteenth century, however, the herring fishery developed most rapidly and successfully along the coasts of the north-east counties of Caithness and Aberdeen.[51] The industry concentrated on particular ports, such as Wick, Peterhead, Fraserburgh, Aberdeen itself and a number of smaller centres. The structure of fishing in these areas ensured that a partnership of mutual benefit could evolve with the impoverished Western Highlands and Islands. The boats were operated through a system of owner-fishermen. The normal pattern was for five or six men, all belonging to the same town or village and often related, to furnish the capital and most of the labour. But they could not provide from their own resources all the extra hands required at the peak season in July and August. It became the custom, therefore, and one which was firmly established by the 1840s, for each crew to be strengthened by the addition of one or two 'strangers'. These were commonly men from the Western Highlands and Islands and from Orkney. The Highlanders predominated. Again, the expansion in output forced up demand for workers in the highly labour-intensive tasks of gutting and packing. It was reckoned that on average three experienced females were required throughout the season to handle the catch of one boat. This demand was partially satisfied by the young women of the north-west Highlands and Islands.

This relationship between the north-east and the north-west was based on mutual needs. The latter region had a surplus of labour but a population with considerable maritime skills. The vast majority of the seasonal migrants to the north-east were natives of Lewis, Wester Ross and some parts of Skye and West Sutherland. These were areas with considerable fishing traditions in their own right. Temporary employment in Caithness or Aberdeen blended well with the customary cycle of fishing activity in the west. The high season in north-eastern waters took place between the earlier herring fishery in the Minch and the later white fishing in the Western Highlands. At the busiest times there was a great migration to the ports of Aberdeenshire and the Caithness coast. One observer reckoned that the population of Wick rose from 6700 to over 16,000 during the fishing season.[52] Official figures revealed that 11,710 people were involved in the Wick fishery in 1846. Of this number twenty-six per cent (2639) were female gutters and sixty-two per cent (7269) fishermen and seamen.[53] Even these totals may understate the true figures. In 1849, for instance, the *John O'Groats Journal* accused the Fishing Board of under-recording the numbers employed by between one third to one half.[54] The Town Council of Wick itself estimated that during the seven weeks of the herring season the port attracted 'a surplus population' of 10,000, many of whom were migrants from the Western Highlands and Islands.[55] A year later, the Council reckoned that 5000-6000 of this seasonal population were 'young, strong and healthy persons from the Highlands of Scotland'.[56] So great was the migration that the Free Church supplied Gaelic-speaking catechists to minister to the spiritual needs of the labourers.[57]

Industry, Construction and Domestic Service

The availability of seasonal jobs in agriculture and fishing indirectly reflected the rapid urban and industrial expansion which had taken place in Scotland since the later eighteenth century. It was the demand for foods and raw materials from the growing towns and manufacturing centres which created the greater opportunities in farming and fishing. Moreover, as industry concentrated in the central Lowlands, peripheral regions, such as the Western Highlands, were rapidly denuded of those weak alternatives to subsistence agriculture which had flourished briefly in the later eighteenth century. One after another, linen manufacture, whisky distilling and commercial fishing went into decline or virtually disappeared altogether as they were systematically crushed by the force of Lowland economic competition. A vast pool of underemployed labour emerged in the Highlands and expanded further as the great sheep farms weakened the old cattle economy. A convenient and cheap supply of seasonal workers for the booming industrial and agricultural regions of Scotland had been created from the economic trauma of Highland society in the decades after the Napoleonic Wars. In one sense, temporary migration simply reflected the fact that the comparative advantage of many districts in the Highlands by the 1840s had become limited to the supply of low-cost labour for the Lowland economy and grazing ground for sheep.

One of the basic features of this form of migration was that its range of diversity increased in the nineteenth century. A whole variety of tasks had a seasonal cycle. Construction work, dock labouring and textile manufacturing tended to expand in spring and summer but fall back in winter. At the same time, the new industrial and urban economy brought into being a series of additional occupations and extended the scope of others which were longer-established. Work on railway construction merged into harvesting and employment on the fisheries was often followed by labouring in the fields. The inhabitants of the parish of Carnoch '. . . contrive to subsist in summer by going in search of work to Edinburgh, Glasgow, Paisley, to railways, harvest work, by driving cattle to the south country markets or by fishing at Caithness'.[58] Men from Avoch in Ross-shire spent the summer at field work and the early winter building roads in Aberdeenshire.[59] Those from Kilmalie in Inverness divided their time between labouring in farms and the Glasgow dye works.[60] This industry where, unusually, employment could be obtained throughout the winter months, was also favoured by the people of Tiree and Ardnamurchan.[61] 'A great many' of the seasonal migrants of Tiree were employed at the famous factory owned by the Tennant family at St. Rollox in Glasgow.[62] The Glasgow and Vale of Leven calico printing works in the early 1840s offered employment to between 4000 and 5000 children. The local factory inspector observed in 1846 that 'very many' came annually from the Highlands and Ireland.[63]

It was common for the young men of Mull, Lochalsh, Gigha and Applecross to go to sea, sometimes for several years on end, while domestic service was probably the most rapidly growing occupation for single females.[64] From around the Tobermory area in Mull 'a considerable number of young women go annually to seek service in Glasgow or other places in the south'.[65] Similar reports came from Islay, Glenelg, Colonsay and other parishes in Mull and Skye.[66] In the early nineteenth century, Hebridean girls employed in the Lowland towns usually returned home during the winter months.[67] Between 1851 and 1891 about a quarter of all women engaged in private households in Greenock were of Highland origin and, in the principal migrant area in central Paisley, sixty-two per cent of employed single females of Highland parentage in 1851 worked as domestic servants.[68]

For men, navvying on the railways had assumed great significance by the early 1840s and was to become even more important during the construction 'mania' of 1846-7. Railway work had two particular attractions. First, it paid better than agricultural employment. In 1845, weekly earnings in railway construction in the south-east region averaged thirty per cent more than harvest rates in the same area.[69] Second, and perhaps more crucially, the period of employment on the railways lasted longer. Even during the winter months operations continued except in the most inclement weather conditions. Thus during disturbances between Highland and Irish labourers in the Linlithgow area the legal authorities counted around 800 men from the Highlands in the district.[70] At Cockburnspath on the Edinburgh to Berwick line, Irish strikers in 1845 were replaced by 300 Highlanders. More than half the 2100 men employed in railway construction in the Lothians in the 1840s were from the Highlands, and in the same period they were also strongly represented among the navvy gangs on the Hawick branch of the North British and on the Caledonian line.[71]

3

There is abundant evidence of a very substantial increase in temporary migration during the potato famine. In 1841 the census enumerators estimated that sixty-two per cent of crofting parishes had some of their inhabitants 'temporarily absent' on census day.[72] By 1851 this total had risen to eighty-nine per cent of all parishes and by 1861 to ninety-seven per cent. The sharp increase between 1841 and 1851 is especially significant because the 1851 census was taken much earlier in the year, in late March, when temporary migration was relatively limited in scale and so under-records to a very great extent the 'real' rate of expansion over the decade. In addition, observations from a number of areas suggest that unusually large numbers went south and east in the later 1840s. Reports indicating this came from Mull, Skye, Raasay, Lochcarron in Wester Ross and Moidart and Arisaig on the west coast of Inverness.[73] The *Glasgow Herald* commented on the exceptional increase in harvest labourers arriving at Clyde ports in August and early September 1846.[74] The same pattern was maintained in 1847. 'Vast numbers' of Highlanders were described as migrating to the east coast for the herring fishery in that year.[75] Such was the scale of the exodus from Skye and Wester Ross that the Central Board reported, '. . . in some parts very few are left behind'.[76] In Kintail, the people 'were going off to the south in every steam boat in great numbers' and, in neighbouring Glenelg, 'as many as can' had left to seek work in the Lowlands. From the estates of Maclean of Ardgour and Cameron of Lochiel multitudes had gone: '. . . every steamer about a score depart'.[77] So extensive was the migration that one government relief official in Skye was becoming concerned that it might have adverse effects on the ability of the people to sustain themselves the following year: '. . . unless a sufficient number remain to till their crofts and cut fuel in April and May, distress next season may be as great as ever'.[78]

The increase in 1846-7 and thereafter had three characteristic features. First, there was an alteration in the age and social composition of the migrant group. Traditionally most temporary migrants were young, single males and females, and the majority of heads of household who were involved seem to have belonged to the cottar class. This pattern did not change radically but more crofters trekked south and east in search of employment than had done so in previous years.[79] Heads of household also participated to a much greater extent than before. Organisations such as the Free Church of Scotland provided aid to the dependants of crofters in order to allow them to go south.[80] Some landlords specifically excluded all able-bodied men between 21 and 50 from relief work in order to induce them to migrate.[81] Second, there was also considerable movement from parishes which had little experience of substantial temporary migration in the past. For the first time, men came in significant numbers from the Outer Hebrides to work at the railways and in the farms of the central Lowlands. At least 107 natives of Barra, South Uist and North Uist were labouring as railway navvies in the summer of 1847.[82] Forty men from Harris, an island whose population were 'always singularly averse to this migration and have never practised it in harvest time like the other Highlanders . . .', stated their intention to go to the mainland in the autumn of 1846.[83] Third, the period of time spent away from home became longer. Government relief officers reported people leaving Mull and Skye as early as February 1847 for work in the Lowlands.[84] In October 1846 the *Inverness Courier* reported that 'a great number of men' who had left their employment at the end of the east-coast fishing season had not returned home as usual but had obtained more work on the railways.[85] Other observers also stressed that in that first year of the potato blight, when the labour market in the south was very buoyant, large numbers stayed away from home as long as possible.[86]

The main reason for the expansion in temporary migration was, of course, the impact of the potato blight and the collapse in cattle prices. The first threatened the survival of many communities and necessitated access to additional sources of cash income to purchase grain. The second further diminished the ability of the Highland population to pay for imported food and was one of the primary reasons why so many small tenants rapidly fell deeply into rent arrears after 1846. The need to obtain cash from alternative sources to acquire meal and, at the same time, maintain rent payments in order to reduce the threat of eviction became pressing. Temporary migration was one of the few opportunities open to the inhabitants of the Western Highlands and Islands as the full extent of the crisis became apparent in the autumn of 1846. One group in particular was likely to be especially vulnerable. As previous discussion has shown, the cottars were most at risk. More than any other class, they depended on the potato. Their patches of land were too small to allow easy conversion to grain culti-vation and, on some estates at least, the tenants were absorbing these plots into their own holdings in order to extend the growing of oats to compensate for the lost potato harvest.[87] There is also evidence that in some cases the tacksmen and larger tenants were less willing to employ the cottars as day labourers because of the deepening economic crisis.[88] Often, too, landlords felt less responsibility to provide relief for them than for their rent-paying tenantry.[89] Cottar families had traditionally been much associated with temporary migration in the past. It is hardly surprising that they now looked to this outlet as their only hope of survival.

Three agencies – landowners, the Free Church of Scotland and the Central Board – did much both to encourage and facilitate the great movement to the Lowlands. Some proprietors provided funds to assist the migration, recognising that to do so was much less costly than maintaining a starving population by distributing meal and providing work at home. Lord Macdonald helped to pay the travel expenses to Glasgow of about 1500 people from his Skye estates.[90] In March 1847, Norman Macleod of Macleod was discouraging the cultivation of land since there was not enough seed and he could no longer supply it. He urged all able-bodied men to seek work in the south.[91] The Countess of Dunmore, proprietrix of Harris, not only provided free passage to the Clyde but gave allowances for one month for the families of those who accepted the offer until they were able to send wages home.[92] But the stick was employed as well as the carrot. In Kintail, Lochalsh and Torridon, proprietors specifically excluded young men from relief works in 1847 and reserved them for married men to induce single people to go south.[93] The policy of the Duke of Argyll both in Tiree and the Ross of Mull was to encourage able-bodied adults to leave home and restrict his own relief programmes '. . . to those who are so circumstanced that they cannot do so'.[94] One also gains the impression that some landowners had a strategy of cutting back on drainage and other works in spring and summer, the period when temporary migra-tion was most popular, and concentrating their relief effort in the winter months when employment was more difficult to obtain in the Lowlands.[95]

A major element in the initiative of the Free Church of Scotland in the early months of the famine was an elaborate scheme to transport more than 3000 people from the distressed region of the north to the labour markets of the south.[96] The plan originated in the winter of 1846 and came into operation in the spring and summer of 1847. Eventually, when the Free Church merged its schemes with those of the Central Board, the programme was administered by the Employment Committee of that organisation. The strategy was significant for several reasons. The level of organisation was impressive. The migrants were to be mainly placed with railway contractors although, in the event, many also found work as domestic servants, harvesters and general labourers. The Church first approached individual railway companies to ensure that jobs were available before sending men to them. This explains why some contractors gave a priority to recruiting Highlanders, even to the extent of refusing work to others until they took up their jobs.[97] The Church's officials were able to exploit effectively their nexus of contacts within the Lowland business community and take advantage of the public sympathy which existed for the inhabitants of the distressed districts of the north-west in 1846 and 1847. In addition, workers were maintained before embarking and their wives and families were supported for five weeks until they were able to send money home. The chances of success received a tremendous boost when James Matheson, proprietor of Lewis, lent his steamship the *Mary Jane* to convey migrants to the Clyde ports from the Hebrides free of charge.

The importance of the Free Church's effort should not be underestimated. It was the one organisation which above all was trusted by the majority of the Highland people. The government acknowledged that its local ministers played a key role in encouraging married men to leave their families at a time of crisis to find work in the Lowlands.[98] The Free Church clearly managed to instil a confidence in many communities that wives and children would be maintained while menfolk were away. Its efforts were probably most effective in those parts of the Highlands where it had been uncommon before 1846 to venture to the south in search of work. The first party conveyed by the *Mary Jane* arrived at the Broomielaw in February 1847. It consisted of 200 to 300 young men from Lewis, Harris and Skye.[99] The steamer returned over a month later with a further 400 passengers, about a quarter of whom were 'females desirous of obtaining country service', and the rest were men recruited by the railway companies.[100] By August 1847 the vessel had brought 2256 individuals to the Clyde ports from the Hebrides.[101] Even this was only a proportion of the overall total which left for the Lowlands in that year, sponsored initially by the Free Church and then by the Central Board.[102]

The Central Board itself also merits consideration in this discussion of the forces promoting temporary migration during the famine. Some contended that its relief measures in the distressed districts actually inhibited movement because it encouraged some who would otherwise have gone south to remain at home and be maintained there.[103] This view, however, is hardly convincing. Even in 1847, when the local operations of the Board were conducted in a more liberal and generous spirit, efforts were made to promote the movement of the young able-bodied to the Lowlands. For the period 1848 to the termination of relief activities in 1850, the argument has even less weight. During this phase, the more rigorous policies adopted by the Central Board acted as an additional expulsive force. From May 1848, all able-bodied single men aged between 18 and 50 and married men with three or less of a family were excluded from relief to induce them to seek work elsewhere.[104] This regulation was tightened further in 1849 by the Edinburgh Section of the Board. Even married men with families of three children or less were now to be debarred from direct relief '. . . beyond a limited assistance to their dependants for two weeks till they can remit a portion of their wages, and the usual assistance to enable them to reach the labour market'.[105] The application of the hated destitution test was enough to ensure that those who could preferred to obtain employment in the Lowlands. In every year from 1847 to 1850 the numbers on the relief lists diminished rapidly between spring and early autumn despite the fact that traditionally this was the time when the pressure of want in the months before the gathering of the new harvest was most acute.[106] It was also, however, the period when the market for temporary workers in the south was most buoyant. The pattern in Skye in 1849 was probably typical. It was reported in June of that year that '. . . owing to the stringent measures adopted by the Relief Committee this season, hundreds of the people have gone out of the country for work which have not done so for the last three years . . . very few of the young people would accept of the Meal on the terms suggested and have left the country in search of better employment'.[107]

It was of major importance that in the first two years of the famine there was a broad coincidence between the needs of the Highland population and the demand for labour in the Lowland economy. At the end of 1846 the Board of Supervision of the Scottish Poor Law reported that '. . . there was an unusual demand for labour at rates of wages probably unprecedented'.[108] The Board had carried out a detailed investigation in the autumn of that year into a representative group of industrial and agricultural parishes and had discovered that 'labour needs are so abundant that every man, woman and child who is able to work, can find employment at good wages'.[109] The main basis of the prosperity was the greatest railway construction boom in nineteenth-century Scotland. In 1846 and 1847, no fewer than twenty-seven separate companies were building permanent way.[110] Three hundred miles of track were under development utilising the labour of 3000 horses and 29,000 men.[111] Table 6.1 demonstrates the huge scale of the demand for labour in the construction gangs. It is impossible to tell precisely how far this was satisfied by temporary migrants from the Highlands. What is clear, however, is that railway employment was of crucial importance for many of the inhabitants of the north in these crisis years. So many Highlanders worked on the Aberdeen Railway that the Free Church appointed a catechist to be responsible for their spiritual welfare.[112] At the end of 1846 this company was advertising for an additional 2000-3000 labourers.[113] In the autumn of 1845 a constant stream of migrants left from Ross-shire for work on the Caledonian, Central and Scottish Midland Railways.[114] In 1847 at least 300 Highlanders were employed on the Caledonian and a further 200 on the Edinburgh and Northern Railway.[115]

In addition, partly because of the impact of the railways on the labour market, employment opportunities in 1846 and for much of 1847 were also widely available in the traditional sectors of agriculture and fishing. Harvest wages throughout Scotland were buoyant in August and September 1846. As the *Inverness Courier* reported: 'Reapers are this year in very great demand and wages are high'.[116] The Government acknowledged that the agricultural labour market '. . . was never better able to bear the influx of Highlanders'. Again, in the spring and summer of 1847 demand for field

Table 6.1. Demand for Railway Labour in Lowland Scotland, 1846-1847

Date	Line	Numbers employed or wanted	Source
Dec. 1846	Aberdeen Railway	Advertising for 2000-3,000 labourers	*Inverness Courier* 9 Dec. 1846
Sept. 1845	North of England Railways	'Highland and north country labourers wanted'	*John O'Groats Jnl* 12 Sept. 1845
20 June 1846	Edinburgh & Northern Railway	3,100 employed	*Edinburgh Evening Courant* 20 June 1846
1 Aug. 1846	North British Railway (Lothians section)	2325; 1300 Scots employed	*Edinburgh Evening Courant* 1 Aug. 1846
1 Aug. 1846	Caledonian Railway (Lothians section)	649; 300 Scots employed	*Ibid.*
27 Aug. 1846	Caledonian Railway (Glasgow-Carlisle)	10,500 employed	*Ibid.* 27 Aug. 1846
3 Sept. 1846	Edinburgh & Northern Railway	5000 men employed	*Ibid.* 3 Sept. 1846
3 Oct. 1846	Various lines in Perthshire	3,900 employed	*Ibid.* 3 Oct. 1846
5 Jun. 1847	Edinburgh & Northern Railway	8,632 men employed, 5000 of whom 'strangers' from Highlands and Ireland	*Witness* 5 June 1847; *Scotsman* 19 June 1847
1 Sept. 1847	Caledonian Railway	'upwards of 20,000 men employed'	*Witness* 1 Sept. 1847
4 Sept. 1847	Scottish Central Railway	4000 employed	*Witness* 4 Sept. 1847

workers remained vigorous throughout Easter Ross, eastern Inverness, Caithness and parts of the south-east Lowlands.[117] The Caithness herring fishery also prospered in 1846. Wages were '. . . at least one third higher than was customary' and demand for hands, despite 'the immense number of Highlanders', was sometimes unsatisfied. Wages which had risen on average from £4 to £6 for a season's work the previous year continued at high levels in 1846. Nearly fifty boats had to remain at Wick for lack of hired men.[118]

Unfortunately, however, the good times did not continue for long. The industrial recession was already starting to take effect in the latter months of 1847, though railway construction was maintained until the autumn and early winter of that year.[119] By October and November, however, as workers were paid off, Highlanders streamed home in large numbers. The press reported 'immense batches' of discharged navvies coming north in the steamships. The arrival of the *Queen* in Wick in November 1847 brought melodramatic comment: 'The dismissal of such multitudes of labourers from the railways in the south threatens to be a serious matter for Caithness . . . in fact as boat after boat came ashore from the vessel with no other passengers on board but "navvies", people began to anticipate a navvy invasion, the more especially as the shrill notes of the national bagpipe seemed to summon them to arms'.[120]

By 1848 the country was plunged into deep industrial recession. The number of casual poor in Scotland relieved through the official Poor Law doubled between 1847 and 1848. Expenditure on relief climbed from £295,232 in 1846 to £544,334 in 1848. By the end of May of that year 227,647 were obtaining poor relief in Scotland, a figure which represented almost twelve per cent of the national population in 1841.[121] In

Table 6.2. *Harvest Wages in Lowland Scotland, 1845-1854*

Date	Location	Wage
Sept. 1845	East Lothian	1/6d p.d.
	Glasgow Cross	1/8d p.d. females
		2/– to 2/2d p.d. males
Aug. 1846	Grassmarket, Edinburgh	12/– to 14/– p.w.
Sept. 1846	East Lothian	12/– p.w.
	Glasgow Cross	2/– to 2/6d p.d.
Sept. 1847	West Lothian	1/4d p.d.
	East Lothian	1/6d p.d.
Aug. 1848	St. James's Fair, Kelso	13/– to 14/– p.w.
Sept. 1848	Grassmarket, Edinburgh	1/– p.d.
Aug. 1849	Grassmarket, Edinburgh	1/2d to 1/3d p.d.
Aug. 1850	East Lothian	7/6d p.w.
	West Lothian	1/6d to 1/9d p.d.
Aug. 1851	Lothians	1/– p.d.
	Glasgow Cross	1/– to 1/3d p.d.
Aug. 1852	West Lothian	1/– p.d.
	Coldstream	16/– to 17/– p.w.
	Berwick	16/– to 17/– p.w.
	Edinburgh	2/3d p.d.
	Dalkeith	9/– p.w.
	Lauder	12/– to 14/– p.w.
	Ayrshire	2/– to 2/4d p.d.
	Berwick	3/6d to 4/– p.d.
Aug. 1853	Wigtownshire	2/–d p.d.
	East Lothian	1/– to 1/3d p.d.
	Midlothian	1/3d p.d.
Aug. 1854	Berwick	2/6d p.d.
	Midlothian	10/– p.w.

Sources: *Scotsman*, 1845-54; *Glasgow Herald*, 1845-54; *Inverness Journal*, 1847-49; *Inverness Advertiser*, 1849-54; *Inverness Courier*, 1845-54.
Notes: p.d. = per day; p.w. = per week. In all cases, the wage quoted excludes food and other perquisites.

such circumstances the outlook for temporary migrants from the Highlands was indeed bleak. On the whole, they were employed in unskilled occupations in sectors of the economy peculiarly vulnerable to the recession. The crisis, for instance, was most evident in railway construction (which had virtually ceased by the end of 1847) where many male Highlanders had found work. Tables 6.2 to 6.4 collate information on two other key sectors, agriculture and fishing, over the period 1845 to 1854. These data confirm a sharp fall in demand for seasonal workers between 1848 and 1850, something of a recovery in 1851 (at least for harvesters) and a brief return to 'boom' conditions, reminiscent of those of 1846, in 1852. In 1853 and 1854, demand for labour in both agriculture and fishing can best be described as moderate. This is not to say, however, that the flow of temporary migrants from the Highlands diminished because of the depression between 1848 and 1851. The Central Board continued to report that large numbers were still leaving in each of these years because of the pressure of want.[122] Again, while wages were depressed on the east coast, the number of men actually employed at the Wick fishery marginally increased from 10,805 in 1847 to 11,512 in 1848, 11,718 in 1849 and 11,846 in 1850.[123]

Table 6.3. Pattern of Demand for Harvest Labour, 1845-1854

1845
Demand in this year appeared 'moderate'. Farmers feared a scarcity of hands because of the expansion of railway construction. But, as in East Lothian, 'there has been no want of reapers'. The marked increase in Irish immigration and the long duration of the harvest prevented any shortage.

1846
Harvest wages rose markedly, because of (a) the railway construction boom, (b) the speedy ripening of the harvest and (c) the decline in the number of Irish reapers. This was explained by demand for railway labour and the late Irish harvest. The *Inverness Courier* concluded: 'Reapers are this year in very great demand and wages are high . . .'. Similar reports came from as far north as Wick and as far south as Berwick.

1847
In this year wages returned to 'moderate' levels. In some districts, notably Lothian, there was an over-supply of reapers. However, in Easter Ross the demand for harvest labour continued at high levels. Elsewhere, the return of large numbers of Irish kept down wage levels.

1848
Details on the labour market for this year are very sparse. Initially, i.e. in early August, demand for labour was brisk but by September it had slumped. Early in that month, male harvesters at the Grassmarket in Edinburgh were being offered 1/– per day without victuals. This was one of the lowest wages recorded between 1845 and 1854. It was likely that the harvest labour market would be over-supplied as the railway construction boom had ended.

1849
Wages were still relatively stagnant although, again, the very meagre evidence makes confident conclusions difficult. Even in the north-east, however, where demand for reapers had been less depressed than elsewhere in 1848, there was 'a lack of demand for shearers and a small decline in wages'.

1850
Supply of reapers was still greater than demand. In East Lothian, 'a considerable number left the market unable to find employers', while in Ayrshire, 'shearers have not been in brisk demand'.

1851
There was some recovery from the depressed levels of 1848 to 1850 but not to any marked extent. In East Lothian at the height of the harvest there was 'an abundance of shearers at low wages'. However, in Berwick demand for reapers was 'moderate' and wages rose above the level of previous years.

1852
This year saw a return to the buoyant market of 1846. In the Lothians, 'the reaping, chiefly owing to the scarcity of labourers, has not kept pace with the maturing of the crops'. From Ayrshire, too, a 'brisk demand' for reapers was reported. Berwick wages, which had stood at 2/6d per day for men in 1851, climbed to between 3/– and 3/6d per day.

1853
By the middle period of the harvest most reports from different districts suggested that supply of labour exceeded demand. However, the market did not fall to the level of 1848-51.

1854
Details scarce but the general impression is given of a 'moderate' level of demand for harvesters.

Sources: Scotsman, 1845-54; *Glasgow Herald*, 1845-54; *Inverness Advertiser*, 1849-54; *Inverness Courier*, 1845-54.

Table 6.4. Pattern of Demand for Fishing Labour at Wick, 1846-1852

1846
Estimated that Caithness rates were 'at least one third higher than customary'. Despite 'the immense number of Highlanders' who came for the fishing season, the *John O'Groats Journal* reported that there had not been a year when there was such a scarcity of men for hire. Fifty boats were described as being unable to sail for lack of hands. Wages, which had started at £4, had risen to £6.

1847
The number of Highlanders arriving seeking work at Wick was 'considerably greater' than before but 'several hundreds' failed to obtain employment. It was reported from Wester Ross that wages gained from the Caithness fishery were 'much below the ordinary average' because of the glut of labour.

1848
Wages lower than in 1846-7; average rate was £4 for the season.

1849
'The market for hired men for the fishing season has been this year so overstocked both at Wick and at the stations along the coast that a good many have had to return home for want of employment. This has arisen . . . chiefly from the want of work at railways in the south. From Skye, Lewis, the west coast of Sutherland, Lochbroom, Gairloch and other Highland districts, the proportion of men has this year been considerably above the average of former seasons . . .'

1850
'We have been visited [in Wick] by a more than ordinary number of Highlanders this year . . . By the latter end of last week [15 July] they began to arrive in boat loads by sea and in droves by land . . . It soon became evident that the supply was much beyond the demand.'
   Experienced hands £5, but 'a great number' at £3 to £3.15s.
   Young, raw hands, as low as 30s. to 40s.

1851
Rate of wages 'much reduced' at Wick. Many had to return home. Some engaged at the low figure of £2.

1852
There seems to have been a dramatic recovery in the labour market. As much as £7 was offered for good hands; the 'general run' was from £3.10s to £6. Scarcity of labour and high wages were reported. Some boats had even to sail for Orkney to procure full crews.

Sources: John O'Groats Journal, 1846-52; *Witness,* 1846-52; *Inverness Courier,* 1846-52; *Inverness Advertiser,* 1849-52; *Destitution Reports,* 1847-50.

4

It is difficult to exaggerate the vital importance of temporary migration during the Highland potato famine. Sir John McNeill quickly became aware of its key significance when he toured the distressed districts in 1851. He recognised that alternative sources of income, such as cattle, were depressed and others, like kelp manufacture and commercial fishing, had been brought to a low level. But the land could not supply all or even the major part of subsistence, especially after the failure of the potato crop. He therefore argued that the population of parts of the Hebrides depended on income earned at a distance for at least one half and more probably two thirds to three quarters of 'their means of living'. He acknowledged the importance of the Central Board in the provision of relief but asserted that temporary migration was much more decisive: 'After obtaining even an imperfect knowledge of the facts, it was impossible to resist the inference, that the relief afforded by the Destitution Fund could have supplied but a small part of the deficiency in the local means of subsistence'. McNeill went on to suggest that those districts where temporary migration was most extensive had suffered least during the crisis.[124]

It is possible that McNeill may have slightly exaggerated his case. He drew much of his evidence from Skye and he failed to fully realise the variation in patterns of migration which could occur both over time and space within the Highland region. Yet it is difficult to disagree with his main conclusion in the light of the evidence presented in this chapter. During the famine, the labour market for temporary migrants probably became the single most important influence on the living standards of the inhabitants of the distressed region. Changing conditions in the Western Highlands clearly reflected the cycle of demand for labour at the railways, in agriculture, and at the fisheries. The massive increase in migration in 1846 and 1847 and the vigour of the southern market for workers released a great stream of income throughout the Highlands. One official of the Central Board referred to the 'unusual amount of hard cash' which entered the north-west in these years.[125] When the sales carried out through the government grain depôts in 1846 and early 1847 were analysed it was found that £24,000 of the £58,000 purchased were acquired 'by consumers for their own use' rather than by landlord intermediaries.[126] Government relief officers in Mull in March 1847 noted that '. . . what is most remarkable, though comparatively few are earning wages, money is always forthcoming'.[127] In Skye, 'the little hoards of the poor', nearly £700 in one month, were being paid into banks by the people on Lord Macdonald's estate.[128] Sir John McNeill himself described how an estimated 20,000 to 30,000 bolls of meal were purchased annually in the distressed districts in addition to supplies distributed by the Central Board. It was also common practice in these years for migrants to bring meal back into the country. In Skye in January 1847, 'numbers of the people were trudging home with meal on their backs', and those leaving the east coast fishery in the autumn of 1846 had spent much of their earnings on grain because of the destruction of the potato crop.[129]

Despite the recession of 1848, the worst effects of the depressed condition of the labour market did not immediately affect the Western Highlands. Some savings had been retained from the two good years which had gone before and were available to buy meal in 1848.[130] This meant, however, that 1849 was probably the worst year of the entire period of famine.[131] Serious destitution persisted until 1853. It is interesting to note that assisted emigration accelerated in these years but declined dramatically in 1852 when the labour market for temporary migrants became more buoyant, a sure sign of its fundamental importance to the living standards of the people.[132] Income from the Lowlands was probably most significant in 1846-7 but retained a continuing importance throughout the famine. Temporary migration, the Poor Law, and, to a lesser extent, the proprietors, were the only major sources of assistance when the Central Board terminated its operations in 1850. Even earlier, both the Board and individual landlords tried to restrict the provision of relief to those groups, such as the old and the very young, who were unable to go south and to periods of the year when the casual labour market in the Lowlands was least active. Temporary movement attracted much less publicity than the efforts of landlords and charities. But its extraordinary scale during the famine not only underlines its importance for an understanding of Highland social history but demonstrates that the people of the region did much to help themselves out of their difficulties. The heavy incidence of migration for work in the Lowlands was the most convincing proof that when the critics referred to a parasitic population, corrupted by charity, they talked utter nonsense.

NOTES

1. Richards, *Highland Clearances*, II, 174.
2. See Appendix 9, Temporary Migration and the Crofting Region: Parish Patterns in the 1840s, for the basis of this estimate.
3. *N.S.A.*, XIV, 194, 213.
4. McNeill Report, xix.
5. *Report to the General Assembly of the Free Church of Scotland regarding Highland Destitution* (Edinburgh, 1847), 1.
6. *McNeill Report*, xiii.
7. *PP*, XXI (1844), *R.C. on Scottish Poor Laws* (1843), Part II, 395.
8. *N.S.A.*, XIV, 308.
9. *McNeill Report*, Appendix A, 59.
10. *PP*, XXI (1844), *R.C. on Scottish Poor Laws* (1843), Part II, 384.
11. SRO, HD21/41, Minutes of the Destitution Committee of Applecross, 2 August 1847; SRO, AF7/85, Survey by R. Lamb, Assistant Inspector of the Fishery, 30 September 1850.
12. *McNeill Report*, Appendix A, 92, 97.
13. NLS, Sutherland Estate Papers, Dep. 313/1173, James Loch to Duke of Sutherland, 4 September 1846.

14. Inveraray Castle, Argyll Estate Papers, Bundle 1529, Report by the Chamberlain of Tiree, August 1845.

15. *McNeill Report*, Appendix A, 33.

16. *Relief Correspondence*, Mr. Loch to Duke of Sutherland, 4 September 1846; to Lord Dunfermline, 4 September 1846.

17. *McNeill Report*, xxiii.

18. *Relief Correspondence*, Capt. Pole to Sir E. Coffin, 19 October 1846.

19. *McNeill Report*, xxiii.

20. See above, pp.25-6.

21. *Destitution Papers*, Report of the Edinburgh Section (1848), H.B. Rose to W.F. Skene, 2 March 1848.

22. For details see Appendix 9.

23. SRO, Riddell Papers, AF49/6, Report of T.G. Dickson for Trustees (1852).

24. *N.S.A.*, VII, 214; Inveraray Castle, Argyll Estate Papers, Bundle 1529, Report by Chamberlain of Tiree, August 1845.

25. SRO, AF7/85, Survey by L. Lamb, Assistant Inspector of the Fishery, 30 September 1850.

26. See above, p.157.

27. *McNeill Report*, Appendix A, Evidence of John Mackintosh, Cotter at Achintraad, 74-5.

28. *Ibid.*, 78.

29. This paragraph is based on Devine, 'Temporary Migration', 344-59; W. Howatson, 'Grain Harvesting and Harvesters', in T.M. Devine, ed., *Farm Servants and Labour in Lowland Scotland, 1779-1914* (Edinburgh, 1984), 124-142; A. Whyte and D. Macfarlane, *General View of the County of Dumbarton* (Glasgow, 1811), 248-9; Gray, *Highland Economy*, 53; J. Knox, *A Tour through the Highlands in 1786* (London, 1787), 60; *O.S.A.*, I, 234; II, 459, 465, 551; III, 24, 329, 565; V, 54.

30. See above, p.161-5.

31. Charles Weld, *Two Months in the Highlands, Orcadia and Skye* (London, 1860), 204.

32. *John O'Groats Journal*, 7 September 1849.

33. G. Robertson, *Rural Recollections* (Irvine, 1829), 383.

34. J. Taylor, 'On the Comparative Merits of Different Modes of Reaping Grain', *Trans. Highland and Agricultural Society*, new ser. 1843-5, 268; E.J.T. Collins, 'Harvest Technology and Labour Supply in Britain, 1790-1870', *Econ. Hist. Rev.*, 2nd ser. XXII (1969).

35. P. Brodie, 'On Green Crops', *Prize Essays and Transactions of the Highland Society of Scotland*, I (1799), 110-111; R.S. Skirving, 'On the Agriculture of East Lothian', *Trans. Highland and Agricultural Society*, 4th ser. V (1873), 19-20.

36. Skirving, 'East Lothian', 19.

37. Devine, ed., *Farm Servants and Labour*, 39-40, 100-101.

38. *PP*, XXXVI (1893-4), *Royal Commission on Labour. The Agricultural Labourer (Scotland)*, Part I, 13-14.

39. *PP*, III (1870), *Royal Commission on the Employment of Children, Young Persons and Women in Agriculture* (1867), *Appendix, Part I to Fourth Report*, 40.

40. Devine, ed., *Farm Servants and Labour*, 110-111.

41. For the conventional wisdom see D.F. Macdonald, *Scotland's Shifting Population* (Glasgow, 1937), 132-3; J. Handley, *The Irish in Scotland* (Cork, 1943) 34; Hunter, *Crofting Community*, 108.

42. Devine, ed., *Farm Servants and Labour*, 124-242; A. Fenton, *Scottish Country Life* (Edinburgh, 1976), 58.

43. *PP*, III (1870), *Royal Commission on the Employment of Children, Young Persons and Women in Agriculture (1867), Appendix, Part I to Fourth Report*, 51, 104.

44. J.A. Symon, *Scottish Farming, Past and Present* (Edinburgh, 1959), 176-189.

45. Devine, ed., *Farm Servants and Labour*, 100-101.

46. *Quarterly Journal of Agriculture*, IV (1832-4), 355.

47. See below, pp.162-4.
48. Gray, *Fishing Industries of Scotland*, *passim*.
49. Lobban, 'Highland Migration to Greenock', 33.
50. Quoted in *Ibid.*, 33.
51. The remainder of this paragraph is based on Gray, *Fishing Industries of Scotland*, *passim*; J. Duthie, *The Art of Fishcuring* (Aberdeen, 1911).
52. Weld, *Two Months in the Highlands*, 52.
53. SRO, AF36/18, Wick Reports and Correspondence, 1839-47.
54. *John O'Groats Journal*, 6 July 1849.
55. *Inverness Courier*, 30 September 1846.
56. *John O'Groats Journal*, 11 June 1847.
57. *Ibid.*
58. *PP*, XX (1844), *R.C. on Scottish Poor Laws* (1843), Part II, 376.
59. *Ibid.*, 68.
60. *Ibid.*
61. *Ibid.*, Part I, QQ. 11633-4.
62. SRO, Riddell Papers, AF49/6, Report of T.G. Dickson for Trustees (1852).
63. *PP*, XV (1847), *Reports of Commissioners, Inspectors of Factories, 1846*, 12.
64. See details and references related to these areas in Appendix 9.
65. *McNeill Report*, Appendix A, 12.
66. See Appendix 9 for details.
67. J. Macdonald, *The Agriculture of the Hebrides* (London, 1811), 150.
68. Lobban, 'Highland Migrants to Greenock', 136; GRO, Census Enumerators' Books, Abbey Parish, Paisley, 1851.
69. *PP*, XIII (1846), *Report from the Select Committee on Railway Labourers*, 10, 16.
70. SRO, Lord Advocate's Papers, AD58/66, Disturbances between Highland and Irish railway labourers in Linlithgow, 1841.
71. *PP*, XII (1846), *S.C. on Railway Labourers*, I, 15-13; *Scotsman*, 27 August 1845.
72. See Appendix 9.
73. *N.C.*, Appendix A, 46; HD20/11, Minutes of Destitution Committee of Duirnish; *McNeill Report*, XIX, 60, 00, 75; SRO, HD6/2, Treasury Correspondence, May to Walker, 22 March 1847.
74. *Glasgow Herald*, 18 September 1846.
75. *Destitution Papers*, Fourth Report by Central Board, July 1847, 2.
76. *Ibid.*
77. SRO, HD6/2, Treasury Correspondence, Mr. Campbell to Sir J. McNeill, 2 March 1847.
78. *Ibid.*, Major Halliday to Sir E. Coffin, 4 March 1847.
79. *McNeill Report*, XII.
80. SRO, Lord Advocate's Papers, AD58/82, Free Kirk Relief Fund, Trevelyan to Lord Advocate, 23 December 1846.
81. Inveraray Castle, Argyll Estate Papers, Bundle 1522, Angus Macdonald to Marquis of Lorne, 8 January 1847.
82. SRO, HD6/6, Note of Men Sent to Railway Contractors.
83. SRO, HD7/28, Correspondence from Highland Landowners, W. Sitwell to Sir E. Coffin, 6 October 1846.
84. SRO, HD6/2, Treasury Correspondence, Robertson to Coffin, 27 February 1847.
85. *Inverness Courier*, 7 October 1846.
86. *Glasgow Herald*, 12 October 1846.
87. *Destitution Papers*, Report of the Edinburgh Section for 1848, 20. See also above, pp.43, 50-51.
88. *McNeill Report*, Appendix A, 65.
89. SRO, HD6/2, Treasury Correspondence, Sir Godfrey Webster to Coffin, 28 February 1847.
90. *Ibid.*, Halliday to Trevelyan, 21 March 1847.

91. Dunvegan Castle, Macleod of Macleod Muniments, 659/28/13, Macleod to Emily Macleod, 8 March 1847.

92. SRO HD6/2, Treasury Correspondence, Capt. Baynton to Coffin, 20 February 1847; SRO, Lord Advocate's Papers, AD58/84, Correspondence of Capt. Sitwell, April/May 1847. See also even more ambitious support provided by the Duke of Sutherland, NLS, Sutherland Estate Papers, Dep. 313/1174, J. Loch to W. Mackenzie, 20 February 1847.

93. SRO, HD6/2, Treasury Correspondence, Mr. Campbell to Sir J. McNeill, 2 March 1847.

94. Inveraray Castle, Argyll Estate Papers, Bundle 1522, Angus Macdonald to Marquis of Lorne, 8 January 1847.

95. *Ibid.*, Bundle 1531, J. Campbell to Duke of Argyll, 9 January 1847.

96. Unless otherwise indicated this account of the Free Church's initiative is based on SRO, Lord Advocate's Papers, AD58/82, Free Kirk Relief Fund, Papers and Correspondence; *Relief Correspondence*, 10-26 December 1846; *Destitution Papers*, Statements of the Free Church, December 1846; *Witness*, 1 January-31 August 1847.

97. Thus, on the Scottish Central Railway in Stirlingshire, '. . . for weeks the gangers had refused work to numerous applicants, both Irish and Lowland Scotch merely that there might be enough room for the Highlanders'. *Scotsman*, 6 March 1847.

98. SRO, Lord Advocate's Papers, AD58/82, Lord Advocate to Trevelyan, 20 December 1846.

99. *Witness*, 27 February 1847.

100. *Ibid.*, 31 March 1847.

101. *Ibid.*, 7 August 1847.

102. SRO, HD6/2, Treasury Correspondence, Baynton to Coffin, 20 February 1847; *Destitution Papers*, Second Report by Glasgow Committee on Employment (1847), 24. Here it was estimated that as many again came without support.

103. *Destitution Papers*, Second Report of Edinburgh Section (1848), 30; *McNeill Report*, Appendix I, 59.

104. *Destitution Papers*, Fifth Report of Edinburgh Society (1848), Capt. H.B. Rose to Relieving Officers in Wester Ross, 1 May 1848.

105. Dunvegan Castle, Macleod of Macleod Muniments, 2/659/2, Alexander Allen to Miss Macleod, 5 May 1849.

106. SRO, HD10/32, Letters from Capt. Fishbourne.

107. Dunvegan Castle, Macleod of Macleod Muniments, 659/11/3, E. Gibbons to Miss Macleod, 27 June 1849.

108. *PP*, XXXII (1847-8), *Second Annual Report of the Board of Supervision*, XV.

109. *Relief Correspondence*, Sir J. McNeill to Sir G. Gray, 25 September 1846.

110. SRO, HD16/108, Note of railways now making (1847).

111. *Edinburgh Evening Courant*, 28 May 1846, quoting a report in the *Railway Chronicle*.

112. *Inverness Courier*, 23 September 1846.

113. *Ibid.*, 9 December 1846.

114. *John O'Groats Journal*, 26 September 1845.

115. *Witness*, 17 March and 5 June 1847. There are also numerous references elsewhere in the press to railway work being the principal employment for male migrants in 1846-7.

116. *Inverness Courier*, 22 August 1846.

117. SRO, HD19/1, Minutes of Destitution Committee of Alness; SRO, HD19/4, Minutes of Destitution Committee of Boleskine, 17 May 1847; SRO, HD19/6, Rev. E. Mackenzie to W. Skene, 14 May 1847; SRO, HD19/19, Statement of Destitution Committee of Rosskeen, April 1847; *Inverness Journal*, 20 August 1847.

118. SRO, HD16/101, Minutes of Committee appointed to watch the progress of events connected with the potato failure (1847); *John O'Groats Journal*, 15 August 1845; 31 July 1846.

119. *PP*, XV (1847), *Inspector of Factories Reports, 1 November-1 May 1847*. For continuation of railway employment see *Witness*, 1 September 1847; *Scotsman*, 3 February 1847; *North British Daily Mail*, 1 May 1847.

120. *John O'Groats Journal*, 19 November 1847.

121. *PP*, XXV (1849), *Third Annual Report of the Board of Supervision*, VII; *PP*, XXVII (1850), *Fourth Annual Report of the Board of Supervision*, XIX.

122. *Destitution Papers*, *Sixth Report of Edinburgh Section* (1848), E.J. Fishbourne to W. Skene, 8 June 1848: 'The numbers going south [from Skye] are quite unusual'; *First Report of Edinburgh Section* (1849), 20; SRO, HD3/10, Portree Letterbook, 1847-50, entries for 8 June 1848; 15 March 1849 and 2 June 1850.

123. SRO, AF36/18-19, Wick Reports and Correspondence, 1839-52.

124. *McNeill Report*, X-XI, XXXVI.

125. *Destitution Papers*, Fourth Report of Edinburgh Section (1848), R. Elliot to W. Skene, 3 February 1848.

126. SRO, HD6/2, Treasury Correspondence, Sir E. Coffin to Mr. Trevelyan, 28 September 1847.

127. *Ibid.*, Capt. Rose to Sir E. Coffin, 28 March 1847.

128. *Ibid.*, Major Halliday to Mr. Trevelyan, 17 April 1847.

129. *Ibid.*, Rev. Mr. Tulloch to Duke of Sutherland, 17 March 1847; *Relief Correspondence*, Major Halliday to Mr. Trevelyan, 10 January 1847; *Inverness Courier*, 16 September 1846.

130. *Destitution Papers*, *Second Report of Edinburgh Section* (1849), Capt. R. Eliot to W.F. Skene, 30 June 1848.

131. *Ibid.*, *Second Report of Edinburgh Section* (1849), 78-9; Capt. R. Eliot to W. Skene, 21 April 1849.

132. See below, p.258.

7

Clearances

In early 1848, William Skene warned that the eventual termination of relief operations would immediately precipitate 'a very great and very extensive "Highland Clearing" '. He went on to describe this as 'a turning out of the population from their holdings without providing any adequate resource' for them. He argued that removals were already underway on a considerable scale but that they would rapidly accelerate and so lead '. . . to a further degradation and impoverishment of a people already too much pauperised'.[1] Skene was describing a phenomenon which had long antecedents in the Scottish Highlands and has come to be regarded as one of the classic themes of Scottish history. The subject of the Clearances has a compelling attraction as a great human tragedy with devastating consequences for an entire culture. For the historian it also offers an unrivalled opportunity to study the processes of agrarian 'modernisation' and their social results. All the great themes are encapsulated within it: the powers of the social élite; dispossession; peasant resistance; cultural alienation; emigration and migration.

The Highland Clearances have attracted a considerable historiography which has extended understanding of several aspects of the subject.[2] But the treatment in the series of books and articles which consider the history of the eviction tends on the whole to be episodic and impressionistic. It is very difficult for the reader to gain an insight into patterns of eviction, how they developed over time, why they concentrated in some regions rather than others and what determined their particular periodicity. The basic weakness in much of what has been written about the Clearances is the failure to adopt a systematic approach to the subject. Studies of the economic background to the evictions abound, as do examinations of particular events, but these lack full impact because the context of time and space is either omitted or described only in superficial terms.[3] The essential problem is that no serious effort has yet been made to quantify the process and nature of clearance. To do so is an exceedingly difficult task and an impossible one for certain periods and some areas. But unless some attempt is made along these lines, the history of the Clearances will always remain a mere catalogue of memorable events. Only through some reckoning of the order of magnitude, even if only in approximate terms, do patterns reveal themselves, spatial variations emerge and developments over time become clear. Only when this task has been carried out can some of the basic questions be tackled: why evictions concentrated in certain periods; what influences governed their spatial variation; how do they tie in with changing patterns of migration and emigration?

In one sense, the paucity of numerical information on the Clearances is not surprising. There are serious gaps in the evidence. Some evictions took place without fuss and have left little trace in the historical record. Public interest in the social problems of the Highlands fluctuated throughout the nineteenth century and contemporary documentation is not always a reliable guide to the real development of events. One source much used in recent work, the national press, can provide graphic detail on particular episodes but too much dependence on contemporary newspapers and journals can easily jeopardise the success of systematic enquiry. Almost inevitably their coverage is biased towards the sensational incident or the exceptional event. The attention the press devoted to Highland problems varied very significantly. Removals which were large in scale, attracted legal investigation, resulted in peasant resistance or occurred in periods when for other reasons (such as the potato famine of the 1840s) the Highlands provoked public interest, loom large in the press. By relying too much on newspapers the historian runs the risk of building his analysis on an inherently biased collection of data assembled from readily accessible sources.

It would be naïve to suggest that a more systematic approach to the Clearances of the type suggested above is possible for all periods of Highland history in the eighteenth and nineteenth centuries. But for the 1840s and 1850s the data available are especially rich and varied and do allow the historian to introduce more precision into an evaluation of eviction. In this chapter, therefore, clearances during the famine are considered in detail. In the first section, the sources used to establish the spatial and chronological sequence of clearance in the 1840s and 1850s are discussed and their strengths and weaknesses described. This is then followed by an assessment of the location and scale of major evictions and of their significance in relation to the history of the Highland Clearances as a whole. The final section concentrates on an examination of the varied reasons why removals seemed to accelerate in both scale and intensity during the potato famine itself.

1

The analysis which follows in much of this chapter is mainly based on the material assembled in Appendix 11, *Principal Evictions in the Highlands, 1846-56*. The term 'principal evictions' refers to removals of entire townships or to those which involved ten or more families. The information which has been assembled is not intended to be a *precise* measure of clearance, because such an index cannot be constructed from the available sources. Some landlords preferred a more extended and less dramatic method of reducing their tenantry rather than instant removal of entire communities at either the Whitsun or Martinmas terms. Thus, in 1849, the Sutherland estate at first decided upon the wholesale clearance of the inland western townships of Knockan and Elphin. It then postponed the plan and opted instead for 'a gradually reducing process' which would eventually accomplish the same result as a major scheme of eviction but over a longer timescale, with less adverse publicity and weaker peasant opposition.[4] In addition, removal was but one of a series of effective sanctions used throughout the famine years to enforce the expulsion of population. In later chapters, evidence will be presented of proprietors consolidating tenancies after either the death or emigration of the occupier, reducing or cutting off relief entirely, confiscating the cattle stock of those deeply in rent arrears, controlling the subdivision of holdings in a more resolute fashion and attempting to limit employment in public works in order to promote migration.[5] The material gathered in Appendix 11, therefore, is restricted to major clearances and to only one, though arguably the most dramatic in its social consequences, of the series of techniques used to displace an unwanted population in the 1840s and 1850s. It aims to provide an interim rough guide to the scale and location of principal evictions in the famine period which can later be modified and extended by local research.

The data have been compiled from five sets of sources: (i) Estate papers, (ii) Destitution papers, (iii) Official and Government papers, (iv) the Census and (v) Contemporary press and periodical literature.

(i) *Estate Papers*

For the period *c*.1840-60 the geographical coverage provided by this source is quite exceptional. The papers for several major properties in the Inner and Outer Hebrides are extant either in whole or in part. Material exists for Lewis (1850-1), North Uist, most of Skye and Raasay, Tiree, parts of Mull, Jura and Islay.[6] For the western mainland and central Highlands, there are the Sutherland Estate Papers, Cameron of Lochiel MSS, Mackenzie of Gairloch MSS, Argyll Estate Papers, Riddell Papers, Breadalbane Muniments, Cromartie Estate Papers and Seafield Muniments, among others. These give information on virtually the whole of the county of Sutherland, parts of Wester Ross, some districts in Inverness-shire and several areas in Argyll.

Estate papers have two principal uses for the historian of the Clearances. On the one hand, the motivation, planning, scale and phasing of eviction is often revealed in detail in factorial correspondence. On the other, time series constructed from rentals provide a guide to fluctuation in tenant and township numbers and when used with other information can indicate the *relative* importance and typicality of particular clearances within the overall population and social structure of a given area. For instance, in the early 1850s, the removal of the two townships of Boreraig and Suishnish on the Skye estate of Lord Macdonald attracted considerable publicity at the time and has achieved even greater notoriety since.[7] Analysis of the Macdonald rentals reveals, however, that clearance of whole townships on the estate at that period was relatively rare and that the elimination of Boreraig and Suishnish was not typical of general policy. In 1847-8 there were 410 tenancies rented at £10 or less on the Macdonald property in the parishes of Sleat and Strath. By 1858 this number had only fallen by six per cent to 387. This puts the infamous Boreraig and Suishnish removals into perspective.[8] These clearances were exceptional; the number of small tenancies on the estate as a whole declined very marginally. At the same time, however, there was probably widespread displacement of cottars on that property and one of the weaknesses of estate rentals is that they rarely provide any guidance on the impact of eviction on this submerged class.

(ii) *Destitution Papers*

The reports of the Central Board occasionally contain general references to the policy of eviction being pursued in certain parts of the Highlands. More valuable, however, is the detailed correspondence of its local officials and committees which often refers to the impact of clearances on social conditions as a factor exacerbating the destitution which the relief organisations were striving to contain.

(iii) *Official and Government Papers*

Within this general category there is a great mass of material:

(a)   Lord Advocate's Papers (SRO), Home Office (Scotland) Domestic Entry Books (SRO) and published reports, such as that by Sir John McNeill in 1851, make intermittent reference to some clearances. This was often the case where authorities became directly involved because of the refusal of the people to accept removal peacefully (such as Sollas in North Uist), or where an offence was suspected (such as Knoydart where allegations were made that those who had been evicted were not receiving proper support from the Poor Law authorities) or when government intervention was sought by the people (such as Strathaird in Skye in 1849).

(b)   The two great inquiries carried out by Lord Napier and his colleagues in 1883 and the Royal Commission of 1892 (the so-called *Deer Forest Commission*) are major sources of information on the evictions of the 1840s and the 1850s.[9] Many of the witnesses who gave evidence lived through the famine and were sometimes themselves victims of eviction. Through their experiences it is possible to obtain an insight into the response of the people which is a perspective very difficult to obtain from any other source. The evidence presented is often detailed and can contain precise information or names of townships and number of families affected by particular evictions. Where estate papers have disappeared or are not otherwise available for consultation, this material is not only the principal, but often the sole guide to events. However, evidence of this type must be handled with great care. It was recorded after *c*.1880 at a time of intense political struggle in the Western Highlands. Several of those who appeared before the two Royal Commissions were among the most active and vocal critics of landlordism. Objectivity in such circumstances was impossible and the historian has to be vigilant when considering the claims of some witnesses. Sometimes, when a form of cross-checking against contemporary sources has been possible, the evidence from 1883 and 1892 has proven to be substantially accurate. On other occasions, however, serious conflicts of fact and interpretation occur which are very difficult to resolve.[10]

(c)   A key source for a study of eviction is the Summonses or Writs of Removal filed among the legal processes in local Sheriff Courts.[11] Curiously they have never been used to any extent in any of the major studies of the Clearances so far published. The material does pose difficulties and cannot be employed as a simple index of removals without significant qualification. An unknown number of small tenants were displaced without the expense of legal procedure. In early 1843, for instance, Macleod of Macleod declared his intention to annex some of the common lands attached to the townships of Roag, Herribost and Griep in the parish of Kilmuir, Skye. He asked the tenants to sign an agreement by which they consented '. . . to place our farms at Macleod's disposal next Whitsunday and bind ourselves to abide by his arrangements whether we receive a legal warning or not'. Thirty-four tenants signed the document.[12] Similarly, in spring 1847 the factor of Cameron of Lochiel tried to obtain signatures from the crofters of the township of Achintore, '. . . binding themselves that they would give up these crofts at Whitsunday first to Lochiel without any legal measures or troubling Lochiel with any expenses'.[13]

Again, summonses of removal were sometimes issued as a form of threat, to try and compel the repayment of rent arrears, rather than to actually force tenants to surrender their lands.[14] This helps to explain why the simple serving of a writ of removal did not always guarantee population displacement. A detailed analysis of summonses issued on the Duke of Argyll's estate on the Ross of Mull was carried out for 1850 and 1851. Thirty per cent of those tenants named in the writs in 1850 had to be served again in 1851.[15] This evidence may also suggest that many tenants resisted the law, not by overt protest and collective opposition, but simply by ignoring the legal demand of their landlord. It is possible that some proprietors at least were unwilling to undertake the additional responsibility of calling in sheriff's officers and the police to enforce the summons by ejecting those who refused to go.

Even F.W. Clark, proprietor of Ulva, who successfully reduced the number of inhabitants on that island by several hundreds in the later 1840s, met stubborn resistance. In 1851 he referred to several 'very refractory and lawless people' on a list he had drawn up of fourteen families to be served with summonses of removal. Some, apparently, had been regularly served with writs for the previous five years but '. . . they laugh to scorn the Sheriff's warrant, saying they will continue to remain where they are independent of either Sheriff or me'. He thought that '. . . he may be under the necessity of resorting to ejection in their case' because several of these truculent tenants 'are in the most valuable part of my sheep wintering ground and are doing much harm to my pasture'.[16]

For these reasons, the temptation to use the material derived from Sheriff Court Processes as a precise index of eviction must be resisted. Nevertheless, when combined with information gleaned from rentals and the census, summonses of removal can provide an invaluable guide to *coercion* and to the approximate spatial variation and chronological sequence of eviction in the region of study.

(iv) *The Census*
The published census offers little assistance to the historian of the Clearances.[17] The printed parish enumerations conceal more than they reveal because both removal and resettlement could take place within parish boundaries, and great changes in population are sometimes hidden behind aggregate figures. The classic illustration of this problem comes from the parish of Farr in Sutherland. Here the major evictions associated with the great clearances in that county are not apparent in the census records for 1821 and 1831. Those who lost their holdings were simply moved to another part of the parish. However, the original enumerators' schedules are more valuable. By analysing those of selected parishes for 1841, 1851 and 1861 it is possible to trace the survival, depletion or disappearance of particular townships. When the information from the enumerators' books is combined with data from estate papers and sheriff court writs of removal, the influence of eviction, relative to other factors in these population changes, can sometimes be determined.[18]

(v) *The Press and Contemporary Pamphlet Literature*
The dangers in relying too heavily and uncritically on press sources have already been discussed.[19] For the period of this study, however, newspapers and periodical literature have a particular value. The potato famine concentrated the attention of the national press on the Highlands. The *Scotsman* and the *Times* both sent special

investigative reporters or 'commissioners' to the distressed districts. An earlier chapter has shown how contemporary newspaper readers had also developed a considerable interest in Highland affairs.[20] This could be more easily satisfied by the 1840s because the development of steamship services to several parts of the western mainland and Inner Hebrides allowed reporters to penetrate much further than ever before in the search for a good story or in order to record a dramatic incident. In addition, by the time of the famine, a regional Highland press, in the form of such periodicals as the *Inverness Courier*, the *Inverness Advertiser* and the *John O'Groats Journal*, had come into being. Each issue contained detailed views on Highland topics. The Free Church newspaper, the *Witness*, also had a special interest in Highland matters. For the early 1850s the *Advertiser*, under the vigorous editorship of Thomas Mulock, and the *Witness*, edited by Hugh Miller, are rich sources of information on some of the more spectacular episodes of clearance.

2

The data derived from an examination of these sources are presented in Appendix 11. There too the reader will find descriptive detail of particular incidents. The regional patterns of clearance identified from the source material are delineated in Tables 7.1 and 7.2. These suggest that the major evictions during the potato famine were concentrated along the western mainland, north of Ardnamurchan, and in the Inner and Outer Hebrides. Only two major incidents occurred in either the central or eastern Highlands, at Strathconan and Greenyards in Easter Ross. But of twenty-two affected parishes, only two were located outside the Western Highlands and Islands. Even the removals in these two areas need to be placed in chronological context. At Strathconon, for instance, the census enumerator observed in 1841 that the population of the glen had fallen since 1831 from 657 to 294. This had come about as a result of 'a systematic plan pursued for many years of ejecting the small tenants and throwing their farms into large sheep walks'. In this district, then, the evictions of the 1840s and 1850s were simply the climax to a much longer process of dispossession, which had begun many years before.[21]

Essentially, the clearances of the 1840s and 1850s, with only a few exceptions, focused on particular areas of the crofting region. When the press and the pamphleteers of the period referred, therefore, to a new surge in *Highland* evictions they exaggerated somewhat. The parishes affected by substantial clearances (as listed in Table 7.1) in the famine years contained a population of 76,523 or about twenty-six per cent of the total population of the four Highland counties in 1841. On the other hand, the number of inhabitants in affected parishes represented forty-four per cent of the population of the crofting zone as defined in Chapter 1.[22]

Within the crofting region, there was also considerable variation in the spatial distribution of major evictions. A broad distinction can be drawn between most parishes in the islands and most districts on the mainland. If the tabulation is restricted to Table 7.1, then seventy-eight per cent of the population in 1841 of affected parishes lived in the Inner and Outer Hebrides. If the calculation is extended to include

Table 7.1. Highland Parishes with Evidence of Substantial Removals, 1846-1856

Parish/Area	Population, 1841	Year of Maximum Population
Central & Eastern Highlands		
Greenyards (1854)		
Strathconon (Contin parish)	1770	1831
Western Mainland		
Knoydart (1853-4) (Glenelg parish)	2729	1841
Morvern (1855)	1774	1831
Ardnamurchan (1852-3)	3025	1831
Lochbroom (1849)	4809	1851
Assynt (1850-)	3178	1841
Edderachillis	1699	1831
Inner Hebrides		
Lismore (and Appin)	4193	1831
Sleat (Skye) (1849-54)	2706	1831
Strath (Skye) (1849-54)	3150	1851
Kilninian (Mull) (1849-)	4335	1831
Torosay (Mull) (1849-)	1616	1821
Kilfinichen (Mull) (1849-)	4103	1841
Kildalton (Islay) (1848-)	3304	1841
Tiree (1848-)	4391	1841
Outer Hebrides		
Uig (Lewis) (1849-)	3828	1891
Lochs (Lewis) (1849-)	2630	1911
Stornoway (Lewis) (1849-)	4804	1911
Barvas (1849-)	4361	1911
N. Uist (1849-)	4428	1821
S. Uist (1849-)	7327	1841
Barra (1849-)	2363	1911
Total Parishes: 22	Total Population: 76,523	

Notes: (i) The source for this and Table 7.2 is Appendix 11, *Principal Evictions in the Highlands, 1846-56.*

(ii) Only parishes where evictions involved removal of townships or c. 10 families or more in the period have been included. The table only provides an interim rough guide to areas where major clearances occurred. It may be modified by future local research and it errs on the side of underestimations of total removals.

(iii) Dates in brackets refer to approximate years of removal.

evidence from Table 7.2, then seventy-two per cent of the population in 1841 of affected parishes resided in the islands. Large-scale removals were limited on the west coast to particular districts. No record of a significant level of eviction in the 1840s and 1850s was found for the Wester Ross parishes of Gairloch, Applecross and Lochcarron. Indeed, evidence presented to the Napier Commission in 1883 specifically comments on the absence of clearances in these districts in these years.[23]

Elsewhere, in parts of western Inverness-shire and Sutherland, evictions did take place but not on anything like the scale of earlier times. Thus the township of Kirkton in the parish of Lochalsh was cleared between 1847 and 1849 but the major population

Table 7.2. Highland Parishes with Evidence of Some Removals, 1846-1856

Parish/Area	Population, 1841	Year of Maximum Population
Western Mainland		
Lochalsh (1849)	2597	1841
Glensheil (1849, 1852)	742	1821
Arisaig & Moidart (1849-53)	3205	1831
Islands		
Harris	4429	1911
Coll (1848-)	1442	1841
Jura	1320	1831
Kilchoman (Islay) (1849-)	4505	1831
Killarow (Islay) (1849-)	5782	1841

Total Parishes: 8   Total Population: 24,022

Note: Parishes and areas described experienced some removals in the period but the evidence examined was too ambiguous or slight to determine overall extent. See Appendix 11 for further details.

displacement had already occurred some years before the famine when the estate was purchased from the Earl of Seaforth by Sir Hugh Innes.[24] Five townships were cleared in Glenshiel from 1849 to 1854 but this was the final stage in a process of eviction which can be traced back to the early decades of the nineteenth century.[25] Similar patterns can be identified in Moidart and Arisaig and on the estate of Cameron of Lochiel.[26] In Morvern, a major removal of 105 people from the township of Auliston took place in 1855. However, most of its inhabitants had already suffered eviction from other settlements between 1841 and 1843. The number who lost land in the famine clearances in Morvern accounted for twenty-five per cent of all those estimated to have experienced eviction in the parish in the nineteenth century.[27] Only in Knoydart (parish of Glenelg) and Ardnamurchan did particularly extensive removals, affecting hundreds rather than dozens, take place in the famine years. At Knoydart, the number of inhabitants was reduced within a timescale of about five years between 1847 and 1853 from 600 to 70 through a combined strategy of clearance and assisted emigration.[28] The Riddell estate in Ardnamurchan was granted 101 summonses of removal in 1852 and began a programme of population redistribution and eviction in the following few years.[29]

That *major* clearances were mainly restricted to the Inner and Outer Hebrides in the 1840s and 1850s is also suggested by the data presented in Table 7.3. This has been constructed from the writs of removal issued at Tobermory Sheriff Court between 1846 and 1852. The jurisdiction of this court included a number of insular and mainland districts in western Argyll. Summonses of removal, as shown earlier, are by no means an exact measure of eviction. Yet the patterns outlined in Table 7.3 are nevertheless suggestive. Of 1558 summonses issued from 1846 to 1852, 1310, or eighty-four per cent, were in favour of island landlords while only 248, or sixteen per cent, were granted to mainland proprietors.

A similar exercise was undertaken for the Duke of Argyll's island estates in Mull and Tiree and the Duke of Sutherland's mainland property in the parishes of Assynt and

Table 7.3. Summonses of Removal and Sequestration, Tobermory Sheriff Court, 1846-1852 (by area)

Islands	Total	1846	1847	1848	1849	1850	1851	1852
Tiree	175	–	24	–	45	78	28	–
Mull	637	40	33	7	122	166	181	88
Ulva	88	6	6	–	12	46	14	4
Coll	93	4	21	–	7	9	30	22
Canna	17	–	–	–	17	–	–	–
Treshnish Is.	15	–	–	–	–	–	11	4
Gometra	4	–	–	–	4	–	–	–
Total	1029	50 (5)	84 (8)	7 (0.6)	207 (20)	299 (29)	264 (26)	118 (12)
Mainland								
Ardnamurchan	211	31	17	–	4	20	15	124
Morvern	37	–	–	–	–	5	22	10
Total	248	31 (12)	17 (7)	–	4 (2)	25 (10)	37 (15)	134 (54)

Source: SRO, Sheriff Court Processes (Tobermory), SC 59/2/4-14.
Notes: Figures in brackets refer to annual numbers as per cent of total, 1846-1852.

Edderachillis in Sutherland. Between 1846 and 1852, 147 writs of removal were granted to the Sutherland estate at Dornoch Sheriff Court, mainly against tenants in the two western parishes.[30] While the Duke of Sutherland obtained summonses at the rate of twenty-one per annum, the Duke of Argyll did so at the rate of fifty-seven per annum over the period.

Substantial evictions, then, in the famine period, took place mainly in the crofting zone and within it were more likely to occur in the Hebrides. The removal of families and the depletion of townships was common throughout the Western Highlands and Islands but large-scale evictions, leading to the disappearance of entire settlements and the movement of many dozens of people, were unusual on the mainland. Only in Knoydart and, to a lesser extent, Morvern and Ardnamurchan was there the widespread uprooting of whole communities on the scale experienced in many parts of the Inner and Outer Hebrides. As far as can be determined from the available evidence, only the islands of Rhum, Eigg, Canna, some areas of Skye and, to a lesser extent, Harris were untouched by the major removals in the islands at this period. Few districts, however, remained entirely immune as the great wave of clearances built up in the wake of the famine. The data collected in Tables 7.1 and 7.2 and Appendix 11 suggest that few substantial evictions occurred in 1846 and 1847 but that thereafter the process accelerated very rapidly from 1849 to 1855 before slowing down again in the later 1850s. By 1860, large-scale clearances had become rare, though the habit of 'weeding out families by twos or threes, or turning adrift the occupants of a single hamlet at a time' continued for many more years.[31]

These clearances, therefore, were very concentrated both in time and space and, as a result, had quite devastating social consequences throughout the Hebrides. One experienced official of the Central Board reckoned that summonses of removal were to be issued against at least 600 families on the island of Mull alone in the two years 1848 and 1849.[32] From 1847 to 1851, the proprietor of Ulva, F.W. Clark, principally through a resolute process of eviction, reduced the total population of his estate from 500 to 150.[33] Between 1847 and 1851, Sir James Matheson, proprietor of Lewis, obtained 1367 summonses of removal against tenants while in 1850 alone, 132 families, numbering 660 souls, were evicted in Barra.[34] Many were shipped to Tobermory from where they dispersed to Inverness and then the cities of the Lowlands. Those who lost their lands in that year were equivalent to a quarter of the island's population of 2363 in 1841.[35] In Skye, in 1852, it was reckoned that eviction was so widespread that many men feared to leave their families to trek south for work. Even the sober and experienced Sir Edward Coffin was alarmed at the sheer scale and speed of clearance. In unusually colourful prose he condemned the landed classes for seeking to bring about 'the extermination of the population'. Eviction was rampant and would inevitably lead to 'the unsettling of the foundations of the social system' as well as to the enforced depopulation of the Highland region.[36]

In one sense, Coffin was correct. The clearances of the 1840s and 1850s, in their pace, extent and intensity recall the great Sutherland evictions of the second and third decades of the nineteenth century.[37] Between c.1810 and 1826, an estimated 8,000 to 9,000 of that county's inhabitants were removed from the interior parishes in one of the most ambitious programmes of social engineering ever undertaken in nineteenth-century Britain. But the evictions of the famine differed from these earlier events in at least three key respects. First, the Sutherland experiment was restricted to one large estate with a population of just over 22,000 in 1821. The clearances of the 1840s and 1850s spread throughout most of the Inner and Outer Hebrides and into several districts on the mainland. They eventually penetrated a region with a total population of over 91,000 people in 1841. Second, the Sutherland strategy was based on the resettlement of the dispossessed communities on the coastal areas and the establishment there of a new maritime economy of fishing and manufacturing which would complement the big sheep farms of the inland districts. The estate apparently initially tried to reduce the social costs of eviction, though their efforts were vitiated by poor planning, the very great insensitivity of some of their agents and the economic crisis emerging in the Highlands of the 1820s. Some clearances in the famine period, such as those in Lewis, the Macdonald estate in Skye and in Ardnamurchan, were associated with limited resettlement.[38] For the most part, however, the strategy in these districts in the 1840s and 1850s differed fundamentally from that of earlier decades. The aim in most of these later evictions became an undisguised and resolute determination to expel the people. In the past, clearance had meant dispossession but not necessarily depopulation. This could not be said of the majority of those which occurred during the famine. Indeed, to ensure expulsion, eviction became combined on a number of properties with elaborate schemes of assisted emigration funded by landlords, in order to rid their estates of the 'redundant' population. This connection between clearance and emigration is explored in detail in Chapter 8.

Third, there was a significant difference in timescale. The Sutherland programme attracted criticism because of the attempt to transform an ancient way of life too quickly through the radical surgery of rapid displacement and movement of population. But the Sutherland clearances took place over a fifteen-year period. The major evictions of the famine only began in *c.*1848-9, reached their peak between 1849 and 1853 and had all but ceased by 1856-7. By any standards, therefore, they were more cataclysmic. These clearances were unleashed on a population already ravaged by hunger, disease and destitution. Few attempts were made to provide shelter for the dispossessed. In the majority of cases the options for most were either emigration or migration, sinking from the status of crofter to that of semi-landless cottar or seeking lodging in overcrowded accommodation in slum villages like Lochcarron, Plockton, Tobermory or Lochaline which continued to grow in size as the evictions intensified.[39]

The famine clearances, therefore, have a special significance in the history of the Highland Clearances as a whole. They were the last in the cycle of great evictions which transformed Highland society from the last quarter of the eighteenth century. They intensified suffering within the Highlands and attracted bitter criticism outside the region. The more notorious episodes of clearances, such as those at South Uist, Knoydart, Sollas in North Uist and Boreraig and Suishnish in Skye, were chronicled in great detail in the national press and stimulated a large and impassioned pamphlet literature.[40] These removals, therefore, had a vital influence on the future political and social development of the Highlands at two levels. They elicited a renewed wave of sympathy for the plight of the Highland people.[41] As has been seen, the failure of the

Central Board to bring prosperity to the region and the partial dependence of the population on outside charity after 1850 brought trenchant criticism of the Highlanders from some quarters both in the Lowlands and in England.[42] The publicity given to the clearances not only temporarily stilled such complaints but stimulated a quite different public response from some sources. In the long run a new mood of support developed which helped to form the political background to the benevolent land legislation of Gladstone's government in the 1880s. Again, though more speculatively, it can be argued that the wave of clearances in the 1850s also helped to forge the developing political self- consciousness of the crofting community. It may well have been these evictions to a much greater extent than those of earlier times which coloured the memories and helped to activate the political will of the land reformers of the 1870s and 1880s. Significantly, more than half of the twenty-six major episodes of eviction documented in Alexander Mackenzie's *History of the Highland Clearances* of 1883, the volume which became a source book of the political agitation, relate to the famine period.[43] Ironically, in trying to solve the daunting economic problems of their estates by such drastic action, the Highland landed classes eventually stimulated a political reaction a few decades later which they proved unable to control.

3

The spatial concentration of the evictions of the 1840s and 1850s reflected the social and economic history of the Highlands in the previous half-century. They occurred in those districts which had suffered the most serious levels of destitution during the famine. By every criterion, estimated levels of mortality, ratio of population to relief applicants and net expenditure on relief, the Hebrides and some districts of the west coast experienced the most acute distress.[44] It was also, therefore, the region where rent arrears accumulated most rapidly and where proprietors feared the costs of maintaining a destitute tenantry either through private charity or the Poor Law.[45]

The area was inhabited by communities of small crofters and cottars who had eked out a precarious existence ever since the collapse of kelp manufacture and the malaise of fishing. Comparison of Table 7.4, which lists the main sources of Highland kelp sold in Liverpool between 1817 and 1828, and Table 7.1, which indicates the parishes where clearances concentrated after *c*.1848, reveals interesting parallels. In both, certain islands in the Inner and Outer Hebrides feature in a prominent way. Moreover, only eight of the twenty-two parishes which experienced extensive eviction reached their maximum levels of population before the census of 1841. These clearances, therefore, can be viewed as an attempt to correct a perceived demographic imbalance which had emerged in the wake of the collapse of the staples of the West Highland economy in the decades after the end of the Napoleonic Wars. In the later eighteenth century many proprietors had built up the croft system to ensure a labour supply for kelping and fishing. This had accelerated the fragmentation of holdings and caused endemic problems of subdivision. The clearances of the famine were a drastic response to these problems. In a sense, over the space of less than two to three generations, estate policy in the Hebrides swung from one extreme to the other. Between *c*.1780 and

Table 7.4. Sources of Highland Kelp sold by W.A. and G. Maxwell of Liverpool, 1817-1828

Source	Volume (tons)	Per cent of total volume
S. Uist	1774	27
Mull	1414	21
Skye	1020	16
Harris	666	10
Jura	621	9
Ulva	256	4
Tiree	181	3
Morvern	119	2
Lochsween	114	2
Fort William	111	2
Lochinver	100	2
Applecross	71	1
Argyllshire (mainland)	61	1
Oban	32	0.4
Glenelg	29	0.4
Gairloch	20	0.3
Totals	6589	100

Source: Dunvegan Castle, Macleod of Macleod Muniments, 2/531, Statement of Kelp sold, July 1817-July 1818 incl. by W.A. and G. Maxwell of Liverpool.

Note: See also Table 9.4, p.215, for a similar correlation between eviction and kelp-producing districts in Lewis.

c.1820 the strategy had concentrated a larger population than could be easily supported by land alone in the coastal crofting townships. In the 1820s and 1830s it moved to dispersal and land consolidation in order that the 'redundant' dense communities of smallholders could be replaced with more profitable pastoral husbandry. The evictions of the famine period accelerated this process and brought it to a climax in the 1850s. As will be seen in Chapter 12, invariably much of the land of the cleared townships was simply added to that of the big grazing farms.[46]

This interpretation fits the spatial distribution of clearance throughout the Highland region. There was no significant level of eviction in the central and eastern Highlands primarily because consolidation of land, the laying down of sheep walks and the creation of a large farm structure had already taken place there by 1840. As the Central Board pointed out after its first survey of the region in 1847: 'In the more eastern and central parts of these districts, the country is partly occupied as large sheep or store farms and partly as small farms and a considerable portion of the country is under tillage'.[47] Their conclusion is supported by the detailed survey of the social and economic structure in this region in the parish reports for this zone presented in Appendix 7.[48] Similarly, the great Sutherland removals before 1830 had reduced the need for further dispersal except in the poorer western parishes of Assynt and Edderachillis.[49] In many of the western districts of Inverness-shire, however, and parts of Wester Ross, the formation of extensive sheep farms in the interior had forced population to collect along the coast. As the Central Board put it: '. . . towards the West, the country becomes more and more exclusively occupied as large sheep-walks and the great mass of the people are clustered round the shores and either occupying small crofts or subsisting by labour, fishing etc.'[50] It was here that the mainland evictions concentrated during the famine.

It would be wrong to assume that the Inner and Outer Hebrides remained insulated from the penetration of the great sheep farms before 1840. Clearances for the purposes of sheep farming had taken place in Harris, Mull, parts of Skye, North Uist and Rhum.[51] But it is important to stress that on the eve of the famine several areas in the Hebrides still remained relatively immune. Only in Harris and Rhum and, to a much lesser extent, North Uist, had the evictions been comprehensive. Lewis, Mull and Skye were still only partially cleared.[52] Major removals had not occurred in Barra or on Tiree and were only beginning in Islay in the early 1840s. During the tenure of the MacNeills of Barra evictions had been restricted to the townships of Roll and Kilbarr but those removed were resettled on neighbouring communities.[53] In 1838 there were 7,600 sheep on the estate but 4,000 of these were to be found on the home farm.[54] The most recent scholarly study of Islay also argues that the process of clearance was in its early stages before 1846.[55] While Mull was already experiencing widespread removals before 1846, it was acknowledged that they were still relatively rare on the Duke of Argyll's large estate on the Ross of Mull. One witness to the Napier Commission, Donald Macdonald, aged 82, of the township of Lee, who had farmed a croft there since 1834, stated that, 'I never heard a complaint scarcely against the Duke or factor until the end of 1846 or 1847'. Such removals as did occur were restricted to 'bad neighbours, not paying rent or being a smuggler'.[56] The famine evictions, therefore, represented in part a massive extension of wholesale clearance in parts of the Hebrides where it had been relatively limited in scale before 1846.

4

Mass eviction was the ultimate manifestation of landlord authority in the Highlands. If, as is often asserted, Scottish landowners were among the most absolute in Europe, the Highland élite had the greatest power of all. Most crofting families depended to a greater or lesser extent on land as the primary source of all the fundamental items of life: food, shelter, fuel and status. Yet, unlike the pattern in various parts of the Continent, peasant ownership of land was unknown. In Europe, it was peasant proprietorship above all which limited seigneurial power.[57] The Highland population relied on land but had no such security of tenure. Long leases for periods of nine years or more, which were characteristic of Lowland agriculture, did exist in the north-west but were restricted to the possessions of the 'tacksmen' (literally 'leaseholders') who farmed land of considerable acreage, invariably rented at £20 per annum or more. The vast majority of tenants, paying £5 per annum or less, held land on an annual basis and so were entirely vulnerable to removal at either the Whitsun or Martinmas terms. Even less secure was the undermass of cottars or subtenants, forming as much as one third to one half of the total population of some estates, who paid no rent at all. On a typical West Highland property, therefore, most of the inhabitants were liable to lose their possessions at the landlord's will. This helps to explain why the eviction of entire communities was common in the Highlands but relatively rare in most Lowland regions. The tenurial restrictions of the south and east only protected the big tenants in the north-west.[58]

However, these formal differences merely reflected the declining economic importance of the small Highland tenantry in the nineteenth century. Their economic value had diminished since the decline in the labour-intensive activities of military employment, illicit whisky-making, fishing and kelping in the 1820s. In the crisis years of 1816-17, 1825, 1836-7 and from 1846 to 1856 many came to depend on the largesse of the landlord class to sustain their very existence. From being an important source of estate revenue many crofting townships rapidly became a drain on landlord resources. Furthermore, the law in Scotland made removal uncomplicated and relatively inexpensive. The basic legislation was an Act of the Scottish Parliament, 'Anent the Warning of Tenants', passed as early as 1555.[59] By an Act of Sederunt of the Lords of Council and Session of 1756 the legal obligations of a proprietor who pursued an eviction were clarified. Consent to a removal could be given if the landlord applied to a Sheriff at least forty days before Whitsun. Such an action 'shall be held as equal to a warning executed in terms of the Act of Parliament'. This rendered eviction in the Highlands much cheaper, quicker and easier than enclosure procedures in England where interested parties often had to obtain parliamentary approval for consolidation of common lands. The Scottish legislation was also comprehensive because, although normally served against a single tenant, the summons affected all persons who lived on the holding. It obliged not only the named individual but '. . . his wife, bairns, family, servants, subtenants, cottars and dependents to flit and remove'. The number of writs of removal which were served, therefore, only give a limited indication of all those likely to be affected by these legal procedures.

It would be wrong, however, to convey the simple impression of a helpless tenantry dependent on the whim of an autocratic landed class for continued possession of land. The people were virtually defenceless but not all landlords were in a powerful position. Several, especially in the Hebridean districts where clearance concentrated, were no longer masters in their own houses.[60] By the early 1850s the three major estates on Skye, including those of Lord Macdonald and Macleod of Macleod, were under trust. So too was the Macdonald estate of North Uist. Sir James Riddell's lands in Ardnamurchan were run by trustees from 1850 and finally put on the market in 1850. Campbell of Islay, who owned virtually the whole of that island, had gone bankrupt in 1849. Five of the smaller estates on Mull were under trust. These properties were administered by the agents of trustees for the creditors of these landowners. Their obligation was to treat the property as an asset, to run it efficiently and, if possible, to bring it to a more profitable condition so that, if unentailed, it could be sold in whole or in part to reduce the debts which were attached to it. Under such a régime, social considerations not only became a decidedly secondary consideration but in law had no relevance whatsoever.

It was, therefore, no coincidence that several of the most controversial clearances of the time took place on estates which were managed by trustees.[61] The major evictions in Ardnamurchan occurred after a detailed survey of the property, carried out by an agent for the trustees, which strongly recommended dispossession of many of the people.[62] Similarly, the bankrupt estate of Islay was administered between 1848 and

1853 by James Brown, an Edinburgh accountant. He enforced removals in the Glen and Oa areas of the island where the small tenants were concentrated.[63] As the *Scotsman* put it: 'When the lands are heavily mortgaged, the obvious though harsh resource is dispossessing the small tenants, to make room for a better class able to pay rent. This task generally devolves on south country managers or trustees, who look only to money returns, and who cannot sympathise with the peculiar situations and feelings of the Highland population.'[64] Even the Ardnamurchan administration recognised the fundamental alterations that trusteeship brought to estate management. They referred to 'the feeling on the part of the Proprietor of concern for the welfare of his tenantry' which disappeared when the property fell under the jurisdiction of trustees: '. . . there being no room for the exercise of these sentiments, the position of matters is entirely changed'.[65]

Financial imperatives could also influence the pattern of eviction in a more subtle fashion. Some estates were so burdened with debt that a significant proportion of income was absorbed in interest payments.[66] In the first half of 1847 interest rates began to rise and the increase sent shock waves through the Highlands. Macleod of Macleod wrote despairingly in December 1846 to his mother:

> Interests for the next half year having risen half a per cent. I am utterly unable any longer to struggle against the load of debt left to me with the estates and in the course of a few weeks you will see the whole of the unentailed lands exposed for sale . . .
> I have never received above £1200 a year clear from the property and now that the interests are raised and the poor people are in such a state that I cannot get from them a third of their rents, it is absolutely necessary this step should be taken . . . My intention is quite unknown here and I much dread the announcement of it for it will cause great lamentation among the people.[67]

The relationship between clearances and financial fluctuations is an unexplored problem. It is, however, interesting to speculate on how far the increasing evidence of eviction in the Western Highlands after 1848-9 reflects the impact of the general economic depression in Britain in these years. The trauma suffered by the people of the crofting region may have been conditioned in part by the rise and fall of the money markets in distant Glasgow, Edinburgh and London.

In one sense, therefore, there was no effective defence against the massive economic and demographic pressures which now gripped the Western Highlands. If 'traditional' landowners avoided or postponed eviction because of paternalistic concern their estates became vulnerable as a result of the fall in rental income and the cost of maintaining a destitute tenantry. In several cases this led to bankruptcy and to a transfer of ownership or authority either to new landlords or to trustees who had less inhibition about implementing policies of clearance on a grand scale.

The catalyst for the great wave of evictions was, of course, the potato famine itself. The sheer length and depth of the crisis seemed to legitimise radical action. It was argued that the famine had finally and conclusively shown the inadequacies of crofting as an economic system.[68] A thinning of numbers was vital, not simply for private gain, but as an essential, if harsh, corrective to the chronic social ills of the region. These public defences of clearance proved influential because they coincided in time with two other factors which made evictions on a large scale both attractive and necessary. Figure 1 reveals the changing price patterns of Cheviot and Blackface sheep. The 1820s and 1830s were both decades of fluctuating fortunes. But from the early 1840s the prices of these breeds recovered and began to rise consistently into the 1860s. At the same time, the main economic support of the crofting class, the trade in black cattle, experienced a phase of prolonged stagnation from *c*.1846. Earlier discussion has shown how prices fell on average by more than a half between 1846 and 1852 and that beasts were often rendered unsaleable by their poor condition during the years of shortage.[69] These changing price relationships powerfully renewed the incentive to consolidate crofting land for the purposes of sheep farming.

It was also argued that the differing market performance of sheep and Highland cattle in the 1840s and early 1850s was not so much a result of short-term fluctuation as a consequence of a deeper structural transformation in British agriculture. Some insisted that the Repeal of the Corn Laws in 1846 might ensure the final ruin of the West Highland cattle business because farmers in more favoured districts of Britain would transfer resources towards mixed and pastoral husbandry as arable cultivation was likely to become more vulnerable to foreign competition.[70] The decline in cattle prices, therefore, was viewed as the symptom of a much more serious malaise. The Highland breed could not compete in the new context. The attractions of converting much of the remaining grazing lands of the small tenantry to sheep farming became irresistible. It was a reflection of the narrowing comparative advantage of the Highland economy. While the rentals of the small tenants slumped on most estates during the famine, income from the big sheep farmers remained buoyant.[71] Even before 1846 it was a much easier administrative task to collect annual payments from a few major tenants than to extract revenue from a destitute host of impoverished crofters.

Figure 1. Sheep Prices, Cheviot and Blackface, 1820-1920

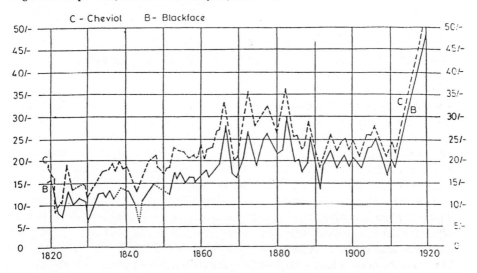

Source: W. Orr, *Deer Forests, Landlords and Crofters* (Edinburgh, 1982), 155.

As the famine persisted, several landlords came under a new pressure to carry out major evictions. The Central Board had undertaken the main burden of relief in the distressed districts. Its activities ensured, as explained in Chapter 5, that the numbers of paupers supported by the official Poor Law did not rise dramatically after 1846.[72] Yet though the potato blight continued well into the 1850s, the Board's operations ceased in 1850. Immediately the numbers of 'occasional poor' in the four Highland counties relieved by the official Poor Law increased sharply. In 1850, 1765 individuals obtained 'occasional' support. By 1852 this number had trebled to 5109.[73] These people became the direct financial responsibility of the ratepayers of the region. The old voluntary system which had lingered in the Highlands longer than in any other part of Scotland had been mainly replaced by c.1850 by a structure of assessment through which landowners and tenants shared the burden of payment.[74] As Table 7.5 indicates, the proportion of 'paupers' relieved to total population in the Highland counties, traditionally lower than anywhere else in the country, had crept much above the Scottish average by 1851-2.

Table 7.5. *Poor Rates in the Highlands, 1851-1853: Proportion Percentage of Paupers Relieved to Total Population*

	1851	1852	1853
Counties			
Argyll	*4.98	*5.41	*5.52
Inverness	*6.20	*6.37	4.70
Ross	*4.89	*6.20	4.73
Sutherland	4.79	4.78	4.74
Islands			
Argyll	*4.97	*5.79	*5.13
Inverness	*7.71	*9.45	3.90
Ross	3.53	3.21	2.16
Scotland	4.85	4.93	4.85

(with exception of above counties)
* = more than Scottish 'average'
Source: *PP*, XLVI (1854-5), *Return of Population and Poor Rates* (Scotland), 1853.

Highland proprietors were now confronted with a horrendous scenario. Even before Sir John McNeill undertook his investigation of the distressed districts in 1851 it was widely rumoured that government was contemplating the introduction of 'an able-bodied poor law' to combat the threat of starvation in the Highlands.[75] This was indeed the logical outcome of Trevelyan's own thinking and the schemes he had encouraged the Central Board to adopt between 1847 and 1850. After the reform of the Poor Law in 1845 only 'paupers' (the old no longer capable of physical toil, widows, orphans and the sick) had a right to relief. An 'able-bodied poor law' would have given the destitute unemployed the legal right to claim support. Since the overwhelming majority of the population of many estates in the Western Highlands were in this distressed condition, the mere suggestion of such legislation was enough to send tremors of alarm through the ranks of the landed classes. One observer alleged in 1849 that such measures were 'being talked of in high quarters as a remedy for the grievances' of the Highlands.[76] Some assumed that McNeill's inquiry would report in favour of a reform of the Scottish Poor Law along these lines to accommodate the problems of the stricken population of the Highlands.[77]

In the event, however, and perhaps not surprisingly given McNeill's own philosophical predilections, he advised instead that the crisis should be solved by a programme of assisted emigration.[78] But before government came to a decision on his *Report* several landlords had come to regard large-scale evictions as the only effective response to the threat posed by an extension of the Poor Law. Sir Charles Trevelyan himself agreed that the possibility of a sharp increase in poor rates '. . . would give a motive for eviction stronger than any which has yet been operated'.[79] Other observers referred to 'the terror of the poor rates' and 'the retribution of the poor law' as the decisive factors in promoting the clearances which swept over the Hebrides between 1849 and 1854.[80] Whether they were or not, it remained true that mass eviction was the culmination of the interplay of powerful demographic, economic and ideological forces which reached a climax in the last years of the potato famine.

NOTES

1. SRO, HD7/47, William Skene to Sir Charles Trevelyan, 21 February 1848.
2. For an assessment of current knowledge on this subject see T.M. Devine, 'The Highland Clearances', *Recent Findings of Research in Economic and Social History*, 4 (1987).
3. See the bibliography in Richards, *Highland Clearances*, I, 508-521 for the range of writing which the subject has attracted.
4. NLS, Sutherland Estate Papers, Dep. 313/877, E. Maciver to James Loch, 8 March 1850.
5. See below, pp.218-19; 235.
6. MS. Diary of J.M. Mackenzie, 1851; Argyll Estate Papers (Inveraray Castle); Macleod of Macleod Muniments (Dunvegan Castle); Lord Macdonald Papers (SRO); Maclaine of Lochbuie Papers (SRO); Campbell of Jura Papers (SRO); Islay Estate Papers (Islay House).
7. For a recent reference see James Hunter and Cailean Maclean, *Skye: the Island* (Edinburgh, 1986), 12-14.
8. SRO, Lord Macdonald Papers, GD123/1, 122/11.
9. The 1892 Royal Commission's *Reports and Minutes of Evidence* are contained in *PP*, XXXVIII-XXXIX (1895).
10. See, for example, the radically different accounts of evictions in Tiree, below, pp.240-1.
11. Those examined in this study were Tobermory Sheriff Court (SRO, SC 59/2/4-14), Stornoway (SRO, SC 33/17/26-33), Dornoch (SRO, SC 59/2), Portree (SC 32/5). These courts cover Mull, Tiree, Morvern, Ardnamurchan, Skye, Lewis and Sutherland. The holdings of other West Highland Sheriff Courts at the time of research (1986) were not available for consultation.
12. Dunvegan Castle, Macleod of Macleod Muniments, Section 2, 228/3, Macleod to People of Roag etc., 16 February 1843.
13. Achnacarry Castle, Cameron of Lochiel MSS, Attic Chest, r.h. top drawer, Bundle 15, Ewan Cameron to Lochiel, 8 April 1847.
14. Inveraray Castle, Argyll Estate Papers, Bundle 1523, J. Campbell to Duke of Argyll, 25 April 1854; MS. Diary of J.M. Mackenzie, 1851, *passim*.
15. SRO, Sheriff Court Processes (Tobermory), SC 59/2/7-9.

16. *Ibid.*, SC 59/2/9, Summons of Removal for F.W. Clark, enclosing letter, Henry Nisbet to F.W. Clark of Ulva, 20 February 1851.

17. Gray, *Highland Economy*, 61.

18. For an example of such an exercise on the parish of Barvas, Lewis, see pp.214-5.

19. See above, p.172.

20. See above, pp.118-19.

21. GRO, Parish of Contin, Enumerator's Schedules (1841). For the Greenyards clearance see *Scotsman*, 8 April 1854, and SRO, Lord Advocate's Papers, AD 56/309/3. For Strathconon, *Inverness Courier*, 15 August, 15 September 1850 and *N.C.* 2260-8.

22. See above, pp.4-9.

23. *N.C.*, 1812, Q.28338; 1832, Q.28511; 1852, Q.28779; 1862, Q.28968; 1886, Q.29223; 1924, Q.29972. See also Conon House, Mackenzie of Gairloch MSS, Black Deed Box, Bundle 53, Correspondence re. estate affairs.

24. *Ibid.*, 1930-47, QQ.30050, 30058, 30245, 30366.

25. *N.S.A.*, XV, 197.

26. *Inverness Advertiser*, 13 November 1849, 4 March 1851; *Destitution Papers*, Ninth Report of Glasgow Section (1848), Appendix II, 28; Achnacarry Castle, Cameron of Lochiel Papers, r.h. top drawer, Bundle 15, E. Cameron to Lochiel, 26 March 1847.

27. *Oban Times*, 20 December 1884; Gaskell, *Morvern Transformed*, 129.

28. Mitchell Library, Letterbook on Highland Emigration of Sir John McNeill, MS 21506, McNeill to Sir C. Trevelyan, 30 December 1852; *Inverness Advertiser*, 13, 27 September 1853; *Scotsman*, 26 October 1853.

29. SRO, Riddell Papers, F 49/6, Report of T.G. Dickson for Trustees (1852); SRO, Sheriff Court Processes (Tobermory), SC 59/2/11.

30. SRO, Sheriff Court Processes (Dornoch), SC 9/7/128-130.

31. Eric J. Findlater, *Highland Clearances: the Real Cause of Highland Famines* (1855), 11.

32. SRO, HD7/47, W. Skene to Sir Charles Trevelyan, 19 June 1848.

33. *McNeill Report*, Appendix A, Evidence of F.W.Clark, 13 February 1851, 10.

34. SRO, Sheriff Court Processes (Stornoway), SC 33/17/26-34. See below, Chapter 9 for a detailed consideration of the Matheson strategy.

35. *Scotsman*, 18 and 21 December 1850.

36. *Destitution Papers*, Second Report of Edinburgh Section (1849), Sir E.P. Coffin to W. Skene, 29 June 1848.

37. The interpretation of events in Sutherland is based on R.J. Adam, ed., *Papers on Sutherland Estate Management* (Edinburgh, 1972), 2 vols. and Richards, *Leviathan of Wealth*, passim.

38. MS. Diary of J.M. Mackenzie, Chamberlain of the Lews, 1851; SRO, Lord Macdonald Papers, GD221/43, Report by Mr. Ballingall for Mr. Brown, 1851; SRO, Riddell Papers, AF 49/6, Report of T.G. Dickson for Trustees (1852).

39. See below, pp.193-4.

40. See, for instance, R. Alister, *The Extermination of the Scottish Peasantry* (Edinburgh, 1853); Findlater, *Highland Clearances*; D. Ross, *The Glengarry Evictions* (Edinburgh, 1853); Anon., *The Depopulation System in the Highlands* (Edinburgh, 1849).

41. Richards, *Highland Clearances*, I, 472-505.

42. See below, pp.249-50.

43. A broadly similar pattern is revealed in much of the evidence to the Napier Commission in 1883.

44. See pp.43-4 above.

45. *Ibid.*

46. See below, pp.277-9.

47. *Destitution Papers*, First Report of Central Board (1847), 10. See also Somers, *Letters from the Highlands*, 10-24 for a perceptive examination of the social and economic structure of the central Highlands in 1847.

48. See below, pp.314-16.

49. NLS, Dep. 313/877, E. Maciver to Tenants of Knockan and Elphin, Height of Assynt, 7 January 1884.

50. *Destitution Papers*, First Report of Central Board (1847), 10.

51. See above, pp.18-20.

52. *Ibid.*

53. *N.C.*, 633, Q.10320.

54. *Ibid.*, 693, Q.10945.

55. M.C. Storrie, *Islay: Biography of an Island* (Port Ellen, 1981), 107-140. However, Dr. Storrie perhaps underestimates the extent of removals before that date. See *N.C.*, 3109-3111.

56. *N.C.*, 2233, Q.35378.

57. Jerome Blum, *The End of the Old Order in Rural Europe* (New Jersey, 1978), 263.

58. These differences are discussed in more detail in T.M. Devine, 'Social Responses to Improvement, 1500-1860: the Highland and Lowland Clearances in Scotland', in R. Houston and I. Whyte, eds., *Scottish Society, 1500-1800* (Cambridge, 1988).

59. These points derive from a study of summonses in the Sheriff Courts referred to above, pp.174-5.

60. See above, pp.85-7.

61. As at Sollas (North Uist) and Boreraig and Suishnish (Skye).

62. SRO, Riddell Papers, AF 49/6, Report by T.G. Dickson for Trustees (1852); SRO, Sheriff Court Processes (Tobermory), SC 59/12/11.

63. Storrie, *Islay*, 135.

64. *Scotsman*, 25 August 1849.

65. SRO, Riddell Papers, AF 49/6, Report by T.G. Dickson for Trustees (1852).

66. SRO, Lord Macdonald Papers, GD221/62, General View of the Affairs of Lord Macdonald, 3 February 1846.

67. Dunvegan Castle, Macleod of Macleod Muniments, 659/23/6, Macleod to Mother, 31 December 1846.

68. See below, pp.202-3 for a detailed discussion of these points.

69. See above, pp.37-8.

70. See, for example, W.P. Alison, *Letter to Sir John McNeill on Highland Destitution* (Edinburgh, 1851), 7.

71. See above, pp.95-100.

72. See above, pp.103-4.

73. *PP*, XXVI (1850); L (1852-3), *Annual Report of the Board of Supervision for Relief of the Poor in Scotland*, 1850 and 1852-3.

74. *PP*, XXIII (1852), *Sixth Annual Report of the Board of Supervision for Relief of the Poor in Scotland*, IV.

75. *Witness*, 16 April 1851; NLS, Sutherland Estate Papers, Dep. 313/1176, J. Loch to Duke of Sutherland, 26 June 1848; SRO, HD7/47, W. Skene to Trevelyan, 21 February 1848; Anon., *Depopulation System*, 23; Alison, *Observations on the Famine*, 30.

76. Anon., *Depopulation System*, 23.

77. *Witness*, 16 April 1851.

78. See below, p.202.

79. SRO, HD7/76, Trevelyan to W. Skene, 26 June 1848.

80. Clark, 'Agriculture of Argyll', 95; Mulock, *Western Highlands and Islands*, 66.

8

The Pattern of Migration and Emigration

1

The approximate scale and regional variation in out-migration during the famine years was established in Chapter 3. The purpose of the analysis in this chapter is to refine and deepen the discussion by evaluating the various forms of migration and attempting to identify their relative significance. As with most aspects of the demography of the Highlands at this period, weaknesses in the source materials make it difficult to come to any absolute or certain conclusion about patterns of migration, though some insight can be gained from estate records and the published and unpublished census into the movement of people within the Highland region itself. It is less easy to identify the global scale of emigration or of migration to the Lowlands and the relative importance of each stream. Deficiencies in the sources mean once again that only provisional and tentative conclusions are possible on these issues.

Statistical materials for the study of Scottish emigration in the middle decades of the nineteenth century do exist.[1] From 1840 the Colonial Land and Emigration Commission was given the responsibility of administering the Passenger Acts. Masters of vessels governed by the regulations were required to deposit lists of passengers with customs before sailing. In addition, records were maintained by emigration officials in colonial possessions overseas.[2] From these two sources, the Commission produced statistics of 'emigration' in its annual reports. These materials distinguish passengers sailing from ports in Scotland, Ireland, England and Wales. Immigrants of Scottish origin are also enumerated in USA and Canadian compilations dating from 1820 and 1829 respectively.

The limitations of these data from the standpoint of the present enquiry are very considerable. They do not record all outward movement or distinguish precisely between migrants and other passengers. They list only the overall numbers leaving Scottish ports, though in this period the enumeration included a significant number of Irish as well as native-born Scots. The Commissioners did not calculate the actual numbers of Irish passengers until 1853 though they did estimate that they amounted to about one third of those leaving from the Clyde ports in the later 1840s.[3] This proportion was, however, likely to change in subsequent years as the pressure of famine conditions in Ireland diminished. At the same time, the figures took no account of the number of Scots leaving from non-Scottish ports. Liverpool, for instance, was a favourite point of departure for many of those emigrating to Australia.[4]

Most seriously of all, the figures are merely *aggregate* statistics of total departures. They do not contain information on the geographical origins of emigrants and so are of little assistance to an enquiry concerned with emigration from *one region* of Scotland. The shipping muster rolls of the later eighteenth century which allowed some analysis of the origins of emigrants do not exist for the middle decades of the nineteenth century. The enumerators' schedules for Highland parishes add little either. In the 1841 returns, enumerators were asked to estimate emigration flows from their parishes in the six months prior to registration. Unfortunately, however, this practice was not followed in 1851. The weaknesses in the aggregate data ensure that we cannot discover the numbers who moved from the Highlands to the Lowlands during the famine, the relative proportion of migrants to emigrants, the total number who left the Highlands for overseas destinations and the relative importance of the various districts in the north-west as sources of emigrants.

Other sources, however, can be used to gain at least a partial insight into some of these important issues. Census enumerators' returns for selected urban parishes and other information, such as poor law and burial records, which supply evidence of the place of origin of Highland migrants, can be employed to construct a provisional analysis of the relative significance of movement from the distressed districts to Lowland centres. Emigration assisted both by private landlords and the Highland and Island Emigration Society is very well documented and so allows for a relatively full analysis of the origins, social class and period of departure of almost 17,000 Highland emigrants during the famine. The contemporary press, though of limited use for aggregate information, contains occasional but vital glimpses of *unassisted* emigration which also help to clarify the overall pattern. Finally, British emigration officials in Quebec took a special interest in Highland emigration in the 1840s and 1850s and their reports include material very relevant to this analysis. These sources form the essential raw materials for this chapter and the three which follow. The discussion here is devoted to the general characteristics of emigration and migration. Chapters 9 to 11 contain detailed case-studies of landlord-assisted emigration from two Hebridean communities and an examination of the great movement to Australia in the 1850s sponsored by the Highland and Island Emigration Society.

2

There seems to have been a general trend during the famine for the population of several of the small towns and villages within the Highland zone itself to increase in size despite the regional pattern of heavy population loss. Stornoway's population expanded by a spectacular forty per cent from 6218 in 1841 to 8668 in 1861. Dornoch in Sutherland rose by ten per cent over the decade 1841 to 1851. From 1841 to 1861 the number of inhabitants in Mull fell by twenty-eight per cent from 10,054 to 7240. But over the same period Tobermory's population increased by about eleven per cent. There were also scattered reports that more people were living in the impoverished settlements of cottars and squatters which existed throughout most districts in the crofting region.[5]

Almost certainly these tendencies, which were against the general trend of acceleration in out-migration, can be explained in large part by the marked increase in eviction documented in Chapter 7. Some of the dispossessed managed to emigrate; others doubtless went south; but many also lingered on either as lodgers in small towns or as squatters eking out an existence on patches of poor land. There were several examples of the latter pattern in Skye.[6] Tobermory in Mull provides a classic instance of the former. In 1847 ninety-six people, 'ejected from the rural parts of the neighbouring districts', settled in the town.[7] Three years later a further seventy-eight removed from the island of Ulva obtained lodgings in overcrowded accommodation in Tobermory.[8] In 1847 Robert Somers wrote a vivid description of the living conditions endured by those who had lost their lands:

> I pushed on to Glenbeg, where I was at length supplied with a boat and three stout rowers, and after two hours sailing was landed safely at Tobermory, the capital of Mull. Having much less time to spend in Mull than I had intended and hearing that the families of cottars ejected from the interior of the island, were taking up their abode almost daily in the village, I resolved to visit as many of the poor in their own houses as possible . . .
> . . . the families of four cottars had been recently ejected from the farms of Ardvergnish, and two of these had taken refuge in Tobermory. I went to see them. They had taken two empty rooms in the upper flat of a back house. In one of the families there were ten children, several of whom were in the room when I entered. The mother, a woman of very respectable appearance, was making thin porridge for their supper; they had got a similar meal in the morning, and this was their whole diet. The rooms were very bare of furniture, containing only a few things which they had carried with them over the mountains. The woman said that her husband had been working some time in Glasgow, that he came home last summer ill with small-pox and had scarcely recovered when this new disaster was prepared for him. The farm on which these families lived as cottars was let at Whitsunday, soon after which time they were ejected, and their cottages pulled to the ground. For six weeks they lived in a tent during the day, but as many as could be accommodated were provided with beds by the neighbour at night. The cold of winter, however, at length drove them out . . . Both of the men, at the time of my visit, were absent at the herring fishing. As soon as they had seen their families safely housed, they trudged away back to Kilfinichen, to make the most of the fishing season, which had been so rudely and cruelly interrupted by their ejectment.[9]

There is also some evidence, as in Lewis and Sutherland, of the redistribution of population within estate boundaries.[10] One of the best examples occurred on the Matheson estate where the population of the parish of Uig declined by five per cent while that of Lochs rose by thirty-four per cent between 1851 and 1861. The estate records show that some of the Uig people were assisted to emigrate, others were resettled in Lochs and their former lands turned over to grazing. Such a redistribution of population had been a characteristic feature of estate strategy throughout the Western Highlands for generations. Almost certainly, however, the pattern was not as common in the 1840s and 1850s as the policy shifted principally towards expulsion rather than resettlement of the 'surplus' population. Nor is there any hard evidence of a significant redistribution of people *within* the crofting region itself. Inward migration from other counties was estimated for seven representative West Highland and Hebridean parishes from data in the enumerators' schedules and the printed census reports for 1851 and 1861.[11] The proportion of those born outside the county of registration rose from 2.5 per cent in 1841 to 3.5 per cent in 1851 and to four per cent in 1861. Of the 878 individuals born outside the county of registration, fifty-two per cent were born in other Highland counties. These figures hardly suggest a major permanent movement of people over long distances within the distressed region.

Professor Flinn and his colleagues argued that during the famine '. . . there was a migratory movement from west to east, from the stricken areas of potato dependency to the slightly more prosperous plain of the east-coast'.[12] The assertion rests on the unproven assumption that an actual gain in numbers in the eastern Highlands between 1841 and 1851 might reflect migration from west to east. A detailed examination of the argument suggests that this thesis is not soundly based. First, there is no evidence in the minutes of the destitution committees of the east-coast parishes for 1846 and 1847 of a large permanent movement of people from the distressed districts of the crofting region. Only occasional comments refer to the traditional movement of migrant workers to fishing and harvest work.[13] Second, the rise in population on the east coast was ephemeral. In the following decade, 1851 to 1861, the total number of inhabitants in the farming region fell by 5.6 per cent, a decline which was almost as great as that experienced by crofting parishes at the same time. Third, an examination of the census enumerators' returns for a sample of ten parishes in 1851 and 1861 in the farming zone failed to detect any major influx from the west. The results of this investigation are presented in Tables 8.1 and 8.2. Only in Tain, where 16.5 per cent of heads of household were from the Western Highlands, is there any suggestion of substantial migration. But the census data indicate that virtually all of these immigrants were from the areas of south-east Sutherland adjacent to Tain and not from the region to the far west which suffered most from the potato blight. It is therefore reasonable to conclude that there was no large-scale transfer of population to the east from the west during the famine.

A much greater movement of people out of the distressed districts to the cities of the Lowlands might be anticipated. Certainly some contemporary observers noted a huge

Table 8.1. Heads of Household born in Western Highlands and Islands but Residing in Selected Easter Ross and Eastern Inverness-shire Parishes, 1851 and 1861

Parish	West Coast and Insular Heads of Household, Totals and Per Cent of Total Parish Households			
	1851	%	1861	%
Cromarty	41	5.8	27	5.2
Resolis	24	6.9	28	3.4
Petty	23	6.1	26	7.0
Daviot	10	2.9	18	3.9
Rosskeen	70	6.1	67	7.3
Tain	131	16.5	100	12.9
Nigg	12	3.6	12	4.0
Kiltearn	22	6.2	27	7.1
Fearn	29	5.8	32	6.3
Tarbet	22	6.9	50	9.5
Totals	384	7.3	387	7.7

Source: GRO, Census Enumerators' Schedules for Relevant Parishes, 1851 and 1861.
Note: 'Western Highlands and Islands' comprise the crofting parishes listed in Appendix 1.

Table 8.2. Detached Single Individuals (not related to Heads of Household) born in Western Highlands and Islands but Residing in Selected Easter Ross and Eastern Inverness-shire Parishes, 1851 and 1861

Parish	West Coast and Insular Detached Single Individuals, Totals and Per Cent of Total Parish Population			
	1851	%	1861	%
Cromarty	47	1.7	25	1.3
Resolis	46	3.0	26	1.7
Petty	44	2.5	23	1.4
Daviot	26	1.4	33	1.9
Rosskeen	94*	1.8	67	1.8
Tain	78	2.2	77	2.3
Nigg	16	1.1	4	0.3
Kiltearn	29	1.9	37	2.3
Fearn	23	1.1	14	0.7
Tarbet	28	1.3	22	1.0
Totals	431	1.8	328	1.6

Source: GRO, Census Enumerators' Schedules for Relevant Parishes, 1851 and 1861.
Notes: 'Western Highlands and Islands' comprise the crofting parishes listed in Appendix 1.
   * 35 of those at Ardross carrying out work associated with the Drainage Act.

increase in the numbers from crofting parishes who, in their view, had fled from hunger and destitution to seek refuge in the large towns. The Rev. Thomas McLauchlan described how some Highlanders emigrated but others '. . . crowd into the towns and add much to the existing mass of pauperism and distress there'.[14] Robert Somers referred in 1847 to '. . . the groups of wretched creatures who crowded into our large towns during summer and autumn'.[15] The Rev. Dr. Norman Macleod, minister of St. Columba's Church in Glasgow and a man of long experience of Highland migration to the Lowland towns, emphasised how, in 1850, '. . . doors were besieged by poor people from the Highlands in a state of destitution . . . the steamboats were frequently arriving crowded with them'.[16] In the same year he wrote privately to the sister of Norman Macleod of Macleod in Skye describing 'the influx of poor starving Highlanders to this city'. He was receiving applications for work 'all hours of the day' and the condition of the people was 'deplorable in the extreme'.[17]

Impressions of this type, even taking into account the reliability of the informant, must be treated with great care. No figures are attached to the claims and, more importantly, no attempt is or can be made to distinguish between the temporary and permanent movement of people. Interestingly, both Somers' comments of 1847 and Macleod's of 1850 refer to those seasons in the year, the summer and autumn months, when temporary migration was at its peak. Their descriptions also aptly fit the impoverished cottar class who formed the majority of temporary workers from the crofting region in this period.[18] Chapter 6 demonstrated that there was indeed a very substantial increase in temporary migration during the famine. Without corroborative evidence we cannot conclude that these valuable contemporary observations indicate a vast *permanent* movement of people from the West Highlands and Islands to the Scottish cities during the subsistence crisis.

It seems reasonably clear at least that there was no such mass influx into the larger towns of the eastern Lowlands. In 1850 a Special Commissioner in Edinburgh, appointed to carry out a detailed survey of destitution in the capital, concluded that '. . . the Highland population is not a miserable population here'. Only a minority were paupers, most migrants had come from the county of Sutherland and they were employed mainly as domestic servants, shopmen, chairmen, porters, policemen and labourers. They numbered no more than 1200 in total.[19] Highland migrants to Dundee, Perth and Stirling were primarily recruited from the central, eastern and southern Highlands rather than from the districts which suffered most during the famine.[20]

In itself this result is not surprising because traditionally the migration trail followed by people of the north-west and the Hebrides was to the towns of the western Lowlands. Even there, however, it is difficult to find numerical data which support the claims of McLauchlan, Somers and Macleod. A source which yields useful information on the destitute poor in Glasgow is the Reports of the Glasgow Night Asylum for the Homeless. These are available for 1849 and 1851 and supply details of the geographical origin of all those who were admitted. Between July and October 1849, only seventy-five individuals or 2.14 per cent of admissions were from the Highland counties, compared with 935 from Ireland.[21] In 1851 the number and proportion of Highlanders was slightly higher at 145, or 3.8 per cent of admissions; 762 or twenty-two per cent of all those admitted were from Ireland.[22] The Highland figures cannot be broken down further to distinguish the relative numbers who belonged to the crofting region. However, work currently in progress in the University of Strathclyde on the 1851 and 1861 census enumerators' returns for the Anderston and High Street districts of Glasgow indicates that the overwhelming majority of Highland migrants in mid-century had been born in Argyllshire and southern Inverness-shire and that only a small minority originated from the Outer Hebrides, Skye and the mainland districts of the north-west coast.[23] These findings are similar to those of previous investigations carried out for Paisley and Greenock for the same period.[24] In the case of Greenock there was a consistent fall in the number of migrants as the distance from the town increased through Argyll, Inverness, Ross and Sutherland.

These conclusions do not prove that the observers of the 1850s were necessarily wrong. There was undoubtedly considerable migration to the towns of the western Lowlands during the famine but much of this was probably mainly of a temporary nature and the contemporary comments may simply reflect reactions to a large influx of poor, transient workers desperately seeking employment. The data from the enumerators' schedules, however, seem to indicate that these movements did not in the long run radically alter the traditional pattern of permanent migration to the cities. Even in 1851 and 1861 the vast majority of Highlanders who took up residence in Glasgow, Greenock, Paisley, Dundee, Perth and Stirling came from the farming region of the Highlands rather than the distressed areas of the far west.[25] Yet, as Chapter 3 showed, there *was* very heavy out-migration from the crofting region during the famine. If no clear evidence of a substantial increase in permanent movement from west to east or from west to south in Scotland itself can be produced, it follows that most of those who left must have left the country altogether.

3

Table 8.3 demonstrates the sharp increase in passenger movement from principal
Scottish ports for North America and Australia between 1846 and 1856. The main
spurt occurred between 1849 and 1853 when sixty-three per cent of departures for the
period took place. Not all of those, of course, were necessarily emigrants and an
estimated one third were Irish rather than Scots. These global figures reveal nothing
about the scale, phasing and direction of emigration from the Scottish Highlands. To
gain a partial insight into those patterns of movement the press, estate records and
other materials have to be utilised instead.

These sources suggest that emigration during the famine can best be divided into
'unassisted' and 'assisted' emigration. The first category includes those who paid their
passage from their own resources or from remittances sent home by relatives already
established in the colonies. The second refers to those supported by landlords, the
Highland and Island Emigration Society and the Colonial Land and Emigration
Commission. Inevitably information on unassisted emigration is rather sparse but
enough has survived to suggest that the diaspora of the famine period was not entirely
confined to the most destitute and poorest members of Highland society.

*Table 8.3. Departures for USA, Canada, Australia (incl. New Zealand) from Principal Scottish
Ports, 1846-1856*

Year	USA	Canada	Australia (incl. NZ)	Total	Annual Per cent
1846	1157	1903	70	3427	3
1847	3782	4219	366	8616	7
1848	7241	3855	282	11505	8
1849	10639	5447	746	17127	13
1850	11488	3025	378	15154	11
1851	10864	10000	541	18646	14
1852	9792	5642	5450	21044	15
1853	7819	5038	4166	16503	12
1854	3534	6941	2699	13307	9
1855	1819	5015	1286	8227	6
1856	2748	–	–	2748	2
	70883 (51 per cent)	51085 (36 per cent)	15,994 (13 per cent)	136304	100

Source: PP, Annual Reports of Colonial Land and Emigration Commissioners 1846-56, PP. XXIV
(1846); XLVII (1847-8); XXIII (1847); XXVI (1847-8); XXII (1849); XXIII (1850);
XXII (1851); XVIII (1852); XL (1852-3); XXVIII (1854); XXIV (1856); XVI
(1857).
Note: 'Principal Ports' are Aberdeen, Glasgow, Greenock, Inverness, Port Glasgow,
Stornoway, Wick. These were selected because the great majority of 'Scottish emigrants'
embarked from them and they were the normal points of departure for Highland
emigrants.

In 1853 press reports revealed that grain shipments from the eastern district of the
Highlands to the west coast and islands had greatly declined. This was explained by

'the extensive migration' involving 'large numbers' from the western mainland and Hebrides. It was also stressed that, except in those districts where landlords or charities had been active, the majority of these emigrants were of the crofter class and consisted of people possessed of some means who had in the past been 'considerable purchasers of oatmeal and good customers to the exporters'.[26] Five years earlier, the *Scotsman* provided further comment on this elusive group of emigrants. In the first six months of 1848, 5165 steerage and 277 cabin passengers left from Glasgow and Greenock. 'Very few' were Irish; the majority were from the Western Highlands. 'A good number' of the emigrants 'were in possession of considerable sums of money and were well supplied with clothes and provisions for the voyage'.[27] In the same year the departure of the *Atlantic* was noted from Ardrossan in July with about 500 passengers. They were 'chiefly' Highlanders and took with them a 'good quantity of property'. Very few could speak or understand English. Nearly 300, it was reckoned, were from Mull and Knapdale, travelling at their own expense. The remaining 200 were from South Uist and had passage paid by their landlord, John Gordon of Cluny.[28]

Another glimpse of unassisted emigration comes from the observations of an anonymous traveller in the Hebrides in the spring and summer of 1847. He recounted how, as the steamship in which he was a passenger sailed south through the Inner Hebrides, it was joined by 'a great many emigrants' on their way to Greenock: '. . . it was heart-rending, as the boats shot out from the rocky headlands every few miles, to see the affectionate leave-takings and hear the cries or rather howls of distress raised by the women on the rock as the steamer again sailed on her course. But the painfulness of the scene was greatly lessened to anyone who had witnessed the hopeless squalor, ignorance and sloth, which the emigrants were leaving behind'. He went on to emphasise that in his experience the number of emigrants had 'considerably increased' in that year but added significantly that they 'were not of the most distressed class being, as I am told, and their appearance suggested, "the better portion" of the poor'. He predicted, with considerable accuracy, that the most wretched would have to linger on until either landlords or government paid for their removal.[29]

There is further partial evidence of considerable unassisted emigration from other parts of the Highlands. Information presented to the Napier Commission in 1883 suggested that 1200 had emigrated to North America and Australia without assistance between 1841 and 1851 from Islay.[30] In July 1847, the *Euclid* of Liverpool sailed from the Broomielaw for Quebec with upwards of 300 passengers from Islay and Kintyre. It was stressed that they were not paupers but 'paid for their passage money, were well-clothed and supplied with the provisions for the voyage'.[31] Some of 'the best conditioned' tenants on Coll emigrated to North America in 1850.[32] Clearances on the estate of Ardmeanach in Mull in 1848 had produced a similar effect. Twenty-six families had raised passage money by selling their cattle, sheep stocks and sparse household effects and emigrated to America at their own expense.[33] Unassisted emigration was especially prevalent from mainland Argyllshire. In the first six months of 1849, 10,560 emigrants left the Clyde. 'Very few' were Irish and the condition of the majority was 'much superior to former years'.[34] It was noted that, according to information received from emigration officers, 'a considerable number of families from Argyllshire' were represented among the emigrants.[35]

This scattered evidence is very fragile but it does suggest certain tentative conclusions. Although no overall estimate of the total of unassisted emigrants is possible, the numbers were clearly very considerable. They belonged in the main to a different social group from those who were supported by individual landlords and the Highland and Island Emigration Society. The descriptions suggest that they generally consisted of middle-rank crofting families of the type identified in Chapter 1 who could finance both passage and resettlement from sale of stock and other assets. Most of the reported emigrant parties came from the western mainland and islands which suffered less privation, such as Islay and mainland Argyllshire, rather than the districts of acute distress in the Inner and Outer Hebrides. The reported departures also tended to concentrate in the later 1840s rather than the 1850s. This may well be significant and perhaps offers a clue to the motivation of the emigrants themselves. The factor of the Maclean estate on the island of Coll stressed that the people were not driven out by fear of starvation but rather by their concern at a serious and rapidly increasing threat to their economic and social position: '. . . from the failure of the potatoes, and the low price of black cattle, they will be unable to preserve their stocks entire and pay their rent; and, finding themselves falling back in the world, they desire to emigrate before their capital is too much reduced'.[36] They were almost certainly also primarily influenced by the pressure of deteriorating economic circumstances at home rather than the attraction of better opportunities overseas in itself. If the press reports provide an accurate guide to the cycle of unassisted emigration, most groups apparently left in the later 1840s when economic conditions in the traditional areas of Highland resettlement in British North America, the maritime provinces and Ontario were poorer than in earlier years though better, perhaps, than those which prevailed in the Hebrides during the famine.[37]

It is also possible that many emigrants may have been supported by funds sent home by expatriates. The major role of such remittances in assisting the mass emigration of the Irish during the Great Famine is well known. Scottish historians have always doubted whether this was ever a significant feature of Highland emigration.[38] The biggest problem is the lack of evidence because it might be anticipated for other reasons that this ought to have been a major characteristic of the Highland exodus to the colonies. The strong kin-ties of the people are well documented and 'chain migration', the forging of a long-term connection between localities in the host and source countries, was also a familiar feature. During the famine itself, many of the assisted emigrant parties settled in townships in Ontario which had long attracted people from the districts of the Western Highlands to which they belonged: Sutherland – Woodstock, Gore and Brock; Lochsheil – Glengarry County; Barra and South Uist – London and Williams townships; Lewis – Lingwick and Sherbrooke.[39] We know too that there was regular correspondence with kinfolk who remained at home which provided information and advice for those contemplating emigration in the future.

Certainly no evidence has come to light in this study of the Irish custom of supplying pre-paid tickets for emigrants. But there are some indications that sums were sent home to assist in the expenses of passage and that on arrival emigrants could anticipate considerable help in the early stages of resettlement. This could markedly reduce costs and lower the threshold of risk attached to emigration. Remittances from Canada to

Britain increased substantially during the years of the famine. In 1844 they were estimated at £4611 but rose to £9744 in 1846 and £15,742 a year later.[40] The government's principal immigration officer in Upper Canada (Ontario) reported that 'The sums remitted by settlers in Canada to enable their relations to emigrate are rapidly increasing in amount; a few years ago such remittances were rare. Now they are becoming almost general'.[41] Moneys were also transmitted from Australia. In the few years after 1852 one observer claimed that £3000 per annum was sent from there to banks in Fort William and that regular remittances to the Lochaber district still continued into the 1880s.[42] Partial confirmation of this statement comes from a press report in 1854 which described the emigration of 100 people from Lochaber to Australia in that year: 'They are principally from the Lochiel district . . . more than £800 were sent from friends in Australia last year to help their emigration.'[43] It was also claimed that emigrants from Sutherland '. . . sent money home to take others out' and that this had been 'the principal way' by which the inhabitants of the estate had managed to cover the costs of passage to Canada and Australia.[44]

4

Emigration assisted by landlords, philanthropic bodies and through public funds is altogether better documented than the exodus of those who supported themselves or obtained help from relatives. Between 1846 and 1857, at least 16,553 Highlanders emigrated with assistance from landowners and the Highland and Island Emigration Society. A further unknown number obtained passage to Australia under the auspices of the government's Colonial Land and Emigration Commission. This section is initially devoted to an examination of the intellectual and economic influence which generated such an increase in both public and private support for Highland emigration. It then moves to a general consideration of landlord-assisted emigration and the movement to Australia supported by the Commissioners. The role of the Highland and Island Emigration Society, which assisted the passage to Australia of almost 5,000 of the inhabitants of some of the most distressed districts, is analysed separately in Chapter 11.

By 1846 it had generally become accepted that a scheme of assisted emigration on a grand scale was required to reduce the dangers of Highland overpopulation. The Select Committee on Emigration (Scotland) in 1841 produced the blueprint for such a programme by identifying the precise numbers of inhabitants who ought to be removed from each Highland district. In the 1820s, and especially from 1838 to 1841, after the harvest failure of 1836-7, there was considerable emigration assisted by landlords, government and destitution committees. The demise of the labour-intensive bi-employments after *c*.1820 in the Western Highlands prompted a transfer in regional resources to the capital-intensive sector of commercial pastoralism. This, in turn, would be facilitated by a removal of the redundant population. But the schemes of the 1820s and 1830s were only a minor prelude to the much more ambitious strategies of the famine period. From 1815 to 1856 an estimated 14,000 persons were assisted by Highland landlords to emigrate to Canada; the vast majority, almost 11,000, left between 1846 and 1856.[45]

Several factors accelerated the existing trend towards assisted emigration during the years of the potato famine. The urge to emigrate undoubtedly became stronger among the people of many districts in the Western Highlands. An inquiry into attitudes towards emigration conducted shortly after the serious harvest failure of 1837 in the region had revealed great diversity between parishes and evidence of considerable reluctance in some districts to accept offers of emigration assistance. Forty-five parishes provided information. In sixteen more than one third of the inhabitants were disposed to emigrate; in twenty-one less than one third. In eight few or none were keen.[46] The detailed analysis carried out in Chapters 9 to 11 indicates that in some areas, such as Lewis and parts of Skye, opposition to emigration persisted despite the trauma of the potato famine and that, in general, the return of better times, even if ephemeral, could quickly reduce the disposition to emigrate throughout the region.[47] Thus, to cite but one example, of the fifty families in Edderachillis in Sutherland who had petitioned for assistance to emigrate in January 1847, only ten were still eager to go by March of that year. Spring weather and better prospects at the fishing had changed the minds of the majority.[48] However, in bad years, and there were of course a whole series of them between 1846 and 1856, destitution undoubtedly helped to loosen the peasant's attachment to his native soil, especially if landlords intensified pressure by threatening evictions or other sanctions.[49]

The scale and duration of the famine also seemed to compel radical remedial action. The only alternative to mass emigration was charity, extension of the Poor Law and provision of public works. By 1851 these options attracted little support. The movement of opinion from a policy based on charity and public works to one which necessitated assisted emigration was both symbolised and encouraged by the passage of the Emigration Advances Act (14 and 15 Victoria, c.91) of 1851. Through this legislation, loans were made available at an interest rate of 6¼ per cent to those proprietors who sought to provide assisted passage for the people of their estates. The Act was passed as a direct consequence of the *Report* written on conditions in the Western Highlands by Sir John McNeill, Chairman of the Board of Supervision of the Scottish Poor Law, after the Central Relief Board ceased relief operations in 1850. The Act demonstrated unequivocally that government planned to prevent a social disaster in the Highlands, not by extending the provisions of the Poor Law to meet the needs of the able-bodied (although this had been widely feared), but by helping to promote more emigration. The Emigration Advances Act made funds available for this purpose from the Drainage Act on the explicit advice of McNeill himself. The Drainage Act, as was shown in Chapter 4, was one of the key foundations of the relief effort in the Highlands in the 1840s.[50] The diversion of its funds to other purposes neatly illustrates the movement of opinion from one which favoured the provision of public and private works as a solution to the crisis to the other extreme of support for emigration schemes as the new panacea for the Highland problem.

The relief operation was finally discredited by 1850. The great programme of the Central Board for economic regeneration had manifestly failed and critics were not slow to point out the implications of this: 'That the Highlanders, after having had a sum of little short of £200,000 expended in their relief, and that under the auspices of a corps of officers of high character, energy and ability, should at the end of relief operations be in a worse condition than at the commencement is so very startling and mortifying a fact as to call for enquiry and explanation.'[51] Three particular arguments were advanced. First, it was asserted that the certainty of relief had actually inhibited emigration and so prolonged the crisis rather than alleviated it.[52] Second, the familiar arguments that the relief schemes had undermined and corrupted the 'moral character' of the Highland population were rehearsed again. Indolence, fecklessness and laziness were still rampant everywhere.[53] The extent to which privation and poverty had affected the 'moral character' of the people was hardly mentioned. Instead all the blame was attached to 'eleemosynary relief'. It is obviously hard to take these claims in any way seriously in the light of the evidence of the meagre pittances dispensed by the officials of the Central Board after 1847 through the labour and destitution tests which were specifically designed to avoid the supposed harmful effects of 'charity'.[54] But it was a viewpoint which was consistently urged on Sir John McNeill in the course of his tour of investigation and after the publication of his *Report* almost became accepted as axiomatic. The *Scotsman* thundered in its editorials that the charitable subscriptions of industrious Lowlanders had been wasted on the support of 'Celtic laziness'.[55] Relief should be ended forthwith and the 'redundant' populations forced to go and earn their bread overseas. Finally, it was asserted that the Irish example dramatically demonstrated the catastrophic effects of overpopulation. To escape 'the Leoprasy of Ireland', as Sir Charles Trevelyan put it, the Highlands must shed people on a significant scale.[56]

By the early 1850s large-scale emigration of Highlanders had much more appeal to those in government who had responsibility for colonial policy. In the later 1840s conditions in Canada had been difficult and were rendered even worse in the short run by the mass, transient immigration of hordes of destitute Irish. The colonial authorities at that time, far from encouraging more emigration, had tried hard to restrict it by raising immigration taxes and port duties to be paid by the masters of emigrant vessels.[57] By the early 1850s, however, the position had changed dramatically. The movement of the Irish had declined to a trickle and the economy of Upper Canada had become much more buoyant. At the end of 1851, for instance, the Emigration Commissioners published a more optimistic appraisal of Canadian economic prospects.[58] Demand for labour had greatly increased; railway work was available; farm servants could readily obtain employment; the lumber business was prospering and the construction of public works, notably the building of the Quebec-Montreal road, was even extending the need for unskilled workers into the winter months. They concluded, therefore, that 'On the whole . . . the present conditions of the colony are most favourable for the reception of a portion of the redundant population of the United Kingdom'.[59] This improvement continued until the end of 1854. The chief immigration officer at Quebec observed in 1853 that 'Canada never presented a more favourable opening for the reception of all classes of emigrants than at present . . .'.[60]

Also of significance was the gold rush in Australia, triggered by the discoveries at Ballarat and Bendigo, which caused a great exodus of the local population to the diggings. Labour shortages in parts of Australia became endemic.[61] A new complementarity was now perceived to exist between the overpopulated Highlands and the underpeopled Antipodes. The expatriation of many of the inhabitants of the crofting region exactly fitted the requirements of imperial policy. Though government took no direct or active part in the emigration programme itself, it was the powerful and influential civil servant, Sir Charles Trevelyan, who became chairman and prime influence on the Highland and Island Emigration Society. Sir John McNeill was his trusted confidant and assistant. In addition, as will be seen in more detail below, the Emigration Commission, a body funded from the public purse, amended their stringent regulations governing assisted passage to Australia to permit more Highlanders to take advantage of the new policy of encouragement to emigration.

Several proprietors acquired the loans made available under the Advances Act to defray their share of the cost of emigration assistance to their tenantry under the auspices of the Highland and Island Emigration Society. In 1852 the Board of Supervision of the Scottish Poor Law, the body responsible for the allocation of funds through the Act, approved loans to Maclean of Coll, Sir James Matheson (Lewis), Sir James Riddell (Ardnamurchan), Macdonald of Lochiel, Alexander McAllister (Strathaird, Skye), Lord Dunmore (Harris) and Norman Macleod (Skye). The following year further loans were authorised for Lord Macdonald (Skye), the Skeabost estate (Skye) and Macdonnell of Glengarry.[62] It is interesting to note that five of the ten properties which obtained financial support were either bankrupt or were under the administration of trustees. Several of the remainder were known to be in considerable financial difficulty. Without government assistance, which itself depended on the political and ideological consensus of the 1850s, assisted emigration from these estates would probably not have taken place on the same scale.

5

Emigration from Scottish ports to Australia accelerated after news of the gold discoveries became known. In 1849 a mere 746 left for Australasian destinations and only 541 in 1851. The following year this figure soared to 5450, 4166 in 1853 and 2699 in 1854.[63] Although many of those who emigrated in 1852 were supported by the Highland and Island Emigration Society, large numbers also obtained their own passages under the scheme administered by the Colonial Land and Emigration Commission. Because of labour shortages in Victoria and New South Wales, families with not more than four children were now admitted to the privilege of free passage. Deposits for single males were reduced to £2, to £1 for women and married men, and to 10s. for children.[64] Even before the great exodus of the early 1850s emigrant parties were leaving the Western Highlands and Islands for Australia. It was reported that while passage there had little appeal in Skye in 1848, 'a great many from Uist have given in their names, also at Roag and Gairloch . . .'.[65] In June of the same year 'large parties', principally consisting of young, unmarried people of both sexes from Lochaber, Strathglass and Strathconon obtained free passage under the auspices of the Emigration Commission.[66] The minister of Iona described how, in February 1846, he read a circular to his congregation both there and in Mull regarding assisted passage to Australia: 'Some of the people have relations in that colony, others seem to prefer it to Canada as the climate is milder, many regard the offer of a free passage as a strong inducement.' Twenty-seven people, on his estimate, indicated their desire to go. Two years later, the factor of the Argyll estate in Mull reckoned 140 'were on the list for Australia'.[67] In August 1849, 150 individuals left Fort William *en route* to Australia: '. . . chiefly tenants of Maclean of Ardgour, with a few families from the lands of Lochiel'. Again, 'a large proportion' were described as 'young, unmarried people'.[68] More than 200 'engaged for Australia' from Sutherland in 1848.[69]

From 1852, however, the scale of the movement increased further. The Highland press began to include stories of fortunate emigrants who had made their fortunes. News circulated of one, Murdo Macgregor from Gairloch, and other Highlanders who shared 70 lbs. of gold between them after less than two months' labour in Australia.[70] The *Inverness Advertiser* reported in June 1852 that 'the tide of emigration to Australia grows daily in volume and magnitude. It has risen to a height hitherto unsurpassed . . .'. The steamer *Martello* left Invergordon in the same month with about 100 emigrants bound for Australia: '. . . many of these were young men – we should say mere boys . . .'. Most were from Sutherland. A further 150 from the same county were planning to embark the following week.[71] In August 1852 'the rush of emigration' to Australia continued. From Inverness 'every week conveys hence numbers who have resolved to try their fortune in the Antipodes'.[72] Complaints were made that those who were leaving were 'chiefly the young and active, the sober and the industrious'.[73] The social composition of this emigration stream was clearly biased towards young, unattached adults. It was complementary to the parties which were assisted by the Emigration Society and which consisted mainly of poor families.

6

The general pattern and composition of those emigrant parties assisted by private landlords from their own resources finally remains to be considered. In this chapter the treatment will be confined to general analysis, leaving more detailed examination to the case-studies of assisted emigration from Lewis and Tiree which are presented in Chapters 9 and 10. Fortunately, this is one aspect of emigration during the famine years which is very well documented. The data relating to it are presented in Tables 8.4 to 8.6 and the sources and details on which these depend are set out in Appendix 10.

The information in the tables suggests several conclusions about the nature of landlord-assisted emigration. There was a specific cycle of movement. The pace of the exodus only began to build up in 1849 and over half the emigrants left in the 1850s. This pattern ties in with the incidence of clearance identified in Chapter 7, with the timing of landlord concern about rising relief payments when the Central Board ceased to operate after 1850 and with the recovery of the labour market in Canada and Australia. Again, there was a close correlation between areas of severe distress and the incidence of assisted emigration. On the mainland, most emigrants came from the two western parishes of Sutherland, Assynt and Edderachillis, Glenelg, Knoydart and Lochalsh. The Hebridean emigrants were natives of districts which had endured much privation during the famine. Only Skye produced few emigrants. This was because the two

Table 8.4. Assisted Emigration to British North America by Highland Landowners, 1846-1856

Estate	Proprietor	No.of Emigrants	Year
Mainland			
Sutherland	Duke of Sutherland	397	1847
Sutherland	Duke of Sutherland	605	1848
Sutherland	Duke of Sutherland	59	1850
Sutherland	Duke of Sutherland	24	1851
Glenelg	James Baillie	344	1839
Knoydart	Mrs. Josephine Macdonnell	332	1853
Lochalsh	William Lillingston	300	1849
Glen Urquhart	Earl of Seafield	'large'	1852
	Macdonald of Lochiel	82	1852
	Miscellaneous	256	1851
		c.2399	
Islands			
Lewis	Sir James Matheson	1554	1851
Lewis	Sir James Matheson	453	1852
Lewis	Sir James Matheson	330	1855
N. Uist	Lord Macdonald	234	1849
Barra & S. Uist	Col. John Gordon	270	1848
Barra & S. Uist	Col. John Gordon	957	1849
Barra & S. Uist	Col. John Gordon	1681	1851
Tiree & Ross of Mull	Duke of Argyll	1101	1847
Tiree & Ross of Mull	Duke of Argyll	627	1849
Tiree & Ross of Mull	Duke of Argyll	533	1851
Tiree & Ross of Mull	Duke of Argyll	18	1853
		7756	

Total, Mainland and Islands = 10,155

Source: Appendix 10.

Table 8.5. Total Emigrants Assisted by Individual Proprietors, 1846-1856

Proprietor	Total Assisted	Percentage of Total
John Gordon of Cluny	2906	29
Sir James Matheson	2279	22
Duke of Argyll	2337	23
Duke of Sutherland	1085	11
James Baillie	344	3
Mrs. Josephine Macdonnell	332	3
William Lillingston	300	3
Lord Macdonald	234	2
Macdonald of Lochshiel	82	1
Miscellaneous	256	2
	10155	Total per cent may not add up to 100 because of rounding up or down

Source: Appendix 10.

Table 8.6. Total Emigrants Assisted by Landowners (Area and Year), 1846-1856

Year	Mainland Emigrants	Island Emigrants	Total	Annual Per cent
1846	–	–	–	–
1847	397	1101	1498	15
1848	605	270	875	9
1849	644	1816	2460	24
1850	59	–	59	1
1851	280	3768	4048	40
1852	82	453	535	5
1853	332	18	350	3
1854	–	–	–	–
1855	–	330	330	3
Total	2399	7756	10155	
Percentage of Total	24	76	–	100

Source: Appendix 10.

largest estates on the island, those of Lord Macdonald and Macleod of Macleod, were under trust and so could not afford expenditure on emigration to the same extent as others. On the other hand, the majority of those who obtained assisted passage to Australia between 1852 and 1857 under the auspices of the Highland and Island Emigration Society, and partly funded on loans under the Emigration Advances Act, were from Skye.[74] In general, however, those assisted by individual landlords belonged not simply to the most destitute districts (with the possible exception of Lewis) but to the poorest classes.

John Gordon of Cluny, proprietor of Barra, South Uist and Benbecula, supported the emigration of almost 3000 people from his estates. They mainly consisted, like the majority of the other assisted parties, of families. For example, of the 1681 who emigrated in 1851, twenty-nine per cent were adult males, thirty-two per cent adult females, thirty-six per cent children aged 1 to 14 years and three per cent were infants. They were all poor in the extreme.[75] One government immigration official in Quebec declared that he had never '. . . during my long experience at this station, seen a body of emigrants so destitute of clothing and bedding'. The wife of the master of the *Admiral*, one of the vessels which carried them, was '. . . busily employed all the voyage in converting empty bread-bags, old canvas and blankets into coverings for them'. He alleged that one fully-grown man passed his inspection '. . . with no other garment but a women's petticoat'.[76] Where evidence of the social composition of the assisted emigrants survives it tends to indicate that they belonged overwhelmingly to the poorest of the small tenantry and, above all, to the cottar class.[77] The next three chapters will demonstrate how those landlords who actively pursued schemes of assisted emigration carefully selected those with the least resources who were likely to require support if they remained at home from either the largesse of the estate or the Poor Law. Relief of this kind would produce a greater drain on estate resources in the long run than the organisation of assisted emigration.[78]

There is also an interesting social distribution among the proprietors who were most heavily involved in assisted emigration. Three were wealthy grandees, the Dukes of

Argyll and Sutherland and the Earl of Seafield. Several others were 'new' landlords who had purchased their estates shortly before the famine. Sir James Matheson had made his money in the East India trade; John Gordon was described as 'the richest commoner in Scotland' at his death; James Baillie was a wealthy Bristol merchant and banker; William Lillingston was also a man of business in London. Matheson had bought the island of Lewis in 1844; Gordon had purchased Barra, South Uist and Benbecula between 1838 and 1845; Baillie had acquired Glenelg in 1837. Ninety-four per cent of those assisted to emigrate by landlords between 1846 and 1856 were supported either by aristocratic grandees or by these new proprietors. It was, therefore, the ebbing of control and ownership from the old, impecunious landed class and the formation of a new Highland élite which in part enabled the development of such a major programme of assisted movement to take place.

Most of the emigrants were conveyed to Ontario (or Upper Canada as the region was known at the time). This implied a significant change in direction from several previous assisted emigrations to British North America, including those associated with the crisis of 1836-7. Then the maritime provinces of Cape Breton Island, Nova Scotia and Prince Edward Island, traditional areas of Highland settlement, had attracted the majority of assisted emigrants across the Atlantic.[79] The explanation seems to be that economic prospects in the later 1840s and early 1850s in these districts were relatively bleak and the colonial authorities were loath to accept any more destitute immigrants who might place an even greater burden on their meagre resources. In 1849, for example, the Duke of Argyll inquired about the possibility of sending emigrants there but was informed that '. . . there is no employment for persons of that class here at present'. Prince Edward Island was in 'a very depressed condition'. The region as a whole had experienced three consecutive bad harvests and a depression in trade. Indeed, there was a cruel but ironical parallel between the plight of the inhabitants of the maritime provinces and that of the Western Highlands from which they had emigrated in previous years. The potato crop, on which most of the poorer settlers depended, had failed and '. . . the people are reduced in many instances to absolute want'. A government official reported that the large numbers who had come to these provinces from Skye and the Long Island between 1838 and 1841 were now 'in a wretched state'. The Duke was therefore strongly advised not to attempt to convey any people there from Tiree and Mull.[80]

The Governor of Nova Scotia reiterated these warnings. Noting that distress in the area was especially great among those who had arrived from the Highlands in previous years, he went on to stress, '. . . this province is in no respect prepared for the reception of poor people . . . and . . . the landing under present circumstances of even a small number in the colony, suffering as it is under the scarcity produced by the failure in the potato and grain crops in the last two seasons, would be seriously injurious to the province itself, while those resorting to it in the expectation of ameliorating their conditions would be grievously disappointed'.[81] So necessitous were the inhabitants that in subsequent years many migrated to other parts of Canada.[82]

The survey of migration and emigration carried out in this chapter suggests a relatively clear pattern of development. There was some movement of people within the Highland region itself due to temporary migration, the impact of eviction and the redistribution of estate populations. However, the idea of a great transfer of population from the distressed western zone to the less deprived eastern districts was discounted. It was also argued that most migration to the Lowland cities was probably of a temporary rather than permanent nature, although it has to be conceded that the distinction between the two forms of movement was always likely to be blurred. Census evidence, however, does not support the notion of a large-scale permanent exodus from the famine-stricken region in the course of the 1840s and 1850s to the large towns of the south and east. This was prevented partly by the activities of the relief agencies in the north-west, the outlets, especially from 1846 to 1847 and 1850 to 1856, which were available for *temporary* migrants in the Lowlands and, perhaps above all, by the fact that much migration was channelled outside Scotland to North America and Australia. Three different emigration streams were identified: the movement of unassisted emigrants with their own means or with help from kinfolk already settled in the host country; the emigration of young, single adults to Australia; the large-scale exodus of poor families of the small tenant and cottar class to Canada and Australia aided by landlords, philanthropic agencies and the Emigration Commission. These three flows combined to ensure that between 1846 and 1856 the Scottish Highlands lost many thousands of its native inhabitants.

NOTES

1. For a discussion of their nature and the problems associated with using them see N.H. Carrier and J.R. Jeffrey, *External Migration: A Study of the Available Statistics, 1815-1950* (London, 1953), 13-20.

2. Those relating to British North America were published annually in parliamentary papers as *Papers Relative to Emigration to the North American Colonies*.

3. *PP*, XVIII (1852), *Twelfth General Report of the Colonial Land and Emigration Commissioners*, 11.

4. SRO, HD4/5, List of Emigrants of the Highland and Island Emigration Society.

5. *Destitution Papers*, Reports on the Islands of Mull . . . etc. (1849), *passim*.

6. See below, pp.253-4.

7. *Destitution Papers*, Reports on the Islands of Mull . . . etc. (1849), 12.

8. *McNeill Report*, Appendix A, 11-12.

9. Somers, *Letters from the Highlands*, 156-9.

10. MS. Diary of J.M. Mackenzie, *passim*; NLS, Sutherland Estate papers, Dep. 313/2737, E. Maciver to Tenants of Knockan and Elphin, Height of Assynt, 7 June 1848.

11. The seven parishes were Strath (Skye), N. Uist, Gairloch, Barvas (Lewis), Barra, Kilfinichen, Lochbroom.

12. Flinn, ed., *Scottish Population History*, 436.

13. SRO, HD19, Minutes and Correspondence of Easter Ross and Inverness-shire Destitution Committees, 1-3, 11-17.

14. Rev. T. McLauchlan, 'The Influence of Emigration on the Social Conditions of the Highlands', *Trans. National Association for Social Science* (1864), 606.

15. Somers, *Letters from the Highlands*, 159.

16. *Witness*, 21 December 1850.

17. Dunvegan Castle, Macleod of Macleod Muniments, 659/24/4, Dr. Norman Macleod to Miss Macleod, 18 October 1850.

18. See above, pp.133-4.

19. *Scotsman*, 13 February 1850.

20. Charles W.J. Withers, 'Highland Migration to Dundee, Perth and Stirling, 1753-1891', *Journal of Historical Geography*, 1985, II (4); *Highland Communities in Dundee and Perth, 1787-1891* (Dundee, 1986).

21. *Scotsman*, 24 November 1850.

22. *Witness*, 19 July 1851.

23. This is being carried out by Mr. W. Sloan, one of my postgraduate students. The districts referred to were among the most popular areas of Highland settlement in the city. I am grateful to Mr. Sloan for allowing me to report some of the early findings of his research.

24. Denis A. Docherty, 'The Migration of Highlanders to Lowland Scotland with particular reference to Paisley', B.A. Dissertation, Department of History, University of Strathclyde, No. 230; R.D. Lobban, 'The Migration of Highlanders into Lowland Scotland with special reference to Greenock, c.1750-1790'. Unpublished Ph.D. Thesis, University of Edinburgh, 1969. For a review of patterns of migration from the Highlands to the Lowland towns in the nineteenth century see T.M. Devine, 'Highland Migration to Lowland Scotland, 1760-1860', *Scottish Historical Review*, LXII (October 1983), 137-149.

25. Some possible reasons why the farming region consistently produced more migrants to the Lowland cities than the crofting districts are explored in Devine, 'Highland Migration to Lowland Scotland', 137-149.

26. *Inverness Advertiser*, 5 July 1853.

27. *Scotsman*, 26 July 1848.

28. *Ibid.*, 21 July 1849.

29. *Ibid.*, 20 July 1847.

30. *N.C.*, Q.44731. See also *Destitution Papers*, Eighth Report of the Glasgow Section of the Central Board (1848), Extract from Mr. Simpson's Reports, Islay, 33-41.

31. *North British Daily Mail*, 17 and 21 June 1847.

32. *McNeill Report*, Appendix A, Evidence of Capt. D. Campbell, 21.

33. *Destitution Papers*, Report on the Islands of Mull . . . etc., 17.

34. *Witness*, 8 August 1849.

35. *Ibid.*, 19 June 1850.

36. *McNeill Report*, Appendix A, Evidence of Capt. D. Campbell, 21.

37. See above, p.208.

38. See James A. Cameron, 'A Study of the Factors that Assisted and Directed Scottish Emigration to Upper Canada, 1815-1855'. Unpublished Ph.D. Thesis, University of Glasgow, 1970, 435.

39. NLS, Sutherland Estate Papers, Dep. 313/2737, Letters from Scourie Emigrants; *PP*, XL (1851), *Copies of Despatches Relative to Emigration*, 33; *Scotsman*, 31 October 1849; *PP*, XXXIII (1852), *Papers relative to Emigration*, A.C. Buchanan to J. Fleming, 26 November 1851, 567; *Inverness Advertiser*, 16 December 1851.

40. NLS, Sutherland Estate Papers, Dep. 313/21738, *Information for Intending Emigrants* (1850).

41. Quoted in Cameron, 'Scottish Emigration', 436.

42. *N.C.*, Appendix A, Statement by Rev. Archibald Clark, Minister of Kilmallie parish, Inverness-shire, 30-31.

43. *Inverness Advertiser*, 12 September 1854.

44. *N.C.*, QQ.38, 348.

45. This estimate is based on PRO, CO 201/101, 102, 113, Petitions from Highland proprietors in aid of Emigration assistance; *PP*, IV (1826), *Select Committee on Emigration*, QQ.639-642; *PP*, VI (1841), *Select Committee on Emigration (Scotland)*, 1841, *passim*; GRO, Census Enumerators' Schedules, West Highland and Hebridean parishes, 1841; SRO, Lord Macdonald Papers, GD221/21, Emigration Papers; Cameron, 'Scottish Emigration'. See also Appendix 10 below for the basis of the 1846-60 calculations. The numbers estimated to have been assisted by landlords to emigrate in the latter period are significantly higher than those indicated in Cameron, 'Scottish Emigration'.

46. Fullarton and Baird, *Remarks*, 128.
47. See below, pp.216-17.
48. NLS, Sutherland Estate Papers, Dep. 313/1512, E. McIver to R. Hersburgh, 22 March 1847.
49. See below, p.260.
50. See above, pp.100-2.
51. *Scotsman*, 18 December 1850.
52. *McNeill Report*, VII.
53. *Ibid.*, Appendix A, 1-2, 46, 11, 14, 74, 99; SRO, HD7/46, James Loch to Sir Charles Trevelyan, 10 January 1848; James Bruce, *Letters on the Present Condition of the Highlands and Islands of Scotland* (Edinburgh, 1847), *passim*.
54. See above, pp.130-2.
55. See, for instance, *Scotsman*, 30 July 1850.
56. SRO, HD7/46, Sir Charles Trevelyan to W. Skene, 2 March 1848. See also SRO, HD16/106, Observations on the Causes of Irish and Highland Destitution and Suggestions for their Removal by Dr. Coll Macdonald.
57. Inveraray Castle, Argyll Estate Papers, Bundle 1535, Donald Campbell, Prince Edward Island to Duke of Argyll, 24 April 1849; *PP*, XXXIII (1847), Governor J. Harvey to Earl Grey, 1 April 1847; *PP*, XXII (1849), *Ninth General Report of Colonial Land and Emigration Commissioners*, 17; *PP*, XXII (1850), *Tenth Report of Colonial Land and Emigration Commissioners*, 3.
58. *PP*, XVIII (1852), *Twelfth Report of the Colonial Land and Emigration Commissioners*, 45.
59. *Ibid.*
60. *Inverness Courier*, 29 March 1853.
61. See below, pp.248-9.
62. *PP*, L (1852-3), *Seventh Report of Board of Supervision*, XII; *PP*, XXIX (1854), *Eighth Report of Board of Supervision*, IX.
63. See above, Table 8.3, p.198 and sources quoted therein.
64. *PP*, XXII (1849), *Ninth General Report of Colonial Land and Emigration Commissioners*, 35. The existing regulations to be observed in the selection of labourers for passage to New South Wales included a preference for married couples below 40, especially those without children, and required 'Agricultural labourers' to pay deposits of £2 per head, if aged 14-40, £6, 40-50 and £11, 50-60.
65. Dunvegan Castle, Macleod of Macleod Muniments, 659/8/1, N. Ferguson to Miss Macleod, 2 June 1848.
66. *Witness*, 14 June 1848.
67. Inveraray Castle, Argyll Estate Papers, Bundle 1522, A. McGregor to ?, 1 February 1847; Bundle 1535, John Campbell to Duke of Argyll, 27 February 1849.
68. *Scotsman*, 12 September 1849; *Witness*, 22 September 1849.
69. *John O'Groats Journal*, 28 April 1848.
70. *Inverness Advertiser*, 17 August 1852.
71. *Ibid.*, 15 June 1852.
72. *Ibid.*, 17 August 1852.
73. *Ibid.*, 5 October 1852.
74. See below, pp.265-6.
75. *PP.*, XXXIII (1852), *Papers Relative to Emigration to the North American Colonies*, 567.
76. *Ibid.*
77. See below, pp.266-8.
78. Inveraray Castle, Argyll Estate Papers, Bundle 1558, Duke of Argyll to ?, 5 May 1851.
79. SRO, Lord Macdonald Papers, GD221/21, Emigration Papers; J.M. Bumsted, *The People's Clearance* (Edinburgh, 1982).
80. Inveraray Castle, Argyll Estate Papers, Bundle 1535, Donald Campbell to Duke of Argyll, 24 April 1849.
81. *PP*, XXXIII (1847), Governor J. Harvey to Earl Grey, 1 April 1847.
82. *PP*, XXXIII (1852), *Papers Relative to Emigration*, 583.

9

Coercion and Emigration: the Isle of Lewis, 1846-1890

1

James Matheson (1798-1878), of the East India trading firm of Jardine, Matheson and Co., bought the island of Lewis from Mrs Stewart Mackenzie of Seaforth in 1844. He is described in Disraeli's *Sybil* as '. . . richer than Croesus, one Macdrug, fresh from Canton with a million of opium in his pocket'. He paid a total of £190,000 for the estate which then had an annual rental of about £9,800.[1] In 1848 the island had 18,359 inhabitants of whom 15,200 lived in the rural districts outside Stornoway. The great majority of the population were crofters paying under £5 per annum in rent; an estimated 577 tenants paid under £2.[2] Due to the enormous wealth of its owner, the estate during the famine years became the focus of the single largest investment programme undertaken in the Highlands. Between 1845 and 1850 a total of £107,767 was spent on 'extensive improvements', or some £67,980 more than the whole revenue derived form the property during the period.[3] Matheson was subsequently knighted for these and other relief initiatives during the famine.

Expenditure on this scale did help to alleviate some of the worst effects of the subsistence crisis. For instance, in 1849-50 the Matheson estate laid out £3,600 on tenants' crofts. The sum was employed in draining, trenching and enclosing. On this expenditure tenants paid interest at the rate of five per cent. The contracts for executing the work were in all cases offered to the tenants themselves and by and large these were accepted. The townships took the contracts for fencing and the individual occupants obtained those for draining and trenching. The sum actually paid for this work was reckoned at £8 to £12 per acre.[4] Yet, while this level of investment reduced destitution in certain parts of the island, it could not entirely insulate the population of the estate from the impact of the potato famine. By 1851 total arrears had risen to £3,376 and 518 families were in arrears to the extent of two years' rental or more.[5] In addition, Matheson and his estate chamberlain, John Munro Mackenzie, recognised by 1850 that the grand scheme of agricultural improvement had entirely failed to bring either an economic return to the estate or lasting material security to the people. They now argued that the root of the problem lay not in the continuing blight and the accumulating impact of a series of bad seasons but in the more fundamental pressure of chronic overpopulation. Mackenzie expressed their pessimistic conclusion clearly and candidly: 'I am of opinion that it is impossible to expend capital on agricultural improvement on this property in such a manner as to make a fair return for the expenditure, and at the same time to provide permanent subsistence for the whole of the present population if the potatoes continue to fail. I state this opinion after a careful examination of the very extensive improvements executed on this property by Sir James Matheson and of the character and habits of the population'.[6]

It is also possible to detect in the statements of Mackenzie and Matheson a deep sense of disappointment, frustration and irritation that their best efforts had come to nought because of the unenthusiastic response of the community to their plans. In 1851, for example, Matheson urged the Chief Emigration Officer in Quebec, A.C. Buchanan, to try to ensure that emigrants from Lewis to Canada should be dispersed rather than remain together in the same communities. Absorbing them within the general mass of the population was, as he put it, 'the best means of eradicating those habits of indolence and inertness to which their impoverished condition must in some measure be attributed'.[7]

The failure of the Matheson scheme and the dismissive attitudes of the two men to the inhabitants of the estate ensured that the emigration solution soon came to be regarded as the only acceptable course of action for the future. Mackenzie, in his evidence to Sir John McNeill's inquiry, could not have been more emphatic: 'I am clearly of opinion that, if the potatoes continue to fail, the inhabitants of Lewis cannot be made self-sustaining unless a considerable number of them remove elsewhere'.[8] Eventually 1554 people were assisted to emigrate to Canada in 1851, a further 453 in 1852 and, after a three-year gap, 330 in 1855.[9] The final total of 2337 (or fourteen per cent of the entire population of Lewis in 1851, the town of Stornoway excepted) represented an unprecedented level of assisted emigration from this island. Between 1838 and 1842 there had been an earlier scheme but only 388 were then supported to move to Canada.[10] The chance survival of John Munro Mackenzie's estate diary for 1851 makes it possible to establish an unusually detailed reconstruction of the events surrounding the emigration, the attitudes of the people and the methods used by the Matheson administration to promote movement.

2

The emigration strategy was the central feature of a wider programme which was designed to renew and stabilise the financial condition of the estate. Levels of investment were to be drastically cut, a vigorous effort to markedly reduce rent arrears was begun and a coherent plan emerged to resettle some areas and vacate others as emigration allowed a redistribution of population. The policy of the estate swung decisively from one which reflected considerable concern for the welfare of the people to a strategy in which the well-being of the inhabitants was rigorously subordinated to efficient economic management. The persistence of the subsistence crisis had hardened attitudes. In the later winter and early spring of 1851, Munro Mackenzie travelled throughout the estate, visited each township and selected those who were to emigrate, those who were to remain and those who were to be resettled elsewhere.[11] The process of selection was carried out with great care. In January 1851 he informed the ground officers of the parishes of Lochs, Uig and Barvas of the '. . . two classes I would propose to emigrate. First of all bad payers, say those two years in arrears of rent if able-bodied and have no reasonable grounds or excuse for being so far in arrears. Secondly, I would propose to clear whole townships which are generally in arrears and are not conveniently situated for fishing and can be converted into grazings, several of which are in the parish of Uig.'[12]

The Great Highland Famine

As the policy developed, a number of other aspects of the selection process became apparent. Communities in areas regarded as potentially solvent or improvable were specifically excluded from emigration assistance. The people of the townships of Breasclete and Garynahine were 'very industrious and their rents well paid. They also have plenty of room'.[13] They were not encouraged to emigrate. On the other hand, Dalmore was '. . . a most unhealthy place . . . there does not appear to be a healthy man in it except an old pensioner who served in Egypt; all seem consumptive'.[14] In general terms, the estate favoured the retention of east-coast townships with established fishing traditions which had survived the famine in much better condition than any others. On the other hand, Mackenzie was determined to reduce those communities which depended on cattle sales to pay rental and had suffered acutely as a result of the slump in stock prices since 1846.[15] Townships such as Arnol, North Bragar, South Bragar and South Shawbost were 'very populous'. Some were to be encouraged to move from them but they 'would be difficult to clear entirely' because of the sheer density of their population. Out of almost 200 inhabitants only thirty-six were therefore to be asked to emigrate from these settlements.[16] Finally, Mackenzie was careful to avoid including in his emigrant list families with several very young children or those whose heads were deemed 'too old'.[17]

Tables 9.1 to 9.4 clarify the process in more detail. Summonses of removal were not issued indiscriminately but, as the tabulation indicates, were served on particular districts. Table 9.3 suggests that the policy of threatened eviction was pursued most vigorously and systematically in Barvas and West Lewis, the poorest parts of the estate. Table 9.4 is especially illuminating because it reveals the clear correlation between parishes where kelp production had concentrated in the 1820s and the locations of removal in the 1850s. On the basis of the evidence, it would be reasonable to argue that the Matheson programme of 1851, like others elsewhere, can be partly explained as an attempt to eliminate those communities now regarded as 'redundant' in consequence of the failure of kelp manufacture.

Table 9.1. Summonses of Removal as Proportion of Number of Households, Parish of Barvas (Lewis), 1848-1853

	1848		1849		1850		1851		1853	
Area	(1)	(2) %	(1)	(2) %	(1)	(2) %	(1)	(2) %	(1)	(2) %
1	–	–	–	–	–	–	25	17.5	–	–
2	3	2.6	58	50.9	–	–	26	22.8	8	9.1
3	–	–	–	–	3	1.7	48	27.7	39	31.2
4	46	48.4	42	44.2	–	–	12	12.6	5	6.0
5	–	–	14	10.1	–	–	26	18.8	–	–
6	3	2.0	6	3.9	–	–	58	37.9	–	–
Total	52		120		3		195		52	

Sources: SRO, Sheriff Court Processes, Stornoway, SC33/17/26-33; GRO, Census Enumerator's Schedules, Barvas, 1851.
Notes: (a) Column (1): Number of summonses of removal issued per area. Column (2): Summonses of removal as percentage of number of households per area.
(b) For areas see Table 9.2, p.215.

Table 9.2. *Census Areas and Population, Parish of Barvas, Lewis, 1851*

Area	Townships	Households	Male	Female	Total
1	S. Bragar, N. Bragar, Arnol	143	304	338	642
2	Bru, Lower & Upper Barvas	114	286	303	589
3	Upper & Lower Shader, Fivepenny & Mid Barve, Melbost, Barve	173	400	449	849
4	N. & S. Galston, S. Dell	95	250	264	514
5	N. Dell, Cross, Swanbost, Habost	138	411	375	786
6	Europie, Fivepenny Ness, Knockaird, Port Caligral, Lionel, Eurodale, Skigersta	153	430	379	809
	Total	816	2081	2108	4189

Source: GRO, Census Enumerator's Schedules, Barvas, 1851

Table 9.3. *Summonses of Removal, Island of Lewis, 1848-1853*

District	1848	1848	1850	1851	1853	Per cent of total 1848-53
Barvas	52	120	3	195	52	30
Tolsta	12	–	–	74	27	8
Stornoway	19	84	–	34	8	10
Eye Peninsula	34	91	–	124	–	17
West Lewis	4	120	90	157	34	28
Lochs	–	11	–	79	5	7
Total	121	426	93	663	126	100

Source: SRO, Sheriff Court Processes, Stornoway, SC 33/17/26-33.

Table 9.4. *Summonses of Removal and Kelp Parishes, Lewis, 1848-1853*

Parish	Summonses of removal as per cent of total summonses, Lewis, 1848-53	Kelp proceeds as per cent of land rental, Lewis estate, 1826
Lochs	7	11
Uig	28	42
Barvas	30	47

Sources: SRO, Sheriff Court Processes, Stornoway, SC 33/17/26-33; SRO, Brown MSS (Temporary Deposit), TD 80/100-4, Statement of Account, Seaforth Estate, 1826.

In essence, therefore, Mackenzie concentrated his attention on 'the most destitute, those most in arrears of rent and who have least stock'. He was aware that they threatened to cause a dramatic increase in expenditure on the poor rates; unless they were moved, 'their families may soon come on the parish'.[18] By the end of his tour of investigation he had identified 518 families whom he wished to send to America. With an average family size of five and a half on the estate in 1851, this suggests a total figure of intended emigrants of over 2,500. Matheson's instructions to Mackenzie had been unequivocal. Tenants must surrender their holdings in cases where two years of rent arrears had gathered and a further year was being added.[19] The arrears of those nominated for emigration stood at £3,376, an average of £6.5 per tenant or just over two years in arrears.[20] The estate made a detailed offer to this group. Free passages to

Canada were promised; all arrears or debts due to the proprietor were cancelled; the right of hypothec was relinquished and if no purchaser was available Matheson agreed to take their stock at valuation. He also indicated his willingness to pay the passage of a minister to accompany them and to provide his salary for two years. On the other hand, '. . . if any one, now in arrear of rent for two years, and who has not the means of subsistence till next harvest, should reject the offer, and be unable to assign a sufficient reason for rejecting it, arising from the age or disability of himself or some dependent member of his family, he will be served with a summons of removal at Whitsunday and deprived of his lands'.[21]

The offer was communicated in February 1851. It met with a very mixed response. From thirty-nine townships examined in the first phase of Mackenzie's investigation, 267 families (1512 individuals) were selected for emigration. Only forty-five, however, (seventeen per cent) were willing to go.[22] This massive shortfall at first astonished the estate officials and then quickly galvanised them into action to ensure that the initial emigration targets would be met in spite of the reluctance of the people. Clearly, there may have been the natural peasant reluctance to surrender land and risk the hazards of life in a strange country. Yet this in itself is not a sufficient explanation. It is apparent, for instance, that in districts as far apart as Barra and Skye there was a general and almost desperate desire for emigration in the early 1850s as the stress of famine, the cessation of the relief activities of the Central Board and a new wave of evictions weakened the grip of the people on the land.[23] Moreover, the estate was intent on directing the emigration towards the eastern Canadian townships of Sherbrooke and Lingwick where the Lewis emigrants of the early 1840s had settled. It was assumed this would help reduce the expected hostility to a long voyage and resettlement in unfamiliar surroundings.[24] Even the experience of serious destitution did not apparently dilute the opposition to emigration in Lewis. Mackenzie noted a widespread unwillingness 'to confess they will be short of food before next crop for fear of being sent to America'.[25] Favourable accounts from previous emigrants failed to have much impact either. John Macdonald, ground officer in Uig, noted that those who left in the early 1840s had prospered on the whole and that their letters home to kinfolk and friends had testified to this: 'but this has had little effect in producing a desire to follow their example on the part of those here'.[26] The estate officials were convinced, like other observers elsewhere in the Highlands, that the poorest were the most reluctant to move: 'The more destitute are generally the most ignorant, and they dread the danger of the voyage, and fear to trust themselves in a new country, and under new circumstances of which they have no accurate notions'.[27] But even this explanation conflicted with other evidence that in Lewis in 1851 successful fishermen were just as opposed to emigration as impoverished cottars.[28]

It is more likely that the prevalent hostility to assisted emigration from Lewis reflected the particular circumstances of the island during the famine. The inhabitants in general seem to have experienced less distress than those of other islands because of the substantial investment programme carried out by the estate and the continued vigour of the white fishery in the Minch.[29] In addition, according to one observer, the Rev. David Watson of the parish of Uig, 'the people generally are under an impression that the proprietor is bound in law to support them'.[30] A number of witnesses agreed that the potato crop was less subject to blight in 1850 in Lewis than in any year since 1846. The grain harvest was above average and there had been extensive seasonal migration to the Caithness fisheries.[31] Evidence from other areas considered suggests that emigration was often a last resort for the very poor and attitudes could radically alter over short periods of time as circumstances and prospects changed.[32] What apparently complicated feelings in Lewis was a sense of outrage among the people that much of the rent arrears which were used to legitimise migration was entirely artificial. In the parish of Uig, where most of the potential emigrants lived, people had received meal on credit from the proprietor in 1846 and 1847. The sums obtained had been added to their rent account and they insisted that this made up most of their debts. They alleged that these had actually been settled: 'The greater number of them deny the quantity charged against them and many assert that they paid the meal when they got it to James and John McKenzie, their ground officers. Neither John nor James can read or write and it was quite impossible they could keep account of the meal given out and from whom they got payment'.[33] Even the estate chamberlain himself admitted, 'I have grave doubts as to all being right in that quarter'.[34]

It was in this atmosphere of stubborn opposition to emigration and great bitterness about the drift of estate policy that Mackenzie and his fellow officials pressed ahead with plans to ensure that their aim of removing 518 families from the estate would be achieved. Notices of removal were formally served upon those selected for emigration.[35] Between 1846 and 1848, 187 summonses of removal were granted to the Matheson estate at Stornoway Sheriff Court. From 1849 to 1851 this figure soared to an astonishing 1180.[36] This number of summonses would inevitably affect many more individuals than the estate wished to expel. Writs were apparently also served on a number of persons who were in arrears of rent but who, there was reason to believe, could find the means of paying the amount due: 'The intention was not absolutely to remove them, but to compel payment by all who were able to pay'.[37] The net result, however, was to inspire intense insecurity in all corners of the estate. Mackenzie had decided to clear four entire townships: Knock (43 inhabitants), Carinish (61), Aird Uig (43) and Dalmore (53).[38] In the event, another three were completely cleared: Reef, Gisla and Ballygloom. Several others, especially in the parish of Uig, suffered considerable depletion.[39]

The policy of eviction and threatened eviction was resolutely pursued.[40] Mackenzie eloquently defined the nature of 'compulsory emigration' at a meeting of Stornoway merchants in April 1851 who were hostile to the emigration, 'on the grounds that, if the people were sent to America, they would lose their debts'. The meeting resolved to detain all in debt to them and, with a cynical eye on their own interests, the merchants denounced Sir James Matheson's 'kind offer' as 'tyrannical and cruel', a flagrant breach of the pledge he made to the parochial boards that 'he would not compel people to emigrate'. Mackenzie stoutly defended his employer: 'I stated that none could be compelled to emigrate and that they need not go unless they please but that all who were two years and upwards in arrears would be deprived of their land at Whitsunday . . . the proprietor can do with his land as he pleases'.[41]

The business classes of Stornoway were almost alone in their vocal protest against the emigration. Local Church of Scotland ministers and a Free Church catechist, interviewed by Sir John McNeill, who visited Lewis in March 1851 in the course of his tour of enquiry on behalf of the Board of Supervision, all acknowledged that emigration was now the only solution to the island's problems.[42] The Free Church supplied the Rev. Mr MacLean to travel with the emigrants.[43] The larger tacksmen also welcomed the policy.[44] Partly because of this widespread support from the propertied classes and influential opinion of the island the estate was able to employ maximum coercion. All those who did not accept the offer of assisted passage were told that 'they need not expect assistance of any kind either in seed or food and . . . they must wholly depend on their own resources'.[45] Those nominated for emigration were also to be refused work on the estate. This was a most potent threat since by this time the operations of the Central Relief Board had come to an end.[46] Those deeply in arrears were also warned that their remaining stocks of cattle would be confiscated.[47]

Even Sir John McNeill became an energetic ally of the estate. Historians have sometimes been doubtful about the objectivity of McNeill's investigation. Sources sympathetic to the people, such as the *Witness*, regarded him as 'bound up . . . in feeling and interest with the ejecting proprietors of the country'.[48] His activities in Lewis in March 1851 confirm that long before the completion of his *Report* he had made up his own mind that the emigration of a proportion of the Highland population was essential. He therefore became a willing and persuasive advocate of the Matheson policy at a critical stage in its evolution. On 31 March he warned the constables of the townships of Arnol and Point 'not to expect help from any quarter'. On the same day he interviewed John Macdonald who had taken ten acres of land two years previously but had been unable to stock his extended holding: 'Sir John seemed pleased to get such evidence as he said the great cry was "give the people more land" which he thinks does more harm than good if they have no capital'. At Bernera on April Fool's Day 1851 he addressed the people, 'telling them they need not look for aid from any quarter' and strongly recommended emigration.[49]

Two further procedures were used. First, in the spring of 1851 the estate prohibited all those served with notices of removal from cutting peat until they had either paid their rent or given satisfactory security.[50] Second, the Poor Law was employed to intensify pressure for emigration. Mackenzie himself was chairman of three of the four parochial boards on the island while the majority of the rest of the board members were greater tacksmen.[51] The Inspectors of the Poor were instructed to grant relief to the 'able-bodied destitute' but only if work was exacted in return and 'to relieve none who had anything of their own till they first disposed of such property'.[52]

There is therefore unambiguous evidence that coercion of various kinds was employed to promote emigration from Lewis in 1851. It amply confirms the statement made by the Rev. Angus Maciver of the Church of Scotland to the Napier Commission in 1883: 'Some people say it was voluntary. But there was a great deal of forcing and these people were sent away very much against their will. That is very well known and people present know that perfectly well. Of course, they were not taken in hand by the policemen and all that, but they were in arrears, and had to go, and remonstrated against going.'[53]

The estate had succeeded in attracting fewer than 250 people to take up its initial offer of emigration assistance. By the end of 1851, however, a total of 1544 embarked for Canada, followed by a further 453 in 1852 and 330 in 1855.[54] This was a tribute to Mackenzie's 'persuasive' powers, the sanctions applied by the administration and the continuing stress of famine. The vigorous collection of arrears by the estate in 1851 – of the total rental of £4,956 due by those remaining, £2,109 was collected in cash *and cattle* by the end of November – must have convinced many to seek a new life abroad rather than continue to endure the hardship and insecurity of an existence in Lewis.[55]

3

Details survive of the embarkation and departure of 787 emigrants in May and June 1851 on the *Marquis of Stafford* (500 passengers), the *Barlow* (287) and the *Islay* (68).[56] John Munro Mackenzie first contacted for advice a director of the Greenock Bank who had been agent for the Duke of Argyll and had been responsible for supervising emigration from the Argyll estates and from Perthshire. The firm contracted to arrange transport and assistance with passage to Canada was Messrs. Reid and Murray of Glasgow, a company which had considerable experience in the emigration trade. On 16 May, the *Marquis of Stafford* arrived in the Sound of Bernera and the emigrants, the greater part of whom were from the upper areas of the parish of Uig, began to load their belongings. Preparations took three days and the emigrants were issued with an allowance of biscuit equal to one pound per adult passenger and tinware for each person who could pay for it. The *Marquis of Stafford* weighed anchor on 20 May and proceeded form Loch Roag to the Port of Ness, arriving there 'after a rather disagreeable passage . . . there being a heavy swell which brought on the sea sickness among the women and children and the appearance in the morning of the decks and fore hold was anything but agreeable'.

The first major problem occurred at this point. The people from Uig were vigorously opposed to allowing any of the Ness emigrants on board, claiming that the ship was already filled to capacity and that there was fever and smallpox in Ness. Mackenzie remonstrated with them but to no effect. The captain of the vessel was ordered to proceed and took on people from Tolsta instead, making a final complement of 500 passengers. The ship then sailed for Troon from where the emigrants left for Canada. It would appear that the Ness people, numbering about seventy, eventually departed on 22 May on a separate vessel, the *Islay*, for Glasgow.

By 2 June, however, the *Barlow*, which was to take on board 287 emigrants from Lewis, was still detained in Sutherland. Mackenzie 'was mobbed by people from all quarters . . . who have become almost desperate'. Many of them had already sold everything they possessed because they expected to have left a month before. The *Barlow* finally arrived on 13 June. It was originally planned that the Rev. Ewen Maclean, a Free Church minister from Harris, would travel with the ship, but he eventually sailed later. Sir James Matheson promised to pay him a salary of £50 per annum for three years on condition he remained with the emigrants as their pastor in the eastern townships of Lower Canada. The Free Church engaged to pay the passage of his family. A week after its arrival the *Barlow* was ready for departure. Mackenzie noted that the emigrants were 'very respectably clothed and seemed very happy and contented'. He had to distribute clothing to a few families only. He was present on board on Saturday 21 June when the ship weighed anchor at 6 a.m.: 'I took leave of the passengers which was very affecting. They thanked me over and over again and, tho' going to part, seemed pleased with the change they were about to make and with the ship and Captain'. No explanation was offered for this extraordinary and radical change in the attitude of the people. On 7 August, Mackenzie received notice of their safe arrival in Quebec.

On the whole the emigration had been managed efficiently. Officials in Quebec complimented Matheson and contrasted the general health and condition of emigrants from his estate and the arrangements made for them with the sad plight of the people from Gordon of Cluny's properties of Barra and South Uist.[57] Even the *Inverness Advertiser*, on most occasions a bitter critic of Highland landlords, was almost fulsome in its praise: '. . . the terms were liberal and such as in every way accorded with the character for distinguished munificence which the proprietor of the island has won'.[58] Only one aspect caused concern. On landing at Quebec, some had made their way to Toronto and from there to the town of Hamilton. Apparently 'they laboured under the delusion that land, to which they should straightway be conveyed, had been provided for them and . . . they expected that they were to be kept in maintenance for the first twelve months of their residence at this new settlement'.[59] The *Advertiser* admitted, however, after conducting its own investigation, that no such promise had been made. Certainly there is no indication in Mackenzie's diary of assurances of this type being given. The party had to be maintained by Scottish charities in Hamilton before eventually finding work on the Canadian railways.

The experience of this group apart, the bulk of the emigrants of 1851 seem to have settled into their new surroundings quickly and comparatively comfortably. Although measles had broken out on the voyage and several children had died, the passage had been comparatively uneventful.[60] In December of that year a series of letters appeared in the *Inverness Advertiser* from the emigrants, all showing satisfaction and optimism:

> Lingwick, 1st Sept. 1851. Dear Friends – I am very sorry because you are not here with us, as this country is promising to be better for poor people than the old and poor country . . . we are working at the railroad for 4s.6d. the first month and the next month 5s. a day . . . there is plenty money here now that we are working.

> Lingwick, 23 Sept. 1851. I am working at the railroad which is passing through the province. 810 miles long and there is plenty of work for many hundreds and good payment too.

> Lingwick, 10 Oct. 1851. . . . provisions are cheap and plentiful and people that are labourers can get through without hardship, as the railroad is going on at Sheerbrooke . . . All that came from Barvas are here.[61]

There is no reason to believe, given the *Advertiser*'s overt sympathy for the people and suspicion of landlord motives, that this was anything other than a fair sample of opinion.[62]

4

The favourable press and government response to the emigration carried out by Sir James Matheson begs two final questions. First, given the fact that coercion, eviction and intimidation were probably as widely employed in Lewis as in any other Highland estate in the 1850s, how is the positive reaction (not least from sources traditionally hostile to landlords) to be explained? Second, did the very substantial assisted emigration from Lewis between 1851 and 1855 help to solve the economic and social problems of the island as the estate officials insisted?

In attempting to answer the first question, three factors must be considered. In the first place, as earlier discussion has outlined, destitution in Lewis was never as oppressive as in some other Hebridean islands. The estate also excluded from emigration assistance families whose heads were too old or which contained several young children.[63] This process of selection and the more favourable circumstances in Lewis may have ensured that emigrants from the island were in a better condition than those from elsewhere to cope with the demands of adjustment to a new life in Canada.[64] Second, the vast majority of the Lewis people, 1997 of the final total of 2334 emigrants, arrived in British North America in 1851 and 1852. In these years, in contrast to the 1840s, the labour market in Canada was very buoyant, due mainly to a remarkable boom in railway construction which helped to provide jobs for many of the Lewis emigrants.[65] Third, the estate administered the process of emigration with great care. The timing of departure was important. The Lewis people arrived in July and August when there was 'an unusual demand' for labourers and at a time when the weather did not impede either travel or resettlement.[66] The majority were directed towards localities where there had been earlier substantial migration from Lewis between 1838 and 1842, and assistance from kinfolk doubtless helped in the resettlement process. The estate also went to greater lengths to reduce the problems of passage than most of those which practised assisted emigration. Not only was a Free Church minister supplied to cater for the spiritual needs of the emigrants but the people were provided with free passage from Quebec to 'any place in the interior which might be specified before departing'.[67] One of the major problems which beset other groups was that this additional but vital subsidy was not always available and many of the destitute only managed to make their way with the assistance of Scottish charities in Canada or with the help of the immigration authorities. It was these less fortunate people who tended to attract the sympathetic attention of the Canadian press and elicited vigorous protest from the colonial authorities against the Highland landlords who had been responsible for sending them.[68]

It is more difficult to provide an unequivocal answer to the second question of the long-term impact of the emigration on conditions in Lewis itself. The absence of estate records for the later period makes it virtually impossible to reach entirely convincing conclusions. Evidence presented to parliamentary and government inquiries and to Royal Commissions is invaluable, but conflicting information and opinion is common and events are often interpreted against the background of the bitter political struggles which took place in the Highlands during the 1880s and 1890s. When John Munro Mackenzie left the island of Lewis in 1854 he took the view that people were 'comparatively prosperous'.[69] One of his successors, William Mackay, contended that the condition of the people had 'vastly improved' between the 1840s and 1880s and pointed to rising standards in their mode of dress, furniture and housing.[70] Whether, however, these changes were directly caused by the emigration is another matter. For a start, a series of other factors, considered in more detail in Chapter 12 of this book, were having a powerful influence on recovery: a very substantial increase in temporary migration to the north-east fishery, the further expansion of the white fishing around Lewis, the recovery both of the potato crop and of cattle prices, and the sharp fall in the cost of the vital grain import from the 1870s.[71] Even more importantly, the population of only one Lewis parish, Uig, fell between 1841 and 1851 as a result of the emigrations. Numbers in the three other parishes continued to rise from census to census until 1911. Even Uig recovered to increase again after 1861. The island as a whole did not achieve its maximum level of population until the early twentieth century; the loss of people which took place in the 1850s was quickly made up (see Table 9.5).

Table 9.5. *Lewis Population, 1841-1911 (excluding Stornoway Burgh)*

Parish	1841	1851	1861	1871	1881	1891	1901	1911
Barvas	4361	4785	5226	5742	6133	6494	6772	6953
Uig	3828	3805	3630	4112	4476	4621	4463	4462
Lochs	2630	3064	3529	4119	4489	4675	4733	4750
Stornoway (landward)	4864	5666	6060	6975	7696	8413	9131	9632

There is little evidence either of a large-scale redistribution of land in favour of those who remained after the great emigration although it would appear that the lots of *some* of those who departed were allocated to crofters moved from other townships. There are also occasional references in the sources to crofts being enlarged through additions made from the land of emigrants.[72] The estate, unlike several others considered in this study, does seem to have made some effort to redistribute rather than simply to consolidate. However, crofters, ministers and local residents who gave evidence to the Napier Commission described how this process was also accompanied by the clearance of whole townships.[73] It was their opinion that the resettlement of some of those who were evicted resulted in further congestion. John Munro Mackenzie disputed this: 'They were in no case crowded on any township where there was no room for them'.[74] But he had himself stated in his diary in early 1851 that entire townships were to be cleared in the parish of Uig in order to form grazing farms.[75] There is subsequent evidence that the lands of Reef and Carinish townships were added to tacksmen's farms as a result of this policy.[76] On balance, then, the acreage available to the people was almost certainly reduced as the population continued to rise. Any recovery could only have come about through higher rewards derived from such non-agricultural sources as fishing and temporary migration. It can hardly have been due to a relaxation of population pressure on the land.

On the whole, then, it is difficult to avoid the conclusion that the Matheson policy of large-scale emigration failed to achieve its stated purpose. While it may have appeared the only possible strategy available to a harassed estate administration in the desperate circumstances of the 1850s, it did not offer a solution to the island's problems in the long run. Indeed, the estate itself contributed to these after 1860 by its unwillingness or inability to control subdivision of land: 'It is against the regulations of the estate to subdivide without the consent of the factor but, as a matter of fact, we do subdivide without his consent'.[77] The Chamberlain contended that 'everything possible was done to prevent subdivision' but admitted: 'Summonses of removal were served but not enforced. In some cases the son was obliged to pull down the house he had built. Notwithstanding, in the course of a year or two, he would commence to build a second house; but the difficulty, if we had obliged him to pull down the house again, what were we to do with him, for we could not drive him out of Lewis'.[78] As a result, subletting continued to thrive. By the later nineteenth century a substantial cottar population had expanded still further in Lewis, complaints of overcrowded townships filled the minutes of evidence of the Royal Commissions of 1883 and 1892, and the island was officially designated a 'Congested District' from 1897.[79] A major subsistence crisis struck once more in 1881-2, as a result of a catastrophic decline in earnings from the north-east fisheries, and again in 1886-7.[80] Memories of the great potato famine were revived.

Ironically, indeed, the strategy of employing maximum coercion to cause people to emigrate eventually backfired with a vengeance. It became virtually impossible to encourage 'voluntary' schemes of emigration because, as even the principal estate factor in the 1880s admitted, 'there lingered in the mind of the people that emigration meant "forced emigration" '.[81] Napier Campbell, a Stornoway solicitor and energetic defender of the rights of the crofters, articulated their own profound hostility to assisted emigration: 'Assisted emigration as hitherto carried out, is the total breaking up of their home, with all its associations. It is dispersal or virtual annihilation *as a race* . . . the factor, they say, gave what he pleased and inadequate value, for their stock, crop and effects. They have a deep-rooted antipathy to compulsory or disguised expatriation'.[82] Far from breaking the grip of the people on the land, therefore, the Matheson policies of the 1850s seem to have induced a resolute opposition to group emigration and a determination to resist any further attempts to promote it. In the next chapter, the remarkably different impact of emigration in Tiree is considered. The contrasting experiences of the two islands demonstrate that the results of population loss were by no means automatically conditioned; but in the final analysis depended on local social and economic circumstances and the different reactions of both landlords and people.

NOTES

1. Cameron, 'Scottish Emigration', 356.
2. *McNeill Report*, Appendix A, Evidence of J.M. Mackenzie, 93.
3. *Ibid.*, ix-xx; Appendix A, 93-5; *N.C.*, Appendix A, 124.
4. *McNeill Report*, Appendix A, 94.
5. MS. Diary of J.M. Mackenzie, 1851, Chamberlain of the Lews (hereafter referred to as Mackenzie's Diary, 1851).
6. *McNeill Report*, Appendix A, 94-95.
7. *PP*, XXII (1852), *Papers Relative to Emigration to the North American Colonies*, Sir J. Matheson to A.C. Buchanan, 10 October 1851.

8. *McNeill Report*, Appendix A, 95; *N.C.*, 3305-6.
9. See Appendix 10 for details and sources.
10. Cameron, 'Scottish Emigration', 358.
11. Mackenzie's Diary, 1851, *passim*.
12. *Ibid.*, 23 January 1851.
13. *Ibid.*, 18 February.
14. *Ibid.*, 19 February.
15. *Ibid.*
16. *Ibid.*
17. *Ibid.*, 17 February 1851.
18. *Ibid.*
19. *N.C.*, 1103, Q.16960.
20. Mackenzie's Diary, 1851, *passim*.
21. *McNeill Report*, Appendix A, 95.
22. Mackenzie's Diary, 1851, *passim*.
23. See below, pp.253-4.
24. Cameron, 'Scottish Emigration', 358; *PP*, XXXIII (1852), *Papers Relative to Emigration to the North American Colonies*, A.C. Buchanan to J. Fleming, 26 November 1851, 568.
25. Mackenzie's Diary, 18 February 1851.
26. *McNeill Report*, Appendix A, 105, Evidence of J. Macdonald.
27. *Ibid.* Average arrears of families 'willing to emigrate' were £6; average of those 'unwilling' were £10.12.2d.
28. Mackenzie's Diary, 27 February 1851.
29. See below, pp.259-60.
30. *McNeill Report*, Appendix A, 103.
31. *Ibid.*, 91-2, 95, 99-100; Mackenzie's Diary, 15 February 1851; *John O'Groats Journal*, 19 July 1850; *Inverness Advertiser*, 22 July 1851.
32. See below, pp.259-60.
33. Mackenzie's Diary, 17 February 1851.
34. *Ibid.*
35. *Ibid.*, 27 February and numerous other entries. See also *McNeill Report*, Appendix A, Evidence of J.M. Mackenzie, 95.
36. SRO, Sheriff Court Processes, Stornoway, SC33/17/26-33.
37. *McNeill Report*, Appendix A, 95.
38. Mackenzie's Diary, 14, 15, 17, 19 February 1851.
39. *N.C.*, 897-898, QQ.13993-13997.
40. Mackenzie's Diary, 21 June 1851.
41. *Ibid.*, 5 April 1851.
42. *McNeill Report*, Appendix A, 89-106.
43. Mackenzie's Diary, 21 June 1851.
44. *Ibid.*, 3 February 1851.
45. *Ibid.*, 24 January 1851.
46. *Ibid.*, 18 February 1851.
47. *Ibid.*, 17 March 1851.
48. *Witness*, 26 July 1851.
49. Mackenzie's Diary, 31 March, 1-2 April 1851.
50. *Ibid.*, 23 May 1851.
51. *McNeill Report*, Appendix A, 97, 99, 101.
52. Mackenzie's Diary, 18 April 1851.
53. *N.C.*, 11, QQ.14301, 16967-8.
54. Mackenzie's Diary, 1851, *passim*; *PP*, XXXIII (1852), 585-8; *PP*, XLVI (1854).
55. Mackenzie's Diary, 1851, *passim*.
56. In Mackenzie's Diary, entries from 21 April-7 August 1851, inclusive.
57. *PP*, XXIII (1852), *Papers Relative to Emigration to the North American Colonies*, A.C. Buchanan to J. Fleming, 26 November 1851.

58. *Inverness Advertiser*, 4 November 1851.

59. *Ibid.*

60. *PP*, XXXIII (1852), A.C. Buchanan to Rt. Hon. Earl Grey, 31 December 1851.

61. *Inverness Advertiser*, 16 December 1851.

62. *N.C.*, Appendix A, 163ff. The long-term effects were more equivocal. J.M. Mackenzie himself admitted that while those who went to L. Canada did 'remarkably well', those who settled in Sherbrooke, N. Canada, did not. See *ibid.*, 3305-6.

63. See above, p.214.

64. The emigrants on board the *Marquis of Stafford* arrived at Oban *en route* for the Clyde and were described as 'generally well clad and had a strong and healthy appearance'. *Inverness Courier*, 12 June 1851.

65. *Inverness Advertiser*, 4 November, 16 December 1851; *PP*, XXXIII (1852), *Papers Relative to Emigration to the North American Colonies*, A.C. Buchanan to J. Fleming, 26 November 1851.

66. *PP*, XXXIII (1852), Buchanan to Fleming, 26 November 1851.

67. *Inverness Advertiser*, 4 November 1851.

68. *PP*, XXXIII (1852), A.C. Buchanan to Rt. Hon Earl Grey, 31 December 1851.

69. *N.C.*, 3307.

70. *Ibid.*, Appendix A, 432, Further Statement by W. Mackay, Chamberlain of Lewis (1884).

71. See below, pp.286-8.

72. Mackenzie's Diary, 23 January, 14 February 1851; *N.C.*, 883, Q.13773; Appendix A, 159-162, Statement by William Mackay, Chamberlain of the Lews, 1848-1854.

73. *N.C.*, 883-884, QQ.13767-13773; 880, Q.13824; 1021, Q.15989.

74. *Ibid.*, 33050, Evidence of J.M. Mackenzie, Chamberlain of the Lews, 1848-1854.

75. Mackenzie's Diary, 23 January 1851.

76. *N.C.*, Appendix A, 159-162, Statement by William Mackay, Chamberlain of the Lews (1883).

77. *Ibid.*, 968, Q.15096.

78. *Ibid.*, 1094, Q.16833.

79. *PP*, LXXX (1888), *Report on the Condition of the Cottar Population of the Lews*; *PP*, XXXIV, 1905, *Report on the Sanitary Condition of the Lews*.

80. *N.C.*, 3315, Q.46056. 24,055 in the Western Highlands received relief in 1881-2 and 'a large proportion' belonged to Lewis. *Report on Cottar Population*, 7. Starvation was once again predicted in 1888.

81. *Ibid.*, 1104, Q.16974.

82. *Ibid.*, Appendix A, Statement by Napier Campbell, Solicitor in Stornoway, 203.

10

Emigration, Social Change and Economic Recovery: the Isle of Tiree, 1760-1890

1

The Hebridean island of Tiree was acquired by the Earls (later Dukes) of Argyll in 1674 from the Macleans of Duart along with the mainland parish of Morvern and part of Mull. It is about twenty-seven square miles in area and the most level and fertile of the Hebrides. The soil in general is light and sandy and the climate less extreme than in other West Highland areas. The island also has a much greater incidence of sunshine and proportionately less rain than is common elsewhere. Of its 13,000 acres, 4000 in the 1830s were considered arable, again a much higher ratio than the Hebridean norm. For this reason and because of its more equable climate, Tiree was considered more suitable for cultivation by small tenants than most other areas in the Western Highlands.[1]

However, despite its physical potential the island suffered as grievously as any of the most distressed districts during the potato famine and before. As early as 1802, a year of crop failure, a detailed report on Tiree by the fifth Duke's Chamberlain, Maxwell of Aros, struck a deeply pessimistic note. Of the 319 tenancies or crofts, most were 'so small that even under better management they were inadequate to support a family'. The productive capacity of the estate could only support the population 'except under conditions of penury'. At a time when it was most unfashionable, Maxwell counselled the need for an emigration of about 1000 of the population to North America, arguing that 'the people themselves have come to wish it'.[2] He reported again in 1822 with even greater urgency: '. . . the families have now multiplied to such an unmanageable degree that the whole produce of the Island is hardly sufficient for their maintenance, and the crowded population on its surface exhibit in many instances cases of individual wretchedness and misery that perhaps are not to be found in any part of Scotland'.[3] His melancholy analysis had been confirmed the previous year when, because of a partial drought on the light, sandy soils of the island, the cattle became so lean as to be virtually unsaleable. A calamity was avoided because of remission of rent and because kelp happened to be in good supply. But as Maxwell complained, no permanent remedial measures were taken and 'matters went on again in the old rut'.[4]

By the 1830s two separate investigations by knowledgeable external observers concluded that destitution was endemic in Tiree. One commentator, Professor Robert Grahame of Glasgow University, estimated that in the spring of 1837, after the grain and potato crops had partially failed, twenty-five per cent of the island's population depended on the charity of others for food.[5] Two other witnesses, Allan Fullarton and Charles Baird of the Glasgow Statistical Society, noted the adverse effects of over-population: 'There can be no question that this is a population much too extensive for these islands [Coll was included in their observations] in their present state of productiveness'. Like Maxwell in 1802 they also thought that the people were very conscious of their deteriorating circumstances and 'are very desirous to emigrate'.[6] The experience of Tiree is a salutary reminder that not even favourable physical conditions could guarantee prosperity in the Western Highlands in the context of an adverse economic and social environment, powerful external forces and inadequate estate planning.

In 1765 the island had a population of 1793 and its agriculture was based on cattle, sheep, horses and the cultivation of rye, barley and oats.[7] Farms were let to individual lessees or tacksmen and through them to the smaller tenants who worked the soil. The initial strategy of the Argyll estate was to consolidate land under the control of 'gentleman farmers' in the custom of the Lowlands and employ the 'supernumeraries', or those who lost their holdings in the process of rationalisation, in fishing, manufactures and the extended farms. The plan failed because of the collapse of the projected industries primarily due to Lowland competition, the reluctance of the people and, above all, because of the more attractive profits to be derived from kelp production. In his estate instructions of 1799, the fifth Duke directed his chamberlain: 'As you inform me that small tenants can afford to pay more rent for farms in Tiree than gentlemen-farmers, owing to the manufacture of kelp, this determines me to let the farms to small tenants which have been and are at present possessed by tacksmen who reside upon farms in Mull'.[8] Immediately thereafter the strategy swung away from consolidation to fragmentation and towards the creation of a croft system. By 1810-12 revenue from kelp exceeded the entire agricultural income. The pressure to divide land was further intensified by the continuing growth in population (which had risen from 1793, c.1765, to 2776 in 1802), and by the Duke's decision to make land available for those young men from Tiree who joined his family regiments during the Napoleonic Wars: 'The minute subdivision of the land was much increased by the family of Argyll having raised three or four regiments for government during the last war, and residences were afforded to those soldiers on their return'.[9] Subdivision of tenancies occurred both as a result of the overt policy of the estate and because of the people's 'systematic breach' of the regulations against subletting. The social effects of the two processes can be seen in the changing population density of particular settlements. Kenovar, Barrapol and Ballinenoch had seventeen tenants in 1769, but numbers had risen to twenty-nine in 1846. In 1769, the estate envisaged the division of the townships of Balephuil and Balemartin into no more than ten holdings. By the eve of the potato famine, however, 'the reckless process of subdivision' had gone so far that sixty-nine tenancies had come into existence, 'all of the poorest class'.[10] Such figures do not take into account the expansion of the cottar population which further added to the remorseless pulverising of the settlement pattern. By 1841, the cottar class comprised thirty-seven per cent of all inhabitants.[11]

From the second decade of the nineteenth century three influences turned a growing crisis into an imminent catastrophe. First, as Table 10.1 demonstrates, the pace of population expansion quickened. In c.1750 the island had 1509 people; by 1801 there were 2776 inhabitants and by 1841 over 4900. This represented an increase of eighty-four per cent between 1750 and 1801 and a further seventy-nine per cent from 1802 to 1841. Again, from Table 10.2 it is apparent that far from slackening as economic pressures escalated, the estimated natural increase rose in the linked parish of Tiree and Coll in the years before 1841, from 542 between 1811 and 1821 to 544, 1821-31, 577, 1831-41 and 583, 1841-51. Table 10.2 also suggests that out-migration was occurring but not before 1841 at a sufficient pace to markedly offset the rate of actual increase. Experienced relief officials during the famine contended that the scale of congestion in the 1840s in Tiree surpassed that of any other area.[12] Certainly the estimated birthrate in the island seems to have been higher than the Highland norm. In the Western Highlands and Islands as a whole the average family size in the early 1800s was 5.5. In a sample of 126 Tiree families who petitioned for assistance to emigrate in 1851 the average size per crofter family was 6.5.[13]

Table 10.1. Tiree Population, c.1750-1841

Year	Population	Per cent change between years
c.1750	1509	+18.82
c.1765	1793	−6.5
1768	1676	+19.15
1776	1997	+5.80
1779	1881	+22.59
1787	2306	+4.77
1792	2416	+15
1802	2776	+16
1808	3200	+39
1831	4453	+11.40
1841	4961	

Sources: E.R. Cregeen, *Argyll Estate Instructions, 1771-1805* (Edinburgh, 1964), xxviii-xxix; Census; Inveraray Castle, Argyll Estate Papers, Bundle 1529, List of Families, Tiree and Ross of Mull.

Table 10.2. Net Out-Migration (estimated) from Parish of Tiree and Coll, 1801-1911

Year	Population	Actual Change	Estimated Natural Increase	Estimated Net Migration	Net out-migration as per cent of starting population
1801	5163	−	−	−	-
1811	5419	+256	516	−260	5.0
1821	5445	+26	542	−516	9.5
1831	5769	+324	544	−220	4.0
1841	5833	+64	577	−513	8.9
1851	4818	−15	583	−598	10.2
1861	3998	−820	482	−1302	27.0
1871	3560	−438	356	−794	19.9
1881	3375	−185	278	−463	13.0
1891	2974	−401	283	−684	20.3
1901	2627	−347	170	−517	17.4
1911	2214	−413	116	−529	20.1

Source: Census

Note: Tiree and Coll formed a single parish for census purposes. For the calculation of estimated natural increase and estimated net migration see above, p.68.

Second, the fifth Duke, who was an enthusiastic improver, was succeeded in 1806 by George, the sixth Duke, who was a spendthrift. As one of his successors put it euphemistically, during Duke George's lifetime 'the restraining and regulating power of a landlord was comparatively in abeyance'.[14] Third, while cattle prices declined and kelp prices collapsed after c.1825, no serious attempt was made to develop alternative and permanent employment for the teeming population of the island. Instead, kelp manufacture was maintained at a loss to employ the people until at least 1837.[15] This practice probably helped to reduce the rate of emigration still further. On the eve of the famine, the bulk of the inhabitants eked out a precarious existence from potato cultivation, fishing, temporary migration to the south and occasional relief from the estate.[16]

It is possible to construct a reasonably clear picture of the social structure and economic conditions of Tiree in the years immediately before the potato blight. The Marquis of Lorne, who succeeded to the estate in 1847 as Duke of Argyll, described in later years how at that time Tiree held 'a vast semi-pauper population'.[17] Between the 1750s and 1841 the number of inhabitants on the island had tripled to 4961; 3123 of this total, or sixty-three per cent, belonged to families of tenants paying rent and 1838, or thirty-seven per cent, to cottar families. Table 10.3 demonstrates that of the 371 rent-paying tenants, 328 had an annual rental of no more than £10 and 232 paid less than £5. That Tiree was an estate dominated by small tenants and cottars is also confirmed when the total rental is scrutinised by class of rent-payer. The smaller crofters were not only supreme in numerical terms but they also contributed fifty-two per cent of the island's rental of £2629. Big tenants paying £50 per annum and above provided only twenty-six per cent of total rent and those exceeding £100 in rental payment a mere thirteen per cent. Plainly, consolidation had made little progress on the island by 1841. Unlike the pattern in many other Hebridean estates, sheep-farming had hardly developed at all. The social problems of Tiree were therefore the direct result of a major imbalance between rising population and declining employment opportunities and cannot be attributed to the impact of clearances related to the expansion of commercial pastoralism.

Table 10.3. Tenant Structure in Tiree, c.1850

Class of Tenant	No. in each class	Aggregate Rental paid by each	Per cent of Total Rental
		£ s d	
(i) Not exceeding £5 p.a. rental	232	706. 2. 5	27
(ii) Exceeding £5 – not exceeding £10	96	656. 9. 3	25
(iii) Exceeding £10 – not exceeding £20	31	359. 9. 6	14
(iv) Exceeding £20 – not exceeding £50	6	194. 3.11	9
(v) Exceeding £50 – not exceeding £100	4	348.16.11	12
(vi) Exceeding £100	2	364. 5. -	13
Totals	371	2629. 7. -	100

Source: Inveraray Castle, Argyll Estate Papers, Bundle 1522, Abstract of Accounts . . . etc., 1843-49.

In 1845 the chamberlain of Tiree reported on the condition of the people.[18] He estimated that about two-thirds of the cottars lived 'in great poverty'. Only those who were tradesmen, shoemakers, weavers and boat carpenters had a relatively secure existence. Tenants paying above £5 in rent were able to live 'tolerably comfortably' as they could raise a crop sufficient to support their families and pay rent. On the other hand, about a third of those paying under £5 were also 'very poor' as the small size of their possessions did not allow them to produce enough for their families. The majority of the island's temporary migrants were drawn from this group and from the cottars. Annually they went to the mainland to seek work at the grain harvests and general labouring. The chamberlain also reported on attitudes to emigration and argued that there was a substantial difference between social groups. There was an inclination to emigrate among tenants 'with some means', the very families whom the estate wished to keep. But the poorer classes in 1845 'had no wish whatever to emigrate'. He explained this attitude by the fact that '. . . they have no hope of bettering their condition, as the accounts sent from those persons who have emigrated to America give no encouragement to persons without means emigrating there'.

If the chamberlain's estimates are approximately correct, 1238 members of cottar families and 1041 of crofter families (a total of 2279 people from a population of 4961) were living in deep poverty. This class would obviously suffer most when the potatoes failed. Indeed in October 1846, when the blight was first becoming obvious, the Marquis of Lorne reckoned that only 400 of the island's inhabitants could be deemed 'independent' of the need for aid.[19] By early 1847 the distress in Tiree was described as among the most severe in the stricken region. John Campbell, the Duke's Chamberlain, arrived in January 1847 and found the people 'in a state of absolute starvation'.[20] The government's relief officials reported that accounts from the island were 'very bad' and noted that disease had broken out and was 'committing great ravages' among the people.[21] Relief came from two main sources. First, from 1847 to 1850 the Glasgow Section of the Central Board was very active on the island. In 1848, even after substantial emigration, the smallest number of relief recipients on the Committee's list was ninety-four, the largest 1590. The average weekly distribution of meal was twenty-eight bolls and those receiving it were employed at road-making, draining, trenching, spinning and weaving.[22] Second, the landlord sponsored a major programme of public works and assisted emigration. Its scale and cost are revealed in Table 10.4.

Relief of destitution by employment rose from 0.4 per cent of total expenditure in 1843 to no less than sixty-four per cent in 1848. Total spending which stood at £502 the year before the famine climbed to £5403 two years later. The balance in favour of the proprietor, which was a positive one between 1843 and 1845, declined dramatically in 1846 and was converted to a deficit of £3173 in 1847. The estate had to borrow 'a large sum' to fund this.[23] The eighth Duke, who was responsible for relief measures during the famine, remembered forty years later, 'During those years, no part of the income derivable from the Island was spent out of it, and the outlays it needed constituted a heavy drain on other resources'. Overall, between 1846 and 1850, £7919 was spent in Tiree and the other Argyll estate on Ross of Mull on gratuitous relief and employment on roads and agricultural improvements. A further £6373, partly financed by a loan of £4250 under the Drainage Act, was laid out on improvements.[24] The information presented in Table 10.5 suggests, nevertheless, that rental income was maintained during some years of the crisis, probably because expenditure on relief through

Table 10.4. Total Expenditure, Tiree Estate, 1843-1849 (£.s.d.)

	1843	1844	1845	1846	1847	1848	1849
Taxes and Public Burdens, Including Poor Law Assessment	957.16. 8 (98%)	610. 9. 1 (74%)	482.19.11 (96%)	600.12. 8 (31%)	908. 0. 2 (17%)	585.19. 7 (22%)	738.17. 8 (18%)
Relief of Destitution by Employment	4. 1.11 (0.4%)	200.12. 9 (24%)	8. 0. 0 (1.5%)	6. 6. 1 (0.3%)	1850.19.11 (34%)	1717. 5.11 (64%)	1709. 1. 2 (41%)
Gratuitous Relief	11.14. 0 (1.13%)	9. 8. 0 (1%)	11. 8. 0 (2%)	1037.10.11 (55%)	2174. 4. 2 (40%)	118.15. 8 (4%)	736. 7. 4 (18%)
Gratuitous Relief for Emigration	–	–	–	215. 0. 0 (11%)	470. 1. 5 (9%)	325. 3. 8 (9%)	1017.10. 8 (24%)
Payments for Draining, Trenching and other Improvements	–	–	–	18.19.0 (1%)	–	–	–
Total	973.12. 7	820. 9.10	502. 7. 1	1878. 8. 8	5403. 5. 8	2747. 4.10	4201.16.10
Balance in favour of Proprietor	1348. 0. 6	1738.18. 5	2226.11. 5	199.15. 0	–	417.11. 3	–
Balance against Proprietor	–	–	–	–	3173.12. 6	–	1314. 5. 7

Source: Inveraray Castle, Argyll Estate Papers, Bundle 1522, Abstract of Accounts . . . etc., 1843-49.
Note: Bracketed figures indicate per cent of total annual expenditure for each category. Normally percentages are expressed in round figures and so may not total exactly to 100.

Table 10.5. Total Rental Actually Paid in Tiree by Each Class, 1843-1849 (£.s.d.)

Class (as in Table 10.3 above)	Rent Payable	1843	1844	1845	1846	1847	1848	1849
(i)	706. 2. 5	637.18. 1	850.16.11	962.10. 8	688.17. 2	688.17. 2	688.17. 2	851.12. 7
(ii)	656. 9. 3	584. 3. 7	737. 4.10	888.18. 5	573.15.10	573.15.10	573.15.10	721. 2. 1
(iii)	359. 9. 6	325. 2.10	360. 4. 1	418.14. 4	318.10. 0	318.10. 0	318.10. 0	480.16. 8
(iv)	194. 3.11	169. 4. 3	198.16. 3	165.14.10	163. 5.10	163. 5.10	163. 5.10	286. 6. 6
(v)	348.16.11	119. 0. 9	232.16. 6	214.19. 2	88. 1. 4	239.10.10	239.10.10	266.13. 5
(vi)	364. 5. 0	486. 3. 7	179. 9. 8	114. 1.11	245.13. 6	245.13. 6	245.13. 6	281. 0. 0
Rent payable	2631. 7. 0	2321.13. 1	2559. 8. 3	2764.17. 4	2078. 3. 8	2229.13. 2	2229.13. 2	2887.11. 3
Per cent of rental actually paid		88	97	104	79	84	84	109

Source: Inveraray Castle, Argyll Estate Papers, Bundle 1522, Abstract of Accounts . . . etc., 1843-49.

employment enabled many crofters to continue payment. However, the financial balance moved decisively against the proprietor from 1847 because of the enormous investment in relief. It was this background of serious levels of destitution and accompanying economic strain which helps to explain the development of an elaborate strategy of assisted emigration in the 1840s and 1850s.

2

The emigration plan was not simply precipitated by the famine since the estate chamberlains had been advising such a policy from the early years of the nineteenth century. Even before the full enormity of the consequences of potato failure became apparent, emigration to Canada from the island had already begun. In spring 1846, 160 left Tiree for that destination, though it is unclear whether this was an assisted emigration.[25] From that year, the estate came under the active and vigorous direction of the young Marquis of Lorne who formally succeeded his father in 1847. The latter, John, the seventh Duke, had been in poor health and his son assumed virtual control of estate policy from the first months of the famine.[26] In a series of revealing letters to James Loch of the Sutherland estate in December 1846, he indicated that he was eager to sell Tiree: 'to us it is an unsatisfactory property from its great distance – and from having enough Island property to manage'.[27] He admitted, however, that the problems involved in marketing it immediately were very great. The 'potato panic' had caused a depreciation in Highland property and the estate was overpopulated. The solution was an extensive scheme of emigration. He stressed to Loch that he was taking 'active measures towards as extensive an emigration as possible. The current has already begun to flow in that direction . . . and I am in great hopes of getting out a much larger number next spring'. If the potatoes recovered and 'a considerable portion of the people emigrate next season . . . Island property will be as saleable as ever'. Only if there was a great exodus in the spring of 1847 would he be prepared to advertise Tiree publicly, but 'if we could find any monied man who was likely to behave well by the people, I would certainly be very glad to see it sold to him'.

The early interest of the estate in emigration is confirmed by comparison with other areas. Apart from the Duke of Sutherland (who assisted 397 to emigrate in 1847), the Duke of Argyll was the only Highland proprietor who supported emigration in 1847. In that year only eight per cent of all emigrants assisted by landlords between 1846 and 1855 left the country, and all of these were from the west coast of Sutherland and the Argyll properties in Tiree and the Ross of Mull.[28] As early as July 1846 the Marquis of Lorne was seeking government aid for emigration and throughout that year was one of the few early advocates of a comprehensive scheme of emigration to relieve Highland destitution.[29] The famine, therefore, certainly prompted the adoption of an emigration strategy in Tiree. But the estate was already disposed towards such a policy in any case and its interest in promoting it was stimulated further by the succession of a young and energetic proprietor.

Previous discussion has indicated that there was a desire to emigrate among certain social strata in Tiree but that some groups, such as the smaller tenants and cottars, were, on the whole, reluctant.[30] In January 1831 the 'inhabitants of Tiree' had petitioned government. As a consequence of the fall in kelp prices they were 'totally without capital or the means of procuring a passage to Canada, where many of their countrymen are now happily settled'.[31] This established disposition in favour of emigration was further strengthened by the potato failure. Early in the winter of 1846 the Marquis of Lorne 'directed the attention of the people most seriously to emigration to Canada' in the following spring. Assistance was promised to those unable to pay their passage. Lorne argued that '. . . less expense will be incurred in aiding the proprietor to send the poorest class out, than will certainly be incurred in aiding by the necessity of keeping them alive, if they remain where they are now'.[32] Over 1000 people from Tiree indicated their willingness to take advantage of this offer.[33] This was a 'voluntary' emigration, in the sense that no evidence exists of coercion being applied directly by the estate.[34] Similarly in 1849 the estate chamberlain, John Campbell, reported that 'there are many applicants both among the smaller crofters and cottars, more particularly the latter, who are ready to go in hundreds to Canada if provided with the means'.[35] Again, in 1851, a 'Petition from Poor Persons in Tiree for Aid to Emigrate' appealed to the Government and the Duke himself for aid on behalf of 825 people.[36] They explained that hitherto they had been employed by the proprietor at drainage and other works during winter and spring before their lands were cropped. During the summer they were supported by the Central Board. With the termination of its operations in 1850 their prospects looked bleak and they had now no alternative but emigration.

This evidence helps to support the Duke of Argyll's later claim that the assisted exodus of 1778 people from his Tiree and Ross of Mull estates during the famine was 'a purely voluntary emigration'.[37] Hunger and the constant pressure of want were plainly the prime influences conditioning the movement. That said, however, it cannot be seen entirely in these terms. The record shows that the Argyll estate, like so many others, was applying coercion in a systematic fashion from 1848 to maintain the level of emigration, especially of the poorest class. A greater sense of urgency is apparent in the estate correspondence as the crisis persisted and relief expenditure remained at stubbornly high levels. The Duke himself stated the strategy succinctly in May 1851: 'I wish to send out those whom we would be obliged to feed if they stayed at home – to get rid of that class is *the object*' [underlined in source].[38] Instructions had earlier been issued to his chamberlain to ensure the complete removal from the family's island estates of those crofters paying under £10 rental and cottars.[39] Increasingly, therefore, the policy of emigration assistance became very selective. In 1846 and 1847 little attempt at discrimination had been made. By 1851, however, a much more careful approach was adopted. In the spring of that year 860 individuals from Tiree indicated that they were 'desirous to emigrate'. John Campbell chose 'all the poorest and those most likely to be a burden on the property'. This group consisted of 490 people, 133 of whom belonged to crofter families 'of the very lowest class', while the rest were members of cottar families. The 370 persons rejected were 'composed of strong individuals who are all to go south and wherewith to defray their own expenses to America if they choose to do so'.[40]

To achieve this end of removing the very poor, a group in the view of the estate traditionally reluctant to emigrate, a variety of sanctions were applied. Campbell stated in evidence to Sir John McNeill that no person was 'forced to emigrate from this property'.[41] But between 1846 and 1852, 174 summonses of removal were issued against tenants on the island. The majority of these clustered in the years after 1849. Only 24 were issued over the period 1846 to 1848, 78 in 1850 and 28 in 1851.[42] These were the years when emigration was heaviest; only 340 departed in 1847 from Tiree and the Ross of Mull but 1420 left between 1849 and 1851. It was also the phase when the estate administration was making an energetic effort to reduce the small tenant and cottar class.[43] In April 1848 Campbell issued 'a goodly number' of removing summonses for arrears of rent but others for 'thieving . . . extreme laziness and bad conduct'.[44] Two years later in 1850 he produced a list of tenants and cottars 'warned' of removal. These totalled 116, of whom 78 lived in Tiree. The main reason given for serving summonses was the failure of tenants to reduce rent arrears but occasionally other causes are mentioned: 'unruly conduct on farm', 'selling whisky' (9 were issued for this reason), and 'neglecting to build their fences within a stated period' (11).[45] Again, in April 1854 'a good many removing summonses' were served on 'the indolent, and bad characters, widows and young men whose fathers died and a few families in small crofts fitted to emigrate'.[46] The extent of eviction at this time was clearly considerable and added a further inducement to leave the island.[47]

Other tactics were also employed. Kelp manufacture was delayed in 1850 in order to stimulate emigration. Campbell observed that 200 had originally applied for assisted passage across the Atlantic but thirty-four withdrew their names because they anticipated that kelp manufacture was about to start.[48] This again confirms the point made in other chapters that, for many, emigration was the last resort and even temporary and marginal improvements in circumstances could cause a change of heart.[49] From 1848 energetic efforts were also made to reduce rent arrears by confiscating cattle stocks.[50] Such a policy eroded the basic capital stock of the small tenantry, reduced them to virtual penury, with little hope of recovery or improvement, and left them vulnerable to eviction at a later date for non-payment of rent. The selection process which John Campbell was able to carry out in 1851 suggests that by that date many more wished to leave the island than the estate was willing to assist.[51] But this movement was far from 'voluntary'. It can more accurately be described as a desperate and despairing reaction to the utterly bleak prospects for the future.[52] As material conditions altered for the better, briefly in 1852, and for a longer period from 1854, the urge to move across the Atlantic rapidly diminished.[53]

From 1847 to 1853, 2279 were assisted to emigrate from Tiree and the Ross of Mull to Canada. A further fifteen left for Australia in 1852 and 1853 under the auspices of the Highland and Island Emigration Society.[54] Of this total of 2294, approximately 1354 or fifty-six per cent were from Tiree. The exodus took place in four main phases: 340 departed in 1847, 364 in 1849, 167 in 1850 and a final major emigration of 465 in 1851. A further eighteen left in 1853.[55] The overall figure of 1354 was equivalent to twenty-seven per cent of the island's 1841 population. It is possible to gain some insight into the social composition of the emigrant parties. In 1847 some were 'respectable crofters . . . in pretty good circumstances'.[56] Of 1059 names given to John Campbell for emigration in April 1847, 241 were either able to cover the cost of their passage entirely or contribute substantially towards it.[57] Yet, even in that year, the majority depended on the proprietor's help. Campbell, however, was convinced that most 'who had any means' came forward in 1847 and that thereafter 'there only remain the really destitute'.[58]

Table 10.6 List of Emigrants from Tiree, on Charlotte and Barlow, June 1849

Total	364 Crofters, 90½ statute adults (26 per cent); Cottars 180½ (74 per cent)
Passage Money:	96½ at £337.15.0. (crofters) at £3.10.0. each 180½ at £631.15.0. (crofters) at £3.10.0. each £969.10.0.

Amount Paid (£. s. d.):

	for Stock	for Crop	for Implements	as Assistance
Crofters	205.11. 0.	127.18.11.	22.0. 2	20.10. 0
Cottars	–	–	4.0. 0.	7.11. 0
Total	387.12.10.			

Total Outlay (excluding returns from crop and stock/sales): £1387. 2.10. = £3.80 per person

Source: Inveraray Castle, Argyll Estate Papers, Bundle 1585, List of Emigrants from Mull and Tiree, June 1849.

Table 10.7. List of Emigrants from Tiree, July 1851, on Conrad, Birnam and Onyx

Conrad	389 souls	313½ statute adults
Birnam	70 souls	58 statute adults
Onyx	6 souls	6 statute adults
Total:	465	377½

Tenants: 21 families; 171 souls (37 per cent)
Cottars: 46 families; 294 souls (63 per cent)
Source: Inveraray Castle, Argyll Estate Papers, Bundle 1805, List of Emigrants, July 1851.
Note: 'statute adults' = one person aged fourteen or upwards or 2 persons aged between one and fourteen.

From 1849, as Tables 10.6 and 10.7 confirm, the majority of emigrants were of the poorest class. Cottars accounted for seventy-four per cent of those who emigrated in June 1849 and sixty-three per cent of those who left in July 1851. The meagre value placed on their crops, stock and implements makes their destitute condition patently obvious (see Table 10.6). This, then, was indeed the exodus of the 'semi-pauper population' which the Duke of Argyll argued had become swollen in the wake of the collapse of the kelping and the persistence of chronic subdivision of land. Campbell characterised the outflow of 1849 as highly beneficial to the estate because it comprised the very poorest of the inhabitants.[59] Again in 1850 they were 'all miserably poor'. He had to supply them with clothing, 'they were so naked'.[60]

It is not possible to be as certain about the sex and age structure of the emigrant parties. The scarce evidence suggests that families dominated in 1847 while in the later emigrations young, single adults became increasingly significant.[61] From Table 10.8, for example, it is apparent that the number of cottar *families* actually increased by seven per cent between 1841 and 1849. Yet the total numbers *in* these families fell by thirty-seven per cent between these two dates. Overall, the number of families on the island dropped by only nine per cent but the population declined by thirty-six per cent. This perhaps implies that the movement of *members* of families was greater than the migration of entire households. The zero values placed against cottars' stock and crops in Table 10.6 may also suggest that many in this group were young single adults rather than heads of households. On the other hand, one cannot necessarily assume that these family members all became part of the emigrant parties. It is highly likely that an unknown number left for the Scottish mainland.[62]

Table 10.8. Population Structure, Island of Tiree, 1841 and 1849

	1841	Per cent of total pop.	1849	Per cent of total pop.	1849 as per cent of 1841
Population	4961	–	3166	–	64
Families	745	–	677	–	91
Rent payers (total population)	3123	63	2004	63	64
Rent payers (families)	469	–	371	–	79
Non-rent payers/cottars (total population)	1848	37	1162	37	63
Non-rent payers/cottars (families)	276	–	296	–	107

Source: Inveraray Castle, Argyll Estate Papers, Bundle 1529, List of Families, Tiree and Ross of Mull, 1841 and 1849.

The famine was the decisive turning-point in both the demographic and social history of Tiree in the nineteenth century. Table 10.2 demonstrates that the position of the united parish of Tiree and Coll (the inclusion of the other island does not seriously affect the calculation because it contained only eleven per cent of total parish population in 1841) rose in a sustained manner to 1841, fell rapidly over the subsequent two decades and continued to decline for the rest of the nineteenth century. An estimated 5867 people left the parish between 1801 and 1901. Thirty-two per cent of this estimated total departed from 1841 to 1861. The estimated loss of population in these two decades was 1900 or about one third of the numbers recorded in the census of 1841.[63] For Tiree alone, population declined from 4391 in 1841 to 3204 in 1861. This latter figure approximately represented the total number of inhabitants on the island in 1808. In effect, the famine emigrations eliminated half a century's growth of population.

Emigration continued at a high level after 1861, with almost twenty per cent of the inhabitants of Tiree and Coll in that year estimated as leaving during the following decade. The great subsistence crisis was therefore not the only force promoting heavy migration in the nineteenth century. Later discussion will show that estate policy after the famine years helped to ensure a continuing pattern of demographic decline.[64] Indeed, it was the impact of this strategy in the long run rather than the potato blight itself which *maintained* a sustained rate of migration after 1861. This differentiated the demographic history of Tiree from areas such as Lewis where, as has been seen, population levels recovered fairly rapidly after 1861.[65] Nevertheless, the famine was a watershed in the island's demographic history. For over a century before the crisis, growth of population had been the norm; after 1846 sustained decline was the common experience.

The evidence does not allow the anatomy of emigration to be carried further into a detailed examination of the relative importance of emigration and migration. It is reasonably clear, however, that those who were assisted to emigrate probably comprised only a proportion, though a large one, of those who left the island in the 1840s and 1850s. Nineteen hundred were estimated to have departed from the parishes of Tiree and Coll and 1354 are known to have obtained assisted passage from Tiree itself. Table 10.8 indicates that, for Tiree alone, numbers fell from 4961 in 1841 to 3166 in 1849, a loss of at least 1795, without taking into account those born in the intervening years and who may have left with the emigrant parties. The migration of at least 1795 was more than twice the total of 784 known to have been granted assisted passage in 1847 and 1849. An additional 106 did depart without the Duke's support in the spring of 1846, before the potato disease struck Tiree, but this still leaves 850 to be accounted for, on the assumption that the estimate is soundly based.[66] Estate correspondence also suggests that from 1848 there was a greater demand for assisted emigration than supply of places. In 1851 John Campbell selected only 490 of the 860 individuals who applied and urged the rest to seek employment on the mainland.[67] It is probable, then, that not all the 'surplus population' of Tiree was channelled across the Atlantic. An undocumented minority may have left for other areas in Scotland.

3

As the famine dragged on, the Duke and his Chamberlain determined to implement a strategy which would improve conditions in Tiree in the long run. Part of this involved the reduction of the poorest class and, whenever possible, assisting them to emigrate from the island. Of the 825 persons who petitioned for emigration aid in 1851, only six per cent belonged to families paying rental of £10 per annum or more, twenty-one per cent were members of poor crofter families paying rent of under £5 but the great majority, sixty-five per cent, belonged to the cottar class.[68] There was little exceptional in this programme of expatriation of the poor. What is distinctive about Tiree, however, is the way in which the proprietor energetically exploited the opportunity provided by the great emigration to carry out a revolution in the social and economic structure of the island. In a publication of 1883 the Duke set out the basis of the policy which had evolved in the 1840s.[69] He argued that the physical endowment and benign climate of Tiree made it very suited to significant improvement. There was, however, a need for a further reduction in numbers and a consolidation of small tenancies if this was to be achieved. The fragmentation of land, which had been occurring at least since the fifth Duke's decision to subdivide tenancies to accommodate a kelp labour force in 1801, was to be reversed. There were four specific elements in the strategy. First, rules prohibiting subdivision were to be strictly enforced in the future. Second, the small crofts should be consolidated as vacancies through death, emigration or insolvency occurred. Third, small farms were to be created out of the unification of crofts. The proprietor emphasised that he was not intent on building up large holdings but rather farms 'of a variety of sizes'. Fourth, substantial investment in fencing, draining and other improvements was planned to take place in parallel with the other aspects of the plan.

Table 10.9. Tenant Structure of Tiree, 1847-1861

Year	Tenants under £2	under £5	under £10	over £10	Total	Rental
1847	97	145	99	45	386	2618
1849	68	141	108	49	366	2867
1852	43	110	108	56	317	2929
1861	4	48	108	102	262	3994
1847-61 (per cent change)	−96%	−67%	+9%	+120%	−32%	+53%

Source: Inveraray Castle, Argyll Estate Papers, Bundle 1539, Tiree Rentals, 1847-1861.

The early consequences of this policy and the effect of heavy emigration on the island's social structure are very apparent from Table 10.9: a reduction in the small tenant class, an expansion in the number of bigger tenants and an advance in rent. The township of Mannal which contained twenty-three crofts in 1846 was possessed by three tenants in 1883. Hillipol had twenty-six on the eve of the famine. A quarter were rented at under £2 per annum. None exceeded £5. By 1853 the proprietor had absorbed the lands of the settlement into his own hands. It was eventually let as one farm. The rental rose from £62 in 1847 to £376 in 1883. Hianish with sixteen 'poor crofts' in 1846 had one tenant thirty years later. The new tenant élite was mainly recruited from the island itself. Of 220 tenants in 1883, only two were Lowlanders and the majority of the rest were natives of Tiree. The Duke stated: '. . . the number of small farms created out of the consolidation of crofts . . . are now held by precisely the same class of men, but who have risen by the opportunities which I have afforded to them'. He described how the process was based on the expansion of possessions under the control of a selected nucleus of families. Hianish gradually fell within the possession of Neil McKinnon, his sons and later his widow: '. . . I have had the great pleasure of enlarging her croft steadily as vacancies occurred around her and of associating with her in the possession of her daughter and her son-in-law'. In his own words, this process of selection was a demonstration of 'the survival of the fittest'.

In 1883 the Duke surveyed with considerable satisfaction the alterations in the social structure of the island which had taken place since the famine. Tiree was more prosperous, rental was significantly higher and the old 'pauperised class', except for a residuum of 300 cottar families, had been eliminated. These he described as 'the *detritus* of the old subdivided cottars and subtenants . . . also in great measure the remains of the old kelp burning population'. He maintained that the social costs of the transformation were slight: 'I had an insuperable objection to taking any sudden step in that direction such as might be harsh towards the people. I thought it my duty to remember that the improvidence of their fathers had been at least seconded, left unchecked, by any active measures, or by the enforcement of any rules of my own predecessors who had been in possession of the estate. I regarded myself, therefore, as representing those who had some share in the responsibility, although that responsibility was one of ommission (*sic*) and not of commission'.

The sheer scale of the revolution which had taken place in Tiree needs little further emphasis. It represented a renewed attempt, and on this occasion a successful one, to develop a 'middle tenantry' of the kind envisaged by the fifth Duke of Argyll in the last quarter of the eighteenth century. In addition, the strategy of rigorous control of subdivision linked with a systematic policy of consolidation helps to explain the sustained decline in population after 1841 which differentiated Tiree from other Hebridean islands, such as Lewis, Barra and South Uist. It is also possible to accept that standards did rise for the community as a whole, although the expansion in external markets after *c*.1856 indicated by the recovery in cattle prices, the development of a regular steamship connection to the mainland, and the rapid increase in a huge export trade in eggs, were probably at least as important as the improvement policies implemented by the estate.[70]

However, the eighth Duke almost certainly underestimated the social costs of his revolution. It was achieved at the expense of a quite massive rate of out-migration with an estimated 3670 people leaving the island between 1841 and 1881 or an average of 17.5 per cent of starting population per decade. Further, Tiree witnesses before the Napier Commission did not take as sanguine a view of the results of the estate's policies as their landlord.[71] The Duke claimed that he had been determined 'not only to avoid anything like what has been called a "clearance", but as a rule, not even to allow any individual evictions or disposal of the existing crofters, except for the one cause of insolvency or non-payment of rent'.[72] But the evidence presented to Lord Napier is full of angry accusations from the people in the island of forced removal, resettlement of cottars on lands occupied by small tenants and withdrawal of grazing from crofting townships.[73] The Duke countered these complaints by referring to their 'exotic character' and claiming that they were simply the product of political agitation and fertile imaginations.[74]

Table 10.10. *Tiree Tenancies, 1847-1881*

Year	Tenants under £5 in Rental	under £10	above £10	Total
1847	242	99	45	386
1861	52	108	102	262
1881	34	68	98	200

Source: Inveraray Castle, Argyll Estate Papers, Bundle 1539, Tiree Rentals, 1847-1861; Argyll, *Crofts and Farms*, 26.

It is impossible, given the paucity and ambiguity of the sources, to come to any clear conclusions on this conflict of evidence. However, consolidation clearly did not take place rapidly and not in the piecemeal manner implied later by the Duke. Of all small tenancies 'lost' between 1847 and 1881, seventy-nine per cent had already disappeared by 1861. A haemorrhage on this scale over less than fourteen years must have caused substantial social dislocation. Evidence from the estate papers of the 1850s which has already been discussed indicates the widespread use of eviction and other forms of coercion.[75] A social revolution of the kind achieved in Tiree could not have come about without considerable social suffering in the short run whatever the material gains for those who remained on the island in the long term.

4

It might finally be worth pondering briefly on the reasons why the social and demographic history of Tiree after the famine differed so profoundly from that of the island of Lewis which was considered in the previous chapter. The history of the two islands from the 1850s demonstrates in microcosm how the long-term impact of the famine was far from uniform and was powerfully influenced by such local factors as landlord attitude, estate policy and the potential of different properties for alternative forms of agricultural development.[76] The post-famine experience of the two communities could not have been more different. In one, the great subsistence crisis created an opportunity for an economic transformation which ultimately led to depopulation; in the other, population recovered quickly and was substantially higher in 1901 than in 1841.

One possible explanation might be the different scale of the famine emigrations from the two islands: 1354 were assisted to move from Tiree while 2334 left from Lewis. Yet though the former figure represented about a third of Tiree's population the latter was only fourteen per cent of the population of Lewis, exclusive of the town of Stornoway.[77] The greater relative exodus from Tiree may have given the estate administration on that island much more scope for rationalisation of the structure of holdings. There were also perceptible differences in attitude to emigration within the two communities in the 1840s and 1850s. Each estate used a variety of sanctions to encourage movement, but in Lewis there was manifestly more reluctance to go than in Tiree. It may be that this reflected differences in economic conditions. The reports of the Central Board show that Lewis suffered much less during the famine. On the other hand, it could also mean that there were divergent social attitudes to emigration and that by the middle decades of the nineteenth century a widespread popular desire for movement had developed in Tiree which was absent in Lewis. If this was the case, the contrasting ethos makes the greater population losses from Tiree in the second half of the nineteenth century more comprehensible.

Yet the primary distinguishing feature was probably the major contrast in the development of estate policy. The Argyll administration was resolutely determined to impose consolidation and proscribe subdivision of tenancies. In Lewis, there was a similar aspiration to control fragmentation of holdings but the policy was implemented with much less conviction and subdivision of crofts persisted on a considerable scale. To some extent, these different responses might simply reflect contrasts in landlord personality and attitudes. But they may also have been related to the differing natural endowment and economic potential of the two islands. The fertile lands of Tiree lent themselves to the formation of medium-sized farms combining cropping and stock-rearing. The smallholding structure which existed on the eve of the famine was in part an aberrant social system brought into existence by the temporary requirements of kelp manufacture. On the other hand, the seas around Lewis were much richer than the land. The estate itself in the 1850s sought to preserve and strengthen the island's fishing commitments.[78] After the famine, too, the scale of temporary migration to the herring fisheries of Caithness and Aberdeenshire expanded to such an extent that the majority of Lewis households began to depend mainly on income from that source.[79] These were the essential supports of the smallholding population and a major source of the rental income of the estate after 1860. Non-agricultural employment on a much greater scale than that available to the people of Tiree allowed the maintenance of the system of small crofts in Lewis, perpetuated widespread access to land and slowed down the rate of permanent migration.

NOTES

1. Fullarton and Baird, *Remarks on the Highlands*, 33-4; *Destitution Reports*, Report on Mull, Ulva etc. by the Glasgow Section, 21-2; The Duke of Argyll, *Crofts and Farms in the Hebrides* (Edinburgh, 1883), 4, 33.
2. Argyll, *Crofts and Farms*, 13-16. This important source reprints vital documents from the Argyll Estate Papers.
3. *Ibid.*, 19.
4. *Ibid.*
5. PRO, T1/4201, Robert Grahame to Fox Maule, 27 March 1837.
6. Fullarton and Baird, *Remarks on the Highlands*, 34.
7. This paragraph is mainly based on Argyll, *Crofts and Farms*, 4-21; E.R. Cregeen, *Argyll Estate Instructions, 1771-1805* (Edinburgh, 1964), xi-xxxviii and 'The Changing Role of the House of Argyll' in N.T. Phillipson and Rosalind Mitchison, eds., *Scotland in the Age of Improvement* (Edinburgh, 1970), 5-23.
8. Cregeen, *Argyll Estate Instructions*, 48.
9. *PP*, VI (1841), *S.C. on Emigration* (1841), 87; PRO, T1/4201, Robert Grahame to Fox Maule, 27 March 1837.
10. Argyll, *Crofts and Farms*, 6-7.
11. Inveraray Castle, Argyll Estate Papers, Bundle 1529, List of Families, Tiree and Ross of Mull.
12. *Ibid.*, Bundle 1533, J. Campbell to the Duke of Argyll, 24 April 1849; *PP*, XXXIII (1847-8), *Second Annual Report of the Board of Supervision for the Relief of the Poor in Scotland*, 27.
13. 'Petition from Poor Persons in Tyree for Aid to Emigrate', in *McNeill Report*, Appendix A, 133-4.
14. Argyll, *Crofts and Farms*, 18.
15. PRO, T1/4201, Robert Grahame to Fox Maule, 27 March 1837.
16. Inveraray Castle, Argyll Estate Papers, Bundle 1529, Report by Chamberlain of Tyree, July 1845.

17. Argyll, *Crofts and Farms*, 18.
18. Inveraray Castle, Argyll Estate Papers, Bundle 1531, J. Campbell to Duke of Argyll, 9 January 1847.
19. *Relief Correspondence*, Marquis of Lorne to Sir George Gray, 17 October 1846.
20. Inveraray Castle, Argyll Estate Papers, Bundle 1531, J. Campbell to Duke of Argyll, 9 January 1847.
21. SRO, HD6/2, Treasury Correspondence relating to Highland Destitution, Capt. Rose to Mr. Trevelyan, 21 February 1847.
22. *Destitution Papers*, Report on Mull, Ulva etc. by the Glasgow Section, 24.
23. Argyll, *Crofts and Farms*, 20.
24. *Ibid.*, Inveraray Castle, Argyll Estate Papers, Bundle 1522, J. Campbell to Duke of Argyll, 21 August 1848.
25. SRO, Loch Muniments, GD268/45, Marquis of Lorne to James Loch, 12 December 1846.
26. Argyll, *Crofts and Farms*, 20.
27. SRO, Loch Muniments, GD268/45, Marquis of Lorne to James Loch, 12 and 14 December 1846.
28. See above, pp.206-7.
29. *Relief Correspondence*, Marquis of Lorne to Sir George Grey, 25 July 1846; Sir E. Coffin to Mr. Trevelyan, 25 September, 7 October 1846.
30. See above, p.230.
31. PRO, CO384/28, ff. 24-6, Petition from inhabitants of Tiree, 24 January 1831.
32. *Witness*, 21 April 1847.
33. Inveraray Castle, Argyll Estate Papers, Bundle 1531, J. Campbell to Lord Lorne, 28 January 1847.
34. *Ibid.*
35. *Ibid.*, Bundle 1335, J. Campbell to Duke of Argyll, 27 February 1849.
36. *McNeill Report*, Appendix A, 133-5.
37. Argyll, *Crofts and Farms*, 20.
38. Inveraray Castle, Argyll Estate Papers, Bundle 1558, Duke of Argyll to ?, 5 May 1851.
39. *Ibid.*, Bundle 1805, J. Campbell to Duke of Argyll, 17 May 1851.
40. *Ibid.*
41. *McNeill Report*, Appendix A, Evidence of J. Campbell.
42. SRO, Sheriff Court Processes (Tobermory), SC59/2/4-14.
43. Inveraray Castle, Argyll Estate Papers, Bundle 1533, Note of Emigrants from Tyree, June 1847; Bundle 1535, List of Emigrants from Mull and Tyree, June 1849; Bundle 1804, List of Emigrants from Tyree and Mull, 1850; Bundle 1805, List of Emigrants, 1851.
44. *Ibid.*, Bundle 1522, J. Campbell to Duke of Argyll, 1 April 1848.
45. *Ibid.*, Bundle 1804, List of tenants and cottars warned of removal, 1850.
46. *Ibid.*, Bundle 1523, J. Campbell to Duke of Argyll, 25 April 1854.
47. This evidence is in conflict with the version of events later given by the Duke in *Crofts and Farms in the Hebrides*, 24-5, published in 1883.
48. Inveraray Castle, Argyll Estate Papers, Bundle 1804, J. Campbell to Duke of Argyll, 29 May 1850.
49. See below, pp.259-60.
50. Inveraray Castle, Argyll Estate Papers, Bundle 1522, J. Campbell to Duke of Argyll, 21 August 1848.
51. See above, p.234.
52. 'Petition from Poor Persons in Tyree for Aid to Emigrate', *McNeill Report*, Appendix A, 133-4.
53. Inveraray Castle, Argyll Estate Papers, Bundle 1805, J. Campbell to Duke of Argyll, 4 May 1852: 'I did all I could when in Tyree to induce some of the Cottar families to give in their names for Australia, but I could not get one . . .'.
54. SRO, HD4/53, List of Emigrants of Highland and Island Emigration Society.

55. See Appendix 10, Assisted Emigration by Highland Landowners, 1846-56, and sources quoted therein.

56. *McNeill Report*, Appendix A, Remarks to the Queries sent by the Commission of the General Assembly of the Free Church, 132.

57. Inveraray Castle, Argyll Estate Papers, Bundle 1531, J. Stewart to Lord Lorne, 12 April 1847.

58. *Ibid.*, J. Campbell to Duke of Argyll, 10 June 1847.

59. *Ibid.*, Bundle 1535, J. Campbell to Duke of Argyll, 8 July 1849.

60. *Ibid.*, Bundle 1804, J. Campbell to Duke of Argyll, 15 May 1850.

61. SRO, HD4/5, List of Emigrants of H.I.E.S.

62. Inveraray Castle, Argyll Estate Papers, Bundle 1805, J. Campbell to the Duke of Argyll, 17 May 1851.

63. For the basis of these calculations, see above, pp.67-9.

64. See below, p.282.

65. See above, pp.222-3.

66. SRO, Loch Muniments GD268/45, Lord Lorne to James Loch, 12 December 1846. It almost certainly exaggerates the rate of net out-migration because it is based on the assumption of a constant level of natural increase during the famine.

67. Inveraray Castle, Argyll Estate Papers, Bundle 1805, J. Campbell to Duke of Argyll, 17 May 1851.

68. 'Petition from Poor Persons in Tyree for Aid to Emigrate', in *McNeill Report*, Appendix A, 133-5.

69. Unless otherwise indicated, all material to the end of the chapter is derived from Argyll, *Crofts and Farms*, 22-71.

70. *N.C.*, 2148-2150, QQ.33702-33737, Evidence of A. Buchanan, Surgeon, Tiree.

71. *Ibid.* The Tiree evidence can be found on pp. 2129- 2175.

72. Argyll, *Crofts and Farms*, 23.

73. *N.C.*, 2129-2175.

74. Argyll, *Crofts and Farms*, 53-61.

75. See above, p.235.

76. This point is developed in detail in Chapter 12.

77. Also there was probably more *unassisted* emigration and migration to the mainland from Tiree than from Lewis. See above, p.238.

78. See above, pp.214-5.

79. Devine, 'Temporary Migration', *passim*.

11

Emigration to Australia: the Highland and Island Emigration Society, 1851-1859

Until the middle decades of the nineteenth century Canada was the preferred choice for the vast majority of emigrants from the Scottish Highlands.[1] Its attractions over the Australian colonies were obvious. The cost of passage was much cheaper, a particular advantage in such a poor society; long-established links existed between areas in Canada and communities in the Highlands as a result of earlier movement from the 1760s; immigration regulations in Canada were not restrictive: for instance, no limit was imposed on age of emigrants or the number of children. However, before 1846 there had already been some movement to the Antipodes from the Highlands. In the 1820s and early 1830s there was limited emigration led by a few Highland tacksmen who sought to acquire land and populate it with their kinfolk and retainers. Secondly, and numerically much more significantly, over 3,000 Highlanders emigrated under the 'government system' between 1837 and 1839. Again, throughout the later 1840s and early 1850s, an unknown number left for Australia under the auspices of the Colonial Land and Emigration Commission.[2] Yet by far the most ambitious scheme to promote Highland movement to Australia by the nineteenth century was that organised by the Highland and Island Emigration Society in the 1850s. This organisation was established in 1852 and over the following few years supported the emigration of almost 5000 people to Australia. In this chapter, the origins, motivation and structure of the Society will be traced. This will then be followed by an assessment of the emigrant group, with particular attention to motivation, social composition and geographical origins.

1

The first major initiative to form an organisation to promote Highland emigration to Australia during the potato famine came from the island of Skye. The termination of the relief programme of the Central Board here as elsewhere seems to have stimulated a search for alternative measures which would go some way to alleviating the alarming conditions of destitution which still prevailed on the island. Towards the end of 1851 Thomas Fraser, sheriff-substitute of Skye, and the heritors, justices of the peace and clergy on the island stated 'in friendly addresses to the inhabitants' that emigration of a part of the population was now necessary for the welfare of the majority. They directed their attention to Australia and explained the facilities available for emigrating there through the Colonial Land and Emigration Commissioners.[3] Fraser had been sheriff in Skye since 1846. He was a man who had deep sympathy and concern for the plight of the people. His evidence to Sir John McNeill in March 1851 had indicated that improvement on the island was possible through reclamation of waste, the granting of leases and some redistribution of pasture lands.[4] He showed himself an acute critic of the relief measures adopted by the Central Board. Fraser was certainly not one of those who believed that massive emigration was the panacea for all the ills of the Highlands. But he did insist that some was necessary, in combination with other policies, to save the society from disaster:

> I am quite satisfied that the Island of Skye might, under improved arrangements, and by the remunerative application of capital to land improvement, be made capable of supporting a much larger population than it can maintain at present, irrespective of the potato crop; and I am not convinced that it might not even maintain a population equally large with that which it at present contains, were that population in a condition of natural and ordinary soundness; but taking into account the existing arrangements of the country, the precarious prospects of potato growing, the extreme poverty of the great mass of the people, the embarrassed position of the principal landed proprietors . . . I am reluctantly driven to the conclusion, that a considerable emigration is indispensable to restore the people of Skye to the condition of a self-supporting population, and that it would not be safe to trust to any system of amelioration, unaided by the alleviation of the burden which emigration could afford.[5]

The situation in Skye seemed to demand a special public effort. As Fraser indicated, assisted emigration on the scale practised by the Duke of Argyll, Sir James Matheson and Gordon of Cluny was impossible since the three principal estates on the island were under trust.[6] According to one source, 'the desire to emigrate to Australia spread rapidly' as a result of the initiatives of Fraser and his colleagues.[7] Finance, however, proved an insurmountable obstacle. Little was likely to be forthcoming from the major proprietors, and the majority of the families who wished to leave were destitute. Passages were only provided to Australia by the Colonial Land and Emigration Commissioners under strict conditions.[8] The deposits required for children and the old were beyond the capacity of the famine- ravaged population of Skye.[9] The authorities were mainly interested in promoting the emigration of young adults with few dependants. They sought to support the passage of the cream of the society rather than large numbers of destitute families.

In these circumstances Fraser and his colleagues formed themselves into a charitable organisation in order to raise by subscription a sum sufficient to enable many more to emigrate under the auspices of the Commissioners. Four hundred families, representing about 2,000 persons, made application.[10] It became immediately apparent that to raise a meaningful level of support the wider Scottish community would have to be approached for assistance. As a result a public meeting was held in Edinburgh on 25 February 1852 under the chairmanship of the Lord Provost. It was reported that the desire of the Skye committee was to promote 'the emigration of unbroken families' and that due to the efforts of Sheriff Fraser the Colonial Land and Emigration Commissioners had extended the preferable age for assistance from 40 to 45 and reduced the deposit for children from £1 to 10s. each. However, 'public benevolence' was still needed to defray the cost of clothing and the expense required for the emigration of the old.[11] Sir John McNeill himself stressed to the meeting that Skye was the one area which could not expect emigration to be sponsored by local landlords. He estimated that seven eighths of the island's population lived on the estates which were now under trust. McNeill added that 'the people are anxious to emigrate and asking for that aid which they are unable sufficiently to obtain from these gentlemen'.[12] It was proposed to advance loans to be repaid in the colony and to call upon both proprietors and trustees in the Highlands 'to contribute sums proportioned to the pecuniary advantages that would accrue to them from the emigration of a part of the population on their properties'.[13] McNeill was appointed chairman to carry out the resolutions and about £600 was subscribed by the inhabitants of Edinburgh. As Chairman of the Board of Supervision of the Scottish Poor Law, a powerful influence on the policies pursued by the Central Board before 1850, and author of the *Report* on Highland conditions which was laid before Parliament in July 1851, McNeill had almost certainly been involved in the initiative from the earliest stages.[14]

The venture, however, was not to remain restricted to Scotland for long. At a meeting held in the Freemasons' Hall, London, presided over by the Earl of Shaftesbury, a Committee was formed 'for promoting Emigration from the Western Highlands and Islands to Australia' with Sir Charles Trevelyan appointed as chairman.[15] This was the logical outcome of Trevelyan's earlier influence on and interest in the problem of Highland destitution. As Assistant Secretary to the Treasury he had been the most powerful figure in government relief measures in the Highlands from 1846 to 1847 and, until 1850, was the principal official responsible for famine relief in Ireland.[16] Earlier discussion has also shown that he had had a significant effect on the formation of policy by the Edinburgh Committee of the Central Board from 1847 to 1850.[17] As he himself put it, 'I have a great deal of experience with the operations of the Edinburgh Relief Board, on every important point of which I was consulted by the Secretary, W. Skene'.[18] Three years before the establishment of the Skye committee he had evinced an interest in Australian emigration as an effective solution to Highland problems, contending that 'whether the Hebrideans made good *Navvies* or not, I am sure they will make good Shepherds'.[19] The failure of the systems of relief to produce amelioration merely emphasised his commitment to the emigration option. Relief had inflicted moral damage: 'The only immediate remedy for the present state of things in Skye is Emigration, and the people will never emigrate while they are supported at home at other people's expense. This mistaken humanity has converted the people of Skye from the Clergy downwards into a Mendicant Community'.[20] He lashed out at those who still sought to provide charity for the Highlanders out of a mistaken humanity. Writing to a Miss Neave and her associate Lady McCaskill who were collecting funds in London for the poor of Skye, he insisted, '. . . the kindest thing in every point of view you and Lady McCaskill can do to the people of Skye is to leave them to themselves, and then they will see the necessity of emigrating and working for their subsistence, instead of living in idleness and habitually imposing upon benevolent persons'.[21]

The appointment of Trevelyan to the chairmanship of the London committee was a decisive step in the development of the policy which had first emerged in Skye in the winter of 1851. On the one hand, it brought to the scene a man of extraordinary energy with powerful connections in the business and political world of Britain and overseas; on the other, his election renewed an old association with Sir John McNeill. Both had 'watched and influenced every step of the process of relief up to the present time' from the point when government assistance first developed in the Highlands in 1846 to the activities of the Central Board thereafter.[22] Now both were enthusiastic supporters of emigration and were to preside over what Trevelyan regarded as the only effective means of solving the Highland problem. He quickly became the fundamental influence on the future development of the Highland and Island Emigration Society.[23]

At first, the idea was that the three committees based in Skye, Edinburgh and London would act, in Trevelyan's words, 'in perfect concert'. McNeill was to be the connecting link between the three. Each body would provide the others with copies of its proceedings and move towards joint planning.[24] However, it was almost inevitable that strategy would rapidly be centralised in the London committee in general and in Trevelyan himself in particular. Apart from his own formidable personality and the fact that he possessed greater political status than any of the other participants, the committee of which he was chairman had much more potential for fund-raising. By May 1852 it included among its members such financial magnates as W.G. Prescott, Governor of the Bank of England, Thomas Baring and Baron Rothschild and had attracted the patronage of Prince Albert himself. It was therefore only a matter of time before the other organisations were absorbed within Trevelyan's committee. In June 1852 the Edinburgh committee was wound up as its funds were exhausted. Instead, four of its members, including McNeill, were co-opted to the London committee and became constituted as a subcommittee in Edinburgh responsible to the main organisation.[25] From that point on the affairs of the Society were primarily managed by McNeill and Trevelyan, with final authority vested in the latter in London.[26] Trevelyan saw the task ahead as a personal mission: 'During the time I have been at the Treasury I have never felt myself justified in giving any share of my time and attention to active management of a private society till now . . . but seeing that the Scotch as well as the Irish Social Revolution is about to vent itself in an exodus, I have felt it to be my duty to assist to the extent of my power in giving a beneficial character and direction to the movement'.[27]

With characteristic energy he launched into a fund-raising campaign. Not only did he have superb contacts – the subscription list was headed by Queen Victoria and her Consort – but the times were propitious. A gold rush had begun in Australia with the rich discoveries at Ballarat and Bendigo. This had created an insatiable demand for labour as employees left their jobs to go to the diggings. It was one of Trevelyan's main arguments that a great Highland emigration could reduce this labour shortage because the intention was to send out people in family groups. One side-effect of this would be that they would be less likely to move *en masse* to the goldfields. Queen Victoria herself saw the point. She wrote: 'The only possible chance against a large portion of the emigrants going to the diggings lies in the system of family emigration, and what are usually considered the prohibitory drags to emigration – the old and the young – are now most useful in forming anchors by which a family would be held to a rural home, with plenty of space and plenty of food'.[28] The pastoral skills and experience of the Highland people were also described as especially useful in the sheep-farming economy of South Australia.[29] These arguments particularly impressed the Yorkshire manufacturing interest who feared a reduction in wool supplies as a result of the rush to the diggings. In May 1852 they were proposing to subscribe enough to send out 10,000 Highlanders, 9,000 under 45 and 1000 over that age.[30] Negotiations were also started with interested parties in Australia. Agreement was reached with Capt. F.S. Brownrigg of the Australian Agricultural Company to send out a shipload of Highlanders direct to the Company's headquarters at Port Stephen.[31] Brownrigg also suggested that Highlanders would find employment opportunities with 'the numerous flockmasters and settlers in the counties of Brisbane, Gloucester and Macquarrie in Liverpool Plains and the District of New England, the Clarence and Darling Downs'.[32]

Establishing an Emigration Society for the Highlanders was also an effective method of taking advantage of the unprecedented level of interest in northern society among polite circles in the south. *The Times* had sent a 'Commissioner' to Skye in 1851 and his reports were full of harrowing details of the scale of human suffering endured by the island's inhabitants after six seasons of potato blight. Philanthropists, such as Lady McCaskill, published highly emotional and graphic accounts of Highland destitution and the *Illustrated London News* ran special features on the plight of the crofting population.[33] There is little doubt either that the new wave of evictions and the critical attention they received at the hands of Thomas Mulock, Donald Ross, Hugh Millar of the *Witness* and others provoked sympathy in many quarters.[34] A subscription in aid of emigration was a much preferred alternative to giving money to support discredited programmes of famine relief. Even Lady McCaskill in her appeal for clothing for the distressed poor of Skye had to recognise the new climate of opinion. She intended '. . . not to ask money to feed a nation of paupers; not to ask money to encourage them in sloth and idleness, but to collect a few pounds and a few coarse clothes for them, to protect their perishing bodies against the approaching severity of the winter'.[35] Similarly, the *Illustrated London News*, in reporting the intention to hold a bazaar 'under most distinguished patronage' in Willis's Rooms in the capital to assist the population of the Highlands, went to great lengths to emphasise that 'mere alms giving is attended with serious drawback and disadvantages; but in assisting to remove industriously-disposed and provident but starving families to a land where honest labour is sure to be rewarded by rude plenty, charity indeed puts on its truest aspect of beneficence'.[36] In short, the Society's schemes suited the public mood of the early 1850s.

They had another attraction. There had been only a slow national recovery from the devastating industrial depression of 1848-9. Increased Irish immigration as a result of the Great Famine had added to a glut of labour in the great manufacturing centres of Scotland and had intensified pressure on the Poor Law. Trevelyan contended that the emigration strategy was vital to sustained economic recovery: 'our object is to prevent the Celtic population from either starving at home or pouring over our Manufacturing Districts where wages are already too much reduced by the competition of the Irish and to direct it to Australia where pastoral labour is extremely wanted and highly productive'.[37] These sentiments found an echo in government policy. As has been noted earlier, by the Emigrant Advances Act of 1851, the power of Highland proprietors to borrow money for drainage and other improvements was extended to cover borrowing to assist emigration. McNeill himself had played a major role in the formulation of this policy. The Society was thus in tune with the political spirit of the times.

Contributions began to come in from a variety of sources. Fund-raising sermons were preached in churches in Scotland. The Court of the East India Co. was approached since it had 'already been in a great part composed of Scotchmen, and a large proportion of the most distinguished servants of the Company are, and have been, Scotchmen and Highlanders'.[38] It was stressed to Australian sheep-farming and Yorkshire textile interests that the distressed districts of the Highlands offered 'an immediate supply of suitable labour on a scale which is not to be found anywhere else'.[39] By April 1853 over £12,000 had been raised, including £1,595 from India, £137 from Mexico, £3,000 from the Colonial Legislature of Van Diemen's Land, an area of extensive Scottish settlement, and £2,498 from the fund subscribed in New South Wales for the destitution of 1846-7.[40] Bazaars and jumble sales were held in both Edinburgh and London; at one in the Scottish capital in May 1852, £170 was gathered for clothing for the poor emigrants from Skye.[41]

The aims of the Society and the conditions under which it would provide assistance were clarified. Its role was to be seen in the wider context of a threefold partnership with Highland landowners and the Colonial Land and Emigration Commission. The Commissioners were to be asked to cooperate fully in providing free passages and, as will be shown below, did respond very sympathetically to the overtures of the Society.[42] Landowners were expected to pay one third of the sum disbursed on account of the emigrants by the Society. Trevelyan regarded this as a central part of the entire operation: '. . . The rule that one third of the sum . . . is to be paid by the Owners or Trustees of the Properties from which the Emigrants are removed is *in no case* to be departed from . . . if the Owner or Agent of a property will not do this, you will give no assistance to Emigrants from that property'.[43] Some indeed argued that proprietors should pay more since they would be the prime beneficiaries of the emigration.[44] Even more controversially landlords were to be directly involved in the selection of emigrants. Once the representatives of the Emigration Commission had made their initial choice, proprietors were to be allowed to influence the final selection: 'they have generally an interest in selecting the poorest'.[45] Trevelyan agreed that even estate factors should be involved as they were 'directly interested in bringing forward the means of the emigrants and have the best knowledge of them'.[46] Because the landlord class was so closely involved in the entire process the Society was bitterly attacked for indirectly encouraging clearance and eviction. It was also condemned for using charitable funds to advance the economic benefit of Highland estates. This, of course, was not the first time such allegations had been made. The Central Board had been vilified in much the same way several years before.[47]

The emigration was to be conducted as far as possible in entire families. This was partly related to a paternalistic concern for the people's welfare and also to a recognition that the great movement which was envisaged would not take place unless the old and the young were also assisted. There was also an awareness that family emigration would limit the dispersal of the people to the gold diggings. If this happened one of the main purposes of the Society, to provide labour for the Australian pastoral economy, would be defeated. At the same time, movement to the goldfields would make it much more difficult to collect loans made to emigrants. As Sir John McNeill argued, '. . . when once fairly set down on a sheep farm with a family I should think our emigrants pretty safe'.[48] Emigrants seeking aid would be required to apply all their available means to defray the expense of their outfits and deposits. They would have to repay to the Society all the sums advanced to them and these would then be applied to promote further emigration.[49] The role of the Society itself was quite specific and complementary to that of the Emigration Commission and the landlords. It outfitted the people, paid their passage from the Highlands to the ports of embarkation for Australia and defrayed the expenses of the children and the elderly, who were not eligible for free passages within the regulations of the Emigration Commission, to the Antipodes. Trevelyan was determined that all advances should be repaid 'to the last penny' in order to establish 'an accumulating fund' to send out many more.[50]

This brief outline indicates how the modest scheme first mooted in Skye by Thomas Fraser and his colleagues in 1851 had quickly grown into a grandiose project. Trevelyan increasingly viewed it as a great programme of social engineering which would provide, in his words, 'the final settlement' of the Highland problem.[51] He reckoned, in a phrase redolent of Thomas Malthus, that the 'surplus population' of the society consisted of 30,000 to 40,000 people. All of them could be transported to Australia at a cost of £100,000 and a fund of this order could and should be collected.[52] His ambition, however, was not limited to solving the Highland problem alone. His plan was 'of a public and comprehensive nature' and, while it was exclusively concerned with the Highlands in its existing form, could be extended 'as occasion required, or our means admit, to any other distressed District or Class in Society'.[53] He envisaged a permanent agency to relieve the demographic pressures which he believed were the causes of so many social ills. His views were also coloured by strong racialist attitudes. To some extent his response to both destitution in Ireland and the Scottish Highlands was founded in his unswerving belief in the superiority of the Saxon over the Celt. He noted the need for 'a national effort' which would 'rid our operatives of the swarming Irish and Scotch Celts'.[54] He wholeheartedly approved of the emigration from St. Kilda: 'By all means send the entire population of St. Kilda to the Antipodes and John Macleod will then have his choice of Celt and Saxon for his future subjects'.[55] He thought more highly of the German peoples than of the Highland Scot and contemplated with satisfaction 'the prospects of flights of Germans settling here in increasing number – an orderly, moral, industrious and frugal people, less foreign to us than the Irish or Scotch Celt, a congenial element which will readily assimilate with our body politic'.[56]

Indeed, as one scrutinises the structure and development of the Highland and Island Emigration Society in detail, it becomes apparent that it was much more than a private, philanthropic agency of the type so common in Victorian times. It can more realistically be seen as a quasi-government organisation carrying out a substantial programme of emigration which the government of the day was unwilling to undertake officially and directly because of constraints of both ideology and cost. Like the Central Board the Emigration Society was intimately connected with officers of the State. A number of pieces of evidence seem to support such a conclusion. The two most powerful men in it, Trevelyan and Sir John McNeill, were both prominent public servants who had been either directly or indirectly involved in the social problems of the Highlands from 1846. McNeill was the author of the influential Report of 1851 which argued strongly for emigration as the only alternative for the Highland population. One result of this was the passage of the Emigration Advances Act of 1851 which allowed landowners to borrow funds to support emigration. Later some landowners in the Highlands used this source to cover the costs of their contribution to the expenses of emigrants assisted by the Highland and Island Emigration Society.[57] Throughout the entire period of the Society's existence all its overseas mail passed through the Treasury Office and was franked there. Treasury police and messengers were used to muster and convoy emigrants and order stores and clothing. Trevelyan even published a *Blue Book* of the Society.[58] The Board of Admiralty agreed to place H.M.S. *Hercules* at the disposal of the Emigration Commissioners for the conveyance of emigrants to Adelaide and Melbourne.[59]

Perhaps most significant of all, however, was the influence which Trevelyan was able to bring to bear on the Colonial Land and Emigration Commission, the government agency which vetted applicants for assisted passage to Australia. It had made family emigration difficult in the past because of its reluctance to fund the passage of children and old people. Trevelyan was able to partially remove some of these obstacles because of his close association with Sir Thomas Murdoch, who had been chairman of the Commission since 1847. In 1852, for instance, he informed Murdoch, unofficially, in a letter containing details of the Highland Society's business, that the Treasury had approved the Commission's application for an increased establishment at the Port of London. By the beginning of 1853 the activities of the Society and the Commission were so closely associated that it was reported 'the Commissioners will not take emigrants from the Distressed Districts except through our Society'.[60] James Chant, an official of the Commission and 'an experienced emigration officer', was deputed to confer with the agents of the Highland proprietors and to make arrangements for the selection and shipment of emigrants.[61] Trevelyan won the vital concession from Murdoch by August 1852 that families with any number of children should be accepted and distributed among several ships so as not to cause excess in individual vessels.[62] In the same month he confided to McNeill that the Emigration Commission would pay the passage of all children who were selected.[63] Trevelyan was well aware that if the Society had not provided assistance 'the Government might have had to do so at a much heavier charge'.[64] At the same time he stressed that what had formerly been 'a small charitable fund' had become 'an extensive social operation'.[65] The enthusiastic participation of public servants, the use of government officials, the role played both by the Colonial Land and Emigration Commission and the Royal Navy, and the support provided through the Emigration Advances Act of 1851 suggest that the 'operation', despite its partial dependence on philanthropic assistance, was a government project in all but name.

2

In 1851 the population of Skye numbered 22,532. It consisted of twenty-seven 'gentlemen's' families, 380 tradesmen and shopkeeper families and forty-one families of farmers or tacksmen, holding thirty acres or above; 184 tenant families possessed lots of eight to thirty acres while 1888 crofting families held land of less than eight acres. There were 1765 families of 'landless' cottars.[66] The last group comprised about 9,000 people. They 'have no regular trade and, it may be added, no regular employment or labour'.[67] Some were kinfolk of the crofters who had benefited from subdivision of land; others were former tenants who had lost their holdings through clearance and had as a result descended the social scale; still others were families who had migrated from other parts of the Hebrides in search of a patch of land.[68] The island was a community which had been ravaged by an accumulation of disasters. In June 1849, for instance, 8162 people or thirty-three per cent of the population of Skye were on the relief lists.[69] When the operations of the Central Board came to an end in 1850 the island was hit by a massive storm on 19 and 20 August of that year which destroyed much of the grain crop.[70] At the same time evictions were on the increase as the trustees of the Macdonald, Macleod and Skeabost estates sought to control the spiral of rent arrears. In the parish of Strath, the Parochial Board imposed the poor-rate assessment with great vigour and was determined 'to sequestrate anything worth a few shillings where payment could not be otherwise obtained. In several instances, arrears of rent as well as of rates were demanded on condition of ejectment, and what between this and the doings of the proprietor's trustees, the people in this parish were sadly oppressed'.[71] In Sleat, most of the crofters were in arrears and 'about a score of them' had been evicted.[72] It was reported from the parish of Snizort that eviction was endemic. Two witnesses, one a local doctor, Alexander Macleod, informed Lady McCaskill during her visit to the island in 1851 that in the Tayinloan district of the parish a total of thirteen families, comprising fifty-five individuals, had been ejected in August and September of that year.[73] Extensive removal of entire townships seems to have been relatively uncommon in Skye at this time, outside the Strathaird estate. The notorious clearance in 1853 of Boreraig and Suishnish, on the McDonald estate, and 'compulsory emigration' from Strathaird were not typical.[74] On the other hand, there is little doubt that ejection of individual families and especially of groups of families of cottars was taking place on a considerable scale. Colonies of evicted crofters and cottars were to be found in many parts of the island. At Struan Mor there was 'a pauper village of evicted tenants' numbering '137 souls living in about six acres of land'; close by, at Coilleor, there was another similar settlement. Sixty-two individuals held about five acres of land among them.[75]

As a result of famine and clearance some observers thought that much of the population of Skye had been brought to the brink of starvation by 1851. Sir Edward Pine Coffin returned to the island in 1851 and was horrified by the decline in both the clothing and physical appearance of the inhabitants which had taken place since 1847.[76] Lady McCaskill visited Skye in the autumn of that year and left some memorable impressions in her published account. She entered one hut, occupied by four or five fishermen: 'cadaverous, hard-featured, thin, wan and diminutive, listless, supine – looking quiet and grave'.[77] In Snizort she witnessed the poignant spectacle of people waiting for the distribution of food: 'At the appointed time and place, these poor creatures troop down in hundreds, wretched and thin, starved and wan. Some have clothing, some almost none and some are a mass of rags, old and young, feeble and infirm. They take their station and await their turn . . .'.[78] The sheer scale of destitution disturbed James Chant , the veteran emigration official who had been sent to the island to select candidates for the Highland and Island Emigration Society: 'I cannot conclude without referring to the destitution of the Island of Skye. It would be difficult, perhaps impossible, to convey to you an idea of the wretchedness and misery I have witnessed. *It must be seen to be understood.* Any description that can be given must fall short of the sad reality. It is not too much to say that many of the swine in England are better fed and better housed than are the poor of this island'.[79]

What also comes through unmistakably from contemporary accounts is that several communities on the island were still being partly supported by southern philanthropy. Although the activities of the Central Board had ceased, informal charity remained relevant to the survival of many in Skye in these years. The crofters at Scouser, for example, were 'assisted by friends in the south' to obtain seed.[80] The Rev. John Kennedy of Stepney discovered in 1851 that at least 750 families in the parishes of Bracadale, Snizort and Strath depended on charity dispensed by local clergymen from funds sent from central Scotland and England.[81] Despite the termination of official relief and the widespread and vocal opposition to charity, small but vital sums continued to be sent north by the Free Church, benevolent organisations and private individuals.[82]

Assistance of this kind, however, could do little more than alleviate hunger and reduce malnutrition. Yet the depth of suffering was such that increasingly the poor were driven to emigration as their only salvation. Conditions deteriorated particularly in the spring and early summer of 1852 when the grain and potato crops were consumed and earnings from temporary migration had not yet been obtained. In May of that year Sheriff Fraser held an emigration meeting. So many attended that his courtroom could not hold them and they had to adjourn to the parish church: 'Many of these people are in a state bordering on starvation; and I have seldom had a more painful duty to perform than to address them without being able to give them any distinct information on the matter, which to them, in their present circumstances, is one of such frightful interest'.[83] There seems little doubt that, in 1852 at least, it was a longing to flee the famine that drove the people of Skye to seek refuge in Australia. News of the gold discoveries in Victoria and New South Wales may have been a significant force changing attitudes to Australian emigration in the long run and in less distressed parts of the Highlands but the desperate urge to escape from destitution and starvation was a much more potent factor in Skye in 1852.[84]

The Highland and Island Emigration Society responded quickly. Arrangements were made through the Emigration Commissioners to despatch 191 emigrants to Victoria in the *Araminta*, then shortly to sail from Liverpool. James Chant was deputed from the Commission to confer immediately with the Skye Committee and the agents of the proprietors to make arrangements for the selection and shipment of future emigrants, the first party of whom were appointed to sail in the *Georgiana* from the Clyde in July. This vessel, with 372 passengers, set sail for Melbourne on the 13th of that month. Other shipments followed in rapid succession[85] (see Table 11.1).

The Society obtained the use of H.M.S. *Hercules* which the Admiralty intended to send to Hong Kong as a floating barracks for troops. It was suggested that she might be employed en route to convey Highland emigrants to Australia. The ship was placed at

Table 11.1. List of Ships Containing Emigrants Assisted by the Highland and Island Emigration Society, sent out to the Australian Colonies during the Year ending April 1853

| | ADULTS | | | | CHILDREN | | | | | | | | |
| | Married | | Single | | Boys | | Girls | | | | | | |
	Males	Fem.	Males	Fem.	From 1 to 14	Under 1 Year	From 1 to 14	Under 1 Year	Totals	Destination	Date of Departure 1852	Date of Arrival 1852	Number of Days on Voyage
1. Mangerton	1	3	1	2	2	–	3	–	10	Victoria	Jan. 26	June 5	130
2. Borneuf	3	3	1	2	5	–	5	1	20	Victoria	May 26	Sept. 3	100
3. Araminta	31	31	19	28	46	1	34	1	191	Victoria	June 20	Oct. 4	106
4. Medina	1	1	1	–	–	–	1	1	5	South Australia	June 25	Oct. 9	106
5. Georgiana	60	60	52	63	63	5	62	7	372	Victoria	July 13	Oct. 16	95
6. Ontario	37	37	58	78	55	3	41	–	309	New South Wales	Aug. 3	Nov. 26	115
7. Ticonderoga	6	6	3	2	10	–	7	–	34	Victoria	Aug. 4	Dec. 22	140
8. Blanche	1	1	2	2	3	–	1	–	10	Victoria	Aug. 5	Nov. 26	113
9. Marmion	35	35	35	26	42	2	35	3	213	Portland Bay	Aug. 28	Dec. 4	98
10. Allison	40	40	51	53	58	3	42	2	289	Victoria	Sept. 13	Feb. 8 1853	148
11. Louisa	1	–	–	–	1	–	–	–	2	Van Diemen's Land	Sept. 24	Jan. 12	110
12. Priscilla	40	40	45	70	43	4	52	4	298	Victoria	Oct. 13	Feb. 24	134
13. Arabian	7	7	11	11	8	2	7	1	54	Victoria	Oct. 27	Mar. 3	127
14. Thames	1	1	–	–	2	–	–	–	4	Victoria	Nov. 3	Mar. 10	127
15. British Queen	1	1	2	–	2	–	3	1	10	Victoria	Jan. 8 1853	May 3	115
16. Panama	5	5	7	3	7	–	10	–	37	Van Diemen's Land	Jan. 8	Apr. 27	109
17. Hercules	110	110	129	150	117	13	112	6	747*	South Australia	Apr. 14+	July 26	103
										Victoria		Aug. 3	111
Totals	380	379	417	490	464	33	415	27	2,605				

Souls
New South Wales 398
Victoria 1846
South Australia 411
Van Diemen's Land 39
                                    2605

* Of these only 380 sailed from Cork in the *Hercules*; the others were forwarded by other ships.
+ 26th December from Campbeltown; final departure, from Cork, 14th April.

Source: Report of Highland Emigration Society.

the disposal of the Colonial Land and Emigration Commissioners by whom she was fitted out to transport a large number of emigrants to Adelaide and Melbourne. The Society obtained the vessel at a lower cost than normal. It was an old line-of-battle ship and, with a capacity for 756 emigrants, could carry more than twice the number of passengers of any of the other vessels used by the Society.[86] The emigrants from Skye, Harris and North Uist embarked at Campbeltown in December 1852. Two contemporary descriptions have survived of their departure.[87] A reporter from the *Illustrated London News* gave a graphic and poignant account:

> Nearly all the females and children suffered greatly from sea-sickness; and when on the afternoon of Sunday the 12th ult. they passed from the *Celt* (on which they had travelled from the Long Island) to the deck of the *Hercules* many of them were still much exhausted . . . It was curious to observe them, as they stepped over the gangway of the great ship. The young women came first – some looking cheerfully round them, some sad and some in tears; but all took pains to adjust their shawls and handkerchiefs, their tresses or their capes, as they made their appearance before strangers. The married women and children followed, the latter skipping and dancing on the broad deck overjoyed at their escape from the confinement of the steamboat; the former so completely absorbed by the care of their children, and the fear of losing them in the crowd that they did not seem to be conscious of where they were or what had brought them there. The men looked dark and stern, like men about to confront danger and not likely to shrink from the encounter, but relaxed into a smile at the first kind word . . .

Sir John McNeill was also there to bid the emigrants farewell. Writing to Trevelyan, he gave a more euphoric report:

> It would have given you great pleasure to have seen the emigrants in the *Hercules* this morning. Cheerful faces met me everywhere. They are surprised and delighted with the accommodation, the bedding, the diet, the kindness they receive – in short with everything. One man said to me: 'We were told of this but we did not believe it'. Their chests were on the deck having this morning been put on board and they were busy arranging their bags. A more joyous group I have rarely seen . . . the barber has been on board and has dipped their heads at one penny per head. The locks on the ladies have been tenderly dealt with . . .
>
> It is no small recompense for the labour and anxiety one has undergone to see how much happiness has already been conferred on these poor people . . . One man with great simplicity expressed his wonder that the Queen could find time to think of all these little things for their comfort. He added, 'well, she must have a kind heart and a clear head. I could not have thought of all these things myself, though I had nothing else to do'. I endeavoured to explain that there were many gentlemen helping to make the arrangements for them.

Tragically, McNeill's optimism was to prove unfounded. The voyage of the *Hercules* turned out to be a long-drawn-out agony for both passengers and crew. Almost as soon as she set sail, the ship encountered a storm which endured for four days: 'the scene on board, from the sickness was painful'.[88] It had to return to Rothesay but soon after departure on 14 January, smallpox and typhus began to rage among the passengers and crew, forcing the vessel to put into Cork harbour where it was detained until 14 April 1853. Fifty-six persons, including the ship's surgeon and matron, died. When she finally sailed again, only 380 embarked; the remainder were mainly split up among twelve other ships. Seventeen were returned home, including orphans whose parents had died. In the process of dispersal whole families were broken up. The voyage itself attracted great press interest and horrific stories were published of the privations of the emigrants. Numerous deaths were recorded, including several attempts at suicide. A young girl from Strath parish in Skye threw herself overboard and was never seen again. After the death of one woman, Ann Macleod, 'no less than eight sharks followed close on the ship, and watching every movement until her body was thrown overboard, when they immediately disappeared after the box containing her corpse was committed to the deep'.[89] At the end of 104 days at sea the *Hercules* reached Adelaide on 20 July 1853. Nine further deaths and five births had occurred.

The adverse publicity given to this particular voyage must have deterred some prospective emigrants. Trevelyan was very much aware that the notoriety associated with the *Hercules* incident could profoundly damage the Society's strategy. In September 1853 he went so far as to write to Messrs. Eyre and Spottiswoode, the publishers, demanding that the type of the journal written by the purser of the ship be broken up without any copies being run off other than the six proofs already sent to him.[90] There was further serious mortality on the *Ontario*, in which thirty adults perished, and the *Priscilla*, in which eleven adults and thirty children died.[91] The overall mortality rate on ships from the Highlands to Australia in the 1840s and 1850s has been calculated at less than three per cent, but on those of the Society it was over four per cent.[92] It was unlikely, however, that this reflected any real inadequacy of organisation. The Society showed great care for the emigrants when they had been selected and went to considerable lengths to ensure their comfort and security. £3,017 of a total outlay of £7,200 in 1852-3 was spent on clothing and a further £43 on Gaelic books and tracts.[93] More probably the higher than average mortality rates on the Society's vessels can be explained by the destitute circumstances of the passengers and the relatively high proportion of children. In the majority of cases the main killer was typhus which thrived amid the insanitary huts and terrible poverty of the Hebrides.

By the end of 1852 a total of 2605 people had left supported by the Society. The majority of these were from Skye but in July 1852 Sir John McNeill was arguing that the problems were now more serious in other islands, such as Tiree and Mull.[94] Subsequently, therefore, operations were extended to these areas and to North Uist and Harris.[95] A number of landlords were approached and McNeill 'inundated the west coast with communications'. Forms were sent to Lord Dunmore in Harris, Dr. Martin in Moidart, the Duke of Argyll, Lord Compton in Mull and the trustees of Maclean of Coll, among others. McNeill feared the possible embarrassment of 'a flood of emigrants' which would 'sweep us off the face of the earth or leave the Society high and dry in some Ararat between Morvern and Assynt. It would be too humiliating to have its remains pointed out as a landmark from Edward Ellice's door in Glenquoch'.[96] Ellice, a Member of Parliament and Highland laird, was an energetic opponent of clearances and assisted emigration. For the most part, however, opposition in the first year of the Society's operation was muted and only became more active in the longer run when some writers, such as Donald Ross, accused the Society of abetting evictions.[97] At national level, both the Free Church and the Church of Scotland were silent although the Society's plans were attacked by some local ministers. Trevelyan recognised that the Free Church itself had acquiesced only with considerable reluctance but that individual pastors were campaigning strongly against emigration. He scornfully linked their motives to those of priests in Ireland: '. . . if the flock go away the shepherd must starve. They will, however, be no more able to prevent it than the Roman Catholic priests can'.[98] McNeill also vigorously denounced those ministers '. . . who for the sake of the few pence they extort from the poor people, are doing all they can to perpetuate the misery of their flocks'. He particularly feared the influence of the Rev. Mr. Maclean of Tobermory in Mull who had stayed in Canada for some years and could therefore speak against emigration from personal knowledge and experience. In exasperation at his efforts and those of his fellow ministers, he declared that he wished they 'were in Canada or at the gold diggings or in any other place where they could get an honest living'.[99]

However, it was more probably the improvement of economic conditions in 1853 than either clerical opposition or the fate of the *Hercules* which explains the sharp decline in the number of emigrants in that year. Only 628 were despatched in four shiploads, mainly to Victoria, in the summer of 1853, and were drawn from the estates of Clarke of Ulva, the Duke of Sutherland, Lord Dunmore, Lord Strathallan, Maclean of Coll, Cameron of Locheil, the Duke of Argyll, Lord Macdonald and the Marquis of Stafford.[100] Activity increased once again in 1854 when the Society assisted a further 1132 emigrants but numbers then declined to 344 in 1855 and 201 in 1857. In March 1856 Trevelyan admitted that 'our emigration undertaking is apparently coming to a natural and happy termination . . .'[101] Two years later, in April 1858, after assisting the emigration of almost 5000 people from the Highlands to Australia, the Society was finally wound up and its residual funds transferred to McNeill and the Board of Supervision of the Poor Law to be employed to help the emigration of needy families.[102]

3

One writer has argued that news of the gold discoveries in Victoria and New South Wales in 1851 'was an overwhelming force for the change of attitudes towards Australia'.[103] In 1852 it was reported from the north-west Highlands that there was much talk about 'the Gold Diggings' and that 'the tenants now read Newspapers much more than they did and they are wonderfully well informed in regard to this discovery lately made in New South Wales'.[104] Letters from successful emigrants began to be published in such northern newspapers as the *Inverness Courier* and the *Northern Ensign* with enticing details about the good life to be had in the Antipodes. Typical was a letter written from Adelaide by W.P. Mackay, who left Sutherland in 1847:

> The time has now arrived when emigrants from Caithness, Sutherland, Ross, Orkney and Zetland, may get a free passage from their own country if they chose . . . to this country which is replete with plenty. Here is no starvation, no seizing of your goods for taxes, no begging for work, but plenty of good meat at 2d. per lb., bread 6d. per loaf . . . To the mechanics and farmers of Caithness I would say, take your ploughs, harrows and

farming implements, and tools and come here as quickly as possible. You, in a few years, will be independent . . . You can worship, as you think proper here. Religious sects for all kinds and persuasions are on equal footing. Government will give them aid if they petition, either for building churches or schools, and also aid teachers. Here are no taxes, the taxes being raised on goods imported.[105]

While it is possible that such blatant propaganda might have spread knowledge of and interest in Australia and could also have contributed to the growth in the number of sailings of private emigrant groups noted in an earlier chapter, it is unlikely that it had a decisive influence on those who travelled under the auspices of the Highland Society. More than half of all the Society's emigrants, 2605 of a total of 4900, left in 1852 before the gold discoveries were widely known. Again, prejudice against Australian emigration lingered on in some parts of the Hebrides to such an extent that the Duchess of Argyll recommended to Sir John McNeill that Gaelic lecturers should be recruited and 'sent amongst them to instruct them in the advantages of Australia'.[106] The Society's own view was that 'desire for Australia' was much more firmly established in the mainland. But it was from the Inner and Outer Hebrides that it drew over eighty per cent of its successful applicants.[107] It also reckoned that the adverse publicity given to the ill-fated voyage of the *Hercules* must have gone some way to further reduce the attractions of emigration to Australia in the Hebridean mind.[108]

When the process of emigration through the Highland Society is considered in detail, it becomes apparent that the primary factor influencing the exodus was the pressure of grinding poverty and a desperate desire to escape from intolerable conditions at home. Two main arguments support this conclusion. First, the long-run cycle of emigration was broadly related to changing conditions in the Western Highlands. The vast majority left in 1852, a year of severe distress (see Table 11.2). In 1853, however, there was a dramatic fall from 2605 emigrants to 628. The officials of the Society were satisfied that this was due to improving economic prospects at home. In autumn 1852 the harvest was more productive and sheep and cattle prices higher than at any time since 1846. The labour market for temporary migrants was also buoyant.[109] By April 1853, therefore, Trevelyan was referring to 'the disinclination to emigrate' and later explained this was a result of improving prospects in the Highlands: '. . . their condition at home is so far better by the increased demand for labour, the high price of cattle and sheep, the abundance and good quality of their crops, especially of potatoes – and the success of the Herring Fishery on the West Coast'.[110] In 1854 conditions in the north deteriorated once more and an increased interest in emigration to Australia was anticipated.[111] By the end of that year over 1130 people had sailed there under the auspices of the Society. However, between 1855 and the termination of the Society's activities in 1857 only a further 545 individuals emigrated. This decline was partly due to the outbreak of war with Russia in 1854 and to the new vigour of the labour market in Canada, '. . . the more accessible colony . . . where so many of the Highlanders have relations and friends . . .'[112] Yet the recovery of the potato crop by 1856 and, even more fundamentally perhaps, the new vigour in the Scottish industries of coal, iron and engineering from the mid-1850s and its effect on general employment opportunities, probably reduced the need to undertake the long sea voyage to Australia.

The Great Highland Famine

Table 11.2. Year of Departure and Destination of H.I.E.S. Emigrants, 1852-1857

Destination	1852	1853	1854	1855	1856	1857	Totals	Per cent
New South Wales	522	15	–	–	–	–	537	11
Victoria	1633	462	1039	–	–	–	3134	64
S. Australia	411	–	93	344	–	–	848	17
Tasmania	39	151	–	–	–	201	391	8
Annual Totals	2605	628	1132	344	–	201	4910	100

Source: SRO, HD4/5, Lists of Emigrants

Second, there was an even more sensitive oscillation in the short run between changing domestic economic circumstances and the spirit of emigration. The desire to emigrate could evaporate at the slightest hope of improvement. There was a classic instance of this on the estate of Macleod of Macleod in 1855: 1,039 persons were enrolled as applicants for emigration from this property. But of these only 237 eventually presented themselves for inspection by the Society's agent, James Chant; 131 were accepted and 116 rejected because of the number of 'young and helpless children'. Chant reported that the remaining 792 had changed their mind between the time of registering for emigration and his arrival to carry out the selection process. He saw this as the direct result of the arrival of a steamer at Dunvegan organised by Donald Ross and other sympathetic parties, freighted with corn and potatoes, and consigned to the Free Church ministers for distribution to the people.[113] This and other examples suggest that the poorest class, who were the prime targets of the Society's effort, only entertained the thought of emigration with great reluctance, departed grudgingly and changed their minds easily at the slightest prospect of improvement in their circumstances.

It was argued at the time that landlord coercion, and eviction in particular, was widely deployed to force emigration. Donald Ross was one of several commentators who asserted that the Society aided and abetted the clearances of the early 1850s because they provided an obvious means of ensuring that those who were evicted did leave the country.[114] It was also claimed that the Society colluded in clearances because landlords were required to pay one third of the cost of the emigration and were closely involved through their agents in the process of selection and recruitment. By their very nature such accusations are exceedingly difficult either to refute or to substantiate. The interaction between destitution, crop failure and removals is so obviously complex that to try to separate out each variable, even for analytical purposes, is to run the risk of following a false historical trail. Again, the pressures making for eviction, as an earlier chapter has shown, were so profound that major clearances would probably have occurred in the 1850s with or without the collusion of the Highland and Island Emigration Society.

On the whole, the emigration cycle seems to have been related more to changes in economic conditions in the region than to the policies of individual proprietors although the urge to evict could also itself concentrate in bad years. The officials of the Society regarded the emigration as 'a popular movement' springing from the desperate circumstances of the Western Highlands.[115] To Trevelyan in July 1852 'the people seem to be all *on the move*. They are *swarming* like Bees'.[116] The authorities could also point to areas such as Iona and St. Kilda where the desire to emigrate was just as evident as elsewhere but where removals were rare.[117] Nor is there any clear indication in the sources consulted of collusive attempts between the Society and individual proprietors to promote emigration through eviction. Such arrangements would have been in total conflict with Trevelyan's own conception of his duty as a public servant and his unswerving devotion to safeguarding the independence of the Society. In the letters of Sir John McNeill it is very evident that the Society's officials were primarily motivated by a desire to secure the welfare of the people. Any benefit for the landed classes was merely the inevitable result of their strategy not its cause. They were spurred on by a sense of paternalistic responsibility rather than a desire to solve the economic problems of Hebridean estates. McNeill stressed that their 'vital consideration' was 'the welfare of the population and their extrication from difficulties which but for our intervention would be insuperable'. He wished, as he put it, 'to keep the doors of escape [for them] open'. The Society had accepted a grave and onerous responsibility: 'the comfort and health of over 1000 human beings will be at stake; men, women and children who rely upon us and are entitled to expect that we shall take every precaution for their safety'.[118] The Society also specifically avoided the direct recruitment of emigrants and abstained from 'inciting' emigration among the people.[119]

It would be naïve, however, to discount all links between the wave of clearances which swept the Highlands in the early 1850s and the activities of the Society. It was not only committed defenders of the people, such as Donald Ross, who saw a connection but individuals associated with the Society itself, like Sir Edward Coffin and Sheriff Fraser, who were both concerned and alarmed that some proprietors and trustees were taking advantage of the existence of an emigration organisation to evict on a massive scale.[120] Even Trevelyan conceded that '. . . a case might no doubt be supposed in which a Proprietor might present to his poor tenants the alternative of *Eviction* or *Emigration assisted by our Society* and so we might come in for a share of his obloquy'.[121] He was, however, sanguine about the inevitability of eviction, especially for the cottar class: 'it does not much matter to the smaller class of under tenants whether they are evicted or not. The process of subdivision has been carried so far that even in the ordinary years they cannot extract a subsistence for themselves and their families from their little holdings; and when the potatoes fail, as they are likely to do this year, they must starve if they are not helped. The choice is between maintaining them at home and sending them to Australia . . .'.[122]

The connection between clearances and the Highland and Island Emigration Society could develop at several levels. First, the Society offered a unique opportunity for landlords and trustees to rid themselves of the poorest population of their estates at minimal cost. The expense of paying for one third of total emigration costs amounted to less than £1 per person (see Table 11.3). Even this outlay could be reduced in the short term by borrowing the cost under the Emigration Advances Act of 1851. The Macleod estate in Skye calculated that 120 souls could be 'emigrated' at an average cost of £3 per head, amounting to £360. The Society paid £240 and the remaining £120 would have to borrowed under the 1851 Act at 6½ per cent interest. This involved an outlay of £7.10.0 per annum for twenty-two years, by which time the debt would be repaid.[123] It was calculations such as these which prompted Lord Macdonald to write to Sir John McNeill that 'It would be absolute insanity not to take advantage of the present opportunity of getting rid of our surplus population and I can hardly believe

Table 11.3. *Source of Emigrants Assisted by H.I.E.S. by Estate, April 1852–April 1853*

Estates	Families	Souls	Total amount advanced £ s. d.	One-third charged to the Proprietors £ s. d.
1. Lord Macdonald	215	1315	3758 6 6½	1252 5 6½
2. Macleod of Macleod	45	277	786 5 1	262 1 8
3. Strathaird	25	148	460 0 10	153 6 11
4. Skeabost	25	130	368 9 3½	111 16 5
5. Waternish	6	41	138 2 3	46 0 9
6. Lyndale	5	37	111 4 4½	37 1 5
7. Dr. Martin	6	31	93 15 1	13 1 0
8. Vice-Chancellor Stewart	2	16	39 3 1	2 15 7
9. Raasay	3	24	8 6 9	76 10 6
10. Lord Dunmore	19	95	229 11 7	56 15 5
11. Sir James Riddell, Bart.	15	90	170 6 5	36 16 0
12. W. Robertson, Esq.	6	46	76 4 5	24 15 5
13. Dr. Martin (Moidart)	4	24	31 11 1½	10 10 4
14. Alex. McDonald, Esq.	1	9	176 16 11	58 18 11
15. Duke of Argyll	11	70	83 6 8	27 15 6
16. Lord Compton	5	34	59 0 7½	19 13 6
17. Mr. McLean of Coll	3	18	208 10 6	69 10 2
18. Mr. Clarke of Ulva	6	37	74 1 10	24 13 11
19. Aros	3	21	238 7 5	79 9 1
20. A. Matheson, Esq., M.P.	10	52	— — —	— — —
21. Mr. Sinclair of Lochaline		47	— — —	— — —
22. Col. Ross	1	7		
23. J.M. MacLeod, Esq., St. Kilda*	7	36		
Totals	471	2605	7220 0 10½	2406 13 7½

* The three last-mentioned Proprietors defrayed the whole expense of the emigrants from their respective estates.
Source: Report of Highland Emigration Society

that my Trustees would allow such a one to slip'. To ensure that he did not do so, he intended to pen 'a very strong letter to him about its [i.e. emigration's] benefit'.[124]

In addition, the factors of landowners and the agents of trustees were so deeply involved in the early stages of the selection of emigrants that there was a constant temptation to use coercion to weed out those deemed most suitable for expulsion. The proprietors were responsible for the distribution of applications, verification of the returns and for making out lists of applicants from the property in due form.[125] Both Trevelyan and McNeill agreed that they had 'an interest in selecting the poorest'.[126] There exists a fascinating document in the papers of Lord Macdonald where those nominated for emigration under the auspices of the Society are listed.[127] The majority were landless or semi-landless cottars, many of whom had often already suffered eviction, and small crofters heavily in arrears.

Finally, there were a series of cases in which the link between clearance and the emigration facilities offered by the Society was especially close. In Sollas in North Uist in 1852 it was alleged that 'an emigrant ship was brought to Lochmaddy, on board of which twelve or fourteen families from the district . . . were prevailed upon or forced to embark for Australia'.[128] These were the remnants of the community which had experienced the highly controversial evictions on Lord Macdonald's estate of North Uist in 1849. It seems clear that the people were reluctant to depart and, as one recent commentator has put it, '. . . there is little doubt that there were ugly scenes when the people were bundled onto the ship'.[129] The vessel in question was the *Celt*, a small steamer which was to take the North Uist emigrants to Campbeltown where they would embark on the *Hercules*. The people from Sollas were among those observed by the reporter from the *Illustrated London News*, in the scene described earlier in this chapter, as they transferred to the larger vessel in Campbeltown harbour.[130] The Macdonald trustees seem to have been especially keen to promote emigration from the North Uist property.[131] Unlike the Skye estates it was not entailed and the trustees for Macdonald's creditors had therefore a considerable interest in a further thinning of the population to make the island marketable.[132] North Uist was successfully sold in 1856.

The Society was also implicated in the Knoydart clearances of 1853.[133] Donald Ross, in his *Glengarry Evictions or Scenes at Knoydart*, alleged that the wholesale removal of the tenantry of the Macdonnell of Glengarry estate would not have taken place if emigration assistance through the Highland and Island Emigration Society had not been available. Mrs. Macdonnell, Glengarry's widow, had written to tenants in 1852 that, 'if they emigrate without trouble or annoyance they will be allowed to remain where they are until the committee are ready to take them . . . Sir John McNeill has promised they shall *all* be removed in *one* ship to Australia'. Ross concluded that if the Society 'had not been so very accommodating, had Sir John not been so very ready with his promise of a large ship the proprietrix might not have been so eager to evict'.[134] Summonses of removal were issued in spring 1853 and the people were offered free passage to Australia or Canada. The cost to the estate of assisting the emigration of the 400 who accepted was £1,700, which was borrowed under the Emigration Advances Act.[135]

The direct involvement of the Society in this affair is difficult to prove. For a start, even if a deal was struck between McNeill and Mrs. Macdonnell the bargain quickly fell through. When the *Sillery* eventually arrived in the summer of 1853 to embark the emigrants it sailed not under the auspices of the Society to Australia but as a private venture to Canada.[136] Evidence also survives of an interview which McNeill had with Mrs. Macdonnell in December 1852 which is relevant to this issue.[137] According to the transcript of the discussion she was indeed eager 'to promote emigration from Knoydart'. The population of the estate consisted of small crofters 'in a miserable state' who had paid no rent for many years: 'their families are growing up in a state of degradation'. The estate itself was under trust. She stated that, 'with a view to the welfare' of the small tenantry, she wished to provide the means of emigrating to Australia. The local priest, according to Mrs. Macdonnell, favoured the measure, 'seeing no other prospect of escape for them'. There is no indication in the record of the meeting whether McNeill agreed to accept her tenants as suitable for assisted passage by the Society. What does come through unequivocally, however, is Mrs. Macdonnell's firm view that whether they emigrated or not 'they must surrender their lands'. Ross's allegations, therefore, seem unconvincing. The decision to carry out the clearance was primarily made independently of the existence of the Society and eventually implemented without its involvement.

The Society, however, was more intimately associated with clearances on the Strathaird estate and the property of Lord Macdonald in Skye. In 1849 Strathaird belonged to Alexander Macalister.[138] It contained a population of over 600 people, 'a very great proportion of whom have paid almost no rent for many years past'. They were served with writs of removal in the summer of 1849 and offered assisted emigration. The tenantry refused and 'because of their resistance the proprietor holds that he has no longer responsibility for them'. The people petitioned Sir George Grey, the Secretary for Home Affairs, to intervene to halt Macalister's 'compulsory emigration'.

> Your petitioners are utterly averse to emigrate to America, on considering their inability to do so arising from their distressed circumstances of potato failure, low prices for cattle, together with the numerous privations to which they will be subjected by being cast pennyless and unprovided for on a foreign shore without any aid from the proprietor to convey them from the place of landing to that part of the country where they could obtain farms.[139]

Grey refused to intervene. He responded that the issue of the writs of ejectment did not constitute a criminal charge. Nor could the proprietor compel emigration.[140] The plight of the Strathaird people is only revealed in the historical record again in May 1852, when the agent for the Macalister estate engaged to pay £600 to the Highland and Island Emigration Society on account of emigrants from the property.[141] In that year twenty-five families, numbering 148 souls, embarked for Australia under its auspices.[142]

The relationship between the operations of the Society and the clearances of the two townships of Boreraig and Suishnish on the estate of Lord Macdonald is more complex. The estate rentals indicate that eight of the Boreraig tenants and nine from Suishnish were settled elsewhere on the property. However, an examination of the tenants of the seventeen holdings allocated to evicted families of these two townships reveals that their names appear on the lists of the Emigration Society. Of the seventeen, seven can be identified with certainty on the lists and there are six other names which were probably those of previous tenants. This does suggest, not surprisingly, that the estate was indeed using the facilities which were offered to advance the process of clearance. Several of the Boreraig and Suishnish people were settled in holdings vacated by those who emigrated through the Society. At the same time, nine families (sixty-nine people) from Boreraig and two (six individuals) from Suishnish were secured passage, under the Society's auspices, in the ill-starred *Hercules* bound for Adelaide.[143]

4

Table 11.4 outlines the geographical origins of emigrants assisted by the Society. In general there was a bias towards the Inner and Outer Hebrides and in particular Skye, Raasay, Harris, Coll and Mull. In all, these areas accounted for seventy-six per cent of the Society's emigrants between 1852 and 1857. Mainland districts, however, were also represented, although these tended on the whole to concentrate along the western maritime districts. There was some, but very limited, participation in the Society's activities by estates in the central and southern Highlands. In essence, therefore, the vast majority of emigrants came from the most distressed districts. Yet, not all destitute areas were well represented. There were few emigrants assisted from Lewis and none at all from Barra, South Uist and Benbecula. Tiree was also under-represented. This pattern is probably to be explained by the fact that the landlords in question, Sir James Matheson, Gordon of Cluny and the Duke of Argyll, had already carried out their own private schemes of assisted emigration on a considerable scale. As men of great wealth they had less need of the Society's support than several others. The Society's operation, therefore, can be seen as complementary to the undertakings of these proprietors. It is significant that its efforts concentrated on such islands as Skye and Harris where landlord-assisted emigration, because of the insolvency of proprietors or because of legal constraints (as in the case of Lord Dunmore[144]), was either limited or non-existent.

Table 11.5 provides a detailed profile of the age and sex structure of the Society's emigrants. It is immediately apparent from this that the Society had successfully accomplished its aim of promoting emigration in family groups. In that sense the composition of its emigrant parties and the majority of those assisted by private landlords was unrepresentative of the 'normal' age and sex structures of nineteenth-century emigrants, which tended to be heavily biased towards young, single adults. As the Society approvingly concluded in its report at the end of the first year of operation: 'The 2605 souls whose emigration is therein recorded are all members of the 380 families who are represented in the column of Married Adults. This is believed to be the nearest approach to "colonisation" which has yet been attempted; each of the ships may be said to form a colony in itself; all the warm affections and hallowed sympathies of home are there, and are borne by the emigrants to their new hearths in the land of

The Great Highland Famine

Table 11.4. Geographical Origins of H.I.E.S. Emigrants, 1852-1857

Area	1852	1853	1854	1855	1857	Per cent of total
Skye	1958	186	514	160	–	59
Raasay	24	–	131	–	–	3
Harris	95	21	5	184	120	6
Ardnamurchan	90	–	23	–	–	2
Moidart	77	–	7	–	–	2
Mull & Iona	168	84	43	–	–	6
Kintail & Lochalsh	52	50	10	–	–	2
Morvern	47	4	20	–	–	2
St. Kilda	36	–	–	–	–	1
Inverness	–	15	–	–	–	0.3
Sutherland	37	82	81	–	–	4
Lochiel/Ardgour	–	88	123	–	–	4
Tiree	2	13	–	–	–	0.3
Coll	10	–	32	–	81	2
Kintyre	–	41	–	–	–	0.8
Rothiemurchus	–	44	–	–	–	0.8
Torridon	–	–	49	–	–	0.9
Lewis	–	–	17	–	–	0.3
Lochaber	–	–	24	–	–	0.4
Glenelg/Knoydart	9	–	25	–	–	0.5
Arisaig	–	–	21	–	–	0.4
Others	–	–	7	–	–	0.14

Source: SRO, HD4/5, Papers of the Highland and Island Emigration Society

their adoption'.[145] The tabulation reveals only one marginal aberration from this pattern. From 1853 the proportion of single females rose from eighteen per cent to around a quarter of all emigrants. This was part of the Society's policy. It soon realised that the demand for unmarried women in Australia was so great that if it could provide a guaranteed supply its dealings with Australian business interests and colonial legislature would be enormously helped. Its capacity to provide unmarried women was stressed constantly when negotiations were being conducted with persons of influence in Australia. Officials of the Society were advised, whenever possible, to bias selection of emigrants in favour of single females. In April 1853 Sir John McNeill urged in relation to Harris, '. . . it is quite indispensable that taken collectively there should be a greater number of single women than of single men amongst the emigrants now to be selected'.[146]

The broad strategy of the Society was to assist in the emigration of the destitute in the Western Highlands, and the social composition of the emigrant groups also reflects this intention.[147] The emigrants from the Skeabost estate in Skye in 1852, numbering 130 souls, were 'of the poorest class'.[148] Those selected in Harris in the spring and early summer of 1852 were so impoverished that they had to be furnished with clothing before they could leave their homes.[149] There is much evidence, too, that the Society, like private landlords, had a special interest in assisting the emigration of the subtenant class.[150] The trustees of Lord Macdonald's estates in Skye were very keen to select cottar families for emigration under the Society's auspices.[151] Despite the massive

Table 11.5. *Age and Sex Structure, H.I.E.S. Emigrants, 1852-1857*

| | Adults | | | | Children | | | | |
| | Married | | Single | | Boys | | Girls | | |
Year	Males	Females	Males	Females	Age 1-14	Under 1	Age 1-14	Under 1	Total
1852	380 15%	379 16%	417 19%	480 18%	464 1%	33 16%	415 16%	27 1%	2605
1853	99 16%	98 16%	92 15%	149 24%	82 13%	5 1%	94 15%	8 1%	628
1854	181 16%	181 16%	197 17%	286 25%	136 12%	15 1%	121 11%	15 1%	1132
1855	48 14%	48 14%	52 15%	79 23%	55 16%	4 1%	57 17%	1	344
1857	28	28	48	44	20	2	29	2	182

Source: SRO, HD4/5, List of Emigrants

exodus from this property for Australia, with 1315 leaving in 1852 alone, the number of crofting townships and the total of individual tenancies on the estate declined only marginally. In the parishes of Portree, Sleat and Strath in 1847 there were fifty-one townships; a decade later the number had only fallen to forty-nine. In the list of crofting settlements only Boreraig and Suishnish disappear from the record. Almost certainly, therefore, the majority of those who were assisted by the Society from this estate were not rent-paying crofters at all but subtenants, cottars and squatters, the very core of the 'redundant population' of the island.[152]

The Society was determined not to send 'men or families that were doing well in any capacity at home or who were not in want of assistance'.[153] But in some cases, notably in 1853 when demand for its services declined, the rule was relaxed. 180 persons sailed on the *Sir Alan Macnab* in October of that year from Coigach, Rothiemurchus and Kintyre, 'of a very superior class, healthy robust people, most of them speak English tolerably well'.[154] In general terms the Society's officials found that mainland emigrants were significantly less deprived than those from the islands, a conclusion which is consistent with the arguments advanced earlier in this book.[155] On the other hand, they were not engaged in the indiscriminate expatriation of the impoverished elements of the Highlands. Careful selection was undertaken by James Chant to eliminate widows with several children, the very old and the infirm. As Table 11.6 demonstrates, the Society's emigrants of 1852 and early 1853 consisted largely of young families with children. Forty-seven per cent were under 14 years of age, ninety-two per cent aged 39 or under and less than one per cent (thirty-six individuals) 60 years or older.

Between 1852 and 1857 the Society played a key role in supporting the movement of people from the distressed districts of the Hebrides to Australia. At times its operations attracted both vigorous controversy and passionate criticism. The Society did not conspire directly with the landed classes but the emigration facilities it provided did facilitate evictions on some estates. Both government, landowners and the Society's organisers had a vested interest in encouraging the emigration of the poorest classes from the Western Highlands. The removal of almost 5000 individuals from the areas of greatest destitution must have markedly reduced the increasing burden of poor rates and relief payments made by proprietors. The Society's operations, therefore, go some way to explain why the number assisted in the Hebrides by the official poor law began to fall from 1853. The great exodus to Australia was of direct benefit to the landlords of the region and, to the extent that the cottar class imposed a burden on the resources of the rent-paying tenantry, also relieved levels of destitution elsewhere in Highland society.

Table 11.6. *Ages of Emigrants Supported by H.I.E.S., 1852 and early 1853*

	0–9	10–14	15–19	20–29	30–39	40–49	50–59	60+	Total
Male	353	204	183	214	139	152	45	10	1300
Female	314	178	175	320	155	137	35	8	1322
Total	667	382	358	534	294	289	80	18	2622
%	25	14	14	20	11	11	3	1	

Source: SRO, HD4/5, List of Emigrants.

NOTES

1. This brief introduction is based on David S. Macmillan, *Scotland and Australia, 1788-1850* (Oxford, 1967), 71-131, 261-303 and Roderick A.C.S. Balfour, 'Emigration from the Highlands and Western Isles of Scotland to Australia during the Nineteenth Century', Unpublished M.Litt. thesis, University of Edinburgh, 1973, 30-86.
2. See above, pp.204-5, for a detailed discussion.
3. *Report of the Highland Emigration Society* (London, 1853), 7; SRO, Home Office (Scotland), Domestic Entry Books, RH2/4/240, H. Waddington to Board of Supervision, 1 January, 1851.
4. *McNeill Report*, Appendix A, 34-6.
5. *Ibid.*, 35-6.
6. These were the properties of Lord Macdonald and Macleod of Macleod and the estate of Skeabost.
7. *Report of Highland Emigration Society*, 7.
8. F.H. Hitchins, *The Colonial Land and Emigration Commission* (London, 1931).
9. *Inverness Advertiser*, 2 March 1852.
10. *Report of Highland Emigration Society*, 7.
11. *Inverness Advertiser*, 2 March 1852.
12. *Ibid.*
13. *Report of Highland Emigration Society*, 8.
14. SRO, Home Office (Scotland), Domestic Entry Books, RH2/4240, H. Waddington to Secretary, Board of Supervision, 1 January 1851.
15. SRO, HD4/1, Letterbook of H.I.E.S. (1), Trevelyan to Sir J. McNeill, 7 April 1852.
16. See above, pp.125ff.
17. See above, pp.130-2.
18. SRO, HD4/1, Letterbook of H.I.E.S. (1), Trevelyan to Miss Neave, 20 January 1852.
19. SRO, HD7/46, Trevelyan-Skene Correspondence, Trevelyan to W. Skene, 5 February 1848.
20. SRO, HD4/1, Letterbook of H.I.E.S. (1), Trevelyan to Miss Neave, 20 January 1852.
21. *Ibid.*, Lady McCaskill, *Twelve Days in Skye* (London, 1852), 38.
22. SRO, HD4/1, Letterbook of H.I.E.S. (1), Trevelyan to Thomas Murdoch, 31 March 1852.
23. David S. Macmillan, 'Sir Charles Trevelyan and the Highland and Island Emigration Society, 1849-1859', *Royal Australian Historical Society Journal*, 49 (1963), 161-88.
24. SRO, HD4/1, Letterbook of H.I.E.S. (1) Trevelyan to Sir J. McNeill, 7 April 1852.
25. SRO, HD4/1, Letterbook of H.I.E.S. (1), Trevelyan to McNeill, 11 June 1852.
26. Mitchell Library, MS21506, Letterbook on Highland Emigration of Sir John McNeill, 1852, *passim.*
27. SRO, HD4/1, Letterbook of H.I.E.S. (1), Trevelyan to D. Mangles, 29 April 1852.
28. *Report of Highland Emigration Society*, 14.
29. SRO, HD4/1, Letterbook of H.I.E.S. (1), Trevelyan to A.P. Simes, 17 May 1852.
30. *Ibid.*, to T. Baring, 19 May 1852.
31. Macmillan, 'Sir Charles Trevelyan', 172-3.
32. *Ibid.*
33. McCaskill, *Twelve Days in Skye, passim*; *Illustrated London News*, 28 May 1853.
34. See, for example, E.C. Tregelles, *Hints on the Hebrides* (London, 1855), 5; Rev. E. Findlater, *Highland Clearances: the Real Cause of Highland Famines* (Edinburgh, 1855).
35. McCaskill, *Twelve Days in Skye*, 38.
36. *Illustrated London News*, 28 May 1853.
37. SRO, HD4/2, Letterbook of H.I.E.S. (2), Trevelyan to J. Cropper, 5 August 1852.
38. SRO, HD4/2, Letterbook of H.I.E.S. (1), Trevelyan to D. Mangles, 29 April 1852.
39. *Ibid.*, to the Earl of Harroby, 19 May 1852.

40. *Report of the Highland Emigration Society*, Treasurer's Account, April 1852-April 1853; SRO, HD4/2, Letterbook of H.I.E.S. (1), Trevelyan to Commissioners of Colonial Land and Emigration, n.d.

41. Mitchell Library, MS. 21506, Letterbook on Highland Emigration of Sir John McNeill, McNeill to Trevelyan, 31 May 1852.

42. *Report of the Highland Emigration Society*, 9.

43. SRO, HD42, Letterbook of H.I.E.S. (1), Trevelyan to Thomas Fraser, 13 May 1852.

44. *Ibid.*

45. Mitchell Library, MS. 21506, Letterbook on Highland Emigration of Sir John McNeill, 1852, McNeill to Trevelyan, 8 July 1852.

46. SRO, HD4/2, Letterbook of H.I.E.S. (2), Trevelyan to Sir John McNeill, 13 August 1852.

47. See, for example, Donald Ross, *The Glengarry Evictions or Scenes at Knoydart* (Edinburgh, 1853), 28. See also above, pp.136-7.

48. Mitchell Library, MS21506, Letterbook on Highland Emigration of Sir John McNeill, 1852, McNeill to Trevelyan, 27 May 1852.

49. *Report of the Highland Emigration Society*, 10.

50. Macmillan, 'Sir Charles Trevelyan'. 169.

51. SRO, HD4/2, Letterbook of H.I.E.S. (1), Trevelyan to Thomas Murdoch, 31 March 1852.

52. *Ibid.*, to John Cropper, 22 May 1852.

53. *Ibid.*, to A. Kingscote, 8 May 1852.

54. Quoted in Macmillan, 'Sir Charles Trevelyan', 174.

55. SRO, HD4/2, Letterbook of H.I.E.S. (2), Trevelyan to Sir J. McNeill, 14 August 1852.

56. *Ibid.*, to Commissary-General Miller, 30 June 1852.

57. For example, the trustees of Macleod of Macleod borrowed £1500 under this Act. Dunvegan Castle, Macleod of Macleod Muniments, Section 2/662, Agreement between Enclosure Commissioners and Macleod's Trustees, 17 February 1853.

58. Macmillan, 'Sir Charles Trevelyan', 180-1.

59. *Report of the Highland Emigration Society*, 12.

60. SRO, HD4/2, Letterbook of H.I.E.S. (2), Trevelyan to Sir J. McNeill, 21 February 1853.

61. Mitchell Library, MS21506, Letterbook on Highland Emigration of Sir John McNeill, J. Chant to McNeill, 8 August 1852.

62. SRO, HD4/2, Letterbook of H.I.E.S. (2), Trevelyan to J. Chant, 18 August 1852.

63. *Ibid.*, to Sir J. McNeill, 23 August 1852.

64. *Ibid.*, to J. Cropper, 5 August 1852.

65. *Ibid.*, to Sir J. McNeill, 26 August 1852.

66. *Witness*, 6 September 1851.

67. *Inverness Advertiser*, 26 August 1851.

68. See above, pp.7-9.

69. *Destitution Papers*, Second Report of the Committee of Management of the Edinburgh Section, 21 June 1849.

70. *Inverness Advertiser*, 25 February 1851.

71. *Witness*, 6 September 1851.

72. *Ibid.*

73. McCaskill, *Twelve Days in Skye*, 19.

74. See above, pp.264-5.

75. *Inverness Advertiser*, 11 February 1851.

76. Mitchell Library, MS21506, Letterbook on Highland Emigration of Sir John McNeill, 1852, McNeill to Trevelyan, 20 June 1851.

77. McCaskill, *Twelve Days in Skye*, 16.

78. *Ibid.*, 35.

79. *Report of the Highland Emigration Society*, 11-12.

80. *Inverness Advertiser*, 18 February 1851.

81. *Ibid.*, 26 August 1851.

82. E.C. Tregellis, *Hints on the Hebrides* (Newcastle, 1855), 15; *Inverness Advertiser*, 10 February 1852.

83. *Report of the Highland Emigration Society*, 10. Another independent witness confirmed that 'the people are anxious and willing to get away'. See Dunvegan Castle, Macleod of Macleod Muniments, 659/7/3, J.D. Ferguson to Madam Macleod, 25 June 1852.

84. The issue of motivation is discussed in more detail above, pp.258-61.

85. *Report of the Highland Emigration Society*, 11-12.

86. *Correspondence relating to Her Majesty's Ship, 'Hercules'* (London, 1853), *passim*.

87. *Illustrated London News*, 23 January 1853; Mitchell Library, MS21506, Letterbook on Highland Emigration of Sir John McNeill, 1852, McNeill to Trevelyan, 13 December 1852.

88. *Correspondence*, 8-11. The subsequent account of the voyage of the *Hercules* is based on this source, SRO/HD4/3, Letterbook of H.I.E.S. (3), Trevelyan's letters, January-February 1853 and E. Richards, 'Highland Emigrants to South Australia in the 1850s', *Northern Scotland*, 5 (1982), 1-30.

89. *Northern Ensign*, 14 April 1853, quoted in Richards, 'Highland Emigrants', 16.

90. SRO, HD4/2, Letterbook of H.I.E.S. (3), Trevelyan to Eyre and Spottiswoode, 9 September 1853.

91. *Ibid.*, to Sir J. McNeill, 15 March 1853; Balfour, 'Emigration from the Highlands to Australia', 157.

92. Balfour, 'Emigration from the Highlands to Australia', 157.

93. *Report of the Highland Emigration Society*, 24.

94. Mitchell Library, MS21506, Letterbook on Highland Emigration of Sir John McNeill, 1852, McNeill to Trevelyan, 13 July 1852.

95. SRO, HD4/5, Lists of Emigrants.

96. Mitchell Library, MS21506, Letterbook on Highland Emigration of Sir John McNeill, 1852, McNeill to Trevelyan, 3 July 1852.

97. Ross, 'Glengarry Evictions', 28.

98. SRO, HD4/2, Letterbook of H.I.E.S. (2), to Sir John McNeill, 17 July 1852. See also Dunvegan Castle, Macleod of Macleod Muniments, 659/11/9, E. Gibbons to Miss Macleod, 17 June 1852.

99. Mitchell Library, MS21506, Letterbook on Highland Emigration of Sir John McNeill, 1852, McNeill to Trevelyan, 15 July 1852.

100. SRO, HD4/5, Lists of Emigrants.

101. SRO, HD4/2, Letterbook of H.I.E.S. (4), Trevelyan to Sir J. McNeill, 26 March 1857.

102. *Ibid.*, Trevelyan to Highland Emigration Society, 14 April 1858.

103. Richards, 'Highland Emigrants', 7.

104. Quoted in *Ibid.*, 7.

105. *Inverness Courier*, 15 February 1848.

106. Mitchell Library, MS21506, Letterbook on Highland Emigration of Sir John McNeill, 1852, McNeill to Trevelyan, 30 June 1852.

107. *Ibid.*, 23 June 1852.

108. SRO, HD4/2, Letterbook of H.I.E.S. (3), Trevelyan to Sir J. McNeill, 6 August 1853.

109. *Ibid.*, Sir J. McNeill to Trevelyan, 21 January 1853.

110. *Ibid.*, Trevelyan to Capt. W. Denison, 4 July 1853; to L. Mackinnon, 25 November 1853.

111. SRO, HD4/4, Trevelyan to T.W. Murdoch, 7 April 1854.

112. *Ibid.*, to Sir M. Denison, 25 October 1854.

113. *Ibid.*, J. Chant to H. Rollo, 30 April 1855. For other instances see Mitchell Library, MS21506, McNeill to Trevelyan, 23 June and 21 August 1852.

114. Ross, *Glengarry Evictions*, 28.

115. SRO, HD4/2, Letterbook of H.I.E.S. (1), Trevelyan to Sir E. Coffin, 13 July 1852.

116. *Ibid.*, HD4/2, to Sir J. McNeill, 17 July 1852.

117. Mitchell Library, MS21506, Letterbook on Highland Emigration of Sir John McNeill,

1852, McNeill to Trevelyan, 12 August 1852.

118. *Ibid.*, to Trevelyan, 26 May, 20 June, 20 August 1852.

119. *Ibid.*, 20 June, 30 June 1852.

120. *Ibid.*, T. Fraser to Sir J. McNeill, 30 December 1851; SRO, HD4/2, Letterbook of H.I.E.S (1), Trevelyan to Sir E. Coffin, 13 July 1852. See also letter to J. Cropper, 5 August 1852.

121. SRO, HD4/2, Letterbook of H.I.E.S. (1), Trevelyan to Sir E. Coffin, 13 July 1852.

122. *Ibid.*, to R. Stewart, 13 August 1852.

123. Dunvegan Castle, Macleod of Macleod Muniments, 659/11/10, E. Gibbons to Miss Macleod, 22 June 1852.

124. Mitchell Library, MS21506, Lord Macdonald to Sir J. McNeill, 9 June 1852.

125. *Ibid.*, McNeill to Trevelyan, 3 July 1852.

126. *Ibid.*, 5 July 1852.

127. SRO, GD221/15, Lord Macdonald Papers, Population Lists of Certain Districts in the Highlands and Islands of Scotland.

128. *N.C.*, 787, 801. That coercion was used in this emigration was confirmed by Charles Shaw, Sheriff-Substitute of the Long Island, who witnessed the events and participated in them. See *N.C.*, 2736.

129. Richards, 'Highland Emigrants', 13.

130. See above, p.256.

131. SRO, GD221/82, Lord Macdonald Papers, Rentals and associated papers, North Uist.

132. SRO, HD4/2, Letterbook of H.I.E.S. (1), Trevelyan to Sir J. McNeill, 4 August 1852.

133. The *Scotsman*, 17 September 1853.

134. Ross, *Glengarry Evictions*, 28.

135. *PP.*, XLVI (1854), *Papers relative to Emigration to British North America*, 79.

136. *Ibid.*

137. Mitchell Library, MS21506, Letterbook on Highland Emigration of Sir John McNeill, 1852, McNeill to Trevelyan, 30 September 1852.

138. SRO, Lord Advocate's Papers, AD58/83, Thomas Ranken to Sir J. McNeill, 8 June 1850.

139. *Ibid.*, The Petition of the Tenants of Strathaird, Isle of Skye, 20 May 1850.

140. *Ibid.*, to Sir G. Grey, 20 July 1850.

141. Mitchell Library, MS21506, Letterbook on Highland Emigration of Sir John McNeill, 1852, McNeill to Trevelyan, 27 May 1852.

142. SRO, HD4/5, Lists of Emigrants.

143. *Ibid.*, Sir A. Geikie, *Scottish Reminiscences* (Glasgow, 1906), 223-7; Mackenzie, *Highland Clearances*, 202-3; SRO, Lord Macdonald Papers, GD122/11, 133/1; SRO, HD4/5, List of Emigrants.

144. SRO, Lord Advocate's Papers, AD58/84, Copy letter W.H. Sitwell to Countess of Dunmore, 1 October 1846.

145. *Report of the Highland Emigration Society*, 13.

146. SRO, HD4/3, Letterbook of H.I.E.S. (3), Sir J. McNeill to Capt. Macdonald, 12 April 1853.

147. Mitchell Library, MS21506, McNeill to T. Fraser, 29 May 1852.

148. *Ibid.*, to Trevelyan, 8 July 1852.

149. *Ibid.*, 26 July 1852.

150. SRO, HD4/2, Letterbook of H.I.E.S (2), Trevelyan to J. Chant, 18 August 1852.

151. SRO, GD221/15, Lord Macdonald Papers. Population Lists of Certain Districts in the Highlands and Islands of Scotland.

152. *Ibid.*, GD2221/43, 70; *Inverness Advertiser*, 26 August 1851.

153. Mitchell Library, MS21506, McNeill to Trevelyan, 18 August 1852.

154. SRO, HD4/3, Letterbook of H.I.E.S. (3), Trevelyan to Sir W. Denison, 5 October 1853.

155. Mitchell Library, MS21506, McNeill to Trevelyan, 21 August 1852. A notable exception was the people of St. Kilda who were described as relatively prosperous.

12

Impact and Aftermath:
the Western Highlands and Islands, 1850-1890

1

By the early 1850s, despite the potato blight and a slump in the market for some traditional Highland products, Highland landowners had not become a debilitated class. True, there were some bankruptcies among them. Rent payments from the small tenantry collapsed and many proprietors incurred substantial costs for both measures of famine relief and programmes of assisted emigration. Indeed, probably their most important subsidy to the crofters on their estates during the crisis was their tolerance for a time of increasing rent arrears in the later 1840s. A later section of this chapter argues that while most of the smaller tenants suffered a decline in the number of cattle, the majority still possessed some stock at the time of Sir John McNeill's inquiry in 1851. In many cases, however, the value of their cattle was less than the total of the arrears they owed in rent to their landlord. In effect, large numbers of crofters were insolvent.[1] Several proprietors tolerated this situation at least for a period, because cattle were difficult to sell before 1852, and to confiscate stock in lieu of rental would have destroyed the capital of the small tenantry and effectively terminated their ability to pay rents in the future.[2] In the short run at least, this course of action would not simply further postpone the possibility of a recovery in estate income but also ran the risk of forcing even more destitute families on to the Poor Law.[3]

In Chapter 4 it was shown that the overwhelming majority of Highland landowners survived the potato famine because many of them had external sources of income; the economies of several estates depended on the market for sheep rather than on demand for black cattle, and the Central Board assumed the main burden of relief provision in most areas from the early months of 1847 until 1850. The loss of income and the rising expenditure which the crisis forced on many landed families should not be underestimated. Yet, in several ways, the potato famine presented as much of a convenient opportunity as a great threat to West Highland landlords. During the 1840s they obtained financial support from two sources which must have gone some way to alleviate their difficulties. By far the more important were the funds released under the Drainage Act.

By the end of March 1847, the overall value of applications from the Highlands for assistance under this legislation had reached the massive total of almost £500,000.[4] Much of the grant which was received was spent on schemes of land improvement, on which the small tenants were not simply required to give the government rate of interest on the loan (which was still being charged in some districts in the 1880s) but were paid wages for their work which then went to pay rents.[5] In 1850, for instance, payment of the Whitsun rents on Lord Macdonald's Skye estates was '. . . facilitated by the wages received for draining and trenching under the Drainage Act'.[6] Campbell of Islay obtained £30,000, and, as the trustees on his estate confirmed, '. . . this money, which was laid out through the tenants, and on which they were bound to pay the government percentage, afforded employment and enabled them to pay their rents'.[7] In the long run, of course, the funds provided through the Drainage Act must have added to the value of of some crofting land and hence to the overall market value of Highland estates. No exact evidence has been found of the areas of land which were actually improved but several observers commented how it had helped to increase the capacity of several crofting townships to grow more grain.[8] Certainly, the investment provided through the Act was a principal reason for the marked increase in cultivated acreage which was an important feature of the economies of some West Highland estates during the famine years.

The second source of subsidy was the relief programme organised by the Central Board between 1847 and 1850. Not simply did it lift the main burden of providing relief from the landed class, either as individual proprietors or as ratepayers, but it also made a significant contribution to the permanent capital of some West Highland and Hebridean estates. The extent to which this occurred in 1847 and 1848 was limited. As was seen in Chapter 5, the roads, bridges and piers which were constructed in those years as part of the labour and destitution tests were sometimes poorly planned, often left uncompleted and, in general, were not designed to maximise the economic resources of the districts where they were built.[9] It was a different story with those additions to the network of communications which were associated with the Cooperative System of 1849 and 1850. They were built in close collaboration with the proprietors and made a key contribution to the development of the internal roadway systems of Wester Ross and parts of Sutherland.[10] How far these routes contributed to the boom in the recreation economy of these districts in the second half of the nineteenth century can only be surmised.[11] At the same time, part of the funds released through the Cooperative System, as with the operation of the Drainage Act, went to pay off rent arrears on some estates. The Parochial Board of the Parish of Gairloch in Wester Ross noted in 1851: 'There was a considerable amount of work on roads on the Gairloch estate last year, under a cooperative arrangement with the relief committee; but a great part of the labour performed went to liquidate the arrears of rent. It was no doubt of great assistance to the people, who were supplied with meal while working, and were also enabled in that manner to pay off part of that arrear.'[12]

A sharp reduction in arrears of rent in all the Highland estates whose records have been examined was one of the striking features of the 1850s. Arrears had stood at £1793 on the Mull property of the Duke of Argyll in 1853. By 1858 the equivalent figure was a mere £74.[13] In the parish of Assynt in Sutherland small tenant arrears fell from sixty-one per cent of rental in 1849 to eight per cent in 1855. In Edderachillis there was a similar decline from eighty-five per cent in 1849 to fifteen per cent in 1855.[14] The pattern was duplicated on the Skye estates of Lord Macdonald which were at the very heart of one of the most distressed districts in the Western Highlands. Arrears were valued at fifty-one per cent of rental in 1850, fell to thirty-three per cent in 1851-2 and sustained a further decline to thirteen per cent in 1856-7.[15]

How far the Drainage Act alone contributed to this process is doubtful. Most drainage funds were spent in the late 1840s before the substantial contraction in arrears began. Nor can the trend be explained by a reduction in the rental charged. No such change took place on any of the estates examined above. In general, there were only occasional references to other landlords giving relief in this way, and alongside these were found other instances of small tenant rents being raised during the crisis.[16]

Three factors more probably help to explain the pattern of falling arrears. First, it reflected the cancellation of arrears on some properties as part of the policy of promoting assisted emigration. Undoubtedly this was a major influence on the decline in arrears in Mull and in Skye, especially between 1850 and 1852.[17] Second, the period of toleration of rent arrears, during the first two to three years of the famine, came to an end by the early 1850s. A determined effort to liquidate outstanding debt seems to have been confined initially to properties which were insolvent or under trust. As early as 1849, for example, such policies were being implemented in estates managed by trustees in Ardnamurchan, Islay, parts of Mull and Skye.[18] But by the early 1850s strategies to reduce rent arrears had been adopted throughout the region. Landlords in Lewis, Mull, Tiree and Wester Ross between 1851 and 1854 were starting to confiscate cattle stocks in order to liquidate the debt of the small tenantry.[19] In the spring of 1854 the Duke of Argyll's chamberlain in Mull and Tiree could write that he expected '. . . the most of the arrears will be wiped off during the year, at last collection I intimated that no partial payments of rent would be received in future, that payment in full must be made at each term'.[20] Third, the three critical influences on the economic condition of the small tenant class changed slowly for the better after 1853. To begin with, cattle markets recovered and prices began a sustained rise from 1853.[21] The potato was more productive in 1855, and from 1856 blight ceased to have the effect which had devastated the crop since 1846.[22] The economic prosperity in the Scottish Lowlands brought a new and more vigorous level of activity to the market for migrant workers from the Highlands.[23]

The reduction in rent arrears had started to take place at a time when many proprietors feared the worst effects of the termination of the relief operations of the Central Board in 1850 and the expected impact that this would have on expenditure on poor-law rates. Several proprietors were once again forced to provide interim relief of the kind which they had abandoned in 1847 after the Central Board came to their aid. In Tiree, in the spring of 1851, it was reported that meal had to be given because some of the small crofters '. . . were actually starving'. Several months earlier, in Mull, the Argyll estate had received a series of desperate petitions for meal: '. . . the worst year they have had yet, the committee funds being at an end and all their little means completely exhausted'.[24]

Despite these strains, however, there was little sign of the widespread panic which had overwhelmed the landed classes in 1846 and 1847. Numbers on the poor roll did rise in 1851 and 1852. The total of 'occasional poor' in the four Highland counties was 1765 in 1850 but thereafter increased to 3103 and 5109 in subsequent years. Most of this expansion, however, was concentrated in the single county of Inverness, which accounted alone for almost half of the Highland increase between 1850 and 1852. In addition, the numbers of 'occasional poor' had returned by 1853 to the level which prevailed in the year before the Central Board had wound up its activities.[25] This outcome did not simply reflect the recovery in cattle prices and the buoyant condition of the market for migrant workers outside the Highlands. It was also a direct consequence of the huge increase in permanent out-migration in the 1850s and conclusive proof of the success of the schemes of assisted emigration which had been adopted since 1849.

As a result many West Highland and Hebridean estates probably emerged from the famine in a leaner and fitter economic condition than they had been before 1846. Since the end of the Napoleonic Wars the great problem for the landlord class had been the lingering presence of a population which had been rendered both destitute and redundant by the terrible consequences of the economic recession of the 1820s and 1830s. This was a population which was a constant drain on resources and a menace to estate solvency because it often had to be fed out of landlord funds during the subsistence crises which occurred at regular intervals throughout these two decades. Chapter 1 demonstrated, however, that though often existing in conditions of grinding poverty, the small tenants and cottars only emigrated with great reluctance.[26] While the exodus of people did gather pace after the Napoleonic Wars, the movement was not yet on a sufficient scale to markedly reduce levels of destitution in all areas. This was especially so because commercial sheep-farming continued to impinge on the sparse land resources of the peasantry at the same time as migration took place and controls on subdivision of holdings were either weak or non-existent in several districts. In a sense, then, the famine in some areas brutally solved the social problem which confronted West Highland landowners. It massively accelerated emigration, not because proprietors cleared the estates, though this gave considerable impetus to the movement in some areas, but because the sheer length and intensity of the crisis, for a time at least, weakened the grip of the people on the land. Large numbers changed their attitudes radically from a great reluctance to move to a desperate urge to get away. Only the potato famine and the associated economic crisis could have worked this revolution in heart and mind and, at the same time, made private, public and philanthropic funds available so that the process of emigration could be accommodated. Before 1846 assisted emigration and clearance did take place, but only a major disaster like the famine could really concentrate the minds of the people and the attention of landlords and government. The fears of a potential catastrophe also allowed some proprietors to behave in ways which seemed to show little concern for the social and human costs of their actions. But they were tolerated for a time because the alternatives to such harsh corrective action seemed likely to have even more appalling consequences. This was indeed the application of drastic surgery to the chronic problems of the Western Highlands.

The landed classes exploited their opportunity with great skill. Much previous discussion in this volume has shown how many proprietors devoted their efforts to ensuring that the poorest of the small tenants and the cottar class were expelled. Assisted emigration, in particular, was carried out in a meticulous and selective fashion. There seems to have been a preference in favour of retaining communities which derived most of their income and employment from the sea rather than the land. Crofting townships which had grown up to service the labour needs of the kelp manufacture were especially vulnerable to clearance and consolidation. The result must have been something akin to 'the survival of the fittest', the phrase used by the Duke of Argyll himself when describing the social revolution which he put into effect in the island of Tiree. Whenever possible the very poorest were shaken out of the tenant structure and the more reliable rent payers were retained. Between 1849 and 1854 a series of careful surveys was conducted on a number of West Highland estates which were designed to separate the weak from the strong in the tenant hierarchy.[27]

Yet fundamental change in estate structure of the kind achieved on the island of Tiree as a result of the famine seems to have been exceptional. No such revolution occurred in any of the other estates for which records are available. The more typical pattern appears to have been a major displacement of the cottar class, a marginal reduction in the number of small tenancies, a net increase in the size of the larger pastoral farms and more effective control of subdivision. On the Macdonald estates in Skye, the number of small tenancies only fell by six per cent between 1846 and 1858, though one suspects that this apparent continuity conceals a considerable turnover in tenant families within the overall structure.[28] In the two western parishes of Sutherland which were most affected by the famine, small tenancies fell by eleven per cent and thirty-one per cent between 1846 and 1855.[29] Some of this, though, must have been due to redistribution of tenancies within the estate as, by the early 1880s, the *total* number and size of crofts in Sutherland as a whole had hardly changed since 1846.[30] On the Riddell estate in Ardnamurchan, where small tenants paid fifty-four per cent of the rental in 1851, '. . . the tendency . . . has been to reduce the number of small holdings, several farms of that class are now under sheep'.[31] There was a similar pattern in Barra and South Uist where, in the later 1840s, '. . . there had been many changes from crofts to grazings of late'.[32] Again, in Strathaird and Skye, emigration and clearance led to the removal of eight crofting townships and the conversion of their lands to sheep runs.[33]

Table 12.1 sets out evidence submitted to the Napier Commission relating to the increased size of the pastoral sector after the famine emigrations. Few of these allegations can be checked against original estate papers but, in the main, they tend to confirm the conclusions derived from those which have been analysed. Sheep-farming was being extended generally throughout the region, but only on a major scale in parts of the Outer Hebrides because in most other areas of the Highlands it was already dominant before 1846. The clearances and emigrations of the famine speeded up the invasion of the last bastions of the crofting population by the Cheviot and the Blackface. By the 1850s the sheep frontier had reached its limit and began to recede from that point in the latter part of the decade as profits fell and deer forests held out more opportunity for commercial gain.[34] In the meantime, however, the extension of sheep pastures left more proprietors poised to exploit the steep increase in the price of mutton and wool which had started in the later 1840s but advanced even more in the following decade. During the famine years the average annual price for Cheviot sheep varied from 16s to 22s. By the mid-1860s, however, the average had climbed to 26s. and 27s.[35]

Table 12.1. Napier Commission Evidence on Redistribution of Croft Lands After Clearances and Emigration, 1846-1856

Ardnamurchan
Removals in early 1850s in Sir James Riddell's time: 'they were removed down to narrow and small places by the shore; some of them have a cow's grass, and some are simply cottars'. Almost

certainly this refers to the relocation of the inhabitants of 'the three Swordles' – townships along the northern coast of Ardnamurchan – to Sanna and Portuairk at the far end of the peninsula. 2282, Q.36018.

Arisaig
Township of Kinloyd cleared in 1853. Now (1883) part of a sheep farm, 'great mass of the land on the estate now held by three tacksmen'. 2080, Q.32852; 2107, Q.33127.

Benbecula
Lands of township of Balvannich, Aird and Nachdar added to three large tacks of Nunton by Col. Gordon. 'Great clearances' of 1849 and 1851 were carried out as being necessary to create sheep walks. 752, Q.11877; 778, Q.12112.

Barra
Township of Castle Bay: lands reduced by three quarters but number of tenants had increased from 10 to 22 plus 30-32 cottars. Township of Bravaig: 4 crofters and 9 cottars are now settled in a place previously occupied by one man. 633, Q.10844.

Glenelg
Factor 'took into his own land the arable lands of the people who went to America'. These were added to his farm in 1851. 2024, Q.31741; 2057, Q.32330.

Glensheil
Removals, 1847-9 at Letterfearn, Drumdaig, West Achanataird. All lands used to extend sheep farms. 2007, Q.31458.

Harris
Crofters in S. Harris did not benefit in any way by 'the sending away of the people to America'. Land used to enlarge tacks. e.g. large farm of Rodel enlarged by removal of crofters. Lands of Borv and Cuidnish townships given to large tacksmen; Big Borv to tack of Scarista-vore. 854, Q.13256; 863, Q.13432.
   Island of Pabbay cleared (26 families); some went to Australia, some to east side of Harris; no attempt made to give the cleared lands to solvent crofters. One witness asserted, 'I never heard of such an attempt being made in this country'. 1173, QQ.17816-17825; 1195, Q.18028.

Islay
Clearances in Kilchoman parish. Four large sheep farms established in it by 1883. Portnahaven had become 'a haven of refuge for the migratory individuals of rural families who had been dispossessed of their homes'. 3111, Q44731.

Lewis
Lands of Carinish and Reef townships went to a tacksman, James Mackenzie. Breanish township congested when the neighbouring township of Molasta was cleared. Six families moved there. In 1849, 'great amount' of hill pasture taken from tenants of upper Shader and occupied by evictees of Galston township. 78 families cleared from Galston and Melbost. Some went to parish of Ness, some 'crowded upon townships in the west'; 'several' went to America. Tacks were enlarged after removals at Belmeanach, Melbost, S. & N. Galston. 108 families evicted. 40 went to America; the rest 'scattered all over the country'. North Tolsta township: 20 families removed to S. Tolsta and their lands converted into a tack. 883,Q.13767-13773; 886, Q.13824; 887, Q.13850; 897, QQ.13993, 13996; 928-9, QQ.14456-7; 991, Q.15311; 995, Q.15465; 1012, QQ.15776-14788; 1023, Q. 15989; 1114, Q.17076.
   These versions of events were challenged by J.M. Mackenzie, the estate Chamberlain, 1848-54; those crofters who did not accept offers of emigration were removed to crofts in other townships vacated by emigrants or to reclaimed land: 'They were in no case crowded on any township where there was no room for them'. 3305-6.

Lismore
Formerly six to seven townships on the island; now only three shepherds and a manager. Crofters only resided on one half of Achanacroigh. 2324, QQ.36849-36857.

Lochalsh
Kirkton township: between 1847 and 1849, nine families emigrated; in 1852 Alton Pan taken from Kirkton and given to 'the late Mr. Mitchell of Attadale who was gradually forming a large sheep farm'. Throughout the parish lands of emigrants 'merely added to large sheep farms'. Only in Ardtoe were crofts extended. 1947, Q.30366; 1986-1987, QQ.31163-31177.

Mull
By 1883, five large farms in Ross of Mull; before 1846, Duke of Argyll's estate there mainly consisted of crofters. Evidence suggests these farms were created after 1850. Ross of Mull: Shiaba township now in the hands of a lowland tacksman where 12 families had formerly lived. 'In all the clearings before 1850 those who had got no land and were not removed were thrown upon the crofters as cottars'.
   Glenforsa estate: after evictions (12 townships, 170 souls) lands let to a Mr. Cameron; removals were 'for the purpose of making large tacks'. All lands (1883) now in tacks or in the proprietor's hands with the exception of a few crofts. 2186, Q.34439; 2198, Q.34695; 2202, Q.34787; 2215, Q.35006; 2227, Q.35260; 2250, Q.35310; 2246, Q.35454-5; 2254, Q.35557; 2255, 35647.

South Uist
Some lands at south end of the island were given to crofters 'by doubling their crofts'. Most lands of emigrants, however, added to the tacks of Askernish and Milton. The lands of the cleared townships of Frobost, Kildonan (27 families) and Bornish (24 families) all added to large neighbouring tacks.
   Tenants of South and North Boisdale township overcrowded by removals from Frobost and Kildonan. In 1883, 19 crofts in South Boisdale but 29 families living in the township. 40 crofts in Milton township added to the large tack held by Mr. Chisholm from Moidart. 701-746, QQ.11039, 1170-11237, 11675.

Skye
Strathaird estate: 8 townships cleared. One was the township of Keppoch, with 44 families; 16 'were sent' to Australia and 5 'placed among' the tenants of an adjacent township Elgoll in 1852. Land was taken from the existing inhabitants to accommodate the newcomers who were relocated as cottars rather than crofters.
   Strath parish: removals in 1852-4 produced increased pressure on other townships, e.g. overcrowding in Drumfearn township. Appendix A, 223, 2789, QQ.5116-5121.
   Raasay: 12 townships cleared; the landlord, Mr Rainy, 'made them into a sheep farm which he had in his own hands'. Appendix A, 223, 278-9, QQ.5116-5121; 440, 448, QQ.7648, 7837, 7858.

There was, however, one important manifestation in several estates along the western mainland and the Inner Hebrides of a decisive break with the past. Proprietors seem to have been much more determined than ever before to control subdivision of holdings and reduce the number of cottars who did not pay rent. Previous chapters indicated how the latter class formed a considerable proportion of the assisted emigration parties of the 1840s and 1850s. It would not be too much to claim that the fall in the number of cottars on certain estates during the famine gave some owners both the incentive and opportunity to ensure that the problem associated with such a large depressed underclass would not emerge again on the same scale. If this hypothesis is correct, it could have significant implications for interpretation of the demographic history of the Western Highlands in the second half of the nineteenth century.

A number of *caveats* should be entered before the argument proceeds. The sub-tenants are commonly among the most difficult groups to identify in the sources of the period because they rarely feature in estate correspondence and never appear in rentals. It is known that successful action to control subdivision was already taking place on some properties, especially along the western mainland, *before* the famine. This probably helps to explain why several parishes in that region had already reached their peak populations by the census of 1841.[36] Again, there are indications that in most areas of the Outer Hebrides *after* the famine, regulations against subdivision were not always implemented as effectively as elsewhere.[37] Nevertheless, for the remainder of the crofting region, there is abundant literary evidence that opposition to sub-division was not only more widespread after the 1850s but that the mechanism for controlling the subletting had become more efficient. The result was that by the 1880s, along the west coast north of Ardnamurchan, in Mull and in other islands of the Inner Hebrides, the cottar class was disappearing rapidly or had vanished entirely from the social structure. The fear of the burdens they might inflict on the poor rates, the memory of the famine, and the assumption that the proliferation of poor cottar families had been a principal and powerful cause of grievous destitution combined to harden opposition to them. These influences ensured that subtenancy was often crushed whatever the human costs. It was yet another sign of the radical change in landlord policy which had taken place since the early nineteenth century. The boom in labour-intensive activities encouraged fragmentation of holdings to *c*.1820; their collapse or stagnation therefore ensured a trend back towards consolidation of holdings which grew stronger during and after the great subsistence crisis.

By the later 1850s mass eviction had virtually come to an end but consolidation and prohibition of subdivision proceeded in a less draconian but equally effective fashion. In theoretical terms, the control of subdivision implied that no additional or separate households could be created within a single tenancy. Only one member of a tenant or cottar family was permitted to set up home after marriage on the lot. Even that could only be done by sharing the father's house until he died. In practice, however, controls were even more stringent than this and were often designed to reduce rather than simply regulate the numbers of households. As one observer put it, 'landlords . . . *weed out* families by twos or threes . . . an absolute veto was placed upon marriage . . . when a young man is guilty of that he may look for a summons of removal'.[38]

These were not the exaggerated claims of an over-enthusiastic pamphleteer. Duncan Darroch, proprietor of the Torridon estate in Wester Ross, admitted to the Napier Commission that the regulations which prevailed on his property meant that the young emigrated '. . . and the elderly members generally go on the poor's roll and, as they die out, the cottages are taken down'.[39] In Arisaig it was alleged that any member of a family who reached the age of 21 had to seek accommodation elsewhere unless allowed to remain '. . . with the written sanction of the proprietor'.[40] There had in the past been a good deal of subdivision of crofts on some parts of the Lochaber estate of Cameron of Lochiel. By the later 1840s, however, these practices were outlawed:

The present proprietor is enlarging rather than subdividing, and his regulations against the increase of population are of the most stringent and Malthusian character. Two families are strictly prohibited from living upon one croft. If one of a family marries, he must leave the croft; and a case has even been brought under my notice, in which the only son of a widow, who is in joint possession of a croft with his mother, has been told that if he marries he will be compelled to leave the estate. Severe penalties are also threatened against the keeping of lodgers. The unlucky crofter who takes a friend under his roof, without first obtaining the consent of Lochiel, must pay for the first offence a fine of £1; and, for the second, shall be removed from the estate.

There is ample evidence in the Lochiel papers that summonses of removal were issued to any crofters who infringed these regulations.[41]

Control of subdivision in Lochcarron meant that '. . . families as they grow up are sent out to shift for themselves. Some of the children find employment at home; some emigrate to the colonies'.[42] In Ardnamurchan and Mull, landlords not only restricted subletting but also pulled down cottages on the death of the occupants in order to cause 'a thinning of numbers'.[43] On the Duke of Argyll's estate in Mull the regulations against subdivision were also rigorously enforced, and by the 1830s the older tradition of subletting to kinfolk had disappeared.[44] Instead, the children of tenants had no alternative but to migrate.[45] At Glensheil, regulations against subletting were regarded as the main reason for the reduction in marriages.[46] Attempts to limit subdivision on the Macdonald estates in Skye had begun before the famine but were only partially effective. From the 1850s, however, it became the 'invariable rule. . . that subdivision of lands by crofters is rigorously prohibited'. Eldest sons were informed that they alone had the right to succeed to the croft held by his father. It therefore was in their interest to prevent the holding from being divided among other members of the family.[47] In other parts of the island, controls were implemented with equal resolution. One tacksman on the Macleod estates ensured that at marriage the couple would have to move. It was alleged that 'If a son married in a man's family, the father dared not give him shelter for a night'.[48]

The results of these policies can be seen in the changing balance between rent-paying tenants and cottars which had taken place by the early 1880s. The Napier Commission selected a number of localities for special study as representative of the crofting region as a whole. These included the parishes of Farr in Sutherland, Uig in Lewis, the districts of Duirnish and Waternish in Skye, and the islands of South Uist and Benbecula.[49] 3,226 families lived in these areas in the early 1880s. Of these only twenty-one per cent were classed as 'landless' cottars and squatters. In the 1840s, by contrast, subtenants of various types formed as much as one half and more of the total population of Skye and parts of the Long Island. The Napier Commission figure, indeed, is biased towards districts which still contained unusually large numbers of cottars by the 1880s. Of the six districts from which their calculations derived, three (Uig, South Uist and Benbecula) were located in the Outer Hebrides where controls over subdivision were more lax than elsewhere. The 'average' depletion of the cottar class elsewhere in the Western Highlands must therefore have been much greater than these data suggest. Not least, then, of the long-term effects of the famine was a sizeable reduction in the relative size of the most impoverished classes in Highland society. This had significant implications not simply for the overall material standards of the society but for an understanding of the forces which sustained a heavy rate of out-migration from most areas for the remainder of the nineteenth century.

2

For the vast majority of the West Highland population the famine did not bring a massive increase in death rates but rather a huge rise in emigration and a profound weakening of the economic structure of crofting. Contemporary observers in the 1850s were of the unanimous view that there had been a progressive deterioration in the condition of the people since 1846.[50] The shortage of potatoes in the first year of the potato failure inevitably forced the widespread slaughter of pigs.[51] Throughout the famine cattle were sold off to buy meal. In Creich, in Mull, half of the small tenants had sold part of their stock by 1851. In Skeabost in Skye, thirty of the fifty-eight crofters paying 50s. annual rent had no stock left. It was reported from Hangarry in North Uist and Uig in Lewis that stock had fallen by more than one half since 1846.[52] Many of the small tenantry in Barra had been entirely stripped of their cattle. Of 230 rent-paying crofters in 1851 on the island, eighty had no stock left of any kind. Only sixteen per cent of families had more than one cow, fifty-six per cent had no horses and fifty-four per cent no sheep.[53] In parts of Wester Ross and the Outer Hebrides boats had even been sold off.[54]

All this represented either the erosion or the entire destruction in some part of the basic assets of the small tenant class. The fact of the decline in stock numbers is especially significant. Traditionally, many were prepared to try to sell clothing rather than market an additional cow in times of difficulty.[55] Partly for this reason assisted emigrants to Canada were notoriously poorly clad on arrival. The Highland and Island Emigration Society had often to issue clothing to those it supported. The small tenantry recognised that the selling of stock was a last and desperate resort, because to do so was to destroy their only capital resource and force their families into chronic and permanent destitution. What made their situation even more parlous was that the Highland cow tended to calve only once in every two years.[56] Even this cycle was not always certain because of the poor feeding which cattle received in some districts during the famine years. Market reports persistently described the under-nourished state of many Highland beasts when presented for sale at the Falkirk trysts and other fairs.[57]

However, two major pressures often made the erosion of cattle stocks inevitable. First, there was the irresistible necessity to sell in order to buy meal. This practice was widely reported in 1846 and the early months of 1847. There is also evidence that in 1848 and 1849, when the market for temporary migrants was depressed, small tenants were also compelled to sell cattle in many Highland districts.[58] The meal trade had increased very significantly during the famine. 34,850 bolls of oatmeal were imported into Tobermory in Mull alone between 1846 and 1850, with annual imports rising from 6184 bolls in 1846 to 8459 in 1849.[59] This was in addition to the provisions made available through the government stores in 1846-7. Much of this grain was paid for by earnings from work carried out under the Drainage Act and, even more significantly, from temporary migration and fishing. But it is highly likely that a proportion was purchased from funds accruing from cattle sales which, given the depressed condition of the market until 1852, had to increase in volume to yield the same return obtained in the period before 1846. Secondly, as has already been seen, landlord tolerance of rent arrears came to an end on some estates in 1848-9 and, in the remainder, after 1850. Throughout many properties a decrease in rent arrears could only be achieved by confiscation of some or all of the cattle stocks of the small tenantry.

But it would be wrong to conclude that the famine reduced all the crofting population to penury and ruin. The evidence indicates a more complex picture. The cottars and those tenants paying rental of £5 per annum or less suffered most. To some extent, indeed, the distinction between the two groups was an artificial one.[60] Small tenants were often reduced to cottar status by eviction, confiscation of cattle stocks and the selling of their few belongings to buy meal. The kinship links between many cottars and small tenants ensured that both groups shared the same burden of destitution through the division which took place of scanty food supplies.[61] But the cottar class was undoubtedly squeezed most. Many lost their potato ground as larger tenants expanded their grain acreage. They probably did not possess much in the way of savings or the cattle and sheep stocks which gave the crofters some degree of resilience. More stringent controls over subdivision also threatened their position and very existence on certain properties.

Yet many inhabitants in the Western Highlands were more fortunate than the cottars or the poorest of the small tenants. Appendix 12 assembles the information recorded on Highland cattle stocks by Sir John McNeill in the course of his inquiry in 1851. The data reveal some quite fascinating patterns. The progressive decline in the numbers of cattle in individual holdings was widely noted, as was the selling of stock to buy meal. However, only exceptionally, in areas such as Barra, parts of Skye and some other localities, had cattle stocks entirely disappeared from a significant number of holdings. More typically, there was a reduction, but not a complete elimination, of the 'normal' number of beasts per holding. Again, there was considerable variation between districts, with the most serious depletions in stock confined to the Outer Hebrides (except Lewis, outside the parish of Uig and the Carloway district of Lochs), Skye, Mull and Coll. By and large, the numbers of cattle were not significantly below the traditional level in Wester Ross and the western parishes of Inverness-shire. These data may support Sir Edward Coffin's conclusion that effective relief had come early enough in 1847 to ensure that most families did not have to sell all their cattle to survive.[62] It could also be, of course, that many cattle were in a half-starved condition and so were virtually unsaleable when market demand was poor. Appendix 3 does indicate that in some years cattle from certain districts simply could not attract buyers.

In addition, McNeill found that the majority of communities which depended on white fishing and, to a lesser extent, those which relied on herring, had not been as adversely affected by the crisis as others. This is consistent with evidence presented earlier that rent payments from fishing townships were more regular and reliable during the famine and that several landlords endeavoured to maintain and consolidate these communities while at the same time removing others by clearance and assisted emigration.[63] It is equally clear that the middling crofters – those renting holdings at £5 to £20 per annum – were also partly protected from the worst effects of the great subsistence crisis. McNeill's evidence strongly suggests that the majority of this class managed to retain most of their stock and that they were rarely threatened with insolvency.

Plainly, this might simply reflect the fact that they possessed more savings than their neighbours. But there were other reasons for their good fortune. Their larger holdings allowed them to diversify cropping more easily after the failure of the potatoes. It was mainly though not exclusively from the medium-sized crofts that the reports came of increasing grain cultivation and the sowing of turnips and cabbages after 1847.[64] These holdings also gained considerably from the extension to cultivated acreage which resulted from the works carried out under the auspices of the Drainage Act.[65] Again, their income did not depend solely on cattle sales. Most small tenants had a few sheep on their crofts but, on the whole, these were probably used to provide wool for clothing for the family. Only the bigger men, however, sold sheep regularly in the market in significant numbers. The average price for sheep sold at market in 1851 varied between 7s. and 9s. depending on age, sex and breed, compared with over £2 per beast for marketable black cattle.[66] Even in the depressed demand conditions for cattle in the 1840s it still required the sale of six to eight sheep to equal the return from one cow. Because of this, only tenants with a fairly large sheep stock could take full advantage of the sharp increase in wool and mutton prices which occurred during the famine years. The middling crofters in the Western Highlands were often in this fortunate position. In Snizort (Skye) a tenant with an £8 holding had eight sheep; in Sorne (Mull), a small tenant paying rental of £9.10s. per annum had twenty sheep; in the township of Bernisdale (Skye) there were 105 cows and followers but 150 sheep in 1851.[67] The view that the crofting class as a whole lost out as sheep prices rose and pastoral farms expanded must be qualified in the case of those who possessed slightly bigger holdings than the majority of their fellows.

It would not be too much therefore to speculate that the famine, in the short term at least, may well have increased economic and social differentiation within the crofting community. No group within the crofter or cottar class could remain entirely insulated from the crisis. But some survived better than others. The condition of the poorest deteriorated dramatically, and for a time in 1846 and 1847, and perhaps also in the early 1850s, they were directly exposed to the dangers of starvation and the threat of disease. On the other hand, the position of the less deprived middle ranks of the small tenantry and several of the fishing communities was consolidated both by their resilience during the famine and by the landlord attempt to get rid of more marginal elements on their estates and control subdivision of holdings thereafter.

3

In broad terms, the period after the end of the potato famine was one of both recovery and considerable change. The purpose of the final two sections of this chapter is to describe these developments, explain them and evaluate their significance.

It was in early 1856, after a full decade of misery, that the first optimistic reports began to appear about Highland conditions in the Scottish press. In that year the *Inverness Advertiser* described how more people were at work in the south and east at 'remunerating wages' and, more significantly, that 'the potato crop succeeded better this year than it did in previous years'.[68] The following year, in western Inverness-shire, '. . . for years there has not been so sound a crop of potatoes'.[69] Very quickly potatoes once more became an important item in the diet of the people. In the early 1870s it could be said '. . . in the Western Isles, potatoes form the principal crop . . . the islanders plant potatoes in all kinds of land. Potatoes and fish constitute the chief dietary of the West Highlanders and Skyemen'.[70] The importance of potatoes in Sutherland was also emphasised a decade later.[71]

But these comments give a false impression of total continuity. The potato remained significant but never again recovered the dominance in the Highland diet which it had attained in the decades before 1846. The exact extent of the change cannot be measured because the Agricultural Statistics which were gathered from the 1850s do not contain returns from occupiers of land of less than £20 annual rental and so do not provide information on the cropping structures of the vast majority of holdings in the Western Highlands and Islands. But there is abundant literary evidence by the 1870s of altered dietary habits in the region. There was a very marked increase in the consumption of imported meal. So significant was this that it became common practice to feed the indigenous grain crop and part of the potato crop to the cattle to sustain them during the winter months while reserving imported meal for human consumption.[72] There was an equally important expansion in the purchase of tea, sugar, jam and tobacco. Until the 1850s these articles were rare and expensive luxuries. By the 1880s tea drinking had become universal in the crofting districts and a familiar part of the domestic way of life.[73]

These alterations in diet were the most obvious manifestations of more fundamental changes in the nature of crofting society in the aftermath of the famine. To some extent, the declining significance of the potato may have reflected the relaxation of population pressure in some districts as emigration persisted and the ranks of the cottar class were thinned in most localities outside the Long Island. But the new dietary patterns were also to be found in the Outer Hebrides where the old problems of population congestion and land hunger remained. The more varied diet, in fact, was simply one part of a wider and deeper social transition which affected *all* areas. In the 1870s and 1880s the majority of the population of the Western Highlands became less dependent on the land for survival and even more reliant on the two sources of income and employment, fishing and temporary migration, which had proved most resilient during the famine itself. They entered more fully into the cash economy, selling their labour for cash wages and buying more of the necessities of life with their earnings rather than producing them themselves.[74]

Manufactured clothes and shoes, 'shop produce' as they were known in the region, steadily replaced the home-made varieties in the two generations after the famine.[75] A new mechanism of credit facilitated these developments. Shopkeepers, merchants and fish curers supplied credit on which meal and clothes were bought until seasonal earnings from fishing and temporary migration became available.[76] The running accounts were then partly paid off on the basis of these returns but more often than not the debts persisted from year to year. In Strath in Skye, 'Every man is in a hurry to get the spring work past and be off to his work on sea and land all through the kingdom and when they return, if their earnings have succeeded well, they pay the shop, and the shopman supplies them on credit, as they require it'.[77] In Lewis, the fishing crews purchased on credit in the curers' shops the meal, clothing and other necessities required for their families. Settlement took place at the end of the season; fishermen were credited with the price of fish delivered by them to the curers and were debited with the price of their purchases.[78]

The entire structure depended ultimately on five factors: the recovery of the prices gained for Highland black cattle; a steep fall in world grain prices in the 1870s and 1880s; a revolutionary expansion in steam navigation in the Western Highlands; the growth of the indigenous fishing industry; and a further increase in the scale of temporary migration and casual employment. These particular influences need also to be viewed against the longer perspective of the decisive change in the economic circumstances of the West Highland population which took place from the later 1850s and continued into the 1860s and 1870s. The period from the end of the Napoleonic Wars to the potato famine had been one of contracting income and falling employment opportunities. The three decades after the crisis saw a significant recovery in both earnings and jobs which was not wholly offset by either rising costs or new demographic pressures. Even given the important qualifications which will be entered below when living standards are considered in more detail, there had been a relative improvement in circumstances.[79]

Price trends, between the 1850s and the 1870s, were to the advantage of the people in the crofting region. This was a dramatic reversal of the pattern before 1846. Cattle prices continued the recovery which had begun in 1852. Crofters' stirks in Lewis selling at 30s. to £2 in 1854 fetched £4 to £5 in 1883.[80] Those small tenants who possessed sheep stocks gained from the upward swing in prices which lasted until the late 1860s.[81] The fact that they were much better fed on grain and potatoes during the winter months added to the marketability of cattle. The principal aim was now one of maximising the potential of stock not simply in the traditional manner to pay rent but as a source of the funds employed to purchase meal and other commodities.

A further expansion in sea transport facilitated both cattle and sheep exports and grain imports. In the early 1850s a single small steamer plied the route between the Clyde and Portree once a fortnight. Three decades later two larger vessels sailed to Skye and Lewis every week and a further three ships visited Barra and North and South Uist.[82] These developments in communications were both cause and effect of the changing way of life in the region and the basis of the close involvement of the people in the money economy. Above all, they allowed the population of more areas to take full advantage of the sustained fall in world grain prices which took place after the opening up of the interior areas of North America by railroad and the new steamship connections established with purchasing countries in Europe. In the early 1840s meal imported from the Clyde sold at an average of £2.2s. per boll in the Outer Hebrides; by the 1880s, average prices were close to 16s. per boll.[83] It was the enormous decline in costs which encouraged the practice of feeding cattle on grain produced at home and allowed earnings from cattle sales and other activities to be devoted to the purchase of cheap meal from outside.

Pivotal to the whole system of increased trade, credit and money transactions was a vast expansion in seasonal employment opportunities. The indigenous white and herring fisheries of the Outer Hebrides achieved a new level of activity and prosperity. Fishing stations were set up at Castlebay, Lochboisdale and Lochmaddy. The number of fish curers increased from seven in 1853 to fifty in 1880. In the early 1850s about 300 small boats were active; three decades later around 600.[84] The organisation and capitalisation of the industry were dominated by men from the east coast but the Hebrideans gained from the new opportunities for seasonal employment. The developing steamer services and the injection of capital from the east had given the winter white fishery in particular a fresh and vigorous stimulus. Casual jobs were also available on the sporting estates as stalkers and ghillies and in the labour squads needed to build the infrastructure of roads and lodges required by the recreation economy.[85] There were seasonal opportunities, too, in sheep smearing which involved working a mixture of butter, tar and grease into the fleece to afford protection against vermin: 'Since one man could only smear about twenty sheep a day and since a quarter of a million were annually smeared in Inverness-shire alone, labour was obviously much in demand. . . During the 1860s and 1870s the wages paid for casual labour of this type rose steadily and more or less doubled between 1850 and 1880.'[86]

Finally, the expansion in temporary migration which had begun during the famine was sustained after it.[87] Virtually all sectors, agricultural work in the Lowlands, domestic service in the cities, the merchant marine, general labouring (such as in the gasworks of the larger towns), produced more opportunities for Highland temporary migrants than before. Because of this, 'seasonal' migration more often became 'temporary' movement with absences extending not simply for a few weeks or month but for the greater part of a year or even longer. The seasonality of different work peaks made it possible to dovetail different tasks outside the Highlands and at the same time alternate labour in the crofting region with work opportunities elsewhere. The classical example of the latter cycle was the interrelationship between the winter white fishery in the Minch, the spring herring fishery in the same waters and the east-coast herring fishery during the summer months. This last was the most dynamic sector and the source of a great stream of income which percolated the entire Inner and Outer Hebrides in the 1860s and 1870s. From 1835 to 1854 the annual average cure in Aberdeenshire and Banffshire increased moderately from 428,343 to 495,879 barrels. In the 1860s and 1870s, however, the industry boomed. The average cure rose from 602,375 barrels between 1865 and 1874 to 902,665 in the period 1875 to 1884. During the same phase the number of herring boats on the east coast grew by fifty-one per cent while the total of fishermen and boys rose by sixty per cent from 1854 to 1884. An increased field of employment opened up in consequence for the population of the Western Highlands and Islands. It was estimated that 30,000 men and women came in a great annual migration to the fishing ports up and down the east coast from the Gaelic-speaking areas of the far west. From Lewis alone 5000 were involved, or about one in five of the island's population: '. . . since 1854 the annual migration from the Lews to the east coast fishing has been steadily increasing till latterly and for a number of years back, every man and woman who was without regular employment went'. Other parts of the Hebrides with only limited connections with the east coast before the 1850s now also produced many migrants. About 500 came from Harris and it was reckoned that most of the young men of Barra also served on the east-coast boats.

4

The issue of the relationship between the famine and emigration from the Scottish Highlands in the second half of the nineteenth century has already attracted scholarly attention. In their study of population history, M.W. Flinn and his colleagues described the crisis as 'the climacteric of the social history of the Hebrides and western Highlands in modern times' and argued that it precipitated a permanent decline in the number of inhabitants in the region.[88] They outlined the process by which the potato had limited the scale of outward movement before 1846, but with its failure '. . . the sheer weight of numbers finally broke the dam, releasing the flood-waters of renewed emigration'. They went further and explored the dynamics of the sustained fall in population after 1851.[89] Emigration had a knock-on effect because it reduced the rate of natural increase by slowing down the rate of marriage. The Flinn team argued that most migrants were single adult males and, when they left, a chronic imbalance inevitably built up between the number of men and women in the marriageable age groups. The sex ratio – the number of males per 100 females – became distorted. As a result, Highland women, in relation to the Scottish norm, tended to marry little and late. Once married, however, Highland females were no less fertile than their counterparts elsewhere in Scotland. The key factor reducing the rate of natural increase was the lower incidence of marriage which was itself induced by heavy male migration. In sum, the thesis advanced by Professor Flinn and his colleagues suggests that the famine was a great turning-point in West Highland demographic history, causing a huge and sustained increase in emigration, which then accelerated the decline in population by further reducing the marriage rate and so the rate of natural increase.

The analysis in this volume suggests a different interpretation. If the crofting region is considered as a whole, numbers did rise to 1841 and declined thereafter. Yet it is not possible on the basis of this evidence alone to see the famine as a 'climacteric' and the cause of an *inevitable* decline in population thereafter. The detailed analysis carried out in Chapters 3 and 8 demonstrated that the subsistence crisis gave a new impetus to an existing trend of heavy emigration. In addition, the discussion outlined the existence of three relatively coherent demographic zones within the Western Highlands and Islands: (i) Sutherland; (ii) Wester Ross, some parishes in western Inverness-shire and most of the Inner Hebrides; (iii) the Outer Hebrides. More people left Sutherland in the 1820s and 1830s than in the famine decades. Zone (ii) fits the Flinn argument best. Forty-four of the forty-six parishes in the region achieved their peak populations by 1851. The demographic history of zone (iii) is, however, in direct conflict with the thesis. All parishes in the Outer Hebrides experienced a great haemorrhage of people during the famine but most recovered and continued to increase in population until the early twentieth century. The example of the Long Island suggests a central weakness in the Flinn approach. Many of the parishes there suffered more grievously than other districts during the crisis and lost more of their inhabitants between 1846 and 1856 than most areas in the crofting region. But the case of the Outer Hebrides demonstrates that the mere fact of large-scale emigration did not in itself automatically result in long-term decline in population. This implies that the close and inevitable link described by Flinn *et al* between migration, sex ratios, marriage rates, natural increase and permanent decline is at least questionable. In 1861 the crude birthrate (live births per 1000 of the population) was 36.7 for Scotland as a whole. The pattern in the Outer Hebrides was very close to the Scottish norm. Lewis had a crude birthrate of 35.1, Barra 33.9 and South Uist 31.3.

The assumptions of a close correspondence elsewhere in the Highlands between emigration, sex ratios and marriage is also doubtful. Sex ratios were indeed very distorted in some Highland areas and in most parishes in the single county of Sutherland. In Farr in Sutherland, for instance, there were only 43 men for every 100 women in the age group 20 to 29 in 1841, in Clyne, 64, in Lairg, 56 and in Rogart, 48. Examples can also be found of equally distorted ratios in parishes outside Sutherland such as Urquhart, Lochalsh and Applecross. These had sex ratios for the 20 to 29 age group in 1861 of 59, 69 and 62 respectively. It must be remembered, however, that the census always underestimated the number of permanent residents because of temporary migration which was already underway at the time of the year when the count was taken. There is the strong probability that many younger males were not recorded as residents simply because they happened to be working elsewhere during the spring and summer before returning home for the winter months.

But even if the census figures are taken at their face value, the premise that sex ratios in the Highland counties *as a whole* were peculiarly imbalanced is unconvincing. In 1861 the ratio of males per 100 females in the crucial age group, 25 to 29, for the Highland counties and Scotland was virtually identical at around 76. In 1871 the Highland ratio stood at 78 while the Scottish average rose to 83. But in 1881, 1891 and 1901 the Highland ratio was consistently more favourable than the Scottish norm (92 to 90; 88 to 87; 101 to 90). Table 12.2 provides a closer perspective on twenty-three districts in the Western Highlands and Islands. It suggests that, on average, the regional sex ratio was not unusually distorted, despite the heavy emigration of the famine decades. In 1861 the Scottish ratio for the age group, 20 to 29, was 76. Seventeen of the twenty-three districts in Table 12.2 had either a similar or a more favourable ratio than this.

Table 12.2. Sex Ratio (Males per 100 Females): Selected West Highland Parishes and Districts, 1841 and 1861

Parish	0-9	0-19	20-29	Age 30-39	40-49	50-59	60+
Assynt	94.2	108.7	81.5	81.8	75.0	92.2	75.5
	113.5	92.9	75.5	82.9	89.5	86.3	80.5
Clyne	100.5	89.4	64.3	65.1	68.1	49.5	89.5
	115.7	92.7	82.3	68.0	79.8	72.3	51.3
Durness	109.5	100.9	83.8	113.0	76.1	100.0	67.7
	89.4	112.5	92.5	84.8	75.0	84.9	73.9

The Great Highland Famine

Parish	Age						
	0-9	10-19	20-29	30-39	40-49	50-59	60+
Edderachillis	119.8	98.9	80.4	100.0	73.6	60.0	57.3
	102.2	102.8	89.0	102.2	81.2	121.1	66.0
Farr	94.0	112.1	43.0	54.6	77.9	56.7	74.1
	97.6	86.7	42.6	62.7	66.7	53.0	69.6
Lairg	117.7	102.8	56.5	83.1	76.0	57.6	65.4
	112.8	113.0	69.6	74.6	69.2	90.6	63.0
Loth	101.3	91.2	73.6	75.1	88.2	72.2	74.6
	133.9	84.0	85.4	77.5	55.6	88.9	66.7
Rogart	113.0	91.4	48.4	52.6	87.7	75.8	63.9
	123.0	85.4	82.6	60.7	64.5	82.6	79.1
Tongue	104.1	102.2	61.3	75.5	60.6	71.6	74.6
	100.0	107.2	48.7	59.0	72.3	87.8	58.9
Sutherland average	103.3	100.1	67.0	74.5	75.2	70.3	72.3
(as above)	107.5	96.5	69.9	73.3	75.3	81.0	67.5
Mull	104.6	105.8	113.0	92.6	88.9	72.4	87.7
	104.3	105.9	114.3	85.7	85.8	99.3	80.4
Coll & Tiree	101.7	102.0	92.0	94.6	83.8	67.0	109.4
	121.0	96.9	85.8	83.6	93.2	110.1	79.4
Argyll average	103.8	104.9	92.7	93.1	87.7	71.2	92.0
(as above)	109.8	102.5	102.3	84.9	88.3	103.4	80.1
Ardnamurchan	105.9	102.7	85.0	95.4	89.7	80.1	83.3
	109.3	93.4	99.8	81.4	85.2	105.9	80.6
Glenelg	106.5	118.9	75.4	82.4	72.9	102.5	65.9
	84.8	96.4	79.9	84.9	83.5	91.4	62.8
Kilmallie	107.6	101.6	108.3	95.6	82.2	80.4	73.0
	97.7	107.6	78.6	65.3	83.1	98.5	73.9
Kilmorach	117.2	87.1	77.2	76.1	76.5	76.1	59.0
	102.8	91.9	85.5	66.5	99.3	76.4	79.9
Kiltarlity	102.1	94.1	69.1	78.0	86.5	69.6	89.0
	94.7	94.6	93.2	90.3	68.1	89.7	80.7
Urquhart &	102.8	93.3	70.9	73.5	70.0	66.7	74.0
Glenmorriston	103.6	108.0	70.5	58.9	67.4	76.7	60.4
Islands	101.8	92.9	73.4	81.7	85.5	79.9	84.5
	101.2	97.6	74.7	77.2	82.6	84.9	78.4
Inverness-shire average	103.5	95.2	77.4	83.9	84.4	80.1	80.1
(as above)	101.2	98.0	78.9	76.7	82.3	87.3	77.5
Applecross	95.6	99.0	90.6	75.4	84.1	91.3	113.4
	93.3	108.1	69.2	80.0	90.5	82.2	75.4
Gairloch	97.1	97.9	88.2	85.2	102.4	88.9	84.1
	99.2	107.2	74.2	84.3	93.8	96.9	83.7
Lochalsh	101.5	98.3	75.9	90.8	78.9	61.8	82.0
	110.5	88.6	62.4	63.0	71.6	100.0	66.7
Lochbroom	112.7	100.0	78.8	99.0	88.7	80.2	84.3
	115.2	91.9	87.9	90.1	89.6	82.9	86.9
Lewis	111.0	103.7	70.2	85.0	88.3	81.7	70.2
	98.2	97.3	82.6	85.1	85.1	88.3	77.9
Ross average	107.3	101.4	76.5	86.6	89.2	81.3	78.4
(as above)	100.7	98.0	79.9	83.6	86.5	89.1	78.9

Sources: Census and RGS.

This result is hardly surprising. Earlier chapters have shown that much assisted emigration during the famine occurred in family parties and was not simply biased towards single male emigrants. The Highland and Island Emigration Society, indeed, specifically tried to support the passage of single females to Australia as well as family groups.[90] There was also a significant and probably increasing demand for female domestic servants from the Western Highlands in the Lowland towns. In the residential districts of the west end of Glasgow, around Park Circus and Kelvinside, the majority of female domestic servants were from the Highland counties.[91] In Greenock, in the second half of the nineteenth century, around a quarter of the women engaged in private households were of Highland origin, the largest single group from any migrant area.[92] The minister of Tobermory in Mull asserted that more young women than men went south for work from his area.[93] Many witnesses questioned by Sir John McNeill in 1851 also drew attention to the outward flow of single females.[94] The argument that migration from the Highland counties as a whole was consistently and generally associated mainly with males to such an extent as to uniquely distort the regional sex ratio remains unproven.

There is, however, another hypothesis which at least has the merit of fitting the regional variation in migration trends more closely. The example of the Outer Hebrides shows that the heavy famine emigrations did not guarantee permanent decline in population. Yet, many districts on the western mainland and the Inner Hebrides did experience a continuous fall in the number of their inhabitants after 1851. The Flinn thesis might help to explain why some areas responded in this way. But it cannot answer the question why rising population occurred in some insular districts and falling population in others in the second half of the nineteenth century. One factor, however, which did differentiate such areas was the varying significance of the controls over subdivision of holdings. Evidence has been submitted earlier in this chapter of a marked increase in the effective implementation of these measures during and after the famine.[95] What requires to be stressed is that the practice *varied* very considerably between estates. There was often an interesting correlation between control and declining population in some areas and lax regulation and increasing numbers in others.

Three particular pieces of evidence are suggestive. First, there seems to have been a much greater reluctance to impose stringent regulation of subdivision in most parishes of the Outer Hebrides. It is not possible in the current state of knowledge to be certain about the reasons for this. Perhaps the boom in the local white fishery from the later 1850s and the increasing scale of temporary migration to the east coast herring fishery allowed the land to carry more people who could be supported by non-agricultural earnings. Landlords, therefore, may have been more willing to tolerate subdivision because it increased the fishing labour force and hence rental income. However, the existence of more relaxed attitudes is more significant to this analysis than the reasons why they came about. In Harris, the estate factor conceded in the early 1880s that it was still the custom for crofters to divide their holdings among their sons when they married.[96] Controls over subdivision had apparently been enforced in Barra and South Uist after the famine but had been abandoned by the time Lady Gordon Cathcart assumed possession in 1878.[97] In Lewis, the position was slightly more complicated. Regulations existed but, as the estate factor admitted, they were universally ignored. Apparently the estate officials were convinced of the need to enforce them but they '. . . could not prevail upon the proprietor in spite of that'. Thus, in the Ness district, for example, it remained the custom at marriage to obtain a sublet of the paternal croft.[98]

Second, the island of North Uist had a distinctive demographic history within the context of the Outer Hebrides as a whole. Unlike neighbouring parishes, it attained its maximum population as early as 1821 and did not experience the same recovery in numbers after 1851. The island was also exceptional in the resolute policy of land consolidation and regulation of subdivision which was adopted by successive proprietors. In 1830 there were 429 separate croft holdings in North Uist. By 1853 the number had contracted by about forty per cent to 283 and subdivision was outlawed.[99] The economy of the island, to a much greater extent than most of the other districts in the Outer Hebrides, was devoted to sheep-farming.[100] The example of North Uist is a compelling instance of the impact of subdivision controls on insular demographic history.

Third, a comparison of the population structures of two island parishes, Kilfinichen in Mull and Barvas in Lewis, reveals some interesting patterns. Barvas' population rose again after 1861 and subdivision regulations were apparently ineffective. The number of people in Kilfinichen fell consistently after the famine and the Argyll estate, which owned most of the land in the parish, adopted a policy of consolidation and prevention of subletting.[101] The enumerators' returns for the two parishes were examined for the census years 1841, 1851 and 1861. Because of the proliferation of certain names in each parish, identification was based on the name and age of household heads and the ages of their children. Having identified the family, it was then possible to follow its progress over the three censuses, recognise 'new' households and document losses of existing households. Perfect accuracy cannot be claimed for the exercise although in the majority of cases the families are unmistakable. Those very few households which consisted entirely of young fishermen, farmworkers or ordnance survey personnel have been excluded. This produces a slight discrepancy between the figures cited below and those contained in the published census. In addition, nephews and nieces of heads of households living with them have not been included in the tabulation of 'offspring'. Where there was an elderly couple or parent in a house with a young couple, the latter have been counted as heads of household. This is necessary in order to monitor the extent of 'informal' subdivision which could have occurred without the specific creation of a 'household' living separately from the home of the original family.

Table 12.3 enumerates the number of households 'lost' either through migration or mortality. Previous discussion has indicated that there was no sustained increase in death rates during the famine, so mortality among heads of household was probably concentrated among the higher age groups. It is also unlikely that temporary migration can explain the disappearance of entire households with heads in the age group, 20 to 49. The main purpose of this form of migration was actually to maintain the family in the holding through the income earned by members elsewhere. When the evidence is examined with these points in mind it becomes apparent that both parishes lost heavily by out-migration but Kilfinichen did so to a greater extent than Barvas.

Table 12.3. *Percentage of All Households 'lost' by Age of Head, Kilfinichen (Mull) and Barvas (Lewis), 1841, 1851, 1861*

Age	K 20 — 29	B	K 30 — 49	B	K 50 — 59	B	K 60+	B	K Total	B
1841-1851	5.7	17.6	20.2	18.0	8.2	15.4	11.8	48.5	45.5	24.4
1851-1861	4.6	26.7	17.2	24.7	7.1	28.6	14.7	28.5	43.6	26.5

Source: GRO, Enumerators' Schedules, Barvas and Kilfinichen, 1841, 1851, 1861.
Note: Kilfinichen excludes Iona but includes Fidden and Kentra districts.

The response to these losses in the two parishes is the central issue here. New households were formed in both. But as Table 12.4 demonstrates, there was little discernible difference between the two parishes in the average number of children in these new families in 1861. Growth in one and decline in the other cannot be attributed to variations in natural increase.

Table 12.4. *Average Number of Offspring, New Households, Kilfinichen (Mull) and Barvas (Lewis), 1861*

Age	0 – 10	0 – 14	10 – 25
Kilfinichen	1.9	2.3	2.9
Barvas	2.1	2.4	2.8

Source: GRO, Enumerators' Schedules, Barvas and Kilfinichen, 1841, 1851, 1861.

A similar pattern is apparent in Table 12.5, which lists the average number of offspring for all households over the entire period, 1841 to 1861. Only in the age group, 0 – 10, is there a discernible difference, with the Barvas average showing a slight increase, while in Kilfinichen there is a marginal decline over the two decades.

Table 12.5. *Average Number of Offspring per Household, Kilfinichen (Mull) and Barvas (Lewis), 1841-1861*

Children aged	K 0 — 10	B	K 0 — 14	B	K 10 — 25	B
1841	2.0	1.7	2.5	2.2	3.3	3.0
1851	1.5	1.4	2.1	2.0	2.8	3.1
1861	1.7	1.9	2.3	2.2	3.1	3.1

Source: GRO, Enumerators' Schedules, Barvas and Kilfinichen, 1841, 1851, 1861.

The main distinction, therefore, between the two parishes is not in the number of children conceived *within* marriage but in the number of *additions* to total households. If the difference between new households and households 'lost' is calculated, a striking contrast emerges. In Barvas, there was a net expansion in the number of households by 8.2 per cent between 1841 and 1851 and a further addition of 5.8 per cent in the following decade. However, Kilfinichen experienced a net contraction in the number of households by 13.6 per cent, 1841 to 1851, and 11.1 per cent between 1851 and 1861. It is not possible to prove conclusively that these differences in household formation were only due to different estate policies towards subdivision of holdings. However, it is reasonable to suggest that some connections may have existed which help to explain the long-term contrast in demographic behaviour between the parishes.

These three detailed examples provide the basis for an alternative interpretation of West Highland demographic history after the famine to that advanced by Professor Flinn and his colleagues. The people of many areas in the region did marry little and late and this was a factor accelerating the trend towards declining population. But the evidence analysed here suggests that it was not the only influence nor was it always a simple or direct consequence of an imbalance between males and females in the marriageable age groups. In many districts it may also have reflected rigorous controls over the creation of new households, constraints which in certain parishes virtually amounted to a veto on marriage itself.

But it would be folly to suggest that such a major social change can be explained solely in terms of one cause alone, no matter how significant it might have been in certain instances and areas. The same pattern of late marriage, but with little alteration in the frequency of child-bearing within marriage, has been identified in Ireland after the Great Famine. Numerous influences have been described to account for this phenomenon but one principal factor may also have a bearing on the problem under discussion here. It is argued that there was a growing conflict between actual and desired standards of life in Ireland after 1850. On the one hand, the expectations of the Irish peasantry rose but, at the same time, their living conditions, while improving *relative* to the years before the famine, remained poor by the standards of other societies: 'More than any other single factor it was the difference between desire and reality and the awesome difficulty of translating ambition into actual achievement, which prompted the rejection of marriage by so many Irish men and women'.[102] Research on the social attitudes of the Highland population in the later nineteenth century has yet to begin in a serious way and so it is impossible to tell whether similar influences were in operation in Scotland. There are, however, some interesting parallels between the two developments. Both in the Western Highlands and in parts of Ireland standards did improve relatively after 1860. Crofters, as was shown earlier in this chapter, became more accustomed to buy clothing, meal and other 'consumer' goods in the market.[103] The outbreak of the Crofters' War in the early 1880s has also been seen as a manifestation of the rising political and social aspirations of the people of the north-west. There are, therefore, enough apparent parallels to suggest that the possible linkages between changing social attitudes and altered marriage patterns in the Highlands after 1860 are a subject which should at least be placed on the research agenda.

5

The extent to which the great Highland emigrations of the famine period benefited those who remained was a question which caused much contemporary controversy. Those who supported the ambitious schemes of assisted emigration asserted that the excess population of the Western Highlands had to be drastically reduced before any long-term material improvement could take place. Others were less convinced. The *Witness* described emigration as a process which '. . . was drawing blood from an already exhausted patient'.[104] Another observer echoed more modern concerns about the social consequences of depopulation: 'The youth and the capital being drained away, and the aged, the poor, and the spiritless being left behind, the consequences must be the general sinking of the condition of the population'.[105]

At first sight, however, the evidence does not support these pessimistic conclusions. The emigration of some of the poorest classes of Highland society did allow a more rapid recovery from the trauma of the crisis than would otherwise have been the case. Cottars and squatters often placed a burden on the over-stretched resources of many crofters and this doubtless diminished when the numbers of these semi-landless people were reduced during the famine and its immediate aftermath.[106] Then, again, the period from 1856 to the later 1870s did appear to be one of considerable material progress in the Western Highlands. Apologists could argue that there was a close correlation between this amelioration and the decline in demographic pressure resulting from heavy migration. Crofting rents on several estates were paid more regularly than before.[107] Consumer goods were imported on a much larger scale. The gathering of shellfish for consumption during the summer months, a practice which had long been one of the principal manifestations of the chronic poverty of the region, seems to have declined though it retained its importance as a source of cash income into the second half of the twentieth century.[108] Numerous contemporary commentators who could recall the deprivation of earlier times were also sure that considerable improvement had taken place in the decades which followed the famine.[109] Even the great crofting agitation of the 1880s can be regarded as a revolt which derived in part from frustrated expectations. The generation of that decade had experienced several years of marginally improving standards which were then threatened by the poor harvests of 1881-2 and the collapse in earnings from temporary migration after 1883.

Two points are reasonably clear. First, in the short run, the famine emigrations because of the social composition of the emigrant parties helped recovery. Second, there was a relative improvement in material standards for much of the period after the effect of the famine receded. What is in dispute is the extent of this amelioration and whether it was mainly caused by a continuation of heavy rates of emigration. On both issues there is considerable uncertainty.

The majority of the inhabitants of the region continued to endure an existence of poverty and insecurity after 1860. Despite relative improvement, life was still precarious and could easily degenerate into destitution if any of the fragile supports of the population temporarily crumbled. Between 1856 and 1890 there was a series of bad seasons which recalled some of the worst years of the potato blight. In 1864, 'the cry of destitution in Skye has been as loud as ever and yet from no part of the Highlands has there been a more extensive emigration'.[110] Conditions in Mull were at that time also briefly reminiscent of the tragic days of the 1840s. On the Duke of Argyll's estate there was a rapid increase in arrears especially among the small tenants and cottars. Food, seed and labour had to be provided for the people who had suffered great hardship since 1862.[111] Four years later distress was again experienced by the population of an island which had sustained a decline in the numbers of its inhabitants from 10,054 to 7,240 between 1841 and 1861. In the Bunessan area, 'many of the poor are actually starving'. Once again meal was made available and public works started.[112] It was successive bad seasons in 1881-2, affecting the whole of the Western Highlands, which not only produced much social suffering but also provided the initial economic impetus for the great crofters' revolt of that decade. Over 24,000 people received relief in these years.[113] Conditions deteriorated once more in 1888. In the Outer Hebrides 'actual starvation' was predicted and the inhabitants once more were supported by charitable organisations from the Lowland cities.[114] The chamberlain of the Lewis estate himself estimated that there had been at least nine seasons between 1853 and 1883 when the proprietor had had to advance varying amounts of seed and meal to the crofters.[115]

At best, then, 'recovery' was modest and was interrupted by years of considerable distress. Typhus remained common in some localities because of poor living conditions and poor sanitation.[116] Cattle continued to share living accommodation with human beings.[117] Domestic squalor persisted and continued to disconcert observers from outside the Highlands. Mass clearances were a thing of the past but insecurity of tenure remained a fact of life: 'Others, not a few, continue quietly evicting by legal process and clearing by so-called voluntary emigration. The lawyer's pen supersedes the soldier's steel.'[118]

In addition, the loss of people was not necessarily the primary cause of such relative improvements as did take place. In the long run, emigration could only be of fundamental benefit if the holdings vacated by the emigrants were redistributed among those who remained. But earlier discussion in this chapter showed that with only some exceptions most of the lands belonging to emigrants were absorbed within the bigger pastoral farms.[119] There is some evidence, indeed, in parts of the Outer Hebrides, that the emigration schemes sometimes increased congestion. Those who were cleared but did not accept assisted passage were moved into overcrowded townships.[120] The example of Tiree, where material improvement was made possible by a combined strategy of emigration, consolidation and redistribution, seems to have been exceptional. The premise of an automatic link between migration, population decline and relative advance in material standards can also be questioned in the case of the Long Island. Most communities there shared in the relative amelioration of the later 1850s, 1860s and 1870s, but this was achieved *in spite of the fact* that population continued to rise and subdivision of land remained endemic. The example of the Outer Hebrides implies that the critical factors in material progress were not depopulation as such but the availability of opportunities of employment, the reduction in the cost of meal and the rise in the price of cattle which took place in the 1860s and 1870s. The condition of the people of the Western Highlands was primarily influenced by the market for labour, whether in the home fishery or in the Lowland economy, and not in the long run by changing patterns of emigration. This was hardly surprising. Those who promoted the 'over-population' theory during the famine had argued on the basis of a false premise. The problem with the Western Highlands, then as now, was not that there were too many people but too few secure economic opportunities for those who lived there.

NOTES

1. *McNeill Report*, Appendix A, *passim*.
2. Inveraray Castle, Argyll Estate Papers, Bundle 1522, John Campbell to Duke of Argyll, 18 October 1847.
3. *Ibid.*, Bundle 1805, John Campbell to Duke of Argyll, 26 April 1851.
4. *PP*, XXXIV (1847), *Return of Applications under the Drainage Act*; SRO, HD7/33, Papers relating to the Drainage of Land Act (1847) including returns. See also Appendix 6, Highland Applications under the Drainage Act, 1846-7.
5. *N.C.*, 783, Q.12229.
6. *McNeill Report*, Appendix A, 60.
7. SRO, Campbell of Jura Papers, GD64/1/347, Report to the Creditors of W.F. Campbell of Islay.
8. *McNeill Report*, Appendix A, 36.
9. See above, pp.138-40.
10. See above, p.104.
11. W. Orr, *Deer Forests, Landlords and Crofters: the Western Highlands in Victorian and Edwardian Times* (Edinburgh, 1982).
12. *McNeill Report*, Appendix A, 82.
13. Inveraray Castle, Estate Papers, Bundle 1523, Arrears and Drainage Interest, Crop 1853; Bundle 897, Rental of Ross of Mull, 1858.
14. NLS, Sutherland Estate Papers, Dep. 313/2283-2303, Sutherland Small Tenant Rentals, 1836-55.
15. SRO, Lord Macdonald Papers, GD221/46, Charge and Discharge, Skye estates, 1849-57.
16. *McNeill Report*, Appendix A, 21, 46, 65; MS. Diary of J.M. Mackenzie, 1851; Inveraray Castle, Argyll Estate Papers, Bundle 1522, J. Campbell to Duke of Argyll, 21 August 1848.
17. See above, pp.201-4.
18. SRO, Riddell Papers, AF 49, Report of T.G. Dickson for Trustees, 1852; SRO, Campbell of Jura Papers, GX64/1/347, Report to Creditors of W.F. Campbell of Islay; SRO, Lord Macdonald Papers, GD221/43, Report by Mr. Ballingall for Mr. Brown, 1851.
19. *McNeill Report*, Appendix A, 80-1; *N.C.*, 1863, Q.28980; MS. Diary of J.M. Mackenzie, 1851.
20. Inveraray Castle, Argyll Estate Papers, Bundle 1853, J. Campbell to Duke of Argyll, 25 April 1854.
21. See Appendix 3 for details.
22. See Appendix 2 for details.
23. *Inverness Advertiser*, 29 January 1856; SRO, HD4/4, Sir Charles Trevelyan to Sir John McNeill, 18 March 1856.
24. Inveraray Castle, Argyll Estate Papers, Bundle 1804, J. Campbell to Duke of Argyll, 19 December 1850; Bundle 1805, Campbell to Duke, 18 March 1851.
25. *PP*, XXVI (1850), XXIII (1852), L (1852-3), XXIX (1854), XLV (1854-5, *Annual Reports of the Board of Supervision for Relief of the Poor in Scotland*.
26. See above, pp.21-5.
27. See, for example, SRO, Lord Macdonald Papers, GD221/43, Report by Mr. Ballingall for Mr. Brown, 1851; SRO, Riddell Papers, AF 49, Report by T.G. Dickson for Trustees, 1852.
28. SRO, Lord Macdonald Papers, GD221/122-123.
29. NLS, Sutherland Estate Papers, Dep. 313/2283-2302, Sutherland Small Tenant Rentals, 1836-55.
30. J. Macdonald, 'On the Agriculture of the County of Sutherland', *Trans. Highland and Agricultural Society*, 4th series, XII (1880), 50.

31. D. Clerk, 'On the Agriculture of the County of Argyll', *Trans. Highland and Agricultural Society*, 4th series, X (1878), 64.

32. *McNeill Report*, Appendix A, 114-115.

33. *N.C.*, 223, Q.4225.

34. Orr, *Deer Forests, Landlords and Crofters*, 12-24.

35. *Trans. of the Highland and Agricultural Society*, 1921. See also Tables 4.1 and 4.2. above, pp.93-5.

36. See above, p.22.

37. See above, p.291-2.

38. Rev. Eric J. Findlater, *Highland Clearances: the Real Cause of Highland Famines* (Edinburgh, 1855), 9.

39. *N.C.*, 2891, Q.42732.

40. *Ibid.*, 2083, Q.32793.

41. Somers, *Letters from the Highlands*, 124-5; Achnacarry Castle, Cameron of Lochiel Papers, Attic Chest, R.H. Top Drawer, Bundle 15, E. Cameron to Lochiel, 7 November 1846; 26 March 1847; Letter of Agreement from Achintore crofters, 1 March 1847.

42. *McNeill Report*, XXVI.

43. Clerk, 'Agriculture of Argyll', 95.

44. Duke of Argyll, *Crofts and Farms*, 23.

45. *N.C.*, 2217, QQ.35050, 35057.

46. *Ibid.*, 2004, Q.31403

47. *Ibid.*, 480; PRO, T1/4201, R. Grahame to Fox Maule, 6 April 1837.

48. *Ibid.*, 343, Q.6169.

49. *N.C.*, 12-13.

50. *Destitution Papers*, Twelfth Report of Glasgow Section (1849), Appendix B, 13-20; *McNeill Report*, Appendix A, 13-14, 48, 59, 67; *Inverness Courier*, 13 February 1851.

51. *Glasgow Herald*, 18 September 1846; *Witness*, 21 November 1846; *Destitution Papers*, Second Statement of Destitution Committee of the Free Church, 16.

52. *McNeill Report*, Appendix A, 7, 45, 112.

53. *Destitution Papers*, Report on the Outer Hebrides (1849), 41.

54. *Glasgow Herald*, 18 September 1846.

55. *McNeill Report*, Appendix A, 11; *PP*, XXXIII (1852), *Papers Relative to Emigration*, A.C. Buchanan to Earl Grey, 31 December 1851.

56. *McNeill Report*, Appendix A, 62.

57. See Appendix 3.

58. *Witness*, 6 October 1847; *North British Daily Mail*, 7 July 1847; *Inverness Courier*, 3 July 1851; *Destitution Papers*, Report on the Outer Hebrides 1849), 9.

59. *McNeill Report*, Appendix A, 25.

60. *Ibid.*, 43, 45, 128.

61. See above, pp.7-9.

62. SRO, HD6/2, Treasury Correspondence, Sir E. Coffin to Sir Charles Trevelyan, 28 September 1847.

63. See above, pp.213-14.

64. SRO, HD6/2, Treasury Correspondence, ff. 233, 272-4; *McNeill Report*, Appendix A, 7, 17; *Destitution Papers*, Tenth Report of Glasgow Section (1848), *passim*.

65. SRO, HD6/2, Treasury Correspondence, ff. 234, 238; *Destitution Papers*, Eighth Report of Glasgow Section (1848), Extract from Mr. Kennedy's Reports.

66. *McNeill Report*, Appendix A, 84.

67. *Ibid.*, 47, 65, 48.

68. *Inverness Advertiser*, 29 January 1856.

69. 'Agricultural Statistics of Scotland, 1857', *Trans. Highland and Agricultural Society*, new ser. (1857-9), 203.

70. W. Macdonald, 'On the Agriculture of Inverness-shire', *Trans. Highland and Agricultural Society*, IV, 4th series (1872), 40.

71. J. Macdonald, 'On the Agriculture of the County of Sutherland', *Trans. Highland and Agricultural Society*, XII, 4th series (1880), 58.

72. *N.C.*, 746, Q.11764; 779; 885, Q.13791.

73. Hunter, *Crofting Community*, 114, 118.

74. Devine, 'Temporary Migration', 344-59.

75. *N.C.*, 43-6, 53.

76. *PP*, C.5265 (1888), *Report on the Condition of the Cottar Population of the Lews*, 5; *N.C.*, 43-6; Devine, 'Temporary Migration', 344-59.

77. *N.C.*, 286, Q.5265.

78. *Report on the Condition of the Lews*, 5.

79. See above, pp.295-6.

80. *Report on the Condition of the Lews*, Statement of K. Smith, Fish-Curer, 36.

81. Orr, *Deer Forests, Landlords and Crofters*, 12-27.

82. *N.C.*, 3308.

83. *Report on the Condition of the Lews*, 6.

84. *Ibid., passim.*

85. Orr, *Deer Forests, Landlords and Crofters*, 107-118.

86. Hunter, *Crofting Community*, 109.

87. For detailed references to this section and subsequent paragraphs, see Devine, 'Temporary Migration', 344-59.

88. Flinn, ed., *Scottish Population History*, 438.

89. *Ibid.*, 318, 320, 327-34, 338-9, 342, 345.

90. See above, p.266.

91. I am again grateful to my postgraduate student, Mr. W. Sloan, for this information derived from his important studies of Irish and Highland migrant experience in nineteenth-century Glasgow.

92. Lobban, 'Migration of Highlanders', 136.

93. *McNeill Report*, Appendix A, 12.

94. *Ibid., passim.*

95. See above, pp.280-1.

96. *N.C.*, 861, Q.13387.

97. *Ibid.*, 659, Q.10420; 662, Q.10467.

98. *Ibid.*, 996, QQ.15484-8; 1004, QQ.15633-4.

99. SRO, Lord Macdonald Papers, GD221/21, 43, 46, 62, 70, 82. North Uist Rentals and Accounts.

100. *N.C.*, 802, Q.1294; 815-816, Q.12734.

101. Argyll, *Crofts and Farms*, 23, 71.

102. N.L. Tranter, *Population and Society, 1750-1940* (London, 1985), 120; R.E. Kennedy, *The Irish: Emigration, Marriage and Fertility* (Los Angeles, 1973).

103. See above, pp.285-6.

104. *Witness*, 26 July 1851.

105. Maclauchlan, 'Emigration and Social Conditions', 610.

106. Inveraray Castle, Argyll Estate Papers, Bundle 1805, John Campbell to Duke of Argyll, 9 July 1851.

107. *N.C.*, 46; Macdonald, 'Agriculture of Inverness', 40.

108. *N.C.*, 52; 247, Q.4685; Alasdair Maclean, *Night falls on Ardnamurchan* (London, 1984).

109. See, for example, *N.C.*, 432; 207; 1789; 3308.

110. Maclauchlan, 'Emigration and Social Conditions', 610.

111. Inveraray Castle, Argyll Estate Papers, Bundle 1763, J. Campbell to Duke of Argyll, 1 February 1864; Bundle 1764, 9 December 1862.

112. *Ibid.*, Bundle 1764, 25 February 1868.

113. *Report on the Lews*, 7.

114. *Ibid.*

115. *N.C.*, 899, Q.14026.
116. *Ibid.*, 733.
117. *Ibid.*, 732, Q.11516.
118. *Ibid.*, 195.
119. See above, pp.277-9; for some evidence of redistribution see *Witness*, 2 January 1850; *McNeill Report*, Appendix A, 127.
120. *N.C.*, 875; 880-884.

Appendices

Appendix 1: Crofting and Farming Parishes, Argyll, Inverness, Ross and Sutherland

(i) Crofting Parishes

Argyll: Ardchattan; Ardnamurchan; Arisaig and Moidart; Gigha; Glenorchy; Inverchaolin; Jura; Kilchoman; Killarow; Kildalton; Kilchrennan; Kilfinan; Kilfinichen; Kilninian; Lismore; Morvern; Tiree; Coll; Torosay.
Inverness: Barra; Bracadale; Dores; Duirnish; Glenelg; Harris; Kilmallie; Kilmonivaig; Kilmorack; Kilmuir; Kiltarlity; N. Uist; S. Uist; Portree; Sleat; Small Isles; Snizort; Strath; Urquhart.
Ross: Applecross; Barvas; Gairloch; Kintail; Lochalsh; Lochbroom; Lochcarron; Lochs; Stornoway; Uig; Glensheil.
Sutherland: Assynt; Clyne; Creich; Dornoch; Durness; Edderachillis; Farr; Kildonan; Lairg; Loth; Rogart; Tongue.

(ii) Farming Parishes

Argyll: Campbeltown; Craignish; Dunoon; Glassary; Inveraray; Kilbrandon; Kilcalmonell; Killean; Kilmodan; Kilmartin; Kilmore; Kilninver; N. Knapdale; S. Knapdale; Lochgoilhead; Sadell; Southend; Strachur.
Inverness: Ardersier; Boleskine; Cromdale; Croy; Inverness; Kingussie; Kirkhill; Laggan; Moy and Dalcross; Petty.
Ross: Alness; Avoch; Contin; Cromarty; Dingwall; Edderton; Fearn; Fodderty; Killearnan; Kilmuir Easter; Kiltearn; Kincardine; Knockbain; Logie Easter; Nigg; Resolis; Rosemarkie; Rosskean; Tain; Tarbat; Urquhart and Logie Wester; Urray.
Sutherland: Golspie.

Appendix 2: Potato Crop Reports, 1848-1856

District	Description of Crop Failure
1848	
Skye	'Renewed and continued failure'
Lewis	Complete failure anticipated
Western Highlands & Islands	General failure reported throughout the region
N. & S. Uist	Total
Morvern	¾ of crop
Mull	⅘
Harris	Same extent as 1846

District	Description of Crop Failure
1849	
Wester Ross	⅔
Mull	'Near complete failure'
West Highlands	Loss estimated at ¼ to ½
Kintail	Partial
Lewis	Almost total
S. Uist & Benbecula	Blight as severe as 1848
1850	
N. Uist	Blight present but not to same extent as previous years
Strathaird, Skye	Almost entire
Mull	Very deficient
Harris, S. Uist, Barra,	
Small Isles, Benbecula	Complete failure
Skye	¼ to ¾ depending on district
West Highlands	Blight 'to a very considerable extent'
1851	
Tiree	At least ⅓ short
Gairloch	Considerable proportion
Lewis	½
Fort William	Only to a small extent
N. Uist	Best crop since 1846
Skye	⅛ to ⅞ loss
Harris	'Poor return'
Mull	Failure greater than in 1850
1852	
Wester Ross	Almost entirely gone
Inverness	Potatoes tainted
1853	
N. Uist	Potatoes exported
Inverness & Ross	Potato exportation beginning again from certain districts
1854	
Skye	Entirely failed
N. Uist	Total failure
Western Isles	Virtually complete failure
Tiree & Mull	Potato disease very bad
1855	
Sutherland & Ross	Good crops
Argyll	'Rather a failure': ¼ of potatoes diseased
Mull, Tiree, Jura	¼ to ⅓ diseased
Western Inverness	½ to ⅓ lost
1856	
Argyll (Cowal)	¼ of crop diseased
Argyll (Inveraray, Knapdale)	Small crop
Mull	¼ to ⅓ of crop diseased
Morvern	⅓ failure
Wester Ross	⅓ to ½ diseased
Lewis	'Much diseased'

Sources: This survey has been constructed from the contemporary press, estate papers and reports of the local destitution committees and their officials. The material consulted is listed in the Bibliography. Lack of space prevents detailed referencing.

Appendix 3: *West Highland Cattle Prices, 1845–1853*

Date	Market	Prices and Remarks	Source
26 Aug. 1845	Broadford, Skye	2 yr. stirks £5 – 8.10s 1 yr. stirks £3 – 5 3 yr. heifers £5 – 7 2 yr. heifers £4 – 6	*Inverness Courier* 26 Aug. 1845
17 Sept. 1845	Falkirk tryst	Argyllshire stirks £2.5s – 4.10s (10-15s up on last year) 2 yr. stirks £4.15s – 6 (10-15s up on last year) 3 yr. stirks £7.10s – 9.11s (15-20s up on last year)	*Inverness Courier* 17 Sept. 1845
17 June 1846	Portree, Skye	'There has not been a better May market at Portree for several years back'	*Inverness Courier* 17 June 1846
15 July 1846	Lewis	2 yr. olds, £3 average. 'Prices were good' 3 yr. olds, £3.15s average	*Inverness Courier* 15 July 1846
21 Oct. 1846	Falkirk tryst	'The last Falkirk tryst, for amount of prices and extent of sales, is the best that has occurred since 1810, both for sheep and cattle'	*Inverness Courier* 21 Oct. 1846. See also *Edinburgh Evening Courant* 3 Oct. 1846
26 Sept. 1846	Sligachan, Skye	'Good demand at fair prices'	*Edinburgh Evening Courant* 26 Sept. 1846
15 Oct. 1846	Falkirk tryst	'. . . for the last 30 years there never was such a clearance effected on the first day of the market' 3 yr. heifers (Skye) £7 2 yr. heifers (Skye) £5 3 yr. West Highlands £7 2 yr. West Highlands £7	*Edinburgh Evening Courant* 15 Oct. 1846

Date	Market	Prices and Remarks	Source
11 Aug. 1847	Falkirk tryst	English buyers scarce because able to obtain cheap Irish cattle in England. 5-10 per cent reduction in Highland cattle	*Witness*, 11 Aug. 1847 *Scotsman*, 11 Aug. 1847
18 Sept. 1847	Falkirk tryst	'. . . most discouraging market for highlanders, They will suffer a loss of 15 to 25 per cent'	*Witness*, 18 Sept. 1847 *Scotsman*, 15 Sept. 1847
16 Oct. 1847	Falkirk tryst	'The small north highland beasts were entirely neglected . . . the losses sustained by north country dealers are immense'	*Witness*, 16 Oct. 1847
8 Oct. 1847	Sligachan Skye	'Prices fell considerably . . .'	*North British Daily Mail* 8 Oct. 1847
13 Sept. 1848	Falkirk tryst	'The numbers from the north were unusually short . . . upon the whole the market was a dull one'	*Scotsman*, 13 Sept. 1848
21 Sept. 1849	Portree, Skye	'Market was a very bad one . . . prices were unprecedentedly low'	*John O'Groats Journal* 21 Sept. 1849
14 Aug. 1849	Falkirk tryst	'Not a worse market for 20 years . . . it is not possible to get the small highland beasts sold at any price' 2 yr. stots (Harris) £2.-9s. 2 yr. heifers (F. William) £2.0s.	*Scotsman*, 15 Aug. 1849
12 Sept. 1849	Falkirk tryst	'About one half of the highland stock, particularly the smaller kinds, left unsold' 20 3 yr. stots from Mull £8.0s. 40 1 yr. sturks from Skye £2.5s. 40 2-3 yr. heifers from W. Highlands £5.0s. 80 2-3 yr. heifers from W. Highlands £3.10s.	*Scotsman*, 12 Sept. 1849

Date	Market	Prices and Remarks	Source
10 Oct. 1849	Falkirk tryst	'West Highland one-year-old stirks about £1 to £1.15s. below last October's prices; 2- and 3-year-old-stots, £2.10s to £3 below'	*Scotsman*, 10 Oct. 1849
4 June 1850	Portree, Skye	'Some sales were effected but at considerably lower prices than previous markets'	*Inverness Advertiser* 4 June 1850
19 Nov. 1850	Fort William	'Small cattle . . . no money offered and many left unsold'	*Ibid.*, 19 Nov. 1850
17 Aug. 1850	Falkirk tryst	'Lean cattle were very stiff to sell' 2-yr-old stots. £3 – 4 six-quarter stot stirks. £1 to £2.10s. six-quarter quey stirks £1 to £2.	*Scotsman*, 17 Aug. 1850
10 July 1851	Lewis	'Prices offered were very low and such as would not remunerate the rearers of stock'	*Inverness Courier* 10 July 1851
24 July 1851	Harris	'Such a bad one was never seen here before'	*Ibid.*, 24 July 1851
16 Aug. 1851	Falkirk tryst	Prices for highland cattle similar to those of last year	*Witness*, 16 Aug. 1851
21 Sept. 1852	Falkirk tryst	Beasts valued at £6 – £7.10s about £1.10s up on 1851. £5 beasts up about £1.5s. £4 beasts up about £1	*Inverness Advertiser* 21 Sept. 1851
19 July 1853	Lewis	Prices 'very high'	*Ibid.*, 19 July 1853
6 Sept. 1853	Portree, Skye	'High prices' for sheep and cattle	*Ibid.*, 6 Sept. 1853

Appendix 4: West Coast and Hebridean Fisheries, 1845–1849

Date	Area	Remarks	Source
17 Dec. 1845	Lochcarron (Wester Ross)	Herring fishery 'more than usually successful'. Rents all paid	*Inverness Courier* 17 Dec. 1845
14 Jan. 1846	Harris	Herring fishing 'complete failure'; cod and ling fishery adversely affected by storms	*Inverness Courier* 14 Jan. 1846
25 Feb. 1846	Loch Torridon (Wester Ross)	Cod and ling plentiful but 'people too poor to furnish lines'	*Inverness Courier* 25 Feb. 1846
28 July 1846	Gairloch (Wester Ross)	'First rate fishing . . . boats averaging 15-20 – crans of excellent quality'	*Inverness Courier* 29 July 1846
23 Sept 1846	Lochcarron	'Herrings and ling fish seem to have deserted the coast this season'	*Inverness Courier* 23 Sept. 1846
21 Oct. 1846	Lochcarron	'Hopes are blighted . . . not a single herring now in the loch'	*Inverness Courier* 7 Oct. 1846; *Glasgow Herald*, 9 Oct. 1846
6 Nov. 1846	Lochs Hourn and Glendhu	'Herrings plentiful'	*John O'Groats Journal* 6 Nov. 1846
22 Oct. 1846	Fort William	'Herring fishery unprecedentedly bad'	*The Times* 22 Oct. 1846
25 June 1846	Lewis	'Not very successful'	*Edinburgh Evening Courant* 25 June 1846
22 Aug. 1846	Skye	'As yet no appearance of a successful herring fishery'	*Edinburgh Evening Courant* 22 August 1846

Date	Area	Remarks	Source
17 Sept. 1846	West Highlands	Herring fishery 'comparatively a failure'	*Ibid.*, 17 Sept. 1846
17 Oct. 1846	Skye	'Great quantities' of herring taken on southern side of the island	*Ibid.*, 17 Oct. 1846; *Glasgow Herald*, 12 Oct. 1846
2 Nov. 1846	Loch Hourn	'Almost unprecedented and highly successful fishery . . . for several days every boat engaged'	*Glasgow Herald* 2 Nov. 1846
6 Nov. 1846	Lochcarron, Loch Glendhu	'Great quantities of herring taken'	*Glasgow Herald* 6 Nov. 1846
14 March 1846	Lewis	Good season for cod and ling off the Butt of Lewis	*Witness* 14 Mar. 1846
30 June 1847	Lochbroom	'Fishing has been backward hitherto'	*Witness* 30 June 1847
15 April 1847	West Highlands	'Cod and ling fishery prosperous this year'	*North British Daily Mail* 14 April 1847
1 July 1847	Lewis	Herring fishery only 'half the catch' of 1846	*North British Daily Mail* 1 July 1847
30 April 1847	Gairloch	Not prosecuted with much success	*John O'Groats Journal* 2 April 1847
5 Jan. 1849	Lochcarron	Herring fishery failed this season	*John O'Groats Journal* 5 Jan. 1849
1 June 1849	Lewis	Fishing 'uncommonly unproductive'	*Ibid.*, 1 June 1849

Date	Area	Remarks	Source
27 July 1849	Lochcarron	'Never in the memory of man was there such an appearance of herrings on the coast'	*Ibid.*, 27 July 1849
10 Aug. 1849	Argyllshire	'Productive . . . almost beyond remembrance'	*Ibid.*, 10 Aug. 1849
7 Sept. 1849	Shieldaig	Nearly 2,000 barrels of herring taken	*Ibid.*, 7 Sept. 1849
17 July 1849	Skye	'Herring fishing exceeds anything that has taken place for the last 40 years'	*Inverness Advertiser* 17 July 1849
7 Aug. 1849	Gairloch	'Great quantities of herring of very fine quality being caught'	*Ibid.*, 7 Aug. 1849
2 Oct. 1849	Kintail	'But partial success'	*Ibid.*, 2 Oct. 1849

Appendix 5: Reports of Sickness and Disease, Highland Districts, 1846-1854

1846	Description	Location	Source
April	Smallpox & fever: '. . . the sickness aggravated by extreme destitution'	Extensive districts of the Highlands	*John O'Groats Journal*, 17 April 1846
August	British cholera caused by eating diseased potatoes. Upwards of 50 people affected	Lochaber	*Relief Corr.*, N. Macleod to Lord Advocate, 27 Aug. 1846
September	'Disease in the most afflictive forms'	'Some of the Islands', esp. Tiree	*Glasgow Herald*, 18 Sept. 1846
	Typhus fever & other diseases 'consequent on underfeeding & of an unwholesome kind'	Argyll	*Relief Corr.*, Minute of Provincial Synod of Argyll, 11 Sept. 1846
	English cholera, 'very fatal in its results'	Parts of Inverness	*Witness*, 9 Sept. 1846
October	'Much sickness of the cholera class . . . attributed to inferior diet viz. bad potatoes'	Raasay	*Relief Corr.*, Capt. Pole to Sir E. Coffin, 14 Oct. 1846
	'A good deal of sickness prevails'	Mull	*Relief Corr.*, Sir E. Coffin to Trevelyan, 5 Oct. 1846
November	British cholera & inflammation of the intestines was 'epidemic'. There were 'upwards of 200 cases'	S. Uist	*Glasgow Herald*, 21 Dec. 1846
December	Increasing mortality as a result of destitution	Mull, Coll & 'some other islands'	*Glasgow Herald*, 21 Dec. 1846
	Fever, dysentery & a 'particular type of typhus fever'. Marked increase in mortality reported	Ross of Mull & Iona. More sickness than elsewhere	*Destitution Papers*, Second Statement of the Dest. Comm. of Free Church, 16-17
	Number of deaths from dysentery & British cholera 'increasing with fearful rapidity among the cottar class'	Throughout the Hebrides	*Scotsman*, 12 Dec. 1846
	Mortality increase due to disease 'from want of proper food'	Bracadale, Skye	*Extracts from Letters to Dr. McLeod*, 8

Month	Description	Location	Source
December (*continued*)	Much sickness prevailing. 'A low typhus fever' & increasing number of deaths	Strath, Skye	*Destitution Papers*, Second Statement of the Dest. Comm. of Free Church, 18-19
	Typhus on the increase	Harris	*Extracts from Letters to Dr. McLeod*, 24
	Mortality in parish unusually great	Snizort, Skye	*Ibid.*, 17
1847 January	'Virulent disease of *purpura* raged in the island . . . deaths occurred every day'	Tiree	*Destitution Papers*, Glasgow Section Reports (1848), Appendix III, 18
	Sickness & mortality esp. among older people. 'Much beyond the common average.	Mull	SRO, HD6/2, Treasury Corr. Coffin to Trevelyan, 28 June 1847
	A great many deaths among old people & children, 'not exactly from want but from poor diet'. 15 funerals in Ross churchyard in one day	Mull	*Witness*, 23 Jan. 1847
	Influenza, dysentery and typhus fever prevalent: '. . . hardly a house free from sickness'	Iona	*Scotsman*, 16 Jan. 1847
	'Greatly increased sickness. Jaundice & diarrhoea due to want of proper nourishment'	Kintail	*Relief Corr.*, Pole to Coffin, 31 Jan. 1847
	Two deaths reported of 'absolute starvation'	Barra	*Scotsman*, 16 Jan. 1847
	Disease 'much on the increase'	N. Uist	*Ibid.*
February	'Fevers, measles & influenza are very distressing on south end of Harris . . . no persons are employed there or allowed to go near the sickly districts'	Harris	SRO, HD20/186, Return from the Island Glass Lighthouse, Jan. 1847
	'Much sickness prevailing'	Strath, Skye	*Witness*, 13 Feb. 1847
	Fever had broken out	Moidart	*Ibid.*, 20 Feb. 1847
	English cholera on the increase. Deaths frequent among the old & children. 'Bloody stools' always present in the disease	Skye	*Ibid.*, 13 March 1847

Month	Description	Location	Source
March	'Disease, the result of insufficient & bad food . . . is committing great ravages'	Tiree & Ross of Mull	SRO, HD6/2, Treasury Corr., Rose to Trevelyan, 21 Feb. 1847
	'Considerable sickness and mortality for last two months'. No. of deaths averaged 40 in population of 4000. Blamed on poor diet. 80 had died in Bunessan area in little more than two months. Treble the same months of former winters.	Ross of Mull	SRO, HD6/2, Treasury Corr., Hope to Coffin, 6 March 1847
	'More than the usual average of deaths'	Tiree	SRO, HD6/2, Treasury Corr., Layton to Secretary of Admiralty, 4 Mar. 1847
May	Purpura prevalent. 'The patient is attacked with great languor and depression, pain of the arms, then ulcers, generally on the legs & body...there is also pain in the mouth & throat'	Tiree	*Destitution Papers*, Reports by Capt. R. Elliot, 7 May 1847
			North British Daily Mail, 8 June 1847
June	'A cutaneous disease called land-scurvy'	A number of Highland districts	*Ibid.*
	Fever	Ulva, Gometra, 'and other places'	*Destitution Papers*, Fifth Rept. by Central Board (1847), Appendix III, 20
	Typhus fever & scurvy	Duirnish, Skye	
			Witness, 8 Sept. 1847
August	Dysentery prevalent	Mull	SRO, HD20/10, Local Committee Repts. H. McAskill to W. Skene, 20 Oct. 1847
September-October	Measles and whooping cough 'now raging among the poorer class'	Duirnish, Skye	
1848 April	151 of population sick with fever & smallpox	Skye	*Destitution Papers*, Rept. of Edinburgh Section (1848), 79
	A number of fever cases terminated fatally. 'Swelling of limbs with discoloration of the skin' also noted. Described as 'a scorbatic affection, arising from deficiency of nutriment'	Tiree	*Destitution Papers*, Ninth Rept. of Glasgow Section, Appendix II, 14

Month	Description	Location	Source
August	Typhus prevalent	Skye	*Witness*, 8 Aug. 1848
	'Last year the virulent disease of land scurvy raged to an alarming extent and deaths occurred every day. But since the introduction of vegetables as food, this disease has disappeared'	Tiree	*Destitution Papers*, Report of the Glasgow Section Nov. 1848, Appendix 18
1849			
May	Malignant typhus fever & smallpox	Skye	Dunvegan Castle, Macleod Muniments, 659/7/8, John D. Ferguson to Miss Macleod, 12 May 1849
1850	No epidemic disease for last two years but much diarrhoea, 1847-9	Gairloch	*McNeill Report*, Appendix A, 80
	No epidemic disease in Uig, 1846-50	Lewis	*McNeill Report*, Appendix A, 91
1852	Typhus fever 'has appeared in more than one locality'	Skye	Dunvegan Castle, Macleod Muniments, 659/7/6, J. Ferguson to Miss Macleod, 23 Feb. 1852
1854	English cholera; 'Prostrate with typhus fever & smallpox'	Portree, Skye, Kilmuir-Dunvegan, Skye	*Ibid.*, 659/11/14, E. Gibbons to Mrs. Ferguson, 6 Oct. 1854

Appendix 6: Highland Applications made under the Drainage Act, 1846-7

Applicant Sept. 1846-1 Feb. 1847	County	Acreage	Amount (£)
Hugh Maclean	Argyll	24,000	1000
Norman Macleod	Inverness	150,000	2000
W.F. Tytler	Inverness	400	3600
Evan Macpherson	Inverness	100	1500
James Baillie Fraser	Inverness	78	600
Lord Macdonald	Inverness	500	6000
Alex Campbell	Argyll	5,260	2900
Duncan Macintyre	Argyll	150	500
James A. Campbell	Argyll	220	3165
Sir K. Mackenzie	Ross	3,200	5000
Walter Frederick Campbell	Argyll	142,000	15000
Alex Maclean	Argyll	2,500	500
William Mackenzie	Ross	20,395	11993

Applicant	County	Acreage	Amount (£)
Hugh Maclean	Argyll	24,000	3570
Norman Macleod	Inverness	500	5000
Hon. Mary Mackenzie	Ross	1,214	8400
Sir Ewan Mackenzie	Ross	17,564	1130
Lord Lovat	Inverness	112	871
Sir James Riddell	Argyll	100,000	4500
Alex Fraser	Inverness	43	314
David Nairne	Argyll	336	3000
Alex Matheson	Ross	57,490	26420
John Fleming	Argyll	1,239	500
Countess of Dunmore	Inverness	1,190	500
James Matheson	Ross	337,855	56000
Duke of Argyll	Argyll	540	2000
Lt.-Col. Macdonald	Argyll	8,000	500
Hon. Mary S. Mackenzie	Ross	58,026	25700
Alex Mathieson	Ross	13,800	7000
James Matheson	Ross	641	2500
Wm. Lillingston	Ross	348	3210
Wm. Forlang	Argyll	-	500
Alex. Maclean	Argyll	2,500	500
James Murray Grant	Inverness	397	4565
Wm. Lillingston	Inverness	800	200
John G. Campbell	Argyll	102	980
Colin Campbell	Argyll	3,000	2000
James Matheson	Sutherland	13,000	2000
Charles Stewart	Argyll	55	550
Sir John Macpherson	Ross	37,133	6500
Lord Lovat	Inverness	552	3138
Alex Campbell	Inverness	350	700
John Campbell of Stonefield	Argyll	14,856	1070
Gordon J. Huntly	Inverness	292	2700
Adam Rolland	Argyll	4,000	7000
Arch. Douglas	Argyll	14,950	4475
David Stewart Galbraith	Argyll	330	2310
Sir J.J. Randall	Ross	37,037	35229
Trustees of Sir Charles Gordon	Argyll	229	1080
Arthur Forbes	Inverness & Ross	2,598	15000
Arch. J. Lamont	Argyll	376	1390
Geo. H. White	Ross	22,000	1040

Sources: *PP*, XXXIV (1847). Return of Number of Applications under the Drainage Act; SRO, HD7/33, Papers relating to the Drainage of Land Act (1847) including returns.

Appendix 7: Removals and Land Consolidation, Highland Parishes, before 1845 (from New Statistical Account)

Parish	Details of Removals and Consolidation
Inverness-shire Urquhart & Glenmoriston	Glenmoriston's population fell from 689 (1811) to 559 (1831) due to introduction of sheep-farming.
Boleskine & Abertarff	Fall in population from 2096 (1821) to 1829 (1831) due to sheep-farming. 30,000 Cheviot sheep in parish.
Kingussie	Greater part of the parish 'now consists of sheep walks'.
Alvie	Most land of the parish in pasture.
Moy & Dalarossie	Decrease from population of 1334 (1795) to 1098 (1831). Proprietors 'in many places have turned away the whole body of their tenantry, and let their lands out in large sheep farms'.
Glenelg	Population 2834 (1801); 2874 (1831). Emigration accounted for by 'letting of large tracts to sheep'.
Small Isles	400 left Rhum in 1826; similar emigration in 1828 from Muck.
Harris	'Some of the most fertile farms, possessed by small tenants have been depopulated and converted into extensive sheep-walks'.
Bracadale (Skye)	Decrease in population, 2250 (1795); 1769 (1831), produced by growth in large sheep farms. 4500 sheep exported annually; 450 black cattle.
Sleat (Skye)	Large sheep farms were being established.
Duirnish (Skye)	1900 acres in cultivation; 3000 once cultivated, now in pasture. Black cattle have given place almost entirely to sheep.
Kilmorack	Population fall from 2318 in 1795 to 2201 in 1831 attributed to 'letting of large tracts of land'.
Pettie	Crofts and small farms 'converted into large ones'.
Laggan	Population decline from 1512 (1795) to 1196 (1831) caused by introduction of sheep.
N. Uist	Considerable extent of land converted from crofts into grazings.
Kiltarlity	Sheep-farming carried on to a considerable extent.
Kilmonivaig	100,000 sheep raised in parish. Population declined from 2869 (1831) to 2783 (1841).
Kilmalie	Decrease in population due to large farms.

Note: 18 of 31 parishes experienced major removals and population loss due to sheep farming. Almost certainly this is an underestimate as details given in accounts for Inverness, Dores, Cromdale, Kirkhill, Daviot are too sparse to permit firm conclusions. Only in the Outer Hebridean parishes of South Uist and Barra is there clear evidence that sheep-farming and large-scale removals had not yet occurred by 1841. Skye represents a transition stage, with some parishes, notably Bracadale and Duirnish, already affected and others relatively undisturbed.

Ross & Cromarty

Kirkmichael	Evidence of extensive consolidation.
Logie Easter	Decrease in population owing to 'letting large farms and thus dispossessing small tenants'.
Killearnan	Large tracts converted into one farm.
Applecross	Torridon estate cleared.
Kintail	Evidence of dispossession as sheep walks expand.
Glensheil	Sheep universal. Class of 'substantial tenants' swept away.
Contin	Several farms stocked with Cheviot sheep.
Rosskeen	Consolidation of farms produced emigration.
Tain	Population decline 'principally due to system of large farm-letting'.
Kiltearn	Rise of sheep-farming system, 1811-21, reduced population from 1616 (1791) to 1605 (1831).
Alness	Land consolidation produced low rate of population increase.
Urquhart	System of enlarging farms general.
Avoch	Decrease due to enlargement of farms.
Kincardine	Extensive sheep-farming and clearances.

Note: 14 of 33 parishes experienced major removals and population loss. This probably underestimates the real total. Details on Nigg, Kilmuir Wester, Dingwall, Lochalsh, Fodderty, Rosemarkie, Fearn, Urray and Eddertoun were too vague or brief to permit meaningful conclusions. However, in all likely cases, except Lochalsh, population either fell, stagnated or rose much less than national average. It can, therefore, be inferred that extensive consolidation had occurred in an additional 8 parishes.

Sutherland

Golspie	Decrease in population due to large sheep farms.
Rogart	More than half the parish under Cheviot sheep.
Farr	Tenants in the interior removed in 1818-19.
Durness	Population diminished since 1815 due to creation of two extensive sheep walks. 1300 acres arable now under pasture.

Assynt	Sheep-farming very extensive.
Lairg	Great decrease in population because of interior let to sheep farmer.
Kildonan	Population decline from 1574 (1811) to 257 (1831). Decline due to sheep.
Clyne	Extensive removals.
Tongue	Much of the population moved to the east to accommodate large farms.

Note: 9 of 13 parishes experienced major removals. Only one parish, Creich, where no sheep farms were established.

Argyllshire

Inveraray	Glenshira depopulated by large sheep walks.
Glenorchy	'Vast tracts . . . exchanged stock and occupants'.
Strachur	Most land in pasture.
Inverchaolin	10,300 sheep in parish; 250 cattle.
Ardnamurchan	60,000 sheep.
Morvern	'the two opposite systems of depopulating and over-peopling are here in full operation'; 29,000 sheep; 690 cows.
Lismore & Appin	Cheviot sheep being introduced, leading to population decline.
Kilfinichen (Mull)	Hills covered with sheep.
Gigha	Decrease of population due to 'enlarging of farms'.
Southend	Mull of Kintyre 'converted into an immense sheep walk'.
Killean	Population decrease and farm consolidation.
Saddell	Extensive clearance and consolidation.
Ardchattan	Fall in population from 1650 (1831) to 1452 (1841) due to 'uniting of farms'. 32,000 sheep.
Kilmartin	Decrease of population due to consolidation.

Note: 14 of 37 parishes experienced major removals, principally, but not solely (cf. cases of Gigha and Kilmartin) due to sheep farms. In 15 parishes, Craignish, Kilninver, South Knapdale, Torosay, Kilninian, Kilfinan, Kilchrennan, Kilcalmonell, Campbeltown, Muckairn, Kilmore, Dunoon, North Knapdale, Glassary, Lochgoilhead information is too sparse to permit generalisation. In 6 parishes, Kilbrandon, Tiree and Coll, Kilchoman, Kildalton, Killarow, Kilmodan (the latter four in Islay) there was clear evidence that few removals had occurred and sheep-farming was either absent or only in early stages of development.

Source: New Statistical Account of Scotland, 15 vols. (Edinburgh, 1835-45).

Appendix 8: Numbers 'Temporarily Absent' at Census, Highland Parishes, 1841-1861

Dates of Census:

Parish	1841 (6 June)	1851 (30 March)	1861 (7 April)
Argyll			
Ardchattan (F)	–	14	12
Ardnamurchan (C)	123+ (S)	35	55
Campbeltown (F)	–	24	65
Craignish (F)	–	10	–
Dunoon (F)	–	45	70
*Gigha (C)	–	17	47
Glassary (F)	–	43	113
Glenorchy (C)	–	53	13
Inveraray (F)	51	–	–
Inverchaolin (C)	–	7	12
Jura (C)	–	20	31
Kilbrandon (F)	'considerable number' (S)	2	19
Kilcalmonell (F)	–	28	28
Kilchoman (C)	70 (S)	–	–
Kilchrennan (F)	–	8	11
Kildalton (C)	'many' (S)	3	27
Kilfinan (C)	–	–	33
Kilfinichen (C)	568 (S)	33	21
Kilmeny (C)	9	2	–
Killean (F)	–	7	31
Kilmodan (F)	c.15	11	24
Kilmartin (F)	–	5	12
Kilmore (F)	c.48	39	26
Kilninian (C)	62–65	65	50
Kilninver (F)	–	6	14
Knapdale (F)	–	–	13
Knapdale (F)	18	18	113
Lismore & Appin (C)	50 (S)	23	24
Lochgoilhead (F)	'several'	16	27
Morvern (C)	c.20 (S)	5	19
Muckairn (F)	c.50	8	3
Saddell & Skipness (F)	–	33	8
Southend (F)	–	–	8
Strachur (F)	–	–	–
Tiree & Coll (C)	495	28	44
Torosay (C)	c.50	11	8
Inverness			
Alvie (F)	'some'	–	28
Ardersier (F)	–	4	27
Barra (C)	c.16	40	31
Boleskine (F)	–	1	26
Bracadale (C)	c.30 (S)	21	12
Croy & Dalcross (F)	–	–	14
Daviot (F)	–	16	11
Dores (C)	c.15 (S)	–	14
*Duirnish (C)	–	120	39
Glenelg (C)	c.30	88	21

Parish	1841 (6 June)	1851 (30 March)	1861 (7 April)
*Harris (C)	–	81	104
Inverness (F)	–	69	153
Kilmonivaig (C)	–	30	69
Kilmorack (C)	–	27	32
Kilmuir (C)	'a great number'	101	29
Kiltarlity (C)	–	32	15
Kingussie (F)	c.40 (S)	29	27
Kirkhill (F)	–	–	–
Laggan (F)	c.50	13	23
Moy (F)	–	13	23
N. Uist (C)	30	36	118
Petty (F)	–	8	6
Portree (C)	49	65	87
Sleat (C)	100	169	102
*Small Isles (C)	–	20	12
*Snizort (C)	–	84	26
S. Uist (C)	–	74	46
Strath (C)	120	245	23
Urquhart (C)	–	–	61
Ross & Cromarty			
Applecross (C)	40–50 (S)	80	119
Avoch (F)	–	–	16
Barvas (C)	50	38	127
Cortin (F)	–	19	16
Cromarty (F)	–	23	1
Dingwall (F)	–	11	16
Edderton (F)	c.200 (S)	10	10
Fearn (F)	–	–	7
Fodderty (F)	–	20	10
Gairloch (C)	c.15	147	110
Glenshiel (C)	7 (S)	18	13
Killearnan (F)	–	8	10
Kilmuir Easter (F)	–	–	13
Kiltearn (F)	–	–	13
Kincardine (F)	–	16	26
*Kintail (C)	–	14	36
Lochalsh (C)	20	79	44
Lochbroom (C)	c.100	203	127
*Lochcarron (C)	–	54	34
Lochs (C)	50	38	127
Logie E. (F)	–	1	5
Nigg (F)	–	5	8
Rosemarkie (F)	–	–	20
Rosskeen (F)	94	16	13
*Stornoway (C)	–	16	156
Tain (F)	45	5	36
Tarbat (F)	–	–	22
*Uig (C)	–	23	66
Urray (F)	–	11	14

Parish	1841 (6 June)	1851 (30 March)	1861 (7 April)
Sutherland			
Assynt (C)	c.96 (S)	41	68
Clyne (C)	c.20–30	25	18
*Creich (C)	–	29	27
*Dornoch (C)	–	8	9
Durness (C)	46	–	12
*Edderachillis (C)	–	2	–
Farr (C)	130 (S)	187	160
Golspie (F)	–	10	7
*Kildonan (C)	–	4	30
Lairg (C)	c.40	14	5
Loth (C)	–	–	5
Rogart (C)	35	10	30
Tongue (C)	83 (S)	120	166

Notes:

C = 'crofting parish'
F = 'farming parish'
S = 'at work in the south'
* = Evidence from other sources that temporary migration was occurring from these parishes in 1841. See Appendix 9.

Source: GRO, Census Enumerators' Schedules for all Parishes above, 1841, 1851, 1861.

Appendix 9: Temporary Migration and the Crofting Region: Parish Patterns in the 1840s

Applecross
'Almost all the young men go to the east coast fishing, and find also other employment there till the season when fishing on the west coast commences, when most of them return'. All the cottars went there.
(SRO, HD21/41, Minutes of the Destitution Committee of Applecross, 2 August 1847; *John O'Groats Journal*, 6 April 1849).

Ardnamurchan
'A very large number of the able-bodied men, especially in Ardnamurchan . . . leave their wives and families for a great portion of the year, go to Glasgow where they get employment in Dye-Works and return to their possessions for only a few months in the summer. In most cases, these parties pay their rents well'.
The *New Statistical Account* stressed this practice was especially common among small tenants and cottars.
(SRO, Riddell Papers, AF49/6, Report of T.G. Dickson for Trustees (1852); *N.S.A.*, VII, 183).

Coigach
In 1841 it was reported that 'many went for the harvest . . . some as far as the Lothians'.
(*PP*, VI (1841), *S.C. on Emigration*, 146, QQ.16l88- 9).

Coll
100 of the inhabitants of Coll went south annually. Extensive migration for harvest employment
also reported in 1842.
(*N.S.A.*, VII, 214; *McNeill Report*, XLVII).

Colonsay
In the spring of 1847 many young men had gone to the Lowlands to search for work. Women had
also left 'to engage themselves as servants'.
(SRO, Treasury Correspondence relating to Highland Destitution, HD6/2, Sir J. McNeill to C.
Trevelyan, 8 March 1847).

Gairloch
Nearly all the young single men and 'many, young married men' went to the east-coast fishery
and Caithness. Those who went to the east were absent about nine weeks. The Caithness men
stayed away for seven weeks.
(SRO, AF7/85, Survey by L. Lamb, Assistant Inspector of the Fishery, 30 September 1850;
McNeill Report, Appendix A, 80, 82-3).

Gigha
Extensive temporary migration as sailors and farmworkers. Those who participated were
generally absent for half the year.
(*N.S.A.*, VII, 4020).

Glenelg
'Many' of the young men had been in the habit of going south for labour.
(*Relief Correspondence*, Resolutions of a Public Meeting held in Glenelg, 25 August 1846).
In the Knoydart area of the parish, the sons and daughters of older people tended to be 'at service'
in the south.
(Anon., *The State of the Highlands in 1854* (Inverness, 1855), 23).

Glenshiel
24 inhabitants had gone south for harvest work in 1847. A further 27 were sent by the
Employment Committee of the Central Board. In 1841, 7 were at 'railway work' in the
south.
(SRO, AD21/17, Minutes of the Destitution Committee of Glenshiel; GRO, Census
Enumerators' Schedules, Glenshiel, 1841).

Harris
200 of the able-bodied men of Harris (population 4250 in 1851) went annually to the Caithness
herring fishery.
    No evidence that the people of Harris were inclined to seek agricultural or other work in the
south of Scotland. But in November 1846, 30 married men left for work on the Central Railway
at Stirling.
(SRO, Lord Advocate's Papers, AD58/84, Copy Letter, W.H. Sitwell to Countess of Dunmore,
1 October 1846; *McNeill Report*, Appendix A, 107; *Inverness Courier*, 14 July, 9 December
1846).

Islay
Labourers in the habit of going to the mainland for harvest work.
    'Many' young men left the island for employment elsewhere in September-October 1846.
'Many' young persons from Oa area 'at service' in south. In 1841, c.70 people from Kilchoman
parish were 'at service' at Glasgow.
(*Extracts from Letters to Rev. Dr. McLeod* (Glasgow, 1847), 27; *Relief Correspondence*, Capt. Pole
to Coffin, 6 and 13 October 1846; GRO, Census Enumerators' Schedules, Kilchoman parish,
1841).

Lewis

'The chief source from which the small crofters of Lewis draw the means of paying that portion of their rent which the sale of stock will not cover, is the Caithness herring fishery, to which a great number of men go yearly . . . Of the class of small crofters there are few families in which there is an able-bodied man who do not send one member to the Caithness fishing'. One observer stated that the migration started when difficulties developed in the kelp industry in the 1820s.
(*McNeill Report*, Appendix A, 92, 97).

Lismore & Appin

In the spring of 1841, c. 30 males and 20 females had left for employment in the south, principally in Glasgow.
(GRO, Census Enumerators' Schedules, Lismore and Appin (1841)).

Lochalsh

'A large proportion of the able-bodied young men and some of the married men went annually to the east coast and returned in time for the fishing on the west coast. Some young men were employed as seamen on merchant ships.' Went away for 'a few years' before returning home.
(*McNeill Report*, Appendix A, 70).

Lochbroom

Parish minister reckoned in 1841 that 'some hundreds' of the inhabitants were away at 'the Caithness deep-sea fishery, at sea and at south country labouring of various kinds'.

The main form of temporary migration seems to have been to Caithness and the Moray Firth. From almost every family at least one person went to the east. They returned in September and spent the winter at home. But some were employed as seamen on trading vessels. Those seeking employment in the herring fishery left home in early July. According to the census enumerator in 1841 'a still greater number' left in the middle of August to obtain employment as shearers in the south of Scotland.
(*N.S.A.*, *Ross and Cromarty*, 83-4; GRO, Census Eumerators' Schedules, Lochbroom (1841); *McNeill Report*, Appendix A, 84, 87).

Lochcarron

The parochial board reckoned that in 1851 about 200 able-bodied men left the parish annually '. . . to work in other parts of the country, especially the east coast, at agricultural work, fishing and harvest'.
(*McNeill Report*, Appendix A, 74).

Moidart & Arisaig

In the spring of 1847 'almost all the able-bodied men' had gone to seek work in the Lowlands.
(SRO, Treasury Correspndence relating to Highland Destitution, HD6/2, Mr. May to Mr. Walker, 22 March 1847).

Morvern

In 1847 'a number of able-bodied men . . . have mostly gone to the low country for work'.
(*Destitution Papers*, Sixth Report of Glasgow Section, Appendix II, D. Boyter to J. Ritchie, 28 August 1847).

Mull

Parish of Kilninian: 'Many young men go to the south for work' (1839). In Tobermory, the census enumerator estimated in 1841 that c. 200 of a total population of 1592 'left for south within the last 3 months'. They were mainly merchant seamen, agricultural labourers and young girls. Most went south though a 'few engaged in the herring fishery'.

In 1851 further information was provided by Rev. David Ross: 'A considerable number of

young females go annually to seek service in Glasgow, or other places in the south. Of the young men a large proportion go to sea. I am of opinion that since 1846 the difficulty of subsisting at home has increased the number of young persons of both sexes who seek for employment elsewhere; but I am not aware that many of them have established themselves permanently in other parts of the country. For the most part they continue to regard Tobermory as their home'.
(GRO, Census Enumerators' Schedules, Kilninian (1841); *McNeill Report*, Appendix A, 12).

Parish of Kilfinichen: In 1851 'a considerable number go annually to seek employment in the south'. John Campbell, chamberlain on the Duke of Argyll's property, noted that 'Few of the able-bodied men from this property have sought a permanent subsistence from labour in the south. They go for a time, but almost invariably return'. The census enumerator in 1841 specifically referred to the movement of younger women: 'a great many females go to the south country for service where they remain generally to the month of November'.
(GRO, Census Enumerators' Schedules, Kilfinichen (1841); *McNeill Report*, Appendix A, 5).

North Uist

In March 1847 some had gone to Glasgow in search of work. But temporary migration had been limited before then. In 1841 the census enumerator indicated that 'Very few can be said to be in the habit of moving from their ordinary place of residence'.
(SRO, Treasury Correspondence relating to Highland Destitution, HD6/2, Capt. Maclean to Sir E. Coffin, 10 March 1841; GRO, Census Enumerator's Schedules, North Uist 1841).

Skye

Parish of Portree: extensive migration to the south by the young. The inspector of the poor noted that more went south in 1847 and 1848, 'the wages then being high'. In 1849 and 1850 fewer went because work was more difficult to obtain. Many went supported by the Central Board and Free Church.

Parish of Bracadale: 40 males and females left the parish annually for harvest work. 60 men went for other forms of employment.

Parish of Strath: 500 able-bodied men (of a total parish population of 3243) left annually for work in the south.

Parish of Sleat: 300 men went south every year (of a total parish population of 2531); '. . . from every family, paying less than £10 of rent one or more member must necessarily go somewhere to earn wages. Of the small crofters, the man who is in the most independent circumstances is he who has able-bodied sons who go south'.
(*McNeill Report*, Appendix A, 32, 36, 57-9).

Sutherland Estate

In autumn 1846 'many young men had gone south from the Dunrobin and Tongue areas of the estate. They were remitting money to the families. However, 'few' had gone from the Scourie area of the far west. Yet it is clear that it was common for the people of Assynt and Edderachillis to have recourse to the east-coast fishery.
(NLS, Sutherland Estate Papers, Dep. 313/1173, James Loch to Duke of Sutherland, 4 September 1846; *N.S.A.*, XV, 104, 129).

Tiree

Temporary migration for harvesting on the mainland was common among the poor of the island. One third of the 278 tenants paying under £5 per annum in rent in 1845 'go to the low country in time of harvest where they can get a little money'.

In 1841 the parish minister reported that 'a great part of the young unmarried population, especially of females' found harvest work in the south: 'Hundreds of these set off about the middle of August, and are generally absent from six to eight weeks'.
(Inveraray Castle, Argyll Estate Papers, Bundle 1529, Report by Chamberlain of Tiree, August 1845; *N.S.A.*, VII, 214).

Appendix 10: Assisted Emigration by Highland Landowners, 1846-1856

N.B. Numbers assisted in each instance are noted at the top left of each entry, followed by the dates of the emigration.

Mainland
Glenelg (James Baillie) 344 (1849)
344 emigrated from this estate on the *Liskeard* in July 1849 for Canada. A petition was presented to the landlord on behalf of 680 individuals praying for his assistance to emigrate. In the event 344 (37 per cent) of the total estate population in January 1849 of 923 actually took up Baillie's offer of assistance and emigrated. All were provided with free passage, clothing and blankets when required plus a sum of money sent to Canada to provide for their initial wants. Rent arrears were written off. Of those who signed the original petition, 36 per cent had 'no land'; 52 per cent one acre and only 5 per cent five acres or more.

This was not a 'compulsory' or 'forced' emigration in the strict sense but the petitioners had been the victims of major clearances in earlier years which had reduced many of them to cottar status. Thomas Mulock visited Glenelg in December 1849 and interviewed 50 heads of families who had declined to emigrate. He asked them if the emigration was 'voluntary': 'With one voice, they assured me that nothing short of the absolute impossibility of obtaining land or employment at home could drive them to seek the doubtful benefits of a foreign shore'. In Mulock's view the emigration was 'the product of desperation'.

Baillie was complimented by the immigration authorities in Quebec because he provided funds for internal transport for the emigrants.

Sources: SRO, HD21/25, Petition of the inhabitants of Glenelg; *McNeill Report*, Appendix A, 66; *Witness*, 21 July 1849; *Scotsman*, 21 July 1849; *PP*, XL (1850), *Papers relative to the Emigration to the North American Colonies*, 12; Mulock, *Western Highlands and Islands*, 68; *Destitution Papers*, Twelfth Rept. of Glasgow Section, Rept. on Glenelg by T. Kier, 25-26.

Glengarry 150 (1852)
'From Glengarry . . . 150 emigrants have gone out, being allowed to sell their stock for their own behoof, having their arrears of rent cancelled and getting the expenses of their passage paid . . .'
Source: *Inverness Advertiser*, 20 July 1852.

Knoydart (Mrs. Josephine Macdonnel) 332 (1853)
In 1847 there were 600 people on this estate. Nominal rental £250 but little or no rent paid for several years; arrears stood at £1500 by 1853. In spring 1853 summonses of removal were issued; all tenants were offered free passage to Canada or Australia. 400 accepted. Clothing and bedding cost £1700, borrowed under the Emigration Advances Act of 1853, but only 332 eventually embarked on the *Sillery*.

Disembarked in September 1853; received free passage as far as Montreal plus allowed 10lbs. of oatmeal when leaving ship. Labour market by 1853 was buoyant in the colony.

Sources: *PP*, 1854-5, XXIV, *Ninth Annual Rept. of Board of Supervision of Relief of the Poor in Scotland, Appendix A, no. 1*; *PP*, 1854, XLVI, *Papers relative to Emigration to the North American Colonies*, 79; James M. Cameron, 'A Study of the Factors that Assisted and Directed Scottish Emigration to Upper Canada, 1815-1855', Unpublished Ph.D. thesis, Glasgow, 1970, 388-9.

Lochalsh (William Lillingston) 300 (1849)
About 300 people left in early July, 1849 for America. W. Lillingston 'helped the poorest with clothes and assisted passage'. Some also received sums from the Destitution Committee. They had petitioned the landlord for assistance.

Sources: *Inverness Advertiser*, 3 July 1849; *Witness*, 3 November 1849; *McNeill Report*, XXVI.

Lochshiel (Macdonald of Lochshiel) 82 (1850)
Probably an example of 'compulsory emigration': 'a number of crofters were ejected' from this
estate in Moidart in 1850 and assisted to emigrate to Canada. 82 emigrants from Oban, assisted
by Macdonald of Lochshiel; were reported as arriving in Canada in 1850.
Sources: *Inverness Advertiser*, 4 March 1851; *PP*, XL (1851), Copies or Extracts of Despatches
relative to Emigration to North American colonies, 316.

Glen Urquhart (Earl of Seafield) ? (1852)
Reference made in *Inverness Advertiser* to 'a large emigration' from Glen Urquhart, assisted by
Lord Seafield. Emigrants left from Glasgow in 1852.
Source: *Inverness Advertiser*, 20 July 1852.

Sutherland (Duke of Sutherland) 1076 (1847-51)
1847: *Serius*, 236 tons; 117 passengers (35 male, 36 female, 46 children under 14 years).
     Panama, 280 passengers (87 male, 73 female, 120 children). Both parties were from the
Scourie district in the far west of Sutherland. The cost to the estate for freight, provisions and
clothing was £1999.14.11.
     In an 'excerpt from a letter' from 'an intelligent Scotch farmer settled in Canada west' it was
reported that the *Panama* had arrived 'without a case of death or sickness occurring on board,
and last week the whole party . . . have reached safely the township of Zorra in good
health . . .'
Sources: N.L.S. Sutherland Estate Papers, Dep. 313/2737, Scheduled list of passengers, 28
May 1847 and emigration expenses, season, 1847; *Scotsman*, 18 September 1847.
1848: *Scotia* departed from Loch Eriboll with 206 souls in May 1848. Arrived Quebec 7 July with
emigrants from Farr and Tongue. Passage provided for them from Quebec to a place 40 miles
beyond Toronto.
     Greenock arrived in Quebec on 28 June from Loch Laxford with 417 passengers.
     During the winter of 1847-8 letters from previous emigrants were printed and circulated by
emigration agents. The estate seems to have been concerned to avoid coercion but offered
assistance to those who wished to move. In March 1849 the Duke was petitioned by tenants from
Clashnessie, Assynt for assistance to emigrate. The petition referred to 'the account which they
have received from Friends in Canada which have led them to wish to emigrate, the poverty and
want of resources at home rendering improvement in the condition and prospects for their
families hopeless'. The Duke replied that, because of cost of transport and the additional estate
expenditure occasioned by the potato failure, he could not pay the entire cost of emigration.
They would have to raise a part.
Sources: N.L.S. Sutherland Estate Papers, Dep. 313/1178, Duke of Sutherland to tenants and
cottars of Clashnessie, 31 March 1849; 313/2822, R. Horsburgh to E. Maciver, 2 June 1848;
John O'Groats Journal, 18 August 1848, 15 September 1848; Cameron, 'Factors in Scottish
Emigration', 375; *PP*, XXXVIII (1849), *Papers relative to British Provinces in America*, 40.
1850: 59 emigrants left in June 1850 on the *Argo*. They were 'from Lochinver and other parts of
West Sutherland'. They had applied to Duke for assistance and he paid passages ((*Inverness
Advertiser*, 25 June 1850).
1851: 24 emigrants sent out on *Vesper* by Sutherland estate from Thurso. Both this group and
that of 1850 were from Assynt, where clearances were carried out in 1850 and people were given
choice of land on the coast or free passage to British N. America (*Inverness Courier*, 26 June
1851; *PP*, XXXIII (1852), *Papers relative to Emigration to the North American Colonies*, 577).

Miscellaneous 256 (1851)
256 sent out by various landlords to Canada in 1851 (*PP*, XXXIII (1852), 578).

Islands
Lewis (Sir James Matheson) 2337 (1851-55)
For a detailed account of the background to the Lewis emigrations to Canada see pp.212-223
above.

Date	Vessel	No. of Passengers
1851	Barlow	287
1851	Marquis of Stafford	500
1851	Islay	68
1851	Wolfville	69
1851	Urgent	370
1851	Prince George	203
1851	Sesostris	7
1851	Birnam	50
1852	Blanche	453
1855	Melissa	330
		Total: 2337

Sources: MS. Diary of J.M. Mackenzie, 1851; *PP*, XXXIII (1852), *Papers relative to Emigration to the North American Colonies*, 585, 8; *PP*, XLVI (1854), *McNeill Report*, Appendix A, 93-6.

North Uist (Lord Macdonald) 234 (1849)

The arrival was reported in Quebec in 1849 of 234 persons from North Uist on board the *Cashmere* and *Water Hen*. They had been assisted by Lord Macdonald. All were described as 'extremely poor'. They had to be provided with food and travel expenses on arrival at Hamilton, Ontario. Were 'sent to the interior at the expense of Hamilton and Toronto St. Andrews Societies'.

Almost certainly these were from the Sollas district in North Uist. The Macdonald estate administrators decided to clear it in 1849 and offer the opportunity to emigrate to the inhabitants. Many refused the terms – free passage and foregoing of all arrears and clothes for the most destitute. Attempts were made to evict them and this led to the notorious clearances at Sollas which produced both resistance from the people, legal action against those who had assaulted police and estate officials and widespread press publicity (see Richards, *Highland Clearances*, I, 420-30). However, it would appear that the estate was partially successful in its 'compulsory emigration'. In September 1850, 70 families lived on in the district but 234 persons (approx. 47 families) had emigrated to Canada in 1849 with expenses paid by the estate.

Sources: *PP*, XL (1850), *Papers relative to Emigration to North American Colonies*, 7, 22; P. Cooper, *An Old Story Retold* (Aberdeen), 1881; *Scotsman*, 28 July 1849; *Inverness Courier*, 12, 26 September 1850.

Barra and South Uist (Col. John Gordon of Cluny) 2906 (1848-1851)

Year	Vessel	No. of Emigrants
1848	Lulan	120
1848	Eromanga	60
1848	Canada	90
		270

Were mainly from South Uist. On arrival, the immigration officers in Quebec noted, 'all those people were in very poor circumstances'. Required assistance to their destination (*Witness*, 16 and 19 August 1848; *PP*, XXXVIII (1849), 40).

Year	Vessel	No. of Emigrants
1849	Atlantic	209
1849	Tuskar	496
1849	Mount Stewart Elphinstone	250
		955

'The most, if not the whole of these people (on *Tuskar* and *Mount Stewart Elphinstone*) were from Col. Gordon's property; he assists them by taking their crops at valuation. The Glasgow section of the Destitution Board also assists some of the more destitute. The people go away quietly and are most desirous to leave, offering to sell their clothes or to do anything to get away'.

On arrival, all but 50 of the passengers of the passengers of the *Atlantic* and *Tuskar* (705) were described as 'destitute' (*PP*, XL (1850), 6; *Scotsman*, 11 August 1849; *Witness*, 27 October 1849; 2 January 1850).

Year	Vessel	No. of Emigrants
1851	Brooksby	285
1851	Montezuma	442
1851	Perthshire	437
1851	Admiral	413
1851	Liskeard	104
		1681

(*PP*, XXXIII (1852), 566-7)

Tiree and Ross of Mull (Duke of Argyll) M = Mull, T = Tiree
For a detailed account of the background to these emigrations see above, pp.220-235.

Year	Vessel	No. of Emigrants
1847	Eliza	c. 140 (T)
1847	Jamaica	200 (T)
1847	?	761 (M)

(Inveraray Castle, Argyll Estate Papers, Bundle 1533, Note of emigrants from Tiree, June 1847; Bundle 1522, List of Emigrants from Ross of Mull, 1847; *Witness*, 16 June 1847)

Year	Vessel	No. of Emigrants
1848	–	–
1849	Charlotte	364 (T) = 627
1849	Barlow	263 (M)

(Inveraray Castle, Argyll Estate Papers, Bundle 1535, List of Emigrants from Mull and Tiree, June 1849; *PP*, XL (1850), 6)

Year	Vessel	No. of Emigrants
1850	Conrad	241 (T = 167; M = 74)
1850	Cumbria	17

(*Ibid.*, Bundle 1804, List of Emigrants from Tiree & Mull, 1850)

Year	Vessel	No. of Emigrants
1851	Birnam	138 (T = 70; M = 68)
1851	Conrad	389 (T = 389)
1851	Onyx	6 (T = 6)

(*Ibid.*, Bundle 1805, List of Emigrants, 1851)

Year	Vessel	No. of Emigrants
1853	Allan Kerr	18

(*PP*, XLVI (1854), *Papers Relative to Emigration to the North American Colonies*, 1854, 31)

Total	2279

Appendix 11: *Principal Evictions in the Highlands, 1846-1856*

It is very probable that the details presented below do not provide a complete record of all major clearances undertaken during the famine. However, they do contain relevant material discovered from a search of a very wide variety of contemporary sources. Space permits only the main outlines of each removal to be described although quantitative data have always been included where available. For more detail, the interested reader should consult the source references listed after each entry. 'Principal evictions' refers to removal of entire townships or a minimum of ten families. The data almost certainly seriously underestimate eviction of cottars. This is always more difficult to trace in estate papers.

Ardnamurchan
Report to trustees in 1852 stressed the need for removals from selected areas of the estate: '. . . the tenants of the farms of Swordlemore, Swordlediorach, Swordlechaol and Kilmory are so deeply in arrears that it is absolutely necessary they be removed . . .' In April 1852 Sir James Riddell obtained summonses of removal at Tobermory Sheriff Court against tenants in the following townships:

Swordlechaol	12 tenants	Branault	6 tenants
Ranachan	6 tenants	Swordlemore	6 tenants
Achnolia	6 tenants	Strontian area	6 tenants
Achoshnik	5 tenants	Annaheilt	12 tenants
Oronsaigmore	6 tenants	Achateny	6 tenants
Ardtoe	8 tenants	Kilchean	6 tenants
		Total	85

Additionally, summonses of sequestration were obtained against 5 tenants at Swordle for arrears due.

Some of those who eventually lost their land were resettled on poor land at Sanna, at the tip of the Ardnamurchan peninsula.
Sources: SRO, Riddell Papers, AF49/6, Report of T.G. Dickson for Trustees (1852); SRO, Sheriff Court Processes (Tobermory), SC/59/2/11.

Arisaig
An official of the Central Board reported in 1849 that 'a considerable number of removals' were to take place in Arisaig. Little further information has been found on the proposed evictions. According to evidence presented to the Napier Commission the township of Kinloyd in Arisaig was cleared in 1853 but the major removals had been implemented by Lord Cranstoun in the early 1840s *before* the famine.
Sources: *Destitution Papers*, Ninth Report of Glasgow Section of the Central Board, Appendix II, 28; *N.C.*, 2082-2107, QQ.32712-3327.

Barra
In a Town Council debate in Edinburgh on evicted migrants from Barra in 1850 it was reported: '. . . in the month of September the Highland Destitution Board suspended relief, when Col. Gordon immediately ordered a large number of his poor tenants to be removed, which was accomplished by demolishing their cottages and then, after they were cast out desolate on the fields, getting them shipped off the island. About 132 families (some 660 souls) were sent in this way to Tobermory. Of these, 37 families had made their way across to Ardrishaig and from that to Glasgow'.

Total population of the island was 2,300 of whom 1809 had been in receipt of relief from the parochial board and the Central Board. The 132 families received notice 'to remove from their houses' in March 1850, but were allowed to remain in them until May 'when they were ejected from them'. These removals exclude those which took place at the time of Col. Gordon's assisted emigrations to Canada.
Source: *Scotsman*, 18, 21 December 1850.

Benbecula
The threat of eviction was widely employed to encourage emigration from the island in 1850 and 1851 and the emigration 'forced in some cases with circumstances of shocking inhumanity . . . emptied townships remained empty, returning gradually to a state of nature'.

'Great clearances for sheep walks' occurred in 1849 and 1851. The lands of the townships of Balvannich, Aird and Nachdar were added to the large farm of Nunton by Col. Gordon.
Source: *N.C.*, Appendix A, 78, Statement of Rev. Donald Mackintosh, Benbecula; 752-779, QQ.11877-12112.

Glensheil
Tenants of Carndubh and Bundaloch deprived of land in 1852 for arrears. 20 families (approx. 100 souls involved). Township of Drindag cleared in 1847, West Achanataird, 1849 and Letter-fearn in 1852. All became part of a large sheep farm.

Major removals in this parish had taken place long before 1846. They were described in the *New Statistical Account*; as a result the parish had already reached its maximum population by 1821.
Source: *N.C.*, 1993-2010, QQ.31380-31256.

Greenyards (Easter Ross)
Concerned 22 families in this township near Bonar Bridge in Easter Ross. They were under notice in 1854 in order to make room for sheep. The eviction attracted widespread attention because the people resisted and scenes of great violence ensued. The events are fully documented in Richards, *Highland Clearances*, I, 460-8.

Harris
At Whitsun 1848, 40 crofters were removed from the island of Bernera, then occupied by 81 families and the lands thus vacated divided among the 41 who remained. With 2 or 3 exceptions, those who were removed were placed on lands previously occupied by tacksmen. In all, 64 families were removed on the Harris estate of Lord Dunmore 1844-51 but the estate factor asserted in evidence to Sir John McNeill that this was 'with a view to improve their own condition and that of the crofters remaining in the farm from which they were removed'. However, this is in conflict with evidence presented to the Napier Commission. There it was stated that removals took place at Big Borv for rent arrears in 1849 and the township's lands added to the large farm of Scarista-vore. Further, the isle of Taransay was cleared around the same period; the evicted 'went to S.W. Harris, some Lewis, some elsewhere'.
Sources: *McNeill Report*, Appendix A, 109, Evidence of J.R. Macdonald, Factor on estate of Lord Dunmore; *N.C.*, 1195-1190.

Islay
The 'cruel process of eviction' began in Islay in 1831. During the decade 1831-41 an estimated 130 emigrants left. A further 1200 were estimated to have been evicted 1841-51: 'the family dispersal policy, begun by the Campbells of Islay, was intensified under the trustees from 1849'. Evictions took place in 'the Glen' and the Oa peninsula (Kildalton parish) and there was a considerable decline in tenancies: 'many changes took place among smaller tenants'.
Sources: *N.C.*, 3109-3111, Evidence of Rev. John MacNeill, Minister of Free Church, Port-na-haven, Islay; SRO, Campbell of Jura Reports, GD64/1/347, Report to the Creditors of the late W. Campbell of Islay; Storrie, *Islay*, 136-7.

Jura
Township of Cnocbreac on western corner of the island was said to have been cleared during the famine period.
Source: Gordon Wright, *Jura* (privately printed, 1983), 16.

Knoydart (Glenelg parish)
This estate was the last possession of the Macdonnels of Glengarry. It was under trust and the trustees and the owner, Mrs. Josephine Macdonnel, decided to clear it with a view to facilitating the sale of the property. In 1847 there were 600 people on the estate; by 1853 this had fallen to 70, the majority of whom lived in townships along the coast. In spring 1853 this remnant received summonses of removal. All were offered free passage to Canada or Australia but only 332 of 400 who originally accepted finally embarked on the *Sillery* for Canada. New summonses of removal were executed against the remainder in August 1853 and their houses were pulled down by sheriff's officers.
Sources: Mitchell Library, Letterbook on Highland Emigration of Sir John McNeill, 1852, MS. 21506, McNeill to Sir Charles Trevelyan, 30 December 1852; *Inverness Advertiser*, 13 and 27 September 1853; *Scotsman*, 26 October 1853; *Scotsman*, 26 October 1853; Anon., *The State of the Highlands in 1854* (Inverness, 1855); *PP*, XLVI (1854-5), *Communications with Regard to the Administration of the Poor Law in the Highlands of Scotland.*

Lewis
A strategy of eviction, assisted emigration and redistribution of population was put into effect on the island between 1848 and 1854. Summonses of removal were employed to encourage emigration. The total number of summonses awarded to the Matheson estate, 1846-53, were:

Year	No. of Summonses
1846	–
1847	66
1848	121
1849	382
1850	141
1851	657
1852	Processes not available
1853	175

As Sir John McNeill reported, '. . . it was indicated to those in arrears and without the means of support till next harvest, if they could not show good reasons, arising from the state of their own health or that of some member of their family for declining to emigrate, they would be required to surrender their lands'. The estate itself admitted that the townships of Reef, Carinish, Hacklete, Ballygloom, Dun Carloway, Dalemore, Melbost, Barve, North Tolsta and Galston were wholly or partly cleared between 1849 and 1853. The inhabitants either emigrated or were removed to other townships, often to take the place of others who had emigrated. In 1851 alone a total of 1993 were assisted to leave the island. For a full account see Chapter 9.
Sources: MS. Diary of J.W. Mackenzie, 1851; SRO, Sheriff Court Processes (Stornoway), SC33/17/26-33; *McNeill Report*, XX-XX1; *N.C.*, Appendix A, 159-162, Statement by William Mackay, Chamberlain of the Lews (1883); 875-1165; 3032, Evidence of J.M. Mackenzie, late Chamberlain of the Lews, 1848-54.

Lismore (Parish of Lismore & Appin)
Clearances began before the famine but intensified during it. Removals occurred from the townships of Rinn-na-fiart, Achanad, Balagrundle, Creaganaich, Gartcharrain, Achanacroigh, Killean. The landlord involved was W. Cheyne, an advocate in Edinburgh with estates in Fife and Linlithgow.
Source: *N.C.*, 2324-2327, QQ.36849-36881.

Lochalsh
Tenants of Avernish township mainly 'expatriated' in 1849. Those who remained 'were allowed a mere fringe of the township, bordering on the rocky sea shore'. Kirkton township: in 1852 Altan Pan taken from it and included in an adjacent sheep farm. However, the major removals in

Lochalsh had taken place earlier during the ownership of Sir Hugh Innes who had bought the estate from the Earls of Seaforth. Evictions during William Lillingston's tenure (i.e., the famine years) were limited.
Source: N.C., 1930-1947, QQ.30056-30756.

Lochbroom

It was reported in June 1847 by Capt. Eliot of the Central Board that Mr J. Bankes of Gruinard estate 'is ejecting 300 souls' from his property. It has not been possible to obtain independent confirmation of this clearance, although evidence presented to the Napier Commission does mention large-scale removals from the township of Drumchork on that estate. What, however, seems reasonably clear (N.C., 1880, Q.29223) is that most of Bankes's evictions were completed before 1846.
Sources: N.L.S., Sutherland Estate Papers, Dep. 313/86, Capt. Eliot to Duke of Sutherland, 19 June 1847; N.C., 1832-1880, QQ.28551-29323.

Moidart

'A number of crofters were ejected last year (1850) from the estate of Lochshiel and were assisted to emigrate to Canada. A few of these have written to their friends at home and given so favourable an account of the land of their adoption as to encourage others to follow them, had they the means of doing so . . .'
Sources: *Inverness Advertiser*, 4 March 1851; Catholic Archives, Columba House, Edinburgh, Oban Letters, OL1/45/8, Ronald Rankin to ?, 4 March 1852.

Morvern

21 families (105 souls) were removed from the township of Auliston on the Drimnin estate of Lady Gordon in 1855. A further 15 families were cleared from Keil and Savary on the Lochaline estate of J. Sinclair between 1841-51. However, only 36 families of the total of 153 estimated to have been evicted in the principal clearances between 1820 and 1868 are known to have been removed during the famine years.
Sources: *Oban Times*, 20 December 1884; N.C., 2293; Gaskell, *Morvern Transformed*, 129.

Mull

The reader should initially consult the table in the text (p.179) where the summonses of removal for Mull are catalogued.

Ardnamurchan estate: 'the crofters and cottars have been warned off . . . 26 families emigrated to America at their own expense, and one at that of the Parochial Board; a good many removed to Kinloch where they are now in great poverty' (1850-1).

Sorne estate: 27 crofters dispossessed when Mr. Forsyth obtained the estate in 1850. A further 52 families (300 souls) were to be removed at Whitsun 1851.

Ulva estate: From 1847 until 1851 a systematic process of removal began which reduced the island's population from 500 to 150 in four years. 350 people were evicted. In 1841 population was 859. 73 families eventually cleared from 16 townships.

Torosay estate: 'removals would take place at Whitsunday next' (i.e. Whitsunday 1852).

Duke of Argyll's estate, Ross of Mull: notice of removal served on 12 families at Shiaba, 1847. 129 summonses of removal granted against tenants in Kilfinichen parish, 1849- 51.

Glenforsa and Morinish estates: removal for the purpose of making large farms. 12 townships cleared; 34 families (approx. 170 souls) dispersed. No exact dates available but mainly in later 1840s.

The above examples contain details from estate papers and literary sources on the scale of eviction on particular estates but they represent only a small proportion of the cases of removal on the island. The table below lists the number of summonses of removal awarded to each landlord in Mull, 1846-52, and extends the information given above.

Landowner	Summons of Removal
Duke of Argyll (Ross of Mull)	154
F.W. Clark (Ulva)	88
Earl Compton (Torloisk estate)	60
D. McLachlan	23
D. Nairne (Aros)	100
J. Stewart	41
Maclaine of Lochbuie	64
Campbell of Torosay	11
W.H. Drummond	24
Arch. Campbell	2
A. Crawford	45
James Forsyth (Sorne)	21
D. McNab	4
D. Macintyre	9
John Sinclair	8
Mull tacksmen	42

Sources: *McNeill Report*, Appendix A, 10, 13, 26; *Destitution Papers*, Report on Mull etc. (1849), 16-17; Inveraray Castle, Argyll Estate Papers, Bundle 1522, Petition of tenants of Shiaba, June 1847; Bundle 1804, List of tenants and cottars warned of removal 1850, SRO, Sheriff Court Processes (Tobermory), SC59/2/4-10.

Skye
Raasay: in 1852-4, 12 townships cleared by the landlord, G. Rainy; 'made them into a sheep farm which he had in his own hands'; 97 families (nearly 500 souls) involved.

Lord Macdonald's estate: 'In 1854, Lord Macdonald's estate was under trust; clearances carried out attended with circumstances of heartless cruelty'; in 1849 it was claimed a large number of summonses of removal had been served on this estate but removal of tenants (as opposed to cottars) mainly concentrated in townships of Boreraig and Suishnish in parish of Strath. In 1850 these contained 22 tenancies; by 1853/4 all had disappeared. A significant proportion of families (8) were resettled in other townships in holdings vacated by those who emigrated through the Highland and Island Emigration Society. At the same time 9 families from Boreraig (69 people) and 2 from Suishnish emigrated through the H.I.E.S. in 1852. 3 tenants from Suishnish were settled in new holdings created at Scullamus. The number of tenants resettled, added to the number emigrating, exceeds the number of holdings originally listed in Boreraig and Suishnish (10 and 12 respectively).

Strathaird: belonged to Alex. McAlastair of Torisdale Castle, Kintyre. Contained 600 people, 'a very great proportion of whom have paid almost no rent for many years past'. Served with summonses of removal in summer 1849 but £1200 made available for emigration. The people refused initially but most seem to have emigrated in 1851-2.
Sources: *N.C.*, Appendix A, 53; 448-449, QQ.7837-7858; Appendix A, Statement by Rev. D. Mackinnon, Strath, Skye, 42; 247-298, QQ.4865-5432; *Witness*, 6 September 1851; *Inverness Advertiser*, 29 October 1850; *Scotsman*, 8 June 1850; SRO, Lord Advocate's Papers, AD58/83; Threatened Eviction of the tenants of Strathaird, Isle of Skye, 1850; SRO, Lord McDonald Papers, GD221/122/4, 11, 19; GD221/123/1.

Strathconon (Contin parish, E. Ross)
21 families, mainly subtenants and cottars, were removed from the Strathconon estate at Whitsun 1849. This represented the final phase of a process of steady attrition of the small tenantry of the glen which stretched back into the early nineteenth century.
Source: The main published details have been collected in Richards, *Highland Clearances*, I, 393-402.

Sutherland

Several townships in the western parishes of Assynt and Edderachillis were partially cleared; in a period of 7 years, one sixth of the population of the Scourie district of the estate emigrated. Throughout the famine 147 summonses of removal were granted to the Duke of Sutherland at Dornoch Sheriff Court.

The clearance of the inland townships of Knockan and Elphin was contemplated in 1849 but never undertaken in a wholesale manner.

Sources: *Witness*, 1 December 1849; N.L.S., Sutherland Estate Papers, Dep. 313/877, Duke of Sutherland to Knockan & Elphin tenants, October 1849; SRO, Sheriff Court Processes (Dornoch), SC9/7/128-130; Richards, *Leviathan of Wealth*, 271.

Tiree

175 summonses of removal granted to the Duke of Argyll against tenants and cottars on his Tiree estate, 1846-52. There is clear evidence throughout the Argyll estate correspondence of a determination to substantially reduce the small tenantry by a process of coercion and assisted emigration. By the 1870s a new estate structure based on medium-sized farms had emerged. For a full account see Chapter 10.

Township	Number of Tenants Removed
Balamartin	32
Scaranish	10
Baugh	5
Kennoway	8
Balephuil	9
Manual	29
Total	93

A further 8 townships were mentioned as suffering major evictions in Napier Commission evidence but no figures of numbers removed were given. The Napier Commission evidence for Tiree is contentious and partly in conflict with the estate's own version of events. It is, for instance, unclear how far the losses referred to above were caused by actual eviction or were mainly the result of consolidation of lands at death of occupiers or after they had left the island.

Sources: SRO, Sheriff Court Processes (Tobermory), SC59/2/4-10; Inveraray Castle, Argyll Estate Papers, Bundle 1522; *N.C.*, 2133-2175, QQ.33475-34252; Duke of Argyll, *Crofts and Farms in the Hebrides* (1883).

North Uist

Sollas district: contained a population of 110 families (603 souls). Served with notices of removal in 1849 but promised assistance to emigrate. There was much resistance (documented in such secondary sources as Richards, *Highland Clearances* I, 422-9); many actually emigrated to Canada in short or medium term. Most of the remainder departed for Australia under the auspices of the Highland and Island Emigration Society in 1852.

Most of the North Uist evictions, despite the notoriety achieved by the Sollas removals, had occurred before the famine. Between 1839-41, 11 townships were cleared and their inhabitants assisted to emigrate. The enormous publicity given to the Sollas clearance shows how press sources can distort the chronological sequence of removals. Essentially, the major restructuring of this estate occurred *before* 1846, despite the impression given in some secondary sources.

Sources: SRO, Lord Advocate's Papers, AD58/85, Evictions of Tenants from the District of Sollas; SRO, GD221/77, Copy of Report by Mr. Ballingall, 1851; *Scotsman*, 28 July 1849; 11 August 1849; P. Cooper, *An Old Story Retold* (Aberdeen, 1881); *N.C.*, 797-801, QQ.12437-12490.

South Uist

40 crofts cleared (approx. 200 souls) in Milton township for sheep farm possessed by Chisholm of Moidart. Frobost, Kildonan (27 families, 135 souls), Bornish (24 families, 120 souls) all cleared, 1848-52.

Source: *N.C.*, 701-711, QQ.11039-11222.

Appendix 12: Cattle Stocks in Crofting Districts, c.1851

Parish/District	Description
(1) Kilfinichen	The small crofters have parted with a great proportion of their cattle, means generally diminished.
(2) Iona	Condition of 'crofter class' deteriorated greatly since 1846; 'many forced to sell part of their stock'. Crofters paying as much as £15 in rent going down in the world. Many small crofters (£3 to £8) forced to sell off stock to buy food. Also incurred debts to proprietor and other parties.
(7) Creich	About one half of the small crofters have sold part of their stock . . . not aware that there is any one of them who has not one cow.
(15) Aros & Mishnish	There are few, even of the small crofters, who have not a cow and half a horse.
(20) Sorne	£10 crofter. No arrears; stock of cattle entire.
(32) Portree	The crofters, on an average, have rather under their usual quantities of stock. £5 crofter = 2-3 cows; 2 year olds; 2 stirks.
(34) Portree (Lord Macdonald's estate)	There are very few crofters who have not some portion of their stock remaining. Not more than five. Most have 2-4 cows.
(45) Skeabost	Of about 58 crofters paying about 50s. rent, 30 have no stock.
(47) Snizort	£8 crofter: stock of 4 cows, 2 stirks and 8 sheep.
(53) Duirnish (Roag)	£3-£5 rent: 2-3 cows and their followers . . . they have still their full number of cows.
(54) Sleat	. . . circumstances of the people have progressively deteriorated, from year to year, since 1846.
(63) Sleat (Sasaig)	£5 crofts. Stock entire. All have cattle stock complete but not the sheep or horses.
(65) Sleat (Ferindonald)	Full stock of £6 lot = 2 cows, 2 year old, a horse, 18 sheep. Present stock is 1 cow, a stirk, 3 or 4 sheep, no horse.
(74) Lochcarron (Kishorn)	2 milk cows for £5 crofters.
(77) Applecross	All the cottars have cows and sheep; with few exceptions, have each two or three cows.
(89) Lochbroom (Ardmair)	Rents from £4.6s. to £2.10s. 14 families. 2-3 have three cows each; 3 with one cow; the remainder have 2.

Parish/District	Description
(93) Lewis (Stornoway)	£5 rent. 5 cows and 1 two year old. £2.6s rent. 3 cows.
(96) Lewis	Except in the parish of Uig and Carloway district of Lochs, the tenants generally have nearly the full amount of their black cattle in stock . . . in Uig and Carloway many of the tenants reduced to their last, and have no sheep stock.
(99) Lewis (Barvas)	£5 rent. Had four milk cows, four young cattle, twelve sheep, besides hogs, and one mare in foal, beside a lame horse.
(105) Lewis (Uig)	£5 rent. 3 cows, of which 2 are young.
(122) N. Uist	£6 rent. 5 milk cows and followers.
(122) N. Uist (Hangarry)	Stock had fallen by half since 1846.
(128) Barra	230 persons paying rent to the proprietor. Of those, there are about 80 who have no stock of any kind.

Source: McNeill Report, Appendix A, *passim*. Numbers in brackets refer to page references in the Appendix.

Bibliography

(i) Manuscript Sources
(ii) Newspapers and Periodicals
(iii) Contemporary Printed Sources
(iv) Parliamentary Papers
(v) Selected Secondary Sources

(i) *Manuscript Sources*
Public Record Office, London
H045/OS. 1794. Papers relating to British Association for the Relief of Distress in Ireland and Scotland
T1/4201. Papers relating to Distress in the Highlands, 1837, including correspondence and report of Robert Grahame
HD45/1080. Potato Famine in Ireland and Scotland, 1846-8
HD45/345, 2351. Relief of Distress in Paisley and Scotland
CO 384; CO 42. Petitions and other Materials relating to Highland Emigration

Scottish Record Office, Edinburgh
AD58/81 (Lord Advocate's Papers). Reports on conditions of various estates in the Highlands and Islands, 1846-7
AD58/82. Free Church Relief Fund, 1846
AD58/83. Threatened Evictions at Strathaird, Skye, 1850
AD58/84. Conditions in the Isle of Harris
AD58/85. Conditions in Barra and South Uist, 1846-9.
AD58/89. Miscellaneous letters re. Highland Destitution to Lord Advocate
AD58/66. Disturbances between Highland and Irish Railway Labourers in Linlithgow, 1841
AD14/47/628. Precognition as to the alleged death of Widow Anne Gillies from starvation, 18 March 1847
HD Highland Destitution. Major collection of government correspondence and all material relating to the activities of the Edinburgh Section of the Central Board, its officers and local committees, 1846-50
HD4/1-6. Papers of the Highland and Island Emigration Society, 1851-9
AF7/85. Reports by the General Inspector (Fisheries) for the West Coast, 1845-52
AF36/18-19. Wick Fishery Reports and Correspondence, 1839-60
CS 279. Court of Session. Petitions in Sequestrations, 1839-56
CS 277. Sederunt Books in Sequestration
SC59/2/4-14. Sheriff Court Processes, Tobermory
SC9/7/128-30. Sheriff Court Processes, Dornoch
SC32/5/1-2. Sheriff Court Processes, Portree
SC33/17/27-34. Sheriff Court Processes, Stornoway
RH 2/4. Home Office (Scotland). Domestic Entry Books
CH2/190/7. Presbytery of Inveraray Records
CH2/230/4. Presbytery of Skye Records
CH2/557/10. Synod of Argyll Records
GD 112. Breadalbane Muniments
GD 170. Campbell of Barcaldine MSS.
GD 64. Campbell of Jura Papers
GD 201. Clanranald Papers
GD 305. Cromartie Estate Papers

GD 208. Loch Muniments
GD 221. Lord Macdonald Papers
GD 174. Maclaine of Lochbuie Papers
GD 1. Riddell Papers
AF 49. Riddell Papers
GD 248. Seafield Muniments
GD 46. Seaforth Muniments
CS 96/1686. Accounts of Donald Maclean and Co., Merchants and Fishcurers, Kyleakin
RH 21/44/1. Roman Catholic Register of Baptisms, Deaths, Marriages, Arisaig, 1839-60
RH 21/48/2. Roman Catholic Register of Baptisms, Deaths, Marriages, Moidart, 1830-55

General Register Office, Edinburgh
Old Parish Registers: Ardchattan (504/2); Ardnamurchan (505/3); Barvas (86/2); Bracadale;
   Campbeltown (507/6); Clyne; Creich (46/2); Dornoch (47/2); Edderachillis (49/2); Farr
   (50/2); Glenorchy (512/3); Harris (111/1); Iona (538/1); Kilfinichen (542/2); Lochs (87/1);
   North Uist (113/1); Portree (114/2); Stornoway (88/2); Strathy (50/2/1); Strontian (505/2);
   Tiree (551/2).

Census Enumerators' Schedules, 1841, 1851 and 1861 Census:
Ardchattan; Ardnamurchan; Arisaig and Moidart; Gigha; Glenorchy; Inverchaolin; Jura;
Kilchoman; Killarow; Kildalton; Kilchrennan; Kilfinan; Kilfinichen; Kilninian; Lismore;
Morvern; Tiree; Coll; Torosay; Barra; Bracadale; Dores; Duirnish; Glenelg; Harris; Kilmallie;
Kilmonivaig; Kilmorack; Kilmuir; Kiltarlity; N. Uist; S. Uist; Portree; Sleat; Small Isles;
Snizort; Strath; Urquhart; Applecross; Barvas; Gairloch; Kintail; Lochalsh; Lochbroom;
Lochcarron; Lochs; Stornoway; Uig; Glensheil; Assynt; Clyne; Creich; Dornoch; Durness;
Edderachillis; Farr; Kildonan; Lairg; Loth; Rogart; Tongue; Campbeltown; Craignish; Du-
noon; Glassary; Inveraray; Kilbrandon; Kilcalmonell; Killean; Kilmodan; Kilmartin; Kil-
more; Kilninver; N. Knapdale; S. Knapdale; Lochgoilhead; Sadell; Southend; Strachur;
Ardersier; Boleskine; Cromdale; Croy; Inverness; Kingussie; Kirkhill; Laggan; Moy and
Dalarossie; Petty; Alness; Avoch; Contin; Cromarty; Dingwall; Edderton; Fearn; Fodderty;
Killearnan; Kilmuir Easter; Kiltearn; Kincardine; Knockbain; Logie Easter; Nigg; Resolis;
Rosemarkie; Rosskean; Tain; Tarbat; Urquhart and Logie Wester; Urray; Golspie; Abbey
Parish, Paisley, 1851.

National Library of Scotland
Dep. 313. Sutherland Estate Papers

Argyll and Bute District Archives, Lochgilphead
CO 6-13. Parochial Board Minutes, Argyllshire Parishes

Scottish Catholic Archives, Columba House, Edinburgh
Oban Letters

Mitchell Library, Glasgow
MS 21506. Letterbook on Highland Emigration of Sir John McNeill, 1852

In Private Hands
Argyll Estate Papers (Inveraray Castle)
Cameron of Locheil Papers (Achnacarry Castle)
Hamilton Muniments (Lennoxlove)
Mackenzie of Gairloch MSS. (Conon House)
Macleod of Macleod Muniments (Dunvegan Castle)
Diary of John Munro Mackenzie, 1851 (Courtesy of Ms. M. Buchanan)

(ii) *Newspapers and Periodicals*
Edinburgh Evening Courant
Glasgow Herald
Inverness Advertiser
Inverness Courier
Illustrated London News
John O'Groats Journal
North British Daily Mail
Scotsman
Times
Witness

(iii) *Contemporary Printed Sources*
R.J. Adam, ed., *Papers on Sutherland Estate Management, 1802-1816*, 2 vols. (Edinburgh, 1972)
'Agricultural Statistics of Scotland, 1855-58', *Trans. Highland and Agricultural Society*, new ser., 1855-7; 1857-9
W.P. Alison, *Letter to Sir John McNeill on Highland Destitution* (Edinburgh, 1851)
— *Observations on the Famine of 1846-7 in the Highlands of Scotland* (London, 1847)
R. Allister, *Extermination of the Scottish Peasantry* (Edinburgh, 1853)
James Anderson, *An Account of the Present State of the Hebrides and Western Coasts of Scotland* (Edinburgh, 1785)
Anon., *The Depopulation System in the Highlands* (Edinburgh, 1849)
— *Extermination of the Highland Clans* (Edinburgh, 1854)
— *Extracts from Letters to Rev. Dr. McLeod* (Glasgow, 1847)
—'The Highlands: Men, Sheep and Deer', *Edinburgh Review*, 106 (1957)
—'Report on the Disease of the Potato Crop in Scotland in the Year 1845', *Trans. Highland and Agricultural Society*, new ser., 1845-7
— 'Reports on the Disease of the Potato Crop in Scotland for the Year 1846', *Trans. Highland and Agricultural Society*, new ser., 1847-9
— *State of the Highlands in 1854* (Inverness, 1855)
Duke of Argyll, *Crofts and Farms in the Hebrides* (Edinburgh, 1883)
Donald Bain, *Observations upon the Potato Disease of 1845 and 1846* (Edinburgh, 1848)
James Barron, *The Northern Highlands in the Nineteenth Century* (Inverness, 1907), 3 vols.
A.W. Blyth, *A Dictionary of Hygiene and Public Health* (London, 1876)
P. Brodie, 'On Green Crops', *Prize Essays and Transactions of the Highland Society of Scotland*, I (1799)
Edward Brown, *Practical Remarks on the Potato Plant* (London, 1847)
J. Bruce, *Letters on the Present Condition of the Highlands and Islands of Scotland* (Edinburgh, 1847)
Duncan Clerk, 'On the Agriculture of the County of Argyll', *Trans. Highland and Agricultural Society*, 4th ser., X (1878)
E.R. Cregeen, ed., *Argyll Estate Instructions, 1771-1805* (Edinburgh, 1964)
J.B. Denton, 'Land Drainage etc., by Loans', *Journal of the Royal Agricultural Society of England*, 4 (ii), 1868
E. Ellice, *Letter to Sir George Gray on the Administration of the Poor Law in the Highlands* (London, 1855)
Eric J. Findlater, *Highland Clearances: the Real Cause of Highland Famine* (Edinburgh, 1855)
Free Church Destitution Committee, *Statements and Reports* (Edinburgh, 1847)
A. Fullarton and C.R. Baird, *Remarks on the Evils at Present Affecting the Highlands and Islands of Scotland* (Glasgow, 1838)
J. Graham, *On the Potato Disease* (London, 1847)
W.N. Hancock, *What are the Causes of the Distressed State of the Highlands of Scotland?* (Belfast, 1852)

John Knox, *A View of the British Empire* (London, 1785)

J. Loch, *An Account of the Improvements on the Estates of the Marquis of Stafford* (London, 1820)

A. Macaulay, *Popular Medical Dictionary*, 11th ed. (Edinburgh, 1852)

Lady McCaskill, *Twelve Days in Skye* (London, 1852)

Dr. John Macculloch, *The Highlands and Western Islands of Scotland* (London, 1824)

James Macdonald, *General View of the Agriculture of the Hebrides* (Edinburgh, 1811)

James Macdonald, 'On the Agriculture of the County of Sutherland', *Trans. Highland and Agricultural Society*, 4th ser., XII (1880)

William Macdonald, 'On the Agriculture of Inverness-shire', *Trans. Highland and Agricultural Society*, 4th ser., IV (1872)

J. Mackenzie, *Letter to Lord John Russell on Sir John McNeill's Report* (Edinburgh, 1851)

A. McGregor, 'On the Advantages of a Government Grant for Emigration from the Highlands and Islands of Scotland', *Quarterly Journal of Agriculture*, XI (1840-1)

T. Maclauchlan, 'The Influence of Emigration on the Social Condition of the Highlands', *Trans. National Association for the Promotion of Social Science*, 1863

J. Mitchell, *Reminiscences of My Life in the Highlands* (1883 reprint, Newton Abbot, 1971)

Thomas Mulock, *The Western Highlands and Islands of Scotland Socially Considered* (Edinburgh, 1850)

New Statistical Account of Scotland, 15 vols. (Edinburgh, 1845)

T. Pennant, *A Tour in Scotland and a Voyage to the Hebrides*, 3 vols. (Warrington, 1774)

Reports of Central Board of Management of the Fund Raised for the Relief of the Destitute Inhabitants of the Highlands and Islands of Scotland (Edinburgh, 1847-50)

Reports of the Edinburgh Section of the Central Board for the Relief of Destitution in the Highlands and Islands of Scotland, 1847-50 (Edinburgh, 1847-50)

Report to the General Assembly of the Free Church of Scotland regarding Highland Destitution (Edinburgh, 1847)

Report on Mull, Tiree, Coll and Morvern by a Deputation of the Glasgow Section of the Highland Relief Board (Glasgow, 1849)

Report on the Outer Hebrides by a Deputation of the Glasgow Section of the Highland Relief Board (Glasgow, 1849)

Report of the Highland Emigration Society (London, 1853)

A. Robertson, *Where are the Highlanders?* (Edinburgh, n.d.)

G. Robertson, *Rural Recollections* (Irvine, 1829)

James Robertson, *General View of the County of Perth* (London, 1794)

D. Ross, *The Scottish Highlanders* (Glasgow, 1852)

—   *The Glengarry Evictions* (Glasgow, 1853)

—   *Real Scottish Grievances* (Glasgow, 1854)

Sir John Sinclair, *General Report on the Agricultural State and Political Circumstances of Scotland* (Edinburgh, 1814)

W.F. Skene, *Celtic Scotland* (Edinburgh, 1880)

—   *The Highlanders of Scotland* (London, 1837)

R.S. Skirving, 'On the Agriculture of East Lothian', *Trans. Highland and Agricultural Society*, 4th ser., V (1873)

Society of Friends, *Transactions of the Central Relief Committee of the Society of Friends during the Famine in Ireland 1846-7* (Dublin, 1852)

R. Somers, *Letters from the Highlands: or the Famine of 1847* (London, 1848)

J. Steill, *The Wrongs and Rights of the Scottish Gael* (Edinburgh, 1854)

W.J. Stewart, *Lectures on the Mountains: or the Highlands and Highlanders as they were and as they are* (London, 1860)

J. Taylor, 'On the Comparative Merits of Different Modes of Reaping Grain', *Trans. Highland and Agricultural Society*, new ser., 1843-5

Lord Teignmouth, *Sketches of the Coasts and Islands of Scotland*, 2 vols. (London, 1836)

E.O. Tregellis, *Hints on the Hebrides* (Newcastle, 1855)

Sir Charles Trevelyan, *The Irish Crisis* (London, 1848)

Charles Weld, *Two Months in the Highlands, Orcadia and Skye* (London, 1860)

A. Whyte and D. Macfarlane, *General View of the County of Dumbarton* (Glasgow, 1811)

(iv) *Parliamentary Reports*

Reports from the Select Committee appointed to inquire into the expediency of encouraging emigration from the United Kingdom, 1826, IV; 1826-7, V

Letters Addressed to Mr. F. Maule by R. Grahame relative to the Distress of the Highlands of Scotland, 1837, LI

Report from the Select Committee appointed to inquire into the condition of the Population of the Highlands and Islands of Scotland, and into the practicablity of affording the People relief by means of Emigration, 1841, VI

Report of the Agent General for Emigration on the Applicability of Emigration to relieve Distress in the Highlands (1837), 1841, XXVI

Report from the Commissioners appointed for inquiring into the Administration and Practical Operation of the Poor Laws in Scotland, 1844, XXVII-XXXVI

Documents relative to the Distress in Scotland in 1783, 1846, XXXVII

Report from the Select Committee on Railway Labourers, 1846, XIII

Colonial Land and Emigration Commissioners, *Annual Reports*, 1845-58

Board of Supervision for Relief of the Poor in Scotland, *Annual Reports*, 1846-56

Reports of Commissioners, Inspectors of Factories, 1846, XV

Papers relative to Emigration to the British Provinces in North America, 1847-60

Return of Applications for Advances under the Drainage Act, 1847, XXXIV

Correspondence relating to the measures adopted for the Relief of Distress in Ireland and Scotland, 1847, LIII

Report to the Board of Supervision by Sir John McNeill on the Western Highlands and Islands, 1851, XXVI

Copies or Extracts of Despatches relative to Emigration to the North American Colonies, 1851, XL

First Report of Select Committee on Emigrant Ships, 1854, XIII

Communications with regard to the Administration of the Poor Law in the Highlands of Scotland, 1854-5, XLVI

Return of Population and Poor Rates, Scotland (1853), 1854-5, XLVII

Royal Commission on the Employment of Children, Young Persons and Women in Agriculture (1867), 1870, III

Reports as to the Alleged Destitution in the Western Highlands and Islands, 1883, LIX

Report and Evidence of the Commissioners of Inquiry into the Condition of the Crofters and Cottars in the Highlands and Islands of Scotland, 1884, XXXII-XXXVI

Report on the Condition of the Cottar Population of the Lews, 1888, LXXX

Royal Commission on Labour. The Agricultural Labourer (Scotland), 1893, XXXVI

Royal Commission (Highlands and Islands, 1892). Reports and Minutes of Evidence, 1895, XXXVIII-XXXIX

Report to the Secretary for Scotland by the Crofters Commission on the Social Condition of the People in Lewis as compared with Twenty Years Ago, 1902, LXXXIII

Report on the Sanitary Conditions of the Lews, 1905, XXXIV

(v) *Selected Secondary Sources*

M. Alamgir, *Famine in South Asia* (Cambridge, Mass., 1980)

A.B. Appleby, 'Disease or Famine? Mortality in Cumbria and Westmoreland, 1580-1640', *Econ. Hist. Rev.*, 2nd ser., 26 (1973)

—— *Famine in Tudor and Stuart England* (Liverpool, 1978)

—— 'Disease, Diet and History', *Journal of Interdisciplinary History*, VIII (1978)

Maurice Aymard, 'The History of Nutrition and Economic History', *Journal of European Economic History*, 2 (1973)

Roderick A.C.S. Balfour, 'Emigration from the Highlands and Western Isles of Scotland to Australia during the Nineteenth Century', Unpublished M.Litt. thesis, University of Edinburgh, 1973

Dudley Baines, *Migration in a Mature Economy* (Cambridge, 1985)

R.D.C. Black, *Economic Thought and the Irish Question* (Cambridge, 1960)

Jerome Blum, *The End of the Old Order in Rural Europe* (New Jersey, 1978)

P.M.A. Bourke, 'The Potato Blight, Weather and Irish Famine', Unpublished Ph.D. thesis, National University of Ireland, 1965

J.M. Bulloch, *The Gordons of Cluny* (Buckie, 1911)

J.M. Bumsted, *The People's Clearance: Highland Emigration to British North America 1770-1815* (Edinburgh, 1982)

W.G. Burton, *The Potato* (London, 1948)

James M. Cameron, 'A Study of the Factors that Assisted and Directed Scottish Emigration to Upper Canada, 1815-1855', Unpublished Ph.D. thesis, University of Glasgow, 1970

G.L. Carefoot and E.R. Sprott, *Famine on the Wind: Plant Diseases and Human History* (London, 1969)

N.H. Carrier and J.R. Jeffrey, *External Migration* (London, 1955)

S.D.M. Carpenter, 'Patterns of Recruitment of the Highland Regiments of the British Army, 1756 to 1815', Unpublished M.Litt. thesis, University of St. Andrews, 1977

Ian Carter, *Farm Life in Northeast Scotland, 1840-1914* (Edinburgh, 1979)

Olive Checkland, *Philanthropy in Victorian Scotland* (Edinburgh, 1980)

K.S. Chester, *The Nature and Prevention of Plant Diseases* (Philadelphia, 1942)

E.J.T. Collins, 'Harvest Technology and Labour Supply in Britain, 1790-1870', *Econ. Hist. Rev.*, 2nd ser., XXII (1969)

S.M. Cousens, 'The Regional Pattern of Emigration during the Great Irish Famine', *Trans. Institute of British Geographers*, 28 (1960)

E. Margaret Crawford, 'Dearth, Diet and Disease in Ireland 1850: a Case Study in Nutritional Deficiency', *Medical History*, 28 (1984)

—'Aspects of Irish Diet, 1839-1904', Unpublished Ph.D. thesis, University of London, 1985

E.R. Cregeen, 'The Changing Role of the House of Argyll in the Scottish Highlands', in N.T. Phillipson and Rosalind Mitchison, eds., *Scotland in the Age of Improvement* (Edinburgh, 1970)

L.M. Cullen, *An Economic History of Ireland since 1660* (London, 1972)

—and T.C. Smout, eds., *Comparative Aspects of Scottish and Irish Economic and Social History, 1660-1900* (Edinburgh, 1977)

—*The Emergence of Modern Ireland 1600-1900* (London, 1981)

F. Fraser Darling, *West Highland Survey* (Oxford, 1955)

S. Davidson and R. Passmore, *Human Nutrition and Dietetics* 3rd. ed. (Cambridge, 1954)

T.M. Devine, 'The Rise and Fall of Illicit Whisky-Making in Northern Scotland, 1780-1840', *Scottish Hist. Rev. 54 (1975)*

'Temporary Migration and the Scottish Highlands in the Nineteenth Century', *Econ. Hist. Rev.*, 2nd ser. XXXII (1979)

—'Social Stability and Agrarian Change in the Rural Lowlands of Scotland, 1780-1840', in T.M. Devine, ed., *Lairds and Improvement in the Scotland of the Enlightenment* (Dundee, 1979)

—'Highland Migration to Lowland Scotland, 1760-1860', *Scottish Hist. Rev 62* (1983)

—(with D. Dickson), ed., *Ireland and Scotland, 1600-1850: Parallels and Contrasts in Economic and Social Development* (Edinburgh, 1983)

—'Pastoralism and Highland Migration', in A. Poitrineau, ed., *Élevage et Vie Pastorale dans les Montagnes d'Europe au Moyen Age et à l'Epoque Moderne* (Clermont Ferrand, 1984)

—ed., *Farm Servants and Labour in Lowland Scotland, 1770-1914* (Edinburgh, 1984)

—'The Highland Clearances', *Recent Findings in Economic and Social History*, 4 (1987)

—'Stability and Unrest in Rural Scotland and Ireland, 1760-1840', in R. Mitchison and P. Roebuck, eds., *Economy and Society in Scotland and Ireland, 1500-1939* (Edinburgh, 1988)

—'Social Responses to Improvement, 1500-1860: the Highland and Lowland Clearances in Scotland', in R. Houston and I. White, eds., *Scottish Society, 1500-1900* (Cambridge, 1988)

Neil Diamond, 'An Evaluation of the Role of the Edinburgh Section of the Central Relief Board, 1847-1850', B.A. dissertation, Department of History, University of Strathclyde, 1986

Denis Docherty, 'The Migration of Highlanders to Lowland Scotland in the Nineteenth Century with special reference to Paisley', B.A. dissertation, Department of History, University of Strathclyde, 1979

J.S. Donnelly, *The Land and People of Nineteenth Century Cork* (London, 1975)

C.L.D. Duckworth and G.E. Langmuir, *West Highland Steamers* (Glasgow, 1967)

J. Duthie, *The Art of Fishcuring* (Aberdeen, 1911)

R.D. Edwards and D.T. Williams, eds., *The Great Famine: Studies in Irish History* (Dublin, 1956)

Charlotte Erickson, *Emigration from Europe, 1815-1914* (London, 1976)

A. Fenton, *Scottish Country Life* (Edinburgh, 1976)

M.W. Flinn, 'Malthus, Emigration and Potatoes in the Scottish North West, 1770-1870', in L.M. Cullen and T.C. Smout, eds., *Comparative Aspects*

—*Scottish Population History from the Seventeenth Century to the 1930s* (Cambridge, 1977)

R. Forster and C. Ramm, *Food and Drink in History* (Baltimore, 1979)

Derek Fraser, *The evolution of the British Welfare State* (London 1973)

Phillip Gaskell, *Morvern Transformed* (Cambridge, 1968)

J.M. Goldstrom, 'Irish Agriculture and the Great Famine', in J.M. Goldstrom and L.A. Clarkson, eds., *Irish Population, Economy and Society* (Oxford, 1981)

Pierre Goubert, *The Ancien Régime: French Society, 1600-1750* (London, 1973)

J.D. Gould, 'European inter-continental emigration, 1815-1914: patterns and causes', *Journal of European History*, 8 (1979)

Malcolm Gray, 'The Consolidation of the Crofting System', *Agricultural History Review*, 5 (1957)

—*The Highland Economy, 1750-1850* (Edinburgh, 1957)

—'The Highland Potato Famine of the 1840s', *Econ. Hist. Rev.*, 2nd ser., 7 (1954-5)

—*The Fishing Industries of Scotland, 1790-1914* (Aberdeen, 1978)

James Handley, *The Irish in Scotland, 1798-1845* (Cork, 1843)

B. Harrison, 'Philanthropy and the Victorians', *Victorian Studies* (1966)

Jenifer Hart, 'Sir Charles Trevelyan at the Treasury', *English Hist. Rev.*, LXXV (1960)

R.N. Hildebrandt, 'Migration and Economic Change in the Northern Highlands during the Nineteenth Century', Unpublished Ph.D. thesis, University of Glasgow, 1980

F.H. Hitchins, *The Colonial Land and Emigration Commission* (London, 1931)

James Hunter, *The Making of the Crofting Community* (Edinburgh, 1976)

—and C. Maclean, *Skye: the Island* (Edinburgh, 1986)

D. Jenkins and M. Visocchi, *Mendelssohn in Scotland* (London, 1978)

D.G. Johnson, 'Famine', *Encyclopaedia Britannica*, 14th ed. (London, 1973)

M.A. Jones, 'The background to emigration from Great Britain in the nineteenth century', *Perspectives in American History*, 7 (1973)

A. Kemp *et al*, *The Biology of Human Starvation* (Minneapolis, 1950)

R.E. Kennedy, *The Irish: Emigration, Marriage and Fertility* (Los Angeles, 1973)

S. Kierse, *The Famine Years in the Parish of Killaloe, 1845-51* (Killaloe, 1984)

E. Le Roy Ladurie, 'L'aménorrhée de famine (XVIIe-XXe siècles)', *Annales*, 24 (1969)

Ian Levitt and Christopher Smout, *The State of the Scottish Working Class in 1843* (Edinburgh, 1979)

R.D. Lobban, 'The Migration of Highlanders into Lowland Scotland, c.1750-1890, with special reference to Greenock', Unpublished Ph.D. thesis, University of Edinburgh, 1969

D.F. Macdonald, *Scotland's Shifting Population* (Glasgow, 1937)

N. Macdonald, *Canada: Immigration and Colonisation, 1841-1903* (Aberdeen, 1966)

Margaret McKay, 'Nineteenth Century Tiree Emigrant Communities in Ontario', *Oral History Journal*, 9 (1981)

Alasdair Maclean, *Night Falls on Ardnamurchan* (London, 1984)

D.S. Macmillan, *Scotland and Australia, 1788-1850: Emigration, Commerce and Investment* (Oxford, 1967)

—'Sir Charles Trevelyan and the Highland and Island Emigration Society, 1849-1859', *Royal Australian Historical Society Journal*, XLIX (1963)

G.B. Masefield, *Famine: Its Prevention and Relief* (Oxford, 1963)

J. Mercer, *Hebridean Islands* (London, 1974)

J. Meuvret, 'French Demographic Crises', in D.V. Glass and D.E.C. Eversley, eds., *Population in History* (London, 1965)

B.R. Mitchell, *Abstract of British Historical Statistics* (Cambridge, 1962)

Joel Mokyr, *Why Ireland Starved* (London, 1983)

—'The Deadly Fungus', in J.L. Simond, ed., *Research in Population Economics* (Greenwich, Conn.)

I.R.M. Mowat, *Easter Ross 1750-1850* (Edinburgh, 1980)

Norman Murray, *The Scottish Handloom Weavers 1790-1850* (Edinburgh, 1978)

C. Ó'Gráda, 'Seasonal Migration and Post-Famine Adjustment in the West of Ireland', *Studia Hibernica*, 13 (1973)

Willie Orr, *Deer Forests, Landlords and Crofters* (Edinburgh, 1982)

G. Ó'Tuathaig, *Ireland before the Famine, 1798-1848* (Dublin, 1972)

Audrey Paterson, 'The New Poor Law in Nineteenth Century Scotland', in Derek Fraser, ed., *The New Poor Law in the Nineteenth Century* (London, 1976)

J.P.D. Post, 'Famine, Mortality and Epidemic Disease in the Process of Modernisation', *Econ. Hist. Rev.*, 2nd ser., XXIX (1976)

J.R. Poynter, *Society and Pauperism* (London, 1969)

Eric Richards, *The Leviathan of Wealth* (London, 1973)

—'Highland Emigrants to South Australia in the 1850s', *Northern Scotland*, 5 (1982)

—*A History of the Highland Clearances*, 2 vols. (London, 1982 and 1985)

R.I. Rotberg and T.K. Rabb, *Hunger and History: the Impact of Changing Food Production and Consumption Patterns on Society* (Cambridge, 1985)

R.N. Salaman, *The History and Social Influence of the Potato* (Cambridge, 1949)

Laurance J. Saunders, *Scottish Democracy, 1815-40* (Edinburgh, 1950)

B.H. Slicher van Bath, *The Agrarian History of Western Europe, 500-1850* (London, 1963)

T.C. Smout, 'Famine and Famine-Relief in Scotland', in L.M. Cullen and T.C. Smout, eds., *Comparative Aspects*

—'The Strange Intervention of Edward Twistleton: Paisley in Depression, 1841-3', in T.C. Smout, ed., *The Search for Wealth and Stability* (London, 1979)

—'Tours in the Scottish Highlands from the eighteenth to the twentieth centuries', *Northern Scotland*, 5 (1983)

Margaret C. Storrie, *Islay: Biography of an Island* (Port Ellen, 1981)

J.A. Symon, *Scottish Farming Past and Present* (Edinburgh, 1959)

L. Timperley, 'The Pattern of Landholding in Eighteenth Century Scotland', in M.L. Parry and T.R. Slater, eds., *The Making of the Scottish Countryside* (London, 1980)

N.L. Tranter, *Population and Society, 1750-1940* (London, 1985)

H.R. Trevor-Roper, 'The Invention of Tradition: the Highland Tradition of Scotland', in E.J. Hobsbawm and T. Ranger, eds., *The Invention of Tradition* (Cambridge, 1983)

Charles W.J. Withers, 'Highland Migration to Dundee, Perth and Stirling, 1753-1891', *Journal of Historical Geography*, 4 (1985)
—*Highland Communities in Dundee and Perth, 1787-1891* (Dundee, 1986)
C. Woodham-Smith, *The Great Hunger* (London, 1962)
A. J. Youngson, *After the Forty Five (Edinburgh, 1973)*

Index